5/20   0803916

ON LINE

LOOKS

LOOKS

Why They Matter More Than You Ever Imagined

GORDON L. PATZER, PH.D.

American Management Association

New York • Atlanta • Brussels • Chicago • Mexico City • San Francisco
Shanghai • Tokyo • Toronto • Washington, D.C.

This publication is designed to provide accurate and authoritative
information in regard to the subject matter covered. It is sold with
the understanding that the publisher is not engaged in rendering
legal, accounting, or other professional service. If legal advice or other
expert assistance is required, the services of a competent professional
person should be sought.

Library of Congress Cataloging-in-Publication Data

Patzer, Gordon L.
    Looks : why they matter more than you ever imagined / Gordon L. Patzer.
      p.   cm.
    Includes bibliographical references and index.
    ISBN 978-0-8144-8054-0
    1. Interpersonal attraction.   2. Beauty, Personal—Social aspects.   3. Body,
Human—Social aspects.   4. Sexual attraction.   I. Title.

HM1151.P36   2008
306.4'613—dc22

                                                                          2007033524

Contents

INTRODUCTION

Looks, Lookism, and the Media

*Far more than meets the eye
and far deeper than skin deep*

She was a former NFL cheerleader with silken hair the color of wild honey, tanned, with flawless skin, a smile from a toothpaste ad, and a head-turning figure that was all original equipment.

With such looks, Melana Scantlin had no difficulty attracting men. But she didn't want just *anybody*. She wanted a special man, one she could start a family with one day, a princely fellow with whom she could spend the rest of her life.

But suddenly she was twenty-six and it wasn't happening. Then Melana, an aspiring actress, was invited to join a kind of video dating service, a unique program designed not only to help find her mate but also to entertain a vast television audience.

As cameras rolled, Melana was introduced to sixteen young men. They were muscular, they were skinny, they were chubby. Some were clean-shaven, others bearded; they wore buzz cuts, fashionable hairstyles, or were balding. They were tall, short, and in between. Line up all sixteen and they were pretty much what you might expect to find at a typical American high school's ten-year class reunion.

According to rules that Melana agreed to, she was obliged to date each man at least once. Immediately she saw that the group included several men in whom she had no interest; in short order, they were gone from the program and from her life. Concentrating on the others, she went on dates or hung out with one or another, getting to know each, learning a bit about their lives, their personalities, their private priorities.

All these men were dubbed "Average Joes," with unremarkable physical attributes, diverse but ordinary occupations, and unexceptional lives. Steadily winnowing the group after a few weeks, Melana finally chose toothy, twenty-eight-year-old Adam Mesh, a husky securities trader with a strong New York accent.

Almost from the moment of birth, each of us is judged—silently, unconsciously, and nearly instantly—on the basis of everything that goes into the mix of qualities known as "physical attractiveness."

Melana said she was sure that she had found her true love—until the show's producers threw her a curve. Suddenly, three young men with looks that would have shamed a Greek god were added to the mix. Would Melana prefer any of them to Adam?

With little hesitation, she left her "true love" for Jason Peoples, twenty-seven, a part-time waiter still living with his parents.

"The eyes, the face, the smile. How could you deny that?" said Melana as she and her Adonis flew off for a honeymoon-like vacation at an exclusive resort.

When this lovely woman abruptly rejected a successful trader who had been the subject of a *Fortune* magazine article to party with a gorgeous slacker, millions of American women, vicariously living Melana's romance, rejoiced. Older and wiser, they might not have chosen the ambition-challenged Jason over one of Wall Street's rising stars—but still, they could appreciate why she had.

That's because for a long time Americans, like people of most other cultures, have allowed what they *see* of a person to strongly influence what they *feel* and *believe* about that person. Almost from the moment of birth, each of us is judged—silently, unconsciously, and nearly instantly—on the basis of our height (or lack of it), our weight and bulk, the shape and symmetry of our facial features, the length and style of our hair, our mode of dress, our grooming—everything that goes into the mix of qualities known as "physical attractiveness."

Sometimes termed "*lookism*"—treating people in ways biased by their perceived individual level of physical attractiveness—the "physical attractiveness (PA)" phenomenon has been studied in depth for decades by social scientists of many disciplines, including psychologists, sociologists, biologists, and anthropologists. They have produced a panoply of sometimes-contradictory research data. But while this subject continues to be studied, a fair appraisal of science's collective conclusion is that in America, more than in most Western cultures, what you look like—or more important, how others perceive you—shapes your life in dozens of often subtle ways from cradle to grave.

As you will see in following chapters, PA affects the way nurses treat newborns in the same way that it shapes the manner in which parents act and react with their children. PA influences a child's self-image and becomes a significant factor in how teachers evaluate, assist, and grade pupils from kindergarten to graduate school. It's a key factor in finding and keeping mates and close friends, in choosing an occupation, in finding or keeping a job, and in defining the limits of an individual's success in a chosen field.

PA's effects permeate such supposedly neutral arenas as courtrooms and elections. Juries, for example, tend to attach more credence to the arguments of a winsome attorney than a less enticing counterpart. Each witness's testimony is unconsciously processed through jurors' perceptions of the individual's PA, and anyone accused of a crime is judged as much on his personal PA as on the facts introduced to a jury.

Since the 1960s, when television finally permeated even the most remote corners of America, it has been nearly impossible for a truly unsightly candidate to win national elective office. And it is almost as difficult for a PA-challenged person to win a local election as it would be to enter a beauty contest.

Just as the rise of the mass media has shaped public perceptions on the parameters of personal attractiveness, PA has reshaped the media itself. Where television news reporters once were unremarkable in appearance, it is now virtually impossible to find an American man or woman reading news copy to a camera who could not be described as attractive or good-looking. Fueled by an explosion of media images that glorify youth and beauty, millions of Americans have turned their waking lives into endless quests for enhanced PA, often at the expense of their health. So powerful are these media images that in the twentieth century, once-rare conditions such as anorexia and bulimia are commonplace throughout the Western world. Literally millions of young people, mostly female, have become so obsessed in the pursuit of attaining a single dimension of PA—body weight—that they willingly endanger their lives by denying their bodies essential nutrition. Other millions exhaust their savings or incur huge debts to pay for one or more cosmetic surgery procedures, often risking their lives. Fed by ever-increasing demand, hucksters, charlatans, and criminals of every stripe prey on vulnerable people, taking their money and leaving a trail of death and disfigurement in their wake.

> Millions of Americans have turned their waking lives into endless quests for enhanced PA, often at the expense of their health.

At the turn of this century, the hottest fad in prime-time television was a raft of "reality" shows featuring young, attractive, and often scantily attired contestants competing for love and money. Whether a "tribe" transported to some remote but photogenic location, couples risking their lives to overcome fear, penniless male hunks presented as wealthy tycoons to clueless female sex objects, or men and women craving cosmetic makeovers, the common denominator is sex appeal: Except as the butt of some joke, reality contestants of average appearance are in short supply.

Even in death PA has news value: If a picture is available, television news directors are far more likely to air the killing or injury of an attractive victim than a plain one.

PA also has a profound influence on the nature and reach of Western culture, including how we define role models, who governs us, what products we buy, and what services we consume. It is a component of the core values that we pass along to our children and of our choice of friends; in short, the PA phenomenon permeates Western society and makes a powerful difference in the lives of hundreds of millions of people.

While PA's effects are amplified by mass media, the phenomenon itself is older than history: There is evidence that some Stone Age women in southern Europe styled their hair. Did they take the time and trouble it must have required 20,000 years before perms, curlers, and hair dryers merely to lure a better class of mastodon to dinner? I don't think so.

History began with the written word—and glamour immediately became an important part of it. For example, in the fourteenth century B.C., Egypt's queen was Nefertiti, whose name means "the beautiful one is come." Did she have other qualifications? Important family connections or diplomatic skills? Management expertise? From her name alone it's obvious that few cared.

Even Aristotle (384–322 B.C.), ancient Greece's premier observer of human nature, recognized the importance of PA. "Personal beauty is a greater recommendation than any letter of reference," he wrote.

And the Hebrew Bible, canonized some 3,000 years ago from far-older written and oral sources, repeatedly describes characters whose appearance affected all around them:

When Abram [later renamed Abraham] entered Egypt, the Egyptians saw how very beautiful the woman [his wife and half-sister Sarai] was. Pharaoh's courtiers saw her and praised her to Pharaoh, and the woman was taken into Pharaoh's palace. And because of her, it went well with Abram; he acquired sheep, oxen, asses, male and female slaves, she-asses, and camels. (Genesis 12:14–16)

This is the story of a stranger in a strange land who becomes rich virtually overnight just because a powerful man admired the way his "wife" *looked*. How many times and with how many variations has this story been repeated throughout history, not to mention in our own time?

In medieval times, affluent noblewomen swallowed arsenic or dabbed bat's blood on their skin to improve their complexions. As recently as the eighteenth century, American women washed themselves in the warm urine of a young boy to erase their freckles. Ever the dispassionate observer of nature, Charles Darwin wrote of a "universal passion for adornment" even when it required "wonderfully great" suffering.

At its root, PA may be the unconscious recognition that beauty serves to attract the opposite sex for the biological imperative of reproduction. Just as plants that use flowers to attract insects to pollinate them and animals to eat their fruit or otherwise spread their seeds are more successful in ensuring the survival of their species, nature commands us to notice the physical characteristics that tell us that a particular human is suitable for reproduction.

> PA also has a profound influence on how we define role models, who governs us, what products we buy, and what services we consume.

In his 1989 landmark study of human mating preferences, Dr. David Buss, now a University of Texas professor of evolutionary psychology, logged mating preferences for more than 10,000 people of thirty-seven cultures and found that a woman's PA was at the top or near it on every man's list. His conclusion: Nothing is more important to a marriage-minded woman than her good looks.

This observation seems to have a basis in reproductive biology. For example, most men find a woman's long, shiny hair appealing, even if they are not aware that hair is a visible history of body health; a woman with unhealthy-looking locks is likely a poor candidate to bear and rear children.

Acknowledging this appeal, to which men are attracted, many

traditional societies, especially in the Middle East, require women to cover their heads in public as a sign of modesty.

In virtually every culture, men find younger women more attractive than older ones, probably because females of our species are capable of reproduction for only a limited period.

Moreover, in most cultures, women are more attracted to older men than they are to younger ones. Could it be because men are capable of fathering children for nearly their entire adult lives, but older men usually have more resources to put at the disposal of their mate and their children?

Humans come in an astonishing variety of shapes, sizes, and appearances, which leads the less physically attractive woman to fret that no one will want her, that she will fail to reproduce and pass on her genes—or that she is incapable of attracting a mate who will have the ability to support her children.

Women compete to attract men; however, men compete for power and dominance, thus to be more attractive to women. These conditions have given rise to such enormous mercantile empires as Revlon, Max Factor, and L'Oréal; created myriad occupations from nail stylists and barbers to cosmetic chemists, liposuction technicians, and plastic surgeons; and contributed mightily to the growth of such industries as advertising and clothing manufacture—all merely to help men and women look better. Pursuit of greater PA has created a $160-billion-a-year global industry ranging from weight-loss preparations, cosmetics, skin and hair care, and perfumes to cosmetic surgery, health clubs, and hormone injections. Americans spend more money each year on beauty enhancements than they do on education.

And it's not merely for powder and paint. Millions of Americans, including many in their supposed "golden years," have gone under the knife to enhance their appearance. Once almost exclusively the province of the wealthy and famous or the hideously malformed, today many Americans of very modest means scrimp and save for cosmetic surgery procedures aimed at making them more attractive.

The following chapters will examine how and why all this happens, and why it is more vital than ever to recognize and appreciate the phenomenon of physical attractiveness.

CHAPTER 1

Older Than Civilization

*A PA tour of the ancient world, from Stone Age
beauty parlors through Pharaonic Egypt and
the Bible to the face that launched a
thousand ships*

Her conception was the consequence of a royal cuckolding: Zeus, king of the gods, took the form of a swan to seduce and impregnate Queen Leda, wife of Tyndareus, King of Sparta. In due course Leda delivered an egg; when it hatched, out stepped the immortal daughter of Zeus, so utterly beautiful that her fame spread to every corner of the ancient world. Helen of Sparta became history's first superstar, famous throughout the civilized West long before the invention of mass media.

According to legend and ancient literature, Tyndareus remained unaware of Helen's true parentage. He forced her to marry the wealthy, middle-aged Menelaus, brother of powerful King Aga-memnon. Helen's subsequent kidnapping by the young, virile, amoral, but oh-so-handsome Paris set off a ten-year war that killed vast numbers and ruined many of the city-states that took part in the hostilities.

And what did Helen think of all this? Never mind the movies. Around 800 B.C., Homer and other ancient Greek poets paid scant attention to the thoughts or feelings of the woman behind the fabu-lous "face that launched a thousand ships." Kidnapped first by Theseus and then by Paris, she was rescued more than once by her brothers and her husband. Snatched back from Paris by an Egyptian king, Helen was later taken from that king's son by husband Mene-laus, as told in *The Iliad* of Homer. And all the while, she seems to have remained nearly oblivious to the tumult and terror around her, to the rise and fall of those who sought to possess her beauty and those protecting her. Was she angry or frightened by her kidnap-pers? Amused? Aroused? Nothing in legend or literature describes Helen's feelings; she scarcely utters a word. Rather, she seems en-tirely neutral toward the men fighting over her, an empty vessel to be filled with the yearnings and aspirations of her admirers.

Was Helen (better known as Helen of Troy) flesh and blood, or merely a fictional plot device? No one can say with certainty. But what matters more is the feminine archetype that she represents. For thousands of years, Helen's abduction—even if, as some hold, she went willingly—has defined the ultimate insult, *casus belli* for any sanction, including war.

To the Greeks and those who embraced their culture, Helen represented the power and potency of human beauty, the immutable cur-rency of physical attractiveness. But ancient Greece's appraisal of PA did not begin and end with Helen.

> "Personal beauty is a greater recommendation than any letter of reference."
> —Aristotle

Plato (427–347 B.C.) called good looks "the privilege of na-ture," while Socrates (469–399 B.C.) described beauty as "a short tyranny." As previously noted, Aristotle (384–322 B.C.) went still further: "Personal beauty is a greater recommendation than any letter of reference." Or perhaps Diogenes (403–323 B.C.) said that, as some scholars insist. Either way, what has come down to us from the Greeks shows a familiarity and deep respect for PA.

The ancient Hebrews also knew of PA and its role in affairs both human and Divine. In the Book of Genesis, Abraham is rewarded with gold, silver, slaves, and livestock because his wife, Sarah, is beautiful.

But there is much more to this story, which begins with a famine in Canaan. On their way to Egypt in search of a better life, Abraham tells Sarah that because she is a "woman of beautiful countenance," when the Egyptians see them together they will understand that they are man and wife, and they will kill Abraham in order to take possession of Sarah. Abraham therefore pleads with Sarah to say that she is his sister, not his wife, so that instead of killing Abraham the Egyptians will treat him well as a means of wooing her!

Soon after arriving in Egypt, what Abraham predicted takes place: Pharaoh's men "invite" Sarah into the palace, where the monarch pitches woo but somehow doesn't connect. When God appears to Pharaoh in a dream, Abraham's ruse is revealed. To stay in Abraham's good graces—thereby avoiding the wrath of God—Pharaoh heaps treasure on him. This story is repeated a generation later, when Abraham's son Isaac and his "very beautiful to behold" wife, Rebecca, place themselves under the protection of King Abimelech of Gerar, a Philistine. Fearing for his life, Isaac tells everyone that Rebecca is his sister, and sure enough, Abimelech's men scoop her up. Again there is a royal dream, and afterward, Rebecca emerges unscathed from the palace and Abimelech posts a warning around his kingdom threatening the head of any man who lays a hand on Rebecca.

PA in men is also acknowledged in the Bible:

Joseph was handsome in form and appearance. (Genesis 39:6)

[David is] . . . a mighty man of valor, a man of war, prudent in speech and a handsome person. (1 Samuel 16:12).

Now in all Israel there was no one who was praised as much as Absalom for his good looks. (2 Samuel 14:25)

To the ancient Hebrews and the Christians who followed in their monotheistic spiritual path, physical beauty was a reward from the Almighty, and its opposite was punishment. As King Solomon put it in Ecclesiastes 8:1–10, "True wisdom, godly wisdom, can even benefit physical appearance. Sin often hardens the face as well as the heart, bringing lines of sadness, despair, guilt, and worry." But wisdom, added the wisest monarch, "brightens a man's face and changes its hard appearance."

PA brought a special burden, however. "As a ring of gold in a swine's snout, so is a lovely woman who lacks discretion" (Proverbs 11:22).

The Bible understood very well the power of PA to shape human affairs, and warned against its temptations:

Do not lust after her beauty in your heart;
Nor let her allure you with her eyelids.
For by means of a harlot a man is reduced to a crust of bread . . .
(Proverbs 6:24–26)

While the Hebrews and Greeks were first to recognize the sway of physical attractiveness over human affairs and to chronicle the ways that PA shapes the human condition, PA was hard at work long before the rise of civilization.

Most anthropologists agree that our species evolved in Africa some 120,000 years ago. The scant evidence provided by the fossil record, however, suggests that until far more recently, the behavior of these anatomically modern humans was little different from that of their more primitive ancestors, which is to say that they spent their time hunting, gathering food, and procreating. If early man spent much time in intellectual pursuits, he left few indications of it.

> To the ancient Hebrews and the Christians, physical beauty was a reward from the Almighty, and its opposite was punishment.

In 2004, however, archaeologists excavating the Blombos Cave at the southern tip of Africa came to an unexpected insight: Clusters of mollusk shells that site workers had discovered over the past decade were found to have been pierced by tools held by human hands, then strung on some sort of cord.[1] In other words, they were not mere shells but *necklaces*—adornment. Definitively dated to 75,000 years ago, the forty-one tiny, orange-and-black beads are the oldest jewelry ever found, symbols of a prehistoric vanity that foreshadows the sort of baubles and bangles worn by women of every station in Helen of Troy's time, no less than in our own.

The Blombos find sent ripples around the world of anthropology and psychology. Experts in these fields concluded that the beads were proof that by expressing concepts of beauty and vanity, primitive humans had a capability for self-awareness. Other experts suggested that the beads were a means of social communication, inferring that these early people used symbolic reasoning—language—and individually felt a sense of group belonging.

Fair enough. But the beads, or necklaces, also suggest that even 75,000 years ago, women wanted to make a fashion statement, to stand out from the crowd. They wanted, in short, to catch a man's eye.

If the Blombos beads are the earliest indication of an appreciation of feminine beauty, they are far from the first proof that prehistoric humans appreciated the power of physical attractiveness. As evidence, meet the most famous femme of the Paleolithic Age, the Venus of Willendorf, a 25,000-year-old limestone fetish. Unearthed in what is now Austria, this figurine of a faceless, Rubenesque woman with luxuriously coiffed tresses demonstrates that at least some primitive women braided and curled their hair. An even earlier ivory object found in France, the Brassempouy Lady, has been dated to approximately 36,000 B.C. and depicts a woman whose hair is covered with a snood or net—an indication, perhaps, that even in the Stone Age, women were concerned about bad-hair days.

But why? How was it that just as many modern people take great pains with hair, makeup, and nails, primitive humans analogously felt the need to compete for sexual attention?

The answer lies in the biology of sexual attraction.

In high school, we learned that male birds boast colorful plumage in order to attract females to mate with; that bright blossoms serve to attract bees and other insects that pollinate plants; and that the males of such species as sheep, elk, and wolves lock horn, hoof, and fang in sometimes mortal combat for the right to inseminate the females of their herd or pack.

Like birds, bees, and badgers, adult humans feel an unconscious desire to reproduce, thereby passing on the unique assortment of genetic material that makes each of us different. The biological purpose of beauty is to attract others of our species for sex. Sex, at least for humans, is usually enjoyable, but its biological purpose is not fun but reproduction. Many animals go far beyond fisticuffs to become more attractive to the opposite sex. Take, for example, the male zebra finch. Because nine out of ten female zebra finches swoon over red-beaked males and may even act like birdbrains for the one with the reddest beak, males cultivate red beaks. How? By ingesting fruits and vegetables such as carrots and tomatoes with the orange and red pigments called carotenoids. As it happens, zebra finches who eat the most carotenoids, which neutralize harmful free radicals and stimulate the immune system, are also the healthiest birds on their branch, proving that once again, Mom was right: If you want to grow up healthy and become a babe magnet, eat your veggies.[2]

If beauty attracts, a healthy, youthful appearance is attractive because it signifies reproductive capability. Men are attracted to younger women because their youth signifies this potential. Women's attraction to slightly older men rests on the assumption that an older man may have more resources to offer her children, enhancing the possibility that they will survive long enough to reproduce themselves.

But biologically speaking, not all men and all women are created equal. Some worry that if they are not attractive enough, no one will want to mate with them. They will not be able to pass along their genes or will not attract a mate capable of nurturing and supporting their children. All this stimulates competitiveness; women compete with one another to attract the best men, while men compete for positions of power and dominance in order to enhance their ability to attract the most beautiful women.[3]

While individual preferences vary, people generally agree about what is attractive in others; if that were otherwise, then the nature of the faces that regularly appear on magazine covers would vary far more widely than it does, and motion picture and television casting directors would rarely require photos before auditioning candidates. But is there an absolute standard by which human beauty can be measured?

The Romans thought so. Their culture, which borrowed liberally from their Greek predecessors, understood the power of PA, but the Romans, at least in their literature, preferred to deal at greater length with the ramifications of its absence. That is to say, while Roman poetry, plays, and polemics abound with passages describing physical appearance, they are almost invariably detailed portraits of people who *lack* physical attractiveness. In other words, uglies.

To contemporary scholars of Roman letters, the Roman ideal of PA was "absence of physical blemishes or flaws" and "a harmonious relationship of parts to the whole."[4] The notion that human beauty is the absence of flaws rather than the presence of attractive features was noted long ago by Cicero (106–43 B.C.). In *The Nature of the Gods,* he concluded that when gods assume the human form, they should be free of blemishes. That being the case, however, they might appear identical to each other. This implies a standard of perfect beauty, where ugliness is measured by how far one departs from this standard.[5]

There might be something to that.

Meet Dr. Stephen Marquardt, a Southern California physician with a specialty in oral and maxillofacial surgery. After some twenty-seven years of surgical practice and teaching at UCLA, he established Marquardt Beauty Analysis, a foundation devoted "to proactively researching human visual aesthetics, including its biological and mathematical bases, and to utilizing the results of that research to develop and provide information and technology with which to analyze and positively modify (i.e., improve) human visual attractiveness." And lots more, about which we will learn later in this book. In short, Marquardt is using science and surgery to make America more beautiful.

So far, he seems to be succeeding, if only by becoming the media's go-to guy on the subject of facial beauty. Marquardt has appeared on dozens of network news and science programs, and his research has been cited in scores of newspaper and magazine articles.

His hands-on, beauty-is-a-quantifiable-property approach has even become the basis for at least one reality TV show, ABC's *Extreme Makeover,* during which men and women undergo a series of cosmetic surgeries designed to radically improve their appearance.

The gist of Marquardt's findings: Human beings find the greatest beauty in symmetry. More intriguingly, Marquardt argues that the basis of the ideal face is a mathematical concept called "phi" that expresses itself both throughout the natural world and in the manifold works of man.

Marquardt's research posits the existence of the "Golden Ratio" of 1.618:1; by itself the number 1.618 is called "phi." The ratio itself has been known by many names, including the Phi Ratio, the Fibonacci Ratio, the Divine Ratio, the Golden Mean, and the Golden Section. By incorporating the phi ratio in some way in triangles, pentagons, and other polygons (two-dimensional figures with more than four angles and sides) and then using these polygons in multiple to assemble progressively more complex geometric shapes, Marquardt has compiled an amazingly sophisticated variety of shapes based on phi components.

He's found these same shapes (and their component ratios) not only in attractive and/or utilitarian man-made objects and famous paintings, but, of course, in the human form. Most intriguingly, the ultimate geometric shape formed by Marquardt's phi-based polygons, which he dubbed the "Golden Decagon Matrix," neatly replicates the exact molecular configuration of the most common form of DNA—the building block of not only human biology but virtually all life forms on earth! Marquardt believes that this is proof that beauty is a biologically programmed component of all life.

Next, by applying mathematics to thousands of faces that neutral observers have deemed "attractive," Marquardt and his researchers constructed a massive database that depicts attractive human faces as collections of phi-based geometric shapes. From this database have come an assortment of patented masks that may be used as templates for comparative diagnosis of facial qualities and, more important, as the basis for cosmetic surgery, which is Marquardt's passion.[6]

If the secrets of facial beauty have yielded to scientific inquiry, what about the rest of the physique? Is there an objective standard for bodily beauty in both men and women?

Ask a group of healthy young men what configuration of a woman's body most attracts them and most would agree that the hourglass figure—a slender waist separating large breasts from generous hips—would fill the bill. And ask a similar number of healthy young women about male bodies and most will agree that the holy trinity is big, balanced (symmetrical), and properly built with a waist-to-hip ratio of about 0.9, which is to say, a hip circumference only slightly larger than waist diameter.[7] According to anthropologist Laura Betzig, like all animals, we humans are programmed to recognize the shape of health: Large, symmetrical, and proportioned humans are usually healthier than those with other shapes.[8]

Moreover, Dr. Peter Ellison, dean of Harvard University's Graduate School of Arts and Sciences and professor of anthropology and an authority on human sexual hormones, has demonstrated a correlation between a woman's hourglass figure and her reproductive ability.[9] Or, as the tabloids put it when this discovery was announced, "Voluptuously endowed ladies are designed by nature for motherhood."

Could it be because women with narrow waists and large bustlines that accentuate the hips are more fertile than women otherwise endowed, and because of higher levels of certain hormones in their bodies, they are almost three times as likely to become pregnant following a single episode of sexual intercourse?

Ellison collaborated in an international study led by Grazyna Jasienska of Jagiellonian University in Krakow, Poland. Her team took measurements from 119 Polish women between the ages of twenty-four and thirty-seven. In particular, her researchers recorded each breast-to-under-breast ratio and waist-to-hip ratio.

High breast-to-under-breast ratios belong to women with large breasts. The three other categories of body shapes used in this study were 1) narrow waist/small breasts, 2) broad waist/large breasts, and 3) broad waist/small breasts.

Jasienska found that compared to the average of all women in the study, the blood of women with both large breasts and a small waist averaged 26 percent more 17b-estradiol (estrogen) during their entire menstrual cycle and 37 percent more during midcycle peak fertility days. These women also had more progesterone than women in all other categories.

According to Jasienska, the presence of larger concentrations of these hormones means that women with large breasts and a small waist are about three times more likely to get pregnant than women of other shapes!

Evolutionary biologists use the term "adaptive" to describe factors that contribute to greater reproductive success. Thus, if most men prefer women with large breasts and a small waist, and if such women *also* have more children than other women, then science concludes that this preference may have arisen for biological, evolutionary reasons.[10]

Therefore, if men subconsciously seek sexual partners with whom they are most likely to reproduce, the preference for big-busted, large-hipped women has probably evolved over thousands of generations.

This study also confirms what the marketing staff at toy maker Mattel, Inc. has known since 1959, when the Barbie doll first hit the market. Soon after introducing Barbie to the world, Mattel became the target of accusations that it was propagating an unwelcome, unrealistic, male-fantasy image of women. More than a billion Barbies later, however, the company can point to Jasienska's research as a reason to continue marketing the doll: Barbie's proportions, while atypical, are pretty much those of the woman most men would like to bear their children.

> Barbie's proportions, while atypical, are pretty much those of the woman most men would like to bear their children.

Not far from Barbie's home in Southern California are the studios of another industry that has long understood that even men who don't know what "adaptive" means are nevertheless attracted to voluptuous females.

When film directors cast such shapely sirens as Marilyn Monroe, Jane Russell, and Sophia Loren, millions of men paid to watch them on the screen. For the same reason, current male moviegoers and television watchers eagerly watch the likes of Jennifer Lopez, Kelly Brook, and Salma Hayek.

But not every woman can be big busted and narrow waisted, and so nature has developed another strategy to help women attract mates.

For example, a 2003 study led by Dr. Craig Roberts, a researcher at the United Kingdom's University of Newcastle, showed that no matter how plain or lovely it may appear at other times, a woman's face is most beautiful and alluring once a month—exactly when she is at the peak of her fertility.

Roberts and his researchers selected some fifty women between the ages of nineteen and thirty-three and took two photographs of each. The first depicted the woman's face eight to fourteen days after the first day of her menstruation cycle, the very time when she was probably most fertile. Two weeks later a second photo was taken. These photo pairs were viewed by 250 men and women, who were then asked to choose the image that showed the woman at her most attractive. Pictures of fertile women were chosen more often—and the 125 female viewers were more sensitive to fertility than the 125 male viewers.[11]

The idea that women are sensitive to other women's cycles is not new. Since the origin of our species, this sensitivity has allowed females to assess their competitors when vying for the attention of males, even if they aren't fully conscious of it.

A related study conducted by Ian Penton-Voak, a lecturer in the department of psychology at the University of Stirling in England, showed that women prefer masculine-looking men when they are ovulating; but at other times of the month, they seek men with the softer features, associated with more social and caring behavior.[12]

If nature has stacked the deck in favor of well-proportioned bodies and symmetrical facial features closely adhering to the Golden Ratio, one might expect that over the thousands of generations in which we humans have propagated our species, most of us should be quite beautiful. Indeed, many of us are. But somehow, quite a few men and women who would never consider entering a beauty contest or pursuing careers in modeling nevertheless seem to be multiplying and making themselves fruitful.

That's because, not long after nature invented mankind, mankind—or perhaps womankind—invented clothes. And cosmetics.

Long before the Romans renamed the pantheon of Greek gods with Latin titles, before even the Golden Age of Greece, Egypt had developed a complex and sophisticated civilization. According to noted author and Egyptologist Joann Fletcher, clothing, wigs, and cosmetics were "employed by the ancient Egyptians as a means of display, social control, and identity, used for their erotic impact and ritual significance as well as their effect on the economy."[13]

Fletcher, who is credited with identifying a previously anonymous mummy as possibly that of Queen Nefertiti (the subject of a Discovery Channel program), cites an abundance of archaeological evidence to show that in ancient Egypt "elaborate hairstyles [including wigs, hair extensions, and false braids], heavy cosmetics, and strong perfumes were worn by both men and women of all ages and social groupings for a wide variety of reasons, not least their practical and often therapeutic value."

The earliest known cosmetics date from about 3100–2907 B.C. Tombs of Egypt's first dynasty contained unguent jars; objects retrieved from later tombs suggest that these unguents were scented. Such preparations, as well as perfumed oils, were extensively used by both men and women to keep the skin supple and unwrinkled. Egyptian women also developed the art of eye decoration; they applied dark green color to the lower lid and blackened the lashes and upper lid with kohl, a preparation made from antimony or soot. References to painted faces appear in the Hebrew Bible, suggesting that the ancient Jews may have borrowed this custom from their neighbors to the south. By the Christian era, cosmetics were used by women throughout the Roman Empire. In addition to darkening lashes and brows and outlining the eyelids, women reddened their cheeks with rouge and dusted white powder on the skin to simulate or heighten fairness.

But why would a woman paint her face?

Perhaps because accentuating the eyes and tinting her cheeks makes a woman's face more closely resemble the coloring Mother Nature provides at the peak of the fertility cycle. In other words, a woman may compete for male attention with those whose beauty has been temporarily enhanced through the hormonal changes that accompany ovulation. Accenting the face with makeup also provides an approximation of the hue women display when sexually stimulated.

Greek mythology and Homeric literature include passages describing women who used not only cosmetics but also clothing, accessories, and jewelry to enhance their ability to attract men. Helen of Troy, no less than the goddesses Aphrodite and Hera, enhanced her natural beauty with dresses, veils, necklaces, arm rings, and belts in pursuit of the seduction of both man and god. In legend as in literature, these female costumes excite admiration and desire; such scenes sometimes are followed by the immediate fulfillment of desire through sexual intercourse.[14]

• • •

The PA phenomenon in antiquity was not limited to the West. While European and African women were using cosmetics as part of their strategies for attracting men, Asian women were similarly interested in maximizing their physical appeal to attract men.

> A woman's face is most beautiful and alluring once a month—exactly when she is at the peak of her fertility.

That Chinese women in ancient eras took the time and trouble to make themselves more physically attractive is widely documented; the Confucian scholar Liu Xiang (ca. 77–76 B.C.) wrote that "[she] takes delight in one's appearance." During the Han dynasty (206 B.C.–8 A.D.), when male-dominated Confucianism established itself as the central ideology of governance, Chinese history records the triumph of a slim, agile, vivacious, and beautiful dancer named Chao Fei-yen who caught the eye of Emperor Ch'en-ti. While she became his concubine, Chao refused to be subservient to any man, even an emperor. Supported by her equally beautiful sister, Chao Hede, she wielded her beauty as a sword against Ch'en-ti, winning the support of powerful courtiers and throwing the palace into a chaotic power struggle. Although the Chao sisters failed to overthrow the ruler, their actions vividly illustrate that the ancient Chinese understood the power of PA.

In fact, to discourage further attempts by women to use their beauty as a way to assert independence of thought and action, the Confucians sought to promote dignity and moral virtue as more admirable traits than feminine beauty. Compiled by Liu Xiang, the *Lienu zhuan* purports to be a biographical compendium of 125 exemplary women. But the book is more polemic than historical, because Liu's text warns women against using their beauty to gain power and argues that external physical beauty is merely a manifestation of internal virtue, defined as adherence to traditional, male-dominated values. To demonstrate the virtues of obedience, several biographies describe several physically unattractive women who nevertheless became empress as a result of inner qualities. Women lacking such virtue are described as schemers who seek to entrap men in sensual pleasures in order to distract them and then fulfill their own selfish plans. Such women, the book concludes, cause disruption in families and contribute to the decay and failure of a state.[15]

Given the biological imperative to reproduce that fuels the PA phenomenon, it's no surprise that over the millennia men and women have learned how to use beauty for personal advantage, and that these techniques have been handed down, generation by generation, as part of the larger culture. And most of us learn how to play the game very early in life.

CHAPTER 2

Pass the Genes, Please: How Looks Drive Dating, Courtship, and Marriage

*The often strange ways that PA drives
social intercourse*

"Never judge a book by its cover."
"Beauty is only skin deep."
"Beauty is in the eye of the beholder."

These maxims, each a comment on the superficiality and subjectivity of physical attractiveness, are ingrained in Western culture and often expressed in literature. Scientific research, however, shows that they are purely myths.[1]

Dr. Judith Langlois, a University of Texas psychologist who has devoted her career to infant research, directs the Langlois Social Development Lab in the Department of Psychology at UT's Austin campus. Her landmark studies show that the polar opposites of these hoary adages are far closer to fact.

Langlois's studies suggest that people *do* agree about who is and isn't attractive, both within and across ethnicity and culture. Beauty is therefore *not* merely in the eye of the beholder. And as we saw in the previous chapter, there are almost certainly universal standards of physical attractiveness.

But do we really never judge a book by its cover?

Were that literally the case, then the work of dozens of art departments and the often brilliant marketing on behalf of the upwards of 55,000 mass-market books published annually in the United States is wasted effort. Clearly it is not! While people buy books for many reasons, a good title and an interesting cover or jacket may strongly influence the buying decision.

However, let's use the statement as the metaphor it was probably intended to convey. In that case, when it comes to deciding about people and their personal qualities, studies show that attractive adults and children are usually judged more favorably and treated more positively than are unattractive adults and children, *even by those who know them.*[2]

And that is—surprise, surprise—because even though both attractive and unattractive people "exhibit positive behaviors and traits, *attractive* people exhibit *more* positive behaviors and traits than unattractive individuals." Beauty, it turns out, goes deeper than skin, hair, and clothes.[3] Beauty is, as Forrest Gump's mom might say, as beauty does.

But this chapter is about dating, so let's slip into some fancy threads, get ourselves all gussied up, and step out into the wild world of one-on-one social intercourse.

The leading predictor in determining whether two people will have a relationship of any sort is spatial contact, also called *proximity* or *propinquity.* That is to say, they must somehow meet, usually often, before they can connect.[4]

Until the twilight of the twentieth century, meeting a possible mate was almost always a face-to-face activity. Even when helpful friends and relatives made introductions and even if a telephone conversation might precede an actual meeting, there was little chance for a meeting of minds, much less emotional engagement, until that face-to-face meeting.

Additional ways evolved to help the mate-minded. Early on, so-called marriage brokers peddled "picture brides" of women living overseas who were willing to come halfway around the globe to marry a man they didn't know in exchange for the chance to live in this new world. Following the disintegration of the Soviet Union in 1989, thousands of Eastern European women sought to become picture brides for an American husband, and many did so.

Not all picture brides were volunteers. Some were forced into the arrangement by desperately poor families hoping to make a little money from the transaction; given their economic circumstances, few picture brides had viable options.

In recent years, however, the rise of the Internet has led to dating services that connect millions of people with others with whom they probably would never have met otherwise. The picture brides of former times have morphed into the online avatars of Web dating sites.

In the first half of 2003, Americans spent $214.3 million on personal ads and online dating, which by 2003 had become the most lucrative form of legal paid online content. In a single month during 2003, 40 million Americans visited at least one online dating site, more than a fourth of all Internet users for that month. They browsed popular sites such as Yahoo! Personals and Match.com, which boasts 12 million users worldwide, as well as far more modest sites focused on ethnic or religious groups or designed to serve those with a strong interest in a particular activity, such as pets, physical fitness, politics, or astrology. A social networking site dubbed Friendster, which encourages people to meet through their mutual friends, claims over 3 million members.[5]

> While shared values and common life goals are important, by far the most important factor is what can be gleaned from the picture accompanying the person's online profile.

Novelist Jennifer Egan, writing about this phenomenon for *The New York Times Magazine,* interviewed dozens of online daters, men and women of all ages. Online dating resembles online shopping in that it involves browsing descriptions or profiles of a seemingly infinite number of possible mates and choosing the few that seem best suited for one's dating goal, whether that's a pal, a lifelong mate, a short-term sexual fling, or something in between. Those who browse are also browsed. The successful online dater strives to write a succinct yet compelling narrative that puts the individual's personal qualities and life experiences in the most favorable possible light.

Egan concluded, however, that while shared values and common life goals are important to those seeking a long-term relationship, by far the most important factor in deciding whether to meet another person face-to-face is what can be gleaned from the picture accompanying the person's online profile. In other words, PA.

"Dating profiles are works in progress," writes Egan, "continually edited and tweaked, fortified with newer, more flattering pictures." Because an inviting photo is so crucial, photographers in major cities have begun to specialize in creating sexy personal profile pictures, usually at rates comparable to those paid for wedding photos. Those who can't afford to hire a professional expend much time and effort in do-it-yourself photography, "trying to take sexy pictures of myself," writes one of Egan's *Times* interviewees. "The good ones have produced lots of responses," he adds.[6]

Even so, online daters often discover that the photo they fell in love with, like the carefully written profile that it accompanies, doesn't tell the whole story. "Most online daters have at least one cranky tale of meeting a date who was shorter or fatter or balder or generally less comely than advertised," writes Egan. She also found that by dropping a year or two off her age, "a forty-year-old woman will appear in many more men's searches." That's because with so many profiles available, screening for the ones that interest a particular browser means making arbitrary choices of such personal descriptors as age, height, and weight. Thus, a man who is, say, five feet ten inches might decide to call himself six feet in hopes of getting past the invisible barrier that transforms a man of average height into a shorty.[7]

> Online daters often discover that the photo they fell in love with, like the carefully written profile that it accompanies, doesn't tell the whole story.

Even if millions of Americans experiment with online dating, the vast majority of us still meet people the old-fashioned way: face-to-face. The first letter of one's family name, if it becomes the basis of, for example, a classroom seating chart, college dorm room assignment, or military transport slot, is an example of how arbitrary determinants give individuals opportunities to meet each other. One classic study of how people meet and make friends was done at the Massachusetts Institute of Technology (Festinger, Schachter, and Back, 1950). According to this study, 65 percent of groups of three closest friends lived in the same building, while 41 percent were next-door neighbors, 22 percent resided only two doors apart, and only 10 percent lived at opposite ends of a hallway.

So it should be no surprise that until 1917, when the United States sent legions of young men to France to fight in World War I, most people who married in this country found a mate among schoolmates, in their small town or city neighborhood, or within their own religious community.

The war changed all that. Some 2 million American soldiers served in Europe, most of them in France. A substantial fraction remained after the war ended to serve as occupation troops in Germany. At least 10 million French, British, German, Dutch, Italian, Russian, and other Europeans, a majority of them young men, died during the war. Many of the women they left behind found husbands among the soldiers of the American Expeditionary Force.

In 1919, songwriter Arthur Fields penned "How 'Ya Gonna Keep 'Em Down on the Farm (After They've Seen Paree)," a popular ditty that took note of the fact that America's returning soldiers, having been exposed to European culture and sophistication, often chose not to make their postwar lives in the rural communities of their birth or childhood. To put it another way, after the Great War, millions of former farm boys moved to the city. So did millions of farmer's daughters, not only to find work in the nation's burgeoning factories and offices, but also in search of an independent life, where they were free to marry whom they chose—or not at all.

America's participation in World War I changed the nation in many ways. In only a few years, the United States made the leap from a sleepy, largely agricultural, developing nation to an industrialized world power. American businesses, great and small, long established and newly formed, prospered during this war; the decade following World War I was a time of rapidly expanding prosperity.

In 1920, American women won the right to vote, and although

this franchise fell far short of full equality with men, it underpinned a heady and liberating time for young American women. This was the era of Clara Bow, the rags-to-riches silent film beauty known as the "It Girl." Foreshadowing the 1960s, the young of the Roaring Twenties staked out new frontiers in personal and especially sexual liberty, throwing off many of the puritanical prohibitions of their forebears.

As America's standard of living increased and its cities boomed, mass media blossomed as never before. Thousands of new theaters offered feature films; network radio became a national phenomenon; and rafts of slick, four-color magazines, all subsidized by the explosive growth of advertising, relentlessly promoted the ideals of beauty, youth, and thinness. The cosmetics industry boomed as never before.

This brings us to the so-called Coolidge effect, named, perhaps in jest, for President Calvin Coolidge, who occupied the White House from 1923 to 1929, just as America was beginning to throw off its puritanical bonds. According to a possibly apocryphal tale, there came a time when President Coolidge and his wife visited a chicken farm. While the president was in another part of the property, a farmer showed Mrs. Coolidge a rooster that, he said, could copulate with a hen all day long, every day.

"Tell that to the president," she told the farmer, who dutifully conveyed this information to Coolidge.

"With the *same* hen?" responded the famously taciturn chief executive.

"No, sir," replied the farmer. "With *different* ones."

"Tell *that* to Mrs. Coolidge," returned the president.[8]

Thus the First Couple learned that males are usually more excited by sexual novelty than are females, a phenomenon confirmed through experiments with several different species. For example, a male rat put into a cage with a previously unknown female rat usually begins their relationship with a frenzy of copulation. After a while, however, the male rat loses interest in sex. Indeed, it is often very difficult to persuade it to copulate with the female. But when a *different* female is put in the cage, the male reverts to stud behavior and again avidly engages in copulation—but again, only for a time. If this process is repeated with new females, the male will continue to copulate until it is totally exhausted, and often even beyond that.[9]

Rats are mammals. Humans are mammals. Does this mean that men are rats?

Judging by their behavior toward women, *some* men clearly are much like rats. But even *they* are merely behaving as male *Homo sapiens*, a species whose psychological sexual preferences and reproductive strategy evolved over many millennia.

Consider the phenomenon of human sexual success strategies as discussed in "Theory of Parental Investment," by Robert Trivers, which notes that while females require only a few matings to fertilize all their available eggs, males can potentially fertilize more eggs than any one female can produce. A female's reproductive success is therefore limited by her access to resources to nourish each of her eggs; male reproductive success is limited by his access to a female's eggs. The difference between male and female mating strategies, then, as perceived by the parents of healthy teenagers, is that while their daughter may become pregnant by the boy next door, their son might well impregnate every girl in the neighborhood.[10]

Is that why so many women support Planned Parenthood and so many men don't?

Well, no. The reason that men of many societies often seem obsessed with impregnating their women is entangled with the history of human evolution.

Until comparatively recent times, we humans competed for day-to-day survival with a host of lethal carnivores, and more than occasionally served as prey for the largest. When climatic conditions or other factors made food scarce—a frequent occurrence for hunter-gatherers—tribes, clans, and individuals competed or warred against each other for survival. In such instances, the young were especially vulnerable. Many starved. Others were killed.

Moreover, until the early twentieth century—a blink of the eye in terms of evolutionary development—when the introduction of antiseptics sharply reduced the risk of infection and the first vaccines were deployed against a multitude of childhood illnesses, women often died in childbirth and many children succumbed to disease or infection long before they reached adulthood.

Accordingly, the Coolidge effect probably became part of human male behavior because impregnating as many females as possible increases the probability that some children, at least, will survive long enough to reproduce themselves. As humans evolved, those men who impregnated more females were more likely to pass on their genes to offspring that survived. Females of our species, however, comport themselves according to a different set of biological imperatives. While they also seek to pass along their genes, once pregnant, the female's goal is to nurture the new life growing inside her. After a baby is born, the mother's agenda is to protect and assist the child until it becomes self-sufficient. This was usually possible only with help from her mate, and so until comparatively recent times, a father who abandoned a wife and child probably doomed one or both to death by starvation. Women of childbearing age are therefore biologically programmed to seek potential mates who will help protect and support their children.[11]

The major difference between the sexual strategies of men and women, then, is that women demand stability and commitment in a relationship, whereas men prefer variety.

> Women demand stability and commitment in a relationship, whereas men prefer variety.

This returns us to the Coolidge effect. If males are programmed to prefer sexual variety, women, who compete with one another for what they hope are loyal and monogamous mates, have been smart enough to find ways to *simulate* that variety by frequently changing their appearance. Using cosmetics to alter or enhance facial features; shortening or lengthening their hair and changing its color; dressing in a different style; accessorizing with jewelry, scarves, hats, and so forth—each technique introduces an element of "newness" into the equation and appeals to the innate male desire for novelty.

But is this a conscious choice? Are women whose dress impresses men with their sexual qualities aware of the effect of their wardrobe choices on men?

To find out, two professors, Ed Edmonds and Delwin Cahoon,

created a study involving forty-four men and eighty-nine women. These college students rated forty pictures of women's apparel in terms of the extent to which they felt men would be sexually aroused by women wearing them. One conclusion: "Females were very knowledgeable concerning the sexual impact of clothing styles on men." Moreover, a second phase of this study showed that women who perceived themselves as "sexually attractive" displayed a marked preference for clothes that men judged to be the most sexually exciting. In other words, women interested in attracting men will dress in ways calculated to excite them.[12]

If the Coolidge effect helps explain why men are attracted to women whose attractive appearance varies, often the "contrast effect" confirms what many people consider their most important high school lesson: If you're an average Joe trying to put the moves on that cute girl in history class, don't do your number while in the company of your handsome, muscular pals from the varsity football squad.

Or, as one research study put it, "When viewed in conjunction with highly attractive others, a person of average attractiveness may be judged less attractive than had the person been evaluated without an immediate comparison group."[13] That holds true even when a person of average or ordinary attractiveness is viewed with people whom everyone would expect to be gorgeous, such as a mob of movie stars or a squad of supermodels.[14]

The contrast effect, moreover, also applies to *self*-evaluation. A man of moderate attractiveness who works, for example, in the fashion industry, and is frequently in the presence of those whose PA is both their livelihood and their identity, will often feel that he is less attractive than he actually is. But the reverse is also true: Comparing himself to less attractive men boosts his ego and makes him feel more attractive.[15]

But it's not just about feeling attractive or unattractive. The contrast effect also influences self-esteem, which is linked to increased or decreased public self-consciousness and heightened social anxiety. In America's PA-shaped cosmos, you *are* as you *believe* you look. And if you are, for example, someone who strongly believes that thin is *in*, but fat is where *you're* at, then merely being exposed to pictures of people of your own gender with an idealized physique can lead to feelings of anxiety and loss of self-esteem. It could even propel you into a depressed state.[16]

Being highly aware of one's PA, whether high or low, may lead to *public* self-consciousness, which is to say a frequent concern with oneself as an object of attention by others. This in turn usually means that such people have more concern for, and are more responsive to, what they believe are the criteria by which others judge their behavior and personal attributes. This differs from *private* self-consciousness, a predisposition to consider only one's own motives, thoughts, and feelings.

According to at least one study, people with public self-consciousness seem to be far more aware of their own PA than others who are less self-conscious—and they will therefore respond more quickly to the ways others judge their appearance. This same study concluded that the *publicly* self-conscious are seen by others as having more PA than those who are less publicly self-conscious, which might simply reflect that this group expends more time and energy enhancing PA.[17]

So, if you're very aware of how other people may judge your appearance, and most of those other people think you're highly attractive, are *you* also aware of their perceptions? Probably not. Several studies designed to answer just that question found no corresponding relationship between people's level of public self-consciousness and their evaluation of their own physical attractiveness.[18]

Some studies conclude that the tendency for those with high public self-consciousness to be more highly invested in their appearance means that they hold themselves to an unreasonably high PA standard. In short, they work hard to stay attractive and often succeed, but that effort does little to ease their deep concerns over their own looks.[19]

PA's significance to interpersonal reactions and to development of the concept of "self" has been noted in many other studies. More to the point, in the world of dating, the cultural emphasis is on not only PA, but the concept that the ideal *female* body is thin. Thus, the contrast effect probably is of most relevance to women.[20]

• • •

Regardless of how involved with one's own appearance a person is, and despite frequent lip service to such factors as personality, intelligence, a sense of humor, and shared interests, a multitude of studies show that PA is by far the most important factor in evaluating both prospective mates and prospective dates.[21] This conclusion was graphically demonstrated in a landmark 1966 experiment conducted at the University of Minnesota in Minneapolis.

A team of social psychologists rounded up 664 student volunteers and asked them to participate in a "computer dance" where their partner of the evening would be selected by a computer. In reality, the partners were matched randomly with a single constraint: Researchers ensured that each man was taller than his female partner.

At intermission, the band took a break and rating forms were passed around. Participants answered questions, such as how much they liked their date, how eager they were to ask the person out again, how attractive they found their date, how attractive they thought their date found them, and so forth.

The researchers wanted to see if the dates' rated physical attractiveness corresponded to how much their partner liked them. The researchers' starting hypothesis was that if personality, intelligence, and other qualities are indeed important, then the linkage of ratings of physical attractiveness to "liking the person" should not be high.

In fact, however, men placed significant importance on PA, as shown by a very high correlation—78 percent—between how attractive male participants rated their date and how much they liked her. For women the correlation was only slightly lower: 69 percent.

While the researchers had anticipated there would be some importance for PA, they were surprised that other factors, which they considered nearly as important, actually mattered so little. For example, the experimenters knew how each subject had ranked in high school and used this as a measure of relative intelligence. Although typical student subjects said that they wanted dates that were intelligent, in reality students' smarts had no correlation at all with how well their dates liked them.

The researchers had also expected that the partners of students with introverted personalities would not like them very much as future dates. Wrong again! Data from the "computer dance" experiment showed that there was no difference between introverted and extroverted personalities when it came to being liked by a date. What mattered was how pretty or handsome the other person was.

The conclusion of this seminal study: The only thing that seemed to matter to these young college students was the physical attractiveness of their date.[22]

In the previous chapter we saw that some standards of feminine and masculine appearance are accepted by nearly everyone in our culture as idealizing physical attractiveness. It is obvious, however, that few people ever attain such perfection or anything close to it. For most of us, PA is less definable, a mixture of what our eyes tell us and what our brain computes. But many aspects of PA have been studied, and it is now possible to say, with some precision, that when it comes to selecting a mate, certain elements of appearance usually attract men to women and vice versa.

Casual, unscientific perusal of personals ads—also called "lonely hearts advertisements" or, in their newest incarnation, Internet dating profiles—reveals that women are most concerned about a potential husband's *height,* while men express the most concern over the *weight* of any possible bride. In other words, men even an inch under average height and women more than twenty pounds overweight may have a tougher time getting a date.

Both preferences are confirmed by scientific studies. In a published study on responses to lonely hearts advertisements and the effects of reported physical attractiveness, Lynn and Shurgot reported that a female's height did not influence the responses she received from her ad, but those who described themselves as slender received more replies. Tall males with dark hair received more replies than did shorter males with lighter hair.[23]

More recently, Daniel Nettle, who divides his time between the departments of biological sciences and psychology at the U.K.'s Open University, studied contemporary populations. He concluded that "tall men have greater reproductive success than shorter men . . . due to their greater ability to attract mates."

Nettle also studied data from Britain's National Child Development Study to examine the life histories of a large, representative sample of U.K. women. These data showed that extremely tall and extremely short women have a high incidence of poor health that affects fertility and childbearing; women between these extremes bore the most children. But the data also showed that "maximum reproductive success was found below the mean height for women." In other words, natural selection of mates favors women selecting tall men and men hooking up with shorter women.[24]

This is probably not news to those who have sweated out an apprenticeship in bodybuilding, but perhaps because of mankind's long evolutionary development as a hunter, women find men with *moderately* developed torsos the most attractive. In several studies featuring silhouettes of differently shaped male torsos, women showed a strong preference for a shape consistent with the ideal hunting physique: strong shoulders, suggesting good throwing ability, but not too much muscle mass, an excess of which negatively affects endurance.[25]

In one study, thirty women were asked to rate the attractiveness of men in color pictures. Each male figure was prerated for its waist-to-chest ratio, waist-to-hip ratio, and body mass index. Waist-to-chest ratio was the principal determinant of attractiveness: Males with narrow waists and a broad chest and shoulders were rated as being more attractive. A more recent 2003 study spotlights a payoff for hours spent in the gym: Men with higher shoulder-to-hip ratios reported having sex at an earlier age and with more sexual partners.[26]

If muscles are not in your present or future, think facial hair. After grooming annual data on British beard fashions between 1842 and 1971, researcher Nigel Barber concluded, in part, that women perceive men with beards as having "the biological and social qualities that would enhance their value as husbands" and also consider them "more potent and more active, suggesting virility as well as physical attractiveness."

Barber cited other studies that concluded that *female* managers, unlike their *male* managerial counterparts, considered bearded men to be more competent. That's right. Female bosses expect the bearded dude to handle things better, while male bosses are unimpressed with another man's facial foliage.

Barber's original research concluded that men have long used facial hair as a way to increase physical attractiveness, especially when they must compete for a limited number of women. "Mustaches and facial hair in general are more frequent when there is a good supply of single men of marriageable age," he wrote. That is to say, when there's lots of competition for wives, men grow beards and mustaches to give them an extra edge.

But what about times when there are more available women than unmarried men? Barber correlated data on out-of-wedlock births with facial hair fashions and concluded that men seemed far less enamored of cultivating mustaches and beards during periods when illegitimate birthrates soared, implying a surplus of possible brides and a shortage of grooms.[27]

A venerable stereotype of American fiction, including novels, movies, and television, is the wealthy older man who marries a beautiful younger woman, the so-called trophy wife. Like many stereotypes, it is grounded in fact, because while physical attractiveness is important to women, as a group they are more willing to trade good looks for socioeconomic status.[28]

> While physical attractiveness is important to women, as a group they are more willing to trade good looks for socioeconomic status.

The basis of trophy wife syndrome is that men express their strong interest in PA by seeking to marry women at least five years their junior. But even with expensive skin and hair care and cosmetic surgery, every woman's PA fades with time—and so, in choosing a mate, the preferred age gap increases as men age.[29]

You're tall, you work out every day, you've got broad shoulders, a lean, manly waist, symmetrical features, and loads of thick, dark hair. Girls and women swoon at the mere sight of you, and even mature women are tongue-tied in your presence. You could be a movie star, but you have other priorities. Is it *inevitable* that the mother of your children will be a living Barbie, a large-breasted, small-waisted woman with womanly hips, long, thick hair, symmetrical features, and skin glowing with good health?

Actually, the mother of your children could be a woman who, by objective standards, has only average PA. Or less.

That's because the two sexes, as already discussed, pursue substantially different reproductive strategies. Women have evolved to seek husbands whose status and power will better provide for their children. So, while women care about men's looks, they don't choose the father of their children on that basis alone.

This conclusion is the fruit of several studies, including an amusing 1990 experiment by John Marshall Townsend and Gary D. Levy. A total of 382 college students, of whom 212 were female, viewed photographs prerated for physical attractiveness, where the ratings were "very attractive," "ordinary," and "only a mother could love that face." Women viewed photos of men, and men viewed photos of women. The photos were matched with three levels of occupational status and income: wealthy, average, and poor. The students were asked to indicate their willingness to engage in relationships of varying levels of sexual intimacy and marital potential with the people in the photos. After analyzing the results, researchers concluded that women are more likely to limit sexual intercourse to relationships involving affection and the possibility of marriage. Women also placed more emphasis than men do on their possible partners' socioeconomic status. Therefore, status, along with the willingness and ability to invest affection and resources in a relationship, often outweighs the effects of PA in a woman's selection of a partner.[30]

Or, as syndicated newspaper columnist Amy Alkon ("The Advice Goddess") put it, women "said they'd choose an ugly man wearing a Rolex over a handsome man in a Burger King uniform—no matter whether they were pairing up for the long haul or the short roll."[31] However, actions speak louder than words when looks actually enter the scene. People do in fact trade the appeal of a potential mate's greater finances for another possessing much greater PA. Examples abound. Of course, all this is influenced by the magnitude of these differences.

But what about choosing between a handsome jerk and a sensitive, average-looking fellow oozing sincerity and kindness—the classic nice guy? Which would most women choose?

Most average Joes will shake their heads knowingly. They've heard a lot of women say that they wish they could date kind, sensitive men—but when actually given that choice, they reject them in favor of a handsome devil with good clothes and a new car. In other words, nice guys always finish last.

But is it really so?

Several studies explore this stereotype. In one, four dozen women between the ages of eighteen and twenty-three (students at a private Northeastern college) read scripts depicting two men competing for a date with a woman in a setup much like a popular TV show, *The Dating Game.* In the script read by test subjects, "Susan" interviews "Todd" and "Michael" and is asked to choose which one to date based on the way they answer her questions. One male "candidate" was randomly assigned one of three conditions. "Nice Todd" gave responses that showed him to be kind, attentive, and emotionally expressive. "Middle Todd" gave more neutral responses, while "Jerk Todd" came off as an insensitive, self-absorbed, macho jerk. Regardless of how Todd acts, he is competing against Michael, whose middle-of-the-road responses are identical in all three conditions. Each female participant read only one version of Todd's responses, depending upon the condition to which she was assigned (the labels "Nice," "Middle," and "Jerk" were omitted). After reading the script, the students were asked to state which man (Todd or Michael) Susan should choose and whom they would choose for themselves.[32]

This study, however, ignored the PA dimension—nothing was said about how Todd or Michael looked. So the researchers undertook a second study, similar to the first. This study considered the responses of 194 young women students between the ages of eighteen and twenty-five from a large Southeastern public university. This time, however, in addition to the varying responses of "Todd" and the unchanging responses of "Michael," a supposed degree of physical attractiveness was presented.

For the PA dimension of the study, twenty female undergraduates who did not participate in the larger experiment rated photographs of men aged 18 to 25 for physical attractiveness. Based on their evaluations, three photos were selected: one of a man judged highly attractive and two rated similarly as having medium to low attractiveness.

In this second study, Todd's "niceness" was manipulated (just as it was in the first study), but participants also viewed photographs of both "Todd" and "Michael" in which Todd's PA also varied. The two photos of men of medium to low attractiveness represented Attractiveness Level One (matching PA); as in the earlier study, one character was called "Todd" and the other "Michael." The third photo, rated *high* in attractiveness, represented "Todd" at Attractiveness Level Two. Michael's photograph, like his responses, always remained the same.

This arrangement yielded six conditions in which "Todd's" attributes varied while "Michael's" remained the same:

1. Nice Todd—Matched Attractiveness

2. Neutral Todd—Matched Attractiveness

3. Jerk Todd—Matched Attractiveness

4. Nice Todd—Mismatched High Attractiveness

5. Neutral Todd—Mismatched High Attractiveness

6. Jerk Todd—Mismatched High Attractiveness

Each study participant was randomly assigned to read a script and view photos in one of these conditions.

While the overall results indicated that both niceness and physical attractiveness were positive factors in women's choices, as well as desirability ratings they assigned each man, the reasons women chose either man varied. When it came to evaluating a man's desirability for a serious relationship, one that could lead to marriage, "niceness" was the most important factor. But if the circumstances were that the woman sought primarily a casual, sexual relationship, PA won the day almost every time.[33]

So handsome jerks get to sow a lot of wild oats, but nice guys get married, have children, and live happily ever after.

Well, no. Researchers Geoffrey C. Urbaniak of Wesleyan University and Peter R. Kilmann of the University of South Carolina also noted a disconnect between what women report in research studies and what they actually do in real life.

> So handsome jerks get to sow a lot of wild oats, but nice guys get married, have children, and live happily ever after? Well, no.

PA was the most important factor in predicting desirability for both sexes, and men consistently acknowledged this fact. Women, however, "rated the desired level of relationship commitment as the most important factor that influenced their mate selection when, in fact, it was one of the least important factors behaviorally," the researchers wrote. "Women were more likely to express a preference for the nice guy if they, themselves, viewed sex as less important, had had fewer sexual partners, and preferred that their dating partners have fewer partners." In other words, despite expressed preferences, many women who participated in this and other such studies actually wanted nice guys only as friends or long-term boyfriends, but preferred "bad boys"—those more physically attractive and willing to manipulate women into sexual activity—as sexual partners.[34]

• • •

Fat or phat, tall or short, buff or puff, by the time men and women pass through puberty they are on the lookout for mating opportunities. Regardless of personal PA, however, and the differing agendas or reproductive strategies of male and female, each person brings a unique personality and outlook to the mix. Some people may be deficient in PA but nevertheless feel entitled to seek a mate of substantially higher PA. Others may reek of PA but remain oblivious to it. Still others may be aware of the effects of their own high PA but have psychological reasons for discounting it.[35]

In other words, there may be very attractive people who would be rated a "10" on a scale of physical attractiveness—where a "1" is Quasimodo (*The Hunchback of Notre Dame*) and a "5" is any of the people we pass in the street every day—and who, for an infinite variety of reasons, might settle for a "6" or even a "4." But why would a "4" believe that any "10" would accept them?

One possible answer lies in the concept of entitlement, which has been studied by Erich Goode.[36] An individual or members of some group or category may feel that they "have a right to certain privileges, that specific rewards should be forthcoming, that the re- sources they covet are rightfully theirs by virtue of what they have done or who they are." Thus, some men feel entitled to sex if they buy their date a nice meal or a few drinks. In decades past, more than a few women felt entitled to a marriage commitment after an exclusive dating relationship had lasted for some commonly agreed upon period of time—say, a year. In like manner, some people feel entitled to have an exclusive romantic relationship with a partner who has a certain value in the dating marketplace, even—or espe- cially—if the partner is far better looking than they are.

Entitlement, according to Goode, exists in two dimensions: There's subjective entitlement, or what the person who feels entitled expects, and objective entitlement, or what society or a given com- munity feels this person deserves. Whether these two dimensions agree with each other is largely a matter of the participants' cultural, social, and economic structures, which define notions of fairness and equity. Thus, for example, twenty-first-century America will toler- ate, albeit with some amusement, a rich but unattractive woman whose mate is considered handsome and virile but comes from a family of penniless immigrants. Each may feel entitled to the other, the man because of his good looks and the woman because of her wealth.

There is also a prestige factor to be gained in dating a physically attractive person. Men, especially, believe that they make a better impression on others by appearing in public with an especially at- tractive date than without one. This is an extension of what some social scientists term "the halo effect," when PA is generalized to other dimensions, such as social or intellectual skills. Research stud- ies strongly suggest that the halo effect makes an impression on perceived social and intellectual competence.[37]

But why would a highly attractive woman agree to date a less attractive man whom she suspects is using her beauty to enhance his social standing? For exactly the same reason: to gain access to a social circle to which she might otherwise not be admitted.

On the other side of the coin, sometimes highly attractive people prefer to date less attractive people. A "10" who wishes to be valued for less obvious qualities may seek dates with far less attractive women who offer the opportunity to display other qualities that transcend PA; in this scenario, a woman with high physical attractiveness might seem superficial.

Power also plays a role in a romantic relationship. In any sort of intimate coupling—parent and child, husband and wife, even close friends—the member of the couple who values the relationship least is in a position to control the other by threatening, either overtly or implicitly, to end the relationship. Thus, a child, lacking the maturity to understand the long-term ramifications, tries to manipulate a parent by withholding affection, and a parent, fearing to alienate the child, gives in to unreasonable demands.

In a romantic relationship, an extremely attractive person may exert power over his or her less-attractive partner by threatening to end the relationship. Those who are endowed with high PA sometimes seek less attractive mates precisely in order to exert that power. Less attractive people may attract more attractive mates by yielding to their whims. While such relationships may not endure, they frequently persist long enough to allow reproduction.

Conversely, less attractive people may avoid relationships with more attractive mates because they fear just such an outcome.

Another factor is availability, which is a factor of both location and chronology. If two people who might seem made for each other never meet, they will never become a couple. The group of possible dating partners for any one individual is called a "courtship pool." At any given time, this pool may or may not contain individuals of opposite sexes with correspondingly high PA. The value of members of a given dating pool to a given person, and that person's value to them, is relative to their numbers and desirability. If a particular pool includes many desirable dating partners, each member of the pool will evaluate any particular other member far more critically than if there are only a few desirable partners.[38]

There is also the issue of rejection, and the fear of it. Seeking to date partners whose PA is vastly greater than one's own is likely to elicit rejection. Similarly, despite high PA, people with low social status—a recent immigrant, for example, or someone with little education or an undesirable profession—may fear rejection by those of higher social status and seek dates with those of a social standing similar to their own. People make dating choices partly based on the probability of rejection. Thus, while most people would prefer to date very attractive others, because rejection is painful, they often choose someone of about their own PA level.[39]

. . .

If good looks are the leading basis for attraction in dating situations, where does that lead a couple whose looks have faded with time? Is PA as the means to launch a relationship a force strong enough to serve as the foundation for a lasting union of male and female?

> If good looks are the leading basis for attraction in dating situations, where does that lead a couple whose looks have faded with time?

"What need, when met, deposits the most love units in one's love bank?" asks Willard F. Harley, Jr., PhD, a psychologist and best-selling author. "If it's physical attractiveness, it should not be ignored," continues Harley. "For many, the need for physical attractiveness not only helps create a relationship, but it continues throughout marriage. Love units are deposited whenever the spouse is seen—*if* he or she is physically attractive."[40]

Some people say that they consider this need for physical attractiveness to be temporary and important only in the beginning of a relationship; others, according to Harley, suggest that those with a need for physical attractiveness are immature, spiritually weak, even lacking in human qualities. These might be the same people who quote Scripture as the answer to every human problem—and if so, good for them.

But Harley takes a dim view of those who denigrate the power of PA: "I don't judge important emotional needs, and I don't think you should, either. The question you should ask is, 'How can I learn how to be an attractive spouse?' "[41]

During Harley's years of counseling married couples, "almost all" complaints voiced about loss of PA were based on relative corpulence. "When diet and exercise bring a spouse back to a healthy size, physical attractiveness almost always returns," he says, with a nod also to choices in clothing, hairstyle, makeup, and personal hygiene.

To end as we began, when it comes to finding the perfect mate, judging the book by the cover is anything but a myth. One study delving into this very subject should be required reading for anyone contemplating marriage or divorce. The study tracks longitudinal changes in values that people consider important for their life partners. After examining data on mate preferences collected in 1939, 1967, 1977, 1984–1985, and 1996, researchers detected major shifts. Between 1939 and 1996, for example, "both sexes increased the importance they attach to physical attractiveness in a mate." Specifically, in 1939, men ranked PA fourteenth on a list of eighteen desirable mate characteristics but eighth in 1996. For the same period, women's value of a prospective husband's PA jumped from seventeenth place to thirteenth.

The study's analysts decided that they could not identify with certainty the reasons for this shift, but they point to "the surge in visual media—television, movies, Internet images, and virtual reality"—as a likely cause.

As PA's importance in choosing an ideal mate grew, the study also found "a general decrease in the valuation of refinement, neatness, and chastity, for both men and women." For these researchers, the sharp decline in chastity's value as a factor in mate selection—it ranked tenth for men in 1939 but sixteenth in 1996—was "one of the most striking cultural changes." Chastity fared no better in women's hierarchy of values: Ranked tenth in 1939, it was next to last—seventeenth—in 1996.

"Clearly, the cultural value attached to virginity has declined over the past 57 years," say the researchers, who attribute the change to the "increased dissemination of birth control devices and the . . . sexual revolution of the 1960s."

The study examined what we Americans value in a life partner, not what causes us to end a presumably lifelong commitment. But the findings require no great leap of suspicion to deduce the influential role of PA. It apparently serves to entice people to *read* the book and even to decide the value of the book's content along the way.[42]

CHAPTER 3

As the Twig Is Bent: How Physical Attractiveness Affects Family Dynamics

What smart parents know (or should know)
about PA

All babies are beautiful.

But some babies are more beautiful than others, especially to their mothers.

A University of Texas study observed mothers interacting with their firstborn infants. The researchers concluded that the mothers of more attractive babies are more affectionate toward their offspring and play with them more often and longer than do the mothers of less attractive infants. A second study by the same researchers concluded that while every mother they observed displayed excellent parenting skills, the mothers of less attractive infants perceived their child as interfering more in their lives than did the mothers of more attractive infants. In other words, even among good moms, the child's PA seems to influence maternal behavior.[1]

These observations help explain why audiences laugh when comedian Tom Smothers whines to his more handsome brother Dick, "Mom always liked you best." It resonates with dimly understood but deeply felt childhood experiences.

> Even among good moms, the child's PA seems to influence maternal behavior.

So, too, does the biblical story of twins Jacob and Esau. As recounted in Genesis 25:19–34, Esau, the older brother, came into the world covered with thick red hair, while Jacob was so ordinary looking as a baby that he is not described at all. Ladies and gentlemen, boys and girls, can anyone think of a small mammal that has two arms, two legs, and is covered with short red fur? It's not hard to see why most mothers would have found Jacob more pleasing to the eye than his simian-like sibling Esau.

When the boys grew up, Esau became a skillful hunter and outdoorsman, while the mild-mannered Jacob "dwelled in tents." Isaac, who had a taste for wild game, favored Esau, but their mother, Rebecca, favored the gentler Jacob. When the time came for Isaac to choose which of his sons would inherit the family business, Rebecca schemed to substitute Jacob for Esau.

Whether one believes that this is God's literal truth, a divinely inspired parable, or merely a story plucked from ancient literature, Rebecca's choice is clear: She liked Jacob best, and while Esau roamed the countryside in search of wild animals to kill, Jacob spent quality time with Mom. The mantle of family leadership passed to Jacob, and in time he fulfilled his mother's genetic expectations by acquiring a quartet of wives and concubines with whom he sired a dozen sons and at least one daughter.

But why should a mother favor her better-looking child? Isn't every baby equally precious to its parents?

It seems not.

As discussed in Chapter 2, female human reproductive strategy requires parents to nurture babies and children until they are able to fend for themselves. From an evolutionary perspective, however, family planning is a very recent development. Until a generation ago, when contraceptives became inexpensive and widely available, few mothers could choose how many children they would bear.

Inevitably, that raises a question: If parents have more than one child to raise, will they invest time and effort equally in all of them? Or do mothers devote more attention and family resources to those who would seem to have the best chance of surviving into maturity, finding a strong mate, and passing along their genes—which, of course, include those of their parents—to the next generation?

Social scientists have shown that parents indeed invest differently in each child, according to their perceived fitness, quality, reproductive potential, and not least, their physical attractiveness.[2] To make sure that the child or children most likely to reproduce survive into adulthood, parents devote more familial resources and personal energy to those siblings who are more attractive.[3] Since PA is an indication of quality and overall health, parents—especially mothers—give their most attractive children better treatment than less attractive offspring by offering more and better attention.[4]

Some researchers even propose that it follows that children with high PA, perhaps because they have more and better parental care, tend to have better traits and exhibit better and more socialized behavior than do children with less PA.[5]

But parents are not the only adults who give better-looking babies preferential attention, care, and nurturing. Another famous study, also done by University of Texas (Austin) researchers, showed that most adults' expectations of infants are based on their perceived PA, rather than on the baby's actual capabilities.[6]

> Some researchers even propose that it follows that children with high PA tend to have better traits and exhibit better and more socialized behavior than do children with less PA.

Aside from their mothers, most newborn American babies get their initial care from hospital nurses. If these nurses are among the first to interact with an infant, it stands to reason that infant-nurse interactions are crucial to each baby's development. Most adults treat more attractive babies better than less attractive ones. When it comes to newborn babies, however, nurses have both training and experience far beyond the average adult. Do nurses apply an equal standard of care to all infants in their charge?

Perhaps not. A 1993 study showed that nurses had a marked preference for healthy infants with normal birth weights. It is widely accepted that an infant's PA is a reliable indicator of how long it will require hospitalization and how quickly it will gain weight. A more recent 2001 study even suggests that the rate of weight gain and decreased length of hospitalization for attractive infants was at least partly a result of their receiving more nurturing care from nurses.[7]

To find out how nurses distribute care among newborn babies with different levels of PA, researchers Janel Rae Crowder and Laurie Sullivan Hunter at South Carolina's Francis Marion University studied the responses of eighty-five nursing students between nineteen and fifty-two years of age; their median age was twenty-nine. The researchers also sought to find out if nursing students' perceptions of infant attractiveness were affected by the wealth and social status of a baby's parents, by the infant's gender and health at birth, and by the student's individual experience in the nursing field.

After being shown photos of infants coded for physical attractiveness, the nursing students were asked to indicate how much time during a normal eight-hour shift they would spend with the infant in the photo and then with each of two other infants who were not described at all.

The results: Nurses perceived an infant's PA in relation to its gender and its health at birth. Boys of normal health at birth were perceived as more attractive than those of low health at birth, but no significant findings were discovered for this variable in female infants; students seemed to expect males to be resilient and hardy while girls were often perceived as naturally delicate and fragile. The nursing students deemed smaller girl infants the most attractive, while the opposite was true for boy infants: The bulkiest and most muscular were perceived as more attractive and healthy.[8]

And how did nursing experience affect these perceptions? Did more seasoned nurses learn to overcome their natural bias toward less attractive infants?

Quite the contrary: The least experienced nurses, those who had never worked in a neonatal ward, reported that they would spend significantly less time with an attractive infant (the median time was 175.70 minutes). That compares to a more experienced group of

nurses with one field clinical rotation, whose median time with attractive infants was reported as 250.01 minutes.[9] The most experienced nursing students also said that they would spend more time
with a normal-health-at-birth infant (median time: 250.67 minutes)
than with a low-health-at-birth infant (median time: 197.50 minutes).

Within minutes of birth, infants in most U.S. hospitals are subjected to a clinical assessment of their heart rate, muscle tone, respiratory effort, color, and reflex responsiveness. The results,
collectively, are called the "Apgar" score. Crowder and Hunter
concluded from their findings that infants with low health at birth
and a low Apgar score got *less* nursing attention and nurturing time
than those with normal health at birth and a normal Apgar score.
They suspected that additional nurturing bestowed by nurses on the
more physically attractive infants led to increased rates of weight
gain, which resulted in shorter hospital stays. "Perhaps if 'at-risk'
infants received a more nurturing environment, they would also
have an increased rate of weight gain and a decreased length of time
in the hospital," wrote the researchers.[10]

But what about the babies? Do they perceive the same sort of
beauty as adults, or do they find Mom beautiful simply because
they're hungry and she's their own private Meals on Wheels?

According to studies in the University of Texas Langlois Social
Development Lab, infants from two to six months of age prefer to
look longer at faces rated as attractive by adults than at faces rated
as unattractive by adults. Assessing babies' preferences for male and
female Caucasian adult faces, African American adult female faces,
and Caucasian infant faces, researchers concluded that one-year-olds
prefer to approach and play with a "stranger" (but *not* a parent or
family member) with an attractive face. In contrast, when a stranger
is unattractive, babies withdraw from them more often—offering
the real possibility that a very ugly person could cause a baby to cry
merely by the sight of them. More to the point, it seems that infants
prefer the same types of faces as adults.[11]

Moreover, as babies grow older, their judgments of facial attractiveness reflect perceptions of their own parents' age and characteristics. The child of a couple in their thirties, for example, tends to see

more beauty in older faces than does a child born to parents in their twenties.

This finding comes from a team of researchers at the School of Psychology of the University of St Andrews in Scotland. Building on research that showed that in many species, mate preferences are shaped by an infant's experience of parental characteristics, the researchers used computer graphics to create faces for children to examine. They found that "women born to 'old' parents (over age 30) were less impressed by youth and more attracted to age cues in male faces than women with 'young' parents (under age 30). For men, preferences for female faces were influenced by their mother's age and not their father's age, *but only for long-term relationships*" (emphasis added).[12]

· · ·

If young children can distinguish between beautiful faces and not-so-attractive ones, and if they prefer to look at the former, do they also link beauty with other favorable human qualities? To a child, does a person's PA suggest someone is a good person?

According to studies at the University of Texas, Austin, that is indeed the case. As children grow older, as stereotypes about attractiveness shape their interactions with others, they tend to choose peers and friends based on PA and the traits they feel this condition of attractiveness denotes in other children.

> To a child, does a person's PA suggest someone is a good person?

Attractive children are liked more, are seen as smarter, and are rated higher on sharing and friendliness and lower on meanness and hitting than are less attractive children. This is equally the case for children who know each other and for those who do not. Studies of young children show that given a choice, they will select prospective playmates on the basis of their PA.[13]

So mothers spend more and better time with their better-looking offspring, nurses give more attention and nurturing to the cuter babies on their ward, and kids prefer more attractive playmates to less attractive ones, whether they are previously acquainted with each other or not. Are these the only childhood advantages for good-looking children?

Not a chance. A study by renowned social scientist Karen K. Dion at the University of Minnesota in 1972 showed that when kids misbehave and must be disciplined, being more attractive usually means escaping the harshest punishment of all, the stigma of lowered expectations.

Dion, then a graduate student, set up her experiment by giving written information about severe classroom disruptions by seven-year-olds to undergraduate women volunteers. The child's supposed lapse in behavior was either mild or severe, and along with the description of behavior came a photo of the kid's face. Some photos were of exceptionally attractive children, others of comparatively unattractive kids.

After reading the "transgression" information and viewing the child's photo, the test subjects completed a questionnaire that assessed the following:

1. The likelihood that the child had done a similar thing in the past

2. The likelihood that the child would do a similar thing in the future

3. The undesirability of the reported transgression

4. The level of punishment the child should receive

Test subjects were also asked to rate the child on the dimensions of their personality traits.

Dion suspected that the results of her study would show that:

1. An attractive child who committed the same transgression as an unattractive child would be judged less likely to exhibit chronic antisocial behavior.

2. An attractive child's transgression would be perceived as less socially undesirable than the same transgression by an unattractive child.

3. The suggested punishment would be less intense for an attractive child than for an unattractive child who committed the same offense.

And that's almost what happened: The subjects tended to blame disruptive behavior on the ugly children, saying that it was easy to see that they were "brats." When the photo showed a beautiful child, however, the test subjects tended to excuse the child's behavior.

Thus, an attractive child's severe transgression was less likely to be seen as a display of chronic antisocial behavior than an equally severe offense by an unattractive child. Mild or severe antisocial behavior by an attractive child was rated as less socially undesirable than the same act by an unattractive child.

The study contained one surprise: Study subjects recommended exactly the same punishments for all children, without regard to PA.

Less surprising, the students rated high-PA kids as more honest and more pleasant than unattractive children who had committed an identical offense.

Dion's study has been widely cited because its results are both strong in evidence and provocative in conclusions, which violate widely held ideals of fairness about evaluating others based on a subject's facial attractiveness. Subsequent studies, however, have validated these findings.[14]

In a related study, Dion and her colleagues showed college students photos of attractive children, average children, and unattractive children and asked their test subjects to rate some twenty-seven personality traits. As expected, the attractive people received the most positive ratings.[15]

Such stereotypical first impressions are not, of course, limited to evaluations by adults of children. Lieutenant Robert FitzRoy, Royal Navy, believed that personality is shown in facial characteristics. In 1831, when FitzRoy was skipper of HMS *Beagle*, a surveying ship, he interviewed a young Anglican minister for the post of naturalist. It was not the candidate's qualifications that gave him pause, but his face; FitzRoy thought that Charles Darwin's oversize nose was a sure sign of a sluggish personality. Fortunately, he was willing to overlook this presumed trait, perhaps because what he really wanted was an educated man who would listen quietly to his own rambling monologues about life and navy service.[16]

Children learn about PA stereotypes in many ways, including the behavior of parents and siblings. Other, less obvious sources are the fairy tales and stories that generations of children hear as very young children.

Such stories as *Cinderella, Hansel and Gretel,* and *Snow White* are filled with messages about beauty and evil. Beauty, these stories tell children, is inherently good and merits reward, while ugly people are wicked, evil, and mean. And that's not all. A 2003 study by Lori Baker-Sperry, an assistant professor at Western Illinois University, and Liz Grauerholz, associate professor of sociology at Purdue University, revealed patterns of fairy tale association between beauty and economic privilege, beauty and race, beauty and goodness, and beauty and danger.

According to Baker-Sperry, "As the only study to offer a historical analysis of the reproduction of a beauty ideal in fairy tales, this research provides critical insight into ways in which children's literature has been shaped by political and social forces over time and yet continues to provide traditional-gendered prescriptions for women. The messages presented in the Grimms' tales portray differing means of status attainment for men and for women, especially white, heterosexual women." She adds, "The pervasiveness of fairy tales in our society, through books and movies, suggest that there are many opportunities for these messages to become internalized."

> An attractive child's severe transgression was less likely to be seen as a display of chronic antisocial behavior than an equally severe offense by an unattractive child.

"Parents need to be aware that all literature is teaching children something," writes study coauthor Grauerholz. "You need to raise questions and have a dialogue with your children about the meaning of these fairy tales. I didn't want my daughters to think they were only valuable for their looks," adds Grauerholz, explaining why she discusses such tales with her children.[17]

Grauerholz and Baker-Sperry analyzed 168 fairy tales by Jacob and Wilhelm Grimm—the "Brothers Grimm." About half these tales from the nineteenth century have found their way into contemporary children's books and movies, including *Cinderella, Snow White, Sleeping Beauty* (originally titled *Briar Rose*), *Little Red Riding Hood,* and *Hansel and Gretel.*

The study found references to PA in 94 percent of the stories, with an average of nearly fourteen such references per story. References to female beauty far outnumbered male references. And the PA-challenged fare very poorly in the Grimms' tales; almost one in five stories make a connection between ugly appearance and evil acts, including many stories describing awful punishments suffered by the wicked uglies.

So, should discerning parents consign these venerable fairy tales to the trash heap, or offer their children another point of view and help them to think about the hidden messages in the stories? Is reading a child a story loaded with hidden symbolic meaning and then urging the child to think about it another way all that different from telling a lie on the TV news and then granting the subject of the lie equal time to respond—when the denial itself may lend credibility to the lie?

A better way might be to learn to think like a Hollywood producer: When circumstances dictate, change the characters, keep the story. Or keep the characters and lose the story. Or both.

Grauerholz concurs. For children too young to read, fix the stories, she says. Make Cinderella a boy, or alter the story's ending so that she decides there's too much of a downside to hooking up with a handsome prince; with her newly minted self-esteem, she knows how to live happily ever after by moving out of her stepmother's house and taking charge of her own life.

Baker-Sperry also thinks that, even for young children, the feminine beauty ideal espoused by fairy tales can provide insight into the dynamic relationship between gender, power, and culture, as well as the cultural and social significance of beauty to women's lives.

But aren't PA messages in fairy tales different from the messages received from television, movies, books, and other popular media? Robin Goodman, a psychologist at New York University's Child Study Center, thinks not. "Media advertising, pop stars, TV, peer interaction—there are so many things" that all reinforce PA and other stereotypes.[18] But, as Goodman points out, not every message in every fairy tale example is negative. In *Beauty and the Beast,* the heroine learns to love the Beast for who he is, not what he looks like.

The ever more pervasive effects of media images on children are not limited to American kids. In this age of globalization, when people in every nation are exposed to mass media images from around the globe, adolescents—and many adults—often attempt to model their own bodies or those of their children on what they have come to believe are ideal—if unattainable—images.

Take, for example, sixteen-year-old Santi. She has three "best friends" who, she says, each weighs less than 110 pounds. "They look so slim, so confident," complains Santi. "I'm the only one whose weight is above 110, and it makes me feel left out."[19] Santi weighs 114 pounds and is five-feet-three-inches tall.

Just another teen who watches too much TV and reads too many fashion publications? Guess again.

"I never saw myself as fat until the day my cousin and my mom told me so," Santi says. "The problem is not magazines or television, because I know it's not real. People are supposed to be thin and beautiful there. But when you hear it from your own parents, then it hurts."

Santi takes diet pills to dull her appetite and eats little more than apples, hoping to reach her goal of 103 pounds, so she can have "a body like a fashion model."

"The current younger generation already has their own concept of an ideal body image," says Dr. Evi Sukmaningrum, an Atma Jaya University (Jakarta, Indonesia) psychologist. And, most disturbing to many people, teens such as Santi "are being pressured to be thin, not only from the magazines and television, but most of all, from their family and friends."[20]

While she may eventually realize that her eating habits are unhealthy and that she's overdoing the diet routine, the issue is not that simple. Stringent dieting to reach a weight target may eventually develop into serious eating disorders such as anorexia nervosa and bulimia that can become life threatening. Moreover, strict dieting in adolescence can lead to serious health problems such as dehydration and irregular menstrual periods. Santi's use of diet pills could even lead to heart disease.

"Adolescent girls need [proper] nutrition for [development of] their hormones," explains Sukmaningrum, suggesting that even truly overweight girls should never starve themselves. Far better, she says, to cut food intake slightly and exercise more. "The most important thing is for parents to make sure that their children follow a smart and healthy living pattern, instead of focusing on an unhealthy body image," adds Sukmaningrum.[21]

You'll find much more about eating disorders in Chapter 9, which includes a discussion of the extremes to which some people will go in pursuit of a "perfect body image." When it comes to children, however, parents and peers should avoid pressuring children to emulate models and actresses, especially when their bodies are still on the path to finding their ultimate form. For too many adolescents, a thin body is not a sign of good health but of unwise nutrition.

CHAPTER 4

Readin', 'Ritin', 'Rithmetic, 'n' Ridicule

*How PA influences teachers, students, success,
failure, and the learning experience*

Mamas and papas do it. Neonatal nurses do it. So how 'bout teachers? When it comes to handing out choice grades, extracurricular assignments, and other school perks, will a pedagogue prime better-looking students at the expense of those less attractive?

Bet the farm that they will. Studies by University of Hawaii psychologist Elaine Hatfield and Illinois State University sociologist Susan Sprecher demonstrated that most teachers *expect* better-looking kids to perform better, and they devote more attention to children they think have greater potential.[1]

And because most school principals, administrators, and counselors cut their professional teeth in the classroom, they, too, have higher expectations for attractive students. Just like teachers, most expect cuter kids to perform better than their less attractive classmates.

But then a funny thing happens on the way to graduation. Because a teacher or counselor *expects* a particular pupil to do better, very often the student actually does: The thought becomes the deed.[2]

Most teachers *expect* better-looking kids to perform better, and they devote more attention to children they think have greater potential.

Dr. Robert Rosenthal at Harvard pioneered work in this field some fifty years ago; it came as a result of a ruined experiment that was intended to complete his own doctoral dissertation. "It appeared that I might have treated my experimental subjects in such a way as to lead them to respond in accordance with my experimental hypothesis, or expectancy," he would later write.[3]

After assessing where his methods went wrong, Rosenthal realized that he had unwittingly raised a question to which no good answer yet existed: Do the *expectations* of a psychological researcher affect the *outcomes* of his laboratory experiments?

If they do, and if Rosenthal's own "unconscious experimenter bias" had led to the puzzling and disconcerting results of his dissertation experiment, then, he reasoned, he could reproduce this phenomenon in his own lab.

A career was launched.

Rosenthal's first studies were conducted with students who were told to rate photographs of people. Half the experimenters were led to expect high ratings and half were led to expect low ratings. Over several studies, those who expected high ratings obtained substantially higher ratings than did those expecting low ratings.[4]

To see if a researcher's expectations would influence the outcome of other kinds of research subjects, Rosenthal and his colleagues set up two more studies that involved laboratory animals. Half the experimenters were told that their rats had been specially bred to perform well in a maze or in a Skinner box (a device used to teach conditioned responses). The others were instructed that their test rats had been specially bred for *poor* performance. Both studies showed that when experimenters *expected* better learning, their lab rats did not disappoint them: They indeed learned better.[5]

If a whiskered rodent becomes brighter merely because a guy in a white coat expects smarter behavior, could a child do the same? Would a kid demonstrate higher intelligence just because his teacher expects it?

To find out, in 1968 Rosenthal and a colleague created yet another study whose findings were published as a book, *Pygmalion in the Classroom*. Each child in a school was given a nonverbal test of intelligence disguised as a test to predict intellectual "blooming." To hide the study's true purpose, the test was given a bogus name: "The Harvard Test of Inflected Acquisition." The school where this experiment was conducted had eighteen classrooms, three for each of six grade levels. Every classroom included children with above-average ability, average ability, and below-average ability, respectively. Rosenthal randomly selected about 20 percent of the student body as his experimental group. Teachers were told by the distinguished Harvard researcher that certain selected children's scores on the test indicated that each of those children would show a surprising spurt in intellectual competence during the next eight months of the school term. Because the children were chosen randomly, however, the only real difference between the small experimental group and the much larger control group was in their teachers' minds.

Eight months later, every child in the school was retested with the same nonverbal intelligence test. The teachers had been led to expect greater intellectual gains from certain children, and those children in fact showed significantly more progress than those in the control group, thereby supporting what Rosenthal dubbed his "Pygmalion hypothesis."[6]

Rosenthal's groundbreaking research was only the beginning; in the years since his "Pygmalion in the classroom" study was published, literally hundreds of other experiments were conducted in this field. Many of these experiments were conducted in classrooms, but others took place in nursing homes, business environments, and courtrooms.

Rosenthal's data led him to conclude that in almost any business

organization, efficiency is increased by raising managers' expectations. Juries will more often return a "guilty" verdict when instructed by a judge who believes a defendant to be guilty.
Depression in nursing home residents is ameliorated by raising their
caretakers' expectations of what patients are capable of achieving.
And, to return to the theme of this chapter, not only in the United
States but in other nations as well, teachers' expectations of student
abilities very often serve as self-fulfilling prophecies, and these expectations may encompass far more than the purely intellectual tasks
associated with classrooms.[7]

So how does it work? What goes on between a kid's ears that
pumps up smarts?

To find out, Robert Hartley carried out a 1986 study into the
problem-solving abilities of a group of disadvantaged children.
These were kids who had been found to be impulsive, poor planners
who rarely checked over their work for mistakes before handing it
in for grading.

When these children were asked to "act like someone who is
very clever," however, their test scores shot up significantly. Why?
Hartley's study revealed that children don't perform at peak ability
by default: Motivational factors affect the degree to which they
apply themselves to a task and ultimately how well they perform it.
His study also showed that when children who view themselves as
low performers step out of this role and assume that of a "clever
person," they then apply themselves to the task more effectively and
thus attain higher scores. This is the root of a philosophical notion
called *constructive alternativism* that posits that all human perception is inherently subjective, and that reality in the form of events or
people may be construed in different ways. Thus, one's understanding of situations and people, no less than of oneself, are *subjective*
constructs that affect how we behave.[8]

So, what's wrong with teachers positively influencing a student's
achievement by raising expectations of performance?

In itself, nothing. But when it comes to physical attractiveness,
the Pygmalion phenomenon has an ugly downside: discrimination
against those with less PA. Sometimes termed "lookism," it exerts

a corrosive effect on self-esteem that can adversely affect children for the rest of their often unhappy lives.

Is this a secret? Ask "Peanuts" creator Charles Schulz, widely considered as history's greatest cartoonist and an astute if untutored observer of juvenile behavior. He once drew a strip featuring Peppermint Patty complaining to Franklin that she failed a school test because "I have a big nose . . . sometimes a teacher just doesn't like the way a kid looks." Franklin then examines her test paper; it's blank. "If a teacher doesn't like your looks, Franklin, there's nothing you can do," she sighs, a truth as plain to Patty as the nose on her freckled face.

Science confirms that, typically, a teacher's first impressions of and reaction to a new pupil are influenced by that child's overall physical characteristics—so less than physically attractive children enter this vital learning relationship with at least one strike against them.[9]

> Science confirms that, typically, a teacher's first impressions of and reaction to a new pupil are influenced by that child's overall physical characteristics.

Many studies have addressed teacher-student bias against less attractive students. Elementary school teachers, for example, associate attractive students with higher IQ, popularity, likely progression in school, and parental interest. Given what we have learned about PA's powerful effects, this finding should not be surprising—except that even when attractive and unattractive students earn identical records, teachers will *still* believe that in the future, attractive students will do better than unattractive students. Moreover, even *outside* academic-related areas, teachers lower their social expectations for unattractive students.[10]

It is shocking, but physically attractive students are often punished only minimally for disciplinary infractions; when less attractive classmates break the same rules, however, their punishment is often more severe than that meted out to better-looking students. In other words, teachers punish children for not looking beautiful![11]

Children are even more susceptible to the power of PA than adults. As we learned in Chapter 3, the renowned social science team of Karen Dion, Ellen Berscheid, and Elaine Walster conducted a now-famous study at the University of Minnesota in 1972 that continues to serve as a basis for much research into the PA phenomenon. The sum of its findings is described by its title: "What is beautiful is good."

In their seminal experiment, Dion, Berscheid, and Walster asked college psychology students to view photos of people and then evaluate their personality traits. Each student opened envelopes containing pictures, respectively, of a person with high PA, one of average PA, and a person almost entirely lacking in PA. The pictures were evenly divided between male and female, but each participant was given photos of only one gender. Students opened one envelope at a time, then rated the person inside on twenty-seven different personality traits. They then used these photos to decide who would be most likely to possess certain quality-of-life characteristics such as marital happiness and social and professional happiness. Finally, the students were asked to decide who they thought would be most likely to enter into each of twenty-seven different professions.

Results indicated that favorable personality and most quality-of-life traits were more often attributed to the highly attractive than to the unattractive; highly attractive people, however, were *not* assumed to make better parents. Gender showed no effect on these results.

Six years later another team of researchers led by Terrance Dushenko built on these findings with two research studies on PA as it relates to age and sex. In one group, the study participants were children aged 10 to 12; the other group was adults aged 55 to 75. The objective was to determine if the strength of the beauty-is-good stereotype varied with age. Participants were presented with pictures of an attractive and an unattractive woman and asked to decide which would display each of nine different personality traits and five quality-of-life elements. While both groups conformed to the beauty-is-good stereotype, children were much more likely to attribute positive characteristics to attractive people than were adults.[12]

In other words, kids react to good-looking adults with all the enthusiasm of a hummingbird sipping nectar—but by the time they acquire serious responsibilities, gray hair, and aching joints, life has taught them that everything that sparkles is not a diamond, that the man from the government is not necessarily there to help you, and that golden tresses are no guarantee of a sterling character. That tiny peep into human nature is the foundation for generations of movie plots, from *She Done Him Wrong* to *The Bad and the Beautiful* to *Catwoman,* all playing to ever-younger audiences.

A year after the Dushenko study, pioneer University of Texas researcher Judith Langlois tested the beauty-is-good stereotype with preschool and second- and fourth-grade children. These kids were shown pictures of attractive and unattractive classmates and asked to decide which they liked and which would be most likely to demonstrate prosocial, antisocial, and socially competent behaviors.

Langlois concluded that attractive girls became increasingly popular as the age of the rater increased. If, however, the rater was over five years old, attractive *boys* became *decreasingly* popular. Overall, unattractive boys were more popular than attractive boys, the reverse of the findings for girls. By age eight, however, *all* attractive peers were better liked than were unattractive peers.[13]

That attractive females were more popular than attractive males was confirmed four years later by another University of Texas study. Children aged 4 or 5 chose three classmates that they "especially liked" from an array of previously rated photos. This study showed that they were more likely to choose attractive than unattractive peers, especially if the peers were girls. While PA was not always an accurate predictor of popularity among boys, researchers also noted that at the start of the school year, when the children in the study were first assessed, it was. By the end of the year, however, this was no longer the case, suggesting that children's initial social perceptions and preferences are PA based.[14] In other words, the more PA a person has, the more likely it is that a child will associate them with positive traits and like them. How they later interact with each other, of course, influences the basis of further friendship.

But how do children come by these behaviors? A 1987 study by Murray Krantz sought to examine the PA dimension of social choices made by kids entering kindergarten. Individual photos were taken just before the school year; children viewed pictures of classmates and were asked to select those they would like to have as friends. Meanwhile, their mothers were asked to predict which class-mates they thought their own child would pick as friends. Five weeks into the school year, the kindergartners were asked to nominate three best friends of their own sex, then rate their remaining same-sex peers. Krantz's results indicated that PA accurately predicts choice of friends among same-sex peers, although mothers and daughters were more likely to use PA in choosing friends and boys placed no emphasis on PA when choosing male friends.[15] Other results of this study suggest that parents play an important role in the development of their child's perceptions.

Are there other factors that influence children's formulation of concepts of what is physically attractive and what is not? According to the eminent social psychology pioneer Albert Bandura, widely known as the "Father of the Cognitive Theory," social behaviors are learned through observing and imitating the behaviors that children observe most frequently: that of parents, teachers, and, nowadays, television programs. If a child perceives that the physically attractive are associated with goodness and treated better than the unattractive, the child

> Children as young as eight take it upon themselves to restrict their dietary intakes because of concern for their own body image.

will adopt this behavior as his own.[16] And so it goes, from one generation to the next.

In a 1980 follow-up study, researchers sought to unravel the interacting perceptions of parents, teachers, and children toward the beauty-is-good stereotype. They showed children and their parents photographic sets of other children and of middle-aged people. The results indicated that parents and teachers expect their own children to make positive attributions and have preferences for attractive as opposed to unattractive male children. While parents did not expect that girls' photographs would be judged on the basis of their relative PA, children made their assessments based on the beauty-is-good stereotype without regard to gender,[17] suggesting that youngsters are predisposed to expect certain behaviors from attractive versus unattractive peers.

Bandura's social learning theory posits that because parents and teachers play such an important role in children's lives, they are a possible cause for this predisposition.[18]

So it should be no surprise that schoolchildren, picking up on teachers' behavior, soon learn to emulate their elders. Indeed, children as young as three years are aware of such physical attributes as weight and use body dimensions and type to match or categorize individuals.[19]

By age five, many children are sensitive to different body types and show a preference for normal weight and build. These youngsters have also developed body-image stereotypes about other children. Even very young children may hold negative views about physical categories to which they do not belong. Children who are of average size or are muscular are seen as happy, kind, smart, neat, strong, and popular. Plump children, however, are perceived as sloppy, lazy, stupid, and likely to cheat. Thin children are considered to be fearful or worried, weak, and lonely. By the time they are six to eight years old, gender differences often appear; girls show more dissatisfaction with their bodies than do boys, more frequently believe that being thin equates to being likable, and thus show more desire to "be thinner" even when their weight is normal.[20]

Small wonder, then, that children as young as eight take it upon themselves to restrict their dietary intakes because of concern for their own body image.[21]

Of all the reasons that a schoolchild in early twenty-first-century America may be seen as unattractive, the leading reason is obesity, which has become a national plague: Two-thirds of Americans are either overweight or obese, including a significant percentage of morbidly obese. Obesity now rivals cigarette smoking as a source of premature death.[22]

As frightening as that is, it gets worse: Children between six and eleven years of age are *three* times as likely to be overweight as they were in 1970, according to Centers for Disease Control statistics.

For those who manage to survive childhood, despite the often severe medical problems associated with obesity, including diabetes and heart disease, growing up with the stigma of unattractiveness may scar their psyches for life. People with early-onset childhood obesity show a greater frequency of psychiatric symptoms as well as higher degrees of psychological distress and symptomatology than subjects who became obese as adults.[23]

It's not that being fat makes you crazy. It's just that less attractive kids, especially the chubby ones, too often become lightning rods for classmate ridicule and teasing, not to mention teachers' prejudices. Sometimes educators even project the dissatisfaction they feel for their own bodies onto students and may suggest that an overweight student diet or pursue fitness activities.[24]

Kids may shrug off the immediate effects of this cruelty, but they tend to internalize adult and peer criticism, which contributes to development of a poor self-image. Overweight students are very aware of their bodies; often they share the same biases toward obesity harbored by their classmates of average weight: namely, that they are lazy, stupid, sloppy, and ugly.

Because peer pressures exert tremendous influences on impressionable young minds, biases experienced in childhood often exert negative influences into adulthood and beyond—even if an overweight child grows into a mature adult of normal weight and average body shape. Some research into the consequences of obesity indicates that overweight young adults remain single more often and have lower household incomes than their average-weight peers.[25]

• • •

Despite its lifetime effects, schoolroom bias toward the less attractive—and toward obese children in particular—seems to have become accepted societal practice.

This is no longer the case with bullying, partly because of its spectacularly tragic consequences. On April 20, 1999, twelve students and a teacher were murdered and twenty-three others wounded in a rampage at Columbine High School in Littleton, Colorado. The shooters, Eric Harris and Dylan Klebold, both Columbine students, then took their own lives. Columbine, alas, was but the bloodiest of a dozen similar shootings during an eighteen-month period in schools from Alaska to Georgia. In each case, the shooters were students, some as young as eleven, who had been bullied because of their physical appearance.

How common is bullying? A 2000 CNN poll of 558 students in a Midwestern middle school found that within the previous thirty days, 80 percent of those questioned admitted to behavior that included physical aggression, social ridicule, teasing, name-calling, and issuing of threats. And being overweight is named, by both boys and girls, as among the five most common reasons for being bullied. Physical weakness is the number-one reason boys say they are picked on by their peers.[26]

> In Columbine and a dozen similar shootings during an eighteen-month period, the shooters were students, some as young as eleven, who had been bullied because of their physical appearance.

Alarmed at how common and destructive bullying suddenly seemed, in 2000 James R. Whitehead and John H. Hoover of the University of North Dakota reviewed scientific literature on this phenomenon, looking for trends or solutions to the problem. Their conclusions echoed that of one of psychiatry's most venerated figures, Dr. Alfred Adler, a student of Sigmund Freud, who in 1932 wrote that "[n]umerous children grow up in the constant dread of being laughed at. Ridicule of children is well-nigh criminal. It retains its effect on the soul of the child, and is transferred into the habits and actions of his adulthood."[27]

Whitehead and Hoover, however, went beyond Adler's observations to link bullying and other behavioral problems with body issues. They found that while at any given time about 60 percent of American women and girls eleven years and older will admit to being on a diet, nearly as many sixth graders of both genders want to weigh less, and one in six had dieted to shed what they considered extra poundage.[28]

Moreover, for both genders, adolescence is both a critical period in emotional development and a time of dramatic physical change as their bodies change shape during puberty. For some teenagers, especially those with depression, this change proves to be a difficult task, and usually it is more difficult for girls than boys, as girls are more concerned about attractiveness and less satisfied with their appearance to begin with.[29]

Asked to choose from a list of body areas, teenage girls, including many who were normal weight or thin, expressed concern that their thighs, buttocks, and hips were too large. Younger girls, however, are far less likely to select areas of sexual attractiveness but are instead dissatisfied with such body parts as teeth, face, and feet,[30] suggesting that the onset of puberty produces changes in body image.

In response to the burden of coping with these adolescent body changes in an atmosphere where PA issues weigh so heavily, more adolescents, and especially girls, experience depression. Depressed girls typically experience their body as less pretty, less interesting, sicker, weaker, clumsier, less useful, less familiar, and more out of control. Depressed girls are particularly dissatisfied with the look of their faces, a primary basis of social judgments on female PA, and with weight, a major determinant of overall body image.[31]

To find out if the pressures that drive young women and girls to be unhappy with their weight and the shape of their bodies come from inner sources—some innate sense that being heavy is wrong or unhealthy—or from experiencing feedback from others, Vanderbilt University psychologists Leslie Morey and Dennis Morey conducted an experiment in 1991. Their subjects, female university students, were asked to estimate their own body weight. Individuals also rated their own level of depression by answering questions on a highly validated test, while their self-estimation of body image was recorded in their choice of comparative body images. In an initial session, subjects were weighed in pounds on a digital scale. In the second session, they were weighed on a scale that read in kilograms. Each participant was randomly assigned a bogus weight either 3 percent lighter or heavier than their true weight.

Morey and Morey found that body estimations of participants who had low feelings of depression were not affected by this weight-related feedback. Highly depressed women, however, became even more depressed by it. The scientists concluded that depressed women are more vulnerable to external feedback.[32] This finding suggests and supports other research that indicates people who are already depressed are driven to further depths of desperation by external images, including idealized media images.[33]

While Whitehead and Hoover found widespread evidence of

negative self-perception related to physical size and appearance, they also found significant ethnic differences. For example, in a study of eating disorder symptoms in girls aged 11 to 16, white girls' dissatisfaction with their bodies increased with age—but the desire to become thinner remained relatively constant in black girls of the same age. While black girls were more vulnerable to developing binge-type eating disorders, white girls were more likely to develop such dietary conditions as anorexia.[34]

Regardless of ethnicity, overweight kids who suffered from decreasing self-esteem were far more likely to be sad, lonely, and nervous than children of normal weight. And if that wasn't worrisome enough, children with low self-esteem are more likely to smoke cigarettes and drink alcohol.[35]

Paradoxically, other studies suggest that attractiveness may also be risky. Women college students with especially pretty faces are at risk for eating disorders if their perfectionism combines with anxiety and hypercriticality. And women are more likely to criticize thin women for their efforts to stay slim.[36]

Far from being prophets of doom, however, Whitehead and Hoover offer hope for the bullied. Their magic wand is no mystery: The most successful prevention and treatment programs combine diet and exercise within a framework of significant behavior change. These programs, they say, should be devised and implemented in coordinated fashion with schools, families, and primary care physicians.

> Paradoxically, women college students with especially pretty faces are at risk for eating disorders if their perfectionism combines with anxiety and hypercriticality.

Whitehead and Hoover caution, however, that it has often proved difficult for schools to maintain such programs. Budgetary limitations and competition for curriculum time make adequate teacher supervision difficult over the long run. Nevertheless, physical education (PE) programs that take into account individual children's needs and sensibilities may serve as a "thread" to reconnect alienated children with caring adults. Moreover, other studies show that physical activity and exercise are just as effective in treating depression as pharmacological interventions—and better than psychotherapy.[37]

But PE programs that actually support those who need it most or children with special physical needs are rarely available in America's public schools anymore. Paradoxically, while educators routinely preach the gospel of fitness and lifelong activity, in practice they often discriminate against the most needy youngsters—the overweight and sedentary. Most schools tailor PE programs to support the most physically gifted students; physical education courses are too often merely feeder systems for interscholastic athletics. And yet it is precisely in physical education classes where individual physiques emerge from camouflaging clothing and body issues become most vexing to the overweight and less attractive of both genders. Many PE departments serve no student's needs quite so well as they do in providing employment opportunities to coaches.[38]

• • •

Another way that physical attractiveness warps the learning experiences of the young is its impact on sexuality. Adolescent psychological and behavioral problems are often traced to a teen's desire to attract the opposite sex. Early and often unhealthy sexual adventures, for example, may be manifestations of a different sort of desire: to have one's physical attractiveness validated by the opposite sex.[39]

A healthier way to get that sort of validation is through participation in sports. A study of 176 girls of high school age explored links between involvement in organized sports, functional body orientation, and self-empowerment. The study concluded that girls who participate in high school team sports are far more likely to avoid the sort of risky sexual behavior that leads to unwanted pregnancy or sexually transmitted diseases.[40]

> No matter how many previous sexual partners a man or woman had been with, the more attractive a presumed new sexual partner was, the less inclined students were to take safe-sex precautions.

As children grow into and beyond adolescence, however, PA issues continue to warp their still-maturing judgments about sexual matters, as demonstrated in a study that showed how the PA of a supposed new sexual partner affects decisions about the use of condoms and other safer-sex practices. For this study, 280 college students (140 of each gender) were shown photos and provided with "biographic information" that included sexual histories of possible sex partners. Students then completed a questionnaire predicated on the assumption that the person in the photo was willing to have sex with them. The results showed that in making judgments about risk and probable future behavior with this person, most participants—but especially men—relied on PA and tended to ignore sexual history information. In short, no matter how many previous sexual partners a man or woman had been with, and no matter what kind of risky previous sexual behavior they had participated in, the more attractive a presumed new sexual partner was, the less inclined students were to take safe-sex precautions.[41]

• • •

We've seen that teachers invest the most effort in good-looking pupils, that students pick up on adult behavior and seek friendships with their cuter classmate—thereby creating schoolwide popularity hierarchies based on PA—and that those with the misfortune to be born less attractive are saddled with heavier burdens in competing for an education.

But what about student attitudes toward good-looking versus "ugly" teachers?

There was a time, not so distant, when as long as a pedagogue appeared in the classroom promptly, dressed appropriately, didn't molest a student or a colleague, and turned grades in on time, America's school boards and the trustees of its institutions of higher education did not much care what students might think of their teachers. Today, however, nearly all college instructors, from tenured professors to temporary lecturers, and many private school teachers as well, must suffer the indignity of periodic student evaluations. In some institutions, a few negative evaluations can lead to teachers being granted the opportunity to "explore other career options" or "spend more time with their families." In nearly all cases, student evaluations are factored into tenure and promotion decisions.

Sounds fair, right?

One venerable scholar and economist tells us that when it comes to student ratings, teachers' looks are actually more important than their instructional ability. Professor Daniel Hamermesh of the University of Texas, Austin, teamed with student Amy Parker to show college-student volunteers photos of ninety-four professors, then they asked them to rate their looks. When Hamermesh and Parker compared those ratings to average student evaluation scores for courses taught by these professors, they discovered that the professors rated most beautiful scored a point higher than those rated least beautiful. A point may not sound like a lot, but student evaluations rarely vary much.

The study by Hamermesh and Parker also disclosed that good looks generated more of a premium, and bad looks more of a penalty, for male instructors. Hamermesh and Parker's data show that the effect of beauty on teaching evaluations for men was three times as great as for women, and that minorities of both sexes earned lower evaluations than white males.[42]

Sound trivial? Not if you're a professor who didn't get tenure because of low student evaluations. Or if anonymous students identify you by name and post criticism of your body shape, wardrobe choices, or complexion on one of several websites dedicated to rating professors, such as www.ratemyprofessors.com, www.profes sorperformance.com, and www.ratingsonline.com.

Nor is this a new phenomenon emerging because of the Internet. In 1973, an audience of professional educators attended a lecture by Myron Fox, PhD, an expert on the application of mathematics to human behavior. He delivered a lecture infused with boundless enthusiasm, double-talk, and contradictory assertions. Afterward the audience was asked to rate the lecture. "Dr. Fox" received very high ratings—and absolutely none of the audience recognized that it was a hoax, that he was not a pedagogue at all but merely a handsome actor with no academic credentials.[43]

An isolated event? Not at all. Several subsequent studies confirmed that students tend to rate their teacher's performance more on the basis of superficialities like PA and clothing style than on the content of their lectures or their ability to communicate.[44]

And now that we've completed our PA tour of the schoolhouse, it's time to go to work.

CHAPTER 5

The Job Is Looking Good

PA's influence on careers and the
workplace dynamic

So you're good-looking. Neonatal nurses nurtured you nonstop upon your arrival in this world. Your parents handed you everything a kid could want, and way more. Teachers from preschool and kindergarten all the way through college and grad school bent backward and forward to cut you every break possible. But now here you are, out of school and about to interview for your first job. So put all that stuff behind you and get real, young sir or miss, because this is the workplace. The gig. The grind. The rat race. Here in Nine-to-Five City, stockholders insist on profits and bosses expect you to work hard to inflate their bonuses. The bottom line *is* the bottom line.

Do you really think that anybody, from the executive suite to the factory floor, gives a flying flip about how beautiful you are?

Well, yes, they do.

And quite a bit.

The fact is, if you are competing for a position against candidates who seem to possess exactly the same qualifications, but *you* are very attractive while the others are average or less in the PA department, scientific studies say that you will get the job and they will not. Always? Well, if you're bursting with PA but could use a manicure or even a minor makeover while the competition is well groomed but so-so looking, relax—you've still got the edge. Your good looks help most when you and your competitors are all otherwise run-of-the-mill candidates: If another applicant is exceptionally well qualified but you're not, you may get a follow-up interview but probably not the job.[1]

> Even though they *believe* that they are able to overlook an applicant's PA, many experienced managers will end up selecting an applicant with high PA whose job qualifications merely match those of a less attractive candidate.

The data and studies that form the scientific basis for this hire-the-handsome phenomenon have been available to personnel managers and corporate management for decades. Most human resource types are well aware that signing the guy with the toothpaste-ad smile or the gorgeous gal with the gams up to *here* isn't solid management practice. An experienced hiring hand will ignore good looks, right?

Not exactly. Yes, the science is readily available and many seasoned hiring executives have actually read it. And no, it doesn't seem to make much difference. Even though they *believe* that they are able to overlook an applicant's PA, and even as they sincerely insist that they ignore such superficialities when making hiring decisions, many experienced managers will end up selecting an applicant with high PA whose job qualifications merely match or parallel those of a less attractive candidate. That's because they think the person with high PA is actually *better* qualified or, if not, will nevertheless turn into a better employee.[2]

And short men, along with all PA-challenged women, no matter how qualified, start any job interview with strikes against them, even when the hiring decision is made by a highly experienced manager or HR executive.[3]

In 2000, British economist Barry Harper examined voluminous data relating to over 11,000 people born in Britain in 1958 and concluded that both men and women "assessed as unattractive or short experience a significant earnings penalty. Tall men receive a pay premium while obese women experience a pay penalty." Harper concluded that while there was evidence that short men and ugly women were on infrequent occasion less productive, "the bulk of the pay differential for appearance arises from employer discrimination."[4]

Oh yes, that's England! But here in the land of the free and the home of the brave? Would an American company really discriminate against a job applicant because he was short? Against a woman who was, shall we say, not so attractive?

Darn tootin' they do, and a pair of Yank professors have the goods to prove it. Daniel M. Cable, a business professor at the University of North Carolina, Chapel-Hill, and Timothy A. Judge, professor of management at the University of Florida, studied data from 8,590 individuals in four different studies in both Great Britain and the United States.[5] These studies followed thousands of participants from childhood to adulthood and examined many details of both their work and their personal lives.

Cable and Judge found no important difference between employees in the United Kingdom and the United States; in both countries their data document a clear linkage between physical height and career success. A person's altitude, they learned, is a significant predictor of attitudes expressed toward them. Height flavors the way people dole out social esteem, invest in leadership, and rate performance, especially in men.

Judge and Cable also examined the relationship between individuals' physical height and their incomes. Overall, their study was among the most comprehensive analyses of the relationship of height to workplace success ever conducted. Their results strongly suggest that tall individuals enjoy many advantages in critical aspects of their careers throughout their organizational lives. How much more? Every inch over average, which for an adult male American is a smidgen over five feet nine inches, means an annual paycheck bonus of some $789.

Even the professors who conducted the research find this information troubling. "With a few exceptions, such as professional basketball, no one could argue that height is an essential ability required for job performance or a bona fide occupational qualification," observed Judge. Yet, if you project the annual paycheck rewards of being tall over the course of a thirty-year career and compound it, "We're talking about literally hundreds of thousands of dollars of earnings advantage that a tall person enjoys," Judge concluded.

"We're talking about literally hundreds of thousands of dollars of earnings advantage that a tall person enjoys."

But how does that work? Why does height make a man more effective on the job? Cable and Judge found that greater height boosted supervisors' subjective ratings of work performance, including their evaluations of job effectiveness, and that, like the expectation phenomenon discussed in Chapter 4, it also elevated such objective measures of performance as sales volume. The relationship between height and earnings was especially strong in sales and management but also found its way into such less social occupations as engineering, accounting, and computer programming.

Cable and Judge speculate that being tall may boost an individual's self-confidence, improving their performance. Other people may also ascribe tall people higher status and afford them greater respect, lending them an edge in negotiating and sales situations. This commanding influence may be an evolutionary remnant from a time when our ancestors lived at the mercy of predators and physical size was an index of power and strength that man used when making "fight or flight" decisions. Primitive humans "ascribed leader-like qualities to tall people because they thought they would be better able to protect them," opined Judge. "Evolutionary psychologists would argue that some of those old patterns still operate in our perceptions today."

• • •

Of all the large institutions found in modern societies, none is more of a meritocracy than the military. Since World War II, at least, individual ability has been the most important determinant of personal advancement. While U.S. armed forces were segregated by race until the Korean War, military leaders have since learned that the talent for leading troops in combat bears no relationship to the color of one's skin or to the occupations or social status of one's forebears.

Yet even the military takes cognizance of each individual's PA. Officers and noncommissioned officers (NCOs) are subject to regular performance ratings, where among the qualities rated by superiors is "military appearance," a subset of PA.

In 1984, Professor Allan Mazur of Syracuse University led a team of social scientists that collected data from the U.S. Military Academy Class of 1950, a cohort that by then was approaching retirement from military service. Mazur and his colleagues found that "facial dominance" (i.e., a handsome, youthful look—another way to parse the PA phenomenon) was strongly related to promotions within the corps of cadets during the class's junior and senior years at West Point. Facial appearance, however, did not seem to have any bearing on predictions of rank attainment after graduation or during an individual's early or middle career path.[6]

What Mazur and his colleagues may have neglected to factor in, however, was the U.S. Army officer promotion system. Barring death or dishonor, military academy graduates who remained in uniform after completing their mandatory five-year service period could be expected to serve on active duty until mandatory retirement age, which increases with an individual's rank until reaching a maximum. In other words, after a certain birthday, it's up or out.

By virtue of having been commissioned on the same day, all members of a West Point class will get their first three or four promotions virtually in lockstep with other classmates. Thus, with few exceptions, every member of the Class of 1950 was promoted to first lieutenant, captain, major, and lieutenant colonel within a few months of each other.

Above the rank of lieutenant colonel, however, the army promotions pyramid narrows sharply. There are far fewer slots for one-star generals than for colonels, fewer still for two-star generals, and only a relative handful of three- and four-star positions. With extremely rare exceptions, these final promotions occur about three or four years before the end of a career. They are usually based on the collective effects of many performance and fitness ratings, as well as personal observations by the army's most senior officers and America's top political figures, including the president.

In 1989, five years after the initial survey of the Class of 1950, Mazur and his colleagues sent out follow-up questionnaires. By then, the highest-ranking generals from the class had reached mandatory retirement age and left the service. To Mazur's surprise, facial dominance—measured from cadet portraits taken years earlier—was now revealed as a significant predictor of promotion to the top ranks of general officer. In other words, owning a face with the right kind of PA was a big advantage even in reaching the top of the military promotion pyramid.[7]

Not only is it more difficult for the short or unattractive to compete with taller or better-looking peers, but, according to yet another study, at the very least among lawyers, simply looking much different from your peers imposes a paycheck penalty.

Ishak Saporta, a professor at Israel's Tel Aviv University, teamed with Jennifer Halpern, an Ithaca, New York, researcher, to study relationships between height, weight, and PA of lawyers and their salaries. Their data suggest that even among those most acquainted with laws prohibiting employment discrimination, individuals who are thinner, heavier, or shorter than peers are penalized with lower salaries and less important jobs, leading to fewer promotion opportunities. They analyzed data from a 1984 national survey of nearly 3,000 American lawyers and found that men who were thin *or* overweight earned less than men of average build. This was not true for women attorneys; in their case, median starting salaries were nearly 10 percent lower than starting salaries for male attorneys.[8] As University of Michigan graduate student Robert Quinn observed in his 1978 master's thesis, PA discrimination toward women lawyers is more subtle. Less attractive women attorneys, whether skinny or fat, are much less likely to get jobs that require face-to-face contact with the public—and these are usually the best-paying jobs in the legal profession.[9]

Those blessed with an attractive countenance gain many workplace advantages collectively referred to as "beauty bias." There is, however, one glaring exception to beauty bias: Exceptionally beautiful women are often at a disadvantage when seeking a job in which appearance is deemed irrelevant, or a job strongly associated with masculine qualities like strength, endurance, and the ability to exercise good judgment under pressure.

A study carried out at Rice University found that while average-looking and attractive men were more often selected for such positions as driving a tow truck or operating a switchboard, beautiful women never won these kinds of jobs when the competition was female and less attractive. The study also found that when it comes to PA, bias is in the eye of the beholder. For example, while *male* employers are usually eager to hire a beautiful woman for a job where face-to-face contact with clients or customers is important, including such occupations as receptionists, dietitians, and public relations, *female* employers are far less willing to do so.[10]

> Exceptionally beautiful women are often at a disadvantage when seeking a job strongly associated with masculine qualities like strength, endurance, and the ability to exercise good judgment under pressure.

The Rice University study also found that for jobs in which appearance isn't considered important, employers of both genders usually opt for a less attractive woman over a more attractive one. One explanation may be that employers think female PA correlates with perceptions of femininity: When a highly attractive woman applies for a traditionally masculine job like truck driver or security guard, she is usually perceived as less capable of meeting the job's requirement for "masculine" qualities. This perception that attractive women lack so-called masculine character traits also extends to supervisory and managerial positions: Attractive females who reach high-level management are more likely to have their success attributed to luck. If a woman is unattractive enough, however, her success in business is viewed as the result of ability.[11]

Yet merely being good-looking is often not enough to get a qualified man or woman a job with frequent public contact. In the twenty-first century, the successful job seeker must also appear youthful. As reported in *Chain Drug Review,* a trade journal, Combe Inc., manufacturer of Just For Men hair coloring, surveyed professional career advisers to determine what personal qualities employers most valued. That survey, "Strategies for Job Success," disclosed that looks are important to workplace advancement: An employee's youthful appearance affects salary and is closely tied to promotions. Almost two-thirds of those surveyed reported that male clients had lost job opportunities because they looked too old. More than three-fourths said that in the economic climate of the twenty-first century, looking younger gives men a distinct competitive advantage. And because job interviewers in many fields tend to be younger than the applicants they screen, they tend to pass over their elders and hire younger workers.[12]

This pattern also extends to *keeping* a job; survey respondents indicated that gray hair undermines job security—bad news for aging baby boomers now approaching the so-called "silver ceiling."

And it's not only American men who face premature retirement or unemployment as they age. In 2003, the management of Malaysian Airlines System (MAS) made public what had long been unpublicized company policy—namely, the company's female flight attendants were forced to "retire" at age 40. (Male flight attendants, however, are allowed to stay on the job until age 55.) Dr. Mohammed Don Abdullah, general manager for the airlines, defended this policy by observing that "customers prefer to be served by young, demure, and pretty stewardesses."

Shocked, a Kuala Lumpur newspaper columnist compared this policy to the treatment afforded ballerinas. "In a nutshell, the simple message from this prominent senior officer is: 'Go home. You are old. You are no longer attractive. We do not need you anymore,'" wrote Vasanthi Ramachandran in the *New Straits Times.* When the MAS general manager was criticized for his stand, he replied that the airline needed "frontliners who are mentally and physically alert; young, pretty, and quick to respond to emergencies, as the safety of passengers is our priority."[13]

In fact, the chief rivals to MAS for transpacific travel, including

Air India, Thai Airways International, Cathay Pacific, All Nippon Airways, and Lufthansa, all allow female flight attendants to stay on the job until age 60 or older. What the MAS official did not say, however, was that like most airlines in a highly competitive environment, its marketing strategy targets business travelers, who are overwhelmingly male. By employing younger and prettier flight attendants than rivals, MAS seeks a competitive edge. Putting aside Malaysian law, local customs, and political correctness, the airline knew that using attractive women to lure male frequent fliers was a winning strategy.

A parallel marketing strategy directed at women was employed by a giant international cosmetics manufacturer, according to a former midlevel manager. In a lawsuit against L'Oréal USA, Inc., Elysa Yanowitz asserts that she was forced out of her job as a regional sales manager after she refused her boss's order to fire a sales associate because she was "not good looking enough."[14]

In a similar vein, in 2004, hip and upscale clothing retailer Abercrombie & Fitch agreed to pay $50 million to settle a lawsuit that accused the chain of promoting whites over minorities, relegating dark-skinned and less attractive employees to store areas where few customers were likely to see them. In addition, in its catalogs and elsewhere, it was accused of cultivating a company image of highly attractive white people. The settlement obliged Abercrombie & Fitch to pay $40 million to black, Hispanic, and Asian employees and job applicants and $10 million for attorneys' fees, and to monitor compliance of changes in its employment policies.[15] The U.S. Equal Employment Opportunity Commission (EEOC) estimated that some 10,000 Hispanic, Asian, and black people would share in the settlement of this lawsuit.

While the plaintiffs and the EEOC claimed victory, Abercrombie & Fitch spun the settlement another way, insisting that it had done nothing wrong. "We have, and always have had, no tolerance for discrimination," said CEO Mike Jeffries. "We decided to settle this suit because we felt that a long, drawn-out dispute would have been harmful to the company and distracting to management."

Former Abercrombie & Fitch managers Dan Moon and Andrea

Mandrick told *60 Minutes* reporter Morley Safer that they were hired for their good looks. They also revealed that corporate supervisors routinely had them reduce the working hours of less attractive salespeople. In their opinion, because the retailer's customer base was young, hip, well-educated white people, the discrimination they saw while working for the chain was more about "lookism" than it was about racism. They added that Abercrombie & Fitch was after a certain "look" in its sales force; the less someone had of this look, the less the salesperson worked. "I was sick of getting my schedule back every week with lines through names," says Mandrick. "I can't look the people that work for me . . . in the eye and . . . lie to them and say, 'Oh, we don't have hours,' when, really, it's because they weren't pretty enough."

• • •

If you are happily among the good-looking and have a job, over the long haul—and most likely, over the short term, too—you will probably be paid more than average-looking counterparts and you will probably rise to a higher level in the organization than those with less PA. Studies show that physically attractive people tend to have better-paying jobs in higher-level positions than do their less attractive counterparts.

How much more? Evidence from studies conducted in the United States, Canada, and China in 1994 and 1999 suggests that highly attractive employees enjoy increased earnings of between 7.5 percent and 15 percent over their average-looking peers.[16]

Why will a bottom-line business shell out more moola to those oozing PA if how they *look* doesn't make any difference in how well they do their job? Is it merely discrimination against the PA impaired, or does hiring good-looking people increase productivity or somehow help to bring in more bucks?

> Does hiring good-looking people increase productivity or somehow help to bring in more bucks?

To find out, economists Gerard A. Pfann of Holland's University of the Maastricht; Jeff E. Biddle, Michigan State University; Daniel S. Hamermesh, University of Texas, Austin; and Ciska M. Bosman of Nice, France, conducted a study focused on the looks of executives in Holland's busy and highly competitive advertising industry.[17] Pfann and his colleagues collected data from hundreds of Dutch advertising firms to analyze the effect of employees' attractiveness, or beauty, on their firms' performance.

They began by assuming that all else being equal, in an industry where employees frequently interact with clients, firms with more attractive workers will face less customer discrimination and thus gain a competitive advantage. But to make a difference on the bottom line of a balance sheet, the beauty of employees must have some measurable positive effect, both on the agency's production of revenue and on its profits after expenses. So, if an agency with beautiful workers pays them *more* than not-so-beautiful workers of equal ability, the company must somehow bring in not merely enough extra income to offset the expense of higher salaries and fringe benefits, but still more income to cover the expense of finding and hiring good-looking people and keeping other, less physically attractive workers motivated—and even more income to increase profit.

The income generated by employee labor is known as "quasi-rents," and according to economic theory, if quasi-rents increase with employee ability, profits may be increased by employing more able or productive workers.

In advertising firms, good working relationships among co-workers and with clients create a type of "human capital," and good ways to create these relationships lower the cost of acquiring this capital. So, more beautiful managers may find it easier to develop relationships with other employees and clients, generating higher earnings for themselves and higher quasi-rents for their company. All else being equal, firms with more beauty capital will produce more and obtain higher revenues. This was the theory that the data would either prove or debunk.

To begin their study, Pfann and his colleagues collected photos of the top management of 289 Dutch ad agencies, and then billing and earnings data from those agencies over a twelve-year span starting in 1984. Collectively, the agencies' sales volume represented about 70 percent of all ad industry revenue in the Netherlands—a very sizable sample.

Executive beauty was assessed using 1,282 black-and-white

photos—head-and-shoulders shots from industry yearbooks—an average of 2.71 pictures per firm. These photos were rated independently by a panel of two men and one woman aged 40 or older, and by a second panel of two men and one woman aged 39 or younger. (The makeup of these panels reflected the age-sex distribution of the ad agencies' clientele.) The people in the photos were rated on a five-point scale, where 5 was "strikingly handsome or beautiful" and 1 was "homely."

The panel rated the average ad-agency manager at 2.80, or just below average in PA. And, as expected, executive beauty had a positive effect on revenue. After taking into account such factors as the size and location of the agency and its experience in the industry, whether small or large, all but a few agencies with better-looking executives reported significantly higher revenue.

But hold on! Does beauty really bring success? What if it's the other way around—success attracts beauty? What if better-looking executives are attracted to join successful agencies *because* these firms bring in more revenue? By tracking employment records, Pfann and his colleagues found no evidence to support this notion: Previously successful firms did *not* attract better-looking executives.

In fact, the Dutch study showed that beauty is highly productive. Among all firms sampled, those with better-looking executives brought in an average of 120,000 guilders more per year in billing revenue. And aside from a handful of tiny agencies operating in Holland's most competitive business region, known as the Randstad, firms boasting better-looking management averaged an extra 188,000 guilders per year in revenue. (The study identified several very small firms, all operating in Holland's most competitive advertising environment, that lacked the financial resources or management ability to capitalize on having a few executives with higher-than-average PA.)

And how much better looking were the men and women who run top-earning firms than those of the average Dutch agency manager? Pfann and friends calculated that the most successful firms employed managers whose beauty was greater than that of ninety out of every hundred Dutch ad executives.

And now to the bottom line. What was the return on this investment of beauty capital? By massaging their Dutch data and estimating individual executive salaries based on industry data, Pfann calculated that good-looking execs created significantly more income from quasi-rents than they cost their companies in higher wages. Even though their own salaries substantially exceeded industry averages, their agencies earned even more. "Beauty capital yields returns to both workers and firms," concluded Pfann and his colleagues.

> Pfann calculated that good-looking execs created significantly more income than they cost their companies in higher wages.

More attractive employees also bring another asset to their employers: According to a 1999 study by Sara J. Solnick of the University of Miami and Maurice E. Schweitzer of the University of Pennsylvania's Wharton School, those blessed with PA tend to have an advantage in bargaining situations.

For many goods and services, the market price is influenced by both market forces and negotiations. In other words, some people or companies will pay more or receive less for the same items or tasks. For example, two executives being considered for similar jobs may get different salary offers but will be expected to perform the same work. The difference lies in the negotiating skills of both the executives and those offering them the job. Similarly, a company purchasing agent may get a manufacturer of, say, spark plugs to throw in a few extra for every hundred the company purchases.

Because many dimensions of business hinge on bargaining, good-looking negotiators may bring their organizations more for less business, which is one way of defining increased productivity. In an effort to see if the bargaining process was influenced by PA or by gender, Sara Solnick and Maurice Schweitzer conducted an "ultimatum game" experiment.[18]

They set up a stylized bargaining situation often used to examine a broad range of behaviors. Stripped to essentials, one player, "the Proposer," suggests a certain split of a monetary sum to the second player, "the Responder," who either accepts or rejects the split. If the proposal is accepted, the money is divided accordingly.

If rejected, neither player receives anything. Thus, for example, a Proposer may suggest a 60–40 split of $100 (the game only works if there is actual money involved) and the Responder either takes the $40 or turns down the offer and receives nothing.[19]

In theory, Proposers offer the smallest amount of money possible and Responders accept it because something is better than nothing. In practice, however, this is rarely the case. Typically, a Proposer offers about half of the available money—but about 10 percent of such offers are rejected. When a Proposer offers 20 percent of the total pie, responders reject it about half the time.[20]

Solnick and Schweitzer's ultimatum game experiment involved men and women selected as attractive or unattractive. In the first stage of the experiment, seventy subjects made ultimatum decisions and were photographed. Afterward, a panel of twenty judges rated the photographs for PA.

The most and least attractive men and women were then selected and randomly ordered into photo books. In the third stage, 108 subjects looked at these photos and made ultimatum game decisions that were resolved by pairing their decisions with those of the photographed subjects.

The study revealed *no significant difference* in decisions made by either the most attractive or least attractive players. In other words, PA had no influence on their judgments. On the other hand, the researchers found very significant differences in the way other players treated both groups. Men and physically attractive women were offered more, while less was demanded from unattractive women and men. The message to business is clear: Don't send an unattractive woman to negotiate on behalf of the firm because probably she will not drive as hard a bargain as a more attractive woman or almost any man.

Sexist? Undoubtedly. And yet that is what science says would provide the most profitable outcome.

• • •

While PA in business can spell "personal asset" to those who have it, those high in PA must also shoulder the burden of their bosses' higher expectations or jealousy—and when the boss is frustrated or disappointed, they pay a higher penalty for personal indiscretions than their more ordinary-looking colleagues.

This was the conclusion of a 2002 study by a psychology professor and a pair of undergraduate students at North Central College, in the Chicago suburb of Naperville. They assembled a group of ninety-eight students, including thirty-six MBA candidates, and asked them to act as "managers" in evaluating the actions of "employees" who violated a company policy against using company computers to access the Internet to shop.

Based on the data, Professor Karl Kelley and students Lori Nita and Brittain Bandura were able to observe how a manager's decision to punish an employee policy violator was affected by the employee's gender and PA. Their data revealed that attractive females were punished most harshly and attractive males suffered the least severe consequences. When it came to employees with low PA, however, the violator's gender made no difference.[21]

What's going on here? Why would managers come down harder on an attractive woman than an ordinary-looking one who had committed the same offense? Probably because business has a sort of love-hate relationship with beauty. Driven by ideals of fairness, or maybe envy, ill will can smolder against coworkers thought to have attained employment unjustly. Better-looking females are known particularly to be the target of such speculations. Managers are not insensitive to these dynamics and, to avoid accusations about preferential treatment, they can feel compelled to mete out stronger disciplinary action when a presumably preferred employee violates company rules. Their doing so is backhanded recognition that their PA opens many doors that remain closed to more average-looking people. Some managers therefore tend to hold their better-looking employees, whom they suspect have always gotten the breaks, more accountable for behaviors that have negative effects on the organization.[22]

When the North Central College researchers conducted a second study that asked a similar group of student participants to decide another employee disciplinary matter, the results were less conclusive. For this study, each participant was provided a section from an employee handbook outlining company policies on vacation, sick leave, and absences. An incident report described the employee's violation of company policy on missing work by repeatedly calling in sick when the individual was not in fact ill; instead, the employee used the time to moonlight for another employer or to address a relationship problem. They also got the employee's personnel file.

All information presented to the participants was identical except for the personnel file, which presented employees as male or female and sometimes included the employee's photo. In some cases, the photograph was manipulated to make its subject appear either very attractive or unattractive.

Students acting as "manager-evaluators" were unanimous in their agreement that the company policy was fair and that what the employee did was a clear violation of the policy. Participants differed, however, in their perceptions of the seriousness of a specific incident, demonstrating not uncommon sentiment against people presumed to benefit unjustly from good fortune, especially if they exploit it. Attractive males were judged more harshly than all others for the bogus sick call incidents, possibly due to a presumption about an unfair advantage in the workplace because of their appearance and sex. These judgments were consistent relative to attractive females as well as less attractive males and females, whether moonlighting or relationship problems motivated the sick calls.[23]

To whom much is given, much is expected. Benefits that come with PA carry higher standards and harsher consequences for violating or not meeting these standards. This might be an example of "expectancy-violation theory,"[24] which posits that while stereotypes often affect people's expectations of others, no two social judgments are ever exactly alike.

> To whom much is given, much is expected. Benefits that come with PA carry higher standards and harsher consequences for violating or not meeting these standards.

Another study, conducted by Comila Shahani-Denning, a Hofstra University professor, and doctoral student Dawn Plumitallo, confirmed this bias against attractiveness in a performance appraisal situation. They gave bank supervisors a memo describing a problem with a male or female employee who was portrayed as attractive, unattractive, or average. The memo asked the manager to assist in disciplining this employee. They found that supervisors were more likely to perceive an attractive employee as failing because of a lack of effort, whereas *unattractive* employees who fail were perceived as victims of bad luck—events or circumstances beyond their control.[25]

. . .

So you're good-looking, and just as your exceptional looks have opened many doors for you, you get this job—even though you were no better prepared for it than other candidates. If you keep your new job, you can expect a bigger salary and faster promotions than the average worker here. If you hope one day to rise to the top of your new company, you've got a good shot—but if you screw up, you can also expect to be treated more harshly than your fellow employees.

And as you get older, you will have to work harder and harder to hang on to your looks. So good luck. And what's this? You've been summoned for jury duty! Well, let's see how far physical attractiveness gets you in a court of law.

CHAPTER 6

Rendering Judgment: How Looks Affect Courtroom Results

How PA testifies in courtrooms, jury boxes, and judges' chambers

"May it please the court, I enter into evidence that my client is a tall, handsome, healthy specimen, as virile a defendant as has ever graced this chamber. Could such a man actually do the terrible things of which he is accused? Plainly, he could not! Furthermore, I pray the court take judicial notice of my own physiognomy, which includes a broad chest and lean waist set off by a head of thick, lustrous hair, pearl-white teeth, unblemished skin devoid of scars or moles, twinkling eyes, and a duo of disarming dimples. Obviously, you must and will believe everything that I say!

"I therefore have no doubt that the court will find that the crime of which my client is accused, though indeed a very serious offense,

could not possibly have been committed by such a splendid-looking
fellow as he. I now move that the court dismiss all charges, so that my
client may at once regain his liberty and return to the pursuit of
happiness to which he is so obviously entitled."

Okay, okay. Let's get real. Would any lawyer really come into court
with such a ludicrous defense, claiming that his client is so gorgeous
that he could not possibly be the archfiend de-
scribed in sworn testimony by a phalanx of
credible witnesses? Or that because the attorney
himself is a hunk, the judge and jury ought to
reject the testimony of a team of forensic experts, ignore a truckload of physical evidence—
and accept whatever the defendant's lawyer tells
them instead?

> Would any lawyer really come into court claiming that his client is so gorgeous that he could not possibly be the archfiend described in sworn testimony by a phalanx of credible witnesses?

You bet. Happens most every day.

Of course, few attorneys are so foolish as
to couch their argument quite so baldly—they
can't actually say such things aloud, much less for the record in a
court of law. But that doesn't stop smart lawyers from using their
own PA, that of witnesses, and especially their clients' own good
looks to influence jury verdicts and judicial rulings. And it's been
going on for a very long time.

Consider, for example, the 1929 trial of theater mogul Alexander Pantages, accused of raping seventeen-year-old Eunice Pringle.
She appeared in court with her long dark hair in a pigtail fastened
with a simple bow and wearing a dark blue, ankle-length dress with
Dutch collar and cuffs, long gloves, flat shoes, and black stockings—as demure an adolescent as ever took the witness stand.

Pantages denied that any rape had occurred, denied that one
was even attempted, swore that no such idea had even entered his
head. Miss Pringle had made an appointment to audition her dance
act, he said, then came to his downtown Los Angeles office. After
chatting for a few minutes, she suddenly jumped up and without
warning tore her clothing, jerked his shirt out of his pants, then ran
into Spring Street screaming that she had been raped.

Pringle told another story. Pantages had shown no interest in her act and had instead pawed her, and when she resisted he apparently became infused with animal lust. With almost superhuman strength, he overpowered her, forced her onto his carpeted floor, pried her legs apart, and had his way with her.

There were no other witnesses.

The case came down to "he said, she said." The jury seemed fascinated with the contrast between the charming, shy, sweet young girl and the wrinkled, scrawny, sixty-something Pantages and his stiff, Old-World manners.

Hoping to show the jury what kind of person Pringle really was, the attorneys for Pantages petitioned the judge to order her to appear for cross-examination dressed exactly as she had been on the day of the alleged rape. When Pringle returned to court the schoolgirl was gone. In her place was a sexy young thing in an adult hairstyle, full makeup, and a clinging, low-cut dress that accentuated every lush curve—an irresistible, full-bodied young woman with the face of an angel.

This was the worst thing that could have happened for Pantages. Now anyone could see how a man with his faded looks and old-fashioned clothing—a man with little sex appeal and few prospects—could have lusted after a sexy morsel like Pringle and lost control of his sexual urges.

The aging showman was convicted and sent to prison.

Two years later, however, on appeal, he won a new trial. New evidence was introduced that thoroughly discredited Pringle's testimony: By her sworn account, Pantages would have required not only superhuman strength but also four arms. New evidence suggested that Pringle had been bribed to bring rape charges against Pantages, paid by her forty-something lover, a mysterious Russian in the employ of an East Coast bootlegger, businessman, and banker named Joseph P. Kennedy. Yes, that Kennedy—the father of the future president of the United States. He coveted Pantages's chain of sixty theaters and wanted to buy them at fire-sale price to turn his start-up film studio into a rival to more established studios and himself into a player.

The second jury deliberated briefly; Pantages left court a free man.[1]

But how could such a thing happen? How could an innocent businessman with a sterling reputation be convicted of rape solely on the accusation of a single witness? Simply put, because the alleged victim was young and beautiful, and the alleged rapist exactly her opposite. Guided by a skilled prosecutor, jurors allowed intellect and reason to bow before emotion and instinct.

But it's hard to blame them: Science and society have struggled for centuries to find connections between human appearance and behavior, especially antisocial behavior.

> Science and society have struggled for centuries to find connections between human appearance and behavior, especially antisocial behavior.

In the sixteenth century, J. Baptiste della Porte (1535–1615) invented the pseudoscience of *physiognomy,* which claimed that judgments about people's character could be made from the appearance of their faces. After studying the cadavers of convicts executed for various crimes, he announced that people with small ears, bushy eyebrows, small noses, and large lips were the most likely to commit criminal acts. Two centuries later, physiognomist Johan Kaspar Lavater (1741–1801) made a connection between "shifty-eyed" people with weak chins and arrogant noses and criminal behavior.

Today, no serious sociologist or criminologist gives the slightest credence to such theories. Yet, until about 1950, respected academics known as "criminal anthropologists" preached that studying the human physique, or body constitution, would eventually show which people were born with genetically determined criminal tendencies, and that the expression of these "bad" genes could be ascertained by expert observation of an individual's facial features and body characteristics.[2]

Such pseudoscience probably rests on superstition, often intertwined with religious teachings, that links evil with ugliness. In antiquity, many people believed that those who consorted with or were possessed by demons, and often their descendants, were afflicted with repulsive appearances—God's way of warning others and of punishing sin. Evil creatures are variously described as the Old Testament's "fallen angels" or the New Testament's "malignant spirits." Many even have names and are associated with such

temptations as lust, mischief, or crime. For example, the demon
Asmodeus could take either male or female form; it filled people
with insatiable desires for sex, leading them to adultery, buggery,
even child molestation. Beelzebub, lord of flies, was believed to inspire murder and cannibalism—anything to do with dead bodies.
Nor were demons limited to Judeo-Christian theology. The Hindi
vampire demon Rakshasas, for example, is associated with murder
lust and was believed capable, for evil purposes, of reanimating dead
bodies.[3]

Even today—in an era of near-instantaneous worldwide communications, where billions of pages of Internet information are
available to anyone with a home computer, and in a time when
robotic explorers beam back close-up images of Saturn's moons and
the dry seabeds of Mars—millions of Americans say they believe the
Bible, demons included, is the literal Word of God. Not many years
ago a substantial fraction of America—not all residing in rural areas
or small towns—believed that when children were born with cere-
bral palsy, a brain disorder mostly afflicting motor skills, it was because of the sin of a parent or grandparent—bad blood, as it was
called.[4]

Still, it's been a while since "experts" opined that when it comes
to guilt or innocence, one's face equates to one's destiny. Surely,
civilization and the application of courtroom justice have come a
very long way, haven't they? Then what could cause a modern juror,
sworn to uphold the law and to determine the facts of a case, to be
swayed by the perception of a witness's physical attractiveness?

To help answer this question, in 1988 Bruce Darby and Devon
Jeffers of Ohio's Denison University created a mock jury to investigate the interaction and effect(s) of hypothetical defendants' PA on
jurors. They recruited seventy-eight college students to serve as
mock jurors and for openers asked them to rate their own PA.

Then photos of "defendants" were shown, "charges" were
read, and "evidence" introduced. The jury was asked to evaluate, in
turn, three categories of defendant—attractive, moderately attractive, or unattractive—and to decide not only the individual's guilt
or innocence but also, after rendering a guilty verdict, whether the

individual was truly responsible for the lawless act. Finally, jurors were asked to rate each defendant's trustworthiness, happiness, honesty, intelligence, and likability, and to recommend punishment for those "convicted."[5]

It should come as no surprise to anyone who has read the first five chapters of this book that attractive jurors were more likely to convict than to acquit an unattractive defendant. And that all jurors in the Darby and Jeffers experiment, regardless of their own personal PA, recommended the least severe punishment for the most attractive defendants. (Less attractive jurors, however, did not seem to factor a defendant's PA into decisions to convict or acquit.) Jurors with high personal PA rendered the harshest verdicts on the least attractive defendants, while jurors lacking in PA were toughest on average-looking defendants. So a smart attorney well versed in the art of criminal defense and representing a good-looking client facing a mountain of incriminating evidence will try to get the best-looking people he can find to put in the jury box. If the accused is PA-challenged, however, that same attorney will try to disqualify good-looking veniremen (i.e., prospective jurors) and seat only the least attractive. And when the client is, like most, only an average-looking person, a smart attorney will try to seat as many average-looking folks as possible.

Sounds pretty simple, no?

Not quite.

Actually, because of the possibility that studying an actual jury trial could affect its outcome, most studies on juror bias have been theoretical, which is to say, they don't involve actual defendants who are in jeopardy of losing life, liberty, or lucre. So any conclusions drawn from them must be tempered by that vital fact.

An important exception is the mammoth study conducted in Chicago in the early 1960s by Harry Kalven, Jr. and Hans Zeisel. They surveyed 225 actual juries and discovered that defendant characteristics, including PA, clearly influenced real-life jury verdicts.

Kalven and Zeisel also employed a questionnaire analysis to determine how judges, if asked to review evidence and determine guilt or innocence without the services of a jury, would have decided a case that had previously been tried before a jury. Their study encompassed nearly 4,000 trials and showed that judges agreed with jury verdicts only 78 percent of the time.

The study also showed that when judge and jury failed to agree, juries were more lenient in 19 percent of the cases while judges showed more leniency in only 3 percent.[6]

Why were juries more lenient than judges? According to this study, sentiment, no less than the need to be certain beyond reasonable doubt, influenced juries far more than it did judges. Juries were more inclined to go easy when a defendant showed genuine regret, had recently experienced life difficulties, or looked physically attractive. Juries also tended to go easier on defendants with a high-status occupation, particularly physicians and members of the clergy; with personal demographics revealing elderly age and widow marital status; or when a likely guilty accomplice escaped penalty through plea bargaining and testifying against the defendant.

Not only are good-looking defendants less likely to be convicted, but when they are, they are likely to suffer less severe punishment than an unattractive person convicted of the same offense.

More recent research confirms and amplifies these findings as they bear on a defendant's looks: Not only are good-looking defendants less likely to be convicted, but when they are, they are likely to suffer less severe punishment than an unattractive person convicted of the same offense.

If justice were PA blind, a person's looks should make no difference to the judge who decides how much bail to assess a defendant awaiting trial in return for liberty. But is this true? To learn if that were so, a pair of British researchers collected data on bail sums assessed defendants in a variety of misdemeanor cases. Then police officers, none of whom were involved with the particular case in question, were asked to rate the attractiveness of the actual defendant in each case.

The data showed that, alas, not even judges are immune to the PA spell. On the average, most judges set bail for attractive defendants significantly lower than for those less attractive.

The same study also examined fines levied by judges against people convicted of misdemeanors. Again, the better-looking defendant usually got off with a smaller fine than did an unattractive offender convicted of the same offense. While this suggests that the legal system operates with a bias for attractive people and against ugly ones, this particular study also demonstrated a much weaker correlation between a defendant's looks and a judge's punishment in *felony* cases.[7]

When it comes to sentencing, most judges are empowered with wide latitude of discretion. Even where there are minimum-sentence laws, a jurist can order a convict imprisoned under very severe conditions, sent to a country club–type minimum security facility, or freed on probation. Often jurists can elect to substitute psychiatric treatment for prison. But when do a defendant's looks provide a reason to hand down less onerous types of sentences?

To answer this question, researchers Stuart McKelvie and James Coley of Bishop's University in Quebec, Canada, recruited 384 undergraduate students for mock juries. For each case, mock jurors were presented with a dozen experimental conditions, including a description of the defendant's crime and a picture of the defendant's face. Then they were asked to make sentencing recommendations. Although the severity of punishment meted out was greater for a murder than for a robbery, it did not differ significantly no matter how attractive—or not—the defendant appeared. A less attractive robber, however, was more likely to get a recommendation for psychiatric care than was a more attractive miscreant. In this study, jurors equated ugliness with bad behavior as it applies to mental illness—but not when it comes to criminal acts.[8]

But a defendant's PA, as well as the appearance of a witness against that defendant, can also warp a jury's perception of guilt. Professor Karl L. Wuensch of the Department of Psychology at East Carolina University in Greenville, North Carolina, and his colleague, Charles H. Moore, set out to see how this theory might work. They enlisted more than 300 student volunteers as mock jurors in a supposed lawsuit in which a man accused his female boss of sexual harassment.

Using several sets of mock juries, Wuensch and Moore manipulated the physical attractiveness of both accused and accuser. Jurors were asked to decide if the female defendant was guilty and then to rate their own "certainty of belief" in the defendant's guilt or innocence.

As it happened, jurors were more convinced of a woman's guilt if the man who brought the charges was attractive than if he was not. It was, in other words, easier for a juror to believe that a woman might cross the line of propriety if the object of her desire was a hunk than if he was ordinary looking.

Female jurors also treated the issue of an *accusing man's* PA as significant only when the woman defendant was *unattractive*. When a pretty woman was accused of sexual harassment, her accuser's looks seemed to make little difference to women on the mock jury.

With male jurors, however, the accuser's attractiveness significantly affected perception of guilt when the defendant was attractive. When accused and accuser significantly *differed* in their degree of attractiveness, women jurors were somewhat more likely than male jurors to conclude that sexual harassment had indeed taken place.[9]

Beyond sexual harassment lies rape, and in many rape cases that go before a jury, verdicts often hang on which party has more credibility, the alleged victim or the alleged rapist. In an attempt to discern whether the PA of these parties affects jurors, in 2001 researchers at Britain's University of Portsmouth set up a two-part study.[10] Alder Vrij and Hannah Firmin first asked volunteers to take a self-exam called Burt's Rape Myth Acceptance Scale (RMA), which correlates an individual's attitudes toward rape by measuring how accepting he or she is of common—but false or erroneous—myths about forcible sexual congress.

Test subjects were then invited to share their perception of a hypothetical rape case. Although every subject heard the same scenario, descriptions concerning attractiveness varied for the alleging victim and alleged offender. Vrij and Firmin sought to determine whether this appearance feature of supposed rape victims and offenders influences their credibility and, if so, whether the effect differs according to a jury member's stance toward legends about rape incidents.

Test results were mixed. Nevertheless, Vrij and Firmin concluded that sufficient PA bias existed that anyone being considered for a jury in a rape trial, or for employment as a police officer, should be required to take the RMA exam.

They might also have concluded that judges who hear rape cases would serve their communities better if they, too, were conversant with Burt's RMA. That's because other studies of both simulated and actual trials indicate that a handsome rapist is more likely to get off with a shorter sentence than an ugly rapist who committed a similar crime. That is to say, judges frequently give more lenient sentences to attractive people convicted of rape.[11]

Moreover, any defendant accused of raping an *un*attractive victim is less likely to be found guilty than one accused of raping an attractive victim.[12]

> Any defendant accused of raping an *un*attractive victim is less likely to be found guilty than one accused of raping an attractive victim.

Jurors also like defendants and attorneys who smile on appropriate occasions more than those who don't.[13]

Not everyone can look like a movie star, of course. But most jury consultants—usually a psychologist who helps attorneys select jurors—agree that even a good suit or a new tie can help make jurors see a defendant as a more attractive person. In fact, a 1968 study of inmates whose appearance was improved by cosmetic surgery before their release found that this group of multiple offenders was less likely to return to jail than those who did not get such surgery. They were even less likely to return than inmates who received rehabilitation services. A decade later, a follow-up study of former inmates found that while the surgery did not affect the chances of someone committing another crime, it lowered the probability that the offender would be returned to prison for that crime.[14]

In summary, unless your attractiveness was obviously helpful to you in committing a crime (something I'll talk about later in this chapter), you are less likely to be convicted and less likely to see the inside of a jail if you are perceived as attractive—even if that requires you to wear dentures, tint your hair, climb into elevator shoes, or wear a Wonderbra. Or, if you have the time and money, get a new nose and do something about those bags under your eyes.[15]

• • •

Physical attractiveness also has an effect on the outcome of civil trials. The PA of witnesses, attorneys, and litigants influences jurors and judges in these proceedings in much the same way as in criminal proceedings.

Nowhere is this more evident than in how juries treat the testimony of expert witnesses. Samuel Gross, a University of Michigan law professor, has written about the paradox of expert testimony. He noted that "we call expert witnesses to testify about matters that are beyond the ordinary understanding of lay people (that is both the major practical justification and a formal legal requirement for expert testimony), and then we ask lay judges and jurors to judge their testimony . . . ."[16]

Expert witnesses are expected to instruct the jury in such complex and often arcane matters as economic modeling, business practices in foreign countries, medical procedures, animal anatomy, physics, chemistry, and a host of other technical or scientific disciplines. In high-stakes civil cases, expert witnesses frequently are called to testify by both plaintiff and defendant, usually offering subtly different but sometimes diametrically opposite conclusions.

Which expert does a juror believe?

Often, it's the one who looks and sounds the most believable. Or it is the expert who is the most likable or the most attractive. Judges, who usually have both legal training and years of experience in courtrooms, are often able to set aside the influences of PA when evaluating an expert witness's testimony. However, jurors as a group are less able to separate their *feelings* about a witness from what that person has told them. This is also true about the way jurors perceive lawyers who introduce evidence, elicit testimony, or cross-examine a witness. Whether male or female, jurors will find the more attractive attorney more likable and therefore more believable and worthy of trust.[17]

• • •

While statutes prohibiting discrimination in such areas as housing, schooling, and employment on the basis of race, ethnicity or religion, gender, or age have been on the books for decades, only a few

U.S. jurisdictions have legislation specifically addressing appearance-based discrimination.[18] One of them is the District of Columbia, where the statute prohibiting employment discrimination includes "personal appearance" as a protected category.

The DC statute defines "personal appearance" as "the outward appearance of any person, irrespective of sex, with regard to bodily condition or characteristics, manner or style of dress, and manner or style of personal grooming, including, but not limited to, hairstyle and beards."

> Only a few U.S. jurisdictions have legislation specifically addressing appearance-based discrimination.

A Santa Cruz, California, ordinance prohibits discrimination based on, among other things, "physical characteristics," defined as "a bodily condition or characteristic of any person which is from birth, accident, or disease, or from any natural physical development, or any event outside the control of that person, including individual physical mannerisms." But while Michigan, for example, prohibits discrimination based on height or weight, it provides no coverage for other aspects of physical appearance.

If "lookism" is still legal in most of the United States, in the English-speaking nations of the former British Commonwealth, where British common law remains the basis for civil codes, physical attractiveness is addressed in unusual ways. In Australia, until November 2002, a woman suing for damages arising from the wrongful death of her husband by another was required to undergo a humiliating hearing where a judge, after considering her age, "warmth of personality," and physical attractiveness, would determine how "marriageable" she was and therefore by how much her damages should be reduced! Australian courts, however, have presumed that few men are financially dependent on their wives, and on the few occasions that such dependency has been demonstrated in spousal wrongful death cases, judges have never required a widower to undergo a similar evaluation of his marriage prospects.[19]

• • •

There is, of course, no truly objective measure of individual PA as it relates to its influence on a jury's determination of guilt or innocence or the harshness or forbearance of sentencing.

If "finders of facts"—judges or a jury impaneled to decide the fate of defendants—tend to discover more mercy in their hearts for those who look more rather than less like they do, will they not also note, for example, such an obvious component of physical attractiveness as skin pigmentation, no less than the size and shape of facial features? In other words, if a defendant of one race comes before a jury of another race, do jurors allow their PA biases to distort justice?

One classic study of this phenomenon, by David A. Abwender and Kenyatta Hough, involved 207 participants chosen from twenty-five regional postbaccalaureate achievement programs at universities across the United States. They were high-achieving college graduates who were first-generation Americans from low-income, ethnic minority groups. Participants had been previously selected for special academic training to better prepare them for completing doctoral programs; they were therefore presumably brighter and possessed more mature judgment than an average American. Because few prospective test subjects were of Asian or Native American ancestry, researchers limited their test group to those describing themselves as African American, Hispanic, or white. The group ranged in age from nineteen to fifty-one years; the mean age was twenty-four.

While several previous studies indicated that PA was a significant factor in jury decisions, no previous study had explored negligent homicide, an unintentional crime associated with poor or lapsed judgment and lacking any implication that a defendant had exploited PA for personal gain. Abwender and Hough sought to learn if a defendant's higher PA would lead a mock juror to expect them to display better judgment. If so, they theorized, then male jurors should be harsher with an attractive woman accused of a crime of negligence, such as vehicular homicide. Because previous studies suggest that women care less about a female defendant's PA, researchers theorized that the expectation of better judgment should be weaker for a female juror.

They also sought to confirm a second hypothesis: that African American jurors would show greater leniency toward an African American defendant than white jurors would, while white jurors would treat African Americans more harshly than members of their own race.

The researchers asked study subjects to read an account of a vehicular homicide that described the facts and circumstances of a killing in an identical manner, except for three particulars: the defendant's PA, which varied between highly attractive and unattractive; the defendant's gender; and the defendant's race, which was variously stated as African American or white. Participants were then asked to rate the defendant's guilt and to recommend a prison sentence.

Contrary to the researchers' expectations and some previous studies, when the crime was negligent homicide, women treated an unattractive female defendant more harshly than an attractive female defendant. In other words, even if women jurors expect a little better judgment from a prettier woman, they still give her a break when it comes to sentencing. Men, on the other hand, were more inclined to give an *un*attractive woman that break, but neither rewarded nor penalized a woman for her good looks. In summary, when an attractive woman screws up big-time, her PA never hurts but could help if there are enough women on the jury.

As for issues of race, Abwender and Hough found that African American participants showed greater leniency when the defendant was described as African American. Hispanic participants, however, dealt more severely with African Americans than with those described as white. White participants, against researchers' expectations, displayed no measurable race-based bias.[20]

The study subjects for this experiment, however, were chosen from an atypical pool. While all were minorities, including those who identified themselves as whites, as potential jurors they were also, like Yogi Bear, "smarter than the average bear." Young college graduates who had been accepted into doctoral programs, individually and collectively they did not much resemble America's pool of potential jurors.

America carries the stain of centuries of racial bias. It was shocking, but hardly surprising, when novelist Harper Lee made this point in her 1960 Pulitzer Prize–winning novel, *To Kill a Mockingbird*: "In our courts, when it's a white man's word against a black man, the white man always wins. They're ugly, but those are the facts of life. . . . The one place a man ought to get a square deal is in the courtroom, be he any color of the rainbow, but people have a way of carrying their resentments right into a jury box."

Forty years later, two University of Michigan scholars set out to learn if the racial biases so blatant and acceptable in 1960 were still operating. On the basis of previously published research reports, Samuel R. Sommers and Phoebe C. Ellsworth hypothesized that during the intervening decades, race relations and related matters had been so widely publicized that in any trial where race was an issue, most white jurors would bend over backward to avoid even the appearance of bigotry.[21]

From previous research suggesting that the character and complexity of race relations in America had changed, they concluded that the elimination of race-based laws and increased economic and social opportunities for minorities, especially blacks, had made racial relations far more nuanced than before the Civil Rights struggle of the 1960s. What they didn't know, and so sought to learn, was if white jurors might be biased against black defendants when the case to be decided had no obvious racial dimension.

Sommers and Ellsworth sent a white male research assistant to the waiting area of an international airport, where he handed out questionnaires to 196 U.S.-born white travelers who ranged in age from eighteen to eighty-three. Their median age was forty-three, and 55 percent were male. Because each traveler had to show a driver's license to pass through airport security, and because in that state driver's license holders are called for jury duty, it was assumed that all test subjects would be eligible for jury duty.

These test subjects were asked to read a brief trial summary and then encouraged to place themselves in the role of juror while answering a questionnaire about legal issues required to resolve a trial.

The trial summary included two paragraphs summarizing the prosecutor's case, two paragraphs summarizing the defense case, and a set of judicial instructions that laid out the legal criteria for conviction. The narrative described a mythical locker-room altercation between two high school basketball players. The prosecution alleged that one player intentionally assaulted the other. The defense maintained that the contact that had caused injury was unintentional: When a third player intervened, the defendant claimed that he panicked, tried to leave the area, and in the process *accidentally* struck the victim.

In the "race salient" version of the trial summary, a witness testified that the defendant was one of only two players of his race (either white or black) on the team and had previously been subjected to unfair criticism and racial slurs. In another version of events, a witness testified that the defendant had only one friend on the team and had previously been the object of obscene remarks and unfair criticism; but there is no mention of race.

Mock jurors received different versions of the trial summary. Some jurors were told that a black male student was accused of hitting a white male student, then the races are reversed in the version told to other jurors. All mock jurors were asked to decide if the defendant was guilty or not guilty, and then, using a nine-point scale, to rate their confidence in this verdict as well as the strength of the defense and prosecution cases. Finally, mock jurors were asked to choose a sentencing option for a person found guilty of assault. The nine options ranged in severity from probation to four years in prison.

When the data were in, Sommers and Ellsworth learned that nearly three-fourths of all mock jurors found the defendant guilty; in this there was no significant difference between male and female jurors. In the race-salient component, the defendant's race made a slight difference to mock jurors (69 percent convicted the white defendant; 66 percent found the black defendant guilty). The largest difference in conviction rates came in the non-race-salient component, where all-white mock jurors convicted the black defendant 90 percent of the time but the white defendant only 70 percent of the time.

The data also showed that when race was *not* a salient component of the case, mock jurors consistently gave higher ratings to the strength of the prosecution's case than to the defense's, and higher ratings to their confidence in their own verdict. When race was salient, however, mock jurors gave lower ratings to the prosecution, higher ratings to the defense, and indicated less confidence in their own verdicts.

From these findings, Sommers and Ellsworth concluded that white juror bias is alive and well whenever there is no obvious racial component to a case against a black defendant. The researchers also suggested that one way to mitigate such antiblack bias is to ensure that all juries include black jurors.

Although attractive defendants seem to have an advantage, researchers have indicated that this situation relates only to such crimes as rape, robbery, and other offenses involving theft.[22] For other types of crimes, and in particular those where someone apparently relied on his or her own PA in furtherance of a crime, being good-looking can cost a defendant dearly.

> Although attractive defendants seem to have an advantage, for types of crimes where someone apparently relied on PA in furtherance of a crime, being good-looking can cost a defendant dearly.

In a 1975 experiment, researchers Harold Sigall and Nancy Ostrove presented sets of mock jurors with a mythical case in which a female defendant was accused, variously, of swindling an unmarried man by convincing him to give her $2,200 to invest in a nonexistent company, or, alternatively, of breaking into his home during the hours of darkness and making off with the same amount of cash.

Half the participants were led to believe that the female defendant was attractive, while the others believed that she was unsightly. True to the PA stereotype, when it came to burglary—a crime where the perpetrator tries not to be seen—the more attractive defendant received a less punitive sentence than that given to the unattractive defendant.

So, when a person uses his or her own elevated PA to help commit a crime, jurors are unlikely to exercise leniency.

There may be no better example of this phenomenon than the infamous case of Ruth Snyder. In the small hours of March 20, 1927, with assistance from her lover, Judd Gray, she killed her husband, Albert Snyder. Ruth and Judd first bludgeoned Albert with a cast-iron window sash weight, then had to finish him off by first strangling him with picture wire before finally stuffing a chloroform-soaked cloth in his nose.

Then—quietly, so as not to wake her sleeping nine-year-old daughter—they ransacked the house to give the appearance of a burglary gone wrong. Before leaving, Judd tied Ruth up and left her in the hallway to give credence to her claim to police that she had been attacked by two "giant Italians."

Police didn't buy it. Ruth was thirty-two, gorgeous, voluptuous, and had a reputation as a party girl who wasn't too particular about whose bed she woke up in. Albert was forty-six, not much to look at, an assistant art editor at a motor-boating magazine, a hardworking, low-paid homebody. And, oh yeah, a few weeks before the "attack of the giant Italians," Ruth had tricked her husband into buying a new life insurance policy that paid twice the normal death benefit if Albert died violently.

Detectives didn't have to lean too hard on Ruth to get a confession. It was, she said, all Judd's doing. She found him irresistible; she was crazed with desire and had to have him. Judd insisted that they kill Albert, and he was relentless, and when she could no longer put him off she gave in and unwillingly went along.

Judd, a corset salesman, was soon in a cell—but telling another story: Ruth was the irresistible one. She had ensnared him with her steamy sexuality and manipulated him into killing Albert. She was the mastermind, he just another victim.

The press mined this gold for every nugget they could dredge up. Ruth and Judd were tried together. Although the venue was New York City, justice moved with the alacrity of a frontier town. The trial began less than thirty days after the murder, and for the next three weeks, fed by the tabloid press and the emerging medium of radio, America followed with fascination as Judd and Ruth took turns testifying about each other's viciousness. The trial was attended by songwriter Irving Berlin, film pioneer D. W. Griffith, and the producers of *Chicago,* a Broadway musical about women doing prison time for murder.

The jury debated a mere hundred minutes before finding both killers guilty. A few months went by while their appeals were heard and rejected. By autumn, New York Governor Al Smith had denied their clemency petition. The lovers perished minutes apart in Sing Sing's electric chair.

But their story lives on in American pop culture: It was the basis for James Cain's *Double Indemnity,* a novel adapted by Raymond Chandler and Billy Wilder into a film starring Fred MacMurray and Barbara Stanwyck as star-crossed lovers and Edward G. Robinson as the implacable insurance investigator who brings them to justice.

As for the real Ruth Snyder, the jury might easily have spared her life. In 1928, few New Yorkers were comfortable with the idea of executing a woman, especially in the then-new and fiendish electric chair. But, no. Ruth came to court in stylish skirts and sheer black stockings that set off her long legs. Her tightly tailored suits and blouses announced an ample bosom. She wore an immaculate coiffure and perfectly lacquered nails. She spoke in low, measured tones. It wasn't hard to see how Ruth could have wrapped first Albert Snyder and then Judd Gray around either of her sinuous little fingers. There were twelve men on the jury and they got it right away: As long as she drew breath, Ruth Snyder could get any man to do her bidding. She was poison—anyone could see it just by looking at her.[23]

CHAPTER 7

Physiognomy and Public Service

How PA influences candidates, elections, policy,
and governance

"A clever, ugly man every now and then is successful with the ladies, but a handsome fool is irresistible." So wrote novelist William Makepeace Thackeray, long before the communications revolution that allows the handsome to reveal themselves as fools to millions in the blink of an eye.

Thackeray wrote of success in romance, implying seduction: lovers fostering feelings that make the object of their affections feel comfortably desirous about surrendering their bodies, their entire being, to the seducer.

What are modern electoral politics if not campaigns of seduction? Isn't an election much like a courtship, where several candidates, instead of competing for the opportunity to pass their genes along through a single mate, vie for each voter's affection, for the opportunity to pass their *ideas* and policies along? If you examine the process, rather than the result, isn't the real objective of an election to get voters—objects of the candidates' desire—to surrender their vote?

Physical attractiveness isn't just important in the sexual arena. Candidates for political office have great concern about optimizing their PA, too. And the higher the office, the greater the concern.

America's last PA-challenged president was elected in 1860. Tall and gaunt, Abraham Lincoln had gigantic hands and feet; oversize ears; asymmetrical features that included a too-prominent nose; gnarled, yellowish skin; thick, unruly hair; an awkward, almost comical gait; and a penchant for careless dress. His appearance inspired churlish jokes and childish ridicule, and not merely among children.

America's last PA-challenged president was elected in 1860.

For example, on March 27, 1861, just three weeks after Lincoln's inauguration, after establishment of the Confederacy but before open warfare began, *London Times* reporter William Russell was waiting in an anteroom when the new president entered. Russell confided to his diary that:

> Soon afterwards there entered, with a shambling, loose, irregular, almost unsteady gait, a tall, lank, lean man, considerably over six feet in height, with stooping shoulders, long pendulous arms, terminating in hands of extraordinary dimensions, which, however, were far exceeded in proportion by his feet. He was dressed in an ill-fitting, wrinkled suit of black, which put one in mind of an undertaker's uniform at a funeral; round his neck a rope of black silk was knotted in a large bulb, with flying ends projecting beyond the collar of his coat; his turned-down shirt-collar disclosed a sinewy muscular yellow neck, and above that, nestling in a great black mass of hair, bristling and compact like a ruff of mourning pins, rose the strange quaint face and head, covered with its thatch of wild, republican hair, of President Lincoln.

The impression produced by the size of his extremities, and

by his flapping and wide projecting ears, may be removed by the appearance of kindliness, sagacity, and the awkward bonhomie of his face; the mouth is absolutely prodigious; the lips, straggling and extending almost from one line of black beard to the other, are only kept in order by two deep furrows from the nostril to the chin; the nose itself—a prominent organ—stands out from the face, with an inquiring, anxious air, as though it were sniffing for some good thing in the wind; the eyes dark, full, and deeply set, are penetrating, but full of an expression which almost amounts to tenderness; and above them projects the shaggy brow, running into the small hard frontal space, the development of which can scarcely be estimated accurately, owing to the irregular flocks of thick hair carelessly brushed across it. . . .

A person who met Mr. Lincoln in the street would not take him to be what—according to the usages of European society—is called a "gentleman," and, indeed, since I came to the United States, I have heard more disparaging allusions made by Americans to him on that account than I could have expected among simple republicans, where all should be equals; but, at the same time, it would not be possible for the most indifferent observer to pass him in the street without notice.[1]

Although a principled man and a brilliant orator, Lincoln had never held national office. He won the presidential election of 1860 only after America's dominant political parties, the Democrats and the Whigs, split themselves along geographical lines over that very issue, while Lincoln's new Republican Party, firmly committed to ending slavery, remained united.

Even so, had most voters been exposed to his physical appearance in the modern manner, it is doubtful that Lincoln could ever have won national office. When he stood for election, however, neither television nor motion pictures had been invented and periodicals of his era were incapable of reproducing photographs. Consequently, few voters actually knew exactly what Lincoln looked like, though many had seen drawings or read newspaper accounts.

We live in different times. On television and the Internet, information circles the planet at a furious pace. Video footage of anyone aspiring to high office is ubiquitous. In such a media environment, PA is more than important—it is vital. As Michael Deaver, an aide to President Ronald Reagan and an enormously successful presidential image manager, famously observed, "In the television age, image sometimes is as useful as substance."[2]

> We live in different times. Video footage of anyone aspiring to high office is ubiquitous. In such a media environment, PA is more than important—it is vital.

But what, exactly, is image?

Image is more than PA. It is both truth and lie, both accurate perception and the gap between reality and perception. It is neither policy nor substance but linked to both. Image is deposited in the ATMs of public consciousness picture by picture, slogan by slogan, slowly gathering value and accruing interest in the bank of public opinion.

Ultimately, our image of the president encompasses his character, talents, worldview, style, family life, and reputed sexual behavior. It includes his use of language, speaking voice, repertoire of facial expressions, and most important, his physical appearance—which in our media era sharply limits who can even be considered a serious candidate for president.[3]

Consider what happened to H. Ross Perot when he ran for president in 1992. A natural leader who had been elected battalion commander and president of his class at the U.S. Naval Academy, Perot was a brilliant salesman and manager who built a billion-dollar company from scratch, a self-made mogul without even a hint of scandal in his life. When his employees were trapped in revolutionary Iran, he spent his own money to hire mercenaries to rescue them. Patriot, shrewd businessman and innovative manager, loyal and decisive leader, Perot was one of the best-qualified people ever to seek the presidency.

But he was short. Very short. He had jug-handle ears. He spoke in a squeaky Southern accent. Although he wore expensive suits, they never looked as good on him as they did on taller rivals. When Perot debated on television, instead of mouthing meaningless but easy-to-recall slogans, he used charts and graphs to make his points. He appealed to people's intellect instead of their guts. He ran against two tall, handsome, well-spoken men and was lampooned without pity by editorial cartoonists from coast to coast. He got a mere 8 percent of the vote.

While America reputedly boasts the world's most obese population, our last truly fat president was the 320-pound William Howard Taft—elected in 1912. In today's America, however, a man that big, regardless of qualifications, has a hard time winning election even to a local office.

Consider the predicament of Montgomery County Executive Douglas Duncan, political leader of Maryland's largest county. Since winning a first term in 1994, Duncan, who stands six-feet-four-inches tall, had steadily gained weight, creeping upward toward 300 pounds. Not only did this have health ramifications—he has a back problem—but he was very aware that voters seemed to want candidates who resemble network news anchors—trim, healthy-looking, and thick-haired. "If Duncan hadn't put on the brakes, he'd be in danger of entering the Taft Zone," a *Washington Post* columnist wrote.

His predicament was driven home during his initial campaign for county executive, when an elderly Leisure World resident, on the way to cast her ballot, stopped and peered up at him.

"What's your name?" she asked.

"Doug Duncan," he replied. "I'm running for county executive."

"Well, I'm voting for you, you big, fat Irishman!"[4]

Thinking about this encounter later, Duncan decided that he might gain a few votes from those who fancy obese Irishmen, but in general he didn't want to be the Big Guy, which is little guy speak for "fatty."

Late-nineteenth-century American politicians were Big Guys and proud of it. As America expanded, so did its leadership. After the Civil War, America boomed; and the most obvious measure of a man's prosperity was the circumference of his trousers—to the point where bursting-at-the-collar politicians were caricatured by the cartoonist of the era. The manly example of virile American manhood was king-size razor blade mogul King C. Gillette. It was barrel-chested financier J. P. Morgan. It was vest-stretching politician Chester A. Arthur.

Power corrupts, as Lord Acton noted. After the inevitable scandals, "industrialists" became "robber barons," while politicians were "fat cats" sucking "pork" from the public "larder." When, one by one, the political bosses were pulled from their pedestals, it did not escape public attention and the new illustrated periodicals that New York's Boss Tweed, Boston's legendary James Michael Curley, and a host of lesser scoundrels were, to a man, unusually well fed.

"Fat politicians are at a particular disadvantage in modern America," says Jeremy Mayer, a Georgetown University professor. "Baldness, ugliness, and even excessively hirsute eyebrows, à la Mike Dukakis, are forgivable sins, because . . . they are beyond the control of the politician. Weight, rightly or wrongly, is seen in America to be a personal, and even a moral, failing."[5]

So when Duncan decided that he wasn't cut out to be the Big Guy, he followed a well-worn path trod by Massachusetts Senator Ted Kennedy, who every six years, just in time for the election, sheds a little of his extra adipose, and President Bill Clinton, who assiduously lost twenty pounds just before his 1996 campaign. Duncan went on a diet, upped his exercise regimen, and sculpted just enough weight from his image to get reelected.

In our media-driven era, image is everything.

In America, estimates of the prevalence of bald or mostly bald men over thirty-five years of age range from 40 percent to 70 percent. Yet the last president without a good head of hair was Dwight Eisenhower—elected in 1952. Of the sixteen men who sought a major party's presidential nomination in 2000 and 2004, none was overweight and all were follicularly gifted.

Of the sixteen men who sought a major party's presidential nomination in 2000 and 2004, none was overweight and all were follicularly gifted.

Since the campaign of John F. Kennedy, the first to make regular use of television in a run for the White House, the trend toward greater presidential PA is clear. The last four chief executives (Ronald Reagan, George H. W. Bush, Bill Clinton, and George W. Bush) were far more attractive men than those who preceded them: Lyndon Johnson, Richard Nixon, Gerald Ford, and Jimmy Carter.

So vital is it to inside-the-Beltway movers and shakers that polit-ical success rest on something less brainless and amoral than simple physical attractiveness that no less a political powerhouse than Sena-tor John McCain could say with a straight face that "Washington is a Hollywood for ugly people. Hollywood is a Washington for the simpleminded."[6] (McCain, of course, has a much younger, looks-like-a-movie-star second wife.)

In reality, looks count for a lot in politics.

But don't take my word for it.

Look at what Professor James N. Schubert witnessed in Roma-nia during a sabbatical from Northern Illinois University. Along with a University of Bucharest biologist, Schubert was studying the political dimensions of the AIDS epidemic. As it happened, Roma-nia was holding national elections at the time, so each of sixteen presidential candidates got equal time on state-run Romanian TV, to the point where almost nothing else was on the tube. Schubert, who teaches political science, found himself watching endless speeches in a language he doesn't understand.

Out of boredom, he videotaped the candidates, and when the election was over, he was struck by the way each candidate's looks correlated with how they fared in the popular vote.

These conclusions, however, were based on his own, unscien-tific appraisal of each candidate's PA. To validate these impressions, he designed an experiment. In 1997 and 1998 he showed still pic-tures and silent videotapes of Romanian candidates to groups across America and Asia. Schubert then asked study participants to rate the candidates' electability. To Schubert's continuing amazement, the winners of the Romanian election were also winners with test sub-jects. Candidates who *looked* the most electable were the most often elected.[7]

In other words, voters don't much care what's in the box as long as it's wrapped well. It's all about packaging.

Or is it?

With help from research assistants, Schubert began to dissect the winning faces, measuring cheekbones, chins, eyebrow ridges, and facial symmetry. His conclusion: Most people, regardless of culture, like male leaders with pronounced lower jaws, sharp brow ridges and cheekbones, and receding hairlines. Tough and strong more than handsome. Schubert calls this look "facial dominance." Think Charlton Heston. Think Steven Seagal. Think Arnold Schwarzenegger.

Turning his attention to American politicians, Schubert focused on forty men and women running for Congress in the 1999–2000 races. He asked test subjects to rate the electability, competence, compassion, honesty, likability, leadership ability, attractiveness, and facial dominance of candidates based solely on photos and video of the candidates. His data showed that attractive candidates rated high on such visceral qualities as compassion and likability. Unless, of course, they were *too* attractive; then many voters wrote them off as eye candy. And once again, those with dominant faces rated high on competence and leadership.

"People aren't aware of it; they don't understand they're doing it," says Schubert. "These are implicit stereotypes . . . when you have little political *issue* information, the kind of information people [do] have access to is what they see in three-second sound bites on the evening news."

In the 2004 U.S. presidential election, hunky North Carolina Senator John Edwards scored high in attractiveness but low in facial dominance. Most people gave him high marks on such qualities as honesty and compassion, but Edwards had to work hard to overcome that baby face, constantly reminding crowds that he was fifty years old, mature and experienced, an able leader.

At the other end of the PA scale was Dennis Kucinich. In the media he was often compared to an elf, a troll, a hobbit, a UFO pilot, and runner-up for most likely to resemble a Home Depot manager. Schubert categorized Senator John Kerry, the eventual Democratic candidate, as the lonely resident of a sort of facial no-man's land, rating neither high nor low on dominance or attractiveness. "He is not distinguished," Schubert opined.

But then there was the former NATO commander and retired general Wesley Clark. Proud owner of the most classically dominant face, he initially led the large field of Democratic candidates for the party nomination. But not for long.

Wait. So it isn't just packaging, after all?

No. Not *just* packaging. Other factors also affect voters' decision-making processes. Even so, as Schubert says, "People are more likely to pay attention to an Edwards than a Kucinich."

One factor that mitigates Schubert's findings is the duration of a political campaign. Unlike in Romania, where campaigning is limited to a few weeks before the election, American presidential campaigns run on for well over a year. General Wesley Clark established a following based on facial dominance early in his campaign, when people knew very little about him. Months later, however, after voters had had ample time to hear and read where he stood on various issues, they decided that facial dominance alone wasn't sufficient, although a determined minority of image-conscious voters kept Clark's hopes alive in the primaries long after most candidates had dropped out—until the very end.

In a short campaign, however, like the one preceding California's gubernatorial recall election of 2004, things might have turned out differently for Clark. In California, hundreds of candidates sought to replace the highly unpopular Governor Gray Davis, a thin, bland, pleasant-looking man.

While Davis had a hard-earned reputation as a brilliant political strategist, a perfect storm of events in part beyond his control, including widespread electrical power shortages, created a groundswell of dissatisfaction with what voters perceived as poor governance. In an ordinary election, Davis would have had an opportunity to explain his policies. But this was a short election. The electorate, as in Romania, had to rely on its gut.

Davis "projected incredible weenie-ism," according to marketing guru Rob Frankel, author of *The Revenge of Brand X*, who told a newspaper reporter for *San Francisco Chronicle* that "anybody who knows Gray Davis knows he's anything but a weenie—he's a fierce, and I do mean fierce, political fighter. But his coloring is off-balance, he's completely without contrast, he has what we euphemistically call an anal retentive stance—trying to squeeze an olive with his buttocks—his shoulders back, his hair groomed back. It all said he was inaccessible."[8]

The winner of the recall election, by an overwhelming margin, was a movie actor with no previous political experience but possessing near-perfect facial dominance and great media presence: Arnold Schwarzenegger.

In a similar manner, in 1997 members of the National Rifle Association (NRA), which functions primarily as the political lobbying arm of the firearms and ammunition industries, selected actor Charlton Heston as first vice president. Two years later, at age 76 and displaying the symptoms of Alzheimer's disease, Heston was elected president and was soon the most visible member of the organization.[9] That Heston was far past the peak of his mental powers was vividly shown in Michael Moore's 2002 Academy Award–winning documentary *Bowling for Columbine,* in which Moore shows up uninvited at Heston's home, convinces the elderly actor to participate in a videotaped interview, and in so doing demonstrates Heston's tenuous grasp on reality and inability to think clearly.

> The winner of the recall election was a movie actor with no previous political experience but possessing near-perfect facial dominance and great media presence: Arnold Schwarzenegger.

Nevertheless, as long as he could mount a stage, wave aloft an antique flintlock rifle, and mouth his trademark slogan, "From my cold, dead hands," Heston was everything the NRA needed in its president: a tall, handsome man with a dominant face, stage presence, and a resonant voice. A man who motivated the rank and file to work toward organizational goals. A man who, despite diminished mental faculties, looked every inch the hero.

• • •

While Professor Schubert stumbled into his initial observations on PA's political muscle, he was neither the first nor the best-known social scientist to make the connection.

Shawn Rosenberg, director of graduate political psychology at the University of California, Irvine, has been exploring the collision of PA and politics for more than fifteen years. When local politicians in surrounding Orange County first got wind of his research, however, they ridiculed it as "moronic."[10]

Rosenberg asked hundreds of subjects to rate real and fake politicians—using only photographs—on competence, trustworthiness, leadership ability, and political demeanor. He concluded that even when candidates weren't especially attractive, they could significantly boost their ratings by manipulating hairstyle, makeup, facial characteristics, camera angles, and clothing. The boost—up to 17 percent for women candidates and 18 percent for men—spanned every political party and was not affected by a candidate's positions on key issues.

Rosenberg tells students that most people think they have a sense of what competence and trustworthiness look like, based on images that are pervasive in our culture. His research showed that U.S. voters liked light eyebrows, almond-shaped eyes with a lot of curvature in the upper eyelid, thin lips, light complexions, broad or round faces, and short hair combed back or to one side. For men, dark, formal clothes are best. Formal blouses and lightly contrasting jackets are best on women, and simple necklaces and earrings work better than no jewelry at all.[11]

"Physical appearance is a significant part of the election equation for voters," says Rosenberg. "Although people will never admit it, appearance can rival issues in the decision-making process."[12] These days, Orange County politicians take Professor Rosenberg's work very seriously.

Another factor for candidates, especially men, is their height, which Rosenberg theorizes is related to the issue of perceived dominance. Others believe that height may also be an expression of our ancestors' evolutionary survival strategy. When a large, hungry bear wants to evict your clan from a cave, which guy would you expect to have the best chance of driving him away?[13]

The so-called "Presidential Height Index"—an unscientific analysis of presidential hopefuls since the dawn of the TV age—shows that the tallest candidate won the most votes in every White House race except a few: In the 1976 contest, five-foot-nine-inch Jimmy Carter beat six-foot Gerald Ford. Ford, however, suffered the handicap of having pardoned disgraced former president Richard Nixon. Even Al Gore (six feet one inch) earned more popular votes than George W. Bush (five feet eleven inches) in 2000.

The 2004 Democratic primary offers a good example of how height dovetails with the phenomena Professor Schubert first observed in Romania. In that election year campaign, Schubert, unable to understand what rival office seekers said about the issues, picked the eventual winner on the basis of overall dominance.

The seven men who emerged from the pack as Democratic hopefuls were in general agreement on most issues confronting America, and they especially agreed that the Republican president was not doing a good job. Where the candidates differed was on who could best lead the country toward solutions to those issues. In speeches and televised appearances, they were all saying the same things: Elect me and I'll do the best job. A few months into the primary campaign, as far as any differences that the average Democratic voter could see, the candidates might as well have been speaking Romanian.

The tallest candidate was John Kerry, who at six feet four inches towered over his rivals. John Edwards was next tallest at six feet. Al Sharpton was five feet eleven inches; Wesley Clark, five feet ten inches; Howard Dean, a shade under five feet nine inches; Joe Lieberman, about five feet eight inches; and Dennis Kucinich, the shortest, stood at five feet seven inches. Because the media habitually mentioned it, several candidates found their height a sensitive issue. For example, much was made of Kucinich's small stature. Lieberman, too, was considered to be altitude-challenged. Moreover, the combative former governor of Vermont, Howard Dean, took great umbrage at a *New York Times* story describing him as "diminutive." Dean insisted that he was almost five feet nine inches, then backed off and settled on five feet eight and three-quarters, then quickly added that he doesn't usually get into the fractional inch thing because it suggests he's touchy about his height, and he's not.

So who won the most delegates?

The tallest man, Kerry. Followed by the next tallest, Edwards. Followed by Clark. Though he's an inch shorter than Sharpton, a black man with a reputation for stirring the racial pot, Clark was white and a retired four-star general and actually stood a chance of getting elected.

The general election was a very long and bitterly partisan campaign. George W. Bush, the incumbent president, defeated the much taller John Kerry. Bush not only benefited from holding office during wartime, but also from proxy groups that effectively, if not always truthfully, attacked Kerry's stature as a war hero. He also had a highly motivated voter base that responded to his campaign. All this rendered traditional if unspoken height issues less relevant. Even so, Kerry won more votes than any Democratic presidential nominee before him.

Many voters won't bother to consider any candidate's positions on the issues until and unless they perceive the person has sufficient PA and media manners to be "electable" based on attractiveness and manner. They presume good-looking politicians are smarter than ugly ones, and they see them as more poised, effective, and sociable.

"Voters will refer to the looks of candidates not as factors in their decisions but as reinforcers of their decisions," insists Roberta Ann Johnson, professor of politics at the University of San Francisco. "Nobody says, 'I voted for Schwarzenegger because I liked his movies.' Instead, they'll say he's a man of action who will get things done—never mind that they drew that impression from the characters he plays in his films."[14]

But while attractive candidates are rated as more competent, honest, and compassionate, and as having more leadership ability than their more homely rivals, appearance holds less sway with people who pay great attention to politics, especially those who could be fairly described as policy wonks or ideological die-hards.

> "Traditionally, voters have a shocking lack of information about the candidates' records . . . so they vote on character. And to discern character, they look to appearances."

To summarize: A candidate's PA matters far more to swing voters with loose party identification who pay little attention to politics than it does to die-hard conservatives, liberals, or progressives. "Traditionally, voters have a shocking lack of information about the candidates' records . . . so they vote on character. And to discern character, they look to appearances," says Rosenberg. "In a sense, we fall back on the most readily available strategy, but the least accurate [one]."[15]

.   .   .

If, as Rosenberg suggests, many, if not most, voters cast their ballots in response to a visceral impression of a particular candidate's abilities—an impression based on the office seeker's PA, including facial dominance and height—does that open the door to trickery and image manipulation? Could winning office in the TV and broadband Internet era be as simple as creating a winning image by enhancing or changing what nature provided?

That's a subject that has long been of interest to Dr. Caroline Keating, a psychologist at Colgate University. Her research has focused on understanding the elusive quality called "charisma." Keating investigates skills, traits, and motives associated with social dominance and leadership. Working with colleagues and student collaborators, she has discovered or confirmed earlier research that we humans convey dominance through facial expressions much like those of other primates.[16]

To learn how voters are affected by perceptions of a candidate's PA, Keating set up an experiment. She began by digitizing facial images of presidents Clinton, Reagan, and Kennedy, then digitally manipulated the images to test whether subtle feature alterations were powerful enough to shift social perceptions of them. Based on previous research, she expected that exaggerating the so-called "facial maturity cues" (tiny details around the edges of major facial features) would lead to shifts in a viewer's perception of "power," defined as the combination of dominance, strength, and cunning, and "warmth," including honesty, attractiveness, and compassion.

Each of these familiar presidential faces was altered to seem younger by enlarging eyes and lips, or made to seem more mature by reducing the sizes of these features. Keating's test subjects, who were undergraduate students, then rated a single version of each face. While these subjects were not aware of Keating's digital manipulation of features, they were affected by them. The first trial, which featured younger or "neotenous" features on a face that once belonged to President Bill Clinton, made him appear more honest and attractive, even to subjects who had not voted for or supported his candidacy in the 1996 election.

The second study manipulated the features of John F. Kennedy, one of the youngest U.S. presidents, to make him appear more mature and hence apparently more cunning. Manipulated images also made Ronald Reagan, America's oldest president, appear less powerful and less warm. Younger features reduced participants' power ratings for both Kennedy and Reagan. In contrast, making Clinton appear younger increased his ratings of honesty and attractiveness without diminishing perception of his power. Keating and her colleagues concluded that even subtle alterations of facial features could be used to manipulate the social perceptions of familiar political leaders.

> One has to wonder how long it will be before politicians get regular surgical makeovers.

In view of these findings, one has to wonder how long it will be before politicians get regular surgical makeovers, perhaps in response to polling information about public perceptions of their looks. Maybe that's already happening.

Keating also discovered that as a group or class, the socially powerful display great acting talent, and the most persuasive leadership performances begin with a leader convincing himself. As a species, she concludes, humans are so invested in facial expression that "if leaders chose to mislead us, their deceptions" are "very difficult to detect."

Finally, let's test Rosenberg's assertion that a person's looks are the least accurate way to gauge his character. One of the most recent studies in this area was conducted by a team lead by Jaume Masip of Spain's University of Salamanca. Dr. Masip, whose field is social psychology, teamed with Drs. Eugenio Garrido-Martín and Carmen Herrero-Alonso, both psychologists at U. Salamanca, to see if an individual's perceptions of the truth of a written statement were influenced by the facial characteristics of its source. In all, 270 undergraduates were shown photos of three people—an adult but "baby-faced" individual, a child, and a mature adult or older person—along with a written statement that was either truthful or deceptive but in all cases was attributed to the person in the photograph.

As researchers had hypothesized, when statements were accompanied by a photo of a baby-faced adult, participants tended to judge them as truthful. The response to photos depicting a child was completely the opposite, however: Participants tended to judge the child's associated statements as deceptive.

On the average, the accuracy of all these character judgments hardly differed from chance—which is to say that if participants had flipped a coin instead of looking at photos, they would have been correct almost exactly as often.

On the other hand, subjects who made judgments (whether correct or not) about baby-faced individuals—but not about the others—felt very strongly that they had made the right choice, especially when they believed the statement was truthful rather than deceptive.[17]

From all this it seems obvious that if American voters took the time and expended the effort to ascertain a candidate's qualifications and positions, if we all went to the polls armed with issues instead of impressions, we might actually elect the candidates best qualified to represent our interests. As we will see in the next chapter, however, few interests are quite so compelling as how things look.

CHAPTER 8

Seeing Is Believing

*How media messages shape PA thoughts
and feelings*

When he was four, Ben Mann of Los Angeles was already such a big fan of the space shuttle that he announced his intention to work for NASA when he grew up. One morning in August 2005, his mother allowed him to watch television while he ate breakfast so that he could see the *Discovery*, under the command of retired Air Force Colonel Eileen Collins, land at nearby Edwards Air Force Base. It was the first shuttle landing of Ben's lifetime, and he was very excited. After he had eaten and while his mother was dressing him for preschool, she asked whether, when he grew up and joined NASA, he would prefer to work at Mission Control or if he might instead want to go into space as a shuttle pilot.

Ben looked confused. "I thought only girls could do those things," he replied.[1]

At his tender age, Ben had never seen a picture of a male shuttle commander. He had never heard a man's name associated with that very particular job description. And so he knew, as utterly as children know things, that the role of space shuttle commander belonged to a woman. Of course, little Ben was dead wrong: Colonel Eileen Collins was the *first* woman to command a shuttle. Her predecessors and peers were men.

Ben looked confused. "I thought only girls could do those things."

While Ben's mother immediately set him straight on issues relating to astronaut pilot gender, this tiny episode serves to illustrate just how powerfully the media, and especially television, influences the individual viewer's paradigm, creating the set of cultural expectations that everyone uses to navigate society or his or her particular part of the world.

And it's not merely the news. Or only in America. It's anywhere and everywhere in the global community where people are immersed in a torrent of media images.

In this early part of the twenty-first century, as it has been for quite a while, media messages are both ubiquitous—hundreds of cable television channels, thousands of magazine titles, tens of thousands of videos and books, over a billion Web pages—and saturated with pictures of physically attractive people.

Does repetitive exposure to such images influence our expectations? Our self-respect? Our cultural references? Scientists around the world have studied this phenomenon for decades. One study by a respected quartet of Florida academics, which concentrated on the effects of media messages targeting children with images about beauty, produced some surprising data.

Researchers analyzed thousands of media messages in magazines, books, videos, and television shows, searching for messages relating to body image. The data showed that messages emphasizing the importance of physical appearance and portraying body stereotypes are present in many children's videos, consistently reinforcing analogous messages throughout most all media. Among the videos they examined, researchers found the most body-image-related messages in *Cinderella* and *The Little Mermaid,* and the least in *The Indian in the Cupboard* and *E.T.*

Children's books, and in particular those with illustrations, were almost uniformly filled with body-image-related messages. *Rapunzel* had the most, while only *Ginger* and *The Stinky Cheese Man* had no such image-related messages.[2]

In postindustrial societies, however, people of every age—but especially the young—get most of their information about the world from television. And if there is one rule governing media images that everyone agrees upon, it is that sex sells.

No group is more aware of this fact than the advertising community. Those who create advertising, those who sell it, those who buy broadcast time or printed-page space to sell their products, services, or ideas, as well as political operatives, media consultants, psychologists, and educators—all are well aware that sexual images are important message enhancers.

Others, however, including many in academia, are concerned that such advertising places inappropriate pressure on people to focus on their appearance. For example, in a recent survey by *Teen People* magazine, 27 percent of responding girls felt that the media pressured them to have a perfect body.[3]

Sure, but teenagers are always complaining about something. What about mature women? In 1996, Saatchi & Saatchi, then one of the world's biggest international advertising agencies with offices in dozens of cities around the world, conducted a poll to see how women perceived the ways in which they were portrayed in ads. Among their many findings was that advertising, which in previous generations aimed to make women feel guilty about having a dirty house, now makes women fear becoming old or unattractive.[4]

Other research suggests that advertising adversely affects many women's body image, which may lead in turn to unhealthy behavior as they strive for the inappropriately ultrathin body idealized by the media (more on this topic in Chapter 9).

Advertising images also promote and idealize a male standard that resembles a bodybuilder rather than the sort of fellow you'd expect to find repairing Ford pickups, building houses, or selling insurance. As a result, men and boys are becoming more insecure about their physical appearance. Researchers are observing in men an alarming increase in obsessive weight training and the use of anabolic steroids and dietary supplements that promise bigger muscles or more stamina.[5]

A study by Dr. Harrison Pope and colleagues at McLean Hospital, an affiliate of the Harvard Medical School, suggests that this pressure to "bulk up" is felt very early in childhood. Pope sees the increasing muscularity of toy action figures as an alarming trend that sets unrealistic ideals for boys in much the same way that Barbie dolls are suspected of providing unrealistic ideals of thinness to preadolescent girls.

> The increasing muscularity of toy action figures is seen as an alarming trend that sets unrealistic ideals for boys in much the same way that Barbie dolls are suspected of providing to preadolescent girls.

"Our society's worship of muscularity may cause increasing numbers of men to develop pathological shame about their bodies. . . . Our observations of these little plastic toys have stimulated us to explore further links between cultural messages, body image disorders, and use of steroids and other drugs," says Pope.[6]

According to various media reports, while 90 percent of teenagers with eating disorders are girls, some experts believe that cases involving boys are steadily increasing but remain underreported because few males are willing to acknowledge a medical condition that is usually associated with females.[7]

Such possibilities aside, most media images stressing thinness are directed at women. Today, the average American woman sees between 400 and 600 advertisements every day; by the time a girl is seventeen, she has received about 250,000 commercial messages. Only 9 percent of these commercials include a direct statement about beauty, but many more implicitly emphasize its importance—especially those aimed at women and girls. One study of Saturday morning television found that half the toy commercials aimed at girls made reference to physical attractiveness—but none of those that targeted boys contained even a single PA reference.[8]

Other studies found that half the advertisements in teen girl magazines and 56 percent of television commercials aimed at female viewers used beauty as a product appeal. This constant exposure to female-oriented advertisements may give girls reason to become self-conscious about their bodies and even to equate their PA as a measure of their worth.[9]

American publishers began using pictures of beautiful women to sell magazines in the late 1890s. They began with illustrations, and later, as publishing technology advanced, turned to photographs. The former medium reached its zenith in 1905 with illustrator Charles Dana Gibson's portraits of the incredibly lovely Evelyn Nesbit, a sixteen-year-old naïf married to one of the world's richest men. She was destined for heartbreak and poverty, but when her likeness appeared on magazine covers, she was billed as the "most beautiful woman in the world."[10]

Color photography as a basis for mass marketing arrived in the third decade of the twentieth century and soon replaced more expensive and less lifelike hand-drawn illustrations. The women photographers selected to pose for advertisements and other commercial images could no longer be ordinary women, however, thanks to the physics of cramming the image of a three-dimensional figure in a two-dimensional space. Unlike illustration, where the artist can modify reality, photos omit the impression of depth while adding the illusion of increased width; the screen or page upon which photographic images are displayed is close to flat and doesn't allow for binocular ("two-eyed") human vision, which after processing by our brains allows us to perceive depth, the third dimension. Flattened by the camera, an average model appears heavier on a screen or a page. The preferred solution is a thinner model, who when photographed looks like a person of average weight.

As a rule of thumb, photographing the average human tends to add about 10 percent to the person's apparent width. So, a 200-pound man looks like a 220-pound man; a 120-pound woman looks like she weighs 132 pounds. But that's only part of the story.

Clothes look better on thinner people because they hang closer to vertical; there are fewer wrinkles and they appear closer to the two-dimensional design from which they originated. Through a century of advertising images, however, thinness gradually became the standard of feminine beauty. The typical fashion model today is not 10 percent lighter than her "normal" feminine counterpart but *23 percent lighter.* So the average American woman between eighteen and thirty-four years of age has only a 7 percent chance of being as slim as a fashion or runway model. Now invert this ratio: A typical fashion photographer's model is slimmer than 93 percent of women her age. Escalate to a so-called "supermodel"—someone whose name is known outside the advertising industry—and you have a creature slimmer than 99 percent of women in her age group.[11]

But I'll make this wager: Ask any supermodel's mom if she's comfortable with how her daughter looks, and if she's a good mother and tells the truth, she'll confess that she wished her daughter would eat just a little more.

Nevertheless, so pervasive and powerful are media images that more than two-thirds of girls interviewed in one study said that magazine models influence their idea of the perfect body shape.[12]

But why do advertisers, who have total control of every ad they sponsor, down to the last comma in the text or script, every wrinkle in a garment, or even the placement of a "mole" on a model's face, so often present such unrealistically thin women to hawk their products?

Some researchers believe that advertisers use models with abnormally thin bodies and beautiful faces to create an *unattainable* desire, because trying to realize the impossible drives product consumption more than trying to attain a realistic goal. "The media markets *desire,*" says Dr. Paul Hamburg, a psychiatrist with the Harvard Medical School. "By reproducing ideals that are absurdly out of line with what real bodies really do look like . . . the media perpetuates a market for frustration and disappointment. Its customers will never disappear."[13]

Whether or not Hamburg's thesis is correct, advertisers have found the thin look fattens their bottom line: The North American diet industry generates between $34 billion and $50 billion in annual revenue, or upwards of $1,000 for every adolescent and adult on the continent.[14]

Women frequently compare their bodies to those they see around them, and researchers have found that exposure to idealized body images lowers women's satisfaction with their own attractiveness. In fact, a 1984 poll by *Glamour* magazine concluded that three-fourths of responding women thought they were "too fat." A larger and more scientific 1997 study found body dissatisfaction increasing at a faster rate than ever before among both men and women. Nearly nine of ten of the study's 3,452 female subjects wanted to lose weight.[15]

> Researchers have found that exposure to idealized body images lowers women's satisfaction with their own attractiveness.

Yet another study found that people who viewed slides of thin models rated their own PA lower than people who viewed average and oversize models.[16]

Registered dietitian and researcher Cindy Maynard believes that body image dissatisfaction is so epidemic in our society that it's almost considered normal, adding that even children in "third grade are concerned about their weight." The most vulnerable, she explains, are teens who are at the impressionable age when people begin to develop self-confidence and self-perception. "About half of female teens think they're too fat," says Maynard, adding that almost as many are dieting. "There is a lot of pressure to succeed, to fit in. One of the ways to fit in is to have the perfect body." Women and girls who responded to Maynard's Web survey indicated overwhelmingly that "very thin" models made them feel insecure about themselves.[17]

But what about women of color?

The ideal of feminine beauty as portrayed on American television is blue-eyed and thin, writes Dr. Carolyn Stroman, who teaches social science at Howard University's School of Communications.[18] What effect does watching an endless parade of such women have on the psyches of young girls who can never hope to look like Britney Spears? What becomes of African American women, for example, as they grow to adulthood bombarded, almost exclusively, with this "all American" beauty ideal?

They "are immediately excluded from what is considered to be 'beautiful,' " writes researcher Karen Perkins of Australia's Key Centre for Cultural and Media Policy. "They have little to no hope of achieving these ideals. As a consequence, historically along the broad spectrum of devaluation of all women, black women have been doomed to the lowest status.''[19]

Perkins's study of television images showed that black females have been deeply and profoundly affected by the politics of skin color, hair texture, and facial features. Their feelings related to self-worth, intelligence, success, and attractiveness are warped by what appears to the greater society as benign and arbitrary physical traits.

It follows that what Perkins describes as an ''insurmountable gulf between herself and the societal beauty ideal'' has an adverse effect on self-esteem. According to Perkins, one study of sixty-six black college women found that 36 percent desired a lighter skin color; less than half that number wanted darker skin.

Stroman's 1991 study documented that young African Americans watch a great deal of television.[20] Yet to be studied in depth, however, are the effects of television's idealized and exclusionary media images on the self-perceptions and psychological well-being of African American women. The Perkins study suggests that until those questions are answered, parents of young black girls should limit their children's television viewing time and substitute interactive activities for TV watching. When parents do allow their children to watch television, they should watch with them and afterward discuss the program's hidden messages. Perkins also recommends that parents push for more responsive media in their respective communities.

> When parents do allow their children to watch television, they should watch with them and afterward discuss the program's hidden messages.

As it happens, that's pretty good advice for all mothers, not just those with dark-skinned children. In 1997, Mary C. Martin and James W. Gentry, professors at the University of Nebraska–Lincoln, created an unusually complex study to examine what happens when young girls—both adolescents and those somewhat younger—are exposed to pictures depicting lovely women in advertisements. Martin and Gentry conjectured that since models used in advertising are selected as image examples of ideal beauty, adolescent girls would compare themselves to these models and find the models to be their superiors in terms of physical attractiveness. They further supposed that if a girl attempted to judge the value or worth of her own PA or body image against that of an advertising model, comparisons are likely to result in lowered self-perceptions and lowered self-esteem.

Previous research by Martin suggested that the interval between the fourth and eighth grade, a time when female bodies go through dramatic changes, is when most girls develop lasting self-images and when adult definitions of beauty become relevant to them as social norms. So, for this new study, Martin and Gentry selected 268 girls all enrolled in the fourth, sixth, and eighth grades of a Midwestern public school (mean age: just over eleven years, nine months), and 261 of them completed the tasks. The girls lived in a region of the country where, in 1997, 98 percent of the population was white and the median annual family income was just over $31,000.[21]

The researchers were careful to note that while their subjects were not representative of all U.S. girls their age, they did represent a segment of the population that other studies had found was most susceptible to eating disorders and other problems linked to PA issues.[22] As an incentive to participate, Martin and Gentry's study subjects took part in a drawing for two prizes of $50 each. In addition, $500 was donated to the local public school system.

The girls who served as test subjects were told that the study was to learn about how people respond to advertising. During a classroom session held at its usual time, students were shown three ads for personal adornment products; then their teacher read aloud a set of questions based on these ads. The girls were asked to fill in questionnaires that rated their own self-perception of PA, body image, and self-esteem. A control group answered the same questions but was shown ads without pictures of models.

For this study, four-color advertisements were created by cutting and pasting from ads in *Seventeen, Sassy, Teen,* and *YM* magazines, the four leading teen U.S. periodicals at the time. These magazines were selected for a second reason as well: They all maintain consistency with respect to the type of beauty they present.[23]

Full-body photos of models from ads and other partial pictures of models were cut from real magazines in a way that eliminated information about their respective sources. These pictures were then used to create ads for fictitious brands of such commonly advertised products as lipstick, jeans, and hair-care products. The ads were very simple and appeared to be professionally executed.

To ensure that the girls tested saw the models in the ads as highly attractive, test subjects were first asked to rate the models in the ads from "very overweight and out of shape, fat" to "very fit and in shape, thin," and from "very unattractive, ugly" to "very attractive, beautiful." The test subjects responses ranged from 5.1 to 6.4 on a seven-point scale, far above the midpoint value of 4, confirming that the girls perceived the models as highly attractive.

Before seeing a set of ads, the girls were shown a drawing of "Amy looking at an advertisement in a magazine" and heard a story about "Amy" comparing herself with a model in an ad. Amy acted for one of four particular reasons, which social scientists call "manipulated motives."

- *Self-Evaluation.* Amy was comparing her own PA with that of models in ads to determine whether she thinks she's as pretty as or prettier than the models with regard to such specifics as hair, eyes, and body.

- *Self-Improvement.* Amy was comparing her own PA with those of models in order to find ways to improve her own attractiveness in such specifics as hairstyle and makeup.

- *Self-Enhancement* (1). Amy was comparing her own PA with the model's so as to enhance her self-esteem by finding specific areas in which she is prettier than the model.

- *Self-Enhancement* (2). Amy was discounting the model's beauty in order to avoid explicit comparison of her own physical attractiveness with that of the magazine model. This reason was presented as an attempt by Amy to protect/maintain her self-esteem.

After looking at the drawing of "Amy" and hearing the four reasons ("motives") why she looked at the ads, the girls were asked to look at the ads as Amy had viewed them. That brought them to the heart of the study: After viewing each ad, girls were asked to list specific ways in which the so-called "manipulated motive" might have happened. For example, when self-improvement was the motive, the girls were asked to look at the model and "list ideas you get on how to improve your looks." The study's intent, of course, was not to gauge naturally occurring motives for social comparison, but rather to look at how the use of various motives changed the girls' reactions to looking at pictures of pretty models.

If a girl completed this listing exercise, the manipulation was considered successful. One of the study's authors analyzed each response to the listing exercise and coded the result to show if the girl succeeded or failed to complete it.

When a girl listed a specific reference to aspects of physical attractiveness she had compared in the ad and gave no indication that another motive was present, it was considered a successful exercise. An example of success in manipulating the self-improvement motive was if a girl listed the ideas she got from looking at the model in the ad: "Use the product. Get a perm. Wear lots of makeup and have as pretty of a face as she does."

Not all the girls bought into the study's premise. For example, when they were asked to list "ways in which your hair, face, and body look compared to the model's hair, face, and body," one girl wrote, "She looks different because I am a different person. I don't really compare to her." Such responses were discarded. In all, seven girls were dropped from the study for failing to complete the listing exercise.

For the final analyses, fifty-one girls (19.5 percent) self-evaluated; fifty-four (20.7 percent) self-improved; fifty-one (19.5 percent) enhanced through downward comparisons; fifty-one (19.5 percent) self-enhanced by discounting the beauty of the models; and fifty-four subjects (20.7 percent), the control group, viewed ads without models.[24]

The Martin-Gentry study yielded hundreds of pages of quantifiable data that the researchers massaged into several tables. For our purposes, however, we need look only at the broad outlines of their findings. As expected, they learned that girls view their bodies differently at different ages; exactly why this is so and how it works in individuals and groups was not a study objective, but the findings help to explain why girls react differently to media messages about their body as they grow up. For example, the fourth graders' self-evaluations produced the lowest self-perceptions of physical attractiveness and the highest (i.e., most skinny) self-perceptions of body image when compared to other "motives." Martin and Gentry suspect that in childhood, girls, like boys, want to get "bigger," and bigger is perceived as being the opposite of skinny.

By the time they are sixth graders, however, girls compare themselves to models and see themselves as too chubby; they want to be skinnier. Perhaps, speculate the researchers, somewhere between fourth and sixth grade a mental transition occurs from "bigger is better" to "skinnier is better."

> Martin and Gentry suspect that in childhood, girls, like boys, want to get "bigger." By the time they are sixth graders, however, girls compare themselves to models and want to be skinnier.

Among all the girls studied, only fourth graders were able to raise their self-esteem by finding features of their own appearance that they could compare favorably with those of the models. The opposite occurred, however, when fourth graders discounted the model's beauty; when that happened, they also lowered their own self-esteem. Martin and Gentry speculate that this might be because fourth graders are so young that they have not realized that they will probably not grow up to be as beautiful as a model.

Overall, the Martin-Gentry study seems to suggest that teachers and parents could use the framework of social comparison to teach children and adolescents about how and when to compare themselves to others. Because previous studies have shown that young girls do not naturally use the self-enhancement tool when comparing themselves with models,[25] getting educators involved would be helpful in teaching young girls how to bolster their self-esteem. If that were to happen often enough, then, as that earlier research suggests, advertisers would have a less socially damaging avenue for peddling their wares, because making consumers feel more physically attractive actually encourages sales of cosmetic and other adornment products.

But is the use of highly attractive models in advertising really the most effective way to sell products and services? Or would advertisers be more likely to convince buyers by using people who looked more like themselves—normal people, in other words?

A few years ago Dr. Amanda Bowers, who teaches marketing at Louisiana State University, and Stacy Landreth, then a doctoral candidate at LSU and now an assistant professor at Villanova University's College of Commerce, sought to find out if using highly attractive models (HAMs) instead of more ordinary-looking people in advertising was truly the most effective way to sell products. They were not the first to tread this road. Several studies that sought to investigate the positive effects of including HAMs in advertising had failed to make a strong case supporting their use.[26]

Bowers and Landreth sought to explore the differences between using HAMs and normally attractive models with different types of products. Their research also explored methods by which matching model attractiveness and product type influenced advertising effectiveness. They began with the long-accepted supposition that selling different types of products often requires directing the sales message to different groups of people. For example, few men purchase such feminine beauty products as lipstick and eye shadow, so an effective sales pitch would address the concerns of women but ignore those of men.

In addition, because the beautiful are often perceived as having better and easier lives with fewer problems than so-called "normal people,"[27] Bowers and Landreth supposed that ads for "problem-solving products," such as dandruff shampoo or acne treatments, would be more effective if the associated model was closer to normal looking.

They also supposed that even with differing products that might appeal to a wide range of potential buyers—soft drinks and foot-care products, for example—the sales pitch would be less enhanced by a beautiful model in the ad than if viewers perceived the model as possessing some expertise about the product. If their premise held up, then an advertiser selling a home insecticide, for example, would be better served by choosing a model who resembles the sort of person likely to use that product—a housewife, perhaps, or an exterminator—than a very pretty model. And if the product was one associated with illness, such as an over-the-counter pain reliever or facial tissues, then a model who appeared to be ill or otherwise uncomfortable—and therefore not attractive—might be the most effective.

In setting up their study, however, Bowers and Landreth took care to avoid comparisons between models with high PA and those who were *un*attractive; several earlier studies have covered that ground. Instead, they sought to differentiate between responses to the sort of models described in previous research as "idealized and unrealistic, haunting images of perfection" and so-called "normally attractive" models, which they defined as of average or moderate weight, height, and facial beauty and more representative of a real woman, attractive but not beautiful. In short, the sort of woman whose picture might grace a woman's magazine in the "makeover" department.

The study sought to learn if matching models that were either "highly attractive" or "normally attractive" with specific types of products influences ad effectiveness either directly, by using a model chosen to make unspoken "arguments" for the product, or indirectly, through the model's perceived credibility.

Bowers and Landreth first conducted two "pretests" to guide them in their choice of products and models. Twenty-five young women were asked to put a list of products into categories; they chose acne concealer and acne medicine to represent the problem-solving category. Next, the same group used a similar process to choose lipstick and earrings as "enhancing" products.

In a second pretest, two judges selected full-color model photos from popular women's magazines. Photos intended to represent "normally attractive models" were selected from Reader Makeover issues featuring moderately attractive women with professionally styled hair and makeup. Two undergraduate classes totaling seventy-two students viewed five photos of normally attractive women, and then sixty-five students in two other classes evaluated five highly attractive model photos. The HAM photo was selected on the basis of the model's extreme beauty and the subjects' previously expressed beliefs that the beautiful model led a less-than-normal life. The normally attractive photo was chosen for its rating of moderate beauty and the fact that the students strongly believed this woman led a "normal" life. Both models had the same hair and eye color.

The main study was based on the opinion of 251 women of an average age of twenty-two; 83 percent were white and 84 percent single. Each subject was given a folder with instructions, an ad including the different products and models, and a questionnaire. Subjects were told to open the folder, view the ad as they would normally view one in a magazine, and then respond to the questions.

The researchers' expectations generally were supported by the first study, suggesting that advertisers should consider that while highly attractive models are usefully associated with enhancing products, there is no advantage in using them to sell "problem-solving products." The study data suggest, instead, that advertising effectiveness is linked with the viewer's beliefs about the model's expertise with a particular problem-solving product.

Bowers and Landreth also concluded that viewers' impressions of a model's beauty had little relation to how much they trusted her; a picture of an extremely beautiful model was perceived as equally trustworthy as that of a woman of average looks.

To validate the results of their first study, Bowers and Landreth conducted a second, almost identical study using different models and different products. This time perfume was the enhancing product, and the problem-solving product was a dandruff shampoo. The same questionnaire was given to a single group of 145 young women ranging in age from seventeen to twenty-two; 99 percent of them were white. Subjects within each row of desks viewed the same ads while those in adjacent rows were shown a different ad.

As in the previous study, subjects were asked to indicate the degree to which they saw themselves as similar to the women in the ads, how important they felt the product was to them personally, and how committed they felt toward buying it.

Again, one of the advertising models was significantly more attractive than the other; subjects rated the latter model as having a much more normal life than her beautiful counterpart. They also found dandruff shampoo much more important than perfume to solving their own problem.

Contrary to what the researchers expected, for those subjects who felt the product was personally important to them, the highly attractive model was perceived as somewhat more trustworthy than the normally attractive model—perhaps because attractive people are often seen as acting from their own feelings without being influenced by others, while unattractive individuals are seen as more easily coerced.[28]

For those subjects who felt that the product was not something they needed, however, model PA had no significant effect on perceptions of trustworthiness. Nor did the subject's perception of how similar her life was to that of either model.

As for how subjects perceived a model's expertise, the data again surprised the researchers. Except for those subjects who felt the product was one they needed, the model's PA made little difference to perceptions of expertise with the product. Those who did feel involved with the product, however, accorded more credibility to the higher-PA model.

Bowers and Landreth concluded that while high-PA models are effective in selling attractiveness-relevant products, they are no better than normally attractive models in selling problem-solving products. They also concluded that marketers need to consider the type of product carefully when selecting a model to hawk it. Finally, to no academic's surprise, they also suggested that more research is needed.

A somewhat more comprehensive study by Hilda Dittmar and Sara Howard of the University of Sussex, Brighton, United Kingdom, sought to replicate earlier findings that showed no difference in advertising effectiveness when the models were thin or of average size. Specifically, they sought to refute the assertion by a spokesperson for Premier Model Management, which represented supermodels Naomi Campbell and Claudia Schiffer, among others, that "statistics have repeatedly shown that if you stick a beautiful skinny girl on the cover of a magazine you sell more copies," and that model agencies merely supply the women their clients, the advertisers, demand. "The [advertisers] would say that they are selling a product and responding to consumer demand," continued the spokesperson. "At the end of the day, it is a business, and the fact is that these models sell the products."[29]

Dittmar and Howard recruited seventy-five women from a London-based fashion advertising company and an equal number of secondary school teachers; about 95 percent of both groups were white. The women in advertising were involved in the creation and promotion of fashion images in administrative, design, or secretarial capacities and had a combined average age of 28.2 years; the teachers had an average age of 37.2 years. Within each group, a third of the women were shown images of thin models, a third images of average-size models, and the remaining third, the control group, ads without pictures of a model.

For this study the researchers created ads for eau de toilette packaged in a perfume flask in one of two "brands" called Water Lily or Red Zest. An image of a red-colored forest was placed behind the Red Zest bottle, while a crashing wave was the backdrop for the Water Lily bottle. Each flask was accompanied by images of women taken from fashion magazines. The models were chosen as examples of the thin ideal—each model's waist circumference was about twenty-four inches and she would fit a U.S. size 2 dress (U.K. size 8).

These same body images (but not the model's head and face) were then "stretched" laterally 25 percent with Adobe Photoshop to represent women of more normal weight. Both models had long hair, which was used to mask the "join" area where a stretched body was joined to its unstretched head. The resulting "normal" models corresponded to women with a thirty-inch waist who would fit U.S. size 12–14 (U.K. size 14).

To confirm that the models were perceived as having different body sizes and that the manipulation of body size did not affect the models' perceived attractiveness, twenty professional women were recruited for a pilot study to rate either the two thin or the two average-size models. Each model was rated on six-point scales, one measuring body size and the other attractiveness. Analysis of body size ratings confirmed that the thin images were perceived as much thinner than the average-size models, while the attractiveness ratings showed that the model in the Water Lily ad was rated as slightly more attractive than the Red Zest model. More critically, this pilot study also confirmed that the thinner models were not seen as more attractive than the average-size models, which is to say that changing the model's apparent body size did not influence her perceived attractiveness.

For the main study, respondents were asked to complete three questionnaires designed to assess whether they 1) internalized the ideal of a thin body, 2) perceived different types of ads as effective, and 3) experienced body-focused anxiety after viewing these ads.

Ideal body internalization was assessed by a series of eight questions, with respondents being asked to indicate agreement with statements such as "I believe that clothes look better on thin models."

Advertising effectiveness was assessed through five questions measuring attitudes toward the ad. Attitude toward the brand and purchase intention was covered with a single question: "If (Brand X) costs the same as the brand that you usually use, how likely would you be to purchase (Brand X) on your next shopping trip?"

Body-focused anxiety was assessed with an eight-item form that asked the women to indicate the degree, if any, of anxiety associated with various weight-related areas of their own body.

Data thus created were evaluated, and the researchers drew several conclusions from them:

- Ads showing attractive average-size models were perceived as equally persuasive as those depicting very thin models, a finding equally true for both teachers and fashion advertising workers.

- Although women in advertising were slightly more critical of all the ads than were teachers, this reaction had no linkage to the model's size.

- Only women who internalized the ideal "thin" body as a personal standard felt anxiety by viewing the images. They showed the most anxiety after viewing thin images and the least anxiety after looking at average-size images.

- This anxiety effect was far more extreme in the teachers than the women working in advertising. The continual exposure to the thin ideal and professional association with thin fashion models may inoculate women working in the industry against these images making them feel bad about their body; even so, the negative impact of thin images on body-focused anxiety was still present, but to a lesser degree. When advertising women viewed the women of more normal appearance, however, they experienced no anxiety at all.

Dittmar and Howard concluded that it is the thinness of the models used in advertising, and not their attractiveness, that creates anxiety in susceptible women viewers.[30]

These were not the only studies on this subject. Researchers in advertising and marketing organizations, whose job it is to gauge the public pulse, now suspect that many women resent ads that insist on presenting unattainable beauty as the norm, and to some extent, the media, and especially advertisers, have warped the public's sensibilities about feminine beauty.

> Researchers in advertising and marketing organizations now suspect that many women resent ads that insist on presenting unattainable beauty as the norm.

• • •

In an effort to ascertain women's sensibilities, Dove, one of the beauty brands owned by Unilever, a behemoth multinational manufacturer of consumer products, commissioned a broadly based and far-ranging study. The stated purpose was to explore empirically what beauty means to women today and why. Dove also wanted to assess methods of talking and thinking about female beauty in ways that were more authentic, satisfying, and empowering.

To enhance credibility, Dove hired Dr. Nancy Etcoff, a Harvard University professor and author of *Survival of the Prettiest,* and Dr. Susie Orbach, visiting professor at the London School of Economics and author of *Fat Is a Feminist Issue,* as principal investigators, with data managed by New York–based StrategyOne, an applied research firm.

Their study, "The Real Truth About Beauty: A Global Report," was published in September 2004. In all, 3,200 women aged 18 to 64 were interviewed between February 27 and March 26, 2004. The women came from ten countries: the United States, Canada, Great Britain, Italy, France, Portugal, the Netherlands, Brazil, Argentina, and Japan.

The report concluded that while few women consider themselves victims of bad looks, and most women are not lost in despair and self-loathing about their looks, few women feel the power and pride of beauty. In fact, according to the data, most women see themselves as below average in appearance, and almost half regard themselves as overweight. Only 2 percent claimed to be beautiful.

In their introduction, these researchers hastened to add context to these findings by citing several other studies that suggest that people in Western cultures (but *not* those of East Asia) rate themselves as "better than average on everything from kindness, intelligence, and popularity." They also rated their parenting, driving, and workplace skills as above average. In fact, "average" is an unusually low rating for such self-evaluations in Western societies.

The Dove study, however, shows that women are less satisfied with their beauty than with almost every other dimension of life, except their financial success. It calls for lifting what the report terms "the quota system on images of beauty," arguing that tall, thin statures; blond hair; fair skin; and blue eyes should not solely define contemporary good looks. The authors opine:

> The diversity of human beauty has been strained through a sieve of culture, status, power and money, and what has emerged is a narrow sliver of the full panorama of human visual splendor. Beauty is diverse and the human eye thrills to new pleasures and fresh sources of inspiration.[31]

More than 100 years earlier, in 1871, Charles Darwin wrote analogously and prophetically about varying determinants of beauty:

> "If all our women were to become as beautiful as the Venus de Medici, we should for a time be charmed; but we should soon wish for variety; and as soon as we had obtained variety, we should wish to see certain characters in our women a little exaggerated beyond the then existing common standard."[32]

In a foreword introducing the Dove report, coauthor Orbach concludes that women "want to see the idea of beauty expanded." She explains that survey data suggest that women perceive qualities of character and individuality and that the emotional component of personality is as much an expression of beauty as the "narrow physical aspects of beauty that currently dominate popular culture."

Perhaps paradoxically, Orbach adds that women nevertheless want to be perceived as *physically attractive,* that their looks are important to how they feel about themselves and how they regard beauty in others.

It may be that men think about beauty in a narrow, linear manner linked to physical attractiveness, while women see beauty in many dimensions. In any case, Orbach concludes that the Dove-sponsored study shows that women also regard being beautiful "as the result of qualities and circumstance: being loved, being engaged in activities that one wants to do, having a close relationship, being happy, being kind, having confidence, exuding dignity and humor. Women who are like this look beautiful. They are beautiful."

The study itself concludes that even when strictly considering only PA, "images of manufactured femininity are rejected as being too narrow, as inauthentic and as insufficient." The study suggests that women want broader definitions of how female PA is depicted. Three-fourths of those surveyed said they wanted much more diversity; they wanted to see images of women of different shapes, in varying sizes and of a broader range of ages than those presently saturating the media.

Orbach also offers her own take on why and how such feminine dissatisfaction has evolved. Over the last half century, she notes, beauty both as an idea and as an ideal has migrated around the world, and what was once the "exclusive province of the Hollywood dream factory, of fashion models and the young bride," is now an essential attribute for women of all ages. Meanwhile, as ordinary women seek to claim beauty for themselves, "there has been an insidious narrowing of the beauty aesthetic to a limited physical type—thin, tall—which . . . excludes . . . millions of women."

Finally, Orbach concludes, democratizing the idea of beauty while, at the same time, sharply limiting its definition has caused women considerable anguish. While most women believe that PA is important, even crucial to finding their place in the world, they feel that conforming to media representations of idealized beauty should not require them to resort to such extreme measures as cosmetic surgery.

In short, according to the authors of "The Real Truth About Beauty," women around the world would like to be considered beautiful no matter their shape, color, size, or age. Women, few of whom think of themselves as physically attractive, insist that PA is only one dimension of beauty, and that they should be valued for the beautiful qualities of their other dimensions. They want to enjoy the benefits of being considered beautiful and resent the media for narrowing beauty's definition to that of physical attractiveness.

> Women, few of whom think of themselves as physically attractive, insist that PA is only one dimension of beauty, and that they should be valued for the beautiful qualities of their other dimensions.

There are, in fact, many things that the media could do to broaden its portrayal of beauty stereotypes. But whether the gatekeepers who have the power to do so will agree remains in doubt. Beauty's less visual qualities are far more difficult to present on page or screen.

Nevertheless, Dove has taken a small step in that direction by incorporating some of the study findings into an unusual and attention-grabbing advertising campaign. Pretty, underwear-clad women of varying ages, all noticeably heavier than typical fashion or advertising models, were featured on billboards and in other advertising promoting Dove lotions and related products. As Dove undoubtedly had hoped, they became a minor sensation, guesting on NBC's *Today,* appearing in a *People* magazine cover story, and sparking opinion articles in major publications, including the *New York Times Magazine.*[33]

It's worth noting, however, that while these Dove Girls did not conform to the fashion model's silhouette, they all had clear skin, lustrous hair, and symmetrical features. In the unlikely event that any of them would ever need to be "fixed up" with a blind date, there is little chance that she would be touted to an eligible man in terms of her peerless personality.

· · ·

The media's influence on American attitudes on physical attractiveness is not, of course, limited to the advertising sphere. Television, especially, provides Americans with idealized images of manhood and womanhood as a component of both entertainment and news programs.

Television as a mass medium was first demonstrated at the 1939 New York World's Fair but did not become publicly available until after World War II. Probably because they were familiar with the use of attractive females on magazine covers to attract readers, the first television producers also used pretty young females to attract viewers. Highly attractive stage or film actresses, usually in full evening dress, announced commercial breaks or delivered program continuity information. Often the women on early television were mere ornaments who silently showed off products on game shows, for example. By the late 1940s, as television's first dramatic programs emerged, the new medium emulated the motion picture industry by presenting women as glamorous objects.

In other words, nothing much has changed.

Today, entertainment programming dominates every station's schedule, a mix of feature films, made-for-TV movies, hour-long dramas, half-hour sitcoms, and so-called "reality" shows. For the most part, all of these programs feature highly attractive actors and actresses, especially in leading roles. With a few notable exceptions, less attractive actors are almost always relegated to supporting roles as comedic foils, dramatic villains, or incidental cast members. In fact, one well-regarded study showed that only 12 percent of prime-time characters were overweight, much lower than the actual percentage of the general population.[34]

No dimension of a television performer's PA is more notable than weight. As previously noted, all people tend to look somewhat heavier when viewed through a camera lens. So it is an extraordinary event when overweight actors are cast in lead roles. Notable examples are John Goodman and Roseanne Barr, who starred in *Roseanne,* a sitcom about a lower-class family struggling with life's essential problems. Until this show appeared on ABC in 1988, Barr was known only as an acerbic stand-up comedienne. Goodman's credits had been limited to a succession of brief supporting roles until he was cast as her husband, Dan Conner, a character conceived as the straight man, feeding the star lines that set up her jokes. The show lasted ten seasons, an extraordinary run, and when it signed off for the last time, Goodman's dramatic talents were widely recognized and his career took off.

But that is not usually what happens for overweight actors cast in sitcoms. Dr. Gregory Fouts, a professor of psychology at the University of Calgary in Alberta, Canada, has studied television for decades. He analyzed the content of two randomly chosen episodes from each of eighteen prime-time sitcoms. Fouts examined body weights for thirty-seven central female characters (92 percent were white, the remainder black), negative comments they received from male characters about their weight or bodies, and audience reactions following the negative comments. He found that, collectively, thin women and girls were overrepresented in these shows; that the heavier the female character, the more frequently and significantly negative comments were made about or to her; and that these negative comments were significantly associated with audience reactions or laughter.

And in earlier research Fouts and colleague Kimberley Burggraf had learned that situation comedies show male characters making positive comments to women according to their body weight: The thinner the woman, the more positive comments she receives.[35] Fouts concluded that sitcoms as a class of programs present males making derogatory remarks about heavier women's weights and bodies, with this reinforced by audience laughter.

He also concluded that the combination of presenting thin actresses in most roles and making derogatory remarks about those who are overweight "likely contributes to the internalization of gender and weight stereotypes which deleteriously affect the health of female adolescents."[36]

But that's about women. Do sitcoms perpetuate the same stereotypes about overweight men? To learn if they did, Fouts conducted a follow-up study. His researchers watched one episode each of the twenty-seven different sitcoms that were available in the Calgary area in February 1999. Fouts observed seventy-five male roles (97 percent white, 3 percent black) identified as central characters who appeared weekly and whose actors were listed consistently in the show's main credits. Fouts and his researchers coded each male character's body weight, the frequency of negative references received from female characters regarding his body weight/shape, the frequency of negative self-references regarding his own body weight/shape, and the frequency of audience reactions to these negative references.

These negative references included, for example, such lines as "You're too fat to wear that in public," and "I'm surprised you could find a belt that fits you." They also included comments by the character himself, such as "I need to go on a diet," and "Geez, this is tight!" There were also negative behavioral references, such as a female character giving the male character a disapproving up-and-down glance or grimacing while pointing a finger at his stomach, or a male character looking with disapproval at his image in a mirror.

Audience reactions were coded by examining each negative reference and determining the presence or absence of an auditory audience reaction such as laughter or "ooh" sounds immediately afterward.

The data Fouts collected showed that 33 percent of the male characters were below average in weight, 54 percent were average, and 13 percent were above average. The 13 percent contrasts with the actual prevalence rate of above-average weight men in North America (approximately 30 percent, according to the U.S. National Center for Health Statistics and the National Institutes of Health). Overweight males are underrepresented in sitcoms and present an inaccurate picture of men's bodies in our society. A previous study by Fouts, however, found that only 7 percent of female sitcom characters were overweight while about one-fourth of North American adult women are considered to be of above-average weight.[37]

All these data suggest that it is more acceptable for men than for women to be overweight on entertainment television.

Moreover, in another study in 2002, Fouts determined that while 9 percent of central male sitcom characters received negative references

> These data suggest that it is more acceptable for men than for women to be overweight on entertainment television.

from female characters regarding their bodies, there was no linkage between the frequency of these negative references and either their weight or audience reactions to the negative references. Fouts concludes, then, that being heavy and male is not associated with receiving punishment by female characters; when it does occur, however, it's not reinforced by audience laughter. He also concludes that this data supports the existence of a double standard that may influence viewers' attitudes about women's and men's bodies.[38]

But wait. If studio audiences find female fat jokes funny, doesn't that suggest, at least, that society as a whole holds a lower opinion of overweight women?

Well, yes and no.

Yes, because network executives won't keep any television show on the air unless it draws a significant audience—suggesting, in turn, that unless viewing audience beliefs are reinforced by a particular show, they won't watch it. So when audiences are exposed to a media message that female fat is funny and thin is not, unless millions of viewers to some extent incorporate such views into their own attitudes, the show will soon fail.

On the other hand, when it comes to television programs, producers leave nothing to chance, including the ostensible reactions of studio audiences. According to Larry Mintz, whose sitcom credits include writing for, producing, consulting for, or creating such sitcoms as *Mork and Mindy, The Nanny, Step by Step, Going Places, Angie, Family Matters,* and *Married . . . with Children,* virtually every sitcom is "sweetened" with a laugh track added in a production studio after the show is filmed. Furthermore, while most sitcoms are shot before a live audience, Mintz explains, these audiences are prepped by production personnel, encouraged to laugh at every joke punch line, and cued to applaud on command.[39]

So when Fouts and his researchers heard a sitcom audience laughing at fat jokes, what they heard was what the show's (usually male) producers wanted them to hear and not a faithful expression of how any studio audience reacted to any particular joke.

• • •

Nor is bias toward PA absent when it comes to television news. Immaculately coiffed, professionally garbed, possessed of perfect teeth and skin, and usually a few pounds under average weight, the men and women who smile guilelessly into a television camera while reporting from the scene or reading text from a studio teleprompter seem to have been cloned from a small, multicultural sampling of idealized Americans. With remarkably few exceptions, they are noticeably better looking than most people who watch them.

Moreover, the television news emphasis on physical appearance is not limited to those who present it. Judging by the quantity of material aired almost any day, news broadcasts often emphasize stories about attractive people at the expense of those who are PA challenged.

Take crime stories: America at the millennium was a nation of nearly 300 million people. Every year, a tiny fraction of one percent of these millions—but still, thousands of people—disappear, many presumably victims of foul play. Many thousands more are raped and/or murdered. Yet few murder victims or missing persons are named in television accounts; in big cities, those few cases that do get reported rarely get more than a passing mention on local stations, even when their killers or abductors are brought to justice.

On the other hand, consider the case of JonBenet Ramsey, a six-year-old whose parents entered her in beauty contests and thus an exceptionally pretty girl, who had been photographed and videotaped in high heels, adult makeup, and professionally styled hair. When she was murdered in 1996, the media went bonkers. The crime was never solved, but even after more than ten years, images of this blonde, blue-eyed first grader in lipstick and eye shadow are still shown on network television.

And in December 2002, when Laci Peterson, eight months pregnant and beautiful to behold, went missing, her story led the evening network news broadcasts for days. Then her husband Scott, tall, handsome, and philandering, was named as a suspect in her disappearance and presumed murder. For months, television news covered the case; it became a national event. Interviews with police investigators, footage of the discovery of Mrs. Peterson's remains and those of her fetus, and the arrest and subsequent trial of Scott Peterson filled thousands of hours on network, cable, and local television. This sordid little tale of an unfaithful fertilizer salesman murdering his pregnant wife had about as much suspense and drama as a *Perry Mason* rerun—yet a made-for-TV movie was hastily cobbled together and aired to respectable ratings even *before* Scott Peterson's trial began.

Isolated cases of media frenzy?

Hardly.

In April 2005, young Jennifer Wilbanks got cold feet on the eve of her Atlanta wedding and hopped a plane. She turned up in Albuquerque a few days later and spun a wild tale of kidnapping and sexual assault. Pretty soon she fessed up: There was no kidnapper, no sexual assault. Jennifer just needed some head time before getting hitched, couldn't find a way to tell her fiancé, and impulsively took off.

Surely this kind of thing has happened before. Surely it will happen again. Yet the "Runaway Bride" story was reported on network news for weeks afterward.

Why?

Because Jennifer is tall, thin, yet curvaceous. Her face is symmetrical, with big eyes and invitingly full lips. In short, Jennifer Wilbanks is one hot-looking babe.

A few weeks later, in May 2005, eighteen-year-old Natalee Holloway, vacationing in Aruba with her mother, disappeared. Foul play was suspected. Once again the evening news was saturated with Natalee stories. There was a problem, however: Even though dozens of journalists and television technicians descended upon tiny Aruba, neither they nor police were able to turn up many clues to Natalee's disappearance. With few developments in a case that went nowhere, there was little actual news to report. Instead of dropping the story and moving on, both the major networks and larger-market stations dug in. Audiences from coast to coast were served conflicting and usually vague stories about suspects, alibis, and clues. As in the Laci Peterson case, as in the "Runaway Bride" case, there was such a paucity of facts that the networks filled valuable airtime with speculation, innuendo, and rehashes of earlier (and often erroneously) reported facts. Almost as often, networks showed one reporter interviewing another about what they had heard or *thought* or even what they *felt* about the case.

Again, why?

Because Natalee was blonde and busty and beautiful. And the networks had pictures showing her in all her glory.

This bias toward the attractive is spreading around the developed world, and at least one European intellectual thinks it's time for a change. "Ugly people should be spotlighted in the media in the same way that the media wishes to emphasize persons from ethnic minorities," says Trond Andresen, who lectures on engineering cybernetics at the Norwegian Institute of Technology in Trondheim. Andresen told *Bergens Tidende,* a local newspaper in Norway, that journalists, photographers, and television producers discriminate against the ugly and emphasize beautiful people whenever possible.[40] This emphasis on appearance, he continued, makes young people insecure and increases their own dissatisfaction with how they look. "If I were chosen for a TV debate I would obviously be assessed by viewers—not for what I had said, but for how I looked," he added.

> Journalists, photographers, and television producers discriminate against the ugly and emphasize beautiful people whenever possible.

But why not give audiences pictures of attractive people on television? What's the harm in that?

When magazines or newspapers sell more advertising than expected, they can add pages and balance commercial pages with additional editorial content. When there is more or more important news to be reported, a newspaper can add pages or put out a special edition. But at the risk of stating the obvious, there are twenty-four hours of sixty minutes in every day, and no television broadcaster can add so much as a minute to any of those hours.

And even all-news channels such as CNN cannot possibly air stories about every event of the day's news cycle. With rare exceptions and only for catastrophic events—the terrorist attacks of September 11, 2001, the Indian Ocean tsunami of 2004 that killed a quarter million people and drove thousands more from their homes, or the drowning of New Orleans by Hurricane Katrina—TV stations and networks limit news programming to about an hour a day, plus a few hours weekly for such magazine-style shows as CBS's *60 Minutes,* NBC's *Dateline,* and ABC's *20/20.*

Put aside the fact that media companies reap billions of dollars from advertising revenues while getting all-but-free usage of a public asset—in this case, the broadcast spectrum. Forget that these companies are licensed to serve the "public interest, needs, and convenience," as the federal licensing statute provides. What's important, it seems, is that the primary role of news executives is to choose which stories to air, which to omit, which to follow up, and which to ignore.

With television news viewership steadily declining, and with the federal government ignoring its former mandate that news programs contribute to fulfilling requirements for public service, news programming is now regarded as no different from entertainment programming: It is required to earn its own way. Accordingly, decisions about which stories to air are no longer made by weighing their relative news values. Decisions are made, instead, by considering each story's ratings possibilities; the more viewers a show attracts, the more the network can charge its advertisers.[41]

Alas, while the networks were filling news schedules and exhausting resources to transmit endless and repetitive stories about physically attractive JonBenet Ramsey, Laci Peterson, Natalee Holloway, and Jennifer Wilbanks, along with celebrities like Paris Hilton, Lindsay Lohan, and Britney Spears, they gave little or no attention to such important matters as:

- *The USS* Liberty *Cover-Up.* After three decades of helping to cover up an aerial attack assault by Israel on the USS *Liberty,* an intelligence vessel, that killed 37 Americans and wounded 174 crew members, Captain Ward Boston, USN, finally confirmed, in 2004, that President Lyndon Johnson and Secretary of Defense Robert McNamara had prevented an investigation.

- *The OSP Intelligence Scam.* A series of articles by a retired Air Force officer revealed that the State Department's Office of

Special Plans (OSP) had cherry-picked intelligence reports to make the case for war against Iraq, and that reporters from the *New York Times* and the *Washington Post* were manipulated into leaking the OSP's fraudulent "findings" to the public.

- *No Iraq Body Counts.* The Pentagon and the White House claimed they could not quantify Iraqi civilian and military casualties, yet have continued to release "estimates" of the size of the insurgent forces.

- *The Ban on Pictures of American Soldiers Killed in Iraq.* Apparently concerned that showing flag-draped coffins returning from the battlefield or footage of the president attending military funerals might pose reelection problems, the White House decided that the sacrifices of the fallen should be publicly ignored.

- *The Mark Rich Affair.* Is America's political class corrupted by financiers who dole out billions of dollars to bankroll political campaigns? Convicted of tax evasion, Rich fled to Switzerland and was later pardoned by President Clinton just before his term expired.

- *The Dot.com Bubble.* Promoters looted millions of dollars from IRA and 401(k) plans before the bubble burst.

- *Official Obstruction of the 9/11 Commission.* Was investigation of the attack on the World Trade Center obstructed by the Bush administration? Many people, including relatives of the victims of 9/11, believe this was the case and that the cover-up continues.

- *Absence of WMDs, Lack of an Iraq/Al-Qaeda Link, and No Evidence Saddam Hussein Had Any Connection with the 9/11 Attacks.* More than two-thirds of adult Americans were persuaded to support the Iraq War based on the belief that all of the above were proven facts after administration officials used television to make their case for war. The TV networks eventually presented information showing that these assertions were untrue, but by then the war had gone on for nearly two years. Television also ignored reporting that when Saddam Hussein used chemical weapons during the Iraq/Iran War, American military advisers helped direct the projectiles to their targets (a story that was reported by the *New York Times*).

- *National Debt.* Tax cuts for the wealthy have added about $700 *billion* to the national debt, by far the greatest acceleration in budget deficits in U.S. history, with enormous implications for future generations.

So what's wrong with showing pretty faces on television? In itself, nothing. But the Founding Fathers did not grant the rights that the First Amendment confers on the media in order that they stupefy the public with mindless stories about the PA-blessed. Our democracy functions because when the checks and balances of the three branches of government fail—as they sometimes do—the press, including television, bring these lapses to public attention so that voters can correct problems at the ballot box. Don't take my word for it. Here's what James Madison said: "A popular government without popular information, or the means of securing it, is but a prelude to a farce or tragedy, perhaps both."

This observation is as true in a small community as it is in a major city. By yielding large portions of their news programs to overblown reports on the lives and times of the physically attractive, local stations leave little time to broadcast news important to their own communities, be that a school board meeting, the misdeeds of a minor public official, or the local effects of a new law. Thus, more often than not, such small but vital items are ignored by television news.

I was left to wonder, like others before me, if most television news executives believe that audiences prefer watching good-looking people to learning important facts, and if the best way to start a news broadcast is not with some unpleasant reality but with pictures of an unforgettable face or a sexy figure.

I wonder no more. Not long ago Les Moonves, who is president and CEO of CBS and simultaneously shares the same duties at CBS's parent corporation, Viacom, made it clear that he makes no distinction between news and entertainment programming. Moonves told a *New York Times* reporter that if hiring an attractive woman to read the news while removing her clothes—in short, emulating the *Naked News* show that titillates watchers in the United Kingdom—would increase news viewership, he would cheerfully do it because his job is to give audiences what they want.[42]

HAPTER 9

The Dark Side of Physical Attractiveness

*Anorexia, bulimia, and other beautifully
unhealthy behavior*

Pity poor Deleese Williams of Conroe, Texas. Her jaw was deformed, crooked teeth crowded her mouth, her eyes drooped, and her breasts were hard to find. At age 30, she looked back on a childhood of endless horror and ridicule by classmates and the agonizing years of an abusive marriage to a man who never let her forget that she was hard to look at.[1]

Then Deleese heard about ABC Television's *Extreme Makeover* show, one of several network "reality" programs that marshal the talents of cosmetic surgeons, professional hairstylists, makeup artists, and wardrobe consultants in order to present severely PA-deficient individuals with the gift of beauty. Of course, there's more to it than that. It's all to satisfy the prurient interests, base instincts, and vicarious pleasures of a nationwide television audience—and, ultimately, for the benefit of advertisers, whose fees feed the network's bottom line.

But never mind all that crass commercialism for now. Williams applied to *Extreme Makeover* in December 2003, an application accompanied by a mandatory full-length video depicting her worst features, the corporeal deficiencies that collectively amounted to one woman's achy-breaky heart. But the show's producers were delighted with that video: Deleese was just the sort of subject they were looking for.

Early in 2004, Williams flew to Los Angeles and met with production executives and the network makeover team. Later, describing this experience, she said that a psychologist and several physicians told her that she needed her eyes "lifted," her ears "pulled back," and implants not merely in her breasts but also in her chin. They also concluded that dental surgery would be required to break and then reset her jaw. But when doctors were finished, producers promised, Deleese would have a Cindy Crawford–like "Hollywood smile." The free makeover would "transform her life and destiny."

But first the network would let audiences see that being ugly is a tough way to get through the day. To reinforce the notion that beauty is good and its absence bad, producers sat Deleese down before the cameras and asked her to describe how her appearance had invited the ridicule that she suffered as a child and then the agonies of her abusive marriage. All that, however, still didn't quite add up to a program segment. So, according to Deleese, producers interviewed her friends and family to talk about her. Up to then, these folks "didn't notice or pretended not to notice" her looks, but once she was picked for the show, they were coached to focus exclusively on Deleese's every physical flaw.

> Producers sat Deleese down before the cameras and asked her to describe how her appearance had invited the ridicule that she suffered as a child and then the agonies of her abusive marriage.

Reluctant to trash her sister, Kellie McGee tried to play up Deleese's good points. But hard-nosed producers "peppered Kellie with questions about her childhood with the ugly Deleese . . . and repeatedly put words in her mouth." Aiming to please the producers, Williams's mother-in-law also laid it on thick, saying things like, "I never believed my son would marry such an ugly woman."

While these comments never aired on TV, Williams sat squirming in an adjoining room listening and watching a monitor as they were taped.

It was tough to take, Deleese acknowledged. Every cruel word pierced her soul. But still, she thought, it would be worth it. After all, when the doctors, cosmeticians, and wardrobe folks were finished, she'd be beautiful. Everything would be better. Her life, her real life, could begin at last.

The episode announcing her selection for a mega makeover aired on January 7, 2004. It included a video emphasizing all her worst physical features. But an extreme makeover would make everything better. Deleese would enjoy a happy ending—isn't that what the program was all about?

Hours before her scheduled dental surgery, as Williams sat alone in a Los Angeles hotel room reading preop instructions, a producer arrived and coolly informed her that everything was off. "You will not be getting an extreme makeover after all. Nothing. It doesn't fit in our time frame. You will have to go back to Texas tomorrow," said the show's emissary.

Williams burst into tears. "How can I go back as ugly as I left? I was supposed to come home pretty," she sobbed.

But Deleese was no longer the producer's problem.

Why? How could this happen?

It seems the doctors, after considering the nature of Deleese's surgery, had advised producers that her recovery time wouldn't fit into the show's schedule.

"The most tragic part is that Deleese is now too ashamed to even go out in public; she is so hurt and humiliated that she grocery shops at midnight," said Wesley Cordova, the Houston-based attorney who filed a lawsuit on her behalf against ABC and its corporate parent, The Walt Disney Company. "She knew that they could drop her at any time, but she didn't believe they would," he added.

Months later, her sister, Kellie McGee, who had, however reluctantly, spoken disparagingly about Deleese and, to please the producers, revealed a long-suppressed disgust at her sister's appearance, became despondent. "Kellie could not live with the fact that she had said horrible things that hurt her sister. She fell to pieces. Four months later, she ended her life with an overdose of pills, alcohol, and cocaine," said Cordova.

Deleese's lawsuit alleges ABC breached its contract, willfully inflicted emotional distress, and was grossly negligent, which contributed to her sister's suicide. The suit claims that producers subjected her to needless humiliation and goaded Kellie into insulting her appearance. Cordova explained that while Kellie suffered from bipolar disorder, it was the experience of trashing her sister's looks that drove her to kill herself.

ABC and Disney offered condolences for Kellie's death but denied that they bore any responsibility because Williams was well aware that the network could end her participation in the show at any time. They had paperwork that said so.

While Deleese Williams's lawsuit works its way through the courts, let's consider that while her ill-fated pursuit of personal PA was tragic, the cumulative effect of the media's relentless focus on the physically attractive in pursuit of ratings or circulation has had vastly more widespread effects on American society. Beyond the tragedy of the Williams case, beyond redefining news as what happens to the best-looking people, PA-centered media messages encourage a raft of unhealthy and often debilitating conditions that threaten the health of millions.

> PA-centered media messages encourage a raft of unhealthy and often debilitating conditions that threaten the health of millions.

• • •

In America, eating disorders have become increasingly common, even in young children. Like their undernourished, famine-oppressed, Third World counterparts, people with these psychological disorders are often preoccupied with thoughts of food and weight, and they share some of the same physical and emotional symptoms as those who have experienced starvation. Many people with eating disorders appear obsessed with food.[2]

Eating disorders affect people from early childhood through young adulthood and are sometimes promulgated between generations within a family. In 2003, a team led by Dr. Hans Steiner at the Stanford University School of Medicine (Division of Child Psychiatry and Child Development) analyzed data to learn that mothers with eating disorders demonstrated greater concern over their children's eating habits; by the time these children were five years old, many of them already displayed the same symptoms found in juveniles with eating disorders.[3]

Steiner and his team were surprised to learn that half of elementary school children wanted to weigh less, about one in eight reported attempts to lose weight, and three-fourths of these children cited their family as the primary source of dieting-related information. In addition, by age 12, nearly one in five girls and one in twelve boys had eating habits associated with fasting and dietary restraint.

There are three distinct types of eating disorders:

1. Binge eating

2. Bulimia nervosa

3. Anorexia nervosa

Binge eating, which is characterized by frequent episodes of uncontrolled eating, is probably the most common disorder. More than a third of obese individuals in weight-loss treatment programs report problems with binge eating. Bingeing is often accompanied by a feeling of being out of control and is followed by feelings of depression, guilt, or disgust.[4]

The *Gale Encyclopedia of Medicine* describes *bulimia nervosa* as a serious, sometimes life-threatening eating disorder affecting mainly young women. Bulimics binge by stuffing themselves with large amounts of food, then try to rid themselves of the food and its attendant calories by fasting, exercising excessively, vomiting, or using laxatives—purging behavior that may reduce stress and relieve anxiety but carries an unhealthy price tag. Bulimia is often accompanied by depression and is considered a psychiatric illness.

Over two million adolescent American girls and young women suffer from bulimia and the associated bingeing and purging activity that often causes severe bodily damage. In rare instances, bingeing causes the stomach to rupture, and purging brings on heart failure from the loss of such vital minerals as potassium. Vomiting causes another set of serious problems, including acid-related scarring of the fingers (if they are used regularly to induce vomiting) and permanent damage to tooth enamel. In addition, the esophagus, which brings food from the mouth to the stomach, is frequently inflamed from exposure to stomach acids. These acids may also lead to swollen salivary glands. Other consequences of bulimia include irregular menstrual periods and severe loss of libido.

An important study of bulimics was conducted by Gary Groth-Marnat and Naomi Michel of Australia's Curtin University of Technology. They asked seventy-six current or former bulimics and a control group of thirty-seven women who had never experienced the disorder to complete a questionnaire about dissociation (a mental state in which some previously integrated part of a person's life becomes separated from the rest of the personality and functions independently) and the incidence and severity of childhood sexual abuse.

Twenty-one participants scored high on the measure of dissociation; they were asked to participate in a structured clinical interview to determine if any of them could be classified under formal criteria for dissociative disorder. Data indicated that dissociation was highest among current bulimics. Those who had put the disorder behind them were less apt to suffer from dissociation than current bulimics—but also more likely to experience dissociation than the nonbulimic control group.

Contrary to the researchers' expectations, however, there was no link between levels of dissociation and incidence of reported childhood sexual abuse. Nor was the incidence of childhood sexual abuse among bulimics higher than among the general population.[5]

Few bulimics are able to stop their behavior without professional help, and while many bulimics recognize that their actions are not normal, they feel that they are no longer in control. Many struggle with other compulsive, risky behaviors such as drug and alcohol abuse. Such psychiatric illnesses as clinical depression, anxiety, and obsessive-compulsive disorder are also commonly associated with bulimia.

Upwards of 90 percent of bulimics are women in their teens or early twenties. While people of every race develop this disorder, most of those who receive this diagnosis are white. Frequently carried out in secrecy, bulimic behavior is accompanied by feelings of guilt or shame. Many bulimics live secret lives, outwardly healthy and successful while carefully concealing feelings of helplessness and low self-esteem.

While bulimia is usually the result of excessive concern with weight control and self-image, its root causes remain mysterious. Researchers now believe that those who suffer from bulimia are at the confluence of both genetic and environmental influences, including their participation in work or sports that emphasize thinness, such as modeling, dancing, or gymnastics. Family pressures also may play a role. One study found that mothers who are extremely concerned about their daughters' PA, and especially their weight, may contribute to causing bulimia. In addition, girls with eating disorders often have fathers and brothers who criticize their weight.

Even more dangerous is the eating disorder *anorexia nervosa,* which amounts to self-induced starvation. Most prevalent among women, anorexics recoil from their phantom fatness by refusing to eat. Even as they grow thinner and smaller, they see themselves as far too heavy. While few anorexics technically starve themselves to death, many incur life-shortening health disorders by starving their bodies of necessary nutrients.

Anorexia brings the highest mortality rate of any psychiatric illness: Somewhere between 6 percent and 10 percent of anorexics die from this condition—a higher death rate than for some cancers. Involving intense physical and emotional issues in conjunction with severe body image distortion, eating disorders are among the most challenging of all illnesses to treat.

Briefing a congressional panel, Dr. Joel Jahraus, a nationally known expert on eating disorders, described an encounter with a lovely young woman named Anna Westin who became his patient. "[She was] twenty-one years old and full of character and charm," he said. "She loved photography and proudly displayed her work, laughing heartily as she told me of the fun she had with her work. But while a healthy side of this young woman wanted to be there [in an eating disorders clinic], there was also a side that struggled with anorexia nervosa."[6]

> Involving intense physical and emotional issues in conjunction with severe body image distortion, eating disorders are among the most challenging of all illnesses to treat.

After years of taking dozens of laxatives and diet pills daily, plus compulsively exercising for two hours each day, Anna's body weight was dangerously low. "Her pulse was forty beats a minute and blood pressure almost imperceptible at times," Jahraus continued. "Her mood would suddenly change and she would cry inconsolably. Her symptoms were so intense and her medical status so compromised that I immediately recommended hospitalization."

But Anna's insurance company balked. "I was told . . . that she wasn't ill enough for hospitalization and that she would be approved [only] for outpatient treatment," recalled Jahraus. After several intense discussions, the insurer relented. Doctors stabilized Anna with intravenous nutrition, then moved on to intensive psychological work and ongoing nutritional therapy. But after only five days, an insurance reviewer declared that Anna's therapy was sufficient and she must now be treated as an outpatient. Jahraus vehemently fought this decision. When Anna discovered that her insurer was insisting that she should be an outpatient, she lost her already tenuous motivation to continue treatment. "The window of opportunity began to close," continued Jahraus. "She told me, 'If an insurance company isn't approving my admission, I can't be *that* bad!'"

A few weeks later, on February 17, 2000, Anna took her own life by intentionally swallowing an overdose of diet pills.

"Her diary spoke volumes of the torture she endured every day from the eating disorder," explained Jahraus. "She wrote, 'My unhappiness continues on. There really is no way to rid myself of this, is there? And who is listening anyway? No one. My life is worthless right now. Saying good-bye to such an unfriendly place can't be as hard as believing in it every day. And essentially my spirit has fled already.'"

Hoping to help others struggling with eating disorders, Anna's parents established the Anna Westin Foundation (www.annawestin foundation.org), dedicated to the prevention and treatment of eating disorders and to raising public awareness of these dangerous illnesses. It includes the Anna Westin House, which combines innovative treatment for eating disorders with cost-effective care. The foundation's website provides some chilling figures:

- Seven million American women and a million men suffer from eating disorders.

- Between 10 percent and 22 percent of those diagnosed with an eating disorder die as a result of that disorder.

- Between 2 percent and 5 percent of those diagnosed with eating disorders commit suicide.

- Of those suffering from eating disorders, 86 percent report its onset by age 20.

- Seventy-seven percent of those diagnosed with eating disorders suffer from it from one to fifteen years.

Treatment for eating disorders is extremely expensive. Inpatient treatment can cost $30,000 or more per month. Outpatient care runs upwards of $100,000 per year, according to the Westin Foundation.

Probably the most famous eating disorder case to be publicized in America was Terri Schiavo. Severely overweight as a teenager, she lost some sixty-five pounds around the time she graduated from high school. Somewhere along the line, however, fitness became her obsession, along with fasting. After a time, Schiavo limited herself to mostly liquids, drinking more than ten glasses of iced tea daily and forcing herself to vomit what little food she did eat. Much later her family would say that while they had worried about her behavior, they had no idea how quickly her health could deteriorate or how dangerous it was to starve herself—so they neither challenged her nor sought medical help for her condition.

In 1990, Terri lapsed into a coma. According to her doctors, this condition was most likely due to an imbalance in blood potassium levels; by taking great quantities of fluids, this vital mineral was flushed out of her body. Eating would have replaced her minerals, but eating was not on Terri's mind.

She never recovered. After spending years in a vegetative state, doctors told her husband, Michael, that she was brain dead—an irreversible condition. Michael then decided to allow Terri to die by removing her feeding tube, thereby depriving her of water and nutrients. Terri's family, however, had other ideas. A lengthy court battle ensued, and one family's sad story became a national tragedy. Around the country, thousands of people who believed that Terri still possessed a degree of consciousness and might one day recover (despite the medical consensus to the contrary), or who were expressing their own deeply held religious or political convictions about the sanctity of life, lined up in support of Terri's parents and siblings, fighting to keep her alive. Asserting spousal privileges and citing her doctors' findings, Michael went to the courts seeking approval for the dignified death that he claimed his wife would have wanted.

The legal battle went on for years amid enormous controversy. Terri Schiavo died on March 31, 2005. She was forty-one.

Issues of law and faith aside, the debate over Terri Schiavo's fate made it clear that eating disorders are still poorly understood by the public. Ironically, over the last fifteen years, science has made much progress in understanding these disorders. Clinicians now know, for example, that those suffering from an eating disorder are best served by early intervention, before their health is endangered through bone loss, reproductive and heart damage, and other serious problems.

Following Schiavo's death, the *Daytona Beach News-Journal* editorialized that state and federal authorities had failed to educate the public about eating disorders. In particular, the editorial argued, government should seek to inform teenage girls, since they are most likely to make unrealistic comparisons of themselves to media images. The editors cited research showing that children as young as five worry about their weight. "Such concern is not evidence of an eating disorder, but it betrays a greater disorder in society's attitude toward weight, on both ends of the spectrum," the editorial stated.

"As Americans grow more obese, the fashion models and actors who represent the ideal of physical attractiveness have become more emaciated. The unachievable ideal, combined with growing concern for health problems related to obesity, has been tied to a significant increase in the number of eating disorders, especially among school-aged children." The editorial went on to suggest that parents and teachers should learn to recognize warning signs relating to eating disorders, and that insurance companies and public health agencies should broaden medical coverage to include treatment for eating disorders.[7]

> "As Americans grow more obese, the fashion models and actors who represent the ideal of physical attractiveness have become more emaciated."

•   •   •

While anorexia and bulimia are primarily female disorders, men have their own set of problems that researchers have termed the *Adonis Complex,* a mostly secret crisis of "male body obsession." Bombarded by idealized male physiques on magazine covers, in underwear ads, and in action movies—all of which feature men with rippling abdominal muscles and bulging biceps, deltoids, and pectorals—many men have grown increasingly insecure about their appearance.

Harrison G. Pope, Jr., and Roberto Olivardia, both physicians and professors at the Harvard Medical School, and Katharine A. Phillips, a Brown University professor, studied pumped-up male bodies from action figure toys to competitive bodybuilders, Chippendale dancers, Playgirl centerfolds, and everything in between. They concluded that the U.S. media presentation of the idealized male has become steadily more muscular.[8]

They began their study with a look at GI Joe, America's first popular action figure. In 1964, they noted, GI Joe had a respectable but unremarkable male physique. If his green plastic figure were scaled up to the height of an average man, or about five feet ten, his waist would have been thirty-two inches, his chest forty-four inches, and his arms on the small side at twelve inches in diameter—a trim, athletic, but otherwise unremarkable fellow. By 1991, however, GI Joe's waist shrank to twenty-nine inches while his arms muscled up to sixteen inches. In short, he was pumped up like a bodybuilder. Likewise, Pope and his colleagues noted that the 1978 Star Wars action figures Luke Skywalker and Han Solo were trim but otherwise unexceptional in proportion. By 1995, however, both appeared to have been pumping iron and gulping steroids.

Next, consider what your own eyes report: Fifteen or twenty years ago, if you wanted the current issue of a bodybuilding or fitness magazine, you probably had to live in a big city where you could mount an expedition to a large newsstand; even then, your choices were limited to no more than two or three publications. Today, a visit to the magazine racks in almost any U.S. convenience store or supermarket will yield half a dozen or more "physique" publications. Now look at the billboards that litter our highways or ride on the sides of city buses: They are filled with hunky, half-naked male models hawking everything from underwear to cars to consumer electronics. Buy a copy of almost any general-interest magazine and you are treated to bare male chests, rippling muscles, and tanned, chiseled, hairless torsos. The Calvin Klein underwear ads. The Soloflex man. The caped and costumed World Wrestling Entertainment performers, all bursting with steroids. There are gyms all over the place, many owned by billion-dollar conglomerates.

Male muscles, in short, are big business.

Pope and his colleagues also examined magazine ads and found that, for example, in the sixties, less than 10 percent of the male models in *Glamour* and *Cosmopolitan* appeared bare-chested or otherwise less than fully dressed. By the eighties, however, that number has nearly tripled. Along the way, male models became noticeably more buff.

In addition to doing a statistical analysis, Pope and his colleagues interviewed dozens of men suffering from what they term "muscle dysmorphia," which they posit as a sort of "reverse anorexia." One of their subjects was "Kevin," whose body bulged with muscles in places where most men don't know they have muscles. Kevin nevertheless believed that his arms were "sticks." Unwilling to chance encountering someone who might disrespect his physique, he became a near recluse. Then there was "Scott," an obsessive bodybuilder whose compulsive commitment to working out cost him his ladylove. On any beach in any country, women would melt at the sight of Scott's rippling muscles—but he was convinced that he looked puny and so he never went near a beach, refusing to display his unclad body out of morbid embarrassment. A man named "Barry" was so disgusted with his "fat" body that he starved himself down to eighty pounds. "Ben," likewise convinced that he was way too fat, surrendered to twice-weekly food binges, swallowing six or seven giant double burgers, an entire fried chicken, and several pounds of fries, then washing it all down with milk shakes—and then forcing himself to vomit up every last bite into a toilet.

Pope, Olivardia, and Phillips conclude that Kevin, Scott, Barry, and Ben are "the tip of the iceberg." American men are being manipulated through the media, "indoctrinated" by exposure to more supermuscular images than any previous generation has ever encountered, all in service to the "male body image industries"—that is, the purveyors of food supplements, diet aids, fitness programs, hair-growth remedies, and countless other products. These industries, the researchers note, "prey increasingly on men's worries, just as analogous industries have preyed for decades on the appearance-related insecurities of women."

"For every severe or dangerous case," say Pope and his colleagues, "there are dozens of less severe cases—men who cope quietly with emotional pain about some aspect of how they look." PA concerns in boys and men "range from minor annoyances to devastating and sometimes even life-threatening obsessions—from manageable dissatisfaction to full-blown psychiatric body-image disorders."

• • •

While muscle dysmorphia seems limited to males, its near relative is not so particular. Body dysmorphic disorder (BDD), formerly termed "dysmorphophobia," was described in psychiatric literature from around the world for over a century but studied systematically in the United States only since the mid-1990s. BDD manifests as an intense preoccupation with an imagined or slight defect in one's appearance and seems to arrive during adolescence or young adulthood. BDD often coexists with such other psychiatric conditions as social anxiety disorder, obsessive-compulsive disorder, and atypical depression.[9]

Symptoms of BDD first show up in the individual at an average age of sixteen years, four months, but the largest study of this disorder shows that it can afflict girls as young as nine and women up to twenty-three years of age. A typical sufferer is someone like the seventeen-year-old white girl I'll call "Maggie." For three months, Maggie refused to leave her house because, as she frequently told her family, she was ashamed of her "big nose," "small breasts," "flat hair," and "bad skin." An objective appraisal of Maggie's looks, however, would conclude that Maggie's perceived "deformities" are virtually invisible; most people would say that she's actually quite attractive. Nevertheless, Maggie spends hours daily critically studying herself in a mirror and repeatedly asking siblings and parents for reassurances. Her once active social life vanished; she started refusing dates and turned down invitations to parties and other social events. In desperation, she consulted a succession of cosmetic surgeons, but none would agree to perform a procedure without parental consent.[10]

When her parents realized that Maggie's condition was serious, they convinced her to meet with a psychotherapist, a fortunate turn of events: The only effective course of treatment for BDD is psychiatric or psychological counseling, coupled with antianxiety medication. Even without therapy, many BDD sufferers gradually lose symptoms as they age, but the untreated often experience a succession of related disorders.[11]

While people who suffer acute, disabling anxiety over their appearance number in the millions, they are nevertheless only a small fraction of the population. Millions more, however, while retaining the abilities to function in their lives and careers, devote an inordinate slice of their waking day to worrying about how they look.

To learn more about this phenomenon, Barbara L. Fredrickson, director of the University of Michigan's Positive Emotions and Psychophysiology Laboratory, assembled 350 young men and women for two experiments aimed at documenting the psychological costs of raising girls in a culture that "persistently objectifies the female body" and "socializes women to adopt a third-person perspective on their bodies."[12]

> Millions, while retaining the abilities to function in their lives and careers, devote an inordinate slice of their waking day to worrying about how they look.

One of Fredrickson's experiments revealed that what a woman wears, even when alone, can heighten her preoccupation with how her body looks—usually at the expense of her critical mental performance skills. And it's not just revealing or low-cut clothes, such as bathing suits or evening dresses, that have this consciousness-altering effect. "Any clothing or circumstances that makes a woman feel self-conscious about how she looks to others, even if she thinks she looks great, might reduce the mental energy she brings to demanding tasks, like solving advanced math problems," explains Fredrickson. She adds that asking herself how she looks, or constantly checking her appearance in mirrors, adjusting a strap, or even tugging on a skirt, diverts mental resources, making the individual temporarily unavailable for more challenging or vital mental tasks.

Men, however, are not affected by their clothing. While women varied widely on their degree of preoccupation with their appearance, "as a group, women scored higher than men on tests of what the researchers call 'self-objectification,'" as Fredrickson and her colleague Stephanie Noll found.

According to Fredrickson and another colleague, social psychologist Tomi-Ann Roberts, the tendency to view one's body from the outside in—that is, by valuing PA and sex appeal as more central to body identity than health, strength, energy level, coordination, or fitness—may have even more harmful effects beyond diminished mental performance, increased feelings of shame and anxiety, and development of eating disorders. Fredrickson and Roberts think that preoccupation with appearance has far-reaching consequences and is probably linked to the high prevalence of depression and sexual dysfunction among American women.

Furthermore, research by Dr. Shanette M. Harris, a professor in the University of Rhode Island's clinical psychology program, suggests that body concerns and dissatisfaction with appearance begin during puberty and remain relatively stable throughout a woman's lifetime.[13] This notion is supported by earlier research done at Cornell University, where researchers found that the cultural ideals represented by thin women are "clearly present" in sixth-grade girls, and that such early establishment of body dissatisfaction is linked to the escalating levels of anorexia nervosa and related eating disorders in adolescents.[14]

Where and how does a young woman learn to objectify herself?

Much has been written about the effect of the mass media on fostering attitudes. The billions of dollars spent annually to advertise products, services, and candidates for public office are testament to at least the strong belief that the images and messages on television, in periodicals, and on billboards are enormously influential. "The mass media force attention to certain issues. They build up public images of political figures. They are constantly presenting objects suggesting what individuals in the mass should think about, know about, have feelings about," wrote Kurt and Gladys Lang in their essay "The Mass Media and Voting."[15]

And if the adults in a family are thereby influenced to form opinions on the nature and importance of PA, could such attitudes influence their offspring during formative years?

To answer that question, a team of Canadian researchers led by Dr. Caroline Davis of York University's Department of Kinesiology and Health Sciences in Ontario decided to see if eating-disordered families are overly concerned with PA and social appearance. Interview and questionnaire data collected from 158 healthy young women were massaged and analyzed. In the end, the researchers concluded that family risk factors have a more potent influence on young women who are easily made anxious, perhaps because they are more sensitive to, or more likely to internalize, pressures and expectations to conform to family values.[16]

Ill health witnessed here offsets beauty benefits. But beauty pays prized dividends, and few people scrutinize transactions beneath the surface veneers. Be it expenditures of health or money, seekers of greater PA abound, investing mightily in pursuits to improve on nature's design. We next peek behind the financial veil and see some not-so-pretty prices.

CHAPTER 10

What Price for Good Looks?

The hidden costs of aesthetic enhancements

The rise of eating disorders and the increase in expressions of body dissatisfaction are not the only indicators of ways that the media's relentless emphasis on physical attractiveness has shaped American beauty values. America's growing obsession with beauty has transformed the cosmetic surgery industry. Only a few years ago a tiny cadre of elite surgeons performed a relatively small number of often secretive and expensive operations for the benefit of the horribly disfigured or to indulge the wealthy. Now tens of thousands of doctors with a variety of medical specialties dispense an astonishing panoply of beauty-enhancing procedures eagerly sought by middle-class Americans of every age.

The most popular, by far, is the injection of Botox, a procedure involving a tiny amount of a purified and extremely dilute solution of the deadly botulism toxin. Injected into the face, it paralyzes muscles, smoothing wrinkles. Side effects may include a degree of loss in facial expression and unwanted facial muscle paralysis in sites near the targeted area and, less commonly, nausea, headache, fatigue, malaise, flu-like symptoms, and rashes.

> Tens of thousands of doctors dispense an astonishing panoply of beauty-enhancing procedures eagerly sought by middle-class Americans of every age.

By any measure, Botox is a hit. In 2004, more than 2.8 million Americans had injections, a 25 percent increase from the preceding year, according to American Society for Aesthetic Plastic Surgery (ASAPS) statistics. A Botox shot for wrinkles is the fastest-growing cosmetic procedure in the country, with women and men flocking to doctors, to spas, to walk-in stores in upscale malls, and even to so-called "Botox parties."

Irena Medavoy advanced beyond such beauty seekers. The attractive forty-four-year-old wife of prominent motion picture executive Mike Medavoy received a series of Botox injections after her dermatologist suggested it might help her cope with migraine headaches. Medavoy told NBC reporter Maria Shriver that while meeting with Dr. Arnold "Dermatologist to the Stars" Klein, she discussed her migraine headaches with him.[1]

"Oh, do you get headaches?" asked Dr. Klein.

"Yes, I get migraines," replied Medavoy.

"Oh, well, you know what? We're using Botox for migraines."

"Really? Wow, I don't . . . you know . . . I don't know."

"Oh, no side effects. It's nothing. It'll definitely help you; it's great."

The Food and Drug Administration has approved Botox for only three medical conditions, including cosmetic application only for the forehead "frown line" between the eyes. Many doctors, however, routinely test new drugs for what are termed "off-label" uses: treatments not yet approved by the FDA. Several off-label Botox uses seem to hold promise, including treatment of migraines.

Irena was well aware of the drug's cosmetic utility and that Dr.

Klein, whose patient roster included Elizabeth Taylor, had been an early Botox booster, touting the treatment for both cosmetic and medical uses. In 2001, Klein took part in an NBC News demonstration of its many applications. Nor can anyone doubt that Irena Medavoy was then among Tinseltown's biggest Botox fans, paying up to $1,000 per treatment to maintain her flawless face. "I don't know anybody who wasn't using it . . . every single friend," confided Medavoy to Shriver and a television audience in the millions. "Absolutely. We all have the exact same forehead. We used to walk around with the same kind of . . . no expression kind of thing."

Before this particular meeting with Dr. Klein, Medavoy's migraines were treated by a neurologist, Dr. Andrew Charles. "Did you think to call [Charles] and say, 'You know what, my dermatologist tells me [to use] Botox for migraines. What do you think?'" asked Shriver. "I didn't," replied Medavoy. "I trusted Klein. I've known him for twenty-five years."

Irena Medavoy accepts responsibility for not asking more questions about Botox. But she blames Dr. Klein for not disclosing that he was a paid consultant to Botox manufacturer Allergan, Inc., and for failing to tell her that injecting Botox for migraines was an off-label treatment. But then again, long before April 2002, when Botox was approved for wrinkles, she had signed Klein's consent form, allowing him to inject her for off-label uses and potentially shielding him from any legal consequences that might arise from these uses.

Medavoy told NBC News that she had experienced no adverse reaction to earlier Botox wrinkle treatments. That changed, she says, with her migraine treatments. According to a medical file that she shared with NBC News, Dr. Klein injected her in the neck, at the base of the skull, with eighty-six units, the largest Botox dose he'd ever given her. NBC spoke with several neurologists who confirmed that both the injection location and dosage were standard Botox migraine treatment.

Medavoy later said that she knew immediately that something was wrong. She nevertheless felt well enough the day following her injections to take her four-year-old and some of his friends to Disneyland. Three or four days later, however, she began to feel strange. At first it was chills and fever, as though she was coming down with influenza. Another two or three days later the roof fell in. "I thought I was having a stroke. I got a headache like I've never had in my life."

Her pain increased and wouldn't respond to the usual migraine medication. So Medavoy called Dr. Klein, who, she claims, admitted that he might have given her too much Botox. The pain, which was *not* like that of her usual migraines, grew worse. "This was an incapacitating, unremitting headache centered more around her neck and shoulders, and didn't respond to any of the medications we tried on her," explained Dr. Charles, her neurologist. Medavoy wound up in the ER, complaining that beyond an excruciating headache, she had trouble breathing, was running a temperature of 102 degrees, and suffered other flulike symptoms. After her second ER trip and a round of doctors' visits, Dr. Robert Huizinga, Medavoy's internist for some five years, was perplexed: His healthy patient had suddenly become very ill.

Mrs. Medavoy sued Klein and Allergan for a number with so many zeroes it would give you, well, a migraine. When the case went to trial in October 2004, however, attorneys representing Klein and Allergan convinced nine of twelve Los Angeles jurors that while Botox might indeed have caused Medavoy's problems, neither Dr. Klein nor Allergan could be held liable for Irena's suffering.[2]

Irena Medavoy is not the only patient to regret choosing Botox. Or what she *thought* was Botox. Because a single dose of this drug is so costly, hundreds of physicians have given in to the temptation of acquiring a substitute from perhaps dubious sources. In 2004, for example, at least 219 doctors purchased an unapproved Botox knockoff from a firm in Tucson, Arizona. Now a dozen physicians in three states face license suspension—and hundreds more are expecting visits by federal regulators—in an investigation into what FDA regulators and federal prosecutors say was the sale of fake Botox and its injection into unsuspecting patients.[3]

> Irena Medavoy is not the only patient to regret choosing Botox. Or what she *thought* was Botox.

As reported in *USA Today,* Toxin Research International (TRI) of Tucson and its affiliates promoted their own version of botulinum toxin as a cheaper alternative to Botox. Despite package labels that said this product was *not* for human use, patients in Florida, Nevada, and Oregon received injections; many were unaware that it was not Botox. Although no injuries were reported among *those* patients, a doctor involved in the distribution of the toxin was not so lucky. Dr. Bach McComb, a Florida osteopath, injected himself and three patients—including his girlfriend—with a solution carrying a far higher concentration of botulinum than found in real Botox. McComb and all three patients were afflicted with potentially fatal muscle paralysis. All four survived extended hospitalization but suffered serious, long-term complications.

TRI's Dr. Chad Livdahl and Dr. Zarah Karim, each thirty-four years old and married to each other, pleaded guilty to mail fraud and conspiracy and could be free in time to celebrate their silver wedding anniversary. McComb pleaded guilty to conspiring to defraud the federal government and to mislabeling drugs. Dr. Robert Baker, professor of ophthalmology and director of oculofacial plastic surgery at the University of Kentucky, also faces federal charges, including conspiracy, in connection with this scheme.[4]

"This deadly toxin . . . wrapped in the guise of medicine represents a grave threat," said Marcos Daniel Jimenez, U.S. Attorney for the Southern District of Florida, who filed the charges. According to prosecutors, Livdahl and Karim marketed their product through brochures mailed to doctors nationwide and in this manner sold over 3,000 vials of the toxin. Their investment of $30,000, including marketing expenses, brought them $1.7 million. A vial of the unapproved toxin, enough for five doses, went for $1,250. In contrast, Allergan's approved Botox comes in a single-dose vial and wholesales for around $560. Each of the knockoff vials cost TRI less than $10.[5]

Based on the latest data from the ASAPS, medical cosmetic procedures in the United States continue to skyrocket. Nearly 11.5 million nonsurgical and surgical procedures were performed in 2006—747 percent and 98 percent increases, respectively, since 1997—with Americans spending just over $12 billion. Botox injections led the nonsurgical list with 3,181,592 procedures followed by hyaluronic acid chemical peel (1,593,554), laser hair removal

(1,475,296), micodermabrasion (993,071), and laser skin resurfacing (576,509). The top five surgical cosmetic procedures were liposuction (403,684 procedures), breast augmentation (383,886),
eyelid surgery (209,999), abdominoplasty (172,457), and breast reduction (145,822). Women account for 92 percent of the 2006
totals, soaring 749 percent for nonsurgical procedures and 123 percent for surgical procedures since 1997. Men received nearly 1 million medical cosmetic procedures in 2006, escalating 722 percent
for nonsurgical procedures and tapering off 2 percent for cosmetic
surgical procedures since 1997.

Because these medical cosmetic procedures are now widely
available and increasingly acceptable socially, they are sought by
ever-growing numbers of people in pursuit of PA enhancement
(whether they can afford the costs or not).
That's *at least* based on ASAPS statistics as collected by surveying board-certified physicians
and surgeons with specialties in plastic surgery,
otolaryngology, and dermatology. ASAPS does
not collect data from other surgeons or from
licensed physicians not certified in cosmetic surgery.

> Because these medical cosmetic procedures are now widely available and increasingly acceptable socially, they are sought by ever-growing numbers of people (whether they can afford the costs or not).

Nor does its data necessarily include the
growing number of off-label procedures performed by doctors whose PA-seeking patients
demand the latest procedures and bring forth the money to pay for
them. Take New York's Dr. Steven Victor, a Madison Avenue cosmetic dermatologist, whose office is stocked with an array of the
newest-fangled body-perfecting and youth-prolonging equipment.
Victor is an advocate of offering the latest technology along with
state-of-the-art pharmaceuticals to his patients, sometimes even
when a particular procedure has not yet gained FDA approval. For
example, Restylane, trade name for a natural sugar present in the
skin called hyaluronic acid, was first used in France, England, and
Canada. Like collagen, it's a wrinkle filler and lip enhancer. Although initially approved in the United States for use in ophthalmo-
logic and orthopedic surgery, it was not approved by the FDA until
late 2003 for cosmetic use specific to facial wrinkles. Restylane lasts

twice as long as collagen, but patients often suffer more pain and bruising, especially in their lips. Victor provided it on request to his most demanding patients long before specific FDA approval.

To Victor, Restylane was old news, already on the road to respectable obsolescence. Interviewed for *New York* magazine in 2003, he said, "By the time Restylane gets approved here, nobody will be using it in Europe anymore. People have been using it in the United States and in other countries for years. We've been hearing forever that it's getting approved by the FDA any day." At that time, even before Restylane was approved in late 2003, the doctor preferred to talk about a hot new wrinkle eliminator called Matridex, for which FDA approval is pending. "Matridex fills instantly and loses only between 30 percent and 50 percent of its correction," he explained, adding that, by contrast, Restylane dissipates entirely in six to nine months, requiring follow-up treatment.[6]

Victor is far from the only doctor practicing and promoting procedures on the leading edges of the aesthetician's art. According to *New York* magazine, many among Gotham's elite cosmetic corps routinely use medicines for off-label treatments. And many see themselves more as part of an international medical community than as strictly American doctors since their patients often have the resources one way or another to travel anywhere for the PA enhancements they crave. So, instead of looking to the FDA, these licensed beauty dispensers follow studies and clinical and anecdotal evidence from European and South American practitioners. Often they voice open resentment of the FDA's measured approval process. Knowing that they are in a global competitive industry driven by high consumer demand, many are willing to venture into gray areas like off-label procedures to attract the sort of well-heeled patients that can turn an ordinary medical practice into a river of cash.

Ethically, such doctors justify use of unapproved drugs under a doctrine called "standard of care," which makes the case that when a considerable number of physicians practice a particular treatment without obviously endangering patients, it tends to legitimize the procedure. In other words, going out on an ethical limb to meet patients' desires for enhanced PA is justified when "everybody does it."

Doctors pursue two legal routes to using a drug lacking FDA

approval: the "off-label" approach (discussed previously), and the use of drugs whose manufacturer has never even sought FDA approval for cosmetic applications.

Other doctors disagree, often heatedly, over the ethics and safety of using unapproved products. To them, FDA regulations are virtually Holy Writ; they think that doctors who ignore government regulations by using unapproved treatments should be subject to losing their medical licenses. "Either we respect the laws or we don't," asserts Dr. Thomas Romo III, a Lenox Hill Hospital official and an influential member of several New York medical societies. "When the FDA says something is not approved at all, it's not 'sort of' against the law if you use it, it *is* against the law," he says. "If it was really necessary for patient survival, like a cancer-curing medicine, maybe one could wink at it, but . . . to fill in a crease? What makes these doctors feel they are above the law?"[7]

Dr. Stephen Bosniak is an ophthalmic plastic surgeon at New York Eye and Ear Infirmary who has used Restylane on patients for years. "Patient safety is paramount," he says, explaining that he used Restylane in animal studies and then at a Brazilian clinic before injecting it into his New York patients. (Apparently, endangering Brazilians is an acceptable risk as long as they're in Brazil.) Yet Bosniak is cautious about off-label usage after treating people who had used certain European-made wrinkle fillers that produced terrible lumps and ugly sores. By way of illustration, he said that when patients ask him for ArteFill, a wrinkle filler that suspends acrylic beads in collagen, he refuses, because the beads often harden under the skin. When patients then ask doctors to repair newly lumpy tissue, cortisone injections sometimes help, but often they don't. "I don't think the FDA will ever approve [ArteFill]," he adds.[8] Despite his handicapping odds, the FDA approved ArteFill in 2006.

Other patients travel to Canada or Europe for treatment—and later regret it. "There have been problems with semipermanent fillers in Canada and Europe," explained Dr. Neil Sadick, a dermatologist. Some people develop persistent nodules under their skin. "They become hard, visible, and inflamed, and many of these reactions can occur years later," continued Sadick, who suggests that people wait at least a few years before using any new product that offers permanent or semipermanent results.[9]

In fact, some doctors believe that even FDA approval doesn't guarantee that a product is safe to use: Over the last few years, many FDA-approved drugs, including painkillers and the arthritis drugs Vioxx and Celebrex, have been yanked from pharmacies or relabeled after patients suffered unanticipated side effects. Another example of poor FDA monitoring: Johnson & Johnson's Duragesic, a prescription patch that delivers fentanyl, a narcotic many times more powerful than morphine. In 2004, pharmacists filled more than 4 million Duragesic prescriptions. Like all opioids— drugs derived from opium—fentanyl controls pain but also reduces respiratory function, and too much fentanyl can cause people to stop breathing entirely. That happens more than occasionally: Between 1999 and 2005, the Los Angeles County coroner's office investigated more than 230 deaths involving fentanyl and classified 127 of these as "accidental," suggesting that victims inadvertently overdosed themselves. Reports from around the country suggest there may be thousands of such cases nationwide. Yet the FDA was slow to investigate hundreds of suspicious deaths associated with fentanyl, or to alert physicians, pharmacists, or patients.[10]

> Some doctors believe that even FDA approval doesn't guarantee that a product is safe to use.

And then there was the widely prescribed fen-phen, a combination of fenfluramine and phentermine. Fen-phen was celebrated, for a time, for its efficacy in promoting weight loss—until 1997, when the celebrated Mayo Clinic reported that twenty-four patients developed heart valve disease after taking it. Dozens of heart-related deaths were reported before the FDA pulled fen-phen from the market. The FDA was criticized for failing to do adequate studies before granting approval.

More recently there's Radiance, FDA-approved for such treatments as thickening bladder walls to deal with incontinence. Made from microscopic calcium particles found in bone and teeth and suspended in a gel, many cosmetic dermatologists inject it, off label, to fill wrinkles or bolster lips. But months or years later some patients develop bonelike deposits in or near the injection location. Just because something is green-lighted by the FDA, opined Dr. Thomas Loeb, a cosmetic surgeon, "doesn't mean that I approve of it. Look at Radiance. People get hard knots in the lip from it."[11]

So what does FDA approval, or its absence, actually guarantee? The agency is vested with the responsibility and authority to ensure that food and drugs offered for sale in America are safe to use. But when the FDA, for example, refuses to allow unrestricted sale of a drug, does that indicate that it is unsafe?

Not at all. Recently, charges of political interference with the FDA approval process were raised by the Government Accountability Office, a nonpartisan congressional watchdog. GAO investigators found that senior officials in the Food and Drug Administration withheld approval of a morning-after birth control pill for over-the-counter sale, perhaps because of pressure from religious groups. The GAO report described "an appalling level of manipulation and suppression of the science," said Representative Henry A. Waxman. The FDA's refusal to approve a pill marketed commercially as "Plan B" followed scientific reviews by three separate FDA offices and two panels of outside advisers. All recommended that Plan B be approved for sale without a prescription. Instead, FDA top management blocked the decision from going forward.[12]

How could this happen? Perhaps because the blocking bureaucrats, political appointees serving at the pleasure of the president of the United States, felt more obligation to political backers than to the public at large. Or because the unrestricted sale of any birth control drug offended their personal morality. Regardless of the reason, if pressures on FDA bureaucrats can get even one of them to ignore scientific studies and block a drug from entering the nonprescription market, where does it stop? Pharmaceutical manufacturers, like every regulated industry, lavish campaign contributions on Washington politicians of every stripe. Could drug makers encourage an FDA decision maker to ignore science and fast-track their product? At least when it comes to trying preparations for purely cosmetic purposes, the wise consumer would do well to recall that pioneers, to paraphrase Hamlet, often suffer the slings and arrows of outrageous fortune.

• • •

While America's enthusiasm for nonsurgical cosmetic procedures soars to new heights, all of cosmetic surgery follows in lockstep. According to ASAPS statistics, in 2006, the latest year for
which full data are available, Americans spent more than $12 billion
on more than 11 million medical cosmetic procedures. As detailed
a few pages back, all the liposuctions, breast augmentations, eyelid
surgeries, facelifts, and so forth add up to a 98 percent increase in
surgical cosmetic procedures and a 747 percent increase in nonsurgical cosmetic procedures between 1997 and 2006.

There is little stigma attached to improving one's looks with a
doctor's assistance these days, and now that cosmetic surgery has
become more of a spending priority, small, specialized clinics have
sprung up around the country. Some of these cosmetic surgery centers attract a steady stream of patients by advertising on cable television; many even offer financing. And the great majority of patients
who avail themselves of such services are pleased with the results.

But many who have blithely plunked down several thousand
bucks for a tummy tuck, boob job, or facelift rue the day they went
under the knife. Like the twenty-three South Floridians who sought
enhanced PA at the Florida Center for Cosmetic Surgery in Fort
Lauderdale. Melanie, a forty-one-year-old woman who declined to
give her last name, said she was so desperate for bigger breasts that
she scrimped for years, finally borrowing the balance of the $4,000
tab by putting up her car as security for a loan.[13]

Melanie doesn't love her new breasts. One is over a full cup size
larger than the other. Her nipples are misshapen. As reported in the
Boca Raton News, a year after her operation, her left breast was afflicted with sharp, chronic pains. "It actually feels like someone is
stabbing me," she complained. "I can only sleep one or two hours
a night because the pain . . . wakes me up."

Melanie said she experienced mild discomfort for weeks immediately following her surgery. During stitch removal, however, a
nurse allegedly stabbed her with scissors. Her left breast became
unbearably painful. "They told me they fixed the problem by firing
the nurse, but they haven't fixed *my* problem. My problem is that
my breast is killing me," she said.

So Melanie, along with twenty-two other patients, asked the clinic to compensate her for pain and suffering, no less than the damage to her figure. Soon thereafter, the Florida Board of Medicine disciplined two of the center's four surgeons for misconduct, according to state records. Oddly, neither surgeon carried medical malpractice insurance, making it difficult to recover damages from their respective medical corporations. When patients tried to collect from the center, its lawyers asserted that the facility exercised no supervision or control over medical services provided by its physicians.

Melanie turned to another doctor at the center for reconstructive surgery. She was injected with steroids to mitigate pain. It seemed to make no difference, so she found a lawyer and sued the Florida Center for Cosmetic Surgery.

While a center spokesperson claimed that over 80 percent of the cosmetic procedures it performs result from patient referrals, the center and its doctors are nevertheless well acquainted with malpractice lawsuits: Since 2000, they have settled with at least eighteen patients; several more cases are pending. Among the latter is Mona Alley, a diabetic, who lost both legs to infection when her intestine was punctured during a tummy tuck at the center. "I just couldn't lose my tummy," she told a local reporter. "I heard a cosmetic surgery ad on TV that liposuction was good for diabetics," said Alley. "I went to the center and the doctor told me it was fantastic and that there would be almost no downtime."[14]

The day after her tummy tuck, however, Alley was so sick she couldn't move. "The pain was unbearable," she said. "But when I went back for follow-up, [the doctor] patted me on the arm and said I'd be fine." After two weeks of complaining to this surgeon, Alley said, he finally listened to her chest through a stethoscope—and immediately referred her to her primary care physician. Tests revealed pockets of air in Alley's abdomen, water in her lungs, and blood clots in her legs. "The liposuction had pierced . . . the abdominal wall," said Alley's lawyer. "The doctor cut her intestine and it was leaking feces into her abdomen."

Alley was required to use a colostomy bag for nearly a year. Both her buttocks required reconstruction. Formerly a champion bowler and always very active, Alley now struggles to perform every-day tasks. "I'm managing, but it was real hard in the beginning," she told the reporter. "If I knew then what I know now, I would never have considered this [procedure] with [the Florida Center]," said Alley. "I would have gone with a good doctor at a reputable hospital. In the center they don't want to do aftercare."

There are other cautionary tales told by former patients of this clinic.[15] One is Adrianna Arroyo of Miami, who nearly died after submitting to a tummy tuck, breast implants, and liposuction on the same day in 1999. For a week afterward she complained of nausea, vomiting, and weakness but received no medical attention until she was taken to Baptist Hospital. There she almost died of kidney failure.

Katherine Kennedy, a North Miami Beach flight attendant, also saw the center's television ads but was persuaded when a friend recommended the center. She chose a "two-for-one special," where she paid $5,000 for breast implants and thigh liposuction. She was left with permanent nerve damage that caused such severe pain she could get temporary relief only from a series of spinal epidurals. Even so, some experts say she was lucky to survive; undergoing two such procedures the same day often leads to deadly complications. Kennedy's case was only one among many: Between 1997 and 2004, at least thirty-six people died in Florida as a result of complications from cosmetic surgery. Two of the dead were patients of the Florida Center for Cosmetic Surgery in Fort Lauderdale: James K. McCormick, a bartender, died on his fifty-first birthday, soon after receiving a chin implant and facelift. And Jacqueline Roberts, an employee of a local newspaper, died three days after her tummy tuck and breast reduction at the center.

On February 11, 2004, the Florida Board of Medicine called for a ninety-day statewide ban on performing outpatient liposuction and tummy tucks within the same fourteen-day period. They also demanded the surgical logs of all Florida doctors who performed these and other cosmetic procedures on outpatients between June 1, 2002, and January 31, 2004.

Bad luck, you say. These unfortunate people, and the hundreds of others who have suffered death or disfigurement from a cosmetic procedure, should have had the sense to insist on undergoing their operation in a real hospital, not a clinic or a doctor's office. In fact, about 20 of every 100,000 patients who underwent liposuction in the United States between 1994 and 1998 died—a higher death rate than for people in motor vehicle accidents. Even so, that's only one-eighth the rate of deaths from liposuction in the 1970s.[16]

So things are getting better, right?

Maybe. But consider the disturbing case of novelist Olivia Goldsmith, at fifty-five years of age the best-selling novelist and author of *The First Wives Club,* who on January 7, 2004, checked into the pricey and highly regarded Manhattan Eye, Ear, and Throat Hospital in New York. Goldsmith was scheduled for what many cosmetic surgeons would describe as minor surgery—a "chin tuck" to remove loose skin beneath her chin.[17]

This procedure was not supposed to be a big deal for the author, who had gone under an aesthetic surgeon's knife on several previous occasions. More to the point, the characters in Goldsmith's pop-feminist novels toss off plastic surgery and Botox injections the way Ian Fleming's James Bond leaves a trail of bleeding bodies and broken hearts in his wake. If there was anyone who should have understood the risks—and perhaps the futility—of burnishing one's outside when one feels ugly inside, it was Olivia Goldsmith.

Yet here she was again with her usual doctor, Norman Pastorek, a well-regarded otolaryngologist (ear, nose, and throat specialist) with what *New York* magazine described as a devoted following. For reasons still not clear, Goldsmith elected general anesthesia instead of less risky and more usual local anesthesia. She knew that while Manhattan Eye, Ear, and Throat is considered one of New York City's best places to get procedures like a chin tuck, like many hospitals purveying a menu of elective surgery, specially trained nurses are allowed to administer anesthesia under an anesthesiologist's supervision. The anesthesiologist, however, is often responsible for supervising multiple operations simultaneously.

Even before Goldsmith's surgeon lifted his scalpel, she had problems. Her entire body began to writhe and buck. As these convulsive spasms abated, she slipped into a coma. Despite many attempts to revive her, Olivia Goldsmith never regained consciousness and died eight days later, on January 15, at nearby Lenox Hill Hospital.

The New York City Medical Examiner concluded that the novelist's death was linked to anesthesia; the operating room staff failed to monitor her respiration and carbon dioxide levels and draped her in such a way that they could not observe her respiratory movements. The official report also said that despite signs of respiratory problems and the fact she was already heavily sedated, Goldsmith was given fentanyl, the powerful pain reliever that acts on the central nervous system but can also interfere with respiration.

Even more distressing to those considering plastic surgery—or whose livelihood is earned in this field—was that the day after the unfortunate Goldsmith expired, a second patient at Manhattan Eye, Ear, and Throat, fifty-six-year-old Susan Malitz of Connecticut also died of complications from anesthesia. The New York State Department of Health attributed Malitz's death to an excessive dose of lidocaine—four times the maximum safe dose for this anesthetic—perhaps complicated by the fact it was injected into her trachea instead of into neck tissue.[18]

New York health department authorities cited the hospital for "serious breakdowns in patient care in its anesthesia and plastic surgery departments" and levied fines of $20,000, or the maximum penalty of $2,000 per violation for each of ten deficiencies. These violations included the staff's failure to complete a thorough preoperative workup for Goldsmith, their lack of adequate monitoring of both patients' respiration and vital signs during surgery, and their unexplained and significant delay in responding appropriately to each emergency.

Americans who can't afford the prices at hospitals like Manhattan Eye, Ear, and Throat sometimes seek bargains abroad, especially in Spain, which has the largest number of plastic surgeons per capita in Europe. Spanish surgeons perform 350,000 procedures a year, trailing only Brazil and the United States. Spanish cosmetic surgery clinics attract not only budget-minded Europeans, but also Arab potentates and developing world dignitaries. People like Stella Obasanjo, fifty-nine, wife of Nigeria's president, General

> Americans who can't afford the prices sometimes seek bargains abroad.

Olusegun Obasanjo, who in October 2005 checked into the ultra-chic Molding Clinic, in the glitzy Costa del Sol resort city of Marbella, for a tummy tuck. Mrs. Obasanjo rose to international prominence in the mid-1990s when, at great personal risk, she successfully campaigned for the release of her husband after he was jailed for allegedly plotting a coup against the repressive Abacha military junta. Mrs. Obasanjo later received several awards for her work on behalf of women's rights.[19]

None of that was of any help when, during surgery, she lapsed into a coma and was rushed from the plastic surgery wing to the ER, where efforts to revive her failed. Her family is said to be considering legal action for medical malpractice.

Far luckier than Mrs. Obasanjo were the patients of fifty-eight-year-old Gregorio Nosovsky. Despite his habit of wearing a white lab coat with "Dr. Nosovsky" embroidered on its breast and the business cards he passed out identifying him as an MD, Nosovsky never finished medical school. That didn't stop him from appearing on TV talk shows as a medical expert or from performing plastic surgery on dozens of women, often with the help of his brother, Isaac, who actually did have a medical license. License or no, Gregorio was a busy fellow. He performed breast enlargements, tummy tucks, nose jobs, facelifts, and liposuction. He made a lot of money.[20]

Gregorio and Isaac Nosovsky saw patients at the Advanced Center for Cosmetic Surgery in an affluent suburb of Fort Lauderdale. Gregorio was arrested in April 2002 after Marta Gonzalez told authorities that she had suffered complications from breast surgery performed by Gregorio. Later, she said, Isaac performed corrective surgery, but that only made things worse. As reported by the *St. Petersburg Times,* once Gonzalez's complaint became public, thirty-five more women came forward with similar stories about disfigurement under Gregorio Nosovsky's scalpel. "These women were victimized," announced Broward County sheriff's spokeswoman Liz Calzadilla-Fiallo. "We by no means think that thirty-six is the final count."

Unlicensed physicians are hardly a new American phenomenon, but the growing interest in cosmetic procedures has opened new vistas for the ethically challenged who believe that even a fake doctor can simply bury his mistakes. One such mistake was made on Maria Cruz, a thirty five-year-old Filipino immigrant who made a six-figure salary at a large New York bank. Maria, described as a chaste and pious woman, sought breast implants from a man calling himself Dr. Dean Faiello. Ten months later, police found Cruz's body folded into a suitcase and embedded in cement outside Faiello's former New Jersey home. Between the time Cruz was last seen alive and her body was recovered, Faiello was arrested for practicing medicine without a license and for illegally possessing medical drugs. He pleaded guilty, was released on bail pending a sentencing hearing, then fled to Costa Rica to evade prison.[21]

Most victims of sloppy surgery find a lawyer; a few, like Theresa Mary Ramirez, seek revenge. She is now serving life in prison for the 1997 murder of Dr. Michael Tavis, whom she claimed gave her leaking breast implants. In Bellevue, Washington, Beryl Challis removed her bandages after a facelift and was so unnerved by the face in the mirror that after killing her surgeon, Dr. Selwyn Cohen, she went home and took her own life.[22]

No discussion of the hazards of aesthetic procedures would be complete without mentioning that a few people find the whole notion of undergoing cosmetic surgery irresistible. And so they spend enormous sums on an endless series of operations, often winding up looking like Frankenstein's monster, but sure that just one or two more surgeries will fix everything.

The world's best-known plastic surgery subject is undoubtedly pop singer Michael Jackson, who has undergone surgery no less than a dozen times—and probably many more. This decades-long metamorphosis transformed him from a dark-skinned, broad-nosed, Afro-haired adolescent into a pasty, slender-nosed, long-haired, dimpled, and androgynous Caucasian whose chiseled features can only be described as grotesque. If Jackson's goal was a singular appearance, he has long since realized it; he now looks so strange that many viewing genuine photographs of him want to believe that the images, and not the man, have been doctored. Dermatologists who have analyzed such pictures speculate that Jackson has had Botox injections in his forehead and plastic surgery on his nose, eyes, and chin. He has probably been injected with a hydroquinone compound (unlawful in the United States) to lighten his skin and has tattooed eyebrows and eyeliner. Widespread rumors have it that repeated surgeries have exacted such a toll that he now sports a prosthetic nose.

Oddly, the world's second-most-famous plastic surgery patient is also both a singer and a Jackson. Cindy Jackson, no relation to the King of Pop, grew up in a small, somewhat isolated Ohio farming community, the daughter of a farmer-turned-inventor. By her account, it was a confined and confining existence that fueled her desire to escape. When she was six, she got a Barbie doll. "In my imagination I dreamed of a happy and glamorous life for my doll. Through Barbie, I could glimpse an alternative destiny," wrote Jackson in her autobiography, *Living Doll*.[23]

Drawn to the Beatles and the so-called music and fashion "British Invasion" of the early sixties, Jackson yearned for London, where everything she wanted to be part of was happening. In her teens, she took up art and photography, but as her awareness of the visual grew, Jackson realized that she could not compete with prettier prom queens and cheerleaders who attracted football players and other campus heroes. After high school she attended art college, while toiling eighteen months in a factory and working a second job in a gas station to save money. In April 1977, Cindy Jackson left for England with two suitcases and $600.

After a few years in London's bohemian scene, Jackson found herself singing backup vocals for a punk band, then writing songs and fronting her own group; for almost a decade she was a fixture on the British rock circuit. In 1988, she came into an inheritance that enabled her to do something about her PA, which she still felt was lacking. She began having cosmetic surgeries, one after another. After nine procedures she looked remarkably like the Barbie doll that invited her childhood dreams. She has written two books, including a memoir about cosmetically improving her PA, and has appeared on a succession of television shows to talk about her surgical transformation, which, she writes, after twenty-eight operations, is nearly complete.

Another of America's most celebrated plastic-surgery subjects is

New York socialite Jocelyn Wildenstein, former wife of a billionaire art dealer. After several surgeries, Jocelyn's face bears a striking resemblance to that of a hairless feline; she is known as the Cat Lady.[24]

• • •

Many Americans clearly are addicted to plastic surgery. Thousands risk their lives and spend millions of dollars in pursuit of artificial perfection; they are sometimes called nip-and-tuck addicts. Many live with grotesque disfigurements yet can hardly wait for their next procedure.

Consider the case of a thirty-four-year-old porn actress who works under the name "Jen X." After multiple Botox injections, a chin implant, and breast augmentation, she began to fear that she was becoming addicted to plastic surgery. "I already have an addictive personality," she told freelance reporter Dan Kapelovitz for an article for *Hustler* magazine. "I'm already in twelve steps. I'm just shifting my addiction from alcohol and drugs to plastic surgery, [which] is way more expensive than alcohol."

> Many Americans clearly are addicted to plastic surgery. Thousands risk their lives and spend millions of dollars in pursuit of artificial perfection.

When Jen X decided that she needed rhinoplasty, she tried to raise the money by agreeing to a porn video group-sex scene, a gig that paid $1,700. The work was so punishing, however, that she wound up with a kidney infection and thousands of dollars in medical bills. She canceled her nose job but still pays monthly for special silicone injections for her lips, an illegal procedure so dangerous that physicians who perform it are considered outlaws. Yet, even knowing the risks, she is driven by the need to compete. "The more surgery everyone else gets, the more I have to get to keep up," she said.

"I do not know any girl who has ever enhanced herself only one time," says Rhiannon, a professional dominatrix who has all but quartered America in her quest for ever-bigger boobs. Rhiannon crams her breasts, which weigh about ten pounds each, into a size 48 triple-M bra. She began her bust-enhancement odyssey in 1991 and has had thirty surgeries on her right breast alone. "I went in for a boob job like some people go to get their teeth cleaned," she told the reporter for *Hustler*.[25] "There's something about my personality that big is never big enough. If I'm going to do it, I'm going all the way," she said, adding that she wants still-larger implants. "You can exercise until you're blue in the face, but your boobies aren't going to grow from that."

The kinky world of transsexuals is full of cosmetic surgery stars, but few have been more forthcoming about their bodywork than Amanda Lepore. Her medical metamorphosis attracted the attention of New York fashion photographer David LaChapelle, who made her an icon of the art world by putting her photo on the face of a watch. Beyond her conversion from male to female, followed by such relatively conventional procedures as liposuction, Botox, and cheek lifts and implants, Lepore had her bottom ribs filed down by a doctor in Mexico, an operation that no ethical American doctor will attempt. "What girl doesn't want a tinier waist?" she asks.

(The hoary assertion that such operations were common among wasp-waisted women of Victorian England is an urban legend; in the absence of sterile conditions and with only the most primitive anesthesia and surgical implements, such a procedure would have been suicidal.)

Not every plastic surgery addict is a performer. Case in point: fifty-something Terry Prone, novelist and public relations executive. Prone described her many trips to the surgeon in *Mirror, Mirror: Confessions of a Plastic Surgery Addict*. She has sampled almost everything in the aesthetic delicatessen: Botox injections, liposuction, tummy tuck, facelift, browlift, cheek implants, arm-lift surgery, laser resurfacing of her skin, LASIK eye surgery, and dental implants. Her eyebrows, eyelids, and lips are permanently tattooed. She had spider veins removed with lasers and even had her hammertoes flattened. "I'm not suggesting that plastic surgery addiction is as out-of-control as alcohol, cigarettes, or heroin," Prone explained. "I'm saying, there's a hell of a high involved. Not a chemical high. A continuous, low-level high."[26]

Of course, not everyone who suffers through the pain and expense of repetitive surgeries is looking for that low-level high. Some are just trying to return their appearance to some semblance of normal. Like Beverly Hills realtor Elaine Young, whose client list, over the years, has included Elvis Presley, Jayne Mansfield, Brad Pitt,

M. C. Hammer, and O. J. Simpson. In 1979, she saw what a silicone injection had done for the face of a close friend and decided that she wanted some. She went to her friend's doctor the next day. "He said, 'I'll make you beautiful,' and that's all I had to hear," said Young. "I didn't check him out. I didn't know anything about him, and I got the injections."[27]

At first, Young was very pleased. But within a year the silicone had migrated and was interfering with facial nerves. Her left cheek expanded until she found it impossible to close her eye. Then she learned that her cheek was gangrenous; if the silicone wasn't removed, the infection would kill her. The removal operation left the side of her face paralyzed for two years. Young blames the injection and subsequent surgery for ruining half of her six marriages and drastically curtailing her career. "I really looked like a monster for years. I would show a house with fifty stitches in my face," she said. Young goes for corrective surgery every six months to remove bits of the silicone.

The doctor who injected Young's face eventually committed suicide. "He hurt a lot of people," said Young, "and unfortunately, yours truly sent a lot of people to him, because he made me look really pretty in the beginning. It's typical insecurity that leads women to [cosmetic surgery]. I don't care what they say; most of the women who do it are either aging, and they want to look younger, or they're very insecure."

• • •

Many, if not all, people addicted to plastic surgery suffer body dysmorphobia or body dysmorphic disorder (BDD). They often come to dermatologists and cosmetic surgeons in search of a way to deal with what turns out to be an imaginary or insignificant defect in their appearance, typically a preoccupation with the skin, hair, or nose. Often they spend an inordinate amount of time and energy picking at their skin or checking themselves in a mirror. Others wear a hat or heavy makeup to camouflage an imagined facial defect. There may be as many as 3 million Americans with this disorder, and among them are tens of thousands of people with the resources to pay for repetitive cosmetic surgeries.[28]

Because BDD is an underrecognized disorder, many plastic surgeons fail to appreciate that some who seek one procedure after another may need a psychiatric referral instead. "There are very well balanced people who have numerous surgeries," opined Dr. Barry Weintraub, a spokesman for the American Society of Plastic Surgeons. "They'll do one, and some months or years go by, and they'll do another and then a third, and so on. Then there's another group of people, and these characters, no matter what you do, are not happy."[29]

Such nip-and-tuck addicts are frequently seen by Dr. Z. Paul Lorenc, a New York cosmetic surgeon whose practice has attracted such notables as Katharine Hepburn (after her encounter with skin cancer) and Fortune 100 CEOs. But mostly his patients are what he calls the Park Avenue Posse—the ultrarich who live in opulent homes near his Upper East Side offices. In his book, *A Little Work: Behind the Doors of a Park Avenue Plastic Surgeon,* Lorenc describes the realities of dealing with a society increasingly obsessed with physical perfection. He finds, for example, that patients may lie about their medical history. "People often hide that they smoke, which affects your face," explains Lorenc. "Others lie about medications they are taking. . . . One male patient was taking steroids but wouldn't tell me. He wanted a facelift and nothing would stop him. I've never seen a patient's face bleed so much in my life. Some people will even tell me that they haven't had plastic surgery before, when it's obvious they have."[30]

In such cases, says Lorenc, "The job of the plastic surgeon is to put on the brakes. Many of these people have body dysmorphic disorder. They're obsessed. I'll never forget one young man who came to me for a scar on his face. He insisted that he had this awful acne scar. I looked through my [magnifying glass] but found nothing there. The worst thing for me to do would be to operate. Because afterward he would have had a real scar."

The wide availability of plastic surgery has distorted what is considered attractive.

Lorenc suspects that the wide availability of plastic surgery has distorted what is considered attractive. "I'm totally against cookie-cutter procedures," he says. "But much of this is media-driven. For instance, the show on MTV, *I Want a Famous Face,* where someone tries to look like Britney Spears—that's insane."

• • •

In their never-ending quest to expand the makeover market-place, some cosmetic surgeons have ventured into previously un-mentionable territory. In 1994, a Toronto physician named Robert H. Stubbs became briefly famous after the news media reported that he had developed a new surgical technique to lengthen a penis, a procedure he said was based on techniques he learned from a physi-cian named Dr. Long. (*I kid you not.*) The publicity brought Stubbs inquiries from legions of men, from every corner of North America, looking for heavier equipment to drive. As more plastic surgeons and urologists learned Stubbs's technique, advertisements for this procedure—along with those for bogus cures—became almost com-monplace. Is there anyone, in this era of the World Wide Web, who has never deleted e-mail spam offering him a thicker, longer penis?

In reality, however, penis-lengthening surgery is no trivial un-dertaking. American Urological Association literature says proce-dures involving the cutting of the suspensory ligament of the penis—the usual lengthening method—has "not been shown to be safe or effective." The operation also requires extensive follow-up. According to Stubbs, the individual must commit to a series of exer-cises involving weights suspended from his organ. After all that, he cautions, results are rarely spectacular. Nevertheless, after treating many men, Stubbs was approached by a series of women who asked him to use his scalpel and surgical skills to enhance their genitalia as well. According to an MSNBC report, Stubbs now sees far more females seeking to enhance their genitals. His specialty: the "Toronto trim," a dual procedure that includes surgical reduction of the inner labia along with a slight "unhood-ing" of the clitoris to enable greater stimulation during sex.[31]

> Thousands of women are now starting to focus their PA perfection-obsession on elective surgeries that promise both a better sex life and more aesthetically pleasing private parts.

But Stubbs operates in Toronto, hardly a center of PA hedo-nism. North America's greatest PA mecca lies thousands of miles away, in Southern California, home of the latest trend in cosmetic surgery, "designer vaginas." Thousands of women who have been nipped, tucked, implanted, and suctioned on nearly every other part of their bodies are now starting to focus their PA perfection-obsession on elective surgeries that promise both a better sex life and more aesthetically pleasing private parts.

Laser vaginal rejuvenation (LVR) is a term coined by Dr. David Matlock, a Los Angeles OB/GYN and plastic surgeon who has performed the procedure since 1995. Since then, he and his surgical techniques have been extensively profiled in the national media. His procedures fall between traditional OB/GYN surgery and cosmetic approaches.[32]

LVR is based on "anterior and posterior repair," a well-established procedure designed to treat incontinence by repairing weakened vaginal walls. This condition is sometimes induced by childbirth and leads to loss of bladder control ("stress incontinence") when laughing, coughing, or sneezing. It's caused by weakened muscle tissues between the vagina and bladder (cystocele) or when the wall between the rectum and the vagina is weakened (rectocele). Anterior (bladder) and posterior (rectum) repair has been used to alleviate this syndrome for decades. Traditionally, such surgical repairs may—or may not—yield a vagina that feels "tighter."

Matlock modified this surgery to focus on tightening the vagina, swapping his traditional scalpel for a laser, which he said reduces blood loss and promotes faster healing. Then he repackaged and marketed the surgery as a cure for mothers who no longer enjoy sex.

Although there is scientific agreement that the clitoris is the woman's primary source of pleasure, doctors who perform LVR often claim that it will improve sex for both man and woman. Matlock hands out literature that states that "as a sexual biological organism, women are superior to men," and claims LVR results in increased friction that increases a woman's sexual pleasure.

One of many American physicians who learned Matlock's technique is Dr. Joe Berenholz, who after twenty years as an OB/GYN opened a small cosmetic surgery clinic grandly styled "The Laser

Vaginal Institute of Michigan" in Southfield, an upscale Detroit suburb. He's doing land-office business.

Berenholz made the transition from conventional medicine, he said, in part because so many of his patients complained about diminished sexual enjoyment after childbirth. He was trained "to reassure a woman, to let her know this [condition] is normal, and to simply go home and live with it."

But that was before many women would pay thousands of dollars to have their genitals sculpted. Berenholz now divides his time between area hospitals, his private OB/GYN practice, and his clinic, where two or three days a week he performs two or three surgeries for fees ranging from $6,500 to $8,500. He also offers a menu of "Designer Laser Vaginoplasty (DLV)" procedures. They include labioplasty (surgery on the labia), hymenoplasty (surgically repairing or replacing the hymen, to give the illusion of virginity), augmentation labioplasty (fat is removed from another part of the patient and transferred to the labia majora for an "aesthetically enhanced and youthful" look), and vulvar lipoplasty (removing unwanted fat from the mons pubis or labia majora, which can "alleviate unsightly fatty bulges of this area and produce an aesthetically pleasing contour"). As with any surgery, Berenholz confirmed that the major risks are infection and bleeding. Prices range from $3,800 to $6,000 per procedure.

According to Dr. V. Leroy Young, chair of the American Society of Plastic Surgeons (ASPS) Committee for Emerging Trends, such procedures are becoming very popular. He has noted that plastic surgeons have performed surgery on the labia for many years, but most use a scalpel. The laser, in his opinion, is "a gimmick." He also thinks that patients seeking LVR will be better off to let an OB/GYN perform this type of surgery.

"Labial reduction is reasonably common among plastic surgeries," Young told one newspaper, adding that current interest seems to be fueled by America's widening acceptance of pornography, and by the lack of understanding of what is normal versus what represents a perceived ideal. "The thing that surprises me," he said, "is how little understanding there is of what normal is."[33]

"There's remarkably amazing patient interest in this," Young told Mireya Navarro, a reporter for the *New York Times*, adding that ASPS, the largest organization of plastic surgeons, does not keep statistics to track doctors whose specialty is "gynecologic cosmetic care" or "vaginal rejuvenation."[34]

Young believes that unless a woman has rectum or bladder prolapse, procedures like LVR are "meddlesome surgery" that pose "the risk that you can end up with loss of sensation or a painful scar." If a patient has a genuine medical problem, "then, sure, there's nothing wrong with the procedures, but they ought to be performed for a legitimate reason."[35]

Outside the bubble of cosmetic surgery practitioners, however, the whole idea of designer genitalia has provoked enormous controversy. Even while many doctors performing these surgeries claim that they are empowering women, others assert that their patients are actually submitting to the sexist notion that desirable women must have a youthfully tight vagina that conforms to a standard look found mostly in porn pictures. And indeed, Dr. Berenholz's website at one point stated that many prospective labioplasty patients arrive with a copy of *Playboy* magazine to show him a centerfold model whose equipment illustrates what they hope their own genitalia will look like.

"Like there's a right way for a woman's private parts to look?" bristles Ophira Edut, editor of *Body Outlaws,* an anthology about women's body image. "I believe the majority of men don't expect women to go out and surgically alter their bodies to look like a *Playboy* centerfold. If a labioplasty is what you really think it will take to make you happy, it might be time to reexamine your idea of happiness."[36]

Berenholz, like many who sculpt designer vaginas, maintains that he is among the majority of physicians who doesn't accept patients for this surgery unless they have a medically necessary reason.

But hold on. Professor Susan Hendrix, an OB/GYN at Wayne State University and director of the Women's Health Initiative, doesn't believe that. She said that pronounced labia hypertrophy is rare; in her sixteen years as an OB/GYN, she has done only "two or three" labioplasties. "Labioplasty is only done in very unusual or rare cases," she explained, adding that complications may include chronic pain and even inability to have sex. She finds the whole notion of undergoing labioplasty for aesthetic reasons "somewhat repulsive" because it implies that women "should worry about how their vagina looks." She added that patients "rely on their doctors. To go out and establish something just for money? That's disgusting that a physician would do that."[37]

Before there were easily available surgical alternatives, women complaining of loss of vaginal sensation during sex were routinely advised to do a simple muscle-training routine, sometimes involving a phalliclike instrument, known as Kegel exercises. Berenholz counters that the Kegel regimen doesn't always work. "The people we see have done millions of Kegel exercises. There is no exercise that can help women recover from torn muscle and damage."

That's true, but Dr. Laura Berman, who runs a Chicago clinic that treats female sexual matters, believes that many women who fail to get help from Kegels aren't doing the exercise correctly, although progress can be monitored by a device available without prescription. According to Berman, Kegels don't strengthen another key area, the transverse abdominal muscles. Just building these muscles isn't enough. "It's learning how to use them during sex," Berman told reporter Sarah Klein of the Detroit *Metro Times*. Often "women have these surgeries because some jerk told them they were too loose, when in fact *he* may have been too small." Berman also said that when a woman learns to strengthen and control her pelvic floor muscles, "she can squeeze around any size she wanted to, even the size of a pinkie."

Then there are women with the opposite problem. "I see a lot of women who have vestibulodynia [pain caused by a vagina that is too tight]," explained Dr. Hope Haefner, director of the University of Michigan's Center for Vulvar Diseases, also speaking with the *Metro Times*. She is skeptical of the value of designer vagina surgery.

> Often "women have these surgeries because some jerk told them they were too loose, when in fact *he* may have been too small."

"I'd really like to see the studies that show this [surgery] really makes a difference in the long-term outcome of relationships," she said. "I'd like to see studies that prove this is beneficial."[38]

Aside from aggressive marketing by cosmetic surgeons (a

Google search for "laser vaginal rejuvenation" turns up over 55,000 hits, the vast majority of them sites offering surgery), the other factor driving the increase in designer vagina surgery is media-fueled fashion influences. It's everything from flimsier swimsuits to bikini waxing, to the ever-growing exposure to nudity in magazines, movies, cable television, and the Web, and the legitimization of pornography.[39]

Catering to this growing desire for physical attractiveness has become an enormous industry. And an enormously profitable one.

CHAPTER 11

The Big Business of Beauty

Give me your tired, your rich, your aging masses
yearning to be beautiful

Boosting or amplifying an individual's physical attractiveness can be enormously profitable, especially for those who have both the ability to devise new products or services and the entrepreneurial chops to market them to a PA-hungry public.

There's no better example than Dr. David Matlock, whose surgery speciality discussed in the prior chapter has propelled him to fame and prosperity through the Laser Vaginal Rejuvenation Institute (LVRI). When Dr. Matlock realized how popular this surgical procedure had become, how many doctors were performing similar operations and how it seemed to be making most of them rich, he decided that he could—nay, should!—profit not only from his own precision applications of the surgical laser, but from anyone using his techniques. Matlock (did I mention that he also has an MBA?) trademarked the terms "LVRI" and "vaginal rejuvenation" and patented some of his procedures.

Then he started a so-called "associate operation"—not, he emphasizes, a franchise. "The doctors are associates of LVRI," he explained. "We taught and trained them in all techniques, and offered them a business model. We also offer support to these associates."[1]

That's nothing like what Burger King does for its franchisees, right?

Matlock's physician-associates enroll in his four-day course to learn surgical techniques to a tune approaching $10,000 and then pay $2,500 monthly fees for two years, totaling about $70,000 per person. By early 2005 he had already enrolled over forty associates in the United States, Canada, Sweden, France, Indonesia, and Australia, adding about three million dollars to his coffers. Always pushing forward, the portion of his website targeted to gain more potential associates (www.drmatlock.com/physicians.asp, accessed August 14, 2007) to supplement his already sizeable surgical earnings, headlines: "No one in the world knows the LVRI business like I do. In 2006, my LVRI practice Gross Revenues were $3,000,000.00 on just 360 cases. This is a normal year for me. David Matlock, MD, MBA, FACOG." As for the many physicians using similar techniques and marketing them in terms that resemble Matlock's trademarked LVRI and "vaginal rejuvenation," as the doctor identifies such practitioners, he dispatches cease-and-desist letters citing his patents and asserting trademark infringement.

> Matlock's physician-associates enroll in his four-day course to learn surgical techniques to a tune approaching $10,000 and then pay $2,500 monthly fees for two years, totaling about $70,000 per person.

Some doctors have expressed shock (or awe) about Matlock's methods, but he stays on message with a rigor that would draw approving nods from any politician or public relations executive. Matlock knows why doctors want to be in the designer vagina business: It's much more lucrative than standard OB/GYN or even conventional cosmetic surgery. In America, if you patent a unique technique for, say, cooking a fowl from the inside out, and get legal trademark protection for "Inverse Cooking," but subsequently learn that others are using your methods and calling them by similar names, you may either use the legal system to bar others from infringing on your patents and trademarks or forfeit further financial interest in your invention. If you don't vigorously protect your intellectual property, you will lose it. So when Matlock tells other doctors that if they want to use his designer vagina techniques they must pay him a license fee, he is merely defending his intellectual property.

And, of course, as Matlock reminds all who care to listen, his mission—and that of his clinic and associates—is not to line anyone's pockets but "to empower women with knowledge, choice, and alternatives."[2]

I do not cite Dr. Matlock to suggest that anything he did might possibly be unlawful. As far as I can tell, he has neither violated any ethical canon nor failed a patient in any way. I choose Matlock only because, in his own way, he is exemplar of a contemporary evolutionary lobe of the colorful New World creature *entrepreneurs americanus,* as much to be admired and maybe emulated as his philosophical forebears Eli Whitney, Thomas Edison, and Bill Gates.

And, of course, as Matlock reminds all who care to listen, his mission is not to line anyone's pockets but "to empower women with knowledge, choice, and alternatives."

Until the middle of the last century, cosmetic surgery was mostly focused on helping the tragically deformed. During World War II, thousands of Japanese were horribly burned by the firebombing of Tokyo and then by atomic bombs dropped on Hiroshima and Nagasaki. A handful of Japanese surgeons and urologists turned their attentions to repairing and reconstructing their faces, but there were too many victims and not enough trained surgeons. Among the most tragic of these victims was a group of grotesquely disfigured adolescent girls dubbed the Hiroshima Maidens; their faces were distorted by thick scar tissue and their hands were bent into near-useless claws. In 1955, twenty-five of these young women were brought to the United States, where they endured a succession of cosmetic operations that helped restore their appearance to a semblance of normalcy.

There were many other disfigured victims of the war, including thousands of American soldiers, and many of them also required plastic surgeons. When the supply of war-related cases began to thin, skills and techniques developed by Japanese and American surgeons were then redirected from therapeutic treatment to enhancing and redefining the nature of beauty.

During the U.S. occupation of Japan, for example, doctors injected young women's breasts with industrial-strength transformer coolant in a primitive and often hazardous attempt to meet the size expectations of American GIs. By the 1960s, topless showgirls in Las Vegas were having liquid silicone pumped into their breasts. By the seventies and eighties, silicone was packaged in gel form and promoted as a cure, as the American Society of Plastic Surgeons so delicately put it, for small breasts, which were defined as "deformities" and "a disease."[3]

Today, more physicians than ever are cashing in on the steadily increasing demand for cosmetic surgery. One of the greatest appeals of this field is that in this era of managed medical care, neither insurance companies nor government health agencies (such as Medicare) will underwrite elective procedures. So any doctor offering pay-as-you-go aesthetic surgery need not bargain with a powerful financial entity over his fee. Some patients bear the additional expense—doctors often charge for the consultation when a patient refuses the procedure—and the embarrassment of shopping for the best price, but aside from that, the plastic surgery candidate's only choice is take it or leave it. And, because they're dealing with individuals who either muster the cash or can whip out a credit card, doctors offering elective surgery don't have to wait months for a behemoth insurer to grudgingly cut them a check. For a piece of the action (a commission from the lender), some clinics even help patients arrange financing.[4]

Moreover, in nearly every U.S. state and Canadian province, any licensed physician can legally perform any medical procedure, including surgeries, whether board certified or not. Whether they have any special training or not. Whether they are surgeons or not.[5]

"When you graduate medical school, you have the ability to practice medicine and surgery," says Dr. Alan Gold, a spokesperson for the American Society for Aesthetic Plastic Surgery (ASAPS), adding that even if he was, say, a specialist in internal medicine or a psychiatrist, in most states, "I'm able to do liposuction, face-lifts, deliver babies, do neural surgery—there's no restriction on my license." So, from coast to coast, more American obstetricians are segueing into liposuction; more ophthalmologists are opting for face-lifts; and more than a few dermatologists are taking on tummy tucks or cheek implants.[6]

And the shift is not limited to physicians: "Now there are dentists who are seeking the ability, in certain states, to do rhinoplasty and face-lift surgery," said Gold. "It's rather scary," he added.[7] In fact, Colorado dentists sought permission in 2003 from the state legislature to perform face-lifts, and almost succeeded. Doubtless they will try again.[8] And, although California Governor Arnold Schwarzenegger first vetoed that state's Senate Bill 1336, which would have authorized oral surgeons to perform elective cosmetic surgeries, he later signed, on October 4, 2006, California Senate Bill 438, which now allows dental surgeons to perform elective cosmetic surgeries.[9]

How do such doctors find new patients? These days, mostly by buying time on TV, often with slick, customized ad campaigns. Among the first uses of modern media marketing techniques to push elective surgery was a richly filmed 1990 video for Profiles & Contours, a budding two-doctor nip-and-tuck practice in New York City. The commercial plays off the hoary advertising tradition of promising consumers a chance to make themselves more sexually attractive. "My husband's in love with a younger woman," sighs a woman in one spot. "Me." Set to a tasteful, new age piano score, the commercial, at first glance, might be confused with an ad to promote Chanel's latest fragrance or a new Procter & Gamble shampoo.

More than fifteen years later, Profiles & Contours, the brainchild of Dr. Mark Erlich, a New Yorker with movie-star looks and P. T. Barnum's marketing instincts, boasts clinics all over New York and Connecticut and offers an enormous range of procedures. It's safe to say that Erlich hasn't time to do most of them personally. It's also safe to say that he's a very wealthy fellow. He owes much of his success to that original top-to-bottom marketing plan devised by professional admen who licensed the same ad to plastic surgeons in six other East Coast markets. It cost each practice a paltry $3,800 per month to use the campaign, plus the cost of buying local TV time. "More and more, consumers are choosing the better marketer—and not the better surgeon," claims a brochure targeting surgeons from Schell/Mullaney, the New York ad agency behind the original TV spot.[10]

> "More and more, consumers are choosing the better marketer—and not the better surgeon."

By 1990, plastic surgeons were spending only about $30 million on ads, plus buying media time to air them.[11] Today, that's not even a drop in the bucket. According to London's respected *Economist* magazine, in 2003 alone the worldwide beauty business spent between $32 billion and $40 billion on advertising—and took in upwards of $160 billion in sales. Nowhere did both advertising expense and sales income account for more bucks than in North America.[12]

For example, although advertising expenditures are not broken down for the cosmetic surgery industry, a March 13, 2007, TNS Media Intelligence (www.tns-mi.com) press release reporting that total advertising expenditures in the United States in 2006 were $149.6 billion was followed by a June 12, 2007, press release projecting $152.3 billion in 2007; and you can bet every corner of the beauty business will be continuing at least its proportionate share. In fact, a July 10, 2007, press release from the Publishers Information Bureau of the Magazine Publishers of America association (www .magazine.org) reported that expenditures for advertising in magazines had already risen for the first half of 2007 to nearly $12 billion ($11,838,362,224.00 to be precise). And, the category of "toiletries and cosmetics" was the number one magazine advertising category for the second quarter of 2007, in which "a boost for cosmetics and beauty aids and personal hygiene and health products accounted for the bulk" of the growth in advertising spending.

All this advertising worked: Cosmetic surgery is now a $20 billion business in America.[13] In 2007, The American Society for Aesthetic Plastic Surgery (ASAPS) lists about 2,400 member surgeons while the larger and older fraternity founded in 1931, the

American Society of Plastic Surgeons (ASPS) (with some overlap in memberships) lists more than 6,000 members. Between 1997 and 2003, the number of surgical cosmetic procedures performed by ASAPS members increased by more than 220 percent, and then by another 44 percent between 2003 and 2004. By 2006, ASAPS members revealed 11.5 million surgical and nonsurgical cosmetic procedures in the United States alone, a whopping 446 percent increase since 1997. And, of course, those figures do not account for procedures performed by doctors who are not board certified in aesthetic surgery and are not therefore ASAPS members. That's right: The work of all those urologists, internists, OB/GYNs, ophthalmologists, and others who have added cosmetic surgery to their repertoires isn't tabulated.[14]

Even so, the ASAPS numbers are amazing. Driven in part by the demand from aging and affluent baby boomers, residents of the United States paid for more than 11 million cosmetic procedures in 2006. To add a little perspective, in a similar year about one-sixth of that number, slightly over 1.8 million Americans, were awarded bachelor's, master's, and doctoral degrees, according to the U.S. Department of Education. And while nearly 85 percent as many Americans underwent liposuction (403,684) as earned a master's degree (481,118), a whopping 660 percent more received injections of Botox (3,181,592) than master's degrees. In fact, tally up the budgets of every sort of education in America and it is plain that we spend more each year on enhancing our PA than we do on education.

In other words, cosmetic surgery is big business. This kind of medicine is no longer about building a relationship of trust between a physician and a patient and learning what's best for the patient. In fact, a cosmetic surgery center today seems more like a restaurant that needs to turn tables over several times each meal to maximize profit. It's about moving a preferably endless line of patients through the company's operating suites as quickly as possible and marketing to those patients additional complementary services, such as skin care and nutrition counseling, as part of a total patient experience. It's about making more and more money.

The boom in cosmetic surgeries has also fueled the rise of

companies that manufacture specialized equipment used in aesthetic procedures. For example, about 1997, doctors learned how to apply intense light to the skin for such cosmetic purposes as removing unwanted hair, wrinkles, tattoos, sunspots, disfiguring acne, and port-wine stains. The first company to get Food and Drug Administration (FDA) clearance on a laser system for hair removal was Palomar Medical Technologies of Burlington, Massachusetts. By 2005, as smaller, cheaper, and more portable devices were developed and more and more doctors became trained to use them, consumers were spending about $8 billion a year on such care. The worldwide market for equipment for these procedures is now sized at some $600 million a year, an annual growth rate of more than 20 percent.[15]

• • •

Few American women today would consider leaving home without carrying makeup in their purses. In my childhood, somewhat after the middle of the last century, when my mother used cosmetics, she limited herself to lipstick, a touch of face powder, and perhaps hairspray. There were, of course, other products available, including skin creams, rouge, mascara, eye shadow, and hair coloring. In that era, however, the only women who regularly painted their faces and dyed their hair were those who performed on a theater stage, for the TV or movie screen, or in a bordello.

Go back a little further, to the early twentieth century, and the beauty industry was a struggling collection of small-time entrepreneurs. One was a Parisian named Eugene Schueller, who in 1909 founded the French Harmless Hair Dye Company. Another was Hamburg pharmacist Paul Beiersdorf. In 1911, he developed the first cream that could chemically bind oil and water. The former company is now known as L'Oréal and is the world's leader in the industry. Beiersdorf's firm became Nivea, which today markets products in 150 nations and is the world's best-known personal-care brand. Both companies compete with Shiseido, a company founded in the same era when Arinobu Fukuhara formulated a skin lotion that was Japan's first cosmetic based on a scientific formula.

In the United States, the beauty industry's rise to prominence grew out of the rivalry between two American women. Elizabeth Arden opened the first modern beauty salon in 1910; a few years later Helena Rubinstein, a Polish immigrant, followed suit. Both supposed that beauty and health were interlinked and combined facials with diet and exercise classes, a holistic approach to which the industry is just now returning. Arden pioneered beauty branding with iconic gold and pink packaging. Together with Max Factor, who initially built his business around the needs of Hollywood film studio makeup departments, Arden and Rubinstein built the foundations of modern marketing, enticing consumers with such innovative tactics as celebrity endorsements and magazine advertorials. In the 1930s, Revlon and then, a decade later, Estée Lauder entered the industry and successfully competed with the pioneers.

> In the United States, the beauty industry's rise to prominence grew out of the rivalry between two American women.

These companies, along with L'Oréal, Nivea, and Shiseido, remain active in the marketplace and together field thousands of beauty products under hundreds of brands, producing billions of dollars in sales. The August 2007 "Personal Products: Global Industry Guide" sold by Datamonitor (www.marketresearch.com) reported the global market for personal care products—skin care, hair care, makeup, oral hygiene, personal hygiene, and over-the-counter health care—grew to $251.1 billion in 2006. It forecasts a 23.1 percent increase to a market value over the next five years of $309 billion in 2011.

Just as the media business has become a competition between a handful of gigantic multinationals, so too has the beauty industry consolidated. Enormous and diversified companies such as Unilever and Procter & Gamble, seeing growth opportunities beyond their traditional household products divisions, have acquired product lines of beauty brands. Traditional beauty industry giants have also snapped up innovative younger brands. A few years ago, for example, Japan's Kao Corporation bought John Frieda as a route into one of the market's fastest-growing segments, hair coloring. LVMH, the multinational behemoth whose diverse brands include Moët Champagne, Hennessy spirits, Christian Dior fragrances,

Donna Karan, Givenchy, and Louis Vuitton, to name only a few, bought Hard Candy and Urban Decay, two funky young makeup brands. Meanwhile, Estée Lauder acquired Stila, MAC, and Bobbi Brown, up-and-coming names at that time in the hotly competitive makeup marketplace. Even though, in the dynamic corporate take-over and buyout worlds, Estée Lauder sold Stila in 2006 while LVMH sold Hard Candy and Urban Decay in 2005, just six multi-nationals currently continue to account for 80 percent of American makeup sales, while eight brands control more than two-thirds of the skin-care market.[16]

So, investing in the beauty business is big business. Industry insiders value the global cosmetics and grooming market at more than $230 billion. Marketing research experts project $13 billion for the beauty market in China alone by 2009, and, already, L'Oréal conducts 35,000 consumer interviews there annually, give or take a few. These efforts pay, big-time. Industry leader L'Oréal, still Paris based and now the world's largest cosmetics merchant, generated annual sales of $15.8 billion in 2006 as it met the ever-demanding market to enhance PA. The company, with operations in more than 100 countries, supports more than 60,000 employees of whom more than 2,000 are chemists. Continuing the pace, L'Oréal regis-tered second-quarter sales in 2007 at $5.86 billion, which, if sus-tained as suspected for the year's four quarters, will at minimum exceed $23 billion in 2007 revenue.[17]

With so much at stake, the beauty industry invests heavily in marketing, including advertising and cross-promotions. And com-panies are not above a little hocus-pocus now and then. While some scientific breakthroughs do happen, the beauty industry's invest-ment in research and development averages only a fifth, or less, of that for pharmaceuticals. They have introduced "cosmeceuticals," new products that blur the line between cosmetics and over-the-counter drugs. L'Oréal's advertisements often stress how many product patents it has filed, and indeed, some new ideas, including face cloths impregnated with cleansers that combine surfactant and paper technology, have come to market.

Other products are more hype than fact, pseudoscience in the service of sales. Shiseido's ads for "Body Creator" skin gel claim that its pepper and grapefruit oil are fat-burners that can melt away over two pounds of body fat in a month without the need to diet or exercise. When it was introduced in 2002, Japanese customers bought a bottle every 3.75 seconds. Not to be outdone, advertising for Avon's Cellu-Sculpt cream claims to take an inch off thighs in four weeks. Other brands play the game different ways: P&G plugged the science underlying development of Olay Regenerist and built Pantene into the world's biggest hair-care brand on the basis of a vitamin B ingredient, despite the fact that vitamins cannot be absorbed through the skin or hair.[18]

But we live in a media age, where every sort of dream is manufactured and sold as reality. All too often, Americans do not stop to realize that there is a vast gulf between what is presented on a flickering screen and the real world. Yet everything, every single item that appears in a picture, every word spoken, every sound heard, is a creation of the production and has some specific purpose in being put before the audience. To forget this is to forget that a movie or TV show is merely entertainment. And while one may sometimes learn valid life lessons from art, it is art, it is artifice, it is not reality—it is a construct from beginning to end.

> All too often, Americans do not stop to realize that there is a vast gulf between what is presented on a flickering screen and the real world.

Still, how many who watched the 1969 film *True Grit* identified with Rooster Cogburn, the character played by the actor John Wayne? In this film Wayne is an aging, overweight hero who, despite deteriorating abilities, redeems himself and overcomes the physical limitations of age. Near the end of the movie, actress Kim Darby, as the lissome Mattie Ross, tells Wayne that he is too old, too rotund, to jump a horse over a fence. "Well, come and see a fat old man sometime," drawls Wayne before galloping his mount and leaping over the corral gate.

Wayne was probably Hollywood's biggest superstar ever. Paradoxically, he earned little critical respect for his acting ability. Yet this single act of cinematic bravado in *True Grit* probably cinched his only Best Actor Oscar, capstone to a lengthy and lucrative career lacking only in award nominations. Surely most in the film industry knew that Wayne distrusted horses and was anything but physically brave; he schemed mightily to avoid military service in World War II and relied on stunt doubles whenever anything risky arose in a script. In *True Grit,* as Wayne wheeled his horse toward the gate, director Henry Hathaway yelled, "Cut!" Wayne dismounted—corset, toupee, and all—and an identically costumed stuntman took his place in the saddle. The cameras rolled and the stuntman jumped the wall. All it took was a bit of cutting-room flimflam for audiences to see The Duke sail over the fence toward his Oscar. There was nothing unusual here; that's how things happen in reel life that can't happen in real life.[19]

The members of the Academy of Motion Picture Arts and Sciences, most of them quite mature and experienced in the ways of Hollywood, surely knew how movies were made. But those who voted for Wayne's Oscar saw what they chose to see and believed, if only for a time, that the movie, not the man, was the myth.

· · ·

The astonishing growth of the beauty industry has been fueled by synergy between the enormous reach and power of the media and entertainment industries combined with the PA phenomenon with its own strengths and dimensions. Each feeds the other: Advertising in magazines and on television depicts beautiful people living glamorous lifestyles, all in an effort to sell consumers goods and services of every sort. Some of the revenues thus generated underwrite the entertainment industry by paying for television shows and movies. Other ad money provides profit margins for publications. In turn, all of this together promulgates the power and persuasiveness of PA.

Meanwhile, entertainment promotes the careers and peddles the products—music CDs, movie tickets, DVDs, television programs, clothing lines, merchandise of every ilk—of beautiful, glamorous celebrities. These worthies, in turn, appear in advertising to hawk consumer products.

In our celebrity-worshipping culture, a youthful appearance is held up as the ideal. Media messages promote the idea that science and technology will allow us to retain our youth, our beauty. Science and technology did not create our fascination with beauty and youth, but they have helped to exaggerate our fear of growing old and of accepting that life is irreversible: Eventually, everyone's body runs down.

And even as advances in PA technologies enhance our struggle to retain a youthful appearance with beauty aids, cosmetic surgery, and hormone replacement, it does so not for our benefit but to promote the beauty industries. To keep the money taps open, the purveyors of youth and beauty products join the media and entertainment industries in seeking to control how we view and measure ourselves, to influence what is deemed important by society, to define what determines physical attractiveness, and to dictate what we must do to achieve an ideal self.

So we are awash in an image tsunami, swimming on a tide of beautiful illusions. It becomes harder and harder to distinguish the reel from the real, to remember that in the end the purpose of all this beauty and glamour, always, is to help somebody make money. Always.

We are genetically programmed to feel and respond to the lures of the physically attractive. We want to look more beautiful. We want to be around better-looking people, watch beautiful people on glowing screens, read about the lives of beautiful people. And yet, even as more and more people spend more and more money on beauty products, as more and more people risk their lives and health to undergo more and more aesthetic surgeries, or struggle to overcome distorted impressions of their own PA inadequacies, it is plain that few people actually feel better about their own PA. In fact, as a worldwide study commissioned by Unilever's Dove brands (to help sell its own beauty products!) shows, few women feel beautiful at all.[20]

And yet. Some people wonder why cosmetic surgery is marketed like makeup and bought as casually as a Wonderbra. Yet we live in a time when in some upscale communities, parents think that breast implants are a good thing to give their daughters as high school graduation presents. Eighty-eight-year-old women choose to undergo breast reduction surgery—and find doctors willing to perform it. Nowadays, too, the "reveal party" has replaced the Tupperware gathering; instead of looking over kitchen products, housewives shriek with joy and shed tears over the result of a friend's "extreme makeover," a personal body renovation project.[21]

And yet. When anthropologists studied northwest Kenya's reclusive Ariaal tribe, an isolated, nomadic community of some 10,000 souls without access to television or magazines, they sought to determine if their body-image stereotypes had been influenced by media from the outside world. One researcher showed the nomads pictures of various men representing a variety of body types. "The girls like the ones like this," he said, pointing to a slender man built much like himself.

Another researcher showed a group of several Ariaal men a copy of *Men's Health* magazine with pictures of impossibly well-sculpted bodybuilders. The nomads admired the chiseled forms. "That one, I like," said an elder, pointing at a photo of a curvy woman who clearly worked out regularly.

Another old-timer gazed at the bulging pectoral muscles of a male bodybuilder and scratched his head. "Was it a man," he wondered aloud, "or a very, very strong woman?"[22]

We live in a time of self-improvement and makeovers. But when we look in the mirror, the image gazing back at us seems so strange and divorced from reality, and so distorted.

Do we need a makeover?

Or is it our culture that needs the extreme makeover?

EPILOGUE

Rising Above the Effects of Lookism

*If you can't do everything, then at least don't
do nothing*

Lookism flourishes. A person's looks have become more important than ever in everything from celebrity-driven media to popular topics in personal conversations.

Good looks make a difference today and most likely always will. This fact translates into rather endless pursuits of greater PA by individuals and encouraged by society. It doesn't matter whether we label it "lookism" when a person's PA impacts the way she is treated by others, or if we use the broader umbrella term "PA phenomenon." Varied adages apply: People do judge people (as well as books) by their covers. Appearances extend far beyond what meets the eye. Beauty may be skin deep, but its effects run much deeper.

What solution can disentangle disparities between people of different levels of PA?

PA is caused partly by nature and partly by nurture, and no simple and easy solution exists to change this reality. It results from a complicated synergy of drives by individuals and influences by our society. Popular culture today often admires extreme makeovers that alter the looks of an individual, but our culture itself could benefit from an extreme makeover of other sorts; otherwise the proverbial playing field of life will never be level for individuals of higher and lower PA.

Whatever our indignities and resolve, we can neither avoid lookism nor eliminate it from society. In life, we interact all the time with people who do—consciously or unconsciously—make judgments about us based on what we look like. Nevertheless, each of us can realistically challenge realities of lookism and rise above it.

For too long, people not affected negatively by discrimination—aligned with differences based on race, sex, PA, and so forth—believed life to be a reasonably level playing field. At best, their insensitivity was inadvertent.

Intentional or not, ignorance, denial, and "turning a blind eye" did not vanish discrimination due to racism and sexism and won't vanish discrimination due to lookism. And, specific to those individuals who possess higher PA, I urge you to keep in mind a pertinent thought from novelist Teena Booth: "If there is one thing worse than being an ugly duckling in a house of swans, it's having the swans pretend there's no difference."

• • •

Evolutionary theory seems to predict eventual disappearance of less than high PA, which would resolve lookism. Dynamics of natural selection en route to survival of the fittest explains this theoretical proposition. It begins with notions that people who possess higher PA also possess greater power to attract more opportunities to produce more offspring than their counterparts. Hypothetically, over zillions of years, fewer and fewer people of lesser PA would be born in this scenario until only people of greater PA would be producing offspring.

Of course, none of us will be around to observe the veracity of such speculative aeonian musings that transcend infinite generations to come. In the meantime, tangible actions currently underway demonstrate corrective steps for our lives today and for the lives of future generations.

Medical and psychological professions now formally acknowledge PA-related illnesses. Official medical diagnoses and treatments address obsessive beliefs and exaggerated focuses concerning a person's looks, such as body dysmorphic disorder (BDD), anorexia, and bulimia. In another development, University of Pennsylvania Health System has established the Center for Human Appearance. It is the first-ever interdisciplinary academic center dedicated to the study and treatment of disorders and quality-of-life issues interconnected with appearance.

At a mass media level and in demonstration of corporate social responsibility, the multinational company Unilever sponsors the Campaign for Real Beauty. That widely disseminated message aligned with Dove personal-care products emphasizes that beauty comes with many different looks, in different shapes, sizes, colors, and ages. A companion program, Dove Real Beauty Workshop for Girls, deals with the impact of looks in the lives of girls eight to twelve years old.

Specific not-for-profit organizations help challenge lookism as well as contend with it. These groups frequently focus on statistically measurable determinants of PA as referenced in their titles—for example, the National Association to Advance Fat Acceptance and the Little People of America.

Face to Face: The National Domestic Violence Project represents another constructive step. It aims to reverse the negative effects experienced by particular individuals due to societal discrimination from lookism. At no cost to recipients, it provides cosmetic surgery to correct PA damage caused by domestic physical abuse.

Parents can and should be conscientious about communications to their children, being careful not to promulgate long-established inequalities aligned with PA differences. This begins with careful presentation of classic children's stories such as *Cinderella, Hansel and Gretel*, and *Snow White*. These traditional classics equate beauty with good that merits reward accordingly, while equating bad, wicked, and evil with people who lack good looks.

Parents need to be aware that actions speak louder than words, and children will internalize value differences, even if a negative message wasn't intended to be communicated. Unhealthy pursuits of greater PA can be unintentionally demonstrated through unhealthy dieting and excessive exercise when the purpose is to achieve better looks rather than better health. Adults who diet and exercise primarily for better looks, and secondarily for better health, send powerful messages that promulgate lookism. The same applies for pursuits of cosmetic surgeries to enhance PA and dinnertime conversations that communicate greater appeal, popularity, and value concerning better-looking friends, neighbors, and media personalities.

Legal options exist. Individuals can work with elected government officials to generate pertinent laws and can file personal lawsuits. Although legal means to alleviate lookism pose difficulties, they do offer possibilities.

The difficulties center on the inability to easily define the physical attractiveness variable. Therefore, plaintiffs usually articulate surrogate measures such as weight, height, and a list of protected-class demographic variables. A 2003 lawsuit against upscale retailer Abercrombie & Fitch initially claimed employment discrimination based on physical attractiveness differences. The plaintiffs later changed their claim to discrimination based on protected-class demographics of race and ethnicity.

Proceedings from the lawsuit against Abercrombie & Fitch identified company employment decisions definitely favorable for persons with high PA and unfavorable for their counterparts. Although employment decisions that discriminate based on PA are not illegal currently, the line is thin between legal and illegal. The decisions become illegal if the PA factor can be proved to be a surrogate bias actually based on age, sex, ethnicity, or disability.

Arguments that the Americans with Disabilities Act should apply to people with less than good looks have not (yet) found favor in court. Existing lookism-related laws apply mostly to tangible aspects of PA and then only in specific municipalities. Santa Cruz, California, outlaws employment decisions based on height, weight, or physical characteristics; San Francisco and the state of Michigan do so for height and weight; and Washington, DC, does so for personal appearance. However, other than officially sanctioned protected classes that might be argued inseparable from appearance features, there are not yet substantive laws to protect discriminatory actions due to lookism.

In conclusion, regardless of what we try to do about it, a person's PA matters in this day and age. Evidence documents that higher and lower PA corresponds with benefits and detriments, respectively. To rise above this reality, people must first know themselves. Beyond that, people need to maintain their awareness of their judgments about others and be sensitive about their corresponding interactions.

And, now that you are knowledgeable about lookism, know that the next time you are drawn to one person over another, your reasons might not be as admirable or as rational or even as fair as you would like to think they are.

RISING ABOVE LOOKISM: CASES OF TWO INDIVIDUALS

Don't overlook yourself as you choose to resist the PA phenomenon and rise above lookism. Look first at your own views, attitudes, and behaviors concerning your own PA. It is an important early step as you move to alter your judgments about others—mates, children, coworkers, friends, politicians, strangers, elected officials, and others—and change your interactions accordingly.

Are you a wannabe Ken or Barbie? Are you overly focused on your looks? Are you pursuing unrealistic levels of PA? Are your concerns and pursuits of PA causing problems in your life, work, and relationships? Are you unhappy with your looks or yourself?

Consider the following two individuals, Jennifer and Douglas. PA phenomenon negatively affects both. It impacts their minds and lives. Although they focus on different physical features, express different thoughts, experience different emotional triggers, and exhibit different behaviors, both of them suffer unhappiness with their looks.

How these two people deal with their unhappiness about their PA produces ineffective results that prove increasingly counterproductive. Jennifer compensates with unaffordable purchases of expensive brands of clothes, hair care, and cosmetics. At the same time, Botox injections register high as a future priority for her, and she has slashed exercise opportunities from her day because others might see her body shape too closely. Douglas responds with much different compensatory behaviors concerning the disliked aspects of his PA. For example, he minimizes valuable work and nonwork interactions when the situations might require him to stand next to taller people. Attitudinally, his self-perceived lack of desired PA causes him to increasingly resent his lot in life.

Jennifer

Jennifer is a pleasant twenty-eight-year-old woman with a college degree, a solid job, and a loving husband. Objective measures confirm her height as average and weight as proportionate. People consider Jennifer to be a nice person who performs her work well, dresses nicely, and looks good. Her husband likes her appearance and occasionally compliments her accordingly.

Jennifer is certainly not clinically obsessive, but substantial difference exists between how the world views her and how she views herself. Picking apart her overall good looks, Jennifer feels neutral about many aspects of appearance that determine her PA, although she feels positive about two of her features: her hair and eyes. However, the dislike she feels about other aspects of her appearance produces an offsetting negative balance.

Although she comments sometimes about displeasing features of her appearance, she hides the extent of her true dislike. Numerous times a week the dislike surfaces in her mind, often triggered by one of several recurring situations. Whenever she steps on a scale, the number exceeds her elusive target weight. As she walks past reflective windows she regularly notices her shape to be different from her ideal. Certain clothing styles make her uncomfortable because they seem, to her, to amplify disliked parts of her body. Her thighs cause the greatest displeasure, and she thinks, "I would die from embarrassment if people saw me at the swimming pool or fitness center. I will never be beautiful with these thunder thighs of mine. I need a potent dose of liposuction."

Almost any time she meets a new person, be it a social or work setting, she attempts to cover or shield less desired parts of her appearance that seem to stand out. Most frequently, it is her mouth, due to the shade of her teeth, which she wants whiter. Advertising has registered firmly in her mind the negative impression a person's smile can make if the teeth are less than gleaming white. Comments by friends about others with unappealing teeth reinforce the message. Similarly, media reports and product advertising for antiwrinkle injections have an influence on Jennifer and her girlfriends, who talk about Botox and Restylane during lunchtime conversations. Potential benefits from these injections rush to Jennifer's thoughts whenever she gets up close to a mirror and sees the start of a visible forehead wrinkle or two.

How does Jennifer deal with her negative feelings concerning her PA? Not well. And it translates into not-good behaviors.

Unchecked, lookism pushes Jennifer into detrimental behaviors. Her attention and thoughts about her PA translate into unhealthy attitudes and actions. The tendency to emphasize negatives about her appearance while forcing out any positive thinking, such as the good she feels about her hair and eyes, pulls down her self-esteem and confidence. She increasingly speculates that people scrutinize her looks with unfavorable conclusions. As a result, she has begun to avoid swimming pools because of the revealing nature of swimwear, and fitness centers because attendees often wear form-fitting clothes, and she stays clear of bathroom scales altogether.

As a solution to alleviate unhappiness with her PA, Jennifer has increased spending beyond her means in three areas: clothes, hair care, and cosmetics. Her latest clothing preferences are loose-fitting styles that seem to disguise parts of her appearance that she particularly dislikes. These purchases increasingly favor more expensive brands because they seem to better enhance her looks. Unreasonably large credit card balances reflect her growing preferences for popular brand-name products when dealing with possibilities to look better. In turn, looming money problems have become frequent points of contention in her marriage.

What does Jennifer need to do to best rise above the influence of lookism within herself?

The answer: She needs to realistically challenge reality. Whether through objective self-evaluation or with the assistance of another person able to be objective, Jennifer needs to reorient her thoughts and behaviors concerning PA. One helpful approach requires her to construct a list of specific statements that organize her thinking and guide her into positive thoughts and behaviors, such as the affirming "I need to . . ." statements listed here.

- "I need to keep in mind that my good job and happy marriage do not depend on looking better."

- "I need to realize that my current looks do not threaten either my job or marriage."

- "I need to admit that my problems with my excessive credit charges are caused by my actions to buy things in hopes of achieving unrealistic, as well as unnecessary, levels of PA."

- "I need to analyze carefully my financial situation before spending even more on my looks by getting Botox or other antiwrinkle injections, which are expensive, temporary, and can produce fake-looking effects."

- "I need to have good thoughts about myself. I need to remind myself every so often about the features I like about my looks, such as my hair and my eyes."

- "I need to reassure myself that my husband loves me and my current looks, and I need to remember that every so often people at work compliment me on my good looks."

- "I need to be more comfortable about my looks."

- "I need to prohibit my looks from dictating whether or not I attend social events."

- "I need to adjust my emotions so that I don't get upset when I see myself in a mirror or when I see my reflection in a store window."

- "I need to stop comparing my looks to those of the beautiful people I see."

- "I need to remind myself that experts in cosmetics apply the makeup and experts in photography and computer technologies almost always alter the photos of famous people in magazines and on TV."

- "I need to stop hating my thighs."

- "I need to be less critical about my weight and body shape."

- "I need to resist my habit of using storefront windows as mirrors."

- "I need to reduce the time that I spend to decide what to wear before going anywhere."

- "I need to get back to swimming because I enjoy it and it is a good exercise."

- "I need to eliminate my recently developed fear of embarrassment concerning what people will think about my weight and shape if they see me at the swimming pool in a swimsuit."

- "I need to improve my diet choices to emphasize foods for overall better health, rather than just thinking about dieting only to look better."

- "I need to get back into the habit of working out at a fitness center. And I need to exercise more for the primary purposes of good health, rather than for purposes of good looks alone."

Douglas

Douglas is forty-one years old and a successful midlevel executive who works as a senior financial analyst. Four years ago, his marriage of nearly ten years ended in divorce. Although he is shorter than the typical American man, his looks appear average and his weight is proportionate, although he has a slight "beer belly" that protrudes moderately.

Despite quite average PA, Doug finds much fault with his looks. His relatively short height of five feet six inches causes the greatest distress. On top of that, his wished-for crowning glory grows less glorious every day. Advancing male pattern baldness shows his substantially thinning hair and receding hairline. And the sight each morning in his bathroom mirror as he prepares for work inflicts another dose of psychological pain. Close-up, he regularly notes each hair lost since last tally.

Physical realities amplified by idealized wants and derogatory self-perceptions provide a recipe for much unhappiness. With more than a little hidden seriousness, he jokes that fate glanced away when it came to him inheriting good looks. He frequently lists specifics: horrible short height, awful thin and thinning hair, terrible elongated nose, and an embarrassing, nonathletic build. Complicating matters, Doug finds no joy in having passed forty. He has started to notice droopy eyelids and pays more attention to media reports about the popularity of cosmetic blepharoplasty surgery for middle-age executives and salesmen.

Anytime that anything displeasing about his appearance enters his consciousness, it quickly sends Doug into a grumpy mood for several days. To worsen his mood, he then spends entirely too much time in front of mirrors analyzing and reanalyzing his features. Accompanying frustration sparks a number of recurring thoughts: "I'm fighting a losing battle. I'm short, old, and balding. Every day things get worse for me: I lose more hair, my gut grows, and my height probably even shrinks."

Torturously connected to his looks, Doug has developed a restrained hostility toward women. He's convinced that he will never again find an attractive woman for a mate because, in his mind, he lacks the necessary stereotypical PA admired on television, in movies, in magazines, and throughout society overall.

Appearances can be deceiving. Despite being a very unhappy camper, Doug exhibits a positive personal veneer at work equal to his achieved professional success. Generally, he functions fine on the job when dealing with the tasks and demands of the position. The bugaboo emerges outside of work and somewhat during free time at work.

How does Doug deal with his negative feelings concerning his PA? Not well, and it translates into not-good behaviors.

Unchecked, lookism pushes Doug toward behaviors counter to success at work and beyond work. With height at the top of his mind, he tends to distance himself physically from taller people. Two specific office situations that he tends to avoid are impromptu water-cooler chats and conversations at business networking events, because in these settings people typically stand while talking. Also, if someone he's talking to seems to stare at his nose, Doug uses his hand to minimize sight of his nose, a sometimes-obvious mannerism that's also employed by people embarrassed by the appearance of their teeth.

To alleviate unhappiness with his PA, Doug endlessly seeks solutions to fix his self-perceived physical defects in pursuit of more handsome looks. Many would-be solutions cost too much or prove ineffective for Doug. Ensuing desperation motivates him to search the Internet too frequently and too long.

Although he has searched top to bottom and head to toe for solutions, he's thus far carried through with relatively few purchases. Things on the back burner for him, for the time being, include a powder spray to darken his balding scalp, a hairpiece in some undetectable form, and shoe inserts to gain an inch or two of height. In the meantime, he dyes his gray hair, spends substantially on ineffective hair-growth products, wears a cap in more situations than reasonable, and has begun to "conceal" his hair loss with a negligible comb-over style that has potential to become increasingly architectural.

What does Doug need to do, to rise above the influence of lookism within himself?

The answer: He needs to realistically challenge reality. Whether through objective self-evaluation or with the assistance of another person able to be objective, Douglas needs to reorient his thoughts and behaviors concerning PA. He can start by constructing a list of specific statements that organize his thinking and guide him into positive thoughts and behaviors. Doug must learn to repeat affirming "I need to . . ." statements. For example:

- "I need to remember that I have a good job and a successful career that I've achieved with my current looks."

- "I need to be honest with myself and remember that I am fortunate to be employed as I am, and that my looks do not threaten my job."

- "I need to stop avoiding conversations at social events in and out of work settings just because I am uncomfortable standing next to taller people."

- "I need to stop dwelling on my height."

- "I need to accept that I am shorter than average, and I need to remind myself about the many successful and popular men who stand with equal or less height."

- "I need to accept that I never was and never will be a muscleman. At the same time, I need to exercise to improve my fitness and, secondarily, to improve or at least maintain my body build."

- "I need to accept my age and the looks that go with it. At forty-one, I am in the prime of my life. I have a great job, excellent health, many friends, and overall I look quite good."

- "I need to start focusing efforts on exercise and diet routines for purposes of achieving better heath, rather than just thinking in terms of better looks."

- "I need to get real about my hair loss. I have more hair than many men my age, and I need to remind myself about the many successful and popular men with equal or less hair."

- "I need to accept the look of my hair. And I need to rule out buying a hairpiece of any sort since high-quality ones cost too much and they still can look fake."

- "I need to be aware of the best hairstyle for my type of hair, which tends to be shorter rather than longer and certainly is not a comb-over style."

- "I need to discontinue considering gimmicks like unproven hair-growth products and powder spray dye to make my underlying scalp less noticeable."

- "I need to avoid analyzing and reanalyzing the length of my nose."

- "I need to reassure myself periodically that not all women are attracted to all men. And I need to reassure myself that women who are not interested in me romantically might very likely feel that way based on factors completely unrelated to my looks."

- "I need to be realistic concerning how 'hot' or 'great looking' a woman needs to be before I am interested in dating her."

- "I need to be cognizant that I have many friends who include attractive women."

- "I need to explicitly remember, particularly when I start criticizing myself, that I've had my share of girlfriends. I've even been happily married to an attractive woman, whom I divorced for reasons unrelated to my looks, and I know that marriage to the right woman will again happen for me."

- "I need to limit my Internet time in regard to searching for the latest, greatest product to improve whatever physical feature that I might be focusing on at the moment."

- "I need to have good thoughts about myself. I need to remind myself every so often about the features I like about my looks, such as my great smile and eyes, which people compliment me on."

• • •

If you can't do everything, then at least don't do nothing! Sure, society reflects the forceful perspective of collective individuals, but individuals can wield much discretion. You can challenge lookism and you can lessen the power and pervasiveness of the PA phenomenon. It begins with knowing yourself. It is followed by your awareness of how you judge others, and becoming more sensitive in your corresponding interactions with other people.

You have already begun. Your knowledge and awareness of the well-documented advantages associated with higher PA and the disadvantages associated with lower PA represent an important positive step.

Notes

CHAPTER 1

1. R. L. Hotz, "With Ancient Jewelry, It's the Thought That Counts," *Los Angeles Times* (April 16, 2004): pp. A1, A15.
2. L. Betzig, *People Are Animals in Human Nature: A Critical Reader,* ed. Laura Betzig (New York: Oxford University Press, 1997).
3. Ibid.
4. J. Erler, "Why Nothing Is Beautiful: Physical Attractiveness in Latin Literature" (paper presented at the American Philological Association Annual Conference, San Diego, CA 2001).
5. Ibid.
6. S. Marquardt, MD, "Marquardt Beauty Analysis" (2003), www.beau tyanalysis.com.
7. Betzig, *People Are Animals in Human Nature.*
8. Ibid.
9. P. T. Ellison, *Ecology, Reproduction, and Human Evolution* (New York: Aldine de Gruyter, 2001).
10. G. Jasienska et al., "Large Breasts and Narrow Waists Indicate High Reproductive Potential in Women," *Proceedings of the Royal Society of London: Series B* 271, no. 1545 (2004): pp. 1213–1217.
11. S. C. Roberts et al., "Female Facial Attractiveness Increases During the Fertile Phase of the Menstrual Cycle," *Proceedings of the Royal Society of London, Biology* 271 (2004): pp. S270–S272.
12. I. Penton-Voak and D. I. Perrett, "Female Preference for Male Faces Changes Cyclically—Further Evidence," *Evolutionary Human Behavior* 21 (2000): pp. 39–48.
13. J. Fletcher, "The Decorated Body in Ancient Egypt: Hairstyles, Cosmetics, and Tattoos" (paper presented at the conference "Clothed Body in the Ancient World," Milton Keynes, UK, 2002).

14. M. Aguirre, "Dress and Female Seduction in Ancient Greece: Litera-
    ture and Art" (paper presented at the conference "Clothed Body in
    the Ancient World," Milton Keynes, UK, 2002).
15. K. West, "Chinese Beauty Through the Changes of Time" (2003),
    http://www.beautyworlds.com/beautychinese.htm#Contenttop.

                          CHAPTER 2

1. J. H. Langlois et al., "Maxims or Myths of Beauty? A Meta-Analytic
    and Theoretical Review," *Psychological Bulletin* 126, no. 3 (2000):
    pp. 390–423.
2. Ibid.
3. Ibid.
4. B. Malle, "Attraction and Relationships, Major Antecedents of Liking
    and Attraction" (1996), http://darkwing.uoregon.edu/~bfmalle/
    sp/L15.html.
5. J. Egan, "Love in the Time of No Time," *New York Times Magazine*
    53, no. 20 (November 23, 2003): p. 66 (Section Six).
6. Ibid.
7. Ibid.
8. M. Sones, "Beauty, Fashion, and the Coolidge Effect" (2002),
    http://www.beautyworlds.com/beautyfashioncoolidge.htm.
9. Ibid.
10. R. Trivers, "Theory of Parental Investment," *Sexual Selection and the
    Descent of Man,* ed. B. Campbell (Chicago: Aldine, 1972).
11. Sones, "Beauty, Fashion, and the Coolidge Effect."
12. D. D. Cahoon and E. M. Edmonds, "Estimates of Opposite-Sex First
    Impressions Related to Females' Clothing Style," *Bulletin-of-the-
    Psychonomic-Society of Augusta College, GA* 65, no. 2 (1989): pp. 171–
    173.
13. R. D. Geiselman, N. A. Haight, and L. G. Kimata, "Context Effects
    in the Perceived Physical Attractiveness of Faces," *Journal of Experi-
    mental Social Psychology* 20 (1984): pp. 409–424.
14. D. T. Kenrick et al., "Integrating Evolutionary and Social Exchange
    Perspectives on Relationships: Effects of Gender, Self-Appraisal, and
    Involvement Level on Mate Selection Criteria," *Journal of Personality
    and Social Psychology* 64 (1993): pp. 951–969.
15. J. D. Brown et al., "When Gulliver Travels: Social Context, Psycholog-
    ical Closeness, and Self-Appraisals," *Journal of Personality and Social
    Psychology* 62 (1992): pp. 717–727.
16. B. Thornton and S. Moore, "Physical Attractiveness Contrast Effect:
    Implications for Self-Esteem and Evaluations of the Social Self," *Per-
    sonality and Social Psychology Bulletin* 19 (1993): pp. 474–480; and
    L. Heinberg, K. Thompson, and S. Stormer, "Development and

Validation of the Sociocultural Attitudes Toward Appearance Questionnaire," *International Journal of Eating Disorders* 17, no. 1 (1995): pp. 81–89.

17. R. G. Turner, L. Gilliland, and H. M. Klein, "Self-Consciousness, Evaluation of Physical Characteristics, and Physical Attractiveness," *Journal of Research in Personality* 15 (1981): pp. 182–190; and A. L. Lipson, D. P. Przybyla, and D. Byrne, "Physical Attractiveness, Self-Awareness, and Mirror-Gazing Behavior," *Bulletin of the Psychonomic Society* 21 (1983): pp. 115–116.

18. T. F. Cash, D. W. Cash, and J. W. Butters, "Mirror, Mirror, on the Wall . . . ? Contrast Effects and Self-Evaluations of Physical Attractiveness," *Personality and Social Psychology Bulletin* 9 (1983): pp. 351–358.

19. T. F. Cash, and A. S. Labarge, "Development of the Appearance Schemas Inventory: A New Cognitive Body-Image Assessment," *Cognitive Therapy and Research* 20 (1996): pp. 37–50.

20. E. Hatfield and S. Sprecher, *Mirror, Mirror: The Importance of Looks in Everyday Life* (Albany, NY: State University of New York Press, 1986); and C. V. Wiseman et al., "Cultural Expectations of Thinness in Women: An Update," *International Journal of Eating Disorders* 11, no. 1 (January 1992): pp. 85–89.

21. E. Walster et al., "Importance of Physical Attractiveness in Dating Behavior," *Journal of Personality and Social Psychology* 4 (1966): pp. 508–516.

22. Ibid.

23. M. Lynn and B. A. Shurgot, "Responses to Lonely Hearts Advertisements: Effects of Reported Physical Attractiveness, Physique, and Coloration," *Personality and Social Psychology Bulletin* 10 (1984): pp. 349–357.

24. D. Nettle, "Women's Height, Reproductive Success, and the Evolution of Sexual Dimorphism in Modern Humans," *Proceedings of the Royal Society of London, B* 269 (2002): pp. 1919–1923.

25. T. Horvarth, "Correlates of Physical Beauty in Men and Women," *Social Behaviour and Personality* 7 (1979): pp. 145–151.

26. D. S. Maisey et al., "Characteristics of Male Attractiveness for Women," *Lancet* 353 (1999): p. 1500; and S. M. Hughes and G. G. Gallup, "Sex Differences in Morphological Predictors of Sexual Behaviour: Shoulder to Hip and Waist to Hip Ratios," *Evolution and Human Behaviour* 24 (2003): pp. 173–178.

27. N. Barber, "Mustache Fashion Covaries with a Good Marriage Market for Women," *Journal of Nonverbal Behavior* 25, no. 4 (2001): pp. 261–272.

28. J. M. Townsend and L. W. Roberts, "Gender Differences in Mate Selection Among Law Students: Divergence and Convergence of Criteria," *Journal of Psychology* 29 (1993): pp. 507–528.

29. S. Sprecher et al., "Asking Questions in Bars: The Girls (and Boys)

May Not Get Prettier at Closing Time and Other Interesting Results," *Personality and Social Psychology Bulletin* 10 (1984): pp. 482–488.

30. J. M. Townsend and G. D. Levy, "Effects of Potential Partners' Physical Attractiveness and Socioeconomic Status on Sexuality and Partner Selection," *Archives of Sexual Behavior* 19 (1990): pp. 149–164.

31. A. Alkon, "Waist Removal" (2003), http://www.advicegoddess .com/columns/column57.html (accessed August 14, 2007).

32. G. C. Urbaniak and P. R. Kilmann, "Physical Attractiveness and the 'Nice Guy Paradox': Do Nice Guys Really Finish Last?" *Sex Roles: A Journal of Research* 49 (2003): pp. 413–426.

33. Ibid.

34. Ibid.

35. E. Goode, "Gender and Courtship Entitlement: Responses to Personal Ads," *Sex Roles: A Journal of Research* 34 (1996): pp. 141–169.

36. Ibid.

37. D. A. Harr, "Halo Effect: The Impact of Differences Between Target and Receiver," *Missouri Western State College* (December 4, 2003), http://clearinghouse.missouriwestern.edu/manuscripts/438.asp?logon =&code=.

38. Goode, "Gender and Courtship Entitlement."

39. E. Berscheid and E. Walster, "Physical Attractiveness," in *Advances in Experimental Social Psychology* 7, ed. L. Berkowitz (New York: Academic Press, 1974): pp. 157–215; and Hatfield and Sprecher, *Mirror, Mirror: The Importance of Looks in Everyday Life.*

40. W. F. Harley, Jr., *His Needs, Her Needs: Building an Affair-Proof Marriage* (Grand Rapids, MI: Baker Book House Company, 2003).

41. Ibid.

42. D. M. Buss et al., "A Half Century of Mate Preferences: The Cultural Evolution of Values," *Journal of Marriage and Family* 63, no. 2 (2001): pp. 491–503.

CHAPTER 3

1. J. H. Langlois et al., "Maxims or Myths of Beauty? A Meta-Analytic and Theoretical Review," *Psychological Bulletin* 126, no. 3 (2000): pp. 390–423.

2. D. M. Buss, *Evolutionary Psychology: The New Science of the Mind* (Boston: Allyn & Bacon, 1999); and M. Daly, "Evolutionary Theory and Parental Motives," in *Mammalian Parenting*, ed. N. A. Krasnegor and R. S. Bridges (New York: Oxford University Press, 1990).

3. J. Mann, "Nurturance or Negligence: Maternal Psychology and Behavioral Preference Among Preterm Twins," in *The Adapted Mind: Evolutionary Psychology and the Generation of Culture*, ed. J. H. Barkow, L. Cosmides, and J. Tobby (New York: Oxford University Press, 1992): pp. 367–390.

4. R. C. Barden et al., "Effects of Craniofacial Deformity in Infancy on the Quality of Mother-Infant Interactions," *Child Development* 60 (1989): pp. 819–824.

5. M. Daly and M. Wilson, "Discriminative Parental Solicitude and the Relevance of Evolutionary Models to the Analysis of Motivational Systems," in *The Cognitive Neurosciences,* ed. M. S. Gassaniga (Cambridge, MA: MIT Press, 1995): pp. 1269–1286.

6. C. W. Stephan and J. H. Langlois, "Baby Beautiful: Adult Attributions of Infant Competence as a Function of Infant Attractiveness," *Child Development* 55 (1984): pp. 576–585.

7. S. Epps, "Labeling Effects of Infant Health and Parent Demographics on Nurses' Ratings of Preterm Infant Behavior," *IMHJ (University of Nebraska Medical Center)* 14, no. 3 (1993): pp. 182–191; and K. L. Badr and B. Abdallah, "Physical Attractiveness of Premature Infants Affects Outcome at Discharge from NICU (Neonatal Intensive Care Unit)," *Infant Behavior and Development* 24, no. 1 (2001): pp. 129–133.

8. J. R. Crowder and L. S. Hunter, "Nursing Students' Perceptions of Infant Attractiveness" (paper presented at the Annual Conference of the Society for Research in Child Development, Tampa, FL, 2003).

9. Ibid.

10. Ibid.

11. J. Langlois, A. Roggman, and L. Rieser-Danner, "Infants' Differential Social Responses to Attractive and Unattractive Faces," *Developmental Psychology* 26 (1990): pp. 153–159.

12. D. I. Perrett et al., "Facial Attractiveness Judgments Reflect Learning of Parental Age Characteristics," *Proceedings of the Royal Society, London, B-Biological Sciences* 269, no. 1494 (2002): pp. 873–880.

13. B. E. Vaughn and J. H. Langlois, "Physical Attractiveness as a Correlate of Peer Status and Social Competence in Preschool Children," *Developmental Psychology* 19 (1983): pp. 561–567; J. H. Langlois and C. Stephan, "The Effects of Physical Attractiveness and Ethnicity on Children's Behavioral Attributions and Peer Preferences," *Child Development* 48 (1977): pp. 1694–1698; and C. W. Stephan and J. H. Langlois, "Physical Attractiveness and Ethnicity: Implications for Stereotyping and Social Development," *Journal of Genetic Psychology* 137 (1980): pp. 303–304.

14. K. K. Dion, "Physical Attractiveness and Evaluation of Children's Transgressions," *Journal of Personality and Social Psychology* 24, no. 2 (1972): pp. 207–213.

15. K. K. Dion, E. Berscheid, and E. Walster, "What Is Beautiful Is Good?" *Journal of Personality and Social Psychology* 24, no. 3 (1972): pp. 285–290.

16. R. E. Fancher, *Pioneers of Psychology* (New York: Norton, 1990).

17. L. Baker-Sperry and L. Grauerholz, "The Pervasiveness and Persistence of the Feminine Beauty Ideal in Children's Fairy Tales," *Gender & Society* 17, no. 5 (2003): pp. 711–726.

18. "Fairy Tales Knock Self-Esteem," Health24.com: Child: Emotions & Behaviour, n.d., available at http://www.health24.com/child/ Emotions_behaviour/833–854,25584.asp (accessed December 12, 2006).

19. D. Santoso, "Teens Struggle to Fit the Picture Perfect Body Image," *The Jakarta (Indonesia) Post* (October 29, 2003): p. 18 (Section 1).

20. Ibid.

21. Ibid.

CHAPTER 4

1. E. Hatfield and S. Sprecher, *Mirror, Mirror: The Importance of Looks in Everyday Life* (Albany, NY: State University of New York Press, 1986).

2. N. Ambady and R. Rosenthal, "Half a Minute: Predicting Teacher Evaluations from Thin Slices of Nonverbal Behavior and Physical Attractiveness," *Journal of Personality and Social Psychology* 64 (1993): pp. 431–441.

3. R. Rosenthal, "Covert Communication in Classrooms, Clinics, and Courtrooms," Psi Chi: The National Honor Society in Psychology, Distinguised Lectures Series, http://www.psichi.org/pubs/articles/ article_121.asp, published in its entirety in *Eye on Psi Chi* 3, no. 1, (Fall 1998): 18–22, published by psi Chi, The National Honor Society in Psychology.

4. R. Rosenthal and K. L. Fode, "The Problem of Experimenter Outcome-Bias," in *Research in Social Psychology,* ed. D. P. Ray (Washington, DC: National Institute of Social and Behavioral Science, 1961).

5. R. Rosenthal and R. Lawson, "A Longitudinal Study of the Effects of Experimenter Bias on the Operant Learning of Laboratory Rats," *Journal of Psychiatric Research* 2 (1964): pp. 61–72.

6. R. Rosenthal and L. Jacobson, *Pygmalion in the Classroom* (New York: Holt, Rinehart, and Winston, 1968).

7. N. Ambady and R. Rosenthal, "Thin Slices of Expressive Behavior as Predictors of Interpersonal Consequences: A Meta-Analysis," *Psychological Bulletin* 111 (1992): pp. 256–274.

8. R. Hartley, "Imagine You're Clever," *Journal of Child Psychology and Psychiatry* 27, no. 3 (1986): pp. 383–396.

9. G. R. Adams and A. S. Cohen, "Children's Physical and Interpersonal Characteristics That Affect Student-Teacher Interactions," *The Journal of Experimental Education* 43 (1974): pp. 1–5.

10. M. M. Clifford and E. Walster, "Research Note: The Effect of Physical Attractiveness on Teacher Expectations," *Sociology of Education* 46 (1973): pp. 238–258; and Adams and Cohen, "Children's Physical and Interpersonal Characteristics That Affect Student-Teacher Interactions."

11. J. Rich, "Effects of Children's Physical Attractiveness on Teacher's Evaluations," *Journal of Educational Psychology* 67 (1975): pp. 599–609.

12. T. W. Dushenko et al., "Generality of the Physical Attractiveness Stereotype for Age and Sex," *Journal of Social Psychology* 105 (1978): pp. 303–304.

13. J. H. Langlois and L. E. Styczynski, "The Effects of Physical Attractiveness on the Behavioral Attributions and Peer Preferences of Acquainted Children," *International Journal of Behavioral Development* 2 (1979): pp. 325–341.

14. B. E. Vaughn and J. H. Langlois, "Physical Attractiveness as a Correlate of Peer Status and Social Competence in Preschool Children," *Developmental Psychology* 19 (1983): pp. 561–567.

15. M. Krantz, "Physical Attractiveness and Popularity: A Predictive Study," *Psychological Reports* 60 (1987): pp. 723–726.

16. E. Aronson, T. D. Wilson, and R. M. Akert, *Social Psychology* (Upper Saddle River, NJ: Prentice Hall, 2002).

17. G. R. Adams and P. Crane, "An Assessment of Parents' and Teachers' Expectations of Preschool Children's Social Preference for Attractive or Unattractive Children and Adults," *Child Development* 51 (1980): pp. 224–231.

18. Aronson, Wilson, and Akert, *Social Psychology.*

19. D. R. White, K. Mauro, and J. Spindler, "Development of Type Salience: Implications for Childhood Educators," *International Review of Applied Psychology* 34 (1985): p. 433.

20. There is a large body of research on the subject of body-image stereotypes in children. See R. M. Lerner and E. Gillert, "Body Build Identification, Preference, and Aversion in Kindergarten Children," *Developmental Psychology* 19 (1969): pp. 856–867; S. W. Kirkpatrick and D. M. Sanders, "Body Image Stereotypes: A Developmental Comparison," *Journal of Genetic Psychology* 132 (1978): pp. 87–95; S. F. Stager and P. J. Burke, "A Reexamination of Body Build Stereotypes," *Journal of Research in Personality* 16 (1982): pp. 435–446; R. Cohen et al., "A Developmental Analysis of the Influence of Body Weight on the Sociometry of Children," *Addictive Behaviors* 14 (1989): pp. 473–476; M. E. Collins, "Body Figure Perceptions and Preferences Among Preadolescent Children," *International Journal of Eating Disorders* 10, no. 2 (1991): pp. 199–208; K. K. Oliver and M. H. Thelen, "Children's Perceptions of Peer Influence on Eating Concerns," *Behavior Therapy* 27 (1996): pp. 25–39; R. Sands et al., "Disordered Eating Patterns, Body Image, Self-Esteem, and Physical Activity in Preadolescent School Children," *International Journal of Eating Disorders* 21, no. 2 (1997): pp. 159–166; S. Shapiro, M. Newcomb, and T. B. Loeb, "Fear of Fat, Disregulated-Restrained Eating, and Body-Esteem: Prevalence and Gender Differences Among Eight-to Ten-Year-Olds," *Journal of Clinical Child Psychology* 26, no. 4

(1997): pp. 358–365; and M. H. Thelen et al., "Eating and Body Image Concerns Among Children," *Journal of Clinical Child Psychology* 21, no. 1 (1992): pp. 41–46.

21. Shapiro, Newcomb, and Loeb, "Fear of Fat, Disregulated-Restrained Eating, and Body-Esteem: Prevalence and Gender Differences Among Eight- to Ten-Year-Olds."

22. G. Critser, *Fat Land, How Americans Became the Fattest People in the World* (New York: Houghton-Mifflin, 2003).

23. J. K. Mills and G. D. Andrianopoulos, "The Relationship Between Childhood Onset Obesity and Psychopathology in Adulthood," *The Journal of Psychology* 127, no. 5 (1993): pp. 547–551.

24. M. I. Loewy, "Suggestions for Working with Fat Children in the Schools," *Professional School Counseling* 1, no. 4 (1998): p. 18; and B. H. Quinn, "Attitudinal Ratings of Educators Toward Normal Weight, Overweight, and Obese Teenage Girls" (doctoral dissertation, Texas Woman's University, Denton, 1987).

25. S. L. Gortmaker et al., "Social and Economic Consequences of Overweight in Adolescence and Young Adulthood," *New England Journal of Medicine* 14 (1993): pp. 1008–1012.

26. J. H. Hoover and R. Oliver, *The Bullying Prevention Handbook: A Guide for Teachers, Administrators, and Counselors* (Bloomington, IN: National Educational Service, 1996).

27. A. Adler, *Understanding Human Nature* (London: George Alan & Unwin, 1932), p. 71.

28. J. R. Whitehead and J. H. Hoover, "The Link Between Body Issues and Behavioral Problems," *Reclaiming Children and Youth* 9, no. 3 (2000): pp. 130–138.

29. J. Rierdan, E. Koff, and M. Stubbs, "Depressive Symptomatology and Body Image in Adolescent Girls," *Journal of Early Adolescence* 7, no. 2 (1987): pp. 205–216.

30. D. Moore, "Body Image and Eating Behavior in Adolescents," *Journal of the American College of Nutrition* 12 (1993): pp. 505–510.

31. J. Rierdan, E. Koff, and M. Stubbs, "A Longitudinal Analysis of Body Image as a Predictor of the Onset and Persistence of Adolescent Girls' Depression," *Journal of Early Adolescence* 7 (1987): pp. 205–216.

32. D. Morey and L. Morey, "The Vulnerable Body Image of Females with Feelings of Depression," *Journal of Research in Personality* 25 (1991): pp. 343–354.

33. A. Moitra, "Depression and Body Image," Psychology Department, Vanderbilt University, n.d., http://www.vanderbilt.edu/AnS/psychology/health_psychology/depressbi.html.

34. R. H. Striegal-Moore et al., "Eating Disorder Symptoms in a Cohort of 11- to 16-Year-Old Black and White Girls: The NHLBI Growth and Health Study," *International Journal of Eating Disorders* 27 (2000): pp. 49–66.

35. C. C. Strauss et al., "Personal and Interpersonal Characteristics Associated with Childhood Obesity," *Journal of Pediatric Psychology* 10, no.

3 (1985): pp. 337–343; and R. S. Strauss, "Childhood Obesity and Self-Esteem," *Pediatrics* 105, no. 1 (2000): p. 15.

36. C. Davis, G. Claridge, and J. Fox, "Not Just a Pretty Face: Physical Attractiveness and Perfectionism in the Risk for Eating Disorders," *International Journal of Eating Disorders* 27, no. 1 (2000): pp. 67–73; and M. Nichter, *Fat Talk: What Girls and Their Parents Say About Dieting* (Cambridge, MA: Harvard University Press, 2000).

37. L. L. Craft and D. M. Landers, "Effect of Exercise on Clinical Depression and Depression Resulting from Mental Illness: A Meta-Analysis," *Journal of Sport and Exercise Psychology* 20 (1998): pp. 339–357.

38. J. Whitehead, "Norman Normal: A Tale of Physical Triumph," *Journal of Physical Education, Recreation, and Dance* 58 (August 1987): pp. 82–87; and Whitehead and Hoover, "The Link Between Body Issues and Behavioral Problems."

39. M. Pipher, *Hunger Pangs* (Holbrook, MA: Adams, 1995).

40. S. J. Lehman and S. L. Koerner, "Adolescent Women's Sports Involvement and Sexual Behavior/Health: A Process-Level Investigation," *Journal of Youth and Adolescence* 33, no. 5 (2004): pp. 443–455.

41. V. B. Agocha and M. L. Cooper, "Risk Perceptions and Safer-Sex Intentions: Does a Partner's Physical Attractiveness Undermine the Use of Risk-Relevant Information?" *Personality and Social Psychology Bulletin* 25, no. 6 (1999): pp. 751–765.

42. D. Hamermesh and A. Parker, "Beauty in the Classroom: Professors' Pulchritude and Putative Pedagogical Productivity," *National Bureau of Economic Research, NBER Paper No. W9853* (2003).

43. D. H. Naftulin, J. E. Ware, and F. A. Donnelly, "The Doctor Fox Lecture: A Paradigm of Educational Seduction," *Journal of Medical Education* 48 (1973): pp. 630–635.

44. L. Rice, "Student Evaluation of Teaching: Problems and Prospects," *Teaching Philosophy* 11 (1988): pp. 329–344; R. Wilson, "New Research Casts Doubt on Value of Student Evaluations of Professors," *The Chronicle of Higher Education* 44, no. 19 (January 16, 1998): p. A12; J. J. Ryan, J. A. Anderson, and A. B. Birchler, "Student Evaluations: The Faculty Responds," *Research in Higher Education* 12, no. 4 (December 1980): pp. 317–333; W. M. Williams and S. J. Ceci, "'How'm I Doing?' Problems with Student Ratings of Instructors and Courses," *Change: The Magazine of Higher Learning* 29 (September/October 1997): pp. 12–23; and P. Selvin, "The Raging Bull of Berkeley," *Science* 251 (1991): pp. 368–371.

CHAPTER 5

1. L. Watkins and L. Johnston, "Screening Job Applicants: The Impact of Physical Attractiveness and Application Quality," *International Journal of Selection and Assessment* 8 (2000): pp. 76–84.

2. T. F. Cash, B. Gillen, and S. D. Burns, "Sexism and Beautyism in Personnel Consultant Decision Making," *Journal of Applied Psychology* 62, no. 3 (1977): pp. 301–310.

3. C. M. Marlowe, S. L. Schneider, and C. E. Nelson, "Gender and Attractiveness Biases in Hiring Decisions: Are More Experienced Managers Less Biased?" *Journal of Applied Psychology* 81, no. 1 (1986): pp. 11–21.

4. B. Harper, "Beauty, Stature, and the Labour Market: A British Cohort Study," *Oxford Bulletin of Economics and Statistics* 62, no. 771–800 (2000).

5. D. M. Cable and T. A. Judge, "The Effect of Physical Height on Workplace Success and Income: Preliminary Test of a Theoretical Model," *Journal of Applied Psychology* 89, no. 3 (2004): pp. 428–441.

6. A. Mazur, J. Mazur, and C. Keating, "Military Rank Attainment of a West Point Class: Effects of Cadets' Physicals Features," *American Journal of Sociology* 90 (1984): pp. 125–150.

7. A. Mazur and U. Mueller, "Facial Dominance," in *Research in Biopolitics* 4, ed. A. Somit and S. Peterson (London: JAI Press, 1996): pp. 99–111; and U. Mueller and A. Mazur, "Facial Dominance of West Point Cadets as a Predictor of Later Military Rank," *Social Forces* 74 (1996): pp. 823–850.

8. I. Saporta and J. J. Halpern, "Being Different Can Hurt: Effects of Deviation from Physical Norms on Lawyers' Salaries," *Industrial Relations* 41, no. 3 (2002): pp. 442–466.

9. R. P. Quinn, "Physical Deviance and Occupational Mistreatment: The Short, the Fat and the Ugly" (unpublished manuscript, Institute for Social Research, Ann Arbor, MI: University of Michigan, 1978).

10. D. Maccarone, "Affirmative Action for the Attractive?" *Psychology Today* 36, no. 1 (January–February 2003): p. 18.

11. B. J. Almond, "Beauty and the 'Beastly Effect,'" *Sallyport: The Magazine of Rice University*, no. 1 (2002), http://www.rice.edu/sallyport/2002/fall/sallyport/beautyandthebeastlyeffect.html.

12. 2007 *Market Wire* news release available at http://newsblaze.com/story/2006020105001100007.mwir/topstory.html.

13. Details of the Malaysian Airlines System case are from V. Ramachandran, "Not Just About Looking Pretty," *New Straits Times* (Kuala Lumpur, Malaysia) (September 29, 2003), http://www.highbeam.com/doc/1P1-82933283.html.

14. K. Ofgang, "Firing Woman for Lack of Attractiveness Violates Anti-Bias Law," *(Los Angeles) Metropolitan News-Enterprise* (March 10, 2003), http://www.metnews.com/articles/yano031003.htm.

15. P. Chavez, "Abercrombie & Fitch to Pay $50 Million to Settle Discrimination Case," Associated Press (November 16, 2004), http://www.billingsgazette.com/newdex.php?display=rednews/2004/11/16/build/ business/40-abercrombie-suit.inc.

16. For more details on the relationship between physical attractiveness

and pay, see E. Diener, E., B. Wolsic, and F. Fujita, "Physical Attractiveness and Subjective Well-Being," *Journal of Personality and Social Psychology* 69, no. 1 (1995): pp. 120–129; D. Umberson and M. Hughes, "The Impact of Physical Attractiveness and Achievement and Psychological Well-Being," *Social Psychology Quarterly* 50, no. 3 (1987): pp. 227–236; D. Hamermesh and J. Biddle, "Beauty and the Labor Market," *American Economic Review* 84 (1994): pp. 1174–1194; and D. Hamermesh, X. Meng, and J. Zhang, "Dress for Success: Does Primping Pay?" *National Bureau of Economic Research, NBER Paper No. 7167* (1999).

17. G. A. Pfann et al., "Business Success and Businesses' Beauty Capital," *Economics Letters* 67, no. 2 (2000): pp. 201–207.

18. S. J. Solnick and M. E. Schweitzer, "The Influence of Physical Attractiveness and Gender on Ultimatum Game Decisions," *Organizational Behavior and Human Decision Processes* 79, no. 3 (1999): pp. 199–215.

19. R. H. Thaler, "The Ultimatum Game," *Journal of Economic Perspectives* 2 (1988): pp. 191–202.

20. C. Camerer, "The Psychology of Strategic Thinking" (working paper, Pasadena, CA: Caltech, 1999).

21. K. N. Kelley, L. B. Nita, and B. P. Bandura, "Evaluating Employee Transgressions: Influence of Attractiveness and Ethical Ideology" (paper presented at the Annual Convention of the American Psychological Society, Atlanta, 2003).

22. C. Shahani-Denning and D. Plumitallo, "The Influence of Physical Attractiveness and Gender on Disciplinary Decisions" (paper presented at the Fifth Annual Convention of the American Psychological Society, Chicago, 1993); and S. D. Farley, R. C. Chia, and L. J. Allred, "Stereotypes About Attractiveness: When Beautiful Is Not Better," *Journal of Social Behavior & Personality* 13 (1998): pp. 479–492.

23. Kelley, Nita, and Bandura, "Evaluating Employee Transgressions: Influence of Attractiveness and Ethical Ideology."

24. L. A. Jackson, L. A. Sullivan, and C. N. Hodge, "Stereotype Effects of Attributions, Predictions, and Evaluations: No Two Social Judgments Are Quite Alike," *Journal of Personality & Social Psychology* 65 (1993): pp. 69–84.

25. C. Shahani-Denning and D. Plumitallo, "The Influence of Physical Attractiveness and Gender on Disciplinary Decisions" (paper presented at the Fifth Annual Convention of the American Psychological Society, Chicago, 1993).

CHAPTER 6

1. M. J. Wolf and K. Mader, *Fallen Angels, Chronicles of LA Crime and Mystery* (New York: Facts on File, 1986).

2. T. O'Connor, "Anthropological Criminology," Lecture in Criminology 301, North Carolina Wesleyan College (2005), http://faculty.ncwc.edu/toconnor/301/301lect03.htm.

3. Ibid.

4. L. H. Goldenson and M. J. Wolf, *Beating the Odds* (New York: Scribner, 1992).

5. B. W. Darby and D. Jeffers, "The Effects of Defendant and Juror Attractiveness on Simulated Courtroom Trial Decisions," *Social Behavior and Personality: An International Journal* 16, no. 1 (1988): pp. 39–50.

6. H. Kalven, Jr. and H. Zeisel, *The American Jury* (Boston: Little, Brown, 1966).

7. A. C. Downs and P. M. Lyons, "Natural Observations of the Links Between Attractiveness and Initial Legal Judgments," *Personality and Social Psychology Bulletin* 17 (1991): pp. 541–547.

8. S. J. McKelvie and J. Coley, "Effects of Crime Seriousness and Offender Facial Attractiveness on Recommended Treatment," *Social Behavior and Personality: An International Journal* 21, no. 4 (1993): pp. 265–277.

9. K. L. Wuensch and C. H. Moore, "Effects of Physical Attractiveness on Evaluations of a Male Employee's Allegation of Sexual Harassment by His Female Employer," *Journal of Social Psychology* 144, no. 2 (2004): pp. 207–217.

10. A. Vrij and H. R. Firmin, "Beautiful Thus Innocent? The Impact of Defendants' and Victims' Physical Attractiveness and Participants' Rape Beliefs on Impression Formation in Alleged Rape Cases," *International Review of Victimology* 8, no. 3 (2001): pp. 245–255.

11. R. Mazzella and A. Feingold, "The Effects of Physical Attractiveness, Race, Socioeconomic Status, and Gender of Defendants and Victims on Judgments of Mock Jurors: A Meta-Analysis," *Journal of Applied Social Psychology* 24 (1994): pp. 1315–1344.

12. M. B. Jacobson and P. M. Popovich, "Victim Attractiveness and Perceptions of Responsibility in an Ambiguous Rape Case," *Psychology of Women Quarterly* 8, no. 1 (1983): pp. 100–104.

13. F. M. Deutsch, "Status, Sex and Smiling: The Effect of Role on Smiling in Men and Women," *Personality and Social Psychology Bulletin* 16 (1990): pp. 531–540; and M. G. Efran, "The Effect of Physical Appearance on the Judgment of Guilt, Interpersonal Attraction, and Severity of Recommended Punishment in a Simulated Jury Task," *Journal of Research in Personality* 8 (1974): pp. 45–54.

14. R. L. Kurtzberg, H. Safar, and N. Cavior, "Surgical and Social Rehabilitation of Adult Offenders," *Proceedings of the 76th Annual Convention of the American Psychological Association* 3 (1968): pp. 649–650; and J. E. Stewart, "Defendants' Attractiveness as a Factor in the Outcome of Trials," *Journal of Applied Social Psychology* 10 (1980): pp. 348–361.

15. H. Sigall and N. Ostrove, "Beautiful but Dangerous: Effects of Offender Attractiveness and Nature of the Crime on Juridic Judgment," *Journal of Personality and Social Psychology* 31 (1975): pp. 410–414.

16. S. R. Gross, "Expert Evidence," *Wisconsin Law Review* (November/December 1991): pp. 1113–1232.

17. D. W. Shuman, E. Whitaker, and A. Champagne, "An Empirical Examination of the Use of Expert Witnesses in the Courts—Part 2: A Three City Study," *Jurimetrics Journal* 34 (1994): pp. 193–208; and R. Hasuike, "Credibility and Gender in the Courtroom," *The Practical Litigator* 11, no. 3 (2000): pp. 19–29.

18. J. J. McDonald, Jr., "Civil Rights for the Aesthetically Challenged," *Employee Relations Law Journal* 29, no. 2 (2003): p. 118.

19. S. Christensen, "The Quest for Equality," *Queensland University of Technology Law & Justice Journal* 3, no. 1 (2003): p. 76.

20. D. A. Abwender and K. Hough, "Interactive Effects of Characteristics of Defendant and Mock Juror on U.S. Participants' Judgment and Sentencing Recommendations," *The Journal of Social Psychology* 141, no. 5 (2001): pp. 603–616.

21. S. R. Sommers and P. C. Ellsworth, "White Juror Bias," *Psychology, Public Policy, and Law* 7, no. 1 (2001): pp. 201–230.

22. Mazzella and Feingold, "The Effects of Physical Attractiveness, Race, Socioeconomic Status, and Gender of Defendants and Victims on Judgments of Mock Jurors."

23. J. Ramey, "The Bloody Blonde and the Marble Woman: Gender and Power in the Case of Ruth Snyder," *Journal of Social History* 37, no. 3 (2004): pp. 625–651.

CHAPTER 7

1. "Views of President Lincoln, 1861," EyeWitness to History, www.eyewitnesstohistory.com (2005) (accessed August 12, 2007).

2. R. Waterman, R. Wright, and G. St. Clair, *The Image-Is-Everything-Presidency* (Boulder, CO: Westview Press, 1999).

3. J. D. Mayer, "The Contemporary Presidency: The Presidency and Image Management: Discipline in Pursuit of Illusion," *Presidential Studies Quarterly* 34, no. 3 (2004): pp. 620–632.

4. F. Ahrens, "Pounds of Political Prevention: Doug Duncan Losing Weight to Ensure an Electoral Gain," *The Washington Post* (November 3, 1997): p. D9.

5. Ibid.

6. Mayer, "The Contemporary Presidency."

7. James Schubert's findings from the Romanian elections study and his other observations on American politics are from J. N. Schubert, "Good Genes and Issue Agreement in Candidate Appraisal" (paper

presented at the Midwest Political Science Association 61st Annual National Conference 2003).

8. V. Haddock, "Here's Lookin' at You, Kid: In the Mayoral Race, the Hunk Factor Is No Junk, Say the Experts," *San Francisco Chronicle* (December 7, 2003): p. D1, http://www.sfgate.com/cgi-bin/article .cgi?f=/c/a/2003/12/07/ING7N3F9H91.DTL.

9. J. Johnson, "Heston Says Famous Line Final Time as NRA President," Cybercast News Service (April 27, 2003), http://www.cns news.com/ViewNation.asp?Page=%5CNation%5Carchive%5C2003 04%5CNAT20030427a.html.

10. T. Sforza, "What You See Is What You Elect. Come November, the Man with the Most 'Dominant' Face May Win. Making an Electable Face," *Orange County Register* (February 22, 2004): p. 1 (cover page).

11. S. Rosenberg, "Facilitating the Development of Political Reasoning in the Classroom: An Experimental Study" (paper presented at the APSA Conference on Teaching and Learning, Washington, DC, 2005).

12. Sforza, "What You See Is What You Elect."

13. D. M. Cable and T. A. Judge, "The Effect of Physical Height on Workplace Success and Income: Preliminary Test of a Theoretical Model," *Journal of Applied Psychology* 89, no. 3 (2004): pp. 428–441.

14. Haddock, "Here's Lookin' at You, Kid: In the Mayoral Race, the Hunk Factor Is No Junk, Say the Experts."

15. Ibid.

16. C. F. Keating and D. Randall, "Dominance and Deception in Children and Adults: Are Leaders the Best Misleaders?" *Personality and Social Psychology Bulletin* 20 (1994): pp. 312–321.

17. J. Masip, E. Garrido, and C. Herrero, "Facial Appearance and Judgments of Credibility: The Effects of Facial Babyishness and Age on Statement Credibility," *Genetic, Social, and General Psychology Monographs* 129, no. 3 (2003): pp. 269–411.

CHAPTER 8

1. T. Mann, and J. Helfert, "Looking up to the Shuttle Commander," *Los Angeles Times* (August 11, 2005): p. B12.

2. S. Herbozo et al., "Beauty and Thinness Messages in Children's Media: A Content Analysis," *Eating Disorders* 12, no. 1 (2004): pp. 21–34.

3. "How to Love the Way You Look," *Teen People* (October 1999).

4. M. Peacock, "Sex, Housework, and Ads," http://femmerevolu tion.8m.com/webpage/HTML/GetInformed/houseworks.htm (accessed August 12, 2007).

5. J. Shalleck-Klein, "Striving for the Baywatch Boy Build," *Silver Chips (Silver Springs, MD, High School) Newspaper* (October 7, 1999).

6. H. Pope et al., "Evolving Ideals of Male Body Image as Seen Through Action Toys," *International Journal of Eating Disorders* 26, no. 1 (1999): pp. 65–72.

7. K. S. Schneider, "Mission Impossible," *People* (June 3, 1996): p. 64; and R. G. Wax, "Boys and Body Image," *San Diego Parent Magazine* (May 1998).

8. R. Miller, "The Plastic Surgery Company Unveils Strategic Shift to Company-Owned Centers," Banchik & Associates Press Release (November 3, 2000).

9. Ibid.

10. C. Kitch, *The Girl on the Magazine Cover: The Origins of Visual Stereotypes in American Mass Media,* 1st ed. (Chapel Hill: University of North Carolina Press, 2001).

11. Miller, "The Plastic Surgery Company Unveils Strategic Shift to Company-Owned Centers."

12. A. E. Field et al., "Exposure to the Mass Media and Weight Concerns Among Girls," *Pediatrics: Official Journal of the American Academy of Pediatrics* 103, no. 3 (1999): http://pediatrics.aappublications.org/ cgi/content/abstract/103/3/e36 (accessed August 12, 2007).

13. P. Hamburg, "The Media and Eating Disorders: Who Is Most Vulnerable?" (paper presented at the conference "Culture, Media and Eating Disorders," Cambridge, MA, 1998).

14. D. Oickle, "Health Matters," *Leeds, Grenville, and Lanark District Health Unit Newsletter* (Spring 2005), http://www.healthunit.org; and Hamburg, "The Media and Eating Disorders: Who Is Most Vulnerable?"

15. E. Dittrich, "About-Face Facts on Body Image" (2000), http:// www.about-face.org/r/facts/bi.shtml.

16. P. Young-Eisendrath, *Women and Desire: Beyond Wanting to Be Wanted* (New York: Harmony Books, 1999).

17. C. Maynard, "Body Image Quiz," available at http://www.etr.org/ recapp/ches/BodyImagequiz.htm (accessed August 12, 2007).

18. C. Stroman, "Television Viewing and Self-Concept Among Black Children," *Journal of Broadcasting and Electronic Media* 30 (1986): pp. 87–93.

19. K. R. Perkins, "The Influence of Television Images on Black Females' Self-Perceptions of Physical Attractiveness," *Journal of Black Psychology* 22, no. 4 (1996): pp. 453–469.

20. C. Stroman, "Television's Role in the Socialization of African American Children and Adolescents," *Journal of Negro Education* 60 (1991): pp. 314–326.

21. M. C. Martin and P. F. Kennedy, "Advertising and Social Comparison: Consequences for Female Pre-Adolescents and Adolescents," *Psychology and Marketing* 10 (November–December 1993): pp. 513–530; and M. C. Martin and J. W. Gentry, "Stuck in the Model

Trap: The Effects of Beautiful Models in Ads on Female Pre-Adolescents and Adolescents," *Journal of Advertising* 26, no. 2 (1997): pp. 19–33.

22. G. I. Szmukler, "The Epidemiology of Anorexia Nervosa and Bulimia," *Journal of Psychiatric Research* 19, no. 2–3 (1985): pp. 143–153.

23. S. Donaton, "Teen Titles Grow Up: Youth Boom Bodes Well for Category," *Advertising Age* 61, no. 24 (June 11, 1990): p. 41; and M. R. Solomon, R. D. Ashmore, and L. C. Longo, "The Beauty Match-Up Hypothesis: Congruence Between Types of Beauty and Product Images in Advertising," *Journal of Advertising* 21 (December 1992): pp. 23–34.

24. Martin and Gentry, "Stuck in the Model Trap: The Effects of Beautiful Models in Ads on Female Pre-Adolescents and Adolescents."

25. T. A. Brown, T. F. Cash, and S. W. Noles, "Perceptions of Physical Attractiveness Among College Students: Selected Determinants and Methodological Matters," *Journal of Social Psychology* 126, no. 3 (1986): pp. 305–316.

26. A. B. Bowers and S. Landreth, "Is Beauty Best? Highly Versus Normally Attractive Models in Advertising," *Journal of Advertising* 30, no. 1 (2001): pp. 1–12.

27. K. Dion, E. Berscheid, and E. Walster, "What Is Beautiful Is Good," *Journal of Personal Social Psychology* 24, no. 3 (1972): pp. 285–290.

28. A. G. Miller, "Role of Physical Attractiveness in Impression Formation," *Psychonomic Science* 19, no. 4 (1970): pp. 241–243.

29. A. Gillian, "Skinny Models Send Unhealthy Message," *The Guardian* (May 31, 2000), http://www.guardian.co.uk/uk_news/story/0,,326440,00.html.

30. H. Dittmar and S. Howard, "Professional Hazards? The Impact of Models' Body Size on Advertising Effectiveness and Women's Body-Focused Anxiety in Professions That Do and Do Not Emphasize the Cultural Ideal of Thinness," *The British Journal of Social Psychology* 43, no. 4 (2004): pp. 477–498.

31. C. Darwin, *The Descent of Man, and Selection in Relation to Sex,* vol. 2 (London: John Murray, 1871), p. 354.

32. N. Etcoff et al., "The Real Truth About Beauty: A Global Report—Findings of the Global Study on Women, Beauty, and Well-Being," commissioned by Dove, a Unilever Beauty Brand (September 2004), http://www.campaignforrealbeauty.com/uploadedfiles/dove_white_paper_final.pdf.

33. R. Walker, "Social Lubricant," *New York Times Magazine* (September 4, 2005): p. 23.

34. L. Kaufman, "Prime-Time Nutrition," *Journal of Communication* 30 (1980): pp. 37–46.

35. G. Fouts and K. Burggraf, "Television Situation Comedies: Female Body Images and Verbal Reinforcements," *Sex Roles: A Journal of Research* 40, no. 5/6 (1999): pp. 473–481.

36. G. Fouts, "Television Situation Comedies: Female Weight, Male Negative Comments, and Audience Reactions," *Sex Roles: A Journal of Research* (May 2000), http://www.findarticles.com/p/articles/mi_m2294/is_2000_May/ai_65306 52 7/.

37. Fouts and Burggraf, "Television Situation Comedies."

38. G. Fouts and K. Vaughan, "Television Situation Comedies: Male Weight, Negative References, and Audience Reactions," *Sex Roles: A Journal of Research* 46, no. 11/12 (2002): pp. 439–442.

39. M. J. Wolf, "Larry Mintz Talks About Sitcom Production," personal communication and interview, Los Angeles, CA, September 21, 2005.

40. J. Tisdall, "Demand for More Ugly People on TV," *Aftenposten: News from Norway* (October 17, 2002), http://www.aftenposten.no/english/local/article419740.ece.

41. L. Hirschberg, "Giving Them What They Want," *New York Times Magazine* (September 4, 2005): p. 30 (Section 6), http://www.nytimes.com/2005/09/04/magazine/04MOONVES.html?pagewanted=1&ei=5088&en=ef2eed3e40ce14d9&ex=1283486400.

42. Ibid.

CHAPTER 9

1. All details of the Deleese Williams story, including comments from her family members and lawyer, were originally reported in M. Caruso, "'Extreme' Tragedy. 'Ugly' Mom Sues ABC for Nixing Makeover," *(New York) Daily News* (September 18, 2005): p. 3.

2. S. Lundahl and C. Vallejos-Bartlett, "BodyWise Handbook: Eating Disorders Information for Middle School Personnel" (Washington, DC: U.S. Department of Health and Human Services, 2005), 3rd ed., http://www.4woman.gov/bodyimage/kids/bodywise.

3. H. Steiner et al., "Risk and Protective Factors for Juvenile Eating Disorders," *European Child & Adolescent Psychiatry [Suppl 1]* 12 (2003): pp. 38–46.

4. Lundahl and Vallejos-Bartlett, "BodyWise Handbook."

5. G. Groth-Marnat and N. Michel, "Dissociation, Comorbidity of Dissociative Disorders, and Childhood Abuse in a Community Sample of Women with Current and Past Bulimia," *Social Behavior and Personality: An International Journal* 28, no. 3 (2000): pp. 279–292.

6. Anna Westin's story as told by J. Jahraus in "American Realities: The Changing Face of Eating Disorders," Congressional briefing before the U.S. Senate, December 2, 2003, http://www.eatingdisorderscoalition.org.

7. The detailed recounting of the Terri Schiavo story is based on the editorial titled "Deadly Diets: Eating Disorders Warrant More Attention," *Daytona Beach News-Journal* (March 31, 2005): p. 4 (Section A).

8. H. Pope, Jr., K. A. Phillips, and R. Olivardia, *The Adonis Complex: The Secret Crisis of Male Body Obsession* (New York: The Free Press, 2000).
9. A. Gurian, "Body Dysmorphic Disorder: An Extreme Distortion," *Letter: Child Study Center* 6, no. 4 (March/April 2002): pp. 1–4.
10. Ibid.
11. E. Stice et al., "Body-Image and Eating Disturbances Predict Onset of Depression Among Female Adolescents: A Longitudinal Study," *Journal of Abnormal Psychology* 109, no. 3 (2000): pp. 438–444.
12. B. L. Fredrickson et al., "That Swimsuit Becomes You: Sex Differences in Self-Objectification, Restrained Eating, and Math Performance," *Journal of Personality and Social Psychology* 75, no. 1 (1998): pp. 269–284.
13. S. M. Harris, "Body Attitudes and the Psychosocial Development of College Women," *The Journal of Psychology* 129 (1995): pp. 315–330.
14. D. A. Blyth, R. G. Simmons, and D. F. Zakin, "Satisfaction with Body Image for Early Adolescent Females: The Impact of Pubertal Timing Within Different School Environments," *Journal of Youth and Adolescence* 14 (1985): pp. 207–225.
15. K. Lang and G. E. Lang, "The Mass Media and Voting," in *Reader in Public Opinion and Communication*, ed. B. Berelson and M. Janowitz (New York: The Free Press, 1966): pp. 455–472.
16. C. Davis et al., "Looking Good—Family Focus on Appearance and the Risk for Eating Disorders," *International Journal of Eating Disorders* 35, no. 2 (2004): pp. 136–144.

CHAPTER 10

1. Details of Irena Medavoy's story are taken from "Battle over Botox: Lawsuit Alleges Malpractice from Hollywood Doctor," NBC News (June 17, 2004), http://www.msnbc.com/news/927823.asp.
2. T. Spee, "Top Defense Verdicts of 2004: Medavoy v. Klein," *Daily Journal Extra: Supplement to the Los Angeles Daily Journal and San Francisco Daily Journal* (January 31, 2005), http://www.swlaw.com/publications/files/Snell_&_WilmerTop_Defense_Verdicts.pdf.
3. J. Appleby, "219 Doctors Purchase Botox Knockoff," *USAToday.com* (February 22, 2005), http://www.usatoday.com/news/health/2005-02-21-fake-botox-usat_x.htm.
4. C. B. Castillo, "Professor of Ophthalmology/Director of Oculo-Facial Plastic Surgery at University of Kentucky Charged in Fake Botox Prosecution," U.S. Attorney for the Southern District of Florida (2005), http://pacer.flsd.uscourts.gov; and A. Fantz, "Physician Couple Enter Plea in Sale of Toxic Botox Knockoff," *Miami Herald* (November 15, 2005), http://www.federalcrimesblog.com/2005/11/mail-fraud-and-conspiracyfake-botox.html.

5. Appleby, "219 Doctors Purchase Botox Knockoff."

6. Interview comments from Dr. Steven Victor are from B. L. Keil, "So What If It's Not Approved? Patients Demand It. Doctors Inject It. But Is It Safe?" *New York* 36, no. 34 (October 6, 2003): p. 49.

7. Ibid.

8. Ibid.

9. Ibid.

10. R. Alonso-Zaldivar, "FDA Slow to Sound Alarm on Pain Drug," *Los Angeles Times* (November 5, 2005): pp. A1, A30, A31.

11. Keil, "So What If It's Not Approved? Patients Demand It. Doctors Inject It. But Is It Safe?"

12. R. Alonso-Zaldivar, "Probe Finds FDA Deviated in Morning-After Pill Decision," *Los Angeles Times* (November 15, 2005): pp. A1, A19.

13. Details of Melanie's case against the Florida Center for Cosmetic Surgery, including all interview comments, are from A. Harrell, "Cosmetic Surgery Clinic Settles 18 Lawsuits, 5 Pending," *Boca Raton News* (April 17, 2004), http://www.bocanews.com/index.php?src=news&prid=8036&category=LOCAL %20NEWS.

14. Details of Mona Alley's case are also from Harrell, "Cosmetic Surgery Clinic Settles 18 Lawsuits, 5 Pending."

15. The stories of Adrianna Arroyo, Katherine Kennedy, and other former patients of the Florida Center for Cosmetic Surgery are from Harrell, "Cosmetic Surgery Clinic Settles 18 Lawsuits, 5 Pending."

16. J. Morelli, "Deaths from Liposuction Too High, Study Shows," *WebMD* (2000), http://www.webmd.com/content/article/17/1676_50256.htm.

17. Details of novelist Olivia Goldsmith's death are from the following sources: R. Gardner, Jr., "Looks to Die For," *New York* 37, no. 5 (February 16, 2004): p. 50; and A. Kuczynski and W. St. John, "Why Did They Die in Cosmetic Surgery?" *New York Times* (June 20, 2004): pp. 1, 10 (Section Nine).

18. Details of Susan Malitz's story are from Kuczynski and St. John, "Why Did They Die in Cosmetic Surgery?"

19. Details of Stella Obasanjo's story are from G. Tremlett, "Spanish Look into Death of Nigerian First Lady After Cosmetic Surgery," *The Guardian* (October 25, 2005): p. 18, http://www.guardian.co.uk/spain/article/0,2763,1599889,00.html.

20. Details of the case against Gregorio Nosovsky were originally reported by the Associated Press in "State Says Surgeon Had Many Patients, No License: A Clinic Where He and His Brother—a Real Doctor—Did Cosmetic Surgery Is Closed After Several Women Complain of Disfiguring Results," *St. Petersburg Times: Online* (May 5, 2005), http://www.sptimes.com/2005/05/05/State/State_says_surgeon_ha.shtml.

21. J. Steinhoff, "Waukesha Woman Dies from Breast Implant Surgery," *(Milwaukee) Shepherd-Express* (March 2, 2004).

22. D. Kapelovitz, "Slaves to the Scalpel: Cosmetic-Surgery Junkies," *Hustler* (November 2002), http://www.kapelovitz.com/plastic.htm.

23. C. Jackson, *Living Doll: Cindy Jackson* (London: Metro Publishing, 2002).

24. Kapelovitz, "Slaves to the Scalpel: Cosmetic-Surgery Junkies."

25. Details of the stories of "Jen X," Rhiannon, and Amanda Lepore are from Kapelovitz, "Slaves to the Scalpel: Cosmetic-Surgery Junkies."

26. Kapelovitz, "Slaves to the Scalpel: Cosmetic-Surgery Junkies."

27. Elaine Young's story originally appeared in Kapelovitz, "Slaves to the Scalpel: Cosmetic-Surgery Junkies."

28. K. A. Phillips and R. G. Dufresne, Jr., "Body Dysmorphic Disorder: A Guide for Dermatologists and Cosmetic Surgeons," *American Journal of Clinical Dermatology* 1, no. 4 (July–August 2000): pp. 235–243.

29. Kapelovitz, "Slaves to the Scalpel: Cosmetic-Surgery Junkies."

30. All interview comments from Dr. Z. Paul Lorenc are from W. Lawson, "In the Name of Beauty," *Psychology Today* 38, no. 3 (May–June 2005), http://www.psychologytoday.com/articles/pto-20050506-000001.html.

31. B. Alexander, "Sexploration: Plastic Surgery on Private Parts," MSNBC Interactive (2005), http://www.msnbc.msn.com/id/813 2227/.

32. Details of Dr. David Matlock's LVR procedure and Dr. Joe Berenholz's practice are from S. Klein, "Does This Make My Labia Look Fat?" *(Detroit) Metro Times* (March 9, 2005), http://www.metro times.com/editorial/story.asp?id=7405.

33. Klein, "Does This Make My Labia Look Fat?"

34. M. Navarro, "The Most Private of Makeovers," *New York Times* (November 28, 2004), http://www.nytimes.com/2004/11/28/fash ion/28PLAS.html?pagewanted=1&ei=5070&en=a53b510cfebfac66 &ex=1165294800&adxnnl=1&adxnnlx=11651621425XeecPlbtKY7 Ce7WmBbTBw.

35. Klein, "Does This Make My Labia Look Fat?"

36. Ibid.

37. Ibid.

38. Ibid.

39. Navarro, "The Most Private of Makeovers."

CHAPTER 11

1. All interview comments from Dr. David Matlock and details of LVRI's business operations are from S. Klein, "Does This Make My Labia Look Fat?" *(Detroit) Metro Times* (March 9, 2005), http://www .metrotimes.com/editorial/story.asp?id=7405.

2. Klein, "Does This Make My Labia Look Fat?"

3. E. Goodman, "The Ugly Truth of Breast Implants," *Los Angeles Times* (November 4, 2003): p. B13.

4. Klein, "Does This Make My Labia Look Fat?"

5. D. Kapelovitz, "Slaves to the Scalpel: Cosmetic-Surgery Junkies," *Hustler* (November 2002), http://www.kapelovitz.com/plastic.htm.

6. Ibid.

7. Ibid.

8. M. Austin, "Dentists Moving Beyond Mouths: Offering of Cosmetic Surgery Draws Intense Complaints from Plastic Surgeons," *Denver Post* (March 23, 2004), http://global.lexisnexis.com (accessed August 12, 2007; fee-paid subscription required).

9. To read the text sent by Governor Schwarzenegger to the California State Senate announcing his veto of Senate Bill 1336 that would have permitted dentists to perform cosmetic surgery see http://www.gov ernor.ca.gov/govsite/pdf/press_release/SB_1336_veto.pdf; and for opposing discussion concerning his later approval of Senate Bill 438 on October 4, 2006, to permit dentists to perform cosmetic surgery see http://www.plasticsurgery.org/medical_professionals/publications/ PSNews-Bulletin-10-4-2006.cfm.

10. The history of Profiles & Contours is from J. Berry, "Tummy Tucks Get a Slicker Sell," *Ad Week* 31 (August 13, 1990): p. 17.

11. Berry, "Tummy Tucks Get a Slicker Sell."

12. "Pots of Promise: The Beauty Business," *Economist* 367, no. 8325 (May 22, 2003): p. 71.

13. Ibid.

14. A. Colbert, "11.9 Million Cosmetic Procedures in 2004: American Society for Aesthetic Plastic Surgery Reports 44 Percent Increase," *American Society for Aesthetic Plastic Surgery* (February 17, 2005).

15. L. D. Maloney, "Just for Appearance Sake: High-Power Light Treatments Target Unsightly Skin Conditions," *Design News* 60, no. 18 (December 5, 2005): p. S13.

16. "Pots of Promise: The Beauty Business."

17. "World Consumer Goods: Key Player—L'Oreal," TMCnet News, August 13, 2007, http://www.tmcnet.com/usubmit/2007/08/13/ 2859289.htm; and A. Lagorce, "L'Oreal Quarterly Sales Rise 10%, Outlook Maintained," MarketWatch, July 13, 2007, http://www .marketwatch.com/news/story/loreal-sales-rise-10-performance/story .aspx?guid=%7BD7325BF6-4B3E-4E92-B4EC- FF2742FBDA9E%7D.

18. "Pots of Promise: The Beauty Business."

19. B. Didcock, "Will the Real John Wayne Please Stand Up? The Hell He Will . . ." *The (Edinburgh, UK) Scotsman* (April 26, 1997), http:// global.lexisnexis.com (accessed October 12, 2007; fee-paid subscription required).

20. N. Etcoff et al., "The Real Truth About Beauty: A Global Report— Findings of the Global Study on Women, Beauty, and Well-Being," commissioned by Dove, a Unilever Beauty Brand (September 2004), http://www.campaignforrealbeauty.com/uploadedfiles/dove_white _paper_final.pdf.

21. Goodman, "The Ugly Truth of Breast Implants"; and D. Fallik, "As Seniors Live Longer, Healthier, Cosmetic Surgeries Get New Look," *The Philadelphia Inquirer* (September 27, 2005): p. 1.

22. M. Lacey, "Remote and Poked, Anthropology's Dream Tribe," *New York Times* (December 18, 2005): pp. 1, 6 (Section One).

References

Abwender, D. A., and K. Hough. "Interactive Effects of Characteristics of Defendant and Mock Juror on U.S. Participants' Judgment and Sentencing Recommendations." *The Journal of Social Psychology* 141, no. 5 (2001): 603–616.

Adams, G. R., and A. S. Cohen. "Children's Physical and Interpersonal Characteristics That Affect Student-Teacher Interactions." *The Journal of Experimental Education* 43 (1974): 1–5.

Adams, G. R., and P. Crane. "An Assessment of Parents' and Teachers' Expectations of Preschool Children's Social Preference for Attractive or Unattractive Children and Adults." *Child Development* 51 (1980): 224–231.

Adler, A. *Understanding Human Nature.* London: George Alan & Unwin, 1932.

Agocha, V. B., and M. L. Cooper. "Risk Perceptions and Safer-Sex Intentions: Does a Partner's Physical Attractiveness Undermine the Use of Risk-Relevant Information?" *Personality and Social Psychology Bulletin* 25, no. 6 (1999): 751–765.

Aguirre, M. "Dress and Female Seduction in Ancient Greece: Literature and Art." Paper presented at the conference "Clothed Body in the Ancient World," Milton Keynes, UK, 2002.

Ahrens, F. "Pounds of Political Prevention: Doug Duncan Losing Weight to Ensure an Electoral Gain." *The Washington Post* (November 3, 1997): D9.

Alexander, B. "Sexploration: Plastic Surgery on Private Parts." MSNBC Interactive (2005): http://www.msnbc.msn.com/id/8132227/.

Alkon, A. "Waist Removal." Advicegoddess.com (2003): http://www.advicegoddess.com/columns/column57.htm.

Almond, B. J. "Beauty and The 'Beastly Effect.'" *Sallyport: The Magazine of Rice University* 59, no. 1 (2002): http://www.rice.edu/sallyport/2002/fall/sallyport/beautyandthebeastlyeffect.html.

Alonso-Zaldivar, R. "FDA Slow to Sound Alarm on Pain Drug." *Los Angeles Times* (November 5, 2005): A1, A30, A31.

———. "Probe Finds FDA Deviated in Morning-After Pill Decision." *Los Angeles Times* (November 15, 2005): A1, A19.

Ambady, N., and R. Rosenthal. "Half a Minute: Predicting Teacher Evaluations from Thin Slices of Nonverbal Behavior and Physical Attractiveness." *Journal of Personality and Social Psychology* 64 (1993): 431–441.

———. "Thin Slices of Expressive Behavior as Predictors of Interpersonal Consequences: A Meta-Analysis." *Psychological Bulletin* 111 (1992): 256–274.

American Society for Aesthetic Plastic Surgery. "Cosmetic Surgery National Data Bank Statistics" (2004): http://www.surgery.org/download/2004-stats.p.

———. "Patient Safety Initiative Outreaches to Hispanics" (2004): http://surgery.org/press/news-release.php?iid=350.

Appleby, J. "219 Doctors Purchase Botox Knockoff." USAToday.com (February 22, 2005): http://www.usatoday.com/news/health/2005-02-21-fake-botox-usat_x.htm.

Aronson, E., T. D. Wilson, and R. M. Akert. *Social Psychology*. Upper Saddle River, NJ: Prentice Hall, 2002.

Associated Press. "State Says Surgeon Had Many Patients, No License: A Clinic Where He and His Brother—a Real Doctor—Did Cosmetic Surgery Is Closed After Several Women Complain of Disfiguring Results." *St. Petersburg Times Online* (May 5, 2005): http://www.sptimes.com/2005/05/05/State/State_says_surgeon_ha.shtml.

Austin, M. "Dentists Moving Beyond Mouths: Offering of Cosmetic Surgery Draws Intense Complaints from Plastic Surgeons." *Denver Post* (March 23, 2004): http://global.lexisnexis.com (access through Lexis-Nexis to this original source requires fee-paid subscription).

Badr, K. L., and B. Abdallah. "Physical Attractiveness of Premature Infants Affects Outcome at Discharge from NICU (Neonatal Intensive Care Unit)." *Infant Behavior and Development* 24, no. 1 (2001): 129–133.

Baker-Sperry, L., and L. Grauerholz. "The Pervasiveness and Persistence of the Feminine Beauty Ideal in Children's Fairy Tales." *Gender and Society* 17, no. 5 (2003): 711–726.

Barber, N. "Mustache Fashion Covaries with a Good Marriage Market for Women." *Journal of Nonverbal Behavior* 25, no. 4 (2001): 261–272.

Barden, R. C., M. E. Ford, A. G. Jensen, M. Rogiers-Salyer, and K. E. Salyer. "Effects of Craniofacial Deformity in Infancy on the Quality of Mother-Infant Interactions." *Child Development* 60 (1989): 819–824.

Berkowitz, L., and N. Frodi. "Reactions to a Child's Mistake as Affected by His/Her Looks." *Psychiatry* 42 (1979): 420–425.

Berry, J. "Tummy Tucks Get a Slicker Sell." *Ad Week* (August 13, 1990): 17.

Berscheid, E., and E. Walster. "Physical Attractiveness." In *Advances in Experimental Social Psychology* vol. 7, edited by L. Berkowitz, 157–215. New York: Academic Press, 1974.

Betzig, L. *People Are Animals in Human Nature: A Critical Reader.* Edited by Laura Betzig. New York: Oxford University Press, 1997.

Blyth, D. A., R. G. Simmons, and D. F. Zakin. "Satisfaction with Body Image for Early Adolescent Females: The Impact of Pubertal Timing Within Different School Environments." *Journal of Youth and Adolescence,* vol. 14 (1985): 207–225.

Bowers, A. B., and S. Landreth. "Is Beauty Best? Highly Versus Normally Attractive Models in Advertising." *Journal of Advertising* 30, no. 1 (2001): 1–12.

Bowling for Columbine. Directed by Michael Moore. Alliance Atlantis Communications, 2002.

Brown, J. D., N. J. Novick, K. A. Lord, and J. M. Richards. "When Gulliver Travels: Social Context, Psychological Closeness, and Self-Appraisals." *Journal of Personality and Social Psychology* 62 (1992): 717–727.

Brown, T. A., T. F. Cash, and S. W. Noles. "Perceptions of Physical Attractiveness Among College Students: Selected Determinants and Methodological Matters." *Journal of Social Psychology* 126, no. 3 (1986): 305–316.

Buss, D. M. *Evolutionary Psychology: The New Science of the Mind.* Boston: Allyn & Bacon, 1999.

Buss, D. M., T. K. Shackelford, L. A. Kirkpatrick, and R. J. Larsen. "A Half Century of Mate Preferences: The Cultural Evolution of Values." *Journal of Marriage and Family* 63, no. 2 (2001): 491–503.

Cable, D. M., and T. A. Judge. "The Effect of Physical Height on Workplace Success and Income: Preliminary Test of a Theoretical Model." *Journal of Applied Psychology* 89, no. 3 (2004): 428–441.

Cahoon, D. D., and E. M. Edmonds. "Estimates of Opposite-Sex First Impressions Related to Females' Clothing Style." *Bulletin of the Psychonomic Society of Augusta College* 65, no. 2 (1989): 171–173.

Camerer, C. "The Psychology of Strategic Thinking." Working paper. Pasadena, CA: Caltech, 1999.

Caruso, M. " 'Extreme' Tragedy. 'Ugly' Mom Sues ABC for Nixing Makeover." *(New York) Daily News* (September 18, 2005): 3.

Cash, T. F., and A. S. Labarge. "Development of the Appearance Schemas Inventory: A New Cognitive Body-Image Assessment." *Cognitive Therapy and Research* 20 (1996): 37–50.

Cash, T. F., B. Gillen, and S. D. Burns. "Sexism and Beautyism in Personnel Consultant Decision Making." *Journal of Applied Psychology* 62, no. 3 (1977): 301–310.

Cash, T. F., D. W. Cash, and J. W. Butters. " 'Mirror, Mirror, on the Wall . . . ?' Contrast Effects and Self-Evaluations of Physical Attractiveness." *Personality and Social Psychology Bulletin* 9 (1983): 351–358.

Castillo, C. B. "Professor of Ophthalmology/Director of Oculo-Facial Plastic Surgery at University of Kentucky Charged in Fake Botox Prosecution." U.S. Attorney for the Southern District of Florida (2005): http://pacer.flsd.uscourts.gov.

CBS Television Network. "The Look of Abercrombie & Fitch." *60 Minutes,* December 5, 2003.

Chavez, P. "Abercrombie & Fitch to Pay $50 Million to Settle Discrimination Case." Associated Press (November 16, 2004): http://www.billings gazette.com/newdex.php?display=rednews/2004/11/16/build/busi ness/40-abercrombie-suit.inc.

Christensen, S. "The Quest for Equality." *Queensland University of Technology Law & Justice Journal* 3, no. 1 (2003): 76.

Cicero, M. T. *Cicero: The Nature of the Gods (De Natura Deorum).* Translated by Harris Racham. Cambridge, MA: Harvard University Press, Loeb Classical Library, 1933.

Clifford, M. M., and E. Walster. "Research Note: The Effect of Physical Attractiveness on Teacher Expectations." *Sociology of Education* 46 (1973): 238–258.

CNN.com. "Are U.S. Schools Safe?" In-Depth Specials, http://www.cnn .com/SPECIALS/1998/schools/ (accessed December 8, 2006).

Cohen, R., R. C. Klesges, M. Summerville, and A. W. Meyers. "A Developmental Analysis of the Influence of Body Weight on the Sociometry of Children." *Addictive Behaviors* 14 (1989): 473–476.

Colbert, A. "11.9 Million Cosmetic Procedures in 2004: American Society for Aesthetic Plastic Surgery Reports 44 Percent Increase." American Society for Aesthetic Plastic Surgery (February 17, 2005).

Collins, M. E. "Body Figure Perceptions and Preferences Among Preadolescent Children." *International Journal of Eating Disorders* 10, no. 2 (1991): 199–208.

Craft, L. L., and D. M. Landers. "Effect of Exercise on Clinical Depression and Depression Resulting from Mental Illness: A Meta-Analysis." *Journal of Sport and Exercise Psychology* 20 (1998): 339–357.

Critser, G. *Fat Land: How Americans Became the Fattest People in the World.* New York: Houghton-Mifflin, 2003.

Crowder, J. R., and L. S. Hunter. "Nursing Students' Perceptions of Infant Attractiveness." Paper presented at the Annual Conference of the Society for Research in Child Development, Tampa, FL, 2003.

Daly, M. "Evolutionary Theory and Parental Motives." In *Mammalian Parenting,* edited by N. A. Krasnegor and R. S. Bridges. New York: Oxford University Press, 1990.

Daly, M., and M. Wilson. "Discriminative Parental Solicitude and the Relevance of Evolutionary Models to the Analysis of Motivational Systems." In *The Cognitive Neurosciences,* edited by M. S. Gassaniga, 1269–1286. Cambridge, MA: MIT Press, 1995.

Darby, B. W., and D. Jeffers. "The Effects of Defendant and Juror Attractiveness on Simulated Courtroom Trial Decisions." *Social Behavior and Personality: An International Journal* 16, no. 1 (1988): 39–50.

Davis, C., B. Shuster, E. Blackmore, and J. Fox. "Looking Good—Family Focus on Appearance and the Risk for Eating Disorders." *International Journal of Eating Disorders* 35, no. 2 (2004): 136–144.

Davis, C., G. Claridge, and J. Fox. "Not Just a Pretty Face: Physical Attractiveness and Perfectionism in the Risk for Eating Disorders." *International Journal of Eating Disorders* 27, no. 1 (2000): 67–73.

"Deadly Diets: Eating Disorders Warrant More Attention." *(Daytona Beach) News Journal* (editorial) (March 31, 2005): 4 (Section A).

DeBenedettem, V. "Two Plastic Surgery Deaths Underscore Risks of Anesthesia." *Drug Topics* (November 3, 2005): http://www.drugtopics.com/drugtopics/article/articleDetail.jsp?id=119402.

Deutsch, F. M. "Status, Sex, and Smiling: The Effect of Role on Smiling in Men and Women." *Personality and Social Psychology Bulletin* 16 (1990): 531–540.

Didcock, B. "Will the Real John Wayne Please Stand Up? The Hell He Will . . ." *The Scotsman* (Edinburgh) (April 26, 1997): http://global.lexisnexis.com (access through LexisNexis to this original source requires fee-paid subscription).

Diener, E., B. Wolsic, and F. Fujita. "Physical Attractiveness and Subjective Well-Being." *Journal of Personality and Social Psychology* 69, no. 1 (1995): 120–129.

Dion, K., E. Berscheid, and E. Walster. "What Is Beautiful Is Good." *Journal of Personal Social Psychology* 24, no. 3 (1972): 285–290.

Dion, K. K. "Physical Attractiveness and Evaluation of Children's Transgressions." *Journal of Personality and Social Psychology* 24, no. 2 (1972): 207–213.

Dittmar, H., and S. Howard. "Professional Hazards? The Impact of Models' Body Size on Advertising Effectiveness and Women's Body-Focused Anxiety in Professions That Do and Do Not Emphasize the Cultural Ideal of Thinness." *The British Journal of Social Psychology* 43, no. 4 (2004): 477–498.

Dittrich, E. "About-Face Facts on Body Image." (2000): http://www.about-face.org/r/facts/bi.shtml.

Donaton, S. "Teen Titles Grow Up: Youth Boom Bodes Well for Category." *Advertising Age* 61, no. 24 (June 11, 1990): 41.

Downs, A. C., and P. M. Lyons. "Natural Observations of the Links Between Attractiveness and Initial Legal Judgments." *Personality and Social Psychology Bulletin* 17 (1991): 541–547.

Dushenko, T. W., R. P. Perry, J. Schilling, and S. Smolarski. "Generality of the Physical Attractiveness Stereotype for Age and Sex." *Journal of Social Psychology* 105 (1978): 303–304.

Efran, M. G. "The Effect of Physical Appearance on the Judgment of Guilt, Interpersonal Attraction, and Severity of Recommended Punishment in a Simulated Jury Task." *Journal of Research in Personality* 8 (1974): 45–54.

Egan, J. "Love in the Time of No Time." *New York Times Magazine* 53, no. 20 (November 23, 2003): 66 (Section Six).

Ellison, P. T. *Ecology, Reproduction, and Human Evolution.* New York: Aldine de Gruyter, 2001.

Epps, S. "Labeling Effects of Infant Health and Parent Demographics on

Nurses' Ratings of Preterm Infant Behavior." *IMHJ (University of Nebraska Medical Center)* 14, no. 3 (1993): 182–191.

Erler, J. "Why Nothing Is Beautiful: Physical Attractiveness in Latin Literature." Paper presented at the American Philological Association (APA) Annual Conference, San Diego, CA, 2001.

Etcoff, N., S. Orbach, J. Scott, and H. D'Agostino. "The Real Truth About Beauty: A Global Report—Findings of the Global Study on Women, Beauty, and Well-Being." Study commissioned by Dove, a Unilever Beauty Brand (September 2004): http://www.campaignforrealbeauty.com/uploadedfiles/dove_white_paper_final.pdf.

Eyewitness to History.com. "Views of President Lincoln, 1861," http://www.eyewitnesstohistory.com/index.html (accessed December 12, 2005).

Fallik, D. "As Seniors Live Longer, Healthier, Cosmetic Surgeries Get New Look." *Philadelphia Inquirer* (September 27, 2005): 1.

Fancher, R. E. *Pioneers of Psychology.* New York: Norton, 1990.

Fantz, A. "Two More Plead Guilty in Fake Botox Case." *Miami Herald* (November 14, 2005): http://www.miami.com/mld/miamiherald/13165368.htm.

Farley, S. D., R. C. Chia, and L. J. Allred. "Stereotypes About Attractiveness: When Beautiful Is Not Better." *Journal of Social Behavior and Personality* 13 (1998): 479–492.

Field, A. E., L. Cheung, A. M. Wolf, D. B. Herzog, S. L. Gortmaker, and G. A. Colditz, "Exposure to the Mass Media and Weight Concerns Among Girls," *Pediatrics: Official Journal of the American Academy of Pediatrics* 103, no. 3 (1999): http://pediatrics.aappublications.org/cgi/content/abstract/103/3/e36 (accessed August 12, 2007).

Fiske, J. *Television Culture.* London: Methuen, 1987.

Fletcher, J. "The Decorated Body in Ancient Egypt: Hairstyles, Cosmetics, and Tattoos." Paper presented at the conference "Clothed Body in the Ancient World," Milton Keynes, UK, 2002.

Fouts, G. "Television Situation Comedies: Female Weight, Male Negative Comments, and Audience Reactions." *Sex Roles: A Journal of Research* (May 2000): http://www.findarticles.com/p/articles/mi_m2294/is_2000_May/ai_65306527/.

Fouts, G., and K. Burggraf. "Television Situation Comedies: Female Body Images and Verbal Reinforcements." *Sex Roles: A Journal of Research* 40, no. 5/6 (1999): 473–481.

Fouts, G., and K. Vaughan. "Television Situation Comedies: Male Weight, Negative References, and Audience Reactions." *Sex Roles: A Journal of Research* 46, no. 11/12 (2002): 439–442.

Fox, R. F. *Harvesting Minds: How TV Commercials Control Kids.* Westport, CT: Praeger Publishing, 1996.

Fredrickson, B. L., T. A. Roberts, S. M. Noll, D. M. Quinn, and J. M. Twenge. "That Swimsuit Becomes You: Sex Differences in Self-Objectification, Restrained Eating, and Math Performance." *Journal of Personality and Social Psychology* 75, no. 1 (1998): 269–284.

Frubeck, G. "Childhood Obesity: Time for Action, Not Complacency." *British Medical Journal* 320 (2000): 323.

Gale Encyclopedia of Medicine. 2nd ed. Edited by Jacqueline L. Longe and Deirdre S. Blachfield. Vol. 1. Detroit, MI: Thompson Gale, 2001.

Gardner, R., Jr. "Looks to Die For." *New York* 37, no. 5 (February 16, 2004): 50.

Geiselman, R. E., N. A. Haight, and L. G. Kimata. "Context Effects in the Perceived Physical Attractiveness of Faces." *Journal of Experimental Social Psychology* 20, no. 5 (1984): 409–424.

Gillian, A. "Skinny Models Send Unhealthy Message." *Guardian* (May 31, 2000): http://www.guardian.co.uk/uk_news/story/0,,326440,00.html.

Gilmore, D. C., T. A. Beehr, and K. G. Love. "Effects of Applicant Sex, Applicant Physical Attractiveness, Type of Rater, and Type of Job on Interview Decisions." *Journal of Occupational Psychology* 59, no. 2 (1986): 103–109.

Goldenson, L. H., and M. J. Wolf. *Beating the Odds.* New York: Scribner, 1992.

Goode, E. "Gender and Courtship Entitlement: Responses to Personal Ads." *Sex Roles: A Journal of Research* 34 (1996): 141–169.

Goodman, E. "The Ugly Truth of Breast Implants." *Los Angeles Times* (November 4, 2003): B13.

Gortmaker, S. L., A. V. Must, J. M. Perrin, A. M. Sobol, and W. H. Dietz. "Social and Economic Consequences of Overweight in Adolescence and Young Adulthood." *New England Journal of Medicine* 14 (1993): 1008–1012.

Gross, S. R. "Expert Evidence." *Wisconsin Law Review* (November/December 1991): 1113–1232: http://global.lexisnexis.com (access through LexisNexis to this original source requires fee-paid subscription).

Groth Marnat, G., and N. Michel. "Dissociation, Comorbidity of Dissociative Disorders, and Childhood Abuse in a Community Sample of Women with Current and Past Bulimia." *Social Behavior and Personality: An International Journal* 28, no. 3 (2000): 279–292.

Gurian, A. "Body Dysmorphic Disorder: An Extreme Distortion." *Letter: Child Study Center* 6, no. 4 (March/April 2002): 1–4.

Haddock, V. "Here's Lookin' at You, Kid: In the Mayoral Race, the Hunk Factor Is No Junk, Say the Experts." *The (San Francisco) Chronicle* (December 7, 2003): D1, http://www.sfgate.com/cgi-bin/article.cgi?f=/c/a/2003/12/07/ING7N3F9H91.DTL.

Hamburg, P. "The Media and Eating Disorders: Who Is Most Vulnerable?" Paper presented at the conference "Culture, Media and Eating Disorders," Cambridge, MA, 1998.

Hamermesh, D., and A. Parker. "Beauty in the Classroom: Professors' Pulchritude and Putative Pedagogical Productivity." National Bureau of Economic Research, NBER Paper No. W9853 (2003).

Hamermesh, D., and J. Biddle. "Beauty and the Labor Market." *American Economic Review* 84 (1994): 1174–1194.

Hamermesh, D., X. Meng, and J. Zhang. "Dress for Success: Does Primping Pay?" National Bureau of Economic Research, NBER Paper No. 7167 (1999).

Harley, W. F., Jr. *His Needs, Her Needs: Building an Affair-Proof Marriage.* Grand Rapids, MI: Baker Book House Company, 2003.

Harper, B. "Beauty, Stature, and the Labour Market: A British Cohort Study." *Oxford Bulletin of Economics and Statistics* 62, no. 771–800 (2000).

Harper, B. L. "Vanity Fair." *Philippine Daily Inquirer* (June 3, 2003): 7.

Harr, D. A. "Halo Effect: The Impact of Differences Between Target and Receiver." Missouri Western State College (December 4, 2003): http://clear inghouse.missouriwestern.edu/manuscripts/438.asp?logon = &code = .

Harrell, A. "Cosmetic Surgery Clinic Settles 18 Lawsuits, 5 Pending." *Boca Raton News* (April 17, 2004): http://www.bocanews.com/index.php?s rc=news&prid=8036&category=LOCAL%20NEWS.

Harris, S. M. "Body Attitudes and the Psychosocial Development of College Women." *The Journal of Psychology* 129 (1995): 315–330.

Hartley, R. "Imagine You're Clever." *Journal of Child Psychology and Psychiatry* 27, no. 3 (1986): 383–396.

Hashimoto, M., and B. T. Yu. "Specific Capital, Employment Contracts, and Wage Rigidity." *Bell Journal of Economics* 11 (1980): 536–549.

Hasuike, R. "Credibility and Gender in the Courtroom." *The Practical Litigator* 11, no. 3 (2000): 19–29.

Hatfield, E., and S. Sprecher. *Mirror, Mirror: The Importance of Looks in Everyday Life.* Albany, NY: State University of New York Press, 1986.

Health24.com. "Fairy Tales Knock Self-Esteem." Child: Emotions & Behaviour, http://www.health24.com/child/Emotions_behaviour/833-854,25584.asp (accessed December 12, 2006.).

Heinberg, L., K. Thompson, and S. Stormer. "Development and Validation of the Sociocultural Attitudes Towards Appearance Questionnaire." *International Journal of Eating Disorders* 17, no. 1 (1995): 81–89.

Herbozo, S., S. Tantleff-Dunn, J. Gokee-Larose, and J. K. Thompson. "Beauty and Thinness Messages in Children's Media: A Content Analysis." *Eating Disorders* 12, no. 1 (2004): 21–34.

Hirschberg, L. "Giving Them What They Want." *New York Times Magazine* (September 4, 2005): 30 (Section 6), http://www.nytimes.com/2005/09/04/magazine/04MOONVES.html?pagewanted=1&ei=5088&en=ef2eed3e40ce14d9&ex=1283486400.

Homer. *The Iliad.* Translated by Robert Fagles. New York: Penguin Books, 1990.

Hoover, J. H., and R. Oliver. *The Bullying Prevention Handbook: A Guide for Teachers, Administrators, and Counselors.* Bloomington, IN: National Educational Service, 1996.

Horvarth, T. "Correlates of Physical Beauty in Men and Women." *Social Behaviour and Personality* 7 (1979): 145–151.

Hotz, R. L. "With Ancient Jewelry, It's the Thought That Counts." *Los Angeles Times* (April 16, 2004): A1, A15.

Hughes, S. M., and G. G. Gallup. "Sex Differences in Morphological Predictors of Sexual Behaviour. Shoulder to Hip and Waist to Hip Ratios." *Evolution and Human Behaviour* 24 (2003): 173–178.

Jackson, C. *Living Doll: Cindy Jackson.* London: Metro Publishing, 2002.

Jackson, L. A., L. A. Sullivan, and C. N. Hodge. "Stereotype Effects of Attributions, Predictions, and Evaluations: No Two Social Judgments Are Quite Alike." *Journal of Personality and Social Psychology* 65 (1993): 69–84.

Jacobson, M. B., and P. M. Popovich. "Victim Attractiveness and Perceptions of Responsibility in an Ambiguous Rape Case." *Psychology of Women Quarterly* 8 (1983): 100–104.

Jahraus, J. "American Realities: The Changing Face of Eating Disorders." Congressional Briefing, U.S. Senate (December 2, 2003): http://www .eatingdisorderscoalition.org / congbriefings / Dec2003 / JahrausSpeech .htm.

Jasienska, G., A. Ziomkiewicz, S. F. Lipson, P. T. Ellison, and I. Thune. "Large Breasts and Narrow Waists Indicate High Reproductive Potential in Women." *Proceedings of the Royal Society of London: Series B* 271, no. 1545 (2004): 1213–1217.

Johnson, J. "Heston Says Famous Line Final Time as NRA President." Cybercast News Service (April 27, 2003): http://www.cnsnews.com/View Nation.asp?Page = %5CNation%5Carchive%5C200304%5CNAT200304 27a.html.

Kalven, H., Jr., and H. Zeisel. *The American Jury.* Boston: Little, Brown, 1966.

Kapelovitz, D. "Slaves to the Scalpel: Cosmetic-Surgery Junkies." *Hustler* (November 2002): http://www.kapelovitz.com/plastic.htm.

Kaufman, L. "Prime-Time Nutrition." *Journal of Communication* 30 (1980): 37–46.

Keating, C. F., and D. Randall. "Dominance and Deception in Children and Adults: Are Leaders the Best Misleaders?" *Personality and Social Psychology Bulletin* 20 (1994): 312–321.

Keating, C. F., D. Randall, and T. Kendrick. "Presidential Physiognomies: Altered Images, Altered Perceptions." *Political Psychology* 20, no. 3 (1999): 593–610.

Keil, B. L. "So What If It's Not Approved? Patients Demand It. Doctors Inject It. But Is It Safe?" *New York* 36, no. 34 (October 6, 2003): 49.

Kelley, K. N., L. B. Nita, and B. P. Bandura. "Evaluating Employee Transgressions: Influence of Attractiveness and Ethical Ideology." Paper presented at the Annual Convention of the American Psychological Society, Atlanta, 2003.

Kenrick, D. T., G. E. Groth, M. R. Trost, and E. K. Sadalla. "Integrating Evolutionary and Social Exchange Perspectives on Relationships: Effects of Gender, Self-Appraisal, and Involvement Level on Mate Selection Criteria." *Journal of Personality and Social Psychology* 64 (1993): 951–969.

Kirkpatrick, S. W., and D. M. Sanders. "Body Image Stereotypes: A Developmental Comparison." *Journal of Genetic Psychology* 132 (1978): 87–95.

Kitch, C. *The Girl on the Magazine Cover: The Origins of Visual Stereotypes in American Mass Media.* 1st ed. Chapel Hill: University of North Carolina Press, 2001.

Klein, S. "Does This Make My Labia Look Fat?" *(Detroit) Metro Times* (March 9, 2005): http://www.metrotimes.com/editorial/story.asp?id =7405.

Krantz, M. "Physical Attractiveness and Popularity: A Predictive Study." *Psychological Reports* 60 (1987): 723–726.

Kuczynski, A., and W. St. John. "Why Did They Die in Cosmetic Surgery?" *New York Times* (June 20, 2004): 1, 10 (Section Nine).

Kurtzberg, R. L., H. Safar, and N. Cavior. "Surgical and Social Rehabilitation of Adult Offenders." *Proceedings of the 76th Annual Convention of the American Psychological Association* 3 (1968): 649–650.

Lacey, M. "Remote and Poked, Anthropology's Dream Tribe." *New York Times* (December 18, 2005): 1, 6 (Section One).

Laennec, C. "Babes on the Box: Women on TV." Sociology professor's university class presentation. University of Aberdeen: Aberdeen, Scotland, United Kingdom (2005): http://www.abdn.ac.uk/womens/ws1504 .doc.

Lang, K., and G. E. Lang. "The Mass Media and Voting." In *Reader in Public Opinion and Communication,* edited by B. Berelson and M. Janowitz, 455–472. New York: The Free Press, 1966.

Langlois, J., A. Roggman, and L. Rieser-Danner. "Infants' Differential Social Responses to Attractive and Unattractive Faces." *Developmental Psychology* 26 (1990): 153–159.

Langlois, J. H., and C. Stephan. "The Effects of Physical Attractiveness and Ethnicity on Children's Behavioral Attributions and Peer Preferences." *Child Development* 48 (1977): 1694–1698.

Langlois, J. H., and L. E. Styczynski. "The Effects of Physical Attractiveness on the Behavioral Attributions and Peer Preferences of Acquainted Children." *International Journal of Behavioral Development* 2 (1979): 325–341.

Langlois, J. H., L. Kalakanis, A. Rubenstein, A. Larson, M. Hallam, and M. Smoot. "Maxims or Myths of Beauty? A Meta-Analytic and Theoretical Review." *Psychological Bulletin* 126, no. 3 (2000): 390–423.

Lawson, W. "In the Name of Beauty." *Psychology Today* 38, no. 3 (May–June 2005): http://www.psychologytoday.com/articles/pto-20050506-000 001.html.

Lee, H. *To Kill a Mockingbird.* 35th anniversary ed. New York: HarperCollins, 1960.

Lehman, S. J., and S. L. Koerner. "Adolescent Women's Sports Involvement and Sexual Behavior/Health: A Process-Level Investigation." *Journal of Youth and Adolescence* 33, no. 5 (2004): 443–455.

Lerner, R. M., and E. Gillert. "Body Build Identification, Preference, and Aversion in Kindergarten Children." *Developmental Psychology* 19 (1969): 856–867.

Levine, M. P. *How Schools Can Help Combat Student Eating Disorders: Anorexia Nervosa and Bulimia.* Washington, DC: National Education Association of the United States, 1987.

Lipson, A. L., D. P. Przybyla, and D. Byrne. "Physical Attractiveness, Self-Awareness, and Mirror-Gazing Behavior." *Bulletin of the Psychonomic Society* 21 (1983): 115–116.

Loewy, M. I. "Suggestions for Working with Fat Children in the Schools." *Professional School Counseling* 1, no. 4 (1998): 18.

Lundahl, S., and C. Vallejos-Bartlett. "BodyWise Handbook: Eating Disorders Information for Middle School Personnel." Washington, DC: U.S. Department of Health and Human Services, 2004: http://www.4woman.gov/bodyimage/bodywise/bp/BodyWise.pdf.

Lynn, M., and B. A. Shurgot. "Responses to Lonely Hearts Advertisements: Effects of Reported Physical Attractiveness, Physique, and Coloration." *Personality and Social Psychology Bulletin* 10 (1984): 349–357.

Maccarone, D. "Affirmative Action for the Attractive?" *Psychology Today* 36, no. 1 (January–February 2003): 18.

Maisey, D. S., E. L. Vale, P. L. Cornelissen, and M. J. Tovée. "Characteristics of Male Attractiveness for Women." *Lancet* 353 (1999): 1500.

Malle, B. "Attraction and Relationships, Major Antecedents of Liking and Attraction." (1996): http://darkwing.uoregon.edu/~bfmalle/sp/L15.html.

Maloney, L. D. "Just for Appearance Sake: High-Power Light Treatments Target Unsightly Skin Conditions." *Design News* 60, no. 18 (December 5, 2005): S13.

Mann, J. "Nurturance or Negligence: Maternal Psychology and Behavioral Preference Among Preterm Twins." In *The Adapted Mind: Evolutionary Psychology and the Generation of Culture,* edited by J. H. Barkow, L. Cosmides, and J. Tobby, 367–390. New York: Oxford University Press, 1992.

Mann, T., and J. Helfert. "Looking Up to the Shuttle Commander." *Los Angeles Times* (August 11, 2005): B12.

Marcotte, P. "Psych Job: Scientists Detect Juror Bias." *American Bar Association Journal* 72, no. 34 (January 1986): http://global.lexisnexis.com (access through LexisNexis to this original source requires fee-paid subscription).

Marlowe, C. M., S. L. Schneider, and C. E. Nelson. "Gender and Attractiveness Biases in Hiring Decisions: Are More Experienced Managers Less Biased?" *Journal of Applied Psychology* 81, no. 1 (1986): 11–21.

Marquardt, S., MD. "Marquardt Beauty Analysis." (2003): www.beautyanalysis.com.

Martin, M. C., and J. W. Gentry. "Stuck in the Model Trap: The Effects of Beautiful Models in Ads on Female Preadolescents and Adolescents." *Journal of Advertising* 26, no. 2 (1997): 19–33.

Martin, M. C., and P. F. Kennedy. "Advertising and Social Comparison: Consequences for Female Preadolescents and Adolescents." *Psychology and Marketing* 10 (November–December 1993): 513–530.

Marvelle, K., and S. Green. "Physical Attractiveness and Sex Bias in Hiring Decisions for Two Types of Jobs." *Journal of the National Association of Women Deans, Administrators, and Counselors* 44, no. 1 (1980): 3–6.

Masip, J., E. Garrido, and C. Herrero. "Facial Appearance and Judgments of Credibility: The Effects of Facial Babyishness and Age on Statement Credibility." *Genetic, Social, and General Psychology Monographs* 129, no. 3 (2003): 269–411.

Mayer, J. D. "The Contemporary Presidency: The Presidency and Image Management: Discipline in Pursuit of Illusion." *Presidential Studies Quarterly* 34, no. 3 (2004): 620–632.

Maynard, C. "Body Image Quiz," http://www.etr.org/recapp/ches/BodyImagequiz.htm.

———. "Can You Live on Junk Food Alone? (Nutrition)." *Current Health* (September 1, 1997): http://www.highbeam.com (access through HighBeam Research to this original source requires fee-paid subscription).

Mazur, A., and U. Mueller. "Facial Dominance." In *Research in Biopolitics* 4, edited by A. Somit and S. Peterson, 99–111. London: JAI Press, 1996.

Mazur, A., J. Mazur, and C. Keating. "Military Rank Attainment of a West Point Class: Effects of Cadets' Physical Features." *American Journal of Sociology* 90 (1984): 125–150.

Mazzella, R., and A. Feingold. "The Effects of Physical Attractiveness, Race, Socioeconomic Status, and Gender of Defendants and Victims on Judgments of Mock Jurors: A Meta-Analysis." *Journal of Applied Social Psychology* 24 (1994): 1315–1344.

McDonald, J. J., Jr. "Civil Rights for the Aesthetically Challenged." *Employee Relations Law Journal* 29, no. 2 (2003): 118.

McKelvie, S. J., and J. Coley. "Effects of Crime Seriousness and Offender Facial Attractiveness on Recommended Treatment." *Social Behavior and Personality: An International Journal* 21, no. 4 (1993): 265–277.

MedKB: Medical Knowledge Base. "Battle over Botox: Lawsuit Alleges Malpractice from Hollywood Doctor." MedKB: Medical Knowledge Base (July 12, 2003): http://www.medkb.com/uwe/Forum.aspx/alternative/127/Battle-over-Botox.

Miller, A. G. "Role of Physical Attractiveness in Impression Formation." *Psychonomic Science* 19, no. 4 (1970): 241–243.

Miller, R. "The Plastic Surgery Company Unveils Strategic Shift to Company-Owned Centers." Banchik & Associates Press Release (November 3, 2000).

Mills, J. K., and G. D. Andrianopoulos. "The Relationship Between Childhood Onset Obesity and Psychopathology in Adulthood." *The Journal of Psychology* 127, no. 5 (1993): 547–551.

Moitra, A. "Depression and Body Image." Psychology Department, Vanderbilt University, n.d.: http://www.vanderbilt.edu/AnS/psychology/ health_psychology/depressbi.html.

Montell, G. "Do Good Looks Equal Good Evaluations?" *The Chronicle of Higher Education: Chronicle Careers* (October 15, 2003): http://chroni cle.com/jobs/2003/10/2003101501c.htm.

Moore, D. "Body Image and Eating Behavior in Adolescents." *Journal of the American College of Nutrition* 12 (1993): 505–510.

Morelli, J. "Deaths from Liposuction Too High, Study Shows." WebMD (2000): http://www.webmd.com/content/article/17/1676_50256.htm.

Morey, D., and L. Morey. "The Vulnerable Body Image of Females with Feelings of Depression." *Journal of Research in Personality* 25 (1991): 343–354.

Mueller, U., and A. Mazur. "Facial Dominance of West Point Cadets as a Predictor of Later Military Rank." *Social Forces* 74 (1996): 823–850.

Naftulin, D. H., J. E. Ware, and F. A. Donnelly. "The Doctor Fox Lecture: A Paradigm of Educational Seduction." *Journal of Medical Education* 48 (1973): 630–635.

Navarro, M. "The Most Private of Makeovers." *New York Times* (November 28, 2004): http://www.nytimes.com/2004/11/28/fashion/ 28PLAS.html?pagewanted = 1&ei = 5070&en = a53b510cfebfac66&ex = 1165294800&adxnnl = 1&adxnnlx = 1165162142-5XeecPlbtKY7Ce 7WmBbTBw.

NBC Television Network News. "Battle over Botox," June 17, 2004: http://www.msnbc.com/news/927823.asp.

Nettle, D. "Women's Height, Reproductive Success, and the Evolution of Sexual Dimorphism in Modern Humans." *Proceedings of the Royal Society of London, B* 269 (2002): 1919–1923.

Nichter, M. *Fat Talk: What Girls and Their Parents Say About Dieting.* Cambridge, MA: Harvard University Press, 2000.

O'Connor, T. "Anthropological Criminology." Lecture in Criminology 301, North Carolina Wesleyan College (2005): http://faculty.ncwc .edu/toconnor/301/301lect03.htm.

Ofang, K. "Firing Woman for Lack of Attractiveness Violates Anti-Bias Law." *(Los Angeles) Metropolitan News-Enterprise* (March 10, 2003): http://www.metnews.com/articles/yano031003.htm.

Oickle, D. "Health Matters." *Leeds, Grenville, and Lanark District Health Unit Newsletter* (Spring 2005): http://www.healthunit.org.

Oliver, K. K., and M. H. Thelen. "Children's Perceptions of Peer Influence on Eating Concerns." *Behavior Therapy* 27 (1996): 25–39.

O'Neil, D. "Early Modern Homo Sapiens." (1999): http://anthro.palo mar.edu/homo2/modern_humans.htm.

Paterniti, T. "Old Beauty Remedies." http://www.webspan.net/~terrip/ cosmetic%20history.htm.

Peacock, M. "Sex, Housework, and Ads." http://femmerevolution.8m. com/webpage/HTML/GetInformed/houseworks.htm.

Penton-Voak, I., and D. I. Perrett. "Female Preference for Male Faces Changes Cyclically—Further Evidence." *Evolutionary Human Behavior* 21 (2000): 39–48.

Perkins, K. R. "The Influence of Television Images on Black Females' Self-Perceptions of Physical Attractiveness." *Journal of Black Psychology* 22, no. 4 (1996): 453–469.

Perrett, D. I., I. S. Penton-Voak, A. C. Little, B. P. Tiddeman, D. M. Burt, N. Schmidt, R. Oxley, N. Kinloch, and L. Barrett. "Facial Attractiveness Judgments Reflect Learning of Parental Age Characteristics." *Proceedings of the Royal Society, London, B-Biological Sciences* 269, no. 1494 (2002): 873–880.

Pfann, G. A., J. E. Biddle, D. S. Hamermesh, and C. M. Bosman. "Business Success and Businesses' Beauty Capital." *Economics Letters* 67, no. 2 (2000): 201–207.

Phillips, K. A., and R. G. Dufresne, Jr. "Body Dysmorphic Disorder: A Guide for Dermatologists and Cosmetic Surgeons." *American Journal of Clinical Dermatology* 1, no. 4 (July–August 2000): 235–243.

Pipher, M. *Hunger Pangs*. Holbrook, MA: Adams, 1995.

Pope, H. G., Jr., K. A. Phillips, and R. Olivardia. *The Adonis Complex: The Secret Crisis of Male Body Obsession*. New York: The Free Press, 2000.

Pope, H. G. Jr., R. Olivardia, A. Gruber, and J. Borowiecki. "Evolving Ideals of Male Body Image as Seen Through Action Toys." *International Journal of Eating Disorders* 26, no. 1 (1999): 65–72.

"Pots of Promise: The Beauty Business." *Economist* 367, no. 8325 (May 22, 2003): 71.

Quinn, B. H. "Attitudinal Ratings of Educators Toward Normal Weight, Overweight, and Obese Teenage Girls." Doctoral dissertation, Texas Woman's University, Denton, TX, 1987.

Quinn, R. P. "Physical Deviance and Occupational Mistreatment: The Short, the Fat, and the Ugly." Unpublished manuscript, Institute for Social Research, Ann Arbor: University of Michigan, 1978.

Ramachandran, V. "Not Just About Looking Pretty." *New Straits Times* (Kuala Lumpur, Malaysia) (September 29, 2003): http://www.high beam.com/doc/1P1-82933283.html.

Ramey, J. "The Bloody Blonde and the Marble Woman: Gender and Power in the Case of Ruth Snyder." *Journal of Social History* 37, no. 3 (2004): 625–651.

Rees, A. "The Role of Fairness in Wage Determination." *Journal of Labor Economics* 11 (1993): 243–252.

Rice, L. "Student Evaluation of Teaching: Problems and Prospects." *Teaching Philosophy* 11 (1988): 329–344.

Rich, J. "Effects of Children's Physical Attractiveness on Teacher's Evaluations." *Journal of Educational Psychology* 67 (1975): 599–609.

Rierdan, J., E. Koff, and M. Stubbs. "Depressive Symptomatology and Body Image in Adolescent Girls." *Journal of Early Adolescence* 7, no. 2 (1989): 205–216.

————. "A Longitudinal Analysis of Body Image as a Predictor of the Onset and Persistence of Adolescent Girls' Depression." *Journal of Early Adolescence* 7 (1987): 205–216.

Roberts, S. C., J. Havlicek, J. Flegr, M. Hruskova, A. C. Little, B. C. Jones, D. I. Perrett, and M. Petrie. "Female Facial Attractiveness Increases During the Fertile Phase of the Menstrual Cycle." *Proceedings of the Royal Society of London, Biology* 271 (2004): S270–S272.

Rosenberg, S. "Facilitating the Development of Political Reasoning in the Classroom: An Experimental Study." Paper presented at the APSA Conference on Teaching and Learning, Washington, DC, 2005.

Rosenthal, R. "From Unconscious Experimenter Bias to Teacher Expectancy Effects." In *Teacher Expectancies,* edited by J. B. Dusek, V. C. Hall, and W. J. Meyer. Hillsdale, NJ: Erlbaum, 1985.

Rosenthal, R., and K. L. Fode. "The Problem of Experimenter Outcome-Bias." In *Research in Social Psychology,* edited by D. P. Ray. Washington, D.C.: National Institute of Social and Behavioral Science, 1961.

Rosenthal, R., and L. Jacobson. *Pygmalion in the Classroom.* New York: Holt, Rinehart, and Winston, 1968.

Rosenthal, R., and R. Lawson. "A Longitudinal Study of the Effects of Experimenter Bias on the Operant Learning of Laboratory Rats." *Journal of Psychiatric Research* 2 (1964): 61–72.

Rowland, R. "Liposuction Blamed in Five Deaths." Atlanta: CNN, May 12, 1999.

Ryan, J. J., J. A. Anderson, and A. B. Birchler. "Student Evaluations: The Faculty Responds." *Research in Higher Education* 12, no. 4 (December 1980): 317–333.

Sands, R., J. Tricker, C. Sherman, C. Armatas, and W. Maschette. "Disordered Eating Patterns, Body Image, Self-Esteem, and Physical Activity in Preadolescent Schoolchildren." *International Journal of Eating Disorders* 21, no. 2 (1997): 159–166.

Santoso, D. "Teens Struggle to Fit the Picture Perfect Body Image." *Jakarta Post* (October 29, 2003): 18 (Section 1).

Saporta, I., and J. J. Halpern. "Being Different Can Hurt: Effects of Deviations from Physical Norms on Lawyers' Salaries." *Industrial Relations* 41, no. 3 (2002): 442–466.

Schneider, K. S. "Mission Impossible." *People* 45, no. 22 (June 3, 1996): 64.

Schubert, J. N. "Good Genes and Issue Agreement in Candidate Appraisal." Paper presented at the Midwest Political Science Association 61st Annual National Conference, 2003.

Schur, E. A., M. Sanders, and H. Steiner. "Body Dissatisfaction and Dieting in Young Children." *International Journal of Eating Disorders* 27, no. 1 (2000): 74–82.

Selvin, P. "The Raging Bull of Berkeley." *Science* 251 (1991): 368–371.

Sforza, T. "What You See Is What You Elect. Come November, the Man with the Most 'Dominant' Face May Win. Making an Electable Face." *Orange County Register* (February 22, 2004): 1 (cover page).

Shahani-Denning, C., and D. Plumitallo. "The Influence of Physical Attractiveness and Gender on Disciplinary Decisions." Paper presented at the Fifth Annual Convention of the American Psychological Society, Chicago, IL, 1993.

Shalleck-Klein, J. "Striving for the Baywatch Boy Build." *Silver Chips (Silver Springs, MD, High School) Newspaper* (October 7, 1999).

Shapiro, S., M. Newcomb, and T. B. Loeb. "Fear of Fat, Disregulated-Restrained Eating, and Body-Esteem: Prevalence and Gender Differences Among Eight- to Ten-Year-Olds." *Journal of Clinical Child Psychology* 26, no. 4 (1997): 358–365.

Shuman, D. W., E. Whitaker, and A. Champagne. "An Empirical Examination of the Use of Expert Witnesses in the Courts—Part 2: A Three City Study." *Jurimetrics Journal* 34 (1994): 193–208.

Sigall, H., and N. Ostrove. "Beautiful but Dangerous: Effects of Offender Attractiveness and Nature of the Crime on Juridic Judgment." *Journal of Personality and Social Psychology* 31 (1975): 410–414.

Snopes.com. "The Fall of Cartilage." (2002): http://www.snopes.com/photos/jackson.asp.

Solnick, S. J., and M. E. Schweitzer. "The Influence of Physical Attractiveness and Gender on Ultimatum Game Decisions." *Organizational Behavior and Human Decision Processes* 79, no. 3 (1999): 199–215.

Solomon, M. R., R. D. Ashmore, and L. C. Longo. "The Beauty Match-up Hypothesis: Congruence Between Types of Beauty and Product Images in Advertising." *Journal of Advertising* 21 (December 1992): 23–34.

Sommers, S. R., and P. C. Ellsworth. "White Juror Bias." *Psychology, Public Policy, and Law* 7, no. 1 (2001): 201–230.

Sones, M. "Beauty, Fashion, and the Coolidge Effect." (2002): http://www.beautyworlds.com/beautyfashioncoolidge.htm.

———. "The Biological Purpose of Beauty." Beauty Worlds, The Culture of Beauty (2000): http://www.beautyworlds.com/beautybiological.htm.

Spee, T. "Top Defense Verdicts of 2004: Medavoy v. Klein." *Daily Journal Extra: Supplement to the Los Angeles Daily Journal and San Francisco Daily Journal* (January 31, 2005): http://www.swlaw.com/publications/files/Snell_&_WilmerTop_Defense_Verdicts.pdf.

Sprecher, S., J. DeLamater, N. Neuman, M. Neuman, P. Kahn, D. Orbuch, and K. McKinney. "Asking Questions in Bars: The Girls (and Boys) May Not Get Prettier at Closing Time and Other Interesting Results." *Personality and Social Psychology Bulletin* 10 (1984): 482–488.

Staffreri, J. R. "A Study of Social Stereotype of Body Image in Children." *Journal of Personality and Social Psychology* 7 (1967): 101–104.

Stager, S. F., and P. J. Burke. "A Reexamination of Body Build Stereotypes." *Journal of Research in Personality* 16 (1982): 435–446.

Steiner, H., W. Kwan, T. Graham-Shaffer, S. Walker, S. Miller, A. Sagar, and J. Lock. "Risk and Protective Factors for Juvenile Eating Disorders." *European Child & Adolescent Psychiatry [Suppl 1]* 12 (2003): 38–46.

Steinhoff, J. "Waukesha Woman Dies from Breast Implant Surgery." *(Milwaukee) Shepherd-Express* 25 (March 2, 2004): http://www.shepherd express.com/.

Stephan, C. W., and J. H. Langlois. "Baby Beautiful: Adult Attributions of Infant Competence as a Function of Infant Attractiveness." *Child Development* 55 (1984): 576–585.

———. "Physical Attractiveness and Ethnicity: Implications for Stereotyping and Social Development." *Journal of Genetic Psychology* 137 (1980): 303–304.

Stewart, J. E. "Defendants' Attractiveness as a Factor in the Outcome of Trials." *Journal of Applied Social Psychology* 10 (1980): 348–361.

Stice, E., C. Hayward, R. P. Cameron, J. D. Killen, and B. C. Taylor. "Body-Image and Eating Disturbances Predict Onset of Depression Among Female Adolescents: A Longitudinal Study." *Journal of Abnormal Psychology* 109, no. 3 (2000): 438–444.

Strauss, C. C., K. Smith, C. Frame, and R. Forehand. "Personal and Interpersonal Characteristics Associated with Childhood Obesity." *Journal of Pediatric Psychology* 10, no. 3 (1985): 337–343.

Strauss, R. S. "Childhood Obesity and Self-Esteem." *Pediatrics* 105, no. 1 (2000): 15.

Striegal-Moore, R. H., G. B. Schreiber, A. Lo, P. Crawford, E. Obarzanek, and J. Rodin. "Eating Disorder Symptoms in a Cohort of 11- to 16-Year-Old Black and White Girls: The NHLBI Growth and Health Study." *International Journal of Eating Disorders* 27 (2000): 49–66.

Stroman, C. "Television's Role in the Socialization of African American Children and Adolescents." *Journal of Negro Education* 60 (1991): 314–326.

———. "Television Viewing and Self-Concept Among Black Children." *Journal of Broadcasting and Electronic Media* 30 (1986): 87–93.

Szmukler, G. I. "The Epidemiology of Anorexia Nervosa and Bulimia." *Journal of Psychiatric Research* 19, no. 2/3 (1985): 143–153.

Teen People Magazine. "How to Love the Way You Look." *Teen People* (October 1999): as cited by Mediascope.org: Body Image and Advertising, June 20, 2005.

Thackeray, W. M. *Catherine: A Story*. London: Serialized in *Fraser's Magazine* for *Town and Country*, 1839–1840.

Thaler, R. H. "The Ultimatum Game." *Journal of Economic Perspectives* 2 (1988): 191–202.

Thelen, M. H., A. L. Powell, C. Lawrence, and M. E. Kuhnert. "Eating and Body Image Concerns Among Children." *Journal of Clinical Child Psychology* 21, no. 1 (1992): 41–46.

Thornton, B., and S. Moore. "Physical Attractiveness Contrast Effect: Implications for Self-Esteem and Evaluations of the Social Self." *Personality and Social Psychology Bulletin* 19 (1993): 474–480.

Tisdall, J. "Demand for More Ugly People on TV." *Aftenposten: News from Norway* (October 17, 2002): http://www.aftenposten.no/english/local/article419740.ece.

Townsend, J. M., and G. D. Levy. "Effects of Potential Partners' Physical Attractiveness and Socioeconomic Status on Sexuality and Partner Selection." *Archives of Sexual Behavior* 19 (1990): 149–164.

Townsend, J. M., and L. W. Roberts. "Gender Differences in Mate Selection Among Law Students: Divergence and Convergence of Criteria." *Journal of Psychology* 29 (1993): 507–528.

Tremlett, G. "Spanish Look into Death of Nigerian First Lady After Cosmetic Surgery." *Guardian* (October 25, 2005): 18, http://www.guardian.co.uk/spain/article/0,2763,1599889,00.html.

Trivers, R. *Sexual Selection and the Descent of Man.* Edited by B. Campbell. Chicago: Aldine, 1972.

Turner, R. G., L. Gilliland, and H. M. Klein. "Self-Consciousness, Evaluation of Physical Characteristics, and Physical Attractiveness." *Journal of Research in Personality* 15 (1981): 182–190.

Umberson, D., and M. Hughes. "The Impact of Physical Attractiveness and Achievement and Psychological Well-Being." *Social Psychology Quarterly* 50, no. 3 (1987): 227–236.

Urbaniak, G. C., and P. R. Kilmann. "Physical Attractiveness and the 'Nice Guy Paradox': Do Nice Guys Really Finish Last?" *Sex Roles: A Journal of Research* 49 (2003): 413–426.

USDE. "Postsecondary: Summary Enrollment." In *Education Statistics.* Washington, DC: U.S. Department of Education, National Center for Education Statistics, 2003.

Vaughn, B. E., and J. H. Langlois. "Physical Attractiveness as a Correlate of Peer Status and Social Competence in Preschool Children." *Developmental Psychology* 19 (1983): 561–567.

Vrij, A., and H. R. Firmin. "Beautiful Thus Innocent? The Impact of Defendants' and Victims' Physical Attractiveness and Participants' Rape Beliefs on Impression Formation in Alleged Rape Cases." *International Review of Victimology* 8, no. 3 (2001): 245–255.

Wadden, T. A., and A. J. Stunkard. "Psychopathology and Obesity." *Annals of the New York Academy of Sciences* 499 (1987): 55–65.

Walker, R. "Social Lubricant." *New York Times Magazine* (September 4, 2005): 23.

Walster, E., V. Aronson, D. Abrahams, and L. Rottman. "Importance of Physical Attractiveness in Dating Behavior." *Journal of Personality and Social Psychology* 5 (1966): 506–516.

Waterman, R., R. Wright, and G. St. Clair. *The Image-Is-Everything Presidency.* Boulder, CO: Westview Press, 1999.

Watkins, L., and L. Johnston. "Screening Job Applicants: The Impact of Physical Attractiveness and Application Quality." *International Journal of Selection and Assessment* 8 (2000): 76–84.

Wax, R. G. "Boys and Body Image." *San Diego Parent Magazine* (May 1998).

West, K. "Chinese Beauty Through the Changes of Time." (2003): http://www.beautyworlds.com/beautychinese.htm#Contenttop.

Westin Foundation, http://www.annawestinfoundation.org.

White, D. R., K. Mauro, and J. Spindler. "Development of Type Salience: Implications for Childhood Educators." *International Review of Applied Psychology* 34 (1985): 433.

Whitehead, J. "Norman Normal: A Tale of Physical Triumph." *Journal of Physical Education, Recreation, and Dance* 58 (August 1987): 82–87.

Whitehead, J. R., and J. H. Hoover. "The Link Between Body Issues and Behavioral Problems." *Reclaiming Children and Youth* 9, no. 3 (2000): 130–138.

Williams, W. M., and S. J. Ceci. " 'How'm I Doing?' Problems with Student Ratings of Instructors and Courses." *Change: The Magazine of Higher Learning* 29 (September/October 1997): 12–23.

Wilson, R. "New Research Casts Doubt on Value of Student Evaluations of Professors." *The Chronicle of Higher Education* 44, no. 19 (January 16, 1998): A12.

Wingert, P. "Young and Overweight." *Newsweek* 135, no. 24 (June 12, 2000): 52.

Wiseman, C. V., J. J. Gray, J. E. Mosimann, and A. H. Ahrens. "Cultural Expectations of Thinness in Women: An Update." *International Journal of Eating Disorders* 11, no. 1 (January 1992): 85–89.

Wolf, M. J. "Larry Mintz Talks About Sitcom Production." Personal communication and interview, Los Angeles, CA, September 21, 2005.

Wolf, M. J., and K. Mader. *Fallen Angels: Chronicles of L.A. Crime and Mystery.* New York: Facts on File, 1986.

Wuensch, K. L., and C. H. Moore. "Effects of Physical Attractiveness on Evaluations of a Male Employee's Allegation of Sexual Harassment by His Female Employer." *Journal of Social Psychology* 144, no. 2 (2004): 207–217.

Young-Eisendrath, P. *Women and Desire: Beyond Wanting to Be Wanted.* New York: Harmony Books, 1999.

Index

"Tending Our Garden " ©2004 Leticia Plate
Limited Edition Bookplate #15 www.bookcrossing.com/artists/plate

I'm a *very special* book. You see, I'm traveling around the world making new friends. I hope I've made another one in you. If so, please go to www.bookcrossing.com, where you can make a brief journal entry with my BCID number (below). You will see where I've been, and my old friends will be happy to know I'm safe here in your hands. Then help keep my dream alive - *READ & RELEASE* me!

BCID:	035- 10480258
First Registered By:	Howdy 81
When & Where:	02-12 / Arlington VA

bookcrossing.com ™
the karma of literature • free and anonymous

Winter Range

Claire Davis

Picador USA   New York

Winter Range

Picador® is a U.S. registered trademark and is used by St. Martin's
Press under license from Pan Books Limited.

Frontispiece courtesy of PhotoDisc Inc.

Book design by Victoria Kuskowski

ISBN 0-312-26140-3

First Edition: September 2000

10 9 8 7 6 5 4 3 2 1

In memory of

Clara and Glenn Davis,

whose love was an act of grace.

And for my son,

Brian Wroblewski

Acknowledgments

I want to thank Judy Blunt, my guide through the heart of these range lands and its people, for her generous gift of time—the numerous nights at her kitchen table, staying up too late, drinking coffee too strong; to Robert Sims Reid for believing in this work and lending me his expertise in the law. My thanks to David Long for his friendship, his selfless mentoring over the years. To Robert Wrigley and Kim Barnes, in whose home, high above the Clearwater River, I wrote this book—thank you for your love and support. My thanks to Mary Clearman Blew for her friendship, her generosity, and to Phil Zweifel, who started it all so many years ago. I also want to thank Sally Wofford-Girand, George Witte, William Kittredge, Mark Clemens, Keith and Shirley Browning, Rudy and Gail Martin. I want to extend my gratitude for the support of the Idaho Commission on the Arts and Lewis-Clark State College.

Finally, thanks to Dennis Held for his support through the years of work, for helping me realize the idea.

Winter Range

Chapter One

The sheriff, Ike Parsons, stood at the curb, zipped his coat closed to his throat, and knocked the snow clear of his hat. A truck rolled past, hit a glazed patch in the street, and did a little sideways slide and jiggle. The driver ducked his head to the sheriff as if apologizing, and then the truck straightened and moved on. It was a year of big snow for this small town, in the corner of Montana, eastern edge of what was known as the hi-line to the locals—a corridor of high desert, along old Highway Two, bisecting the northern tier of the state. Just a jump from Canada to the north and the Bearpaw Range, the Little Rockies to the distant south. Dry land farm and ranch country—wheat, cattle.

Parsons tucked his hat over his ears, tugging the brim to a beak above his nose. The snow fell haphazard out of the bright blue overhead, papered alike the streets and hydrants, hats and shoulders of his fellow townsfolk. Across the street, the vet Purvis was angling his way over a snowbank, cutting a diagonal toward Ike. He was a tall man in his early sixties, graying, but like many out here, ropy-muscled and fit from dealing with livestock. He hopped the curb and a foot dipped under him so that he bobbled a moment and the sheriff snatched him under an arm and steadied the older man.

"I meant to do that," Purvis said.

Parsons shrugged. "And I meant to let you fall on your ass."

The two men grinned. Purvis looked up, dodged a clump of falling snow, said, "Ain't this a sight? Once in a generation."

Come spring the land would be rich with water, and with any luck it would signal the end of seven years of drought, but now, late winter, it was snow, burying the streets. Just outside of town—a flat-open slab of white over hardpan and scrub, a scattering of sage and cactus and greasewood punching through, a skiff of tumbleweeds dashing over the icy surface, swooping about in the wind.

"You off to work?" Purvis asked.

Ike stepped away. "My day off."

Purvis fell in alongside. "You get those? What the hell's the law coming to?"

Ike shook his head and a clot of snow flopped down from the brim. "World's gone to the dogs, I guess." Parsons glanced in a storefront window, sucked his stomach in. At forty-two he was still a solid man, but softening at the edges and he did not take kindly to it. Too many sedentary hours behind the desk, too many miles on the roads.

"So, your day off—what you got lined up?"

"Hardware store." Ike shoved his hat back, tugged at his hair. "Steve's for a trim. Get lunch. Find my wife." Ike tipped a finger to his hat as Lucy Mattick ducked past. Some few people lived in town, but most, like Lucy, drove in once a month, or twice, and their families had done so for two–three generations, so that everyone knew each other as well as the vehicles they drove in. A far cry from his former life as a police officer in Milwaukee, Wisconsin, where, with any luck, he was able to keep all the faces anonymous, and where, on his old beat—downtown to the near north side, the projects rambling down Cherry and Vine, the entrenched North Avenue—there were more steel bars over doors and windows than in a jail.

Lucy walked with her shoulders braced forward as if against a headwind. Her son Joe scuffed behind at about ten feet—a sullen teenager who'd already been into enough trouble to look the other way as he passed the sheriff.

The vet doffed his hat, said, "Morning, Lucy." And after she'd passed, he leaned into Ike's hearing. "One damned fine-looking woman, that Lucy Mattick. But nervous."

2

"Purvis, don't you have some sick animal to go look after?"

The older man shook his head. "Think *I'll* take the day off," he said, "think I'll just keep you company till you find Pattiann. See if I can't talk her out of a home-cooked meal later." He grinned at Ike. "*She* likes me, you know."

They crossed the street at the courthouse, turned right toward the mercantile. A good-sized town, by western standards, seven parallel blocks east–west, four north–south around a central square. Building fronts were brick and wood, two-storied with western faces, free-swinging shingles, and hand-lettered signboards: post office, grocer, mercantile.

The bell over the hardware door saluted their entry. Ike found his way between tall shelves of pipe joints and plungers, nuts, bolts, and chain, samples of barb and insulators. The fir floor dipped in the center of the aisles where a hundred years of boots had worn a groove. He found a new float for the toilet, a spare ball and chain just in case. And damn but he hated this business of home repair, hoped he had the right parts, already dreading his awkwardness in the confines of the tank, at odds with balls and washers, how easily undone he was by overflows. At the counter he paid for the parts. Purvis lifted a cigar from the display case and tipped it toward the cash drawer. "On my bill," he said. The young clerk smiled and nodded.

Back in the street, Ike squinted against the white light of sun on snow, the spangling of chrome and windshield. He took a deep breath, caught himself hoping for a glimpse of his wife Pattiann, her red hair as bright and buoyant as the air itself.

At the end of Main Street and Third, Purvis lit his cigar, took a great puff, and hummed as he released the smoke. They stopped to read the signboard on the Unitarian church: *Here today* . . . In the sky behind the Unitarian's stunted steeple, Ike could see the grain elevators where birds convened and squabbled. No songbirds for this place, nothing fancy, just starlings—black on black so deep the sun couldn't shine bright enough to light their feathers.

Across from the courthouse was Steve's barber shop. Purvis stepped in ahead of Ike. Five men were spread out among the row of seats against the wall and the sofa backed to the front window. Ike's father-in-law Bill was seated on the sofa, neck clean-shaven, his dark hair clipped close and scalp pinked as a shorn sheep. Pattiann sat kitty-corner to him, her booted feet raised and resting on the low table that magazines were rifled across. When Ike entered she smiled, lifted her face to him.

"Jig's up, Pattiann," Purvis said, walked over and gave her a smacking kiss on the lips. "Sheriff's here."

"Oh good," she said. "You got the handcuffs, honey?" She smiled at Ike, a toothsome grin.

Her father was extending his hand to Ike, and a deep flush moved up his neck and over his face. He looked over at his daughter. "I don't know that a father needs to hear this," he said.

Pattiann snorted. "Really? And what about those dress spurs hanging on your bedroom wall?"

"Those, Missy, were your grandfather's," Bill said, his color rising.

Rob, Pattiann's brother, seated in one of the three barber chairs, fended Steve off with a hand and sat forward. "Believe he's right, Sis. The spurs were Grandpa's. But the lasso next to them is Dad's."

Purvis knocked the ash from his cigar into a sink. "Used to be I knew a few lariat tricks myself."

Steve leaned over, flushed the sink clear with cold water. "You know an ashtray when you see one?" he asked. Steve was a long-shanked man with a ripe, pear-shaped belly. A birdly man who had a peckish way of combing and cutting, his elbows winging over the heads of bibbed customers. "You here for a cut Sheriff, or to shoot the bull like this other bunch?" he asked, his scissors stabbing the air toward Aaron Wolfgram, Wes Long, and John Fonslow.

Wes clucked his tongue, said, "Well, now I *am* hurt. You hurt?" He turned toward Aaron, then, "You, John?"

Both men nodded.

Ike slung his hat up on the coatrack.

Steve eyed Ike's hair. He nodded, satisfied. "A trim," he said, pointed to an empty barber chair, wagged his finger in Rob's direction. "And you could take a lesson. Sheriff here may be the only man in town hasn't come in asking me to salvage his head after some botched-up, ham-handed home haircut."

"That's 'cause the only way Pattiann's likely to cut anything is with a livestock clipper," Rob said.

"Well," she said, "I like to go with what works. Why, the other day, when I was doing my legs . . ."

Ike eased into the chair, enjoying the men's laughter, the pride in his father-in-law's eyes as he cocked his head to a side and winked at his daughter. There was no getting ahead of Pattiann for long. She could keep the best of them treading water. Steve flapped a bib over Ike, and the cloth billowed down slow as a sheet over a bed. Ike leaned back, the sunshine warm, reflecting brightly off the pin-striped cloth. Steve bustled back to Rob and Ike let the men's chatter fall about him. Let himself enjoy this moment in the company of his good friend Purvis, the friendly town men, Pattiann and her family. He let his gaze drift to where Patti-ann lounged, a booted foot crossed over the other, wagging a slow three-beat rhythm, waltz time. Her head tipped back and her red hair, kindled in the wide swath of midmorning sunlight, lit the ocher wall behind her. And on the wall over her head was the gallery of old photographs that Ike loved next best about this place, next best to the friends and jokes and tall tales. The row of photos, framed with handwritten notes Scotch-taped below and alongside—the who and where and when of each.

Pictures of the town's boom era, 1910 through 1917, when in that narrow window the high desert was blessed with years of water and the dry lands became great waving prairies of grass: blue grama, needle and thread, redleaf sedge, bluestem, buffalo, plains muhley and barley. A savannah of green under a breakneck blue sky. And there were the rush of homesteaders, Midwesterners mostly—farmers, merchants, newlyweds, and mavericks, greenhorns all, clutching full-color brochures, and ready to cash in on their own free three hundred and twenty–acre parcel of land. A little bit of paradise. A homestead of their own.

And then the rains ended, this little bit of paradise, after all, being part of the Great American Desert.

Damn but they were a scrappy bunch, their wagons and trucks strapped high with furniture like a presage of the Great Depression caravans. Young men trailing mismatched teams, a hobnob collection of this and that they'd mustered up, or brought along. Ill-prepared, ill-informed, downright lied to by the railroads trying to people this great wasteland. A photo of the train depot—a clutch of men and women in fine but rumpled clothing, an unlikely crop of parasols blooming overhead. Ike's favorite picture was the front of the old boardinghouse, a line of men in cocked bowlers, waistcoats, and bow ties, arms over each other's shoulders grinning into the camera, ignoring the sweat, the heat of the day. And others. Women with bibbed and knickered children in front of tar paper shacks. Or women in long dresses, in the field, great shocks of wheat bundled under their arms. And what Ike thinks most telling, perhaps, is their gaze, not the brash head-on stare of the men, but a distant kind of seeing, their focus directed somewhere clear of the camera's lens, some other place on the far horizon. Some other time.

And truth was, most all of the locals were descendants of that raw-boned, greenhorn stock, savvy with the accumulated breaks and mistakes of three and four generations. It was true of Bill and Rob. Pattiann was a third-generation Montanan—a rancher's daughter raised to be a rancher's wife who had instead married a Midwest boy turned sheriff. Sometimes he marveled that she chose him. But what choice had he given her, really, appearing out of nowhere with his hat in hand, *Pattiann, will you marry me?* Like some orphaned calf. How that must have appealed.

He shut his eyes, drifting in the warm sun, the bantering, the soft chatter. He and Pattiann had been married three years now, had known each other for two years before that. He met her in a night class in criminology at the university back home in Wisconsin, the one and only semester Ike had ever agreed to act as a visiting instructor. She sat in the back of the classroom, by the door, on the edge of her seat as though she might bolt.

The first time they made love was in his single bed in an efficiency apartment. He'd turned on a portable cassette player to cover the neighbor's TV. She took off her blouse, and he said, "I'm a lot older than you." She slipped the bra straps from her shoulder, and he said, "I don't think cops should marry." When she shrugged out of her jeans and panties, he shut up. Afterward he said, "We probably shouldn't be doing this." She offered her bed the next night.

She earned a C in his class. She might have done better, but she never got assignments in on time. Six months later, she had left to go back home. Montana. A place, at that time, he could hardly conceive of. A place she'd talk about only reluctantly. A year later, he'd followed.

He heard the chair next to him tip forward with a squeak, and opened his eyes to see Rob stand up, then duck his head to glance in the mirror as Steve whisked his shoulders with a small hand broom.

He caught the tail end of a conversation between Wes and Aaron. The words "stubble," and "field," and then, "Well, if I ever turn that stupid, shoot me, put me out of my misery." This from Aaron, who ran a tidy ranch, great-great-grandson of one of those early homesteaders. Then silence. Pattiann was staring down at her lap, her hands capping her knees, and her father Bill was turned sideways on the sofa, looking over his shoulder and out the front window. He seemed distracted or uneasy. Purvis came out of the washroom, wiping his hands on a paper towel that he tossed into a basket under the sink. The stub of his cigar was clamped between his lips and he knocked a full inch of ash into the porcelain sink. He scooted over to Pattiann, out of the range of Steve rinsing the bowl once again, with a great splashing gesture.

"You must be wondering what I'm doing here," Purvis said to her.

She patted his hand, her lips twitching to a side. "My guess is you need a haircut or a home-cooked dinner."

"You know," he said, dousing his cigar in the clean ashtray, "if just one other woman knew my heart half as well as you—"

"You mean stomach."

"Whatever." He waved his hand in front of her. "I'd snatch her up."

Rob grabbed his coat off the rack, threaded his arms into the sleeves. "Knew this guy—Phil Zweifel was his name—trail cooked for us one season. Best chow I ever ate."

"Well," Purvis said. "He still around?" He laced his fingers behind his head, grinned up at the ceiling. "He more than half ugly?"

Pattiann pumped him in the ribs with an elbow. Bill stood and gathered his coat and hat. "I am taking my leave now, while I still have a high opinion of you all." He tipped a finger to the group, leaned over Ike in the chair, studied the right side of Ike's head, the left, returned to the right, and asked Steve, "That look even to you?" After which he backpedaled for the door. The bell chimed and a cool whiff of snowy air brisked in and was as quickly snuffed as the door clamped shut behind the two men.

Steve was fussing over Ike's right side now, and Pattiann was laughing into her fist, while Purvis named off a list of dinner favorites. Ike basked in the warm sunlight coming through the wide windows, the soft laughter and chatter making him drowsy with pleasure. The bell rang again, and then again as more men filed in while others took their leave. Greetings were exchanged, news of weather and livestock, bad jokes and good-natured ribbings. He studied how his wife joined in the banter, how easily she moved in and out of this most male arena with wit and grace. He watched the faces around her light with humor. He knew them by name, their spouses and children, and a good number of them, their histories. The scissors snicked in the air beside him and there was a crow of laughter and in the far corner a pocket of quiet conversation. He watched the give and take between the men, the conversations, the gestures, all the delicate connections between strangers that make up community, family. Sometimes, he thought, it was unaccountable. How we found ourselves so far afield from our expectations. And even more surprising, how right it could feel. He lifted his gaze, and outside the large window in the waning light of morning was the weightless fall of snow.

Chapter Two

A set of headlights picked out the indigo road ahead of the white-on-blue Bronco, sheriff's insignia on both door panels. Inside, Ike popped his knuckles, cracked open the side window. Below the full moon and peck of clouds, the swale of land sprawled flat and blue as far as the eye could see. He drove slowly, headlights a rogue star moving countercurrent to the swarm overhead.

The night was cold, startlingly clear. He kept his down jacket open and the shearling earflaps slapped up on his cap. The air stung his nostrils so that he pinched them twice to keep from sneezing. He was watching for the Mattick boy, reported missing by his mother. What had Purvis said about her the other morning? A fine-looking woman but nervous. And yes, she was—chewed her nails to the quick, chewed the quick till it was bloody—but that didn't mean she hadn't cause. Joe was a troublesome kid, but mostly petty stuff, more irritating than anything. And chances were they'd find him by morning, holed up with a friend or in a shed drunk on Thunderbird. Still, he felt compelled to check.

Jackrabbits paced him, white, long-shanked, mule-eared, and hurtling down the headlights with a sudden veering and then a small *whump* under a rear tire, and the Bronco would shift like an old man accommodating a full stomach before settling back onto its course. Lucy'd said Joe had a friend out this way. The fence line scrolled past, and in the distance he could see running forms. Coyotes, he thought, but slowed anyway.

He pulled the Bronco over, switched off the headlights to let his eyes adjust. His concern was the boy wandering drunk in the cold, trying to make it on foot. The radio was on scan, picking up the county's cross-chatter. So far, all he'd heard was a lot of useless talk from Harley, a whey-faced deputy who was dating the dispatcher. In the morning, he'd have *another* talk with Harley. Wished his young deputy would marry the girl, nothing quenching chatter as quickly as marriage.

Though, to be fair, Pattiann had never been given to unnecessary speech. And marriage only made her predictable in small ways—her rowdy hair in the mornings, or the way her shoelaces came untied and she would tie the right before the left whether it needed it or not. Marriage had not answered the look she shot him at odd moments, her eyes narrowing while the focus drifted and he wanted to know what or who it was she saw. In those times, it was like living with a stranger. But maybe that was true of all women. A Goddamned mystery. Their nature, secret as the womb. Damned confusing. Still, it would be good for Harley to marry. It settled young men down, wised them up, taught caution where the job couldn't. He stretched back in the seat, the springs creaking.

Out in the field, blots of black moved against the snow—cattle. Through the cracked window came their plangent lowing, a sound he could not hear without being reminded of his father's farm, and the barn—two-storied oak plank with a fieldstone base. And perhaps his belief in the orderliness of the law came from being a child of the fifties in a central Wisconsin farming community, with trim stone walls where fields were plowed in days instead of weeks. Just the other side of the fence, cattle huddled, ropy tails to the wind.

He stepped out, crossed the road. The fields were crisp with moon-light, flat to the horizon but for drifts and mounds that gave the land-scape an ingenuity it lacked in summer. The winds had crafted the snow into waves and skiffs of powder snaked through the troughs, or lofted off the crests in fine whiffs like sea spume. Ike's skin burned with the cold. It was not something he could explain—the way this land humbled and terrified him. The cattle made soft grunting noises. There was one horse, and it nickered, a sound like chestnuts knocking in a pocket. It walked with a nodding gait, then leaned over the fence, its breath frosting whiskers and the eyelashes over the round dark eyes. It was a piebald, face wide and white. Stark as honesty. Ike reached over and the horse nosed the gloved hand, then offered its head.

He'd seen winter-poor stock, but these might be the worst. Ike ran his hands over the horse's wither, down the ribs, fingered the dips between accordioned bone like a knacker. He reached through the barbs, thumped the horse on the chest. He gazed over the small clot of cattle, looking and not looking for the boy.

Land, more land and more of the same. The year he'd first come west, he'd find himself imagining roads quartering the vast sections, homes sprouting in suburbs, malls convening on the highways. It would happen, he believed. Not that he wanted that change, no, but you couldn't stop a train by standing on the tracks.

He peered into the dark and saw the coyotes, blackly silhouetted, body heat rising from their backs like smoke from snuffed candles. There was a bark, an answering yip, and they loped away.

Curious their being so near house and herd. Ike hoped to get another glimpse, but close at hand there came a bawling sound and one of the cows staggered. The animal rocked like a boat anchored in choppy water, then dropped. It tried to lift itself, and failing, rolled back with a grunt. Ike glanced down the road then at the barbed wire. None of his business. He eased between the fence wires, caught his pant leg on a barb, and cursed his clumsiness. Alongside the cow, he settled on one knee, hands against the spine to roll her to her feet. The animal's nose drooped into the snow. He pushed, but it would not be roused. He knew the way it would happen: the animal too weak to rise, the snow drifting up over the hide. In an hour, maybe two, the cow would be shrouded. By morning, it would be a mound—like any other in the field. Ike braced his legs and tugged at the head, its eyes large and black, an odd intelligence in them, as if resigned to the way the body fails. He stopped with the head between his hands. He released it slowly.

A mound. Like any other in the field.

The horse nudged at Ike's jacket, and he elbowed it aside. He waded over to a drift, whisked the snow clear, and ran his hand down the outline of a cow. He looked over the acres of mounds and drifts. As he walked farther in, the horse followed, nosing at his hair, its breath friendly on Ike's neck. Every now and again, Ike lifted from his task, resting his arm over the horse's back, grateful for the company, to stare across the distance to where Chas Stubblefield's house watched over them, lights dim in the windows like a well-banked fire.

Chas Stubblefield liked to believe himself a self-made man. His daddy had preferred to think him a kid, right up to five years ago when Chas turned twenty-eight and his father had died at seventy-nine. Chas stood over the stove, his shadow skittering across the walls as the overhead fluorescent coil sputtered its blue-white light until he reached up and ticked the bulb. When it stopped fluttering, he turned back to the counter, prodded the steak with a fork. His stomach griped. He dropped the meat into a cast-iron pan and watched the edges crimp. Through the back porch windows, the quartered cow, silhouetted by moonlight, hung from hooks. Torso tall as a man. The best cuts nearly gone. Didn't matter. Tomorrow or the next day he'd bring in another, hoist it, skin and quarter it. As long as the cold stayed and the cattle kept dying, he had all the food in the world. It was all a meat locker now. He lowered his face to the pan, inhaled. Meat. That was what was left him.

Accustomed to living alone, he ate with conspicuous relish, a swath of meat through potatoes and gravy. He swabbed the plate clean. He was not a man normally given to waste, but encouraged to these ends by men he'd trusted. Such as Taylor at the bank. Best friends as kids. But Taylor had put distance between them these days with his three-piece suits and immaculate nails.

"We've known each other a long time," Taylor had said at their last meeting a month ago. Chas took note that for all Taylor's high-handedness, there were no windows in his office, and the bathroom was far down the hall. He wondered if Taylor rutted with the secretary in there, skirt hitched up and nylons hobbling her ankles, like he'd taken the girls in the back of Chas's pickup as teenagers. Taylor, always the one the girls chose, and it was Chas, the awkward one no one really cared to know, who was reduced to chauffeuring them down some bucketing road deep into the breaks where Taylor would assure them, "Old Chas don't mind," and, "He won't look." Though he had watched the first couple of times, through the rear window, saw the buttocks rising and falling, a breast flattened in a mouth, but for the most part, Chas would stretch out across the seat with his boot heels hooked on a window, hopping one cigarette off another, convincing himself it made no difference to him, convincing himself he needed to be alone because he had a future in mind with no room to accommodate anyone else. Just then.

"A loan. Just enough to tide me over," Chas had said. He was pieced together in clean jeans, white shirt, and string tie. He'd taken a scissors to his blond hair and the ends looked chewed over his forehead. It gave him a boyish appearance. He sat straight.

"You needed to unload some livestock, Chas. There isn't another soul here didn't see this coming."

"My dad survived worse. I come from a long line of survivors." He shrugged.

"Your daddy made it because he had *half the herd*." Taylor wiped his forehead with a handkerchief, folded it into neat squares, and lifted a cheek to tuck it in a rear pocket.

Taylor leaned over his desk, the blotter under his elbows the green of freshly minted money. He rested his hands on the desk, screwing his wedding band up to the first knuckle and down. He shrugged the cuff on his wrist. He slumped back from the desk, as if coming in from a long day. And, of course, it was hard work, this turning away, ignoring old ties: *I knew you when*. Hard work. *A real piece of work*. Taylor stood. He sighed, put a hand on Chas's shoulder. "You already got a payment coming due. You understand? Much as I'd like to, I can't. . . ." He crossed over to the door. "Sorry, Chas."

But Chas stayed seated, a smile on his face—sweet and quirky. "We done then?" He lifted a picture of Taylor's wife from the desktop and squinted until his blue eyes were a slit. "You remember we used to run the back roads? Stinking drunk until even God wouldn't claim us?"

From the doorway, Taylor nodded, taken by charm as easily as he had always been—the first misled and the last disabused. Seeing what he wished to—that Chas was the young rube he'd always been, and bad things did not happen to bankers in the light of day, in their offices.

"And all those times in the back of my pickup?" Chas asked. "I remember," he said, "her dimpled ass."

"Get out."

"You two should come out for dinner. I got steak and more steak."

Taylor stood in the doorway. "Don't come back, Chas."

That was one short month ago when his cattle were the other side of desperate, back when Chas still believed salvation was for the asking. He ran water over a dishrag and the rag turned slick and the counter clouded with each swipe.

He could still smell the steak. And something else. Yes. The house still smelled like the old man his daddy had become. Isn't that the way? All the shed hair and bloody noses, farts and cigarette smoke, the stink of old shit and bad breath stayed on in the wood, the furniture. Sometimes it was like living in another man's skin.

Pattiann woke to the sound of the downstairs door opening. She turned on the bedside lamp, letting her long copper hair shield her eyes from the first light. Their house was on the edge of town, a white two-story bungalow with narrow clapboards and green trim that could have been lifted whole from the Midwest, a concession she'd made in buying this particular house, knowing how its familiarity comforted her husband. She greeted Ike on the stairwell. "I'll make us coffee," she said, and led him back to the kitchen. She was dressed in flannel pajamas, throat buttons open, socks—winter sleepwear of choice. She bent to the sink, sloshed water through the pot and ground fresh beans while he told her about searching for the Mattick boy and what he'd found instead. He told her how after uncovering one carcass he'd gone on to another,

another, and another, and stopped only after he no longer had the stomach for it.

The coffee dribbled into the pot, dark and strong, the fragrance thick as humus. She kept her back to him. What to say? She turned to him. He was changing—his skin aged, his hair hinting at salt and pepper, but his heart? Still in the right place, warm and so easily damaged. Some days she had little tolerance for it.

She set him in the chair, poured them coffee. He sipped the strong brew. "It's been a hard year," she said.

"No," he said. "This is a slaughter."

When she did not answer, he stood and left. She counted his steps, five to the first landing, turn, and the last five. She heard him cross overhead, past the small hall table with its Chinese-lacquered box, a Christmas gift from his mother, past the family photos on the wall: a portrait of her father and mother. More pictures: her brother Rob, wife and kids. A picture of Ike as a kid—buzz haircut, eyes pinched against the sun, behind him the barns of the old farm. In the next picture is his mother, her smile short on patience. His father always behind the camera except for the one small print that shows him glancing over a shoulder, surprised in the act of milking. He's a slender man, with a face gentler than his wife's, a softer version of Ike's own. It was Pattiann's favorite picture: the young man caught with his own camera in the intimacy of milking.

She closed her eyes, heard the soft thuds as Ike sat on the bed, releasing one shoe, then the other. Setting his gun in the bedside table drawer. She rinsed the cups, unplugged the coffeepot, and turned out the lights. In the dark, she felt her way along the Formica countertops, coming to know this place as she had known her father's house—late at night after long hours of calving, feeling her way to the bathroom where she washed in the dark, feeling competent and discovering the aches in her arms and back strangely comforting—as if finding the smell of blood, the dark house, the land and animals, were all pieces that completed her.

She'd heard about Stubblefield's trouble, early on, from hired hands at her brother's. "Goddamned cattle are starving," they said, and, "Flopping dead like flies." And she'd heard about it again the other morning, at Steve's shop. But they were rumors, after all. You didn't tell the law rumors, particularly if the law was your husband. She'd waited like everyone else for the issue to resolve itself. And it would. Painfully. This sort of thing shamed them all, and no one liked to hear about it. She kept her hand on the banister, wound her way up to the second floor, down the hall.

And as for Chas? She was startled by the glitch she felt in her breathing. This would finish him with the community. Light seeped from around the bedroom door. She braced herself. Tried to think of what she could say to Ike that would make this reasonable. Or acceptable? She was tired of apologizing for the intractability of the land, its people, for the distances that wore at him, the endless driving. She reminded herself: he had followed her here. Landless and loving and too damn good to be true.

She sat on the edge of their bed and waited for him to come out of the bathroom. He would leave a slough of water on the sink that he would ineffectually mop up. She still thought the small mess endearing. He returned, toweling his neck, his face, as if he could rub it clean of the windburn, clear down to the Midwest shine.

"This sort of thing is rare," she said, "but it happens."

He looked at the towel, at his hands. Sometimes, at night like this, they would cramp from the long hours on the wheel. When he looked up, she was composed on her side of the bed and he wanted something else from her. "If you'd seen it," he said. But she didn't answer. He knew he was being willfully naive, for of course she'd seen it before, other places, other times. Hard winters. He knew how he looked to her: foolish. He hated that. He balled the towel and pitched it into a corner. "You ranchers act like nobody can understand anything out here but you. You act like I don't live here."

He wished he'd kept silent, that he'd come home to find her frowzy with sleep, when her lack of presence was a thing in itself, so utterly distinct from the woman she was by day—a force to be reckoned with. It was the way she had been raised. She could string fence, pull calves, cook for a crew of ranch hands, balance books, and take insult if you thought that exceptional. She took gain and loss with the same levelheaded shrug. Sometimes Ike believed she could lose anything but her way.

She snapped off her bedside lamp. "Sometimes, Ike, you *don't* live here. You're still back on some little farm where corn can't help but grow and the cattle die fat and happy."

He hated that, too. The way she could ambush him, put him back where he belonged.

"There's no pleasure in it," she said, snugged her feet under the covers and rolled over. "No rancher wants to see his stock die. You're taking this too personal."

She looked small in their bed. She was thirty-three years to his forty-two, and slimmer than when they'd first met. Weren't wives supposed to gain weight, grow complacent? And wasn't there something comforting in that? Not Pattiann. No soft edges in her old age; she'd chip them off herself, if she had to.

"They're *his* cattle," she said.

And that was the problem here, he thought, their inherent belief in property as a "God-given right." For them the law protected property, didn't infringe on it. She'd settled under the covers. He slipped into the far side, reached up, and drew aside the curtains. Her breathing was shallow, but it would soon change; she always fell asleep so easily. Even on a fight. He could hear the wind sheering around the corner of the house. He craned his head back and saw the snow in sloping ledges on the mullioned windows. Moonlight fired the iced glass, spread onto the sill, the headboard, his body. He looked over to where Pattiann lay on her side, the rise and fall of the bedding, her body adrift, and he was hit with the familiar fear that he'd missed some *thing* that could not be regained. He put his hand on her hip. Never let the sun set on your anger—his mother's creed, sparked, he thought, from that childhood dirge, *If I should die before I wake,* as if death were the consequence of sleep, or the dark. Pattiann's hand shrugged out from under the quilts and covered his, an abeyance for the night and that was enough.

Ike sat at the counter of the Dig-In Diner, still mildly peeved with Patti-ann. He picked at his sandwich as if it were a bone. The single-roomed diner had a wide thermopane that looked out on Main Street where men tugged hats against the wind and women herded children ahead of them. There was counter seating for eight where Ike sat, three chrome and Formica tables behind him and two window booths hoarded by teenagers on hot summer nights, the underside of the tables lumped with gum. Roy, the owner, worked the grill; his wife Mary made salads, desserts, and kept the place as clean as weather and working cowboys allowed. Today's special—meatloaf sandwiches and split pea soup. Ike left a two-dollar tip for Fran, his waitress, who rented an apartment in town so her kids could go to the only school in two hundred miles, sixty miles distant from where her husband worked their ranch, where she spent her weekends—weather allowing—restoring order. He stepped out onto the diner porch. He rolled the brim of his Stetson, a hat he tended to hold more than wear.

Lucy Mattick's car was parked across from the mercantile. That morning her son had surfaced, hungover and with sixty unaccounted-for dollars in his pocket, of which his mama relieved him and delivered to Ike's office in a plain white envelope. "I ain't saying he took it," she said. "But you hear someone lost some money, misplaced it, maybe, you give it back. No trouble."

Ike stopped at Coker's feed mill. It was one of those queer blue days with a mist of snow falling through bright sunlight. Next door, the steel-sided grain elevators marched in an imposing row. He parked his Bronco alongside the loading dock, hefted himself up the boardwalk. Sunlight streamed through the bay doors over stacked bags: hog feed, chicken, sheep, dog, horse, rabbit, cat, cattle. To the left, through the store window, shelves of coat conditioners, hoof varnishes, salves, calf and colt formulas, tack. A young clerk, apron rucked up between thighs, stocked shelves. Overhead a country tune buzzed through a blown speaker in the warehouse and the wind gusted and eddied. Down the feed rows, tucked beneath and between the pallets, were bits of silver paper with chocolate-colored cubes displayed like party favors. He angled through the building and out the back door where he found Sam Coker seated on a bench. When he saw Ike, he shrugged. "Rats," he said. "Rats, cats, skunks." He offered a cube to Ike. "Poison. Smells just like those French chocolates." He looked smug. "Rats are fools for chocolate."

Ike wondered how he had arrived at such insight into the rodent mind—this curious little man with droopy trousers and suspenders. "Won't own a belt," he'd once said. "Pinch your gut. Won't own a wife, either," and left the town to wonder if the same reasoning applied.

"Chas Stubblefield?" he said, answering Ike's question. "Gave him barley cakes on credit a couple months ago. Told him to make it last." He clapped his hands over ruddy ears; his thin hair looked sprung in the wind. "He's going down and taking a bite of me along." Then he seemed stricken with the indelicacy of his words and he picked at Ike's sleeve. "Don't go spreading it about."

Late afternoon, Ike drove past Coker's again, saw the big bay doors battened against the wind. He turned down the street bordering the cemetery with its small stone chapel and a rick of brush where black-birds huddled. He drove down residential streets quiet on this a work and school day. He slowed past the vet's pole barn clinic, a horse and cow drowsing in separate holding paddocks, then turned onto the high-way, and although the land looked flat, it was the sheer scope of dis-tances that leveled the eyes instead. A half-hour or an hour between ranches and connecting roads. The intersecting county roads had lad-dered signs with names scrawled on the crossbars: Macley, Zito, Har-rington, Forman, Maresca. An hour out, he turned down Beaver Creek Road, Pattiann's family's ranch at the far end, five miles of ranch road, dead-ending on the Missouri Breaks in their thirty thousand–acre spread with all but nine thousand leased from the Bureau of Land Manage-ment. Here she could locate her way by a boulder in the field, or the stunted juniper, having named them, as children of this place did: Indi-anhead cliff, painted rock, the old Jonas tree, as if naming gave the thing substance, though what it really did, he suspected, was give the *people* substance for the span of their or their children's memory. A small place in history. And who could deny the need for that where the land so easily swallowed accomplishments, so blatantly wore its age in the bones of the prehistoric inhabitants lumped in the hardpan?

Stubblefield's spread was near the end of the road, just after the turn-off onto private road. Ike stopped on the shoulder. The piebald horse paced the fence and cattle huddled in small groups. Chas stood at the water trough. A rifle, a Marlin, lever-action .30-.30, was propped against the tank. He was bending over one of the cows, a surprisingly reverent posture, an attentiveness Ike found familiar—his own father had done this, moving among his cows, leaning into their guts to hear the rumbles or silence. Chas watched as Ike approached.

"Who died?" Chas asked.

Ike stopped. And then he nodded. "Must seem that way to folks when a sheriff stops—somebody dead."

Chas was a man of medium height who carried his weight in his chest and arms. He wore a Stetson punched low over his forehead, the brim dipping toward the nose he scratched with a gloved finger. He looked clean, his clothes laundered. He waited patiently.

"You got a problem," Ike said.

"No," he said, and his eyes were the unperturbed blue of the sky. "I don't have a worry in the world. Bank's got about two hundred," Chas said. "And more every day." He prodded one of the weakened cows with an elbow.

"You out of feed?"

"Out of money. Out of credit. Out of luck. All I got left is patience. I got patience to spend."

"Sell some of them."

Chas tugged on his hat. "Why you could be my own father come back from the dead," Chas said. "You're that farsighted." He clapped his hand over the spine of a cow and the animal shuffled away. "Not enough meat to pay what I owe and nobody to buy. No. These animals are going to die." He turned away, lifted a sledge, and brought it down on the skin of ice in the water trough. He knocked the ice loose and sifted it off the surface. When he turned around, he looked surprised to see the sheriff still waiting. He wiped his hands on his jacket.

"What do you want? You think it's me doing this, you're wrong. Talk to the bank. Let Sam at the feed mill come out. Let all of them come see it up close. Come spring, let them *smell* it." He picked up his rifle.

"This isn't about the bank, Chas. This is about you."

Chas winged the rifle stock up under his arm, barrel swinging around. Chas was smiling again and shaking his head as though he were just another of the stunned cattle. "Maybe what you mean is everyone wants everything neat and odorless, you, Taylor, and Coker . . . and you got the law to make it so. But these animals are mine." He raised the rifle to his shoulder, drew a bead on a cow. Then he turned his face toward Ike, his cheeks dimpling, and Ike caught a glimpse of what the man must have looked like as a boy. Then he fired. The animal stood a moment, blood spraying an outline of its forequarters in the snow, a curiously liquid sound in the frozen landscape, and then it dropped, its eyes still open as though contemplating life with no regrets.

"I can shoot that cow because it's mine," Chas said. He raised the rifle, levered another bullet, aimed it at another cow. "This one. That one. You tell me what difference it makes if they're shot, pole-axed, or starved." He lowered the rifle. "They're meat and meat," he said, leaning into the sheriff's face. "You just think they're something else."

Chapter Three

C lear and simple, Ike believed there was an order to the world—a sensibility that man could comprehend: boys became men, the moon followed the sun, stars were birthed and collapsed, environment determined its inhabitants and their numbers. And order—the need for it—inspired law, both moral and social. What bothered Ike in Stubblefield's case was the manner in which the animals were suffering, the waste. Ike thought of his father measuring feed into bins, the cows yielding a marvel of milk. He ate meat like a sacrament.

Not that Ike was the sentimentalist his father had been. No. What it came down to for Ike was respect. We were human, with the ability to construct order, to make choices, and a conscience that demanded we bear the consequences of our actions. It raised us above the animals. It was a matter of humanity. Dignity.

Bullshit.

It was the cow dropping, the grunt as it hit the turf, and Stubblefield's smile.

Ike crossed town on foot. He turned down a block, crossed through the cemetery, and out the other side. He found Purvis working on his '57 Chevy in the garage connected to the clinic. A good vet but an unlikely mechanic, who believed he could master anything if the problem were presented in the correct frame of reference. When they'd first met, he'd endeared himself to Ike by comparing a fouled carburetor to an impacted anus. Ike had asked if the exhaust wouldn't be more like an anus, after which they'd retired to the house to mull the problem over whiskey. It was clear to Ike the Chevy would never run properly as long as Purvis was under the hood. It was equally clear Purvis knew as well.

The Mattick boy was on a stool, stripping electrical wire. He was a handsome boy, dark, and Ike supposed that's what fed the rumors about the Indian blood. The boy was a heller and folks were apt to seek an excuse for whatever dark inclinations moved within them, preferring to believe there was good blood, bad blood, and what constituted bad blood often came down to what skin color wasn't yours. So damn much out there you *couldn't* know: weather, disease, government. It inspired a reductionist kind of thought—find a name and face to place the blame. The boy shifted on the stool.

"Ike," Purvis said. Coming out from under the opened hood, he offered his hand. "Come to help?" He pointed to the boy. "You know Joe?"

Joe's eyes passed over Ike's face, rested briefly on his badge. Guilty, Ike thought. Of what he didn't know, but suddenly he worried for his friend Purvis. This boy was trouble in the making. Ike pointed to the car. "What's it this time?"

Purvis wiped his hands down his coveralls. "A problem with the synapse," he said.

"Careful or that synapse is going to electrocute you," Ike said.

The young boy snorted and looked away.

Next to the car was an enameled tray with wrenches and sockets lined up on a surgical towel. Joe set the snips down. "I got to go. Back tomorrow, okay?" At the door, Joe hesitated. "You won't do anything," he said, waving a finger toward the wires.

Purvis smiled. "Tomorrow."

The door heeled open against the wind. The boy eased himself through and the door blew shut. Outside the walls, the wind whistled—a constant with all that land and no purchase for the wind, no mountains, or forests, instead, the elements of land and heaven skittering loose, chaff, sticks, stones, rain, hail, snow, and sleet, bearing down and down until buildings canted and what few trees there were grew one-sided as a limp. People rode their animals or stood in the fields pitched forward until it was a part of them, ligaments shortened, tendons stretched. Even in churches, halls, and homes, still they leaned in bodies remade by the fervor of wind.

There was the patter of corn snow on the roof. Purvis watched the door. "Joe's a good boy," he said. "He worries too much, though. Thinks I might hurt myself." Purvis motioned Ike closer. "What happens if I hook this up here?"

"Epilepsy," Ike said.

Purvis nodded, set the wires down. "I need a drink."

"I'm on duty."

"Didn't say nothing about you drinking. Make you some coffee."

They crossed through the pole building with its pens and chute where people dropped off livestock, and at the barn door a head catch arrangement with side panels that swung out of the way. Inside the heated building, block and tackle hoists ranged on the overhead beams to remove the dead, or drag unconscious animals clear. Along the wall were stacked portable corral panels. In one corner, hay bales loomed fragrant and stacks of rubber pans teetered against bedding straw. At the far end was the surgery—a concrete floor with a center drain. Boxes of sterile packing lined shelves on one wall. Cabinets stocked with antibiotics, tranquilizers, anesthetics that could reduce a thousand-pound animal to cataclysmic dreams, or dust and bones. Art consisted of diplomas and an anatomical chart of a pig done by Purvis during his van Gogh period.

They crossed through a connecting passage to the main house, entered the kitchen transformed into a small-animal surgery, then into the living section—kitchenette, dining, and parlor all in one, with a bed and bath off to the side. Ike thought it eccentric, even for a bachelor. And what woman could live with this? Pattiann. Put it on some land and Pattiann could. She'd welcome the challenge. Her pioneer great-grandmother had raised five boys in a tar paper shack not much bigger than a one-car garage.

They sat at the table, pushing aside dishes and dog-eared magazines.

Purvis poured Ike a cup, which he used to warm his hands, having learned long ago about Purvis's coffee. Purvis ran his thumbs down a glass of whiskey, took a sip, and swiveled in his chair. "I know what this is about," he said. "And it isn't as bad as you think. He's a little misdirected, let's say."

Ike was beginning to believe he was the last person to have found out. "Misdirected," Ike repeated.

"He's young. We worked it out. He's coming over two days a week." Purvis crossed his arms over his chest and rocked back. "If he shows any aptitude, I'll send him to a good pre-vet program." He studied Ike over his glasses. "Trouble with the law is it doesn't recognize potential."

"What the hell are you talking about?"

Purvis rocked forward, braced his hands on the table. "What are you talking about?"

"Stubblefield."

Purvis ducked his head. "Oh shit." And it came out that Purvis and Harley had had breakfast at the diner with Harley mentioning the sixty dollars found on the kid, and Purvis admitting he was "missing some money." Eighty dollars Purvis had "sort of forgotten and left on the table in the garage." Which money just "up and disappeared" after the Mattick boy and a friend stopped by to admire the car. Purvis had asked Harley not to make an issue of it.

"They bought a case of the dry heaves—twenty of the eighty—with wine, cigarettes, and donuts. Couldn't ask for a more fitting retribution, could you?"

Ike sipped the coffee. His stomach quailed and then stilled. The lull before the storm. Christ. "Maybe I ought to go out and heal some cattle," Ike said.

Purvis shook his head. "You wouldn't like it. Prolapsed uterus, mastitis, hoof rot. Makes me wonder why I left small-animal practice." He finished the whiskey. "No. Poodles were the worst. Can't take a decent shit. You got to pick the hair off their ass and squeeze their rectum." His fingers pinched the air and Ike's buttock flinched. "Do you have any idea how many years of selective breeding it took to produce an animal that

can't take a crap?" His hands spread open before him. "So now all I got
to deal with are cows bred too young to bulls too big. Or steers dropping
dead from heart attacks in the feedlots for the marbleized beef market. I
should have been a mechanic."

"Purvis, I don't give a good Goddamn about constipated poodles or
fat cows. I'm talking about respect."

"Respect."

"For the law."

"Right and wrong." Purvis poured another shot. "You're so single-
minded. Say I bring charges," he said, and waved his hand, "and I won't,
but say I do. He's a minor. He goes to juvie, gets a record and community service. So instead, the kid helps me—knows more about engines
than either of us. Hell, third son on a ranch—he's been tinkering on the
damn things since he was a baby. He keeps me from electrocuting
myself. I'm the only vet for a hundred miles. That's community service,
and I save the citizenry some taxpayer money."

"Purvis, you're a real hero." And even as Ike joked, he suspected it
was true. There was something large and generous in the old vet. His
stomach clenched, a stabbing in the gut. "But you can't make coffee to
save your life," Ike said. "I'm going to have to use your bathroom—no, I
don't need you to squeeze my rectum—then we're going for a drive. Just
you and me."

It was midafternoon, and from where Chas stood in the door of the mercantile, he could see the sheriff's Bronco pulling away, tires sluicing a
rooster tail of grit and snow. He stepped into the street, watched the turn
signal *blink, blink, blink.* The vet was in the passenger seat.

Chas had come to set matters right. Explain things to the sheriff. But
even as he'd stood watching them pull away, he knew there were no
words that could detour the events of today, or tomorrow or yesterday.
He felt doomed, and there was a relief in that, as if his head had just
rolled free of his body, taking its imponderable weight with it. And
maybe this was what death was, when the soul fled the body.

But what did he know of that? What his mother had told him? *Unto thee O Lord, do I lift up my soul.* Daughter of a Baptist minister, a tall, earnest woman who favored the psalms: *O, keep my soul and deliver me . . .* Who, of certain evenings, would retreat to Chas's room, settle herself bedside with her long brown hair knotted as tightly to the back of her neck late at night as it was first of the morning. An educated woman who picked through the handful of books she had salted away, a woman who favored the lyrical, whether it was the psalms or Milton, Dante . . . *for I put my trust in thee.* And she would read to Chas, her voice rising and falling, but so softly, a patter of sound like rain on the windowsill, that he would quiet his breathing, hunch forward to hear the words as insubstantial as the things they spoke of: the fall from grace, love, redemption. The soul.

No.

More memorably, it was what his father believed. It was the spring of Chas's tenth year, a hot day in May, and they were branding and cutting. Chuting young calves through the corrals narrowing in a bottleneck where Chas branded them and ending in a calf table with an iron gate that vised over their necks. Chas's father stood on one side of the table. His left hand clamped the squeeze catch and the restraining bars pressed into the calf's side. His right hand, large and pale as a slab of cooked pork, held the knife. He depressed a foot pedal and the table tilted, the locked-in calf keening over onto its side, and then Chas looped the catch rope around the calf's upper hind hoof, pulled it back, exposing the testicles, bearing down with his weight to keep the animal from kicking. His father ran a slit from the underbelly of the sack to the top and stripped the small balls out with a pinch of thumb and forefinger. A few cautious knife strokes frayed the cords, and then he swabbed the empty sack with Lysol-water. Then Chas flipped the table upright, loosing the animal. Now and again, his father would swipe at the sweat under his hat brim.

Chas goaded another calf through the chute. It balked. Chas kneed it in the rump, hot, dirty, and angry at the calves with their rolling eyes, dull hooves, and burned flesh. The calf reared in the pen and trapped itself sideways. His father turned, asked, "What the hell's wrong?"

"Just scared to the soul," Chas said, shoving the animal clear.

His father had spat into the dirt. "And suppose you tell me what a soul is, boy?"

And for all his mother's talk—of winged insubstantial things, a light in the hollow of your chest, or a thread tangled in your body like a second intestine tying you to God—he could not.

The calf was locked in, the table careened, and the animal lay supine. Chas's father slit the sack and held out the matched balls. "Here's all the soul you'll ever see. The only afterlife there is. Animals fuck. People fuck and anything worthy of regard is passed on to the offspring." He drew the handful close to his eyes. "Think on it. My daddy living in me, and his daddy and his daddy before him, and me in you." He tossed the testicles into a bucket. "Or not. And that's as much of an afterlife as this youngster's ever going to know."

The sky was clear overhead, and even in the stink of the stockyard Chas could smell the sweet tang of sage. Magpies squabbled on the rail and a few stock flies buzzed in the offal bucket. And that was as much soul as his father would credit any creature. He'd never been a generous man—least of all in opinion.

Chas walked back to his pickup. There was nothing to keep him in town. And then he spotted Pattiann, the sheriff's wife, striding down the walk. She was dressed in a long gray coat and jeans, a bright spark of hair escaping a watch cap. The only real color among the shabby buildings, drab sky, and slowing snow. When he thought of her, if he thought of her at all, these past years, it was of the heft of that hair and how it used to curl around his hand with a life of its own. He unlatched the cab door, stepped out, and aimed for her. Would she be pleased? After all this time? Probably not. They'd managed to avoid each other so thoroughly. But then it only seemed just, after all, the sheriff at his place and Chas with the sheriff's wife. Why not? Might as well be hung for a fool as a coward.

They took the highway west. Purvis stretched out on the seat, his arm looped over the backseat. A standard-issue shotgun racked next to him. Ike thought he looked as amused as a child by a ride in a squad car.

"You going to tell me where we're going?" Purvis asked. "No. Don't. A little mystery in the afternoon is good for the soul." He pulled his coat open, the snaps rifling. He shrugged a cigar from his shirt-front pocket, slipped off the cellophane and rolled open the window. "Nothing like a good cigar after whiskey unless it's whiskey after a good meal and a good woman waiting at the end of it all. Speaking of which, how's Pattiann? Good, good," he said, as if he'd given Ike time to answer. "I was pleased that little girl took up with you. Get her out of the damn ranching business."

He lit the cigar, looked out the side window. "This way of life's going to end. Mark my words. Another fifty years, the fences'll be down. The government will reintroduce bison to the plains with a command to be fruitful and multiply. Tourists will pay to be trampled. Wolves, elk, antelope, movie stars—they'll press the prairie flat with their numbers. 'Home . . . home, on the range, Where the deer and the antelope play,' " he sang.

Ike flipped his Stetson into the backseat. "Purvis, I knew you'd smoke your stinking cigars like I knew you'd talk my ears off, and I came prepared to pay the price. But I draw the line at singing."

Purvis drew on his cigar and leisurely released the smoke. "So I suppose you want to know why I became a vet."

"No."

"It's a vocation, like a call from God—"

"The Mattick boy—he get this call too?"

Purvis waved off the question. "Heard it while riding an eight hundred-pound sow on my daddy's farm. Southern Illinois. I was nine."

Clouds rankled in the east, a high wide billowing like the thunderheads of summer, but overhead was blue sky, and Ike flipped his sunglasses on, the snow and the world turning deeper, more vibrant, the

30

light polarized and somehow more true so that the distant cuneal hills were compressed, and the plains became dimples and swales, gullies and hollows, brushed blue and bluer, cobalt and indigo.

Purvis was speaking of his childhood, of hogs, and his father's farm that would eventually perish under rising land prices, and corporate farming.

"A prize sow, a prime specimen of Yorkshire cultivation, ears like the wings of a dove, shanks broad as the hills that spawned her breed, a nose of absolute grace. My father's pet. He'd have called it daughter if God and my mother could have abided it. Naturally, I hated that pig." He rolled an inch of ash into the ashtray, clenched the cigar between his knuckles.

"We had cows," Ike said.

"Lucky you. Pigs stink. It's a natural fact. Even the pearly pink ones. My brothers and I rode them every chance we had, though my father forbade it. But it's human. That old saying you only hurt the ones you love? Doesn't say half enough about the ones we hate.

"It must have been a hundred degrees the day I took it into my head to ride that sow. My brothers cornered her and I hopped on. I rode her like a bronc. She spun and bucked, torqued and trotted. Scraped me along the fencing. But she never squealed. And I never let go." He held his hands up. "My knees locked over her belly and she ran so hard, I didn't know who rode who anymore." Purvis was laughing, wheezing like that winded pig. He wiped his eyes, took a deep breath.

"When she began to stagger, I believed I'd won. And then she did the only thing left her. Her hocks buckled up and her snout shoveled a three-foot-long trench. She lay there, eyes open, sunlight pinking through her ears. Dead. In the mud—spiteful—getting the last word in after all. And maybe fear of my father had something to do with it, but more than that I knew I had killed her—you know, that instant when you *see* you'll never again be who you once were? Life, even for pigs, is no small matter. Call it shock, or my first reckoning with an irrevocable action, but when my brothers took off, I hauled that head into my lap, clamped her mouth shut, and fit my lips over her snout. I blew into that pig like God blew breath into Adam. I blew into that pig, and I blew and blew, even when lights swam in my eyes. Until I passed out. And that's how my father found me, passed out in the pig yard."

Purvis leaned his head back, took a haul off the cigar, and smiled. Ike exited the county road, past the old Grant homestead, foundation drifting, razed by rodents from the inside out. It was a half mile of silence before Ike gave in. "Well, did you save it? The pig?"

"What do you think? I was a snot-nosed kid with pig dirt in his mouth. Of course I didn't." Ike started to laugh and Purvis clamped a hand on his arm. "No, you don't laugh at this part. This is a matter of the miraculous and it requires respect. In all my father's grief for that pig, he still found it in him to love me. And though I learned I could kill, I could not resurrect. A heady and humbling experience, as the miraculous commonly is. But it was clear what I wanted from the rest of my life, it just required I set my sights a bit lower than bringing back the dead. So, where we headed?"

"Thought you wanted to be surprised."

"All my life, I've opened presents before Christmas. Can't keep a secret either."

"Chas Stubblefield's." Ike watched to see if that registered, but the vet was resting his head back on the seat again, eyes closed, mouthing the oily cigar stub.

"Knew his father," Purvis finally said. "Avery. Avery Stubblefield." Purvis eyed the cigar stub regretfully and stobbed it out in the ashtray. Ike picked it up and flicked it out the window. Purvis grinned. "My father used to say, you can't hate a man. You can hate the things he does, *but you can't hate the man.*"

Purvis leaned against the side window, crossed an ankle over his knee. "There's all kinds of mean. I've studied this. I've known men mean to their wives who can love a Goddamned mangy dog. I've known men who sing in church and rob their neighbors blind. It's as if people can't bear to be all of one thing—good or bad.

"But Avery . . ." Purvis shook his head, settled deeper in the seat.

They were nearing Stubblefield's, the road flat and straight as a razor slice. The snowbanks were gritty reliquaries—bones and skin, slivers and fragments of jackrabbit, skunk, deer.

"You believe the sins of the father can be visited upon the son?" Ike asked.

"I believe in the process of distillation. You can cook and cook a thing, reduce it, skin and bone, until you find the thing you desire. With Avery for a father, I believe Chas must have spent a lot of time in the pot."

Ike pulled over onto the shoulder across from Stubblefield's lot.

"Why bring me?" Purvis asked.

"I need a second opinion."

He leaned with his back against the window, staring across the seat at Ike. "Is it bad?"

Ike opened his door. There was roughly the same grouping of animals as on his last visit. He felt strangely relieved to see the piebald horse. "You tell me," he said.

That morning, Ike had waited for Pattiann to say the first word. She suspected he wanted an apology. Some teary response. Not a chance. Pattiann almost felt sorry for him. At twelve years of age, Pattiann's old horse Jubilee had died. It was the animal she'd learned to ride on at three, had hung on to her over younger horses, a sense of loyalty perhaps, or that streak in her that would not let go what she believed was hers. It was a clear, sweet day, land trampled green, the reservoir blue as an eye. Branding time, the neighbors and family gathered, calves milling in the corral, irons hot on the fires, and in the middle of work the horse had simply folded under her. After her father had touched an eyeball for response and found none, she unbridled the horse herself, unbuckled the chin strap, and dragged it from under the head, pried the bit from its teeth. Her father watched, offering a soiled handkerchief, for although he strove to inspire stoicism in his children, some part of him believed a lack of tears unnatural in a woman. Her mother knew better. That evening, at bedside, her mother had asked, "Will you cry when I die?"

"Would it do any good?" Pattiann had asked in return.

33

Her mother had laughed at that, straightened the bedsheet, snugged it between box spring and mattress, then kissed Pattiann goodnight. Turned out the light.

She studied the barber shop window, snatched a quick glimpse of her hair, embarrassed as she so often was by its . . . *redness*. She waved to Steve sitting in his own barber chair, reading the paper. Steve waved and then the paper fluttered up over his face again. It was a good morning, she decided. Never mind Ike's picking at his eggs and slopping his coffee only to wipe it up with a dish towel, even though he knew that that would anger her. *Because* he knew. But she'd ignored it, finished her own breakfast in silence.

She checked her pocket for the grocery list. She hurried on, feeling, oddly enough, guilty. Her silence had pushed Ike, as she knew it would, and she admitted some small pleasure in that. She'd confounded her father with her composure more than once.

When she looked up, she saw Chas Stubblefield crossing the street in her direction. She thought to turn away. Instead, she smiled politely.

He tugged his Stetson down on his brow. "Afternoon, *Mrs.* Parsons—Pattiann?"

"Chas."

"That's encouraging. You can still speak to me."

"No reason not to."

"*Some* might find reason. We didn't part so well, did we?"

Pattiann straightened her shoulders, while Chas shifted from foot to foot, each smiling, but at a point over the other's shoulder. "Well, I have to go, Chas." Pattiann fished out the grocery list and started to leave, but he caught her sleeve.

"Thought we might talk. But if you're in a hurry . . ." His voice was apologetic, and he hung on to her coat. "Been a rash of that this morning. Drove all the way in to speak with the sheriff," Chas paused, "but he's gone with the vet. That mean anything to you, Pattiann?"

Across the street, Kathy Grieger looked at them briefly before turning back to her own business. Cars drove by, pickups. Pattiann cocked her head toward Chas. "I can't help you."

He shook his head. "You think I'm going to ask you to talk to your husband. You think I'm going to call in old friendship—"

"That's history, Chas."

He flinched, and it made her feel petty. He looked vulnerable and she found that embarrassing. Foolhardy.

He released her arm. He turned away, stepped off the curb.

She was tempted to call out, apologize. No excuse for incivility, not in public. But chance encounter or not, people would improvise scenarios. *Saw Stubblefield cozying up to the sheriff's wife. Those two? Again? His cattle dying out there, the whole damn shooting match from what I heard—*

In the grocery store, she took her time, browsed the breads, tipped each egg in its cup, broke one and felt compelled to buy it. When she finished shopping, he was waiting at the door. "All right," she said, tucked the bag of groceries higher on her hip. "One cup. I'll buy."

Ike and Purvis stayed roadside. Chas's pickup was gone and Ike wondered where he might be. The piebald strained its neck over the fence as if they were old friends.

Purvis studied the herd, squinting into the snow's glare. His breath chugged. He rocked back on his heels, eyes skimming the drifts and the nearby patches of brown where coyotes had scavenged, a hank of fur, bone splintered like greenwood. Then he shuffled back to the truck, and seated himself. Ike offered his open palm and the horse licked it for salt.

Forty-five minutes into the return ride, when Purvis started speaking again, it wasn't about the herd. "Why the law?" he asked. "Was it like a call from God?" He was fading to a silhouette against the early darkening. "I've often thought the law's like the priesthood. A contemplative life on the applications of morality. You mete out punishment: three Our Fathers, a Hail Mary, two years in jail, and grant absolution."

"I don't deal in punishment or absolution. That's for the courts."

"You don't turn away sometimes? Give a warning instead of a ticket? You don't judge the perpetrator by means and motive and intent?"

"You saying I should forget this?"

They turned east onto the highway, heading into the early moon. In the rearview, Ike saw the last of the sunset, a slim band of red and umber hazing into the darkness. He tapped the high beams on and waited for the first of the inevitable jackrabbits.

"What was your father like? I imagine he was a principled man."

The fields lapped into the horizon, snow dunes cresting under the moon. It could be a lake, broad and handsome, and the cruiser, a skiff troweling through. He thought of his childhood. "Back home," Ike said, "a lake bordered our farm. Nothing big, just a pockmark with a swamp on one end where ducks and mute swans nested. Our side was rocky. Couldn't dive in. Had to tread water until you were exhausted. So, my father got this idea. He was a man of ideas." Ike raked his fingers through his hair. "You remind me of him sometimes. You and that Chevy."

Purvis grinned. "But principled."

"Yes," Ike said.

"I knew it," Purvis said.

"His idea was to build a beach, but this was midwinter and the lake was closed in ice. I was ten. I spent three successive Saturday mornings with him in our old stake truck at the quarry—a mountain of sand crusted six inches thick with frost and snow. Pickax first, then by the shovelful we loaded the truck. Oh, yes, come summer, my father said, we'd wade to our knees in sand. At home, he backed the truck onto the ice and we shoveled it out. He'd say, 'You watch, the ice will melt, the sand will drop and we will wade in our wisdom.' " Ike dimmed his brights, slowed. Deer stood off to the side of the road. A buck, two does.

Purvis's head reclined against the headrest. His eyes were closed and he was smiling. It could have been he'd drifted off to sleep, dreaming of home and bed, or of the good woman he was always pining for, but then he asked, "Did you get your beach?"

"Come spring the ice melted, all over that lake, except for the hundred or so feet insulated by sand. And then the winds came up and blew it to the middle of the lake, a huge dirty iceberg. It sank in sixty feet of water. We watched it. We were up in the pasture clearing rocks." Ike tapped the wheel with his fingers, glanced at his side mirror to where the sun had set, now pearling gray. "He laughed until he had to sit down—right there in the dirt. He laughed until I thought he'd gone crazy. All that work for nothing. I told him so. I was a practical child."

"Surprise, surprise," Purvis said.

" 'It's not every day you catch the Lord jesting,' my father said." And this was, Ike thought, the essence of his father—unaccomplished dreamer, undaunted in the face of midwestern icebergs and a scrub rock farm, one of God's good fools. Ike could smile about it now. As a young boy, he had walked away disgusted. He could still imagine how his turned back must have looked to his dad.

"He still alive? Your dad?"

Ike shook his head. "Died of a heart attack when I was eighteen. He'd sold the farm, oh, a good two years before. He got a job at a factory—Allis Chalmers—working on turbine engines. I think he'd have preferred the tractor division. He died on the assembly floor."

"Sometimes God's jokes leave something to be desired. So, you went into law enforcement?"

Ike nodded. "It was a job. Turned out I liked the work. Went back to college, got a degree in criminology, moved to Milwaukee, worked in the police department, taught a night class, met Pattiann"—he grinned over at Purvis—"lived happily ever after."

"You off work yet? I could use a beer."

Ike nodded. "I'll call in."

"So, why take me to Stubblefield's? You knew what you'd seen. It's a formal complaint you want?" Purvis rapped his knuckles on the side window. He watched the land slide by in the dark. "Nights like this, I know why God bothered with eastern Montana."

"It would make it official," Ike said.

"But you *could* file it yourself." He looked over at Ike and waited. "Cowardice is an unlikely virtue in a sheriff, don't you think?"

"I prefer to call it caution."

"I'll bet you do. It's an issue of property. Nothing else puts their backs up like property. Fact is, whoever calls the alarm on this one's not going to be popular. And you're elected. You got to consider that. I understand. As for me. They haven't much choice, have they? And I've been here longer." Purvis looked down into his lap, mumbled something. He had the look of a man about to flip a coin. Then he turned to Ike. "Give me *your* reasons."

"I'm in office because they voted out Art. You know it, I know it." The old sheriff, impeccable in his appearance, had been slovenly with the law. He was a native Montanan. A tall, silver-haired man who did not gain weight and so had developed appetites without restraint. Stockpiled snack food—Fritos, donuts, chips, and crackers; lotions he swabbed on his coddled skin, colognes that lingered in the squads to this day. He'd had a taste for young girls as well, it turned out. But Ike had come into his office, asking for a job, and the man heard out his credentials and gave him one. He must have thought Ike traitorous for running against him two years later. But Art Anders was a rogue cop, an outlaw in even the kindest terms.

"I'm the outsider here—I mess with a man's cattle, they'll take that seriously."

"Still strikes me as cowardice. And that's not your style. No. It's something else."

Ike kept his silence. This could be a pleasant drive in the moonlight, a good friend at his side, the Bronco casting off miles of clean road, past the solitary prick of lights where ranchers and families settled down to meals, their cattle watered, fed, and lulled into believing by the good life—the vale of stars overhead and the wide land—that the slaughter trucks never roll for them.

"It's gotten personal, hasn't it," Purvis said.

Pattiann slipped the bridle over the horse's head, tweezed the ear through the leather eye. The roached mane bristled in her palm. The barn was empty. Earlier, her brother had come upon her while she was currying the mare. Rob gave her a loving knock on the shoulder before slouching off to another of the chores that kept him moving all day and tossing in his sleep. He was of medium height, shorter than their father, with the width and breadth of chest and shoulders their father had had when young. Rob's arms were wedges that split shirt seams. And like her father, he was a man who got over things quickly. He ran emotions like running hurdles—impatience, anger, love.

He did not ask why she was there, though he must think it strange, leaving her husband and home to drive out at all hours. But he would not ask. What she would say might be more than he cared to hear. And Pattiann credited her brother for his discretion and his generosity that had nothing to do with guilt. It wouldn't have occurred to him there might be cause—this ranch, now mostly his, was to be *all* his on the day their father would decide to hand it over. She was the eldest, but he was the eldest son, and that's the way it was.

She led the horse out into the yard, ran her hands through the cinch strap, raised her knee into the horse's belly, and pulled. The horse farted, and Pattiann secured the cinch. They walked past the house through the squares of light that wicked from windows, pausing to hear her niece practicing the fiddle. Pattiann's father played too, though less now with age crabbing his fingers. It pleased her to think of her niece learning the instrument, that plump girlish hand curling around the wooden neck. She was trying a jig, and Pattiann could almost see the way it used to be, her father on the fiddle while a young Rob—in his father's boots, tops over his knees and hat falling across his face— clowned and danced for their mother as he would for no one else, not then or ever again.

Across the fields, due west a mile and a half, was the main house, where her parents still lived. She clucked to the mare, picked her head up, and urged her down the utility road, along the fence line. At the gate, she released the come-along latch, swung it open as they rode through, and kicked the horse a quarter turn to close the gate behind them.

She wore a fleece-lined denim jacket, jeans, lined leather gloves, and a canvas navigator's hat with the earflaps snapped beneath her chin. The horse minced in the snow and she slapped its flanks, drew back the reins until the walk flattened out. They left the road, wading into the snow;

heat rose through the horse's shaggy coat and its breath was a rapid chuffing like the trailings of a steam engine, its heart stoked.

She'd come for silence, solitude, but for another reason as well—to reassure herself that the herd was safe. It all had to do with Chas, their talk over coffee.

"You didn't expect to find yourself here," he'd said, "with me. Maybe the last thing you expected, huh?"

"It wasn't an idea I woke up with." She looked off across the diner's tables, toward the door and the street beyond where even now, had she been wise, she would be walking homeward with a sack of groceries in arm. "It's been a long time, Chas. You're not in town very often."

"And if I was, would you notice?" He stalled her off with a hand. "I don't mean to make you uncomfortable. You got to understand, I'm not in the habit of friends." He shrugged. "Making or keeping."

"What do you want, Chas?"

"Just this." He waved a hand around the room. "A cup of coffee. Some time away from everything dead or dying. Someone to hear my side. Someone else who's got something in this world to gain or lose in the hearing."

"And you think I have a stake in this?"

"Don't you?" He looked genuinely confused. He shook his head. "I just want *you* to understand. For old times' sake."

Her cup was half empty, and she covered the top with her hand when Fran skimmed by. Chas tugged at a shank of blond hair fallen over his forehead, an old habit she'd once found endearing, and it was strange how familiar the gesture still was, and how she had to squelch the urge to comb the lock back from his face with her fingers. Emmylou Harris sang on the radio in the kitchen. Acquaintances, friends came and went, politely and observantly ignoring the two seated in the back booth. She felt weary. This was an old business she'd long thought herself done with, and here he was, playing on her sympathy. She sat straighter. "What's to understand?" she said. "Too many cattle, too little feed, cash, and equity."

"No. Yes," he said. "Of course." He leaned back in his seat, the coffee mug cradled in his hands. "They came to me, the banks. Drove out to my spread shortly after my old man died. Wanted to set all the business straight, what debts I'd inherited—few enough. 'Your daddy was not a person to take advantage,' they said, 'of opportunity.' "

"I've heard this song and dance," she said.

He pursed his lips, blew out his cheeks with a sigh. "They walked my place and *showed* me what it was capable of. And of course, I'd dreamed that very thing myself, all those years ago as a boy, when I imagined the ranch mine. More land, more cattle spread over the hills, the hills greener.

"Machinery. Work. A few good years. All it would take was money, they said. Jesus, I was fresh-faced." He shook his head and laughed, then stopped abruptly.

"I was set up. A patsy."

Pattiann leaned back into the booth. "No," she said. "It's not that easy. The bankers believed, too. They're businessmen and they believed there was a profit to be had. They don't make money out here on foreclosures. Imprudent, maybe, their advice, but not intentionally bad."

"Imprudent." He snorted. "You've changed. I never knew you to be so *careful* in your opinions. God damn," he said. "It was like a fire, those bank loans." He stared over her shoulder. She lifted the cup to her lips and sipped, set it back down.

"Starts with a spark," he said. "Sure your hands strike the match, but the spark—it's an independent-minded thing. Sets about its business of living, feeding. Ever set a fire, Pattiann?" He was studying her, watching her hands, her eyes.

He brought his cup back up to the table and perched forward on the seat. "How one minute you think it's in hand and next thing it's eating everything around you until there's nothing left but you and by now it's a whole lot bigger than you, than anything you imagined. It's eating your house, your cattle, and it'll take you too, you know, but still you stand there holding your hands out to it, like it might just warm them." He leaned back and stirred his coffee; the spoon chattered against the sides. There was an intensity in his eyes that bore through her into the booth behind her, the wall, and the streets beyond. She knew what he meant. She understood how things went out of control, how easily, even naively, we tendered our own downfall.

The mare shifted her hindquarters, cocked a leg. They had stopped in one of the near pastures. In the dark, the cattle were a pale smudge, a fog of breath and body heat. They had congregated like the spokes of a wheel, their heads forming the hub. In another month or so, they'd be brought in for calving. Pattiann gripped the pommel and eased her numbed feet up out of the stirrups, then to the ground. She tossed the reins over the mare's head, ground-tying her. Pattiann walked to get the circulation in her feet started again. The area had been roughly plowed so that feed would not get trampled into the snow. Horses would paw and forage. Cattle wouldn't. There were dark streaks where Rob had lined out long running cuts of hay so that the cattle would not bunch and injure themselves.

When the needles in her feet turned to a warm flush, she pulled herself back up into the saddle, pocketed her feet in the stirrups, and goaded the animal forward. The land comprised long dips and rises, deceptively flat to the naive eye. She followed the trampled path.

Coyotes howled in the distance, yips and yodels, the love of that sound a heresy all cowhands shared, even knowing what coyotes did to calving herds, the sickly, the wounded, the very young. The mare balked, but Pattiann gigged it in the ribs and scolded. The mare's head complied with a droop.

There'd been nothing overtly threatening in Chas's conversation. No tactless reminders of their time together—back when they were young and headstrong as range animals.

The herd was dozing, their bellies full. Barring catastrophic weather, and you could never exclude that possibility, Rob and her father would do well this year, this abundance of snow turning to much-needed water. The families would thrive. And even as she was thinking of him, Rob's oldest son rode up. "Evening, Pattiann," he said. All wisdom and courtesy at the ripe age of fourteen.

"Your papa send you, Justin?"

"No, ma'am." He snugged his horse closer, let the reins drop, and picked out a wad of chew, a vice he enjoyed well out of his parents' sight. He offered her some, a solemn gift, which she declined.

"I'd have a smoke if you had one," she said, knowing he didn't. It had been a long time since she'd wanted a cigarette, and having said it, she knew the young boy would find one and keep it pocketed, somewhere, so that he could oblige her in the future, and whether she ever asked for another or not, it would be there. He was that kind of boy.

"Thought you might like some company."

And that was like him too, giving her the hour of privacy before checking on her. Justin, with his child's body and man's heart, could not be rebuked. He leaned over the other side of his horse and spat.

"So, where's Orion?" she asked, although she could have picked it out on any given night, even those stumbling drunk nights as a young woman and she believed she felt a yearning for that again too—that sweet, unreasonable state.

The boy raised his arm dutifully. It was a ritual they both enjoyed—pinning the heavens at fingertip, naming the constellations. His finger riveted Orion, then his arm dropped. "Leo?" he asked her. She raised her arm. "There, there, there," she said, and outlined the stars. The horses' heads lowered, their eyes lidded, breath evening out. They shifted from foot to foot, while the cattle, crowded for warmth, sank to their knees as if in genuflection and drifted into sleep. Pattiann felt the fierce joy she found only in these odd moments, outside her usual life, and then she remembered Chas's parting remark: "Your husband and I should talk. Only common courtesy. Don't you look a steer in the eyes before you shoot it?"

And then he was gone, out the door, down the street and into his pickup. And Pattiann was left to wonder what he meant and who he believed was holding the gun. She looked at Justin, nailing constellations, the elaborate sweep of his arm, and she felt frightened again, as though Chas were there with them, and in a way he was, her cheeks burning now as they had at the diner, at the shame of it—his dying cattle—his failure become hers.

This was a community that knew each other's families and histories and shared the same jokes, and one person's grief became another's. Shame ran deepest. All of them were stung by Chas's shameful act, the cruelty of it, because that worked at the fabric of their lives—these animals, this *way* of life—all of it dependent on a basic respect for what was given into your hands, and for the first time she wondered if her own hands would have been any stronger.

The cattle drowsed. She heard the chuffing of their horses, the squeak of saddle leather, and despite the cattle calmed in sleep, their shadows pilloried in the snow by a steady moonlight, she sensed events in motion beyond their control. She watched the shining face of her nephew, followed the pointing arm, and it seemed to Pattiann that the stars overhead turned perilous.

Though Ike had gotten home late, he'd only had one beer with Purvis, the remaining hours spent on paperwork in the office. He came home to find the bedsheets spread back, pillows plumped like airy pastries. He'd apologized, but she'd dismissed it, saying she'd been at her brother's and it was only a matter of luck she'd gotten home first. But would he have thought to prepare for her? He doubted it. Kept a meal warm in the oven? Probably not. Be honest. No. Not that he wouldn't, should he *think of it,* but that was the rub; it just wouldn't occur to him, those small attentions that were more a part of her, not because she was a woman—no, she would not be accused of that, no girlhood lessons on how to temper or please your man—but because it was her nature to trust action over words.

They ate a quiet dinner, then Pattiann ran a bath for him. She sat tubside, soaping his back, and seemed mildly amused by his erection, though she declined his offer to join him. Instead, she waited in the bedroom while he dried off. Another woman might have put on music. But Pattiann preferred the quiet, the jounce of bedsprings, and that was fine to his way of thinking. She was naked on the bed, a book, *Dry Land Ranching,* spread open in her lap. A candle flickered in the window.

"Pretty dark to read," he said.

She turned a page. "I don't want to appear anxious."

He looked down at himself. "I could use something myself, maybe a *Life* magazine." He measured his erection like a trout, and as he drew his hands upward, they moved wider apart. "Full spread."

She held her thumb out in a painter's measure, notched her knuckle with a nail, shook her head.

"Your perspective is screwed," she said, and he lay next to her.

"And the rest of me?"

"In good time."

They laughed, and when they leaned together to kiss, they bumped heads. And this was the best of it, holding each other as laughs turned to small talk until that dissipated like the weather they grumbled about. They held each other as friends. Their toes fidgeted under the sheets and she lay in the crook of his arm, her red hair spread among the peppered hairs on his chest. When they made love, it was Ike taking her each step, beyond her own surprised embarrassment—as, after all these years, she was still reluctant to lose that fine control she held over her emotions, slow to bare them, or perhaps trust them. He laid his hand on the hairs that furled into the ditch between her thighs. He eased her legs apart and touched her here, and here, watching the focus in her eyes come back from that place she always went to, come back to him, the iris opening even as she had, and he cautioned his own impatience, kissed her in the hollow of her throat, amazed as always at how soft that flesh felt to his lips, and when at last she reached for him, it was with an unfamiliar gesture, kissing the tips of his ears, drawing his fingers to her mouth, and when her own hands clasped his arms, his shoulders, buttocks, he entered her with a sweet quiet and held still to feel her close around him and he wondered how it must be to open yourself like this to another person, to take him into your body, and the vulnerability of the act was both appealing and appalling, and he moved slow, and then quicker, enjoying how her skin moistened like the bed of a leaf in early morning and how the white span of flesh between her chest and neck flushed red, and when at last she came in a cry, his own orgasm caught

45

him like a blow to the spine, a jolt rising from his groin through his chest and arms carrying him over that brink where he let go, as he would in no other part of his life, the order he so carefully maintained.

When he slumped to his side, he took her with him down into the deep folds of quilt, the candle guttering. When they parted, it was to spoon her back to his belly, his right hand tucked under her breast and eyes closed to the reassurance of his breath in her hair, and while they slept the wind continued its low complaint over the house and into the fields, and snow fell from the starless sky, great dollops of snow that broke the wind's back at last in bundling sheets, blanketing the land, crowning fenceposts with top hats and transforming coyotes, cattle, and horses into snow creatures, and in all that land the only movement was of smoke lifting from chimneys, snow falling from the sky.

Chapter Four

Chas dug the book out from under his old bed, a youth's bed, still blanketed and pillowed as if waiting for its occupant to step back across the years and rest his head. He flipped the yearbook open. There was no writing in the book, no well wishes or jokes, the only signature his own printed on the fly of the front cover. He always printed. He believed printing gave nothing away.

He flipped to the senior class, and found Pattiann. She wore a crew neck sweater, her hair in a flip with a shelf of bangs across her forehead. No smile, her lips narrowed, clenched. In her eyes, he believed he could see her old wildness. He found it intriguing that she seemed softer now—steel gone malleable. He flipped past the school clubs and activities pages—she wasn't there, as he wasn't, another similarity, a kinship. But then there were the rumors of her drunkenness, her promiscuity, and he believed no one better appreciated the power and efficacy of rumors than he, nor how they pale against the truth. He tore the page out and folded it around her picture. He put on coat, hat, muffler, and gloves, and opened the door.

It had snowed, a wet, heavy snow that cleaned the air, submerging fences, the land, until even the calling of cattle was muted. The overhead casters rumbled as the barn door rolled back. Starlings racketed off the eaves. He was struck by the static colors of the pickup, the barn, sky, fields: red, gray, blue, white, and then the sudden chattering flight of black. And it seemed if ever there was a time to curse God, it was at this moment, with starlings reeling overhead, and a woman's picture cozied in his pocket, this was the time to curse Him, His benevolent, malevolent face. He loaded a couple of the too few remaining feed sacks into the pickup, switched on the hydraulics, and the plow whined into place. He set the blade and cleared a lane to the pasture. He plowed a space for the gate, pulled through, closed it behind him. In the field, he opened a twenty-foot corridor, and the cattle in the far corner swung their heads like bell clappers and bellowed. They stumbled in single file, one or two trying to run, crowding him while he opened the sacks. Some of the cows fell to their knees, some butted heads, some stood dazed in the background. These he roused with kicks to the shanks. He chipped ice from the trough and ran new water. The last of the rationed feed he reserved for the piebald, his father's old horse, that stood its distance. The horse nickered when he approached and ground the feed in the bucket with its teeth.

He hauled bridle and saddle off the back of the truck while a few cattle hung their heads over the truck bed huffing the chaff to the far corners with strangled breaths. He saddled the piebald, cinch strap looping long and trailing. He roped a pickax to the cantle. When he mounted, the horse staggered and planted its feet wide. But it moved off well enough, and they set out at a slow walk, skirting the heaviest drifts, wading up to its canon bones through the wet snow.

An hour to cover a half-hour's journey. They stopped at the reservoir, and though he saw no living cattle nearby, he chose to believe some might have survived on scrub. He ground-tied the horse and fetched the ax, teetered across the bank's edge on snow-covered ice. A crease ran down the center—like a wound, like a woman's sex—where he had picked the trench two days past. He set to work, absorbing the blows with his muscles, feeling useful again with this pain. He thought of his talk with Pattiann. She'd listened, her heart driven by the same needs as his—land and cattle—and had despaired of the same failure: she was a woman, he was incompetent. He drove the pick: water sloshed over his boots, a sulfurous smell. He moved down.

They'd been so young the first time. Seventeen? It was late summer, in the field, wheat buckling in the wind, his knee cocked against the sky, and the sky a black platter overhead so near he believed he could raise up on an elbow and touch it. Closer, it seemed, than Pattiann staggering over him, tipping a bottle up, up until almost gone. The bottle he'd bought with the money he'd been saving for a new pair of boots. But it was worth every cent to see her, so much more than he'd dared imagine all those times he'd watched her driving cattle, or across the school corridors. Or listening to the other boys talk—none of what they said deterring him, but rather believing the thing that drove her drunk from one boy to another was the same emptiness he'd so often felt. And when he'd seen her at the dance, he'd sidled up to her, and when she turned to find the boy she'd arrived with, instead she found him—all one and the same to her in those days—and he was grateful for that.

He'd struggled with his jeans, the zipper, the condom that seemed easy enough when he'd practiced all those times, alone. She kicked her jeans aside and he halted his fumbling to take it in, skin and wheat and stars. He tried to roll the condom down, like a sock on a foot, but his penis was unsteady, wavering between rampant and retreat, and the rubber ring tweaked and pinched, tweezing pubic hairs, his breath in winces. She was standing over him, straddling his torso, and he said, "Oh yes," and then, "Just a minute."

He was still on his back when she mounted him, and the condom she'd flung like a spent snakeskin dangled from the trampled edge of wheat. A wind sock. And then Pattiann had him in hand and then inside of her, and sex was as much a thing as he'd imagined. He'd seen sex before—Taylor with his procession of girls in the back of the pickup—and from a small boy on he'd seen sex among the animals, and heard about it from friends in jokes, mostly about sheep, and so this is something he'd never admitted to anyone, how he'd masturbated as a young boy, imagined nestling his crotch to the woolly behind, lanolin waxing his belly. Because it was what he could picture back then, never this. But now it was happening and shocks rippled down his legs so that his toes curled. Her breasts swung over his face. She was lovely and he made himself breathe. I could marry her, he thought. Make this right. He let himself imagine this. He was that young and foolish. He was that drunk.

She was on him, rocking, and then something changed, the tenor of the stars or the complications in the way her hips cradled him because it began to chafe and she was grinding down as if she'd reduce him to rubble. She kept him inside her in a distracted way so that he became embarrassed, fearful he would shrivel inside her.

"Let me up," he said, but she wasn't listening, her eyes closed, a clicking noise in her throat, and she began to ride him up and back again. He understood then that this had nothing to do with him, and was it then he'd promised to change that? To make her see *him* as someone.

"Let me up," he said again. But she'd turned sweet, and so he wasn't sure he meant it, though by then he was sore and getting sorer, wishing she'd come, or he would so that he'd be excused like a young boy from the dinner table.

It ended as it began. She was suddenly standing over him and he was startled to see his cock still full and poised, and while he couldn't bear the thought of risking her again, he was already anticipating the unaccomplished ache that would settle in.

She stood contemplating the stars through the bottom of the bottle, holding the mouthpiece to her eye so that when some liquid dribbled down her cheek, she swiped at it and licked the hand. "Big Dipper," she said. She swung the bottle west, "Big Dipper," oriented the bottle on him, his penis, "Little Dipper." She dropped to a squat, and the suddenness of the action tilted her off her feet, landing her at his side.

When she lifted herself from the dirt, she struggled to put on her jeans, hopping one-legged, falling, scuffling in the dirt. "Damn stupid," she said.

He watched as she struck off across the field alone. Her daddy's field. Where she'd insisted they come. She reeled her way through the wheat like a haywire combine. He thought to follow, but instead walked back to the road, to his pickup parked down by the coulee where he sat with the door open to the cooling night, contemplating the act of sex, the stinging rawness of it.

They were meant to be together.

He'd believed that way back then. And he was startled to find some part of him, after all this time, willing to forget how she had cut and run, willing to believe that again.

He stepped farther out onto the ice. He'd had plenty of women since. Some few from town or neighboring ranches. Nowadays, he mostly drove to Lewistown, or Havre, dressed in his best, prosperous with distance. He met them in bars, paid the motel bill up front.

He preferred the dark where they were one and the same, this one, that one, skinny, tall, fat. Their skin yeasty beneath his fingers. And in most he found relief, for at least a little while. More than men, he thought, women carried God inside them, ejaculated His names in orgasms, oh Jesus, oh God, oh Christ, oh sweet Lord.

He niched the trench deep and the water wept over the snow, yellow, as if hounds had pissed the length of the cut. He fastened the pickax across the back of the saddle and mounted, his leg swinging over the point, nestled his feet in the stirrups, and nudged the horse. He followed the trail they'd cut and returned in shorter time to see the sheriff's Bronco pulled alongside the highway. The door swung open and Parsons was crossing the road.

Chas unstrapped the pickax, carried it to the truck bed, and leaned it there. He returned to the horse for the saddle.

The sheriff called, "Stubblefield." Then again, "Stubblefield." Chas glanced over. He looked stocky in his sheriff's jacket and Chas wondered what it was Pattiann saw in the dark of their bedroom and if she too cried, *oh Jesus*. He felt strangely privileged thinking of them like that, as if he could see them as they couldn't see themselves. He thought of her picture in his pocket, the raw-boned younger Pattiann, and then he thought of her now and saw her marriage to a landless man, an outsider, for what it was, a penance.

"All right if I come in?" the sheriff asked.

"Hasn't stopped you before." Chas slung the saddle over the tailgate. "You got a warrant?"

"This isn't court business." The sheriff shut the gate and strode to where Chas was unbridling the horse. The sheriff laid a hand on the horse's back, rubbed at the sweat and salt streaks. It was a proprietary laying on of hands and Chas paused until the hand withdrew. That done, he slapped the horse's neck and the animal pivoted, ran a few steps with a coltish kicking.

Ike laughed, and it seemed to Chas the sheriff's eyes went softer. And Chas knew then that he was already a gutted man. The sheriff would have it all—meat and gristle. Chas tossed the bridle into the bed.

"I could buy that horse off your hands."

Chas pulled his Stetson down so that the brim of his hat cut short the sky and all he could see was the white below and the horse. "If I was selling."

"You could use the money. I'd pay a fair price."

"Fair." Chas sank his chin on his chest. "Buy my cattle, too? The ranch, my truck, my tack?" He lifted one foot at a time. "How about these old shit-heeled boots?" He looked up, saw the way the sheriff's eyes grew guarded. Chas laughed to put him back at ease. "Why don't you tell me what you *think* is fair?"

Parsons looked relieved. "I'll go nine hundred."

Chas glanced up into the sky, watched the first edge of a new snow-fall tumble toward them, slowly, from feet up, or miles, he couldn't say, but it was coming at him with the inevitability of hard luck. "Then you're a fool, and I don't deal with fools." Chas started to walk away, felt a hand on his arm. He shook it off.

"Another few weeks there won't be enough money to save that horse. Nine hundred now," Ike said, keeping his distance, "could buy enough feed to pull some of the cattle through."

Chas looked over at the milling cows, knowing that this was all the herd that might be salvaged, and if there were any cattle left standing in the backcountry it was just another grudging gesture of Providence, too little too late.

"I'm just trying to help—"

Chas felt for the picture in his pocket. Found, instead, a coin, a pill of lint that rolled between his fingers, but no picture. Lost, he realized, somewhere back on the trail, moments ago, no years before, actually. It didn't really matter, did it? Chas walked over to the truck, raised the pickax overhead, and sank it into the truck bed with a clang so that the handle stood upright like a masthead. "You can open the gate. Close it when you leave." He started the truck. He waited, windows shut, staring out over the hood past the sheriff, who swung the gate wide, and driving out never looked back to see if Ike closed it after him.

Ike spent the afternoon in the office on reports, then to the courthouse for three DUIs and a break-in while marshaling crews to deal with stranded cars on the drifting county roads, in the middle of which he'd dispatched Harley to a domestic squabble. The snow kept falling. Late afternoon, while Ike was wolfing down a tuna fish sandwich, coffee, and an eclair in his office, he'd asked Troy, the desk sergeant, if Harley'd checked back in.

Three hours. No word. They tried the radio. No answer. No phone. Ike hauled on his jacket, snatching the address from the counter. "Call if you hear anything." And then he was out into the cold, the eclair and tuna fish swimming in his belly, and he was thinking about the dinner Pattiann would already be cooking, which he would probably miss and maybe just as well, because he wouldn't be able to eat anything anyway for a long time. Fish and custard. Good God. He turned on the lights, and the town's snowy face was stricken blue with each sweep. He accelerated past his house even while wanting to slow and pull in, her tenderness last night still with him like an aftertaste.

When he hit the highway, he kicked the Bronco into four-wheel drive. He was headed to Tom and Emily Millan's trailer home, eighteen miles south down the highway, five miles east on gravel that might or might not be plowed. He cruised by a vehicle in the ditch. The driver was standing alongside his car, smoking a cigarette, disgusted with himself probably, the weather, the sheriff's car that blew past. Ike called it in. He thought of Pattiann and how she turned in his arms, her breasts rolling onto his chest, her legs hitched about his groin. He let in fresh air. What did it say about a forty-two-year-old man who finds himself lusting like a kid again for something as simple as a good fuck with the same woman he's slept next to for years? Was he that easy?

He slowed for the county road, skidded, and steered to compensate. Farther down the highway a plow approached, its headlights fuming in the snow while sparks off the blade fired the undercarriage with a cobalt light. It would be a long five miles, and Ike drove slowly, trusting the road was straight.

The snow drove at a hard angle into the windshield. To a side, a column twisted into the air; it whirligigged across the road, buffeting the front end of the Bronco, and then was gone. For not the first time that day, he questioned what this place had to recommend itself, the long burn of summer, when the land fried to tinder, or spring when the roads turned to gumbo—six inches, ten inches deep, compact clay saturated to a vast wallow. Flash floods that drove burrow owls, deer mice, and prairie dogs shooting for the surface and curled scorpions into balls to roll like pennies down culverts, turning the high desert into an ocean, inches deep, that glutted reservoirs, rushed over the jumps and breaks— a confluence of water, mud, rocks, and small mammals—down to the Missouri and its tributaries.

Though he believed none of the seasons had the better of winter, whose storms varied like a catalogue of ailments: sleet, wind, whiteouts, arctic freights.

He turned into the Millan drive. In a makeshift corral, two horses and a handful of cattle. Harley's cruiser was pulled up alongside. The trailer door was cracked open, and somewhere behind a television yammered, canned laughter. To a side stood Tom Millan, a man in his seventies given over to long underwear and semizipped pants. He held a gun to his own head. His wife Emily stood in front of him, in a pink housedress and matching mules. She had a kitchen knife in her fist. Jesus H. Christ.

54

Ike walked to the side window, stretched up on toes to look in. Harley sat on the sofa. His gun was drawn and resting on his knees. Ike could swear Harley was watching the TV. He looked sour.

When all else fails, be polite. Ike knocked on the door.

"Come in," Emily called.

Harley lurched to his feet, and Tom slid the gun to his temple. "I'll shoot," he said.

"You do, I'll cut my throat," Emily said, and the wattle of her neck shook.

Ike stopped, kicked the snow from his feet, and stepped in carefully. Harley had dropped back into the sofa, though his gun was still out. "Put that thing away, Harley. We got enough weapons here already." He turned to Tom, took in the phone cord pulled from the wall. "Would someone like to tell me what's going on? Tom?" he asked.

The old man looked away.

Ike turned to Emily.

"The IRS. They say we owe seven hundred dollars from 1994," she said. "For seven hundred dollars he's going to blow his head off. Like it's worth it, you old dope." She pointed the knife at her husband. "I tell him, fine. But he's not leaving me to deal with the mess."

Harley sighed. "So he calls us, thinking we'll take her off his hands so he can get on with it. She won't leave, he won't drop the gun–"

"So you pull yours?"

"I thought–" he said, and stopped. "They could have–" He waited.

"Why don't you go radio the folks back home. Tell them we're fine." Ike took his coat off. "Warm in here. Didn't think it of you two–a domestic squabble."

"We ain't fighting," Tom said.

"The heck we aren't," Emily said.

Ike lowered himself into a chair, a vinyl and chrome thing that wobbled. The kitchen was a four-foot galley papered in old calendar pictures: canyons and gorges, steam-fired locomotives trundling over trestles. Their dishes were a secondhand mix. There was the sweet smell of starch and the ironing board was still out. These people lived by their own scratch and scrabble. A small retirement fund maybe, a few head of cattle, some chickens. What could the IRS want of them? What needs of this community, or this nation, would be met by that piddling amount, $700, still more money than these two had in the world right now? He felt guilty, as though his role as sheriff gave him some part in this. "We could talk to an accountant; Ben Johnson would do it," Ike said.

Tom's spine stiffened, and the gun skidded to the hairline. The old man's hand whitened. "Number shifters. Next thing you know I owe him, too."

His hand was shaking. And Ike feared a mistake might happen. "All right," Ike said, his hands inching closer to his own gun—*getting as bad as Harley, what are you going to do, shoot the old man?* "Just give me a minute," Ike said.

Tom nodded, eased himself into the chair across from Ike, rested his elbow on the table. The gun pinned to his temple took on a deadly steadiness. "A pound of flesh. You mail it to them, Sheriff."

Then Emily seated herself and there they were, the three of them. It might have been a stage play, theater of the absurd—the old man with the gun to his head, his wife with a knife, and the sheriff.

Emily leaned toward Ike. "You tell me if you think seven hundred bucks is worth killing yourself and your wife?"

"I'm not killing you," Tom said. "Just myself."

"Yes, you are." She reached over, patted her husband's free hand as she must have comforted their children many years ago. "It would kill me," she put the knife down; "and wouldn't need this to do it, either. Forty years together and this is what I get." She turned to Ike. "My husband kills me. It'll be on his soul."

"Hear that, Tom? The IRS won't even sneeze at losing seven hundred dollars. Who wins?"

Tom closed his eyes and beneath the thin lids his eyes fretted and he sat so still that Ike could almost believe he had fallen asleep except for the sighs—one, two, and then two more. When he opened his eyes again, he lowered the gun, his hand shaking. "Cripes." He pushed it across the table to Ike. "One year I take a lousy part-time job. Pays a few bills, buys some good meat for a change, maybe a new set of long johns, some things for Emily. Two thousand dollars and now they want seven hundred back that was gone and spent years ago.

"I don't bother them. No welfare, no handouts, no gimme, gimme, gimme. I was in the war." He shook his head.

"How about this?" Ike asked. "You pay them five bucks a month for the next one hundred and forty years and the hell with them."

Tom was nodding. "I could do that."

They talked awhile longer, about the government and their grown children and the weather outside. Emily sliced thick slabs of homemade bread, doled pats of butter on them, and set plates before the men. "Where's the mercy?" she asked. "Where's the milk of human kindness?" She looked around. "Where's that other young fellow, maybe he'd like some bread?"

Harley would not be coaxed back in. Ike ate, though lunch still warred with his stomach. When he left, he took the handgun. "Next week, I'll bring it back."

Tom shook him off. "That's all right, I'll pick it up next time I'm in town. I got another." And Emily closed the door softly as Ike stepped out into the yard. He nodded to Harley, started up his own vehicle, and pulled out.

Nearing the town limits, Ike called Harley over the radio and told him to stop at the diner. They took a side booth. Harley wasn't talking and Ike felt talked out as well. They drank a half cup each.

"I nearly pulled *my* gun," Ike offered and stirred his coffee. Black coffee. His stomach already felt soiled.

Harley looked up in surprise, blushed. "God damn," Harley said. "Those old fools."

Ike reached under his jacket, shrugged his gun to the side. Some years were enough to give men a load of wisdom, but Harley, at a tender twenty-five, hadn't seen that year yet. That was clear. It was beyond Ike to instruct him, but Ike had no doubt it was coming. Today, tomorrow, next year or the next, somewhere down the pike a semi was rolling and painted on its side was the message: *Here to break Harley's heart and make him a better human,* and Ike didn't envy Harley that moment of impact. He hoped it would come while Harley still had a young, tough hide. It had happened to Ike the year his father died: the world had gone out of true, and it'd seemed to Ike that all the orderliness of his own world had finally hinged on a man with skinny legs and a weak heart. "This wasn't one of the Millans' better nights."

"Jesus."

Ike laughed. "But still," he took a sip of coffee, grimaced, "it was a hell of a gesture." More than Ike had managed with Stubblefield, his ploy to buy the horse at double its worth. But sometimes, Ike believed, that was all you were left with, the gesture.

"How'd you get the gun away?" Harley slopped coffee on the table, swiped at it with a napkin. "I tried everything. The old man ripped the phone out. I couldn't leave them to go radio in—"

"By that time, Tom was looking for a way out." Ike finished his coffee. "Damn, they're a prideful people."

Harley cleared his throat. "You going to tell them"—he nodded toward their office—"about tonight? About me?"

"Yup."

"Shit."

Harley left and Ike stretched his legs under the table and gripped his belly. He ordered an Alka-Seltzer and Fran dropped two tablets into a glass of water, seated herself across from him. She was Pattiann's age, or close to it. She looked worn as Pattiann rarely did, but Fran had three children, and children were something Ike and Pattiann had discussed at length long ago and rarely since. "I'm not ready," she'd said, and truthfully speaking, Ike had been relieved, believing that if ever he'd been ready, it had been years before, when he was younger, some green and earnest years he'd overlooked taking care of his mother, taking care of his career after his mother had remarried and moved on, and then Pattiann had come after he'd despaired of marriage, used to dating women who had tried commitment and found it stifling, or could not bear the prospect of their husband wearing a gun every day. And he'd seen enough cop marriages and divorces to understand their fears. When he'd met Pattiann, he'd expected the same. He was wrong. And when she'd left the Midwest to return to Montana, she'd said, "I love you. But I can't stay." It had nothing to do with him but everything to do with *home*. He'd followed a year later, just showed up, got a job in the sheriff's department. There were days of late, he admitted, when he thought they should have had children, might yet. A daughter, maybe. A son. He glanced up. Fran was shaking a finger at him.

"I warned you about that lunch," she said.

"What is it about women makes them love to say I told you so?" The seltzer was expanding in his gut.

"Being right, I suppose," she said. She slipped her shoes off, rested her heels on the bench next to him; her feet were narrow. "You'd feel better if you belched."

He belched, nodded. "Maybe it's because they're always stating the obvious."

She loosened her collar button. "How you suffer." She closed her eyes, sat dreaming a moment.

She was beautiful, her face slack and clean, the dark under her eyes like soft thumbprints, brown hair escaping the hairnet. To a stranger, she might look frail, and that would be a misapprehension. Just maybe Fran held reserves deeper than Pattiann or Ike, because she'd risked children, and, so that her children could be schooled, lived a life separate from her husband's, even though she was a young woman, and he found himself thinking of her, alone, in restless nights turning to find comfort where there was none—her husband sixty miles away dreaming of the next day's ranch chores. He shook his head, looked down at his hands. He belched again.

Fran smiled. "Did Stubblefield find you yesterday? Came by early afternoon, asking for you. Came back later with Pattiann."

His stomach clenched. He looked over her shoulder to the darkened picture windows where the diner was reflected—the fluorescent lights, stools, and counter, the couple at the booth, elbow to elbow with their reflections, lifting twin sandwiches to lips, the young woman turning her head, hand wavering toward the glass as if she meant to reach into the reflection. "I was out of town in the afternoon," he said.

Fran eased a foot over her knee and massaged it. "With Purvis. Word gets out. I was a little surprised to see Pattiann with Chas. Been awhile."

But Pattiann hadn't told Ike about seeing Chas. He thought about the previous evening, the dinner, bath, the way she took him into her.

Fran settled her feet back into her shoes. "Been years, so I was kind of surprised to see them together.

"I always thought Stubblefield was trouble. Never could see what Pattiann saw—Chas kept to himself mostly." She tapped the tabletop with a fingernail. "They were wild, those two." She looked up at him. "But you've heard all this?"

Ike shrugged and smiled. "There's little I haven't heard before," he said, which was mostly true, for Pattiann had spoken of her own troubles, her drunkenness, her anger, but never in detail. Never any particular man.

"Thought so," Fran said. She kicked back in the seat. "They were into pranks, general rowdiness, like the time they painted Browning's dun mare in camouflage and it took that man with his lousy eyes a week and a half to find her out on the range. Though I never believed Pattiann capable of meanness—did see her lay Chas flat one night with a bottle upside the head, and never had a doubt he deserved as much. You need any more?" she asked. And for a moment, Ike thought she meant of the history, until he noticed her finger pointing at his coffee cup. He shook his head.

"Her dad hated Chas."

"Not a good catch?" Ike asked.

"Not as good as she got," Fran said. Her smile dimpled and she winked.

"Ah, but he had land."

She wrinkled her nose. "And look where it got him. Land without sense." She rolled her eyes. "Might as well own a horse without feet."

"He doesn't strike me as stupid."

She sat forward, plumped a fist in her back, and stretched. "It's as much intuition. Something that can't be taught. Maybe it's an astuteness that he lacks. Or maybe he's just a sonofabitch."

She leaned forward. She smelled of soap, and hamburgers and fries. "It's just that Pattiann did all right by herself, and I guess I'd hate to see her mess that up."

Ike waited, but he could see Fran had crossed some line and was regretting it. She fetched her order book out of a pocket, flipped out the bill. She patted his hand and stood up. "Seltzer's on me."

Ike drove past their home without slowing. The lights were on. He mulled over what Fran had told him. Quite a surprise. Pattiann hadn't mentioned a word about Stubblefield. Ever.

He drove just to drive, and ended up where he'd known he would. He stood roadside. The lights in Stubblefield's house were out, but smoke puffed from the chimney. The truck was parked next to the shed. What had he thought to do? Roust Stubblefield? Ask what he and Patti-ann talked about?

It was so still. The land and house and even the stars seemed frozen in place. The cattle were a darker piece of the night, as though the evening had congealed in solid fragments on the snow. Ike pulled a pail from behind the seat.

The bucket swung at his side, loaded with pellets and grain he'd bought at the mill that morning, back when he'd believed this whole mess could be resolved with the purchase of a horse. He watched the house to see if Chas had the second sight that told him someone was out there. Ike had had it while working the city beat, and he wondered if it was an acuity that fled with disuse. All *he* could feel was the wide night. All he could hear was the cattle blowing in their sleep, the *plock, plock* of the horse ambling across the packed snow. The house was still, and he imagined Chas deep in sleep, or sitting in the dark with his feet propped on the woodstove while embers popped and dimmed. The horse nosed the air, snuffled, and banged its muzzle into the feed pail.

This was what he'd come for—the simple act of feeding this horse. What this horse had come to mean he didn't understand yet, but Ike knew he must go through with it. He'd keep it on its feet with feed at night, and then once the animals were confiscated, he'd pay for the piebald's keep until he could buy it at auction. Maybe, in the next few years, he and Pattiann could get a few cattle, more horses—and land—her own small spread. Not that she would ever ask. No. And wouldn't it be better unasked for—a gift? Life would go on. Standing in this doomed place, he felt it was essential he believe that.

The night drew closer, the stars squandered in the black canopy, and the horse snorted in the pail, lipping the sides, the bottom. When finished, the horse swiped its head on Ike's arm in a long leisurely scratch. It nickered, then stood watching the distance over Ike's shoulder as if dreaming of buffalo grass, blue joint, silver sage and cats paw, a swale of fescue to bunk in, the smell of green and greener: a feast of air.

Ike's arm hooked over the horse's neck, fingers scruffing behind the ears. He looked at the house, and it seemed unchanged, although Ike sensed something. He watched the field, the calm night, the sleeping cattle. The horse stretched its neck over the barb, hooking a straggle of mane as it lipped at Ike's sleeve.

Ike walked to the Bronco. He sat behind the wheel and shut the door with a thud. He tucked his hands under his armpits to warm them. Stubblefield's yard light was off and the yard was a haphazard clutter of disabled cars and pickups, old farming equipment, a warren of waste. Little enough to admire here even in the forgiving dark, but Ike believed he could understand Stubblefield—stumbling deeper into the tangle of hope and luck with loans, believing each wrong step was the right one. Not so unlike those last years before Ike left Wisconsin, marking time, hoping there would be more in his life than the usual suspects, the faceless crimes, the succession of wounded—not joy, he couldn't hope for that, but some contentment perhaps, just the ability to lay aside the day's despair, go home at night to the sound of his own footsteps in the rooms, and not hear the echo as loss.

Ike snicked the key into the ignition, turned the engine over. He wanted to be home. He'd felt stung to hear secondhand of Pattiann and Chas—their meeting. Their *history*. This was a complication he hadn't counted on, would not have dreamed of. Though he knew something of Pattiann's trouble as a young woman, he didn't have the details: *Wild*, she'd said. *A lot of drinking. I got around.* And he would no more have considered asking for the details of her sexual past than she would have considered asking about his. And that seemed natural enough. The safest path. Until now. And what did he want now?

He turned into Stubblefield's drive with his headlights off, idled a moment. In the deep of the porch, he saw a spark, an ebb and glow. He waited. Then again, the glow and ebb, an ember hopping in the dark. Then the cigarette arced out over the porch and onto the snow. In the shadows something moved, the door opened and closed, and Stubblefield was gone. Ike hit a switch and the front of the house was washed with light. He rolled the vehicle back onto the highway and was gone.

Chapter Five

Stubblefield drifted in and out of his house with a new aimlessness that disoriented him at odd moments so that he was uncertain what task followed another, or even what hour of the day or evening it was. He'd find himself standing on the threshold of his bedroom, or hovering over the kitchen sink trying to remember why he was there. He had never appreciated the length of a day, until he'd run out of work. He plowed the feedlot as though there were bales to put down, and chipped the ice from the reservoir. What little feed was left, he rationed to the horse and the few standing cattle, enough to keep them upright—a week? Maybe. Did he care?

Avery Stubblefield would have. He'd never wanted to give Chas the ranch. Wouldn't have, except he'd died before he could sell it off and move to Arizona where he'd planned to finish his life withering away to a shank of leather. But there he was seized up in bed, already in his winding sheets, his heart squeezing in his eyes and telling Chas, *Get me to a doctor.*

And Chas took that old man up into his arms, carried him out the door fully intending to get help. But on the porch, he stopped. The old man had no more substance than a bird. The moon was a spit of light in the west and the yard lamp out front burned a hole into the night. Each time a pain hit Avery, Chas could hear the old man's leg bones grinding in their sockets, the old body knotting and breath coming, but so thin, so far gone, it was as if Chas could see right through the sheet and bone to the knotty pine floorboards. Was it then, Chas wondered, that he came to know what was just? Chas willed the heart to clench, and it did; the old man's eyes strayed, one up, one left. His bladder voided. Chas raised his head to clear his breath and the stars were a rapture; the cattle knelt in the grass lowing over their cud and his father's piebald horse loped the length of the fence. All this and more would be *his*.

The old man's breath piped, and the space about them grew still. He set his father in the dirt, went to the truck and turned on the radio, tuned in the national ministry and cranked the volume. He dragged the body up under the yard light. And to give Chas credit, he'd waited at his father's side, the long hours it took before taking himself off to clean up and go to bed.

And perhaps that was where it had started wrong. The land never properly given. Perhaps Avery's ghost lingered, a skinflint in everything but grief, even now. Tonight, Chas went out of his way to drive past Pattiann's old home. Smoke lifted from the bunkhouse chimney, the hay mows in the feed yard were tall and solemn with snow. He doubled back, drove into town, past Coker's mill, doors bolted on the feed. Chas slowed at Coker's house where he thought he saw Sam's shadow on the drapes.

Chas stopped at the filling station where he bought ten dollars worth of gas for the truck. In the back of the truck was a five-gallon can of kerosene from home. He drove to the bank, parked in front, lit a cigarette, and waited.

He fired up the engine. It choked, sputtered, and caught. No traffic. His truck wavered in the street-front windows, awnings clamped shut. The diner, concrete block with cedar trim, CLOSED sign in the window. He circled the square. The grocery, one bank of lights lit, the grizzled guard dog napping behind the glass door. Past the courthouse—white, squat as a mortician's slab. Past the sheriff's quarters, two lights burning. The parking lot: a car, three squads, and a pickup. A bank of dirty snow. He drove on. The vet's with horse trailer backed up to the loading bay. Barn lit. The sheriff's house. Lights out. Driveway empty. He pulled up to the garage, left the motor running. He thought of Pattiann: her snorting laughter, how she used to chew the inside of her lip when anxious, the way she used to balance on his hips. He thought of the sheriff, offering to buy that broken-down old piebald.

No one home. And me come to visit.

The clapboard house sat like tinder. He pressed his forehead against the window, humming a tune whose name he could not remember.

He turned back toward town, left at the junction, one mile, swung a hard right down the gravel lane. Taylor's house. A sprawling two-story affair. Lights out. Chas parked off the road a quarter mile down. He walked back; the can of kerosene hung like a plumb bob from his arm. He stepped lightly. No stars. Clouds thick as smoke damped back down a chimney.

As he walked the road, the small birds that inhabited the pines shifted on their perches and snowshoe hares squatted in snowy depressions. There was darkness and the air smelled as if it had been peeled clean, and here and there a bed of animal musk, a whiff of woodsmoke, wet bark, the streambed choked with snow and ice, and Chas believed he knew as animals did a world brighter in detail for lack of sight, and that the musk of him was a thing still traveling the road behind, trailing like a spirit.

He walked the plowed driveway leaving no prints and found the front door locked. He circled to the back and that door opened. It was cooler inside, cluttered with smells: gas, oil, and cat piss. His eyes adjusted and he picked out the hood of a car, two bicycles hanging from the ceiling, their front wheels crooked like mounted heads. He crossed to the door connecting the house and opened it. A night-light was on next to the stove. The kitchen was clean, counters cleared, table scrubbed. Chas stepped onto the threshold. The stove's digital clock notched a luminous green moment and another. He stepped forward and the floor creaked. There was a thin yapping overhead and Taylor's voice, "God damn it, shut up," and the dog did, and then mumbling, then silence.

Chas backed into the garage, easing the door shut. The car sat humped in the dark and Chas slipped into the driver's side. A big car, new. He imagined starting the engine—the computer dinging to life and a seat belt wrapping across his chest as though he were precious. He checked the ashtray, no butts. The interior smelled of cologne. Leather. No vinyl for old Taylor. He'd come a long way from those days in the back of Chas's pickup.

Chas stepped out of the car, removed his glove, and unscrewed the cap from the kerosene can. He leaned in, tipped the can, and emptied it over the front bench seats, the carpeted floors. Splash and gurgle. There was a thick oily smell in the garage now. He could have used gasoline with its quick hot *whoomp* of conflagration, but kerosene burned slower, dirtier. He stepped back, fished in his pocket for his glove and lighter.

Paused. It was all too easy.

He thought of Taylor falling back into dreams. That easily. When had Taylor suffered his last sleepless night? Chas cocked his head to a side. There was a lesson to be learned here. He slipped his glove on, tucked the lighter in his pocket. Looked around the garage one more time and passed back through the door where the night waited.

Chas drove home rejuvenated. He drove past the sheriff's home, honked and waved as though someone were there to receive it. He passed Coker's and turned onto the highway. Like a kid he gunned it so that the headlights wheeled a circle on the empty roadway, and another, and then the truck was bumped up against a snowbank like a compass for home. He engaged the four-wheel drive and relaxed as the road drew him away, and behind him the town with its sleeping, careless people vanished.

The elderly woman at the table had been a stunner in her day. Proof was in the old photograph on the table in the living room—Martha in jeans and boots, cowboy hat, brim hawk-nosed over her face. There's a quirt in her hand, at a jaunty angle to one hip. She looks like trouble standing next to a large raw-boned bay. Hard to believe she would shrink from five foot three to four foot ten, her back humped, spine collapsing, bone to bone. Always small. But not like this.

No one would have actually *called* her small. She was a presence, an only child who refused to be spoiled, though her father tried, and her mother let him because of all the miscarriages since. And finally surgery settled the question once and for all.

Did Martha know this? Too young, surely. And yet after the surgery, when her mother took months to recover and Martha came in from the range, wild and headstrong as her father had encouraged, she settled herself in to cook, clean, and tend. Ten years old and she did well enough, though she was a failure at breads. She bulldogged the dough on the counter, her arms and hands smelling yeasty even in bed. The chickens grew peevish on the hard loaves and still she worked. There was nothing to explain it, and her mother moved from the bedroom to the sofa while her father moved his cattle farther out to range, distancing himself from the commotion of flour.

When did it end? When did that prize-winning loaf first appear? Martha herself could not say. But somewhere in the span of a year her attention turned inward. It came finally like a gift, that reserve of quiet, and the day indoors came to be as wide and various as the open range she'd loved.

Her mother got strong and Martha rejoined her father working the range when he needed the help and her life took on a pleasurable wandering between house and fields. She raised bread and cattle with equanimity, and when at last the neighbor's son came to court, she studied his eyes and hands as if that were all there was of the man. They married, and her father, as an old man, died happy, having seen the properties joined and a son-in-law to tend the herd he'd started.

The stuff of family history. Pattiann perched on a stool a little ways from the table. She caught a smile her mother aimed at Ike across the table, a small wink, as intimate a gesture as Martha was likely to give. It surprised Pattiann, the affection between her mother and husband. Martha turned to listen to her husband Bill, who sat at the head. Pattiann's brother sat across next to their mother. Her sister-in-law Harriet shuffled dishes into the dishwasher. At a stool next to Pattiann, Justin was braiding a hackamore, working the bosal, the noseband that, when fitted to a bronc, cut the wind until the animal behaved. The braiding was her father's craft, taught to his grandson as he'd taught it to Rob and Pattiann.

The boy was configuring an eight-string braid over a core of rawhide, half-inch by two yards in length, cured and twisted for endurance. The eight ends of outer braid, soaped and pliable, splayed over his lap. His fingers caught each up, turned it under, released it to his other hand, and moved on. He was deft. Such a serious boy. As a young woman, she'd imagined evenings like this at the ranch—though she'd always imagined it her home, her son. She'd never imagined a daughter.

"Place is changing," her father said. "Look at Bozeman. Christ. People lived there three, four generations, bought up, moved out. Livingston. For Christ's sake. Used to be a town you could get shit-heeled in—"

"Bill," Martha said, tossed a look toward Justin.

Pattiann's father leaned over, his elbows thumping the tabletop. "You think he ain't heard worse? You heard worse, son?"

Justin turned a rawhide strand under. "Yes, sir. Heard the price of tit's gotten out of hand, so to speak."

Harriet slammed the dishwasher closed. "That's Odell, isn't it? You been hanging with Odell."

Rob quietly changed the subject. "Won't happen here, not like there—"

"Well, this is still a Christian household, isn't it?" Harriet cut in.

"You got any more coffee, Harriet?" Martha asked, attempting to rise. Harriet waved her off.

"Sit. Anybody else?" There were nods and shakes and the conversation moved on.

Sometimes Pattiann felt sorry for Harriet. She had married Rob just after high school, had Justin during Rob's first year at Montana State: agribusiness. She was town people, her father an accountant. Pattiann suspected conversations ran differently there—sentences carried through, ideas completed. Not the starts and stalls, the dodging of issues, silences saying more than words. Ike had never had a problem catching on to the elliptical nature of these conversations, their wariness, but was often unwilling to partake. He was bullheaded. Curiously, she loved that in him for its familiarity.

"Wolves," her father was saying, "cannot be confined to one place, unless it's their hide tacked to a wall."

"Read somewhere, long time ago," Rob said, "Wilt Chamberlain had a blanket made of wolf snouts."

"What's to admire? He didn't shoot them, did he?" Bill asked.

"Don't know I'd want to sleep under it," Rob said.

"Point is, the world's gone to hell and suddenly it's our fault—as if this ain't the least altered place on God's good earth." Bill dared each in turn to contradict him.

"Maybe that's it," Ike said. "A toehold. Some ground to turn around on."

Bill rubbed his jaw. "For some hundred years those big city folks been sitting in their own crap. Now they wake up surprised to find their bottoms dirty. So what's that make us? A place to come clean 'em off in? Missile silos, nuclear dumpsites, toxic landfills. Ain't nothing we done to this land they wouldn't do worse given half a chance."

"Will Angela play for us tonight?" Martha asked. The fluorescent light buzzed overhead. The coffee had cooled and on cue, they heard Angela in the living room tuning.

"You bring your fiddle, Dad?" Rob asked.

Martha pushed her chair back, braced her hands on the table. "He'll say no, but of course he did. Justin, it's out behind the truck seat. Now, you excuse me, I'm going to creep off, settle into the softest seat in the living room while the rest of you plead and beg this old coot to play until he finally breaks down and does exactly as he'd planned to all along." Her steps were crabbed.

Bill looked stricken. Martha patted his arm as she walked past him. "Sometimes, dear, the bullshit gets just too deep to wade through."

He smiled at her tweaking, laughed deep from his belly, said, "You heard her. Start begging."

Pattiann stayed in the kitchen with Harriet. She could hear her father's voice rasping in the living room. Then more tuning. There would be coffee at the end of it and some cake that Harriet had stashed out of reach of Rob and the hands and the kids.

"You need help, Harriet?" Pattiann asked, picked at a length of damp rawhide, thinking she should take it up again. Make a braided quirt, like the one her father had made for her mother as a fifth wedding anniversary present. The one her mother held in the photograph. The leather felt good in her fingers.

"No," Harriet said. She turned to Pattiann, her hands dropped to her side. She looked faded in the overhead light, the table cleared, sink clean, her hands empty. It wasn't that Pattiann didn't like Harriet, but she'd truthfully never felt much need to make a friend of her.

"I'd like to ask you something." Harriet rushed on, "I'm thinking of moving to town with the kids. Justin starts high school next fall. But Angela wants to stay in school here, stay on the ranch, though the change might do her good."

"Might," Pattiann said.

"It's Justin. You heard him tonight."

"Won't be any less of that talk in town."

Harriet shook her head. Lowered her voice. "It's him falling in with *them* all the time. Without a chance to think differently."

Them. Pattiann's hands stilled. It was *us* and *them* and Harriet clearly saw Pattiann in her camp. Pattiann dropped the rawhide strip back onto the bench. "What's Rob say?"

Harriet pulled a chair up. "He doesn't want me to go."

"He'd miss you."

Harriet nodded. "And who'd feed the hands, do the chores?"

"Other men survive."

"Who'd take care of Martha? I'm over there two, three times a week keeping their house up."

Of course. She could see it, Harriet stopping to visit and later on, after Harriet had left, Martha would find the wash done, or some dusting, or a floor scrubbed, or meals in the freezer, and neither would say a word to each other about it, or to Pattiann. Least of all Pattiann. If Harriet moved into town, it would be three households. "I could help," she said. "Come out every few days—"

Harriet was picking at her sweater, pilling the fuzz and gathering it into a nest in her lap. "I didn't mean that. Rob says Justin can make it on his own in town. Get a place, a part-time job, just like he did at Justin's age."

Just as Pattiann had. Moved out from the only place she knew or understood into town. And how frightening it had seemed back then, at fourteen, just off the ranch. All the noise, the cars. The town kids who bawled as she went by, calling her "new stock." She spent the first months ducking, or fighting. She lived in a one-room apartment, over the mercantile. Worked as a waitress part time, minimum wage for lunch money. Home weekends and holidays. How she'd hated it. Grew up fast.

"It's easier on boys," Pattiann said. "Justin'll be fine."

Harriet's breath hissed. "That's what Rob says. I didn't argue when he had Justin out on roundup and branding before he could keep his drawers dry." She stood up. "It's not like I knew what I was getting into."

Pattiann should say something of comfort, but she wanted, more than anything, to change the subject. She didn't want to know her brother's life wasn't what she'd believed it was. There was laughter in the next room, then the sound of a fiddle. Angela, a little unsteady, off pitch. Another fiddle joining, slowed from its usual pace. It was a kindness her father was capable of, but rarely showed. He was not a patient man.

Harriet's eyes studied Pattiann's, looking for some imagined sisterhood, assuming another woman would understand, a woman from town, as if Pattiann's ranch history were an aberration in some larger, more meaningful story. She sighed. "I'd better get the cake and coffee ready." She stood and turned away. She worked quietly at the sink. Her body looked as if it had sustained a blow.

Pattiann drove, and it was a treat for Ike, being the passenger, kicking back in the buzz of coffee and the leftover glow of Jim Beam while the road slipped by. Snowing again. It fell in clumps, a giggling clumsy descent. White on white. Not a break for miles, no barns, homes, trees. White, more white. A person could get lost out here. A person could go mad. But at least it wasn't blowing.

"I miss trees," he said. "Deciduous: chestnut, maples, hickory, oak–something to turn color in fall. Something to stop the snow, the damned wind."

"The wind gets to everyone," Pattiann said. "*Something* gets to everyone here." She turned onto the plowed highway, disengaged the four-wheel drive. "I need to spend more time at Rob's."

Ike snorted, leaned his head back and closed his eyes.

"With Harriet. Help out at my folks'."

He cracked an eye open. Pattiann didn't go to her old place, Bill and Martha's. Rob's house was as close as she got. It was why the family gathered there now, with Martha's frailty, too weak to entertain, supplying the excuse. Typical. Don't mention it, just move the gatherings. He waited.

"Justin's entering high school come fall. He'll need to move to town."

Sometimes there was just no following. They conversed as if they were herding cattle, circling, driving in, backing off. Listening was a Goddamned art. They dodged real talk with jokes and silences, as though words were blunt objects in their hands. He opened his jacket, turned the heater down. Ahead of them, the snow pitched into the head-lights, the fields were a billowing white and seemed to glow as if the earth beneath were lamp-lit. They hadn't seen another car on the road, which suggested to him that people were staying in. His pager hadn't beeped. Another good sign.

She cleared her throat. "We got that spare room downstairs. I was thinking Justin could use it. He'd go home some weekends, holidays, summer."

And this was a surprise. He reached down, turned the radio on, swung the dial listening for a weather bulletin. "A kid in the house makes a difference. Loud music. You'll have to close the door when you take a bath." His mouth ticked into a smile.

She was watching the highway, hands fixed on the wheel.

Ike sat straighter. Packing snow, wet and heavy. There would be heart attacks in the morning—the elderly town man shoveling his sidewalk. The older rancher who walked too far out into the deep drifts, or seized up while cutting a path to the shed. How were you supposed to know? "We haven't talked about children in awhile," he said.

Pattiann nodded. "Have we avoided it?"

"I don't know. You go from day to day. You don't think of it." He paused. "Maybe I have avoided it."

"You'd make a good father," she said.

They were passing Stubblefield's. The lights were out. No truck in the drive. Ike leaned against the glass. There was the lower corral and the field, the few standing cattle, maybe fifty head. Skinnier by now. The piebald horse, holding its own with Ike's help. And Ike wished he'd brought grain. They could stop and the horse, its back hi-hatted in snow, would trundle its way to the fence, dip its muzzle in Ike's palm. Pattiann would be startled by their easy familiarity. He'd confess how he'd been feeding the animal. He'd tell her how he'd tried to buy the horse. She wouldn't laugh.

"I don't know," he said. "I'm not around much. Things can happen to a man in my job." Ike sat up away from the window. "My dad was a good father, I guess. But damn, he *loved* the farm. Silos packed with silage. Calves in spring. Milk pouring from teats. Bulls mounting cows. No artificial insemination for his cows." He looked over at Pattiann. She was watching the road. "He was a sensual man. Does that surprise you?"

"No." Pattiann laughed.

"He used to embarrass the hell out of my mother, the way he'd moon after her. There couldn't have been a more unlikely pair. She kept the farm going, the bank off our back. She shipped the cows out when they went dry. Sold the veal calves. My father—he'd have kept them all, the sick, the old, the worthless, and starved us doing it." And that, Ike knew, would be beyond Pattiann's comprehension. Sentimentality past the age of six.

"Did he hate her for it?"

And what surprised Ike was that he hadn't wondered the same thing.

He took out a cigarette, tamped it on his watch. He lit it and took a deep breath. Air whistled through the window he'd opened to a slit. After the rendering truck would pull away, or the veal calves were loaded on transports to the slaughterhouse, his father would hide out in his study. He'd come out three, five, twelve hours later—when he was good and ready to. Then he'd fold himself behind the wheel of their old Rambler station wagon and drive off. He'd be gone for days, a week, leaving the farmwork to Ike and his mother. His mother never made any move to find out where he was or what he was doing.

When his father returned, he brought flowers. He told jokes, took to his chores as if he'd never abandoned them. "No," Ike finally said. "He didn't hate her."

By the time they hit the outskirts of town, the snow had eased. Ike thought he could make out a new opacity in the cloud cover, a thin umbrus of light that might be the moon. It was late, and he wondered if he would hold Pattiann in his arms, beneath the bedroom window, under the light of moon on snow. If she would respond. He wondered if it was the talk of children that prompted his interest.

"We could try it with Justin," Ike said. "If you'd like. Might be nice to have a kid in the house." Watching her face, he had the feeling that it was the possibility of enjoying it that frightened her.

The next day, late afternoon, Ike found Chas sitting in a booth at O'Brian's. Ike seated himself across from Stubblefield, who didn't bother looking up. There was an empty shot glass next to a coffee cup.

That morning, Ike had been over to Taylor's to investigate the vandalism on his car. Taylor looked hard rode. Insisted it was Stubblefield. "You got any reason to believe that?" Ike asked after inspecting the car.

"Turned him down for a loan."

"That something new for you? I expect you've got more than one person pissed." Ike glanced over at the doorway, saw Taylor's wife wavering there. "Excuse me, ma'am," he said, though she did not look offended. She slumped against the doorjamb, her hands pushing at the hair tightly pinned back from her face. She was a handsome woman, though this morning it looked an effort. He told Taylor they'd keep an eye on his house and check out Stubblefield.

The bar was dim; a thin edging of sunlight squeezed under the drawn shades. The length of the walnut bar was gouged where the clientele scored the wood with the edges of quarters, or silver dollars in the old days. Nothing personal or intimate to the act, one hand taking up where another left off. The back bar reared up through the dropped ceiling to the old pressed-tin ceiling, oxidized from smoke, too fussy in those modern sixties for the management's taste. A Goddamned shabby place, but you had to admire them clinging to the 1960s while the more savvy towns conjured up the 1880s and cashed in.

Chas looked rested. His hands were scrubbed and he held the coffee cup as if his fingers were sensitive. "Your phone out of order?" Ike finally asked.

Stubblefield grinned. "You know, funny thing, I get these letters from the phone company, next thing the damn phone don't work. Good thing I didn't pay, hey?"

Ike tried again. "You all right, Chas?"

He looked over Ike's shoulder. "Is it snowing yet?" And when Ike shook his head, Chas went on, "It will. Just won't stop this year." He leaned back. "Like in the ninth circle of hell. That's the *Inferno,* you know. Read it. Read *Paradise Lost,* too. When I was a kid. Those two books up there on the shelf butt-ending the Bible like last-minute scripture. My mama's books.

"But there's this ninth circle of hell, and it's all snow and ice and shit with sinners buried up to their necks in it." He waved a finger to the bartender Barry and pointed to the shot glass. "You?" he asked Ike. "No? Anyway, I have this dream last night, and there I am buried up to my neck in frozen cattle, hooves and eyes and teats and balls, and I'm thinking it's so fucking cold, ain't there supposed to be fire? What burns hotter, fire or ice?"

Ike wasn't in the mood. "Last night, someone broke into Taylor's garage, poured kerosene over the front seat of his car." He watched

Stubblefield's eyes, waiting for a flicker, amusement, nervousness. Nothing. "He and his wife were asleep in the house at the time."

Barry brought the drink and refilled their coffee. Chas saluted with the glass and gunned the shot. He sat back. "So there you go," he said. "It could have been worse. Seems to me whoever did it was downright Christian."

"Taylor thinks it was you." Again Ike waited.

"Well, I am a Christian. I think."

Ike stood up to leave. "I don't have time for this. I'm watching you, Stubblefield."

Chas reached across the table, grabbed Ike's wrist in his hand, held tight. "You come in here to talk, or what?" His hand relaxed, drew back around the coffee cup.

Ike thought there was something in Chas's eyes, so that Ike hesitated, thinking to see at last a side of Chas he could understand if not trust.

Ike sat and Chas asked, "You meet Pattiann back east? Your family from there?"

Ike didn't like the sound of his wife's name in Stubblefield's mouth.

"They farmers?" And when Ike nodded, Chas asked, "Dairy?"

"Sixty head."

"So'd you lose the farm or what? You didn't want it?"

"We sold it, just before my father died." Ike opened the last two buttons on his coat. "The sale kept us comfortable until I got work."

"Comfortable. I like that thought. With the police."

Ike eased back in his seat.

"I knew there was a reason you got elected. I mean an outsider and all, but you'd been here a couple of years, married Pattiann." He stirred more cream into his coffee. "You come from a farming background, had all that experience, a diploma, and you didn't diddle none of the ranchers' daughters like the old sheriff used to. You'd think that sorry old sonofabitch would have known. It's like a rule: *You don't diddle the ranchers' daughters.*"

"Or mess with their property," Ike added.

78

Chas crooked his head and laughed. The afternoon light shone hot on the shades, a warm amber glow that deepened the gloom in the rest of the room. The bell over the door jangled and the first of the early evening regulars stepped in.

"Don't fuck with the daughters, or property." Chas wiped his eyes and straightened up. "So why you doing it? We both know I'm going down either way—quick your way, or slow mine."

"As slow as the cattle?" Ike asked.

"Just so." He held his hand out over the table, ticked one finger down, another and another. "One piece at a time. Come on, Parsons. You never seen cows die on your father's ranch"—he corrected himself—"farm? You don't know all things have their seasons?" Stubblefield straightened his fingers, rubbed his palm across the table. The skin of cream trembled in his cup.

Ike rested his head on the backstop and turned to look at the bar where Barry sat talking with old Charlie Sandovar who'd lost his wife and only son in a car wreck. It had been Ike's first year here. He'd had to go tell him. It was one of the difficulties working with so small a population. You knew the face of the wounded and they were always there to haunt you. And then there was Chas, a whole different kind of spook, asking the question Ike wasn't comfortable with himself. Why? Because animals were suffering? That's where it'd started. But now? Had it gotten personal? Slippery grounds for a man with a badge and a gun. But Chas was in the wrong, after all, and it was Ike's *job,* and enforcing the law wasn't arbitrary, turning a blind eye when it was convenient or things got too uncomfortable. And then, between one breath and the next, it seemed to Ike as if he were missing some *thing,* some reasoning outside of logic essential to the heart of his work, a dim reckoning that was almost physical, like the memory of taste or smell.

Conversation at the bar picked up with the *ding* of the door opening. Chas was watching him. Ike shook his head, weary with the only answer he could find it in himself to offer. "Stubblefield, what I'm concerned with here is the law dictated me by the state of Montana. You break it, I'll nail your ass. I don't care if it's for starving cattle or vandalism." He stood to leave. "Keep clear of Taylor."

Ike was almost out the door when Chas called, "You say hi to Pattiann for me?" Stubblefield waved to Ike's back as he stepped out and then raised a finger for another shot. "There'll be a tip in this for you, Barry," Chas said.

The crowd was picking up, two more people at the bar. Chas took a sip of whiskey, and followed it with cold coffee—a lousy chaser, but free. His mind slowed; his limbs jigged. He paced himself, keeping track of drinks like a loan payment. And they were. A dip into the small store he'd set aside. Not enough for much of anything, just a little something, good-faith money. But there was no good faith in this world, only sheriffs, feed suppliers, and bankers . . . driving kerosene-soaked cars. He snorted and eased further down into the seat, pulled out a pack of cigarettes. Chas flicked back the cap of his old lighter, thumbed the wheel. There was a spark, a flame, and the smell of lighter fluid. He lit a cigarette.

A mistake mentioning Pattiann. Making the sheriff angry. But he'd sensed it was what was sitting between them, and wasn't it interesting that she should sit, a phantom third party at the table, that each begrudged the other. What the hell, he was going down, anyway. Wasn't nothing going to stop it. He took another sip to keep the spin in his head going, the buzz, the lovely stall before the fall.

Smoke trickled off the burning cigarette, script in the air. He heard the *ka-chink* of change, the whirr of the jukebox selection, and then Willie Nelson was singing "Blue Eyes Crying in the Rain." The door opened and another body shuffled in. He ordered another shot.

Barry dawdled, served two, three other folks first, but when Chas called a second time, spread a five-dollar bill on the table, Barry delivered. He made change, hovered. "You sure you can afford this?"

Chas shrugged. "Can't afford not to."

He sipped the shot. The door opened and it was darker outside than in. Chas guessed that it was a weekend, maybe. Or Friday. Payday. Maybe. The bar was filling with groups of men, a few couples, a cribbage game set up at a near table, men slapping cards, *fifteen-two, pair is four,* at the pool table a young kid sighted down the cue. Chas wet a finger in the shot glass and wrote his name on the murky tabletop. When he looked up, Purvis was standing next to him.

Chas grinned. "This a house call?"

Purvis pointed to the empty seat across from Chas. "You waiting for someone to come and play catch-up?"

"I'm waiting for the floor to open and swallow everything but me, this handful of change and barful of drinks."

Purvis set his beer down and seated himself. "Don't see you out much."

"Yeah, well," Chas said and downed the shot. "We're a private people. Come from a whole line of folks nobody's ever seen or heard of."

Purvis shrugged. "Knew your daddy."

"You count yourself a lucky man?" Chas tipped his empty shot glass, rolled it in a circle under the palm of his hand. "You really here to talk about my old man?"

"I've seen your cattle."

"You and the sheriff, and anybody who hasn't, has heard—old lady Carver drives by in her Studebaker like she's still queen of the 1940s, sees a cow drop on my place, and next thing people in two counties know my herd's dying. And soon as they hear it's starvation and not disease, they breathe a little easier and turn the dogs out to watch the hayricks. Maybe one of them sonsofbitches comes along in a pickup with a load of hay, shuffles his feet at my door, and says it's the Christian thing to do—ain't much, mind you, 'cause times are tight and he's got his own, and it's been a bad stretch of years, but it's the least a God-fearing man can do. And so I show him the gate and tell him to take his charity with him." He raised his shot glass to Barry for another drink.

Purvis took a swallow of beer. "You need to put those cattle down, Chas. Way it is, they're suffering and not likely to be brought back."

"No," Chas agreed. "But that's the point."

Purvis looked confused.

"You think I'm the only one had a hand in this? Tell you what, you get Taylor, Sam Coker out to my spread. You get them to shovel shit and blood for awhile—and I'll think on it. That'd be a sight, hey?"

"Christ, Chas." Purvis thumped his glass down on the table, a skud of foam rose to the lip. "I don't give a rat's ass about any grudge match between you and them. And I don't give a good Goddamn about what all went wrong, or some sorry-ass song about how you tried your best. Those animals are suffering and you can stop it now. It's the decent thing. Before the law steps in."

"Parsons." Chas smiled. "He's got his own agenda."

"I'll help you do it, Chas."

Barry delivered Chas's drink, then stood there, as if reluctant to take another of the dwindling bills on the table. Barry's head was back-lit, his face in shadow so that it was hard for Chas to read the pity he knew was there. Chas turned to Purvis. "You want to help? Buy this round."

Purvis slipped out of the booth. He handed Barry money for the drinks and walked out the door.

"Now that's what I call Christian," Chas said and sipped the whiskey. He settled in, parsing out dollars and cents to last the night, or for how-ever long it took. He drank until the edges softened. The jukebox played the same tunes over and over, but Chas found himself humming along now. The overhead light turned liquid the faces at the bar. Bottles were stacked on the back bar like a firing line among barrel-bellied jars in which floated pickled pigs feet, sausages or eggs in a rusty brine, and on first glance it reminded him of the traveling freak show he'd seen as a young boy in Havre, with its array of jars: jellyfish, a two-headed eel, six-legged frog, a lamb with a leg growing from its stomach—phantasms of heavy metals, inbreeding, and mythological creatures hatched of taxi-dermy. And the finishing touch: on a creaking turntable, one human fetus floating in alcohol, making its own slow revolutions in the fluid, butt cheeks bumping against the glass in pale eggish ovals.

He would order one now, he thought, an egg, if he could, and he rested his head against the seat cushion and listened to the talk: football and kids, cattle and crop forecasts. He saw old Jerry Tallwell canting on a barstool and suddenly Chas had a clear picture of him, a year or two

82

distant, heeling end-over-end in a combine while the blades still thrashed, the wheat and dirt rising skyward in a plume. And then Chas found himself in the latrine, the urinal clogged with plugs of chew that rose and floated as he relieved himself and even in the dark and stink he *was* relieved, with the music thumping at the door, the voices raised in laughter so that he laughed too while fumbling with the zipper. And when he made his way back out to the bar, he saw his table cleaned, found the last of his money tucked in his pocket. He was sidetracked by the black-haired, middle-aged, recently divorced daughter of one of his father's old cronies, and though he could not come up with her name, she was offering to buy him a drink, and then she was leading him in hand through the maze of tables, past the politely turned backs of the other men, and out into the dark behind the bar.

Chapter Six

Ike sat in Judge Costello's home study. The judge thought the situation unfortunate. "It happens," he said, wheeling back his office chair. "Back in the snow of '49–'50, the whole state stank—cattle putrefying in the fields." He shrugged. "This Stubblefield . . . a bad judgment call. Pride goeth before—" The judge was a small man, made smaller by the mahogany desk, his head so bent that Ike could see where the black hair tint had leached onto his scalp. "Haven't you ever made a bad call?"

His legs were delicately crossed, one argyle sock shucked down around an ankle. "And they are, after all, *his cattle*. Our constituents are particular about what belongs to them and who fools with it. They've mortgaged their house, their land, barn, and equipment for the cattle. They got ledgers in their heads saying what cow birthed what calf and when, and sometimes they can trace it clear back to their grandfathers' stock. It's awful personal.

"The rains don't come, prices drop, the wife fools around, but they can still run their finger down a book and tell you what quarter this steer is in and how long till market." He wagged his head but the hair didn't move.

"Ike, nothing happens on this earth hasn't happened before. They are used to dealing with it their own way. The man's an anomaly and there isn't a member in this community won't condemn him for it, won't hesitate to turn their back when he comes around. But you take his cattle away and who do you think they're going to turn on?" The judge dug out a small sheet from a bundle of loose papers on his desk.

"Now I got attorney McLeod's memo, but I don't think she's committed to this. Says given a choice, the county generally ignores this sort of thing. Too expensive, no chance of recovering the expenses. I could talk to her."

"What isn't dead is dying," Ike said.

"Yes. He's a fool."

"With a gun," Ike added.

"That's not against the law," the judge said.

"But starving livestock is," Ike added.

"Only if it's brought to the attention of this court."

The late afternoon sun shone through the French doors, and the judge's hair gleamed blue. There was the smell of fried chicken coming from another part of the house. His stomach growled and he had paperwork to do. Ike stood. "Consider it brought."

The judge sighed, nodded slowly. He offered his hand across the desk to Ike. "I'll get the paperwork started. We'll meet in my chambers with Stubblefield, see if we can't clear this up outside of court." He walked Ike to the door. "Gets any untidier than that, no one will thank you for it."

Ike stood at the stove next to Pattiann, lifting pot covers and peering in. Purvis had invited himself to dinner, walking the mile and a half to their house through a mixture of rain and snow to stand in the back doorway, dripping onto the hooked rug. Pattiann toweled his hair and face, an intimate gesture she bestowed on no other guest. "He's such a great shaggy dog," she'd once told Ike.

"You need a wife," Pattiann said.

"You find me one can stand me."

"Amy Schumacher?"

Purvis ducked his head. "If I offered her my heart, she'd eat it."

"Purvis," Pattiann scolded.

He raised three fingers in front of her face. "That we know of. She's a widow maker." He bobbed out of Pattiann's arms and over to the stove next to Ike. "Spaghetti?"

"Lasagna," Pattiann answered, "once I put it all together. So why don't you two pour me a whiskey ditch and let me work?"

Ike and Purvis sat in the dining room while pots clattered in the kitchen. Sometimes Ike could see Pattiann as she crossed to the pantry. He thought how comfortably ordinary a thing it was—this time spent anticipating dinner, his wife's shadow flirting in the doorway. He rolled the glass in his fingers, sipped the drink, and listened to the ice cubes clink. Purvis sighed. "She could almost convince me to marry."

"Worked for me," Ike said.

"That's not the way I heard it," Purvis said. "Heard you had to follow her fifteen hundred miles and take hostages."

Ike smiled and lifted his feet onto an adjoining chair. "No hostages."

A kettle banged in the background. The oven door yawned open and clamped shut. Pattiann brought another setting for the table, lit candles, and slapped the overhead light switch off.

"*Miss* Pattiann," Purvis said, "candlelight?"

In the doorway, she looked over her shoulder at the pair. "Covers a multitude of sins."

Purvis nodded. "You should have married someone handsome."

"The bread didn't raise properly," she corrected and strolled back into the kitchen.

"What, you don't think I'm pretty, Purvis?" Ike asked.

"There ain't a light that forgiving." He scuffed at his drying hair. "Got a call from Judge Costello today."

Ike waited.

"So you went and did it," Purvis pushed. "Got an order on Stubble-field."

"You make it sound like I shot my best bird dog."

"My daddy used to say—"

"Christ, Purvis. None of your homespun wisdom. The man's gone off half-cocked, it's time I put an end to it."

Purvis tipped back in his chair. He looked older than he needed to. "Heard about Taylor's car," he finally said. "Think Chas did it?"

"I think he's capable of it." Ike tipped the bottle, refilled his glass and Purvis's. "I don't want to find out what more he's capable of."

Ike looked up and Pattiann was standing in the doorway. The kitchen light on her hair was a pale red corona. He knew Pattiann didn't want to talk about Stubblefield's troubles, and in that way she was a barometer of the locals, her disapproving silence.

Ike patted the chair next to him but Pattiann stayed where she was, caught in the half-dark where he could not read her face, just the shape of her breasts and hips, her feet planted on the threshold. She ran her hand down a kitchen towel draped from a jean pocket, a nervous gesture. She was a woman any number of men might have fallen for, still would, but he was the lucky one. And what were the odds of that?

Purvis rocked his chair forward, landed his elbows on the table. "Judge wanted my opinion. Three days ago, I might have kept hands off. Now, I think maybe you're right. Up and down I hear talk, folks taking sides. People feeling sorry for him. Think he's gotten a drubbing from the bank. Nothing they enjoy more than to bad-mouth banks.

"My father bought everything with cash. A man made by the Depression. Never got past it. 'When the banks closed their doors,' he'd said, 'they gave back the people ten cents on every dollar. But come time to collect, they'll empty your pockets—a dollar ten and more for every one you borrowed, and there's no door you can close against them.'" Purvis rolled the glass in his hand. "People carry a grudge a hell of a long time.

"And I think Chas has grudges to spare." He sipped the whiskey. "Pattiann," he called to her in the doorway. "Where's dinner?"

"In the oven," she said.

"Good." Purvis slapped the place next to him. "Bring your pretty little good influence over here and set it down next to me."

He poured her a fresh drink. "What I like about you—you got that lasagna timed? good, good—is that you smell like God intended woman to." He inhaled deeply. "Sausage and onions and Roma tomatoes."

"Christ, Purvis, you make every woman sound like a deli?" she asked.

He wrapped an arm around her shoulder and buffed her cheek with a kiss. "Only the best. A vet makes more money than a sheriff."

"That much, huh?" Pattiann shoved Purvis's glass a little farther out of reach.

Ike laughed. Pattiann could nose-lead just about any man she met. Years of dealing with ranchers and cowhands and other stiff-necked animals.

"Rejected again," Purvis said, snagging his glass.

"You expecting sympathy?" Ike asked.

But Purvis was puffing out his chest. "I can take it." He turned back to Pattiann. "So what do your folks think about Stubblefield?"

Pattiann took a long, slow drink, started to rise. "I should check the meal."

Purvis snorted.

Pattiann sat back down. "They don't think much of him, or his management of finances. They don't like to see cattle starve, but they've seen it before." She looked them both over.

"Their own cattle?" Purvis pushed.

Pattiann looked slapped. "Not in my recollection."

"Never happened," Purvis said. "Never will. Because there's something infinitely more decent in your father and most of the other folks hereabouts than in Stubblefield. Money might have started this, but it isn't money keeps him from putting those animals out of their misery.

"No," Purvis continued, "he's in the spotlight, and where most people might duck with shame, he's taking a bow."

"That's a little rough, don't you think, Purvis?" Pattiann asked. Her lips were pinched. "Don't you think there's more to it?"

Ike watched out of the corner of his eye the way her back straightened, her chin tipping up and elbows braced—a fighting stance. He felt the glow of the candles and talk and whiskey fading. He felt irritated and was surprised to realize it was directed mostly at Purvis, his turn of conversation, and Ike wondered what that said about his own silences these days, his avoidance of the problem, about what the town was thinking, or even how Pattiann felt about it all. About Stubblefield.

Purvis pushed back in his chair. "Well, *of course* there's more to it. More than I or Ike, or Stubblefield himself can fathom. I don't mean to reduce the thing it is—a tragedy—but neither will I choose to ignore what I sensed when I ran into him the other night at the bar. And maybe it was just the booze, or my own faulty intuition, but I believe he's pleased with the suffering of his cattle, the discomfort of decent people, and even the clumsy offer of help from a country vet. You know," he said, shook his finger, "I have seen animals worry a healing wound because they *like* the taste of blood."

They sat in the fulsome air: garlic and roasted tomatoes, a peppery backbite of basil. The candle flames wavered as the furnace fan kicked in and Purvis's whiskey glass cast a watery circle of amber light onto the white dinner cloth that he fingered as if it were a stain. They did not look at one another, until Purvis cleared his throat.

"Had an interesting case the other day," Purvis said. "This rancher comes in, wants me to do a vasectomy on him. Says all the doctors he's talked to want an arm and a leg along with his nuts. I tell him I'm not a physician, I'm a vet. All I do is castrations. He says, 'Hell, if I'd wanted that, I'd do it myself.' "

Ike laughed. Pattiann sat quietly a moment, then smiled at Purvis. "Is that supposed to provide a lesson about Stubblefield's problem?"

Purvis smiled back evenly. "Doesn't it?"

She patted his hand. "Purvis, it's a good thing you're a vet and not a preacher."

The conversation moved more easily after that, like breathing after a hard swim, though there was one small glitch when Ike asked about the Mattick boy. "Fine," Purvis said, his eyes evading Ike's. "Promising." And he'd said no more about it. Purvis ate two large plates of lasagna and was offered and accepted a ride home. He carried his belly in both hands out the door.

When they went to bed that night, Pattiann was fidgeting, punched her pillow, slid a leg up over the quilt. She sighed.

Ike raised on an elbow. He ran a finger down her exposed leg, and the limb jerked. "Something wrong?" he asked.

She turned toward him. "Dinner was all right?"

"Purvis ate like two men."

She waited a beat in the dark. "About Stubblefield," she said, "I have the feeling you expect something from me. You and Purvis both."

Ike kept silent.

"Which is curious, because, you see, Chas seems to expect something from me as well. I saw him, you know. Last week. Had coffee with him."

Ike nodded in the dark. "I'd heard."

"What else have you heard?" she asked. "Never mind." She pushed the covers back and sat up. "Nothing that isn't true, I'm sure. Chas says he just wants someone to talk to. Someone else with something at stake."

"Like?"

"My marriage, maybe."

Ike nodded.

"This could get ugly," she said.

"It already is," he answered.

"Not between us. Not yet."

"But you see that as part of a natural progression?"

She sighed. "I think it's a distinct possibility. Don't you?"

Ike laced his fingers behind his head. "I'm disturbed that Chas seeks you out, thinks to use you. That it took you this long to tell me."

Pattiann sighed. She tucked the quilt around her legs. "Chas and I started out as kids together, both of us wild and holding grudges. The first time Chas stopped over at my folks', we were eighteen. He arrived in his best pair of jeans and a clean short-sleeved shirt—buttoned to the neck—entered the house, hat in hand, hair slicked back, a good-looking young man. It damned near broke my heart . . ."

And Ike could believe that, remembering the way he'd been fooled by Chas's smile, how young it had made him look, how strangely vulnerable, and how Ike had thought, just maybe, there was something in Chas a person could like, could call friend.

"My dad met him on the stoop, stopped him before he ever got past the door. Looked him up and down like he did breeding stock at a sale. You could see it—I know Chas could—the way my dad backed up even as he offered his hand. Took one look and judged Chas like meat on the hoof, too shallow in the chest maybe, or weak in the haunches. My father built his ranch on the accuracy of his eye, and Chas sure as hell didn't make the grade." She stroked the quilt, patted it down like a temperamental horse. "Which was reason enough for me to stay with Chas, at least early on."

"And later?"

"It's hard to imagine now. Never mind that I don't want to think of it, and a lot of it's just gone. I can't deny there came to be more than just willfulness and spite on my part. A genuine . . . regard."

It was dark in the room and Ike wished he could see her face. He tried to read the pitch of her voice, but that felt as if he were trying to catch out a suspect. "Regard. Makes it sound like you two were shaking hands." She laughed and leaned into him. His arm snugged around her and she turned her face into his chest, kissed the narrow spot where his arm conjoined his chest, a light airy touch that allowed him to breathe again. This is what saves us, he thought, these gestures deeper than reason.

"I never loved him. Even back then, when I thought up any number of reasons for the things I did, that was never one of them. He was there. He was lonely and hurt. And so was I." She snugged down deeper next to him. "I wanted his anger." She exhaled deeply. "To sustain mine.

"Purvis is right." She tugged the quilt up under her chin. "About Stubblefield. The cattle. They're an end to his means," she said.

Ike looped a strand of her hair over his hand, stroked it between thumb and forefinger.

"You know that look in Stubblefield's eyes?" she asked.

He wasn't sure he did. He quieted his hand a moment and waited.

"Vengeance," she said. She turned, positioned herself in the crook of his elbow. "And it scares the hell out of me." She was quiet a long beat.

"But you know the really crazy part?" He felt her head turn up toward him. "Something in me still feels like his friend."

Early morning at the courthouse people arrived one at a time, holding coats closed against the wind. Sidewalks were shoveled and the two-foot mounds on either side had taken on the glaze of a newly frosted donut. Chas was sitting on the steps so that people navigated around him as if he were a stone gargoyle. He'd been in the building already, while it was mostly empty, radiators just then clanking and hissing to life. The secretary, a middle-aged dowd in a black dress, raised a powdered face and told him the judge was readying himself in chambers, asked, would he care to wait? He turned on his heel and walked out. Chas had dressed for his appearance. Wore his mucking boots.

He sat with his head pitched forward, so cold that the nerve endings in his cheeks ached. When the door at his back opened and the dowd's voice called, he didn't turn, but stared out over the square where pigeons squatted in a gazebo while a hawk wheeled overhead.

He heard her descend the stairs, her breathing labored, and then her hand was on his shoulder and he swatted it away as if it were a fly.

Her hair had blown loose, the ends yellow as straw and thin as a gleaned field. He stood and passed her, letting the door racket on its hinges. Her stubby heels clacked counter to the chunk of his boots, and when they arrived at the office, she hurried ahead, alternately tugging at her skirt and hair before opening an inner door. "He's here," she said, then ducked out.

Chas scraped his boots on the threshold, ignored the judge's hand, and took a chair in the center of the room.

The judge seated himself. "Good to see you, Chas," the judge said. The vet sat in a corner. Parsons watched from the side of the room, his eyes connecting with Chas's. He nodded and Chas thought there was something new in the sheriff's posture, something different. As if a new distraction had set in. Chas smiled back, ignoring the judge. "You the cat that swallowed the bird, Parsons? You think you can do it in one bite?"

"Chas," Purvis said. "Don't make this—"

"Shut up," Chas said.

The judge stood. Chas turned his smile on him.

"We're doing you a favor here, Mr. Stubblefield."

Chas laughed.

"I expect you to return the courtesy," the judge said and picked up a sheaf of papers. "Got a complaint here, that you have neglected your cattle to the point of abuse. That said herd is dead or dying, offending all sense of human dignity and posing a serious health risk to the community. Now we're just here to try and resolve this with as little embarrassment to you as possible."

The room was warm. He could smell his boots heating up, a sweet, rank odor. "Where's Taylor?" Chas asked. "Coker?"

The judge set the papers down. "Sheriff Parsons filed the complaint and Purvis here has verified the problem. It's common sense, man. Simple decency. You have got to do something about those animals." He leaned back in his chair. "Would you like a cup of coffee?"

"You got any whiskey?"

The judge sighed. Purvis was rolling his head on his neck as if it ached. Parsons walked over to the window overlooking the courtyard.

"That hawk still out there?" Chas asked, and Parsons looked skyward, nodded.

"This is what we'll do," the judge cut in. "We agree, neighbor to neighbor, that you clean up this mess or hand it over and we do it for you."

"And if I don't agree?"

"You go to court, lose the herd, you pay court fees, a fine, and jail."

"I can't pay no lawyer."

"I'll appoint one."

"I can't pay no fines."

"You go to jail longer."

Chas thrummed his fingers on his pant legs. Books lined the walls, gold-lettered spines. He guessed they were law books. Tomes of the quick and the dead.

"You considering what I've said?" the judge asked.

"I'm considering the quick and the dead," Chas said. "And the quick are quickly enough dead, so I guess it's all one and the same thing." Chas stood, dusted his hands down his pants. He looked around. He walked down the row of bookcases, finger bumping the spines like a stick on a picket fence, the soft *tha-bump, tha-bump.* He knocked into the back of Purvis's chair, kept going until he'd stopped short of Parsons at the window. "I never been here before."

"We didn't bring this on, Chas," Purvis said.

Chas turned on him. "No. You're just the warm bodies that operate the machine, and it's a Goddamned complicated piece of work, that machine. Parsons here's just a grease monkey and you"—he pointed to the judge—"you turn the key. Like to keep your hands clean, don't you?" He stepped back into the center of the room. "I got to go," he said. "I'm a busy man."

The judge was standing with an effort. Chas thought to walk over there, behind that desk, and pinch the bony elbow in his own strong hand—help the old man understand that for all his books and robes and wide desks, what he *really* was was just so much flypaper even as Chas's own father had become.

"Is that it then?" the judge asked, his voice rising.

"Unless you got a gavel or something you want to pound." Chas walked to the door, opened it, and stood with his back to them. When he turned, they were each held to their private occupation: the vet with his mercy, the sheriff with his law, and the judge with his clean hands. "I'll think on it. Let you know in a day." He shut the door behind him. The secretary was still out. Hiding maybe.

When he stepped into the wind again, Taylor was waiting, coat collar turned up, hands muffled in his pockets. His face was puffy, his eyes wedged in skin, as if he hadn't been sleeping well. There was a pleasure to this, Chas thought.

"Stubblefield," Taylor said. "You sonofabitch. I'm onto you."

"You drive here, Taylor?"

Taylor's hands balled in his coat pockets. But they were soft hands tied to weak wrists and scrabbly arms. Chas kept his own hands loose at his sides. Didn't feel the cold for calluses. He almost pitied the poor fat fuck.

"I got a gun, Stubblefield. You step foot on my property again, I'll kill you."

"Ain't that the way?" Chas asked. He looked out over the town square, people shoved down the sidewalks by luck and wind. Like so many cattle. He turned his attention back on Taylor. "Man gets a gun, next thing you know, he's turning it on his friends." Chas stepped past him. "Gun's a dangerous thing, Taylor. You don't want to keep it loaded in the house. Who knows, that little dog of yours might take to playing with it and blow a hole clear through its ass."

Taylor's face had gone tight. "Maybe I'll just get a bigger dog then." He raised a fist out of his pocket. Chas snatched it on the rise, turned it back.

"Easy," Chas said, twisting it. He let go.

Taylor looked chastised. A whipped dog himself. "Chas, damn you, it's not my say who gets money and who doesn't. There are guidelines—"

"Well, why don't you take those guidelines to bed with you, see how much sleep you get."

"Don't come near me again, Chas."

"Taylor." Chas shook his head and leaned into Taylor's ear. "I didn't search you out." He whispered, "You put yourself at my door, and as Jesus once said, you just got to knock to enter the kingdom of heaven." He backed away, cupped a hand to his ear. "What's that I hear? Someone knocking?"

He stepped clear of Taylor and strolled off, the wind at his back as if they were old friends.

Maybe it was the paperwork that put Ike in a bad mood, an unending stream of reports and requests, a chore he had dreaded but had never fully comprehended when he ran for the office. An eight-hour shift at the desk made even driving the back roads in snow appealing. Or maybe it was spending the morning in a closed room with Stubblefield and his stinking boots. And of course, it had everything to do with his talk with Pattiann, her confusion over her loyalty to Chas. The last straw was Harley dropping in late with a battery of excuses that came down to his lollygagging with the dispatcher.

Ike handed him a radar unit, told him to set up in Dodson—there'd been complaints about speeders on the main road out of the small township. An hour there. Three hours on radar. An hour back. It would keep him out of Ike's hair and off the dispatcher's desk the rest of the day.

Harley looked down the radar gun tube. "What the hell am I supposed to clock up there this time of year? Birds?" Harley followed Ike back into his office.

Ike sat in the chair, eyed the mound of papers. His mood grew blacker.

"That new kid, Dan Roehe, could take it. He ain't doing anything."

"Harley," Ike said, took a deep breath and waited.

"Well, this is a damned snipe hunt." He waved the radar gun at Ike.

Ike closed his eyes. He was hungry and he could smell manure on his clothes, as if the stink of Stubblefield had taken residence. When he opened his eyes again, the gun was limp at Harley's side. "How far you want to press this issue, Harley?" he asked.

Harley gave a sullen nod and walked out of the room. He shut the door softly behind him though, and Ike gave him credit for that.

Ike took his work to the diner. Fran settled him into the far booth. "You look like varmint bait," she said.

He plopped the papers on the table. "Your tax dollars at work."

"You'll want the chicken. A green salad on the side—keep you regular. And a nice glass of milk."

"How about you take my temperature and write me a note?" he crabbed. "I'll take the meatloaf special, heavy on the gravy, extra mashed potatoes, and all the black coffee you can pour."

"You want an eclair to finish you off again?"

"You give your husband this much shit?"

Her face whitened and she took a step back. She turned away, turned back, and settled into the seat across from Ike. She folded her hands on the table, looked him in the eye. "My husband eats the meals I freeze, calls Fridays to make sure the kids and I can get home for the weekend, and when I can't he drives the twelve miles to Jolene Peck's trailer home where he's taken very good care of, I'm sure."

She raised her chin and her fingers locked tighter so that the knuckles shone. A country jig piped from the kitchen radio and a pot clattered, an oven door closed. A customer dropped a couple singles on the counter, some change, stood, and took his leave.

"I'm sorry," Ike said. And he was, and he was at a loss for what more to say. He looked at her hands, the fingers curled in a tired fist, and he wished he could say something, do something. He wondered how a man married to her could look at another woman. And he wondered at how easily life is altered—one day he's living alone, working in a big city police department, grabbing the meatloaf special night after night. And suddenly he's here, in this small-town diner, trying to edge his way around Fran's heartbreak. Trying to feel his way through Pattiann's mixed loyalties. In another life, he could have been Chas with his world collapsing about him. Ike closed his eyes. Fact was, he *understood* the pity Pattiann must feel for Stubblefield, but he could not *feel* it. He looked across at Fran. "He's a fool," Ike said. "Your husband."

"No. He's a practical man. Most particularly when it comes to his *needs*. And I," she pointed a finger at herself, "am a practical woman. I've got three children. Whom I love and who love their daddy. Cripes, you really needed to hear this." She tapped a finger on the stack of paper— "Like you haven't got enough crap to deal with"—and she bustled out of the booth.

"Meatloaf?" she asked.

"Chicken," he said. "Green salad on the side."

She nodded, slapping open her order book.

"But coffee. A man's got to draw the line somewhere."

He ate his lunch in silence, and the chicken was good, the salad tasty. As Ike was finishing, the front door opened and Joe Mattick came in with two others: one school age; the other was Lester Colcox, a cowhand from one of the ranches, a decent hand when he was sober. Which he didn't look to be at the moment. Bad company. And Ike remembered how Purvis had balked at talking about Joe. He looked at his watch. One-thirty. Seemed a little late for a school lunch hour.

The chicken was bones on his plate. He considered a wedge of pie, reconsidered. Fran brought the check. He shuffled his papers into a manageable heap and started to rise, but her hand fell on his shoulder. Gently. Just a squeeze.

"How's Pattiann? She getting on all right?" She smiled, the corners of her mouth turned up nervously. She wasn't asking about Pattiann but about herself. She was a young, healthy woman. Trying to come to terms with betrayal. Testing the waters.

"Yeah," he said. "She's fine."

"Good." She dropped her hand. "Good. Just thought I'd ask." She stepped away, looked down at her shoes, over her shoulder, then back at Ike. "You let her know I said hi."

He nodded, but she was already off for one of the other tables. At the counter, the Mattick boy hunkered in his stool. Lester was humming under his breath.

"You on lunch break from school?" Ike asked Joe.

The young boy next to Joe giggled. "Suspended," he volunteered. "For the week." He elbowed Joe in the ribs, and Joe slapped at the boy's arm. Lester was singing an old tune made famous by Rex Allen, "The Last Roundup."

"Well, it's true." The boy was bright and fidgety. "Last Friday. For drunkenness." He giggled again.

"That right? You were drunk?" Ike asked.

Joe shrugged.

"Lester here didn't have nothing to do with it?" Ike reached over and snatched Lester's collar. The singing stopped.

The man's eyes slid over to the sheriff, widened. "Why, it's the sheriff."

The boy giggled again. It was getting on Ike's nerves. He blessed Fran for the quiet in his stomach. "You boys been into some of Lester's liquor?" he asked the youngster.

99

"We're clean," the boy said, his voice a squeak.

Ike turned back to Joe. "Saw Purvis. He says you're doing fine work."

Joe looked pleased. "That old Chevy's close to running," he said. "He thinks I'd make a good vet." Joe seemed as clearly confused by the logic of that as Ike was. "Says he'll let me help in surgery. Nothing big, just fetch instruments, prep animals."

"That all right by you?" Ike asked.

"Yeah. I guess so. Said he'll pay me."

"You could do worse," Ike said. He looked at Lester. "You got a job, Lester?"

"Lazy K. For now, for a while, forever." His head rolled on his neck.

"Good. Hate to hear you were out of work, just bumming, or giving kids booze."

"Gotcha," Lester said. "Milkshakes all around. Chocolate, right?" The boys nodded. And he took up another chorus of "The Last Roundup."

Chas dropped by Coker's feed mill. The clerk said Coker was "indisposed."

"Is that like he's hammered to a toilet seat with the shits?" Chas asked.

"Sir? I don't know. He's not here. Can I help you?"

"Sure. See that pickup out there. Why don't you fill the back with feed cakes." Chas tipped on his heels, scanned the aisles to see what was interesting.

"Is that for cattle, sir?"

"Do I look like a pig farmer to you? Or sheep?" He bounced forward on his toes. The boy backed up. Just a whip of a kid. Gangling and gawky.

"How many sacks?"

Chas thought on it, picked at his chin. "Stack them tight, make it twenty."

The boy smiled. His big sale of the day. "Cash or credit?"

Chas cocked his thumb at the speaker overhead. "Coker know you play that stuff when he's not around?" Chas shuffled an awkward dance step, gave up. "An abomination." He stepped toward the door. "You go about your business. Seems I forgot to bring cash. You tell Coker I said hi."

"Who do I say, sir?"

But Chas was already in the warehouse stepping toward the open bay doors. The sun was shining. It was turning into one of those bright days with the sun hooked high in the wide blue. He looked over his shoulder and the boy had gone back to the shelves, hips twitching to the music. Chas looked around. Feed. Feed and more feed. And then his eyes alighted on the thing he was looking for but hadn't realized until this moment. He snatched the small box under his coat and jumped off the loading ramp. He tossed the box under the seat. When he backed the truck out, the sun struck off the glazed windshield, a blinding white, and as quickly gone. But he felt like he'd been riven from the head through the heels by a bolt of lightning, bored clean in a single stroke of inspiration. If he opened his mouth now he would speak in tongues.

Chapter Seven

In the kitchen, at the plank table swept clean with the heel of his hand, Chas sliced cubes of meat. Tenderloin. For each cube he slit a pocket, ran his finger back and forth inside, cleaning a nice tight space. He hummed "Rock of Ages," a tune his mama had been fond of. On the table in front of him was the box he'd lifted from Coker's mill. Twenty-five silver-foil packets of rat poison, stacked in fives. He unwrapped one, sniffed. Good enough to eat. He tucked it into a meat pocket, squeezed the opening shut behind the treat, and set it aside. He worked at a leisurely pace.

"Big dogs, little dogs. Here, Fido." He practiced whistling, imagined a dog, any one—fat-bellied, long-legged, parti-colored—creeping up to filch the treat, gobble it down. He tucked two in for good measure. Set it to the left, earmarked for a big dog, a very big dog.

He thought of Taylor's yapping little mutt. Coker's heeler on a short chain. The assorted town dogs. One night's work.

He had no use for dogs, nor did his father, who also had no use for cats, women, or children, though he'd saddled himself with a wife, and with her fathered a child. What delight in that? Like feeding poison to a dog. Only draw it out over years. He pictured his mother, the sincere, ineffectual woman she was—hope-chest linens bleached and soured, bleached and soured—taking Avery into herself like every hurt he ever doled out.

Until the hundred daily doses took their toll, and she walked with her hands cupping her stomach, as if they held a cancer. Though by nature a tidy woman, she became meticulous, windows glossy with polish, the corners of the wood floor picked clean. He supposed he should have known by the way the bun of hair at the nape of her neck was strung tighter and tighter, until the hairs pulled loose from her temples, trailing down her back or over her shoulder, and she snatched them out and burned them in the woodstove, a stinging stink that marked the hours that last day.

He shook his head. He should have known that in the deep night she would steal herself away to the barn, so that in the morning, when he went out to chores, Avery would find her hanging plumb from the rafter.

Chas set another large dose aside. Some creatures were born to be martyrs: cattle, hogs, sheep, goats, dogs, chickens, women. When he'd used up the last of the silver packets, he slung the prepared meat into a paper sack.

Outside, the night was black under the new moon and the stars pulsed with a light so clear and close that when Chas put his head back, it seemed as though the heavens were falling, and his arms spread out to check his sudden dizziness, the paper bundle in his hand swinging back and forth until Chas tucked it close to his side, as a hand might steady a racing heart. The truck windows were sealed with frost and he waited in the cold while the defroster raged, his breath building a white rime on eyelashes and brows. He planned a route. He'd save most of it for the town dogs, but with nearly two dozen doses in hand, he could afford to be generous.

He wheeled down the highway in a state of near giddiness. It was not the act of killing itself that enthused him, but the sense of purpose once again, direction, if even so fleeting as for these brief hours. He'd found again an urgency that set the clock moving forward on real time, and wasn't that what terrified him most these days, how he'd discovered his life to have become nothing more than a string of odd moments that turned into hours that turned into days that amounted to nothing? Sometimes he felt like the dead in waiting.

Outside of town, Chas turned his headlights off and angled down side streets. He parked in back of Truman's shop, the town's mechanic, always a changing group of cars and trucks awaiting maintenance back there. No one would notice another vehicle. Chas set out on foot, found he could generally pitch the meat the distance to where the dog was chained. He came across a stray in the grocer's back lot, foraging at the base of a Dumpster. A midsized long-haired mongrel, asymmetrical white and black coloration—heeler cross, maybe. It padded up to Chas with its nose narrowing in on the bag. Chas moved into the building's shadow. The dog followed. He told it, "Sit." The dog sat, tail wagging. "Down," he said, and the animal slumped to its belly. "Good boy." Chas patted the wide dome of its head. Its dark eyes were raised, trusting. Chas reached into the bag, pulled out a cube of meat. The dog sat up. Chas drew the meat back. "No," he said. "Down." And the dog complied.

"Better," Chas said. He stroked the striped black and white brows. The dog's breath warmed his knuckles and the tail gently thumped the asphalt. He cupped the jaw in one hand, held the meat at a level with the dog's eyes. Chas could almost swear the animal smiled. "I believe it will be fast," he said, surprised at how much that sounded like an apology. No difference, he told himself, one death or another, cattle or dog. Still he held off and the moment passed into another and another, longer yet. Just minutes ago, two blocks away, it had been easy enough tossing the meat over a fence, staying to hear the gabble of a chained hound as it wolfed down the treat. And it wasn't as if he were foreign to the sound of dropping bodies, and despite the reasons he might give others or himself on a more resourceful day, he *was* aware of his own part in the *cause* and *manner* of his cattles' deaths. The dog rested its head on its paws, eyes steady on Chas. Finally, it was all about the killing itself. Because he could. Because he wanted to. For although they might believe him a fool and helpless, still he was, after all, not really *harmless*.

The dog shifted, creeping toward the bag on the ground, masking its motives with a gesture of affection—it laid its head on Chas's knee. Chas smiled. It was in the nature of dogs to be fools for man. He ruffled the dog's neck, feeling a keen sense of regret. He wished there was someone he could talk to about it. "Stay," he said, and perched the cube of meat on the dog's nose. The dog sniffed delicately, but held in place, its eyes alert on the meat. It would be a matter of self-determination. "You be a good boy now, and we'll just see . . ." He took his hand away from the dog's muzzle, the meat floating in the dark on top of the dog's nose. "Stay," he ordered. He would give it a minute, maybe two more, and if in that time the dog held faith . . . well, then . . .

Chas crouched back on his heels admiring the way the dog balanced its split nature—heart against gut. The temperature was dropping and Chas flipped his jacket collar up, muffled his hands in pockets. A hoar frost was building, and over the parking lot, beneath the arc of a street lamp he could see a shimmering mist rising in the light, like powdered glass. By morning the overhead wires would bristle with frost and the scrub brush, the tumbleweed and sage would thicken, grow coats of crystal, like coral conceived in a sea of air. Chas lifted his face, closed his eyes, and imagined the utter stillness, the long night of dreaming it would take to grow a coat of ice. It was so quiet, he believed he could hear the crystals forming and that he could hear the shush of tires on the highway miles away, the bang of a pot in a kitchen nearby. And then the distant bark of a dog roused him like an alarm, and when he looked down to the dog at his feet, it lay there waiting patiently in the dark with its eyes trained to Chas. The chunk of meat was gone.

"Good boy," Chas said, and felt neither joy nor disappointment, but relief as if the dog's willful act were an affirmation of Chas's own. One way or another we were all made to swallow our own death.

Ike left the office midmorning. He'd called the courthouse. No word from Stubblefield and the judge wasn't about to rush it. Ike parked outside Purvis's barn, let the heater warm him before stepping into the cold. He was getting soft. As a kid, he'd worked long hours outdoors and in the barns with January temperatures averaging in the single digits and snow to the eaves. But here, the difficulties were of a different nature. Here, in the open, snow traveled, always shifting, and with no buildings as referents you didn't know how deep until you were in it. So easy to become lost. It all came down to getting lost. You were or you weren't and he felt himself continually stumbling between the two. A hell of a thing to admit if you're sheriff.

Ike found his friend in the pole barn. There was a row of dead dogs, assorted by size, muzzles clenched over teeth, tongues distended. "Been coming in all morning," Purvis said. "Joe's out, picking up more." He nudged a stiff terrier with a toe.

"What's going on?" Ike asked.

Purvis peeled back a dog's lips—a shepherd gone fat and too soft to ward off that last unfriendly hand. "Strychnine. Not a pretty death. Run-of-the-mill rat poison. Whole world's gone cockeyed. Nine dead dogs and more on the way." He stopped for breath, gripped his stomach. "And I haven't had breakfast yet."

Ike led the way into the living quarters. He opened the refrigerator with a familiarity, already knowing what he'd find—plastic bags filled with the odds and ends of animals. Tissue samples in wafered slices. Vials of blood and urine. "Purvis," Ike said, "no wonder you don't eat at home."

"What?" He turned with his hands dripping, reached for a towel, smelled it first, then wiped his hands. "Perfectly safe. They're all contained. I keep the semen in the freezer." He joined Ike, brought out a dozen eggs, a quart of milk, two pork chops, and some leftover green beans which Ike pitched into the garbage.

Ike fried the chops, salvaged some potatoes for hash browns, and topped it with four eggs. They cleared a space at the kitchen table and sat to eat. Purvis made the coffee so Ike drank water.

Ike spooned up more eggs and potatoes. "Joe's been suspended from school, you know that?"

Purvis nodded again. "He told me."

"For drinking. Been hanging out with Lester Colcox."

"Didn't tell me that."

Ike took a bite of the pork chop, chewed it slowly. "I thought you might like to know is all."

Purvis finished the plate of food, shoved it back. "Thanks," he said.

He looked to the door that led to the surgery and the barn. "There's more out there than a man wants to know or can deal with. You know, Joe could do well. He could be a vet. Or a lawyer, or doctor, or I don't know what, don't really care. But he could *be* someone, given a chance."

"You sure he wants one?"

Purvis looked down at the empty plate. "Best breakfast I've had in this kitchen. I don't know. He comes around, we work and talk. He's got my Chevy running. Did I tell you that?"

"No." Ike smiled. "When's the unveiling?"

"Spring. When the ice's off the roads. I'm going to buy a Panama hat and a good cigar, and I'm going to drive Main Street on a warm night with the windows down and wave at everybody, like I was my own parade."

Purvis rubbed his belly. "Maybe I'll drive clear to Illinois, pull into Leroy's Custard stand, order a double thick malt, cheeseburger, and fries, and be the envy of every sixteen-year-old there."

"You miss Illinois?"

Purvis smiled. "Sometimes. When I'm picking cheat grass out of an animal's eyes and there's not a quarter of shade for miles and the water tastes like piss. But mostly when you come around asking questions like that. You got a case of it, don't you?"

"Winter blues is all."

"Well, I put myself here and I'm bullheaded enough to stick with it. And truth is, I've come to love it. Imagine that, come to see a whole lot of nothing as beautiful." A truck pulled up outside. "That's Joe," Purvis said, rising from the table, and they both went to see what the boy brought.

He looked young but comfortable behind the wheel—driving ranch rigs since twelve, licensed at fifteen. They pushed young boys to adulthood out here, Ike thought, or maybe elsewhere they were coddled too long? Who was to say? He didn't understand children and maybe that had to do with being an only child. And maybe that had to do with his discomfort about having children of his own. But now, come fall, it looked like Justin would be moving in, turning tables every which way.

And here was the old bachelor, Purvis, taking Joe under his wing. What was it that made middle-aged men believe they could raise a child better than they could have as a younger, fitter man? Discipline. Reserves of patience. Or something more selfish? A last stab at making a difference.

There were two dogs lying in the back of the truck—a heeler and a border collie. "Picked this one up just outside of town. Coker's dog," Joe said.

Ike prodded it with a finger. "How do you know?"

"Saw him dump it." He turned to Purvis.

Ike lifted the dog off the truck bed. Joe carried the other dog. Purvis opened the door for them and Joe moved up alongside Ike.

"Hard to believe somebody would do this." Joe shook his head. "Think it was someone we know?"

Pattiann pulled into her parents' drive, four miles of frozen road, snow-banks scalloped by the wind. She didn't remember a winter with this much snow. Good for the soil come spring. They were still a long way off on the water table and it would take years of good snows, wet springs to make up for it. A beneficent decade or two—and that's the way you had to see it out here—a generation spent keeping even, or catching up for your children's time on the land.

A kestrel on the fence, neck feathers ruffled, watched for movement—mice bulldozing snow tunnels, a system of veins bulging on the other-wise flat white surface. And if she stepped out of the truck and walked across the snow, she'd see where mice had rooted up to the surface, their small freckled prints. Or maybe she'd see the scoring of wings where hawks and prairie chickens made their floundering takeoffs. And jackrabbit tracks like exclamation points. Pockets where elk bedded. Fox spoor. Raccoon—a pestilence of them these past years, decimating the prairie chickens. What had tipped the balance, upset the numbers. Something new, a crop, fertilizer? Or was it a matter of accretion? Because somehow, each minor change seemed to snowball. Take out the buffalo. The wolves, ferrets, fox, hawks, eagles. Introduce roads and towns, fireweed, cheat grass, cattle, people, and garbage, and watch it all turn topsy-turvy, slowly, over a hundred years, until it never seemed to be anything other than it was right now and you're confounded by the way prairie dogs colonize in numbers out of proportion and raccoon invade and there aren't enough bullets, traps, or people on God's green earth to answer for it. But it's always been tough out here, and at least, by God, you don't have the wolves to contend with. And here is where she was torn, because this was all she had ever known, and didn't want to see it change either, could not bring herself to leave, could not argue for the return of wolves and buffalo and unpopulated grasslands because she believed herself as native as the trees and rocks and snakes. It was not something she could undo. She had tried.

Rob's truck was parked next to the barn, but the horses were out, so she assumed they were checking the herd, fence, or both. Or bringing the cows down for calving, short weeks away. And that was what she'd enjoyed most. Late nights alone in the barn. The warm pen. The cow's grunting, the crick of wood. The first earnest pushes.

She set her foot on the driveway, found the familiar strange. It had been a long time since she'd come to her parents' house. Anger? Avoidance? Or just more comfortable to leave things where she'd left them.

The door was unlocked, as always, even when they drove into town. *A hell of a way to drive for little enough worth taking,* her mother'd always said. The living room was unchanged, though less managed. A quiet dishevelment. Rugs needed vacuuming, tables dusting. Her father's spot was neat, papers folded, his reading glasses clean and on the table where he'd reach over and swing them up over his nose, screw them down tight on his ears as if he faced a brisk wind. She pictured him, feet in a pail of Epsom Salts water, *Rancher's Quarterly* or *Horse and Tack* or his private addiction *Field and Stream* propped open on his lap, though she couldn't remember the last time he'd taken off for a pack trip or fished. She supposed it had to do with her mother's health, his own aging.

As a younger man, twice a year, he'd take a four-day weekend with friends: Bill Baxter, Charlie Potts, Blair Oliver, Jason Fales. They'd meet at the ranch, horse trailers loaded, supplies tarped down in pickups, and they'd plan in the kitchen while it was still dark outside, stewing over maps they knew by heart. Her mother packed lunches and waited for them to be gone, for her own vacation to begin, one less mouth to feed—two when Rob got old enough—and time in the evening to read, put off the dishes until morning, or drive herself and Pattiann to Lewistown for dinner, a movie, and a night in a motel where someone else made the bed. A second-rate adventure for Pattiann, who had wanted, more than anything, to be with the men on horseback in the mountains.

Pattiann called out, hoping it wouldn't startle her mother too badly. She called again, and from the bedroom her mother answered, "Be right there. Give me a moment."

When her mother came into the room, she acted as if her daughter stopped regularly, as if years were days. "Got some coffee on." She headed into the kitchen. Pattiann poured, cut the cake, and served them on the unchipped china—*company* plates. "I was just driving by," she said.

Her mother nodded. She wouldn't question it any more than she'd believe it. "Your dad and Rob are bringing the cows in. There's going to be a bad blow yet. Something's coming. You laugh, but I can feel it. Don't I sound like one of the old men? Age makes you a believer. We're never far from the clay God formed us from." She sipped the hot coffee. She set the cup down gently. "I'm hardpan gone to gumbo. You'll have to excuse the mess." She thumbed toward the dishes, stacked and waiting. "I get to them, just not as quick as I used to."

"You could use a dishwasher," Pattiann said.

"Never as clean as hand-washed. And work keeps a person motivated. Damned if I'm going to do less than I can. And I *can* do it. Just not as quick."

Their coffee cooled. Tenderness had never been an easy thing between them.

Martha tapped a finger on the table. "Ike's well?"

Pattiann nodded.

Martha smiled. "He's a good man for a hard job."

"Husband or sheriff?"

"Ha," Martha shouted. "When you were a baby, you gummed my teats like you wanted it all—milk and meat." She leaned forward, propped her chin on a hand. "Never lost that appetite, did you?"

Pattiann waited.

Martha looked around the kitchen. "My mama would have said I had it all. Married to the neighbor boy, properties buddied up. Deeded over the home place day after my father's funeral. Now don't go mistaking me, I loved your daddy, would have married him land or no, but it pleased my mama to see the place grow. The day we bulldozed the homestead, she stood with us. Said she wanted to see the place as she'd first seen it. 'Prettiest piece of land in God's good eyes,' she said, 'before we put up that butt-ugly tar paper shack.' The same shack she raised me in, addition by addition.

"Right up to the moment the last wall fell, she seemed pleased. Walked in the cat's treads where the living room used to be. It was the strangest thing I've ever seen come over a person. There was my mama, her feet planted on those rocking walls, crazy happy one minute, and then you could see her whole body shift, at odds with itself. And her eyes wandering like they'd lost their focus. As if she didn't know where she was anymore. The land had reclaimed it all—her place and history. Just that easy." She snapped her fingers.

"I must have thought about that day a hundred times since. Imagine discovering you can be wiped out so easily, so completely. Or that the one thing you believe you want out of this life can undo you. The house was gone and then so was she." Martha picked at her cake with the fork.

"I wish I'd known her," Pattiann said.

"Well, hell, you're enough like her. She died just before you were born, and sometimes I've thought, if there is such a thing as reincarnation, she didn't wait long or look far."

Pattiann laughed, but Martha stared down at her cake and took a small bite. "Ike's a good man," she said again.

Pattiann nodded.

"Hasn't been easy for him, making his way in here, being sheriff and all. You appreciate that? I mean, sure Art booted himself out of his job, but Ike's earned it. Isn't a person out here knows him or of him and doesn't speak well of him. That's no easy chore."

"It could change," Pattiann said. She slid her plate to a side. Refilled her cup and her mother's.

"Is changing," Martha said and nodded. "Stubblefield. I may be old, but I still get around. I've overheard."

"And?"

"Nobody's pleased. But Stubblefield comes from a long history of not making friends. His daddy, Avery, was a step below coyote in the social register. His daddy, they say, was mean enough to starve the animals for spite. But Chas? They think he's been forced into it by the banks." Martha snorted.

"Chas got in too deep with the banks," Pattiann agreed. "But it was of his own choice."

"I believe that's what your daddy said."

And that surprised Pattiann. Her father taking Ike's side, the law's side, the bankers'. It went against grain.

"Anymore, the small ranchers have trimmed to the bones or sold out. Chas's father doomed him years ago. Chas took on Avery's debt and added his own without a lick of sense. Without an inkling of what was coming down the hi-line.

"These days, ranching's a business, not a way of life. Probability forecasts and money management. Rob's facing it, and I pray to God he makes it, but I won't lay odds, not over the long haul, not for Justin. Maybe it's for the best. I don't know." She reached across the table for her daughter's hand. "But I don't want to be here when the bulldozers wipe it out again. I don't care what the land looked like without us. Is that selfish?"

She shook her head. "The others feel sorry for Chas. But mostly they're thinking it could have been them, might be yet. And that makes it personal. I feel sorry for Chas. It's only natural." She reached up and touched her daughter's cheek, an uncommon gesture between them. "It's going to be harder for you." She lowered her hand. "To know what it is you feel."

Pattiann cleared her throat. Wanted to speak. But it was not something she could put that easily into context, that mix of feelings, love or friendship, pity or guilt.

Martha sighed and ate her cake in silence. When they did talk again, it was of safer things: the ranch, the coming spring, tidbits of town news, the grandkids, and when the kitchen turned warmer with late afternoon sunlight, Pattiann rose from her chair, stacked the dishes. "I've got to go," she said.

"You could stay for dinner. Your dad will be home soon; he'd hate to have missed you."

"I don't think so." Pattiann carried the dishes to the sink. Her mother stayed seated. The dishes in the sink were a reproach. It would have killed her mother as a younger woman to have her kitchen seen this way.

"You don't give your father enough credit. He loves you, always has. He's just not a vocal man."

"I remember him being pretty damn vocal," Pattiann said.

"I remember you could be pretty damn deaf."

The two women looked at each other across the kitchen. Long shadows tilted across the floor, over the checked linoleum still buckled at the doorway. The refrigerator hummed softly. Pattiann suddenly felt the poor daughter; she was the stranger she'd always thought Harriet to be. She lifted a clean dishrag from a drawer. "You want help with these dishes?"

Martha waved her off. "I can do them later. I can still do for myself."

Pattiann smiled down at her hands. It was never easy. "You want me to stay?" she asked. "Then give me a reason."

"All right." Martha labored over the words, as if chipping them out of hardpan. "You wash. I'll dry."

By the time Pattiann drove out, the sky was a bruised light paling to gray. When her father'd come back with Rob, he hadn't seemed surprised to find her there, or the dishes cleaned, the floor mopped, and the house tidied. And that was like him—more likely to question the ways of

God than women. Pattiann took her leave before she could be talked into dinner. Easy enough. She used Ike as an excuse. "He'd starve without me," she said, which was unfair to Ike, but her father seemed to find that idea reassuring.

She wound out through the private road, onto county, flicked the headlights on. In this twilight, with the roads straight as furrows, distances were abbreviated, the sky and land fused gray on gray. The temptation was to let the rig steer itself down the straight and narrow. She could drive this road in her sleep. The bump of tires over cattle guards, then the quick hitch over Beaver Creek Bridge where as a child she'd caught carp and hell from her father for calling them trout.

She thought about her grandmother watching the bulldozer wipe the slate clean and herself with it. And then she was approaching Stubblefield's and found herself slowing. As a family, they'd had little to do with Stubblefields, though their proximity might have dictated otherwise, would have in any other case. What did she remember of Chas as a boy? Not much, a kid riding fences. She thought she remembered the mother, a tall, slim woman, snatching clothes off the line. A blur as they trundled past in the old pickup, she and Rob piled in back, shouting open-mouthed into the wind.

And then like a memory called up, there was Chas, his truck stalled on the side of the road, and he was waving her down. She hit the brakes even as she knew she shouldn't. She came to a stop twenty yards farther on. Stubblefield loped up.

He leaned against the closed window, hands cupped around his face. He smiled, and there was the boyishness she'd always found so attractive. He tapped the glass with a forefinger. She rolled down the window.

"You need help, Chas?"

"I need to see the judge on business, and my truck's down. You headed to town?"

She paused and saw this amused Chas.

"Just a ride," he said. He hooked his fingers over the door, the nailbeds scoured and red.

"Why don't you phone?"

"It's turned off. Thought you'd heard—my life's gone to shit and back."

And he did look lost, befuddled by the calamity his life had become, and Pattiann felt a twinge of guilt, a certain culpability in how she'd abandoned him. But no, that wasn't the truth of it, was it?

"Jesus, but that heater feels good," he said. "You going to give me a ride? Honest to God, I'm going to drop with cold if you don't say yes." He crossed his heart, and the gesture struck her like a blow. That old joke between them. She reached over and unlocked the passenger door.

Chas bolted around the front of the truck, slapping the hood so that it banged, the sound still jolting through Pattiann as he clambered in. He slid his left arm over the bench seat to rest behind her neck. "I am not a prosperous man, but in friends. I'll tell you what—" He opened the door again, swung his legs out. "You wait. I got something." And he was running toward the house.

Out in the yard a knot of cattle stood, sides stoved in, and she realized that in all the times she'd driven past his spread she'd avoided looking, and even now it was just a glance, as if at a shameful thing she had a part in, something nasty. She shifted on the seat, tapped the wheel with her fingers. She could leave. Yank the door shut, throw the truck in gear, and haul ass. Which was only common sense. It would be dark before she got to town. She was thinking of driving down the highway alone with Chas. Her foot dropped the clutch, she slipped the stick into gear— the path of least resistance—but then she was back in neutral. She couldn't just leave. Mostly she didn't want Chas knowing he had disturbed her enough to send her running. Again.

She looked across the yard with its covey of junk to the house with its boards weathered to a dark gleaming. It might have been a nice place at one time, a trim little construction with generous windows bracing either side of the door and fronted by a covered porch with many of its spindle rails missing, a gap-toothed look that was strangely charming. The door opened and Chas swung it shut behind him. He jumped off the porch, tripped, slid to a knee. He limped to the truck door, his cheeks a high red with cold and embarrassment. He raked a hand through his hair, tossed a wrapped parcel on the floor, and stepped in. "Meat," he said. "Sirloin tips."

"Thanks, Chas, but—"

"I got more beef than I can eat." He laughed and looked out at the pen where a few cattle milled. The horse pawed at the snow, moved on. "They ain't much to look at," Chas said, "but they're all mine. Raised every mother one of them. You got a minute? You want to meet them? Pay your respects to the dead?"

"Look, Chas—"

"Your husband does that, you know. Comes out late at night to visit that old horse out there, feeds it when he thinks I'm not looking. Even offered cash for it—down to three legs with age and less with hunger— imagine that. Only neighborly to turn him down. Good thing he's a sheriff, your husband, don't know shit about livestock."

"Ike?"

Chas nodded. "Wants my horse. Maybe the whole spread. You'd like that. Always wanted a place, didn't you?"

She looked stung. "You don't know what I want, Chas."

He slung his arm back over the seat. "Knew you once," he said, and his hand bundled her hair gently. "Know you still." He rubbed her hair between his fingers like coins.

Pattiann didn't move. She could feel his hand on her neck, and the heat rising in her face. "You'd better step out," she said.

"No." Chas shook his head. He released her hair, moved his hand back to his lap. "It's a cold, cold walk to town, and no telling when someone else might come along. I got business with the judge—news he and your husband have been waiting on. Now I understand that we've got some unfinished business you might be uncomfortable with, so you *could* order me out of here and get along with your life . . . or you could help me get this over with."

She punched in the clutch, put the truck in gear, and pulled out. Chas settled his hands on his knees. "Nothing like a proper truck," he said. "Mine's a good old heap. Runs all right, except now and then."

They drove in silence.

Chas shifted, toed the packaged meat to a side. "It's good meat, you know. Fried some up for myself the other night." He whistled softly, stopped. "Damn," he said, looked out the side window. "I find myself with a shitload of time now, you know?" He turned to her. Her face was grim. "Find myself thinking on the strangest things. Things I haven't thought on for years—like you. We're two of a kind, you and me. Two sides of the same coin—your daddy trained you for what you can't have, and mine left me what he didn't prepare me for." He fidgeted in his pocket, pulled out a dime. He flipped it, let it drop. "We'd have made a good couple."

Pattiann flicked him a sidelong glance. "Chas, we made a lousy couple."

Chas turned back toward the window. His legs were splayed and the one kneecap was dark with wet and dirt where he had fallen. It was touching, like a dirty knee on an errant child. She wondered if the skin was scuffed beneath. She looked away, up the road for the town lights she knew were miles and miles away yet. The sky had darkened and the road spun out broad and white in the headlights.

"Well, good or no, it's always been a mystery what brings two people together. I used to wonder about what my mother saw in my father. She was a woman of no particular talent, except faith, and maybe that was enough. You know, faith sets you up for things like that. Believe long enough in the fall and, by God, you'll fall. Head over heels for a man who hit rock bottom and liked it there. What is it Satan says in *Paradise Lost*—better to rule in hell than serve in heaven? Think he had Montana in mind?" He rolled down the window, bent his head into the cold air. His hair, bright as flax, whipped from one side to another as he turned his face to and fro. Then he pulled back in; he looked up at the overcast sky. "Not a star in sight. Clouds. More clouds." He closed the window.

They turned onto the highway and Pattiann relaxed, drove a bit faster on the plowed pavement.

"Want to know what I've decided to tell the judge?"

He surprised her with that. And, yes, she did want to know, but didn't find it in herself to ask.

"No? It's no secret, leastways it won't be. Hey, say what, I'll tell you a *real* secret and then you give me one. Like best friends."

"I don't think there's a thing I could tell you, Chas."

"No?" He scrubbed at his cheeks with the palm of his hand. "What to tell?" Then he slapped his hand back on his knee and took a deep breath. "One time, when I was about five, I found this cat. A small scruffy thing. My daddy was gone for a few days, cattle sale, or some such excuse, so I carried it home to show to my mama. She says we'd keep it, *just for the time being,* because we both knew he wasn't going to stand for no cat. But after a day or two, she'd taken a real liking to the animal, and so when my father returned, we kept it hid, she and I. For a day and a half, we fed it leftovers, tucked it under the quilts with me at night." His face lit. "By God, she liked that little beast, though by then I'd about come to hate it, the fleabites and claws. But that seemed a small enough price to pay. She wasn't happy often, and it was a thing to see.

"Until my father smelled it out. He had a nose on him; I give him that. He could smell out anything. Told me once, he could sniff out my mama's woman parts in a whorehouse. 'Sanctimonious,' he'd call them— 'the smell of God with dirty hands.' " He looked over at Pattiann to see how she was taking it. He wished he could see if she were blushing, but she stared at the road, concentrating as though the highway might veer where it never had before. And that seemed reasonable to Chas. Having seen firsthand how the familiar shifts and cants under your feet—one day prosperous, the next day a hundred less cattle, no two mornings alike no matter how many you woke to. "Now," he said, "I hope you're not offended, but the hard part about secrets, you understand"—he leaned toward her, rested his hand on the space between them—"is that you got to tell it all or nothing."

She nodded.

"Anyway, by the second morning, he found the cat in my room, hauled it out by the scruff of the neck. I've never been able to figure it, I mean, it had clawed me often enough—but in my daddy's hands it went limp as a hung man. And even when my daddy shook it in my face, all it did was blink. 'Where'd you get this?' he asks me.

"To give my mama credit, she said, 'No, Avery,' maybe once, twice. But he was not a man to be deterred, and so he asks again. I can hear the cat panting. And then he lays his other hand on the back of my neck like he does the cat."

He paused and in the silence there was the hum of the tires on the highway and her steady breathing with which he willingly fell into step. The indicator lights in the truck dash gave off a dim, green glow that buffed the knuckles of Pattiann's fingers, the point of her chin and cheekbones. The highway markers closed in the dark behind them. He pinched his eyes shut. Opened them and picked the story back up.

"My daddy's hand tightens on my neck, cricks my head over to a side. I hear the cat yowl.

"Then I hear a snick from his left hand and the cat stops blinking. He hands me the body. 'Bury this.' And I did. Took the cat to the manure pile, dug a space with my own hands, and stuffed it in. I wasn't about to question my daddy ever again."

Chas took a deep breath, eased it out between his teeth. Pattiann stared ahead. She reached over, turned the heater down. He thought he could smell sweat and perfume, wondered what it would be like to take her in the cab of the truck, or in the flatbed, the cold iron against her back tempering his heat. He wondered if she'd feel different now, all these years later, wondered if her bones had grown longer, or looser, if her flesh were still dimpled so sweetly over her ass. He looked out the window so she wouldn't see it on his face, but he slung his arm once again over the back of the seat, his fingers behind her neck.

"That old man kept things lively." He laughed. "The old coot. Lived longer than he had a right to." He paused. "Wasn't about to give the ranch over to no one, especially not me. But then there he was, dead at last. Do you have any idea what it feels like to find the thing you've stopped believing can happen, suddenly has, and the porch you're standing on is yours, and all the land becomes particular to you, every stone and shrub, and all the creatures on it, and even the Goddamned stars are at attention and the night's not big enough? And I wouldn't have been more surprised," he said, "if the sky had opened up and trumpets sounded." He giggled. "I half expected the world to end."

"But it didn't," she said.

Chas leaned his forehead against the side window. "No," he said softly. "Not then." He watched the road wheel away beneath them. He looked over at her, saw in the tilt of her head, the way her face softened, something reminiscent of that time between them, and it moved him so that he believed he could risk asking. "Why'd you leave?" His voice nearest a whisper. "Run off like that? Sometimes I think if I had a chance at all in this world, it was with you."

Her hands tightened on the wheel. She shook her head. "Damn you, Chas."

He had stung her and there was a pleasure in it, not exactly happiness, but something deeper, more integral, like releasing a long-held breath.

Her voice was calm. "This is a pretty time to dump this load of crap on me. All these years later. I've got to wonder if you're remembering the same time I am. I mean, how do you see us as being so *good* together? Because we could drink each other under the table, and we never hurt one another beyond a slap or two. I guess that's on the plus side."

She swiped at her face, as if some microscopic bug pestered her, a nervous habit that usually signaled the beginning of a blowout between them. It was a gesture he'd come to hate, seeing himself as that invisible gnat flinching about her face.

"But what were the good times, really? When we rolled the car and neither of us remembered who was driving? How about the time I came to in my own vomit, on the side of the road, twenty miles from town, and you were gone and so was the car? I mean, this is all just so much crap—if you cared to be honest at all, you'd admit the only thing we were good for with each other was trouble. And that has a pretty limited appeal in the long run."

"We were young, reckless," he said. "It would have changed, if you'd given it time."

"No," she said. Her eyes narrowed. "You think if we'd stayed together, everything would be different—your ranch intact, your cattle healthy. But the truth is, had I stayed, it would have still turned out as badly as it has, because all we had between us was an interest in self-destruction. As long as we could hurt each other or ourselves, we got on fine. But it couldn't stay there, between us, could it? That kind of hurt spreads."

She cracked the window a moment, let the air rouse her, then cranked it shut. "My secret," she said. "Why I left in such a hurry."

Pattiann downshifted for the curve in the highway and the engine whined. This was something it had taken her years to let go. Except in dreams. And sometimes she woke up sweating, heart pounding, the air thick as smoke. It had been a long time since she'd allowed herself to think about those years—her drinking, the hurt she heaped on her family. And taking up with Stubblefield. Mostly to get back at her father. How he'd laughed when she'd asked which half of the ranch would be hers. *Honey, you* know *the ranch will be Rob's. Hell, someday you'll have a husband with his own spread, and if he's any part smart, you'll be his right-hand man.*

"You and I, we'd been to the Stockmans' earlier on, bought a bottle and drove out to my folks' place."

He nodded, grinned at her. "You were wearing jeans and a shirt with little flowers, blue ones."

She tried to call that evening to mind with a clarity that matched his. But it was difficult. She'd spent so much time trying to forget.

Chas started in again. "In the wheat," he said. "Same place I'd first bedded you, back of your pa's place, south field. Damn, but we were eager." His voice was almost reverential, as if surprised at the ambitions of the body, the heedless way the young take in life like air into lungs. "Barely time to unzip."

Pattiann's eyes were focused on the road. Her jaw worked, clenching and releasing. "We fucked. We finished and I left. Not a pretty sight."

Chas laughed. "Not half so bad, way I remember it. You shed of your shirt, walking away wearing nothing but sex, sweat, and the night air." He wanted to tell her he'd kept the shirt. For the long six years she was gone. And even the first year she was back, like a token, a promise, as if she'd return, if not for him then for that thing she'd left behind—a shirt with small blue flowers on it.

"Drunk or no, I managed to stumble home, right into the house in front of Rob and a couple of the hands, and my mama," and she could see Martha as she was then, staring at Pattiann's breasts, gaze sliding down to the dirty knees on her jeans, the wheat chaff stuck to skin. "Didn't say a word."

"And your daddy?"

"Sent Rob and the men outdoors. Then he walked right up to me, not really looking at me but over my right shoulder. He was making this noise, like his wind had broke. Then he was talking about killing you, and Mama was wrestling with him. I stood there laughing until they stopped. And then he swung back his arm and laid me flat."

"And so you ran away," Chas said.

"They locked me in that night," she said. "I was still higher than a kite and strong. Proud because my dad had knocked me flat and I'd stood back up. Middle of the night I climbed out the window, went to the barn, then walked back out to the south field."

"What'd you get in the barn? A gun?" He raised his head, sniffed intently. "Gasoline," he guessed, and smiled.

"You were gone. It was me and the wheat—the crop I'd helped plant. Before that moment I'd have never believed I had it in me. It was mid-summer, the crop still green but filling out. I splashed the gasoline around, struck a match, and it blew me off my feet for the second time in a night."

He threw his head back. "Whoowee," he said. Rubbed his hands together as if before the fire. "It must have been something," Chas said.

"Fire took a good hold for awhile. And then the lights were coming on in the house—I could see them: bedroom light, hall light, living room, kitchen, porch." What she hadn't seen, she knew, her mother at the phone and Rob stumbling into jeans cranky with sleep, scared, and her father loading wet burlap sacks into the back of the pickup and hustling the men to ready the tractor, plow a break around the fire. And in awhile men from other ranches arriving to help, to contain the blaze before it reached the barns, the house.

"I was drunk and sick and scared. I left before they got out there, holed up with a friend for a day, pulled what savings I had, and hitched a ride out."

"And nobody ever knew how the fire started."

Her parents had known. And perhaps that was the thing that had really chased her from her home and town, coming to the realization that her father had always known what she was capable of. Had, in fact, been right to give the ranch to Rob, because when it came right down to it, she'd risked it all—livestock, crops, land and buildings, her family's home and history—in a drunken tantrum. And she'd seen then, the long years she and Chas had been feeding off each other's anger had less to do with love and much more to do with ambition—a staging ground, bolstered by their petty violences, for just such an act of meanness.

They hit the outskirts of town, the first homes snug with light in the kitchens and dining rooms. Ike would be waiting dinner. She had no appetite left. "I burned the land," she said.

"Yeah, well," he said. "You were drunk."

She gripped the wheel, downshifted to the speed limit. She had no answer. Her act was an offense against land, family. But Chas would never see that—his heart as flawed as hers. She stopped at the courthouse. The building was dark. "You could leave a note, I suppose," she said.

He shook his head. "No. I got to see the judge. I'll walk over to his house." He laughed. "Maybe he'll invite me in to dinner."

Pattiann snorted at the idea.

Then Chas was reaching for the door and then he stopped, his hand on the handle. He turned the palm of his free hand up. "None of this talk will change things. You're married now and I understand that." He looked out the side window, then back at her. "But I'm not willing to let it go as easy as this either." He leaned over, spoke softly next to her ear. "We had *some* good times," he said. He buffed her cheek with a kiss. "I remember how you would cry out in my arms." He winked at her, pushed the door open. "Need to thank you, Miss Pattiann, for the ride and talk."

"How you getting home?"

He shrugged, tipped back his hatless head, and studied the sky. He pointed out the North Star. "I'll direct my feet and hike my thumb." He closed the door, bent down into the open window. "I'll threaten to camp out on the judge's sofa. Bet he'll find me a ride then." He stood back, slapped the hood with his hand. He started walking away, turned. "You tell your husband, I'm handing the cattle over. He might forgive you the ride." He turned on his heels and walked off.

Ike came home to an empty house. It was beginning to feel normal. Like everything else in this Goddamned place, a dozen dead dogs, Harley whining because he was on call, and then the only woman deputy complains about sexual innuendoes made by another deputy, Jim Parker—a man Ike's age who sprouted a handlebar mustache, wore his Stetson like a second crop of hair, and lived in another Goddamned century.

"I was just being nice," he'd said, slumping in a chair. He perched his hat low over his eyes. Ike's office door was closed, but shapes congregated outside the frosted glass for an earful.

"Telling her she should go braless so you can see her titties better."

"Maybe I didn't say that."

"Then what?"

He shrugged. "I don't remember." He was smiling now. "Nothing I said ain't been said a hundred times."

"Not by my officers," Ike said, and Jim snickered, so Ike knew he had an afternoon ahead of him with the men. One of those man-to-men chats about respect for fellow officers and workers, one of those friendly commands to stow their juices or he'd have their badges. "You're suspended. Two weeks without pay."

Jim sat up. "You can't—"

"The hell I can't. You're just damned lucky she's not pressing charges, because I'd back her up. *Do you understand?*" Ike kept himself in check. He was angry and you didn't mix anger with discipline.

Jim stood. "Two weeks?" he said. He walked to the door. "Maybe I'll check out the bulletin board for openings elsewhere."

Parker was a good deputy, knew the county, the people, better than any other on the force. Ike didn't want to lose him, but if he pushed it . . . Ike sighed, shrugged.

"You ain't making friends," Parker said. "People here know me."

Ike was tired. He had paperwork to finish. "Two weeks."

Which left him the rest of the day, tied to the office—a flubbed robbery out in Shono, vandalism at the elementary school in Derby, and some drunken boys picked up for driving down the wrong side of the street, and finally, a late afternoon call from Parker's wife calling Ike a sonofabitch and "Just how the hell do you think we'll make truck payments, mortgage, and groceries without two weeks' pay?"

Which finally sent him home, that last call, with his back and head aching, and hungry and in no mood to turn on the lights as he walked through the empty house. So he didn't. He sat in the dark, sipping Dickel, getting lightheaded on the way to drunk if he didn't eat soon, but he wasn't inclined to find his way through the dark for cold chicken or old cheese and bread.

When the phone rang, he was tempted to let it ring. It might be Parker's wife again, or another dead dog. But he picked it up, because it might be Pattiann, and drunk or no, he couldn't leave her out in the dark. It was his mother, long distance from Florida, where she'd moved after marrying Raymond, a retired colonel from the armed services. She'd been thinking of Ike these last several days, and it was probably her turn to call, though who was counting?

Ike lowered into his chair, rested his head against the back, and sipped the whiskey, nodding into the dark, saying yes and fine when necessary.

"Pattiann's not there? You drinking, Ike?"

"Some."

"You want her to find you that way?"

"Yup."

He could hear her breathing into the phone. "Maybe you think I should take it elsewhere?" he said, and thought he was drunker than he'd known. His dad had been a binge drinker who liked his privacy. And yes, he'd loved his dad, but it was his mother he'd believed in. And now he'd hurt her, too. Chalk it up to the fitting end of a perfect day. "I'm sorry. Listen, everything's fine. I had a difficult day at work," he said.

"That's no excuse," she said, as tough at seventy-five as she'd been at forty-three, or thirty-two. He could picture her hands spidered around the receiver, her left leg bouncing as it always did, setting the floor, the ground quivering. As a child he'd found it comforting, and wasn't that a queer thing, the way he could feel her presence alive and leaping through the floorboards, while his father was a quiet absence. "Listen," she went on, "I didn't mean to scold. This is obviously not a good time to talk. Just wanted you to know we're well."

"Good to hear that, Mom. Listen, I'm sorry, too. What say I call you back in a day or two, my nickel."

"Give Pattiann our love," she said and was gone. Always the efficient one, even at good-byes. He thought about filling his glass again, but he wasn't in the mood anymore. As a young man, on the rare times he drank to excess, he was always careful to do it away from home. Like his father before him. His family hadn't been so different from folks out here. What you didn't see, you didn't have to deal with. It made for polite company. He was woozy and closed his eyes, and when he opened them again, perhaps he'd slept a bit. He felt stiff and his tongue thick. There were sounds in the kitchen.

"That you?" he called out.

She peeked in the doorway. "You were asleep, thought I'd wake you for dinner. Got some nice beef."

"Surprise, surprise," he muttered. A cattleman's daughter. He pushed himself out of the chair. His headache stirred and he made his way blinking into the kitchen to douse the beginnings of a hangover. He drank a glass of water at the sink in a few large gulps, came up panting.

"Celebrating?" she asked.

He seated himself in a kitchen chair, poked at a wrapped package. "What's this?"

"Some meat," Pattiann said. "Beef. Chas gave it to us."

"Stubblefield." He hefted the unopened package and studied it. "Giving us gifts now." The package was solid in his hand and he lofted it, trying to guess the weight. Substantial. His mouth had gone dry. He found he had to ask, "You two getting chummy again?"

"For Christ's sake, Ike. He needed a ride, and I was there."

"Convenient." Even as he said it, he knew it was petty. Trite. But his head was pounding and so was his heart and he believed he recognized in her eyes something that hadn't been there that morning. She was avoiding him. He moved in on her, the meat still chilling his palm. He meant to crowd her, push her. Into what? An admission of guilt? Confession?

She cocked her chin high. "How bad do you want this fight?" she asked.

He balanced the meat in one hand, looked at her, then walked to the back door and lobbed it like a football, a long pass into the dark. He heard the thump as it hit the dirt, could see the pale wrapping turn end over end into the bushes. There was the snapping of small twigs and then nothing. The night air was cold on his skin and the shock of it was invigorating. Like a cold shower. Like a good fight. There was silence at his back, and then he heard her long, exasperated sigh.

"That was good meat you just threw to the neighborhood dogs, Ike."

"The neighborhood dogs," he said, and turned back toward her, "are dead. Long live the coyotes." He closed the door. She was standing with her back to the sink, the distance of the kitchen between them. A careful space. And he suddenly believed, as he hadn't to this point, that not only was he was capable of losing her but was capable, in fact, of driving her away. Right into Stubblefield's arms. Again. Maybe that had already happened. And that realization started like a small tic in his gut, a sudden need for caution, that triggered instead something more resembling anger. A part of him was alarmed, how quickly it had escalated to this, tried to clamp down even as another part of him wanted to let it get out of control. Wanted to hurt her in whatever way it took to put her as much at his mercy as he was at hers. With all his years in law enforcement, he believed he understood the attraction of violence, the satisfaction of it, how you became submerged in the act, became the impulse. He did not think himself a violent man, but knew he was susceptible to it, the way the game face you put on before kicking in the door *became your face,* violence begetting violence. And sometimes Ike believed he could smell it when cuffing them, or transporting them away from the scene, could smell it on himself as well, a musk on the skin, a sweetness that quickly turned bitter and soured after the fact.

"What's wrong?" she asked, and touched his hand, and his arm startled out from under her fingers.

He settled his hand in his pocket to cover his surprise at how she had crossed the distance to him in his distraction, and at the same time he tried to resurrect that edge he'd been so carefully walking. "What's wrong? I have the original day from hell and come home to an empty house and you ask what's wrong. Somebody's poisoned half the dogs in the county, I have to suspend my best officer who's threatening to leave me in a lurch in the middle of this . . . this dog killing." He hooked his thumb toward the yard. "And Parker's wife wants to know who's going to pay for groceries and maybe, just maybe, we ought to take that hunk of meat and give it to them." He walked past Pattiann, sat heavily at the table. He was more sober than he wanted to be.

"You suspended Parker?"

"Fuck Parker."

Pattiann stepped away, put the kettle on to simmer. She busied herself at the stove and then she stopped as if to say something, shook her head, and took the lid off the kettle to prod at the contents with a long fork. She tried again. "In case you're wondering, we're having stew, tonight." She waited, put the lid back on. "If you'd turned on a light and read the note I left, you'd know that. It was in the fridge. All you had to do was pop it on the stove to simmer."

"No," he pointed a finger at her. "All I had to do was sit in an easy chair and unwind from a day at work while all you had to do was be here and pop that Goddamned stew on the stove. Instead, you're off wandering around with that half-cocked psychopath, Stubblefield, who's giving you presents now, meat off his half-rotted cows."

He thought she'd blow, and he looked forward to it, an honest fight, some good clean anger to settle the air between them instead of this skulking about. But she eased back into a chair, blinked into the overhead light, and then crossed her hands before her.

"I spent the day at my mother's," she said. Her voice got smaller. "I haven't been much help to her."

And that was so Goddamned unfair of her. Turning him upside down. Making him feel the lout, and worse yet, never intending to. He dropped his head into his hands, felt the headache bloom, the day's frustrations, Parker and Harley. And Stubblefield—the one who made the whole thing personal as the law was never meant to be. "We got any aspirin?" he asked. She brought him two and another full glass of water.

She sat across from him after he swallowed the pills. "I was coming home when Chas waved me down. His truck was stalled on the roadside."

She got that look in her eyes that came at rare moments, so that they lit a little sharper and her brows drew tighter. She took a deep breath and leaned back. "And I knew you wouldn't like it, but he *needed* a ride, so I gave him one, and as a thank-you, he gave me the meat. Nothing more, nothing less. He's going to turn the cattle over. He came in to tell the judge." She waited.

Tomorrow would be no better, he thought. Except that maybe they could begin to put this Stubblefield business behind them. He wanted to reach across the table, take her hand in his, but he didn't trust himself yet. "How's your mama?" he asked instead, and, "When do we eat?" Though he wasn't sure he could swallow a bite.

As it happened, the judge patted Chas on the back. "Good, good," he said. "Better this way."

Chas said how happy it made him to come out a hero in this sorry mess. They stood in the foyer. Over the judge's shoulder a door opened on the living room. Beyond that, in the next room, was a table laid out in dinnerware. "Well, I just wanted you to know there ain't no hard feelings. Smells good. Pork?"

He could swear the judge cringed. Chas smiled. "Got beef at home. Good cuts. A little on the lean side, but only does the heart good, right?" He slapped the judge on the shoulder and the old man rocked. "But it's a cold night, and a hell of a walk on an empty stomach. Truck broke down, had to hitch a ride in. Don't know how I'm getting home. Maybe I'll hang till morning, find a *neighbor* with a spare room. Surely God will provide for His stray lamb? Though this being cattle country, *our* God don't abide sheep. Pork, you say?" And that was when the judge made the phone call. Moments later, a squad drew up and Chas was on his way.

The ride home was silent. The thin-lipped young deputy, Harley, insisted Chas sit in back, behind the cage, beyond reach of the shotgun, and maybe that was a smart move, because Chas was feeling churlish, up to his craw with bigger-and-better-than-thou types, and Harley was just another example, fiddling with the radio, rolling through stops and flipping on the overheads at the one traffic light in town, as though this were a real emergency. God suffered more fools than He had a right to.

At home, Chas moved the horse into the barn, gave it the last of the feed cakes. As for the cattle, they were out of his hands now and there was nothing left he could do for them, except maybe put a hole through somebody's head—Sam Coker, or Taylor.

He'd resigned himself to what would inevitably happen. When the sheriff and his helpers came, they would find what they'd find—cattle good as dead anyway, anemic and developing coughs that laid them lower than hunger did. Cattle that had long ago stripped the jack pines, needles greening their tongues, to abort their fetuses. What protein they burned came from the liver, spleen, and muscles. Did Parsons know this, that they stop pissing after awhile? What was spared was the heart and brain. Nature's questionable taste in jokes—the heart keeps beating so the brain takes it all in, all the hope and pain.

The piebald nickered, snuffing the bare floor for more feed, rocked against the stall. His daddy's old horse. Down to its last legs anyway, but fitter than the rest of his stock. The sheriff had kindly seen to that. And that was why Chas hid the horse now. Call it one small blow. Let the nag starve. He still had that right. He'd given them the cattle, but the horse was his, and in case they meant to argue it—what they didn't know they wouldn't miss. He leaned over the stall and the piebald crooked its muzzle toward him. "Now you get hungry, you let me know," he said to the horse and laughed. He walked to the house. The sheriff would take the cattle out of Chas's hands in a day or two. He would take another piece of Chas's life away, even that last piece, and call it humane, and then he'd go home and warm his feet against Pattiann's back cheeks. And that picture proved too much to imagine, so that Chas could not use it, not even to prick his anger. Instead, he thought of her riding the long miles in the truck with him, how, willingly or not, she made him feel as if there was still something left for him. And he did not know whether he meant to thank her for that or curse her.

He stopped in the doorway. He turned to the yard, gazed out over the bones of cars, rusted fenders and gaping doors, discarded balers, an old wagon bed, the odd hubcap eyeing him from the shrinking snow. He lifted his sight, beyond the corral where the steaming breath of cattle fogged the air, to the open land that appeared, even now, as it had the night he'd held his dying father, to invite dreams, so generously expansive it was. Enough land to make a man itch with possibilities. *It could have been,* he thought. He stepped in and closed the door behind him. *Could have been,* but for all the things in this world beyond a man's knowing, all the slights stacked up against him. No. This was no accident, no casual catastrophe of nature. It was a trail of culpability: the mill, the bank, the government. And by whose higher hand the drought, then winter? It was provoked. And it occurred to him, that if there were any *real* justice in this world—if God were a man, He'd come down again, just so Chas could put a bullet in His head.

Chapter Eight

I t took three days to arrange and another two days stalled by bad weather, but on the sixth morning the sun shone whole and faultless in the blue. People waved to each other from the streets, and raised their fingers on steering wheels as they passed on the highway, cracked windows to the air and shucked coats. Ranchers tuned in futures markets, plotted crop strategy, and anticipated rolling up their sleeves in the calving pens. Soon. Everything about this morning said *soon.*

It seemed a curious contradiction to Ike, standing in Stubblefield's feedlot, everything around him quickening to life again while he watched the front-end loaders make tidy work of it, the buckets scraping cattle free from the ice and snow, lifting another carcass, or a half, a quarter, to be stacked in the waiting trucks, WESTERN BIPRODUCTS, wide red letters. It wasn't that Ike could hear the bodies being snatched free over the whine of hydraulics, diesel, the rumble of tracks grinding up the ragged turf, but somehow his mind supplied the details, the chew and tear, bone and muscle—everything still frozen, nothing liquid anymore.

The judge had had the papers ready, his only questions being cost and who got charged? And so Ike knew the judge was covering his ass, had talked to the commissioner's office, assayed the economics of moving and disposing of nearly two hundred head of cattle, sniffed out the potential voter response, and scrubbed his hands in public. Ike reassured him. The rendering company had been only too glad to take the problem off their hands.

They'd hauled off the first three truckloads. The hands from his brother-in-law's ranch were there. Ike had phoned Rob to call in a favor—men to ride the back pastures, locate cattle, lend a horse so he could ride out with them. He would do what killing was necessary. That was as it should be, wasn't it?

Pattiann was with them. She'd insisted. Still, Ike wished he could send her home. Protect her. No, be truthful. Protect himself, from how she would see him, clumsy in the saddle, exposed in all that land and shooting another man's cattle. No better than a rustler.

Purvis had trailered his own horse to the site. He'd brought along cattle markers—fat, colored grease sticks—to mark the cattle with a bright red X like a stand of trees to be thinned. But the herd was too far gone. They'd given up marking them. "Ah, Jesus," Purvis had said. "They're standing on dead wood—not enough protein to keep the blood circulating. Come a good thaw, the legs'll turn black and rot. What a waste." He looked away.

Harley was in the far corral helping load the cattle. In a passing cruelty, Ike wondered what Harley would say about his day to the dispatcher tonight.

Chas had yet to put in an appearance, and though Ike supposed he should be grateful for that, especially with Pattiann here, perversely enough, he wanted to see *them* together, to hear her voice, see if she ducked her head with annoyance or blushed with pleasure. Chas's house looked peaceable, squat and square. The windows were corniced with snow and a plume of smoke pulled out of the chimney. Just so damned domestic and sensible-looking. Ike warned Harley to stay put, keep his eyes open, mouth shut, and his temper in check.

They rode out the north fence line, over Beaver Creek, past the cut banks and buffalo jump, to where the trail climbed the rising hills to a high plateau. They took it slowly, single-file, staying to the high ground where the winds had blown clear the snow, and alternating leads in the hollows, sparing the horses who plodded through it, heads lowered, as do all good cow horses. Ike thought about the piebald. Had they found it? Hauled it away while he hadn't been looking? Would they find it yet, out here? Or had it turned like the other animals to frozen turf? He thought of that first night in the field, that graceless beast with its honest face and how it had followed him. He was ashamed he'd forgotten the animal. Maybe it would have been the one thing worth saving. The animals they were riding were groomed and well fed. They snorted into the sweet wind.

"Chinook," one of the men said and opened his parka.

Pattiann rode ahead. Her back was straight, her seat tucked well into the saddle. He envied her ease and he was proud of her. She'd once told him, as a child she used to ride out where no one might see, ride her horse *breakneck and far from chores*. Her words. Until one of the hands saw and told her daddy. He took her horse from her. Ground-tied her to the house, cooking for ranch hands, working with her mother, a sullen union that held for nearly five years. "Two women in the kitchen," Pattiann had said. "Better he should have beat me."

At the top, the men rode off to plant flags where they found cattle submerged in snow, and already the draws were dotted with bright scraps of red perking in the chinook. The surviving cattle were too far gone to herd down, a number of them blind with starvation, bumping into each other or the horses as they milled a moment before settling into a sullen stillness. Ike sidled his horse alongside Pattiann's.

"You shouldn't have come."

"I won't embarrass you," she said, and tugged her horse clear before he could tell her it was not *her* competence he feared. And then he was not sure he could have said that anyway.

Fewer than thirty cattle still stood on the high plateau. When they walked, the hooves clacked against each other like a chorus of wooden spoons. They would never survive a drive down to the waiting trucks. Ike pocketed his gloves, curled and uncurled his fingers, wiped the palms on his jeans. He unsheathed his Winchester 30.30.

He looped the reins over the horn. "Easy, girl," he said to the horse, and hoisted the rifle to his shoulder. It was a mercy, he told himself. He concentrated on a small patch of hide, the soft area behind the ear. Black Angus had damnable bony heads. He *could* risk a shot between the eyes, just below the frontal plate, but he imagined the trajectory of the bullet slowed through bone, shredding, imploding—the agonizing damage. No.

Behind the ear and out through the eye. One shot. A neat snick and pop, the cow dropping, that easy, and damn Chas Stubblefield. He worked the lever action, snugged the maple stock into his shoulder, held his breath, and sighted on the small flap of flesh.

He focused on the black, the snow burning a frame for the animal. He squeezed. A recoil against his shoulder and the cow dropped. The horse flinched but stood steady. "Good girl," he said, and kneed her forward lining up another black scrap. He cocked the lever, aimed, squeezed. The spent cartridge flicked waspish into the air. He didn't have to hear the cow drop; instead, he listened for the bang winging out over the plateau to where coyotes denned, and beyond where the land dropped to the valley floor and cottonwoods grew in a snarl on the riverbank. By the fifth shot, the horse no longer flinched. A tenderness set into Ike's shoulder. By the tenth, the ache was bone deep. He changed rifles. Still Ike distanced himself from the cattle, imagining himself instead down in the breaks where the sound of the killing would have long faded, following the distant river, listening to the water's muffled current beneath the icy shelf where trout flashed out of the deep.

By the eighteenth shot, his shoulder felt compressed, his arms sore. He could no longer trust the careful shot behind the ear. He resorted to the point between the eyes, his attention wrenched back to meat and bone. He heard the concussion like a blow to his head and he lowered the rifle to his lap. His shoulder had numbed and his cheek tingled. There was a ringing of brass in his head. He stopped to let the commotion quiet.

Pattiann approached. She reached over and touched his knee. The men were scattered about the plateau. Purvis looked politely away. "I could take over," she said.

He *wanted* to hand it over, but this was his work. It no longer mattered how he'd come to it. Good intentions or not. There was a penance here he'd meant to inflict and it had come back on his own head. "No," he said. Then he touched her fingers. Sheathed the rifle. He dismounted and dropped the reins. He waded through the snow. Slipping the handgun from his holster, he approached a cow. It turned to him with eyes that were wide and unfocused as if in a rapture. Ike aimed and shot.

There was nothing distant anymore, it was up close and personal. He was surprised to find how little he felt besides gratitude for not feeling more. He shot them. They folded. One after another.

Pattiann and the other hands worked on around him, planting flags like a flock of cardinals on the snow, marking the buried carcasses for the rendering crews that would join them after they'd finished below. Purvis sat astride his horse gazing over the valley.

The actual killing took less than an hour. In the end, both Pattiann and Purvis helped. Purvis had been the first to step in. Pattiann had followed. Some of Rob's hands rode out farther, to check for animals still standing. What few were left were fodder for the coyotes, their numbers small, and nature was meticulous: coyotes, buzzards, magpies, beetles.

None of the riders had seen a piebald horse. "It's pretty damned big out there," one had said. "The only thing moving is slinking."

Pattiann and Purvis stayed on as the hands turned their horses back down the trail. The three of them stood in a loose group, surveying the flags, the downed cattle. "It was a mercy," Purvis said.

"Once before," Pattiann said, "I've seen it this bad. A blizzard—lasted two, two and a half days. My dad lost cattle. They all did. But Goddamn it, he tried so hard. Blamed himself for years because he wasn't stronger than the weather. But this . . ." She turned her back to them. "Can Chas sleep at night? You have to pity him."

Ike wanted to tell her she should save it. Chas had gotten off easy. But he kept his quiet, looked at her across the distance of a few feet. Her hand raised to her horse's chin strap, fingers looped through it.

"Pity?" Purvis said. "Maybe I'm just too sick of this business to think properly. I *want* to believe I'm a man who can turn his cheek if the occasion calls for it." He lowered the reins, lifted his foot to the stirrup, and hefted himself into the saddle. The leather creaked and the horse huffed as Purvis shifted the saddle under him. "But at this moment, Pattiann, if you can talk about pity, you're a better person than I am." He swung his horse toward the trail at a slow walk.

Ike scanned the area one last time. He raised his foot into the stirrup, bounced twice on his standing leg, an embarrassment that he couldn't do it in one faultless swing like Pattiann, or even the older Purvis. He headed down after Purvis and soon he heard her coming up behind.

The snow in the low spots was already pooling from the chinook. They caught the odd jackrabbit lapping at the standing water. In less than a month, barring another heavy storm, the snow would be gone. The range would turn to gumbo, followed by lush green shoots, and the ranchers would breathe easier with calves coming in, cows and the range both freshening. Ike lifted his face to the breeze, let the reins swing with the horse's nodding. *Soon.* All spring and summer would stretch ahead as if it had no intention of ending, except in the designs of men who plotted crops and planned from the lessons learned this winter and all the preceding winters. And he wondered how long could a man learn, unlearn, and relearn before he came upon the thing that undid him? Storm. Drought. Age. The market. One year you're at home and the next—a stranger to the place you'd made for yourself. And maybe the best you could hope for in those instances was to find yourself, like Chas, still young enough to start over at something else.

When they got back down, they found the rendering crew in good spirits. This was a windfall. Meat for the taking, enough to make it worthwhile. The lower feed yard was cleared, scraped. Workers milled around machines. Harley was in the cruiser, on the radio. He clicked off when he saw Ike. A half-dozen cars and pickups lined the roadside, people sitting in cabs or bunched by the fence. Spectators. Neighbors with a nose for misfortune.

"Harley," Ike called. "Tell them to leave."

"I tried," Harley said. "Don't get pissed at me. I kept them behind the fence, didn't I?"

Fred Timbers was there, Ben Joust, Paul Lange and his wife, Letta. Old Tom Millan stood by his truck. Still carrying his grudge with the IRS and probably seeing this as just another example of big government squeezing the little guy. Ike could read it in their faces. A lynch mob. Who they wanted to lynch remained to be seen.

"You see a horse?" Ike asked Harley. "A piebald, white face? Stubble-field's horse?"

Harley shook his head. "Shit. I've seen more cows today than I ever wanted to see in my life, but no horses other than what you rode in on."

"Check the barn," Ike said.

Harley looked at his watch. "I was hoping to get out—"

"Then it's a good thing I'm only asking you to check the barn."

"Guess so," Harley said. He smiled.

"And while you're at it, check the shed." He pointed to the far corner of the yard.

Ike handed the reins to Harley and approached the gathering of bystanders. He seated his hat, nodded to Letta still in the pickup. "You men here to help?"

Joust snorted. "Don't seem the bank needs any more bully boys than what's here already."

"That how you see this, Ben? Hired guns? Just like the bad old days, huh?"

"Government kill-ers," Millan said, his voice breaking on the last syllable.

"Tom," Ike said, holding up a hand, "this is me, Ike Parsons, and that there is Harley, and Purvis, and there isn't a soul here you don't know by first name."

"That include Stubblefield whose cattle you just killed?" Joust asked.

Ike nodded. "He signed the cattle over to dispose of as best we could, a merciful act, don't you think . . ." He held his hand up, tipped back his hat. "But you all know that already, and have come in a good community spirit, to support Mr. Stubblefield in his time of need. I'm sure he appreciates it, watching as he must be from his window, knowing you all came out of friendship and not out of a need to gawk and gossip."

Letta laughed from inside the pickup cab. "Right between the eyes," she called. Paul leaned down and hushed her. "Ha," she said, and again louder, "Ha."

"Now, if you got any questions, I'm in my office, regular hours." But Ben was already stepping up into the cab.

They pulled out one by one. Tom Millan was last to leave. "Blood-sucking government," he called out.

"Yeah, Tom. You drive careful."

Tom smiled, waved as he pulled out onto the highway and rumbled off in his Studebaker pickup. Ike turned, looked over at Stubblefield's house. Blank-faced windows. No chickens, cats, or dogs. Machinery rumbled in the yard and men called to each other. He could hear Harley laughing. Pattiann and Purvis were loading the horses, and once it was done, all the trucks and men with their noise pulled out, Ike tried to imagine this place. There would be nothing. Just Stubblefield. And all the silence he could ever hope for.

Pattiann rode back with Purvis. She would have stayed until the last truck left, but she sensed Ike didn't want that. He wanted her far from Stubblefield, and maybe from himself as well. She'd stepped in it for sure. Pitying Chas, but there it was. She wasn't about to take back the truth. Purvis drove slowly, checking the trailer in the sideview mirrors. The horse shuffled, leaned to a side, and the truck hitched and meandered over the line. "Damn cob-headed beast," Purvis said.

"Your horse likes to lean," she agreed as the truck wandered a few feet left.

"I'm talking about the truck. Not made for hauling something more determined than it is. But it'll settle down in awhile."

"The truck?"

"The horse. Always spooky the first couple miles. He'll get a comfortable lean—I'll compensate—and sleep the whole way home. The horse, not me."

"I'm relieved."

"You're tired. You want, you can rest your pretty head." He patted his shoulder. "Take a nap."

"No," Pattiann said. "I'm tired, but not sleepy." She watched the road spindle away in the sideview mirror. It would be dark soon. How was it, she wondered, that in fall the days shortened so much more quickly than they lengthened in late winter. Or maybe winter days were so gray, it seemed like dusk from dawn to nightfall. But today had been brilliant, the chinook making you believe the end was at hand. Perhaps her mother had read her bones wrong and they were done with the worst, the last big blow come and gone. An early spring. Something they never tired of praying for. She rubbed a cramp out of her thigh. She hoped Ike would be home early. She wanted to make it up to him.

"You think Ike's upset with me?" Pattiann asked.

Purvis ducked his head. "You know him better than I do."

Pattiann laughed. "You believe that? Or just dodging the question?"

"Both." He corrected for the lean. "I think Ike's out of sorts with the world right now, understandably, and you stand front and center in his attention, always. It's a condition of marriage—to judge the weather by each other. I'm not saying you're responsible, but he sees you pitying Chas, he reads you as the community. *They* see you pitying Chas, it feeds the fire."

"So I shouldn't care?"

Purvis sighed, hunkered down in the seat. "You confound me, Pattiann."

"Chas hasn't got a friend in the world," she said.

"He's got himself," Purvis snapped. "Fitting company."

Purvis stared at the road, his hands fixed on the wheel. Pattiann looked out over the snow, the small pools of meltwater cupped on the surface that shone a deeper gray, like so many tossed coins. How the hell could this have happened? Really? A bad year for snow, yes. And last summer, yet another summer of drought. But others had managed, laid away feed, sold off stock. And that was the pinch. She could imagine it as Chas must have. More land, turn it over to pasture for quick profit, turn the profit into more cows banking on a mild winter, banking on God Almighty, a last-minute miracle.

Not the God Pattiann knew. Her God was a distracted presence whose attention wandered, did His best work over millennia. She did not pray for miracles. Her God was larger than a last-ditch miracle. And if it was true that in the early days God walked with man, He'd long since grown bored with their questions.

Purvis broke the silence. "So maybe I'm wrong. Maybe you know something about Chas I don't?"

Pattiann shook her head. "Who knows Chas but Chas, or any of his family? No one cared to know Avery, and that was fine with him. I barely remember Chas's mother, Abbie. I do remember she was a seriously religious woman, and I don't mean the type who wears it like a new skin." Pattiann looked out the window. "She was"—she looked over at Purvis—"what's the word?"

"A fanatic?"

"She was too *distant* for that, know what I mean? Always staring off at some other place, or plane. Not that we saw her that much. Maybe my mama knew her best, and if you asked her she wouldn't claim much more than a passing acquaintance. Otherworldly, that's the word."

"Died young."

"Suicide."

"And Chas must have been what, about twelve? That's a lot for a young kid to bear up under. Then of course there were all those years alone with Avery." Purvis leaned his head back, closed his eyes a moment, and when he opened them again he gazed up into the rearview mirror and held his focus there, as if at himself. "But isn't there a time when a person has to say, all right, now this is the *rest* of my life? And I'm accountable for that?"

He looked over at Pattiann. "Chas was offered help. He *chose* not to take it. Now you can shrug that off to pride, some people might even admire it, 'Well, he come on hard times and wasn't a man to take what he couldn't pay for,' that sort of thing. But then he wasn't the one starving, was he? He ate the dead like it was his just meets, and maybe it was. Point is, I can't look into his soul. I got only his actions to judge by, and if there was suffering in his past, that's not what I see now. He's taken a pleasure in this business."

"Is that the way you see it?" Pattiann leaned over to Purvis. "Christ, maybe he's just trying to find his own damn way."

Purvis's foot lifted from the gas pedal. He shifted and the engine whined down. He pulled to the roadside, sat with the truck idling. The horse shuffled awake in the trailer, the truck jolting softly. Purvis pulled a cigar from his jacket pocket, slid the cellophane wrapper clear, nipped the cigar end, and lit it. He inhaled, held it, exhaled. "You're pretty touchy when it comes to Chas."

"So I should just shut up and keep house."

"Damn it, woman, I'm not saying that. Now if you insist on pitying Chas, all right. But it's a thing any self-respecting man would detest. Now, *understanding* is another thing." His cigar bobbed in the darkening cab. "Compassion. Yes. And I think those require a right-minded thinking. A considered and deserved emotion. But pity—"

"Semantics," Pattiann said.

"Hell, yes, semantics. It occurs to me, you haven't examined what you're feeling or why—pity's what Chas is tweaking right now—self-pity and no thought about those animals, or what he's done to this community. Pity is mindless, invoked by the self-pitying. It's an emotion that calls for no direct action. We are *salved* by pity—'nothing I can do but feel sorry for the poor bastard.' And you, soft-hearted as you are, and mind me, I'm not saying I'm not in favor of that, God spare me the hard-hearted woman, but he's taken you in hook, line, and sinker."

His eyebrows raised, cigar smoke curling through his hair and drafting out the window. Purvis clamped the stub between his teeth, put the truck in gear, and pulled out slowly.

"I'm not saying you're entirely wrong in this," she said softly. "But I think Stubblefield's hurting. And if someone had been there earlier for him, this wouldn't have happened."

Purvis clucked his tongue. "This is the worst kind of spilt milk," he said. "Whatever you did or didn't do, you can't take back, and no amount of beating your breasts is going to make Stubblefield any more or less than he is right now."

"So we let it ride?"

"For now. This passes, hopefully, and we offer what help he'll accept." Purvis shuffled his cigar to the other side of his mouth. He blinked in the smoke, eyes watering.

"You know, one day, smoking's going to kill you."

"You worried or hopeful?"

"I'm thinking how there wouldn't be a soul left in this world to lecture me."

She studied him in the last light, a graying man, his chunky fingers wrapped around the cigar, who did his work quietly and took his friends seriously. Good humor and a true heart his only defense. The sides of his hands and jacket sleeves blackly inked by grease sticks. Got more on him than the cows. She turned away, looked out the side window at the last miles before town.

It was dark by the time they drove the front-end loader onto its trailer. "You need help again," the rendering company foreman said, "give us a call. You ever in Helena, stop by for a beer. Want a tour of the plant, we'll take you through. It's a good setup. Clean. We feed the nation's dogs, feed yours—you got one?—no? Well, we do good work. Hell, we ain't ghouls," he said, spreading his hands like an apology. "It just looks that way."

He smiled and shrugged, and after he'd driven off, Ike stood in the exhaust and the scraped yard believing he still smelled death and wondered if that man carried it home with him to his wife and children, set it at the table alongside the aroma of potatoes and green beans. Ike sniffed his own hands, his jacket. Gunpowder, all in all a clean business. The last semi trucked down the road, the crews gone off for beers and home, and still no sign of Chas, though a light had come on in the house, moved from room to room like a hand-held kerosene lamp, and Ike wondered if Chas's power had been cut, too. But no, the yard light was on and it sketched intricate shadows amid the tangle of old car parts and machinery.

He stood in the scoured lot, turned his head aside from the wind that brisked across the field. First time he'd smelled death, it was back in an apartment building, apartment 4D, Sutter Street, Milwaukee. Mid-August, ninety-eight degrees. Humid. He was twenty-two, and it was his first bad one. A retired school principal who'd lived alone, dead four days when a neighbor complained. At the scene, just outside the apartment door, his partner Bassette lifted his nose into the air, sniffed, and stepped back. "This ain't going to be amusing," he said, and signaled Ike to go first.

The apartment was clean. Everything in a predictable place. That was the first thing that struck Ike. All the lamps had ruffled shades and the tables had clean tops. The sofa was chintz-covered and there was one worn cushion, as though she'd lived her life in that one spot. It was an orderly apartment but for the corpse that had bloated until the skin had split. Her dress was hiked up over wallowing thighs and it seemed indecent to Ike so that he started to rearrange the skirt when Bassette stopped him. "Leave it be. Ain't nobody embarrassed here but you. We make the report first, call in the coroner." They wandered through the apartment, waiting for the meat truck to arrive, and when it did, the attendants gripped their noses with one hand and folded her into a rubber sheet with another. She was fluid. She rolled like jelly, emitting great vaporous farts. Bassette seemed disappointed that Ike didn't get sick, but afterward, in the shade of the oak-lined street, he said, "You did good, kid."

Ike stood in the lot, staring at the fields, the fences, the house cozied into the night. It came to him like a premonition that it was not over, a foreboding that rooted him in place until his skin burned with cold, felt as raw and scraped as the yard around him. And then he was crossing the lot, passing through the gate he no longer bothered to close, and stepping onto Stubblefield's front porch. He knocked twice. He wasn't sure why he was standing here, except he knew he couldn't steal away into the dark. There was a reckoning he hadn't made yet, but what it was he wasn't sure.

Stubblefield opened the door a crack, peered out. He gestured with a cupped hand, turned his back, and disappeared. Ike followed. To the side, he could see a light in the kitchen, but Stubblefield moved into the dark of the living room where he settled into the shadows. Ike seated himself on the sofa adjacent. A bar of light from the kitchen doorway sliced across the back cushions and over his lap.

"Thought you'd want to know we're done." Ike nodded toward the door. "It went quick. Purvis said there was nothing to save—"

Stubblefield sighed, a sound like the last breath issuing out of a corpse. Ike waited. He should have let matters ride. He should have driven off and not looked back. He spread his hands out in the slab of light and the gesture seemed clumsy, as if his hands had become out-sized in the small room. "I just thought I should tell you."

"You want a drink, Sheriff? I got a last bottle here somewhere." There was the chink of glass, then Stubblefield leaned into the light with a half-emptied bottle.

Ike took a sip and handed it back. Stubblefield drank deeply before settling back.

"We are, all of us, a sorry lot." Chas paused. The sound of liquid sloshing, another dark swallow. "Last year, when I was still young, I believed I would make this land and it would make me."

It got so quiet, Ike thought Chas had fallen asleep, but then he said, "I had ambitions." He giggled and then it turned softer, more like a kind of crying and perhaps it was.

"Whooee," Chas said when finished. "I'm on my way to drunker. Care to make a night of it, you know, like old friends, partners in crime?"

He pushed the bottle into the light, but Ike shook his head. He should get back. He should get on to doing what he'd come here for. But that escaped him still, what it was he expected of himself. He pushed forward, perched on the end of the sofa. There was a pair of clean socks bundled in the corner of the couch, and in the dark, Ike thought he could make out a line of shapes—shirts with arms up in surrender, pants, underwear. And although it must have been there all the time, only now did he hear the *drip, drip*. Ike smelled detergent and bleach. Laundry.

"Maybe you could start over," Ike said.

"Sure, sure," Chas said. "Work cattle for someone else, save up. Buy a few head, find some land, hit my old buddy Taylor up for a loan at the bank, buckle down, pull myself up by my bootstraps, marry well. Any number of things could happen. I am a man rich in potential."

"Do something else," Ike said. "People change their lives all the time."

"Attaboy," Chas said. "Reborn—a grocery clerk." He got up, walked over to the window where the moonlight broke over him, his pale skin tinted blue as new snow. "What do you want? Really? Ain't neither of us interested in holding the other's hand. What *more* do you want?" He pressed open palms to the window, leaned his head against it, stared out.

Ike looked down at his own hands. What did he want? His assurance that this was the end of it. That it stopped here. But Ike could not find the words, or maybe he was just unwilling to give Chas the pleasure of knowing how much he disturbed Ike.

Chas looked over his shoulder, his palms still spread on the cold glass. "Fact is, I gave it over to you years ago."

Ike sat still on the sofa, waiting to see what turn Chas would take next. He gripped his knees with his hands.

Chas slouched against the sill so that he was back-lit, a pale corona blueing his hair, the moist palm prints shining from the window on either side of his head. "When Pattiann first came back home, I thought all I had to do was give her time. Just bide my while and she'd come around." He was laughing and shaking his head. He looked across the room to where Ike sat. "Can you believe that?"

Ike found himself shaking his head. No. Pattiann would never be the first to come back around. Ike knew her better than that.

"And by God, I *knew* her better than that," Chas said.

Ike sat back. His own thoughts echoed by Chas in a voice tender with grief, a level of intimacy he didn't want to share, and just as suddenly given an insight into the couple they'd once been, and maybe it wasn't just haphazard fucking, or the youthful wildness Ike'd wanted to believe, but something deeper that had more to do with the territory of love than lust.

"Queer, isn't it? Here's you and me talking like old friends, and all we got in the world to hold us together is dead cattle, and the same woman."

"No, Chas," Ike said. "She's not the Pattiann you knew."

"Hah!" His laugh came out like a bark. "You think you know her differently?"

Ike shifted to the edge of the sofa. He kept his hands on either side of his body, locked on the cushion. This was going bad. He could feel his heart laboring as if his blood had thickened, though his arms and hands felt strangely light and he gripped the worn cushion tighter. The butt of his gun goaded him in the ribs. He was a professional, he told himself.

No room for the personal in his job. Ike stood, rolled his hat brim in his hand, stopped.

"I didn't come here to talk about my *wife*." He felt angry and just as suddenly foolish for being pushed into this by Chas, the man who had, after all, lost everything, who spent his day doing laundry while another man shot his cattle. It was pathetic, really. And just as suddenly Ike was aware of what it was he'd really needed to say, even though it would be a bitter thing. "I'm sorry. It's what I came to say. I'm sorry it had to be this way."

Stubblefield moved. The bottle landed on the floor, rolled the small distance between them, and stopped. Chas giggled again, the pained little sound. "Want to know what I learned?" he asked. "What I learned is there ain't enough time left us in this world to be sorry for all our transgressions. Little ones, big ones, cattle, *friends,* fuck 'em all, I say." He leaned into the light. He giggled. "That means fuck you too." He fell back into the dark.

There was a snicker from the shadow and Ike left the house feeling he'd wear that sound on the long ride home, but the clear air made him feel buoyant again. He drove to town strangely unburdened and he drove quickly, the window open so he could savor the last of the chinook.

He stopped by the diner after checking in with the office. He told himself it was because he was hungry. Just a bite, another hour before going home. He didn't examine it too closely. He took a corner booth. There were five people seated at a table near the front and a couple at the stools. He could smell the special—fried liver and onions, a dish his mother had made him eat until he'd acquired a tolerance. He hadn't eaten it since.

Roy was in the kitchen, singing a monotone "Stairway to Heaven." Fran was working the front alone, and when she came to his table she smiled as if it cost her.

"Long day?" he asked.

She glanced over her shoulder at the table of five. "Three hours to eat three specials, two fried chickens, a swill of black coffee, and a quick run through the dessert list. They'll pay their bill and leave. No tip. Every Wednesday night. This ain't home. Does this *look* like home?" She sighed. "But my shift ends in ten minutes. What the hell." She stripped her apron off, tossed it onto the seat. "Cup of coffee?"

She brought a pot and two cups. She looked serious about relaxing, propped her feet on the seat next to Ike, pulled out a pack of cigarettes and lit one. The five were shuffling to their feet, pawing through pockets and purses. "Have a nice day," she called over her shoulder and took a long pull on her cigarette. "You look pretty done in yourself. That Stubblefield business? Heard about it."

Ike nodded. "The usual malcontents?"

"This Goddamned county is malcontent. It's the winter. Brings out the worst at a time when you don't want to see it." She made a face. "I should have brewed us a fresh pot." She poured in a dollop of milk, added sugar. "Am I being crabby? You don't need crabby." She waved the cigarette at him. "How'd it go?"

And he found himself telling her. He told her about the cattle. He told her about his bruised shoulder, the ringing in his ears. He imagined he could tell her damn near anything and she'd make sense of it. He told her about Stubblefield.

"Well, there's reasons enough in this life to get drunk. Having your herd destroyed is one of them," she said. "Having to do another man's job and shoot that herd's another one. But here you are, drinking coffee. You did your job, you'll do it tomorrow and the day after. It's what separates you from Stubblefield." She sipped her coffee and paused, looking at the window where they sat stiffly reflected in diner light. She picked up her cigarette and snubbed it out.

She stood up. "This coffee's terrible. No wonder I don't get tips. I got to get home. Sitter's waiting. Want to walk me?" She stood tableside, bunching up the apron in a hand. She looked small, hanging on to the strings.

"You get ready," he said. "I'll finish this. Bad or not, it's the first warm thing I've had today."

She smiled and stepped through the kitchen door.

A few minutes later she returned, wearing a coat and mittens. Her face looked pink and scrubbed. She breezed out the door ahead of him, throwing a good-bye over her shoulder to Roy, who grunted from the counter. He nodded to Ike and Ike could already imagine the word spreading through town, but that was unfair because Roy was a man of few words who kept his nose in his own business. The streets were empty, scrubbed clean by wind. Water from the day's warm spell glittered in a frozen runoff down the gutters. Fran lived two blocks west, a block south, the small residential section.

Fran kept in step with Ike. "This is kind of you," she said. "You got your own troubles and here I hand you mine as well. But in all this town there isn't a soul I can talk to. It happens. You grow up with these folks, make a fool of yourself at their parties, fight and get past it because who the hell else is there? But tell them something and you live with it the rest of your life."

Ike knew what she meant. Sometimes he thought even their faces came to resemble one another's as married couples do over a long time. Cottonwoods lined the street, spindly limbs fretting in the wind. He lifted his coat collar over his ears.

She slowed her pace. "You know how I told you I thought that Dave was seeing Jolene, on weekends I couldn't get home? Well, he moved her trailer onto our back acreage, out of view of the house. He called a couple nights ago to tell me. Said he was just being neighborly. The poor girl *can't make it on her own,* but don't take this wrong, understand? Just being kind. He thinks we could be friends. Thinks I'm that kind of fool. And why not? All this time and I didn't say a word."

It felt at that moment as if Ike were cursed to spend his life apologizing for sins he had no hand in. "I'm sorry," he said.

"Ah, don't be. There'll be enough of that once word gets out. You know the thing that absolutely beats me? When I told him I knew he'd been shacking up with her off and on for the past five years, he didn't deny it. He said, we could work it out. Like it was a sliver. And then the sonofabitch cried. In fifteen years, I never heard him cry and now . . . *now* he cries."

"What will you do?" Ike asked.

"Get a divorce. Raise the kids and try to be out of the house when he picks them up. Isn't that the way? You know what *really* hurts him—all those tears—this is going to cost him big time, he figures. He's afraid he'll lose the ranch."

"The courts won't ruin a man," Ike said, but then he thought of Stubblefield. The laundry dripping in the dark.

"They can come damn close. He knows it, and I know it, and right about now he probably thinks I'm angry enough to go for his throat."

"But you're not, are you?"

"Oh, I'm angry enough. But he's still the kids' dad and I can't destroy that, can I?"

They walked the last steps to her house. Lights were on throughout the first floor. They stood in the dark of the street.

She tipped her head. A tinny sound came from the house, voices and music. "Why is it kids turn up the volume so they can hear it all over the house, like they'd miss something otherwise? It's all so much garbage. Garbage in, garbage out. I wish we'd called it quits earlier, but there were the kids and there was the ranch. I hate that he thinks I'd sit out there with his girlfriend and take it, but mostly I'm relieved." She laid a hand on his arm. "And scared, I'll admit."

He folded his hand over hers. He touched her face, wiped the tears with his thumb, and he imagined kissing her cheek and then imagined her lips, and in the quiet of the familiar street, under the honest cottonwoods, the strangeness of her mouth would be exciting, shocking, and he wished he could forget who and where he was. So easy, he thought, and then he stepped back.

She smiled, glanced over at the lit house. "I'd better get in, turn down the television before the neighbors call the sheriff." She leaned into his ear. "Thank you, Ike," she whispered. "You tell Pattiann, hi." Then she pivoted on her heel and crossed the walk to her front door. She waved good night and disappeared inside.

The house was spotless. Pattiann was restless and it translated to washing the kitchen floor, scrubbing counters, tables, cleaning the glass on the pictures that hung in the hallway. She tried a book. Turned the television on for background, turned it off. She settled into the kitchen to make spaghetti, something that would keep late and heat easily. She shaped meatballs, sliced onions, tomatoes, peppers, seasoned the Dutch oven and thought about Ike.

It was a nasty job and no rancher relished it—putting down the odd steer that broke a limb, or the old cow that prolapsed or wouldn't freshen, destined for the canning jars—a meat gamey with age and pressure-cooked until it was chewable. She'd been raised on it. On those mornings her father would sit at coffee a little longer before he'd slap his hat on and suggest Martha check her jars. And Martha would not have to ask which animal—she knew the stock as well as he did—but would instead kiss him on the cheek and thank him for his work, suggest the meat would taste good come winter. When they were ten years of age, the children helped dress the animal out. At fourteen, Pattiann was handed the gun.

"Make it clean," he'd said and she had. There was no lecture on respect beyond what she'd witnessed all her life—ranchers gave their lives over to the care of livestock, and the meat was a kindness returned.

She set the sauce on at a low simmer, threw her coat over her shoulders, and stepped out onto the porch. She perched on the top step and pulled the coat closed. The street was quiet, and she leaned from under the porch roof to see the stinging points of starlight in the black. The snow had disappeared, save a few baleful patches against garages and in ditches. In a month or less, the air would smell new with rain and thaw. Children would scramble in spring games in the school yard while the town people resurrected flowerpots.

A cat stalked the curb, a large gray and white tabby, its paw fishing the gutter. When she moved, it crouched and then startled off into the dark. Pattiann rested her back against a post; she looked up the street. Small town. Down the block, windows glowed. The half-dozen houses rucked up against each other, boundaries picked out by split-rail and picket fences that children hurdled and adults tended as though fearful their neighbors might break free to range elsewhere. She wondered at her being in this place, tucked in among houses and neighbors instead of coulees and breaks. Married to a town man, who liked the orderly lawns and fences, the streetlights. She thought of the midwestern cities with all the confinement of a side rail feedlot. On sidewalks, streets, the ceaseless movement—she knew a herd when she saw one and she'd ridden them too long to become part of one. She eased back on the step to brace her spine. There was comfort to this house, and as far as compromise went, it wasn't a bad one, but sometimes even this small town seemed to close in on her, and then she found herself dealing with it the only way she knew how, retreating deeper into her own territory, spending more time at the ranch, longer hours on the road between here and there.

The cat was back, playing with its own shadow. She called to it and the animal stopped, moved nearer on the points of its toes. It sidled within inches of her outstretched fingers, and then a door slammed down the street and the cat was gone.

By the time Ike came home, the sauce was done. She hoped the fragrant house made him feel welcome. He hung his coat up, washed at the kitchen sink as he preferred, a holdover from his youth, and she found that endearing, as though she were seeing him as a young boy again, ladling water over his neck. He raised his dripping face. Pattiann lifted the towel from a rack and pressed it to his cheeks, then his nose and eyelids, his forehead and the tuft of hair that always fell unchecked over his brows, dried them all carefully. "I'm sorry," she said. "What I said earlier . . . about Chas. It was thoughtless of me."

He stood with his face in her hands, then he put his arms around her. She could feel his wet palms through the back of her shirt, his thumbs cradling her wing bones. He smelled of horses—unfamiliar on him but comforting to Pattiann. "It's been a day for apologies," he said.

"Sshh." She tamped the towel over his lips, followed it with a kiss, and she wanted him to be ardent, to clench her blouse in his hands and bury his mouth in her hair, but he was tired and hurt and she was, according to her nature, a practical woman, so she sat him down in a chair and spooned hot spaghetti onto two plates. He ate slowly at first, but after he cleaned the first plate, he served himself another the same size and finished that as well. She pulled out an apple cobbler, scooped ice cream onto it. When he worked the spoon into the cobbler, she asked, "Did it go all right after I left?"

He nodded, swallowed a bite. "Didn't think they'd get it done. But it was a good team, and they were grateful," he said. "Invited us to tour the plant, have a beer with them. Can't think of anything I'd rather do, can you?" He smiled. "Chas stayed away." He stopped eating. "Stayed in the house. From another man, I'd believe he was embarrassed and hiding, but not our boy, Chas."

Pattiann sat waiting. She'd flinched over the way he said "our boy" with a tenderness she hadn't expected. She was embarrassed by her own surprise. It was one thing for the town to believe Ike did his business without feeling, it was another for her to do so. She knew how much the law meant to him. She also knew how much he labored over the consequences it dealt to people's lives. Sometimes, she thought, he was too human for his job. But of course, that's what made him right for it.

"I stopped in afterward, to let him know we were done. He was on his way to drunk. Offered to take me along."

"You must have felt ready for one," she said.

He stopped eating. He shifted his eyes away from Pattiann's. "Well, I didn't." He pushed the plate aside and stood up. "Think I'll go to bed."

"Want someone to join you?" she asked.

He shrugged. "If you're tired."

He was walking away and Pattiann wasn't sure how to stop him, so she followed. He climbed the stairs like an old man and she wanted to offer her arm, say something that would lift his steps or his heart, and it always came to this, she thought, this simple loss of words, some tenderness lacking in her.

"I'll turn down the bed," she said, and he closed himself in the bathroom. When he came back, she was tucked in and waiting. He turned off the light and felt his way to bed. "We could use some time to ourselves," she said.

He didn't answer. She moved over to snug at his side. "You've been working too hard."

He sighed, moved an arm under her head. "Is this what you wanted? From your life?" he asked. "This place? Me?"

She reached up for his hand, pressed it against her cheek. "I don't know what else to ask for." She should say more. Do more. She wanted to wipe the day away. Take him into her body and rock him as she would a child in her womb. She ran her finger down his arm, felt the muscle tight beneath the skin. His shoulders were bunched and she wanted to knead them, straddle his belly with her legs and stroke his chest, feel his cock grow erect beneath her. She raised on an elbow. She should take him, tired or no, pull him inside of her and carry him to someplace beyond this room, this small house and town, let him feel how the land grows large beneath your feet and the sky crimps at the edge of your heart. She should do all this with her body as she never could by speaking of it. She wanted him to know how much this place was a part of her and he a part of it all now.

But he was tired. The small furrow between his brows eased; his breathing deepened. His foot kicked as he struggled into sleep and she eased herself down beside him. She moved her arm over him as if she could safeguard his dreams, cradled her ear to his chest, and closed her eyes.

Chas had watched the sheriff pull out of the drive, taking his sad act of guilt and repentance off somewhere where it might do him some good—to bed with his wife maybe. There was not a thing in this world Chas felt required to grieve over. Certainly not the cattle. They were raised to die. Chas flipped on the lights, stoked the woodstove fire with paperwork from a generation and a half of ranching. His father's accounts, printed in his crabby script. What would that old man feel? Not surprise. Proved out, that's how. Proved out and gratified to see it. There wasn't anything that old man liked more than being right. "Pleased to oblige you, Daddy," Chas said, and fed another stack to the fire. He slipped on his coat, strung bootlaces, and walked outdoors. Smoke purled down from the chimney. A hot, dirty smoke—paper, ink, ambition.

He drew a bucket of water at the pump and carried it into the shed. He'd move the horse back into the barn tomorrow. There'd been a moment this afternoon when Chas thought he'd been found out. Harley had come snooping around, had headed for the shed. It had been close, but all he'd done was stand in the lee of it and light a smoke, so God-damned full of himself, just feet from the piebald, the last living thing on this spread save Chas himself. And then again when the sheriff stopped in. Chas had waited for the question, *Where's the horse?* but nothing came of that either. And so it was still here, alive for now and safely his. Wasn't no one coming anymore, not until spring, and then it would be bankers, auctioneers, and acquaintances who would ring him around to say, *Sorry to hear of your trouble,* and, *Yes, I'll take that tractor thirty cents on the dollar.* And the banks would be distressed to have to take such measures, but appeased. And his neighbors and friends, oh, they'd be sorry to do it, but you understand how tough it's been.

His father used to say, "You're a fool if you think you can get rich in this business." But Chas had come close. What? Three, four weeks short of a break, a damned month or two of feed and he'd have had cows calving, then summer pasture, a crop of steers and the market for it.

Well, he'd made a killing all right.

He turned on the overhead light, a single bulb screwed into the plank ceiling. The shed was a tight fit with the horse in it, discs and harrow, rake and baler, and in the far corner, the horse bumped tight against the wall. An ugly thing, but his. "You are the last word in the argument," he said to the horse. "And I spoke it." He set the bucket on the dirt floor and the horse nosed over, snuffing at his pant legs, dropped its muzzle to the water, and drew in guzzling draughts.

"Fill your belly," he said. "Suck it up till you slosh like a canteen, then drink some more because it's all God's provided." He laughed. He felt good and knew it was the booze, but more than that it was a curious feeling of relief. His life reduced to this last knowable thing.

The horse nosed the bucket over. Water dribbled out and beaded on the dirt floor. The shed was a history of ranching details: bailing twine, a roll of double-barbed fencing, a broken ax handle, posthole digger, wire stretcher, an old milk crate filled with empty oil cans, and a coffee mug with its handle broken off. Shovels, pick and hoe, wedge and ax hung on the wall, and below, in the corner, there was a hole where a pack rat had burrowed in, lived its life, and deserted or died. Chas had to admit a begrudging fondness for the creatures. Given a chance, the little thieves would steal the buckle off his belt while he slept. He cursed their thefts with an animation born of admiration. He'd set out poison and traps, collect the carcasses like a tithe, fling them into the manure pile where they festered in the heat or froze in winter.

But there would be no more of that. And no more pulling calves, breaking ice, honing harrow blades. He could see it. The house gone, the well seized up, the fences lapsing back into the land. And himself? He squinted as if he could see beyond the canting clapboard, the hoes and rakes, the barren fields, to some place where he walked in cleated heels on concrete, past houses and cemeteries, beneath skyscrapers where pigeons cooed and swooped alongside the clatter of trains, the hump of turn buckles, following the endless lines of freight to some other place where the dirt was red and crusted his face while he worked another man's land with nothing he could call his own but sweat. But he could not *see* it. Could not call to mind a tangible future. He was a hole in the city, a lapse in some other man's bright red earth. He was nothing, beholden to nothing. Accountable to no one. A wisp. A puff of air no more substantial than the breath of this horse.

He wondered what he would do tonight. Tomorrow. The next day and the next. There was nothing left here but this last piece of work. What he had been was no more and what he would become was mystery. He was, it seemed to him, a piece of God's whimsy. But if he was no more than a whim, look what a whim could do: fire, flood, hurricanes, drought, tornadoes, disease, plague. God made man to have something to destroy. He fashioned man's will to bend it. And *then* came the kicker—after all was said and done, the judgment rung in, He exacted eternal praise from this lot He'd buggered from cradle to grave.

Chas picked up the bucket and the horse snapped its head away from the swinging metal. The handle creaked and sawed, creaked and sawed.

He watched the horse and the horse watched the bucket swinging in smaller and smaller arcs.

"Hear that?" he asked the horse. Its ears flicked toward him, settled back. "Might as well be a clock winding down. And maybe all the time you got left in this world is the swing of this bucket." He stopped it with his free hand, set the bucket down. He laid his hand on the horse's belly, lowered his ear to the stomach wall and listened for the rumbling, but it was still. Quiet as the shed and the reaches beyond it. He stayed that way, and after awhile, the horse crooked its neck over his back and rested its head on Chas's flank, as it would a companion horse in the fields.

Chas listened for the thump and lub of the horse's heart. Waited for the small squeezings of stomach or intestine and imagined the landscape within, awash with water, feeding on itself while time spindled on and on. That was all that was left. Time. He would have whole days to take account, rack up the scores against Providence and man. Given enough time, whimsy brought down buildings, rearranged the land, fed the flames, triggered fear, grew bold and terrible.

The piebald shifted and Chas stepped away. And just as suddenly, Chas doubted what it was he planned to do. He thought of the sheriff and his fondness for the old sway-backed animal. He thought of Patti-ann and just as quickly pushed her from his head. Amazing, how she could still evoke in him feelings he could no longer afford. Hope. Salvation. But that was flogging a dead horse, wasn't it? And he laughed, a harsh little sound that surprised even him. The horse snorted, lowered its head to the empty feedbin that would only get emptier. Chas turned his back on the animal, shut the door behind him, and stood on the threshold of the land. He had never much liked the horse, all that white, like God Himself had laid its face open to blame.

Chapter Nine

Seven in the morning and Ike was at the Brandt place—trailer home on a thousand plus acres of low-yield scrubland. Lila Brandt had called in a shooting. She was the daughter of the lately departed Asa Brandt, lifelong practitioner of subsistence living. Fifty head of cattle and a three hundred square-foot pole barn. Also a believer in the theory that homes didn't build barns, but barns built homes. So a year ago he died at the age of fifty, finally having achieved his dream of a respectable barn and still living in the trailer house at the door to which Ike now stood. In the front yard, her new boyfriend mourned his motorcycle.

She was telling Ike about her former boyfriend, Eddie Bacon, of Absorokee, who worked for the Millers. A round-faced man, barely twenty; Ike would have thought he lacked the imagination for this.

"He came rapping at the door, six a.m., with a rifle under his arm." She nodded at the man in the yard. "Henry took one look and shut the door."

"He's armed," Ike said.

"Didn't I just say that? Shoots a hole through my porch roof, jumps onto his horse, ropes Henry's motorcycle and drags it around the yard. Hollering." Her face turned thoughtful.

"He shot my bike," Henry said. He had a small voice, out of place in his large body. He wore tight jeans with pockets worried thin and an undershirt stained in the armpits. He toed the sprinkle of chrome and glass, what remained of his headlight. "He dragged it around the yard, then he shot it in the head. Took off on his horse, leading a fresh one."

Ike had an outlaw on his hands. Getaway horse and all.

He caught up to the desperado where the road hitched north. Ike hit two short blasts on the siren and picked up the mike.

It was a short, spirited chase. When Eddie dismounted, he looked a little chagrined, and proud. Ike was amazed by the willful naiveté of it all. Eddie, the young fool, romantic and in love, reverts to the silver-screen cowboy, the West's own Don Quixote lassoing motorcycles on the lone prairie.

"You going to cuff me?" he asked.

And there was Eddie, five foot seven, trying to look bigger than life, wearing a long-rider coat, Mexican spurs that clanked when he walked, cowboy hat with a white neckerchief, for Christ's sake, knotted around his throat. The horse shook its head and the bit chimed. Ike stared over Eddie's shoulder, to the land that ran low and level as if it couldn't get to the horizon quick enough. How could you not half-admire this? All the grandiose schemes it hatched in people.

Eddie wanted to be a legend in his own time. As if there weren't enough already. A pain in the ass. That's what legends were, a pain in the ass.

"No," Ike said, and walked over to Eddie's rifle. Ike picked it up and put it in the back of his Bronco. "You've been enough of a damned nuisance. You take those horses home, get a ride down to the office by early afternoon, or I'll issue a warrant."

As Ike pulled away, he could see Eddie mounting. He'd turn himself in first thing. Ike had no doubts about that. Eddie would make his apologies and pay the damages. He'd see his story in the newspaper and hope his mother didn't read it, and if she did, she'd mention it once and never again. The other hands would make his life hell for awhile with jokes, but he would survive that. Someday, when he married, he *might* tell his wife. He'd never tell his kids. Because by then, of course, he'd be an upstanding member of the community.

Ike called dispatch. The Brandt woman and Henry could come down and file charges. He'd be in soon. Had some things to check on first.

He headed out toward his brother-in-law's place where Pattiann was helping, bringing the cows into the lower yards, preparing for calving. He'd be seeing less and less of her for a few weeks and he remembered resenting it early on in their marriage. But the resentment had passed until now—and he wasn't sure what he'd feel this spring calving; indifference? some—but truth was, he still loved Pattiann, and he wanted it to be as easy again as those first fumbling nights back in his small apartment, where crowding with Pattiann was a delicious kind of constraint, a hand-to-hand combat so that they fell into each other more deeply, heedless of the close wall, the single bed. And what had come of those early days? Only this—the certain knowledge that all the room he'd ever needed was in her.

He turned onto the county road, the snow mostly gone, and slowed the car, cranked down the window hoping to hear geese overhead, or the drum of prairie hens mating, some indication that they'd turned a corner into an early spring. But the air still had the edge of snow in it and the wind whistled aimlessly. He found himself speeding toward Rob's ranch, wanting to put the miles behind him, see this place in a different light, discover he still gave a damn.

The Stubblefield place shunted past. It had been close to a week now since they'd cleared his yards of cattle and no one had seen or heard from Chas. Partly the reason Ike drove out this way, he supposed. There was no sign of Chas. He felt a small regret when he thought about the horse. Nobody had seen it, and he wondered again if the crew had scooped it up from the snow, or if it had ranged off onto higher grounds scrabbling for food, or fallen to coyotes, and that seemed the most likely scenario and so he'd let it go—just another guilt he couldn't afford to live with.

In the distance, the seamless land ran helter-skelter to the breaks and beyond to where the Little Rockies were etched clear against the sky. A few more miles and he'd be at Rob's, for no other reason than he wanted to see Pattiann.

Harriet was on her knees scrubbing the kitchen floor. "You can come in," she said, waving the sponge at him. "It's dry. I'll be done soon." The kitchen was warm, and Ike could smell chicken in the oven. "You'll stay?" she asked. "All my recipes feed a troupe. Anymore, off season or not, I can't seem to cook less. They'll be in shortly, I'm sure . . . chores always manage to end around an empty stomach."

"Who's working?" Ike asked.

"Bill, Rob, Pattiann, Justin. Martha's in the barn to see the new horse Rob bought Angela. She drags everyone she can out there to see the beast. Ugly brute, a gelding with a head like a bass fiddle." She shrugged, pushed her hair back, sopping the ends with soap. "I meant to go rescue Martha myself, but"—she threw the scrub brush back in the bucket, water sloshed and stilled—"maybe you could? Make sure Angela hasn't worn her down?"

He was glad for the excuse. He liked Harriet, but she was a woman who spoke in abstracted segments, her attention wandering so that you were never sure if you were talking just to hear yourself talk.

The barn was fragrant with hay and droppings—musky with fresh manure and urine, the feral hints of cat, rat, starling, and magpie. Back home it had been barn swallows and pigeons. The pigeons flapped wings with a slap like dealt cards and cooed garbled messages his father translated. One afternoon, he'd pulled Ike to his side and said, "Hear that? That's the plump one. Imagine being raised in *her* downy breasts. Then one day," and he booted Ike gently in the seat, "out of the nest, into the wide, cold world and all your life you wander, seeking a nest as sweet as the one she fashioned. Someday . . ." His eyes raised to the hard window of light, the single shaft spilling over the loft's slotted floor, and his father had stood there in the shattered light and dust, hands sunk into the breasts of his bibs, eyes lit with a look between glory and grief so that Ike did not know from which to turn away.

He could hear Angela prattling, her small girlish voice piping clear. "Don't you think he's handsome?" she asked. "I learned this in 4-H."

Martha was in the aisle, seated on a milking stool. She looked frail in the half-light, her spine curved, ankles crossed one over the other. She was studying the wide rump of a horse across from her. In the far stall, their milk cow shifted from foot to foot, its ears cocked to the young girl's voice. Ike took off his hat, slapped it gently against a thigh. Martha looked up over her shoulder, smiled, and nodded toward him, and he could see Pattiann's vigor in her, but also a quiet he'd never yet seen in his wife. She was strength and heart where her daughter was still nerve. Ike longed to believe that in the years to come, Pattiann would find a similar sweetness of her own and that he would be with her to see it.

"Ike," Martha said, and beckoned him over with a finger, "come take a look at Angela's new horse. He's a big one, but she can handle him."

"Oh, he's kind, Uncle Ike. Even you could ride him," Angela said, and turned back to curry the animal's coat.

Martha reached up for his hand, gave it a squeeze. "Good to see you, Ike. What brings you out?"

"I heard you were in a cold barn at the mercy of a young girl in the first throes of love. Thought you could use rescuing. Harriet's about done with the floor, lunch is heating. I'm invited."

"Angela, you're going to wear a patch on that horse's back before you ever put a saddle to him. Why don't you see if your mother needs you?"

Angela blew out a gust of air that flopped her bangs off her forehead. "You just want to get rid of me."

"Yes," Martha said.

"Brother," Angela said, but put her tools away. She rubbed her horse's forehead one last time and slowly walked to the barn door, looking back over her shoulder twice. She paused at the door.

"I forgot—"

"Your manners. Your horse will be here after lunch. Go on."

"But isn't he beautiful?" she asked.

"He's a rare, beautiful beast," Martha said. The young girl shut the door quietly behind her.

"Pattiann was just as bad," Martha said. "Pull up a sawhorse. Can't stand to have people hovering up there." Ike sat. "Been meaning to ask how you're doing," she said. "I worry, you know."

He waited, unsure what she had in mind. He ran the brim of his hat through his fingers. She plucked it away.

"You look like Rob used to when I caught him taking shortcuts with chores. This Stubblefield business. Isn't over yet. You know that?"

"Haven't heard a thing from him in almost a week. Looks over to me."

"There's talk. Always talk. Here and there. Won't say much to us, you being related, but I hear it and you ought to know. People are saying Art would have handled it different."

"No doubt." Ike smiled.

Martha picked at her jeans. "Oh yes. Art had a way. What he didn't know about . . ."

"And if it had been brought to his attention?"

"Oh, he'd have slapped Stubblefield around a few times and called it even. He could get away with that. You could have, too. Slap a man around for being a jerk and they'll say he had it coming. But take away his cattle?"

"I didn't take them. I shot them."

"Yes, well." She leaned back on the stool, her hand propped against her spine. She stretched. "Someone, I'm not saying who, but *someone* with maybe an eye on your job is saying there might have been money involved."

"Jim Parker."

She crooked her mouth in a tight smirk. "You didn't hear me say that."

"It'll blow over."

"Maybe. If the weather turns and folks get busy with other matters. Then Stubblefield will be forgotten and so will the rumors and Parker will be back as your deputy and glad for it. And maybe in a year and a half he'll forget this barb up his ass and not bring it up in a bid to defeat you."

Ike eased his buttocks on the wood, braced both hands on the beam. "Assuming I don't hand the whole shitteree over to him or someone like him before then and skip town with all that money I made off Stubblefield's scrawny herd."

"That isn't funny." She shook her finger at him. "Parker's a good old boy from way back and if he hadn't felt Art's scandal a little too closely he might have run for the job and gotten it."

"And he might have done all right by this community. Do the jobs they want him to and ignore the ones they don't. It's what they want. A homespun boy who'll spit with them and wrangle the pesky cayuse when necessary."

She sat resolute on the stool. "Do we look that small to you?" She studied her feet, kicked them like a schoolgirl. "I suppose we must appear unworldly sometimes. But don't mistake that for stupid." She pointed a finger at him. "You're a good sheriff and we've needed one. That'll sink in. Give it time . . . and a little judicious self-defense right now. Sue the sonofabitch for slander."

He sighed and leaned his elbows on his knees, his hands clasped in front. He looked around him. "Maybe I'm not cut out for this place."

"You thinking of leaving?" She crooked a fist and rubbed her lower back. "She won't follow. It's not in her."

"You know your daughter that well?"

Martha stood from the stool and offered her hand. "Let's start up to the house. Used to be," she said, "I could outstride any cowhand on the place, outwrangle, outride. You should have known me then. Pattiann got the best of me and her father, that one. And the worst."

They stepped out into the bright afternoon light. Martha squinted against the sun. Her skin was freckled, liver-spotted, tanned, and worn fine. "This is what Pattiann wanted." She waved her hand over the ranch. "And the hard truth of it is, she could have done it. She had it all: smarts, talent, drive, stubbornness—a whole lot of that. At ten she killed a rattler that bit her, hung on to the damn dead thing the whole ride in to the doctor's. Bill couldn't take it away, not the doctor or the nurse. I didn't try. Why? Because I knew her that well. She wanted us all to know—the family, the town, God, and the snake—that she'd gotten the upper hand." Martha slowed to a stop, took a deep breath. "If there was one failing in that child, it was a lack of humility. Took her until her early twenties to learn that. And then she left."

"She came back," Ike said.

"She came back when she was ready. After she'd met you and come to realize there were other possibilities to life, even out here. Before that, she was a young woman going to seed who ran off every eligible bachelor in a hundred-mile radius, to hang with that worthless Stubblefield. And I knew what was behind that, too." She crooked a finger at the house. "Harriet's a good woman, don't get me wrong. She's what a rancher needs. Keeps house, helps out, raises a brood of kids, and generally stays out of the way. Pattiann wasn't about to set herself up for that. She didn't see it could be any other way. So she picked Stubblefield, the one man it wouldn't happen with." The focus in Martha's eyes softened. "Pattiann didn't get to see me in my glory days."

"You must have been hell on a horse."

She tugged at his arm. "And don't you forget it." She stopped and looked over her shoulder. "This is not something a mother should say, but I'm going to. Whether you go or stay, Pattiann will survive. She'll work the ranch for a hand's wages, move in our house when we die. She'll be a canker in Rob's side, and you, dear boy, will be well out of it.

"She's a survivor. I'm not saying I like the picture I painted. What I want to see is her having a decent life with you. Some kids to keep her occupied; she'll wean herself away from here, given time. Maybe the two of you will find your own small spread and it'll be hers. Not mine or Bill's or Rob's. Her own." Martha picked at his hand, shook it hard. "You should stay. It'll get better. It's just this damn winter gets to folks."

He ushered her onto the back porch. "And you want me to stay."

She perked her head into the wind, listened a moment. "Misery loves company, son." She opened the door, stuck her head into the kitchen. "Get the food on the table, Harriet. They're back."

The first head of cattle made their lowing entrance into the feed yard and behind them the young Justin, looking older on his mount, then Rob and Bill, and trailing them all, Pattiann. Clear across the yards and the milling cattle, the tired, dismounting men, Ike saw the smile that spread across Pattiann's face at the sight of him. Her wave was lighthearted. He thought he loved her more than he could bear, and as he turned away, he saw that Martha, standing at the side of the door, had read it on his face.

Purvis sat on a stool in the empty garage. The Chevy was gone. He'd had a full surgery, pets. They carried his business through the slack winter months, before tuberculin testing and calving and the usual assorted ailments of working, range horses. There'd been a cat with ringworm that had dosed a passel of children.

There'd been some distraction with the one case of indiscreet digestion in a Great Dane. They'd lumbered the animal up onto the X-ray table, he and Joe, while the owner, Lois Varner, wrung her hands and baby-talked: "Oh my precious, my sweetie-umpkins." The dog snarled, snapped at Joe.

Purvis twisted the hindquarters up for a side view, told Joe, "Throw a blanket over sweetie-umpkin's head so he doesn't take your arm off."

The woman swore the dog was gentle and a finicky eater. "He won't touch anything but what we give him in his doggie bowl," she insisted. "He's a good boy. But such a picky eater. You don't know what I've gone through to bring him to size. It's a tumor. I just know it's a tumor. Cancer runs in my family," she said.

The dog's stomach was belled with bloat, and before operating, Purvis wanted to see what the dog had gotten into and if the spleen was still in place or had rolled under the stomach. Bloat wasn't uncommon among dogs that ran free on large spreads. They ate whatever presented itself until their stomachs swelled and rolled with gas, twisting the stomach, intestines, and displacing the spleen—if not corrected surgically, the animal died. He'd read about a case of it in humans once. Fellow ate so much roast corn, it packed the stomach walls, then brewed enough gas to float him like a buoy. Ruptured the stomach. Corned to death.

They snapped two plates, side and belly-up. A real feat. When they put the film on the viewer, the owner sucked in her breath and sidled up to it. She fingered the illumined stomach contents—traced one bone and another, her finger filling in the details. "He ate one of my goats. *He ate one of my goats.*"

Purvis remembered then, her State Fair, grand champion, dwarf

Nubian goats. And yes, here one was, the tiny skull still mostly intact and curled against a fetlock as though it were asleep in its mother's womb.

"Jesus," Joe whispered. "Would you look at that." He glanced over at the bloated dog as if it were a miracle. "He swallowed it whole."

Purvis steered the woman away from the picture. "Let's get you out front," he said. Then, to Joe, "Put her on the couch. Set her feet high, her head low. Get her signature on an operating form, then come back and help prep."

The dog survived, but with a newly acquired taste for Nubian goat. In all, a day of small emergencies among the mundane. Joe left the clinic before five. Purvis had come out into the garage after dinner to bask in the glow of his carnauba-waxed, fully operating car, to find it gone.

He'd walked around the garage, as if another angle might reveal the car. He sidestepped the grease-spotted concrete. He sat. He didn't want to think it was Joe. But Joe had a key. Purvis had the other one in his right hand. So this was what it was like, he thought, to be a parent. Your best shot rolling down the highway behind the wheel of a stolen '57 Chevy. What could he have been *thinking*? How could he explain what he'd seen in the Mattick boy that had sounded off him like an echo of himself at fifteen, that made him want to see in himself the kindness, the steady hand and level heart of his own father? And perhaps to be given one last chance to save something in this world besides some goat-eating dog.

He scuffed his heels on the cement, snatched up an oil rag and rubbed his hands on it. Still trying to resurrect the hog. His wife Babs had recognized it early on, threw up her pretty little nineteen-year-old hands after a quick year of marriage, and absconded with his favorite Stones album and a jeweler's apprentice for the good life far away from veterinary schools and one-room apartments. And what the hell, she'd been right to go. He was a budding young doctor, not the real kind, but the kind fit for animals, who would scrimp and save and work his whole damned life to cash it in on a small clinic in the badlands of Montana.

"Good for you, Babs," he said. Got out long before it came to what it would have between them, this moment where he'd want more out of his life and turned to her for it. It was more than a person could ask of another, a wife, a friend, or a fifteen-year-old boy named Joe Mattick. Had Joe ever *said* he wanted to be a vet's assistant, or a vet or an auto mechanic? Hadn't Ike warned him, hadn't he?

His stomach tightened. He should call Ike. His chest hurt and he sat quickly back on the stool, tried breathing through his nose.

He could see the chase, the car rolling down some bank, end over end, a dull *whump, whump, whump*. Purvis was shaking. He didn't give a shit about the car. He just wanted to know he hadn't done something irreparable this late in life.

He stood, turned a slow circle around the garage. What he should do is call Joe's parents, or get in his truck, go looking for the boy. He wadded the oil rag and flung it at the far wall, but the cloth billowed open and fell short and soft. Goddamn it. Give me something I can do.

Just after a late dinner with Pattiann, Ike's phone rang. "More dead dogs, Purvis?" he asked, half hoping that's all there was to it. "We're still working on it," he said, and they were, sort of, a low-priority investigation. He'd given it to Harley.

"Forget the damn dogs. This is about Joe."

Ike waited, could hear in the pause how reluctant Purvis was, and at the same time how desperate. "What?"

"The car's gone. Joe's got a key. He needed one, you know, working on it . . ."

Ike could hear Purvis blaming himself, and hadn't Ike known somewhere down the line it would come to this. "Maybe he's just out on a test drive."

"No."

"You're sure it's Joe? Have you called his parents?"

"Yes, yes, of course. They thought he was with me. I told them not to worry, I said I'd talk to you. I told them you'd make sure Joe was all right. You will, Ike, won't you?"

"Cripes." He looked up at Pattiann, who was near; she perched herself on the edge of the dining table. "I'll do what I can. I'll have the officers keep an eye out."

"I'm just asking you, no high-speed chases, okay? Let him ride the damn thing out of gas."

Dan Roehe was a rookie on the sheriff's force. It showed in his work hours: graveyard shift on backcountry roads, worked in tandem with the Highway Patrol. The local drag strip, lover's lane. The straightest route between reservation bars. He spent his nights running people through the DUI drill. Walk a straight line, backwards, heel to toe. Say the alphabet slowly, distinctly. Arms out, touch your finger to your nose alternating right and left. Close your eyes and stand with one foot raised. The other. He stocked Breathalyzer kits by the caseful.

But a good portion of the night, especially this time of year, after the worst of winter, he spent hours daydreaming into the dark fields, or spotlighting coyotes, the occasional elk herd, an antelope and his harem. His favorite, oddly enough, were the jackrabbits, leggy, mule-eared beasts that bumped their way across the land in vast numbers. Once or twice an evening he liked to open his squad door quietly, then slam it, and a hundred heads would jerk up into the night, ears lifted in surrender. On a really good night, when the ground was pounded hard with cold, he'd turn the car into the field and part the sea of rabbits, like Moses delivering the Jews. He'd cut the engine and roll the window down to hear the stampede. The small thundering of a thousand paws. He'd have liked to pick a few off, but the sheriff was fussy about spent bullets. Like they came out of his own pocket. Accountability, he called it. But what the fuck was a guy supposed to do out here, at night, with nothing but time on his hands, and rabbits?

The car blew past him before he realized it. And then it was just a streak of taillights fading. He looked at the radar. He tried to keep it at a distance—everybody knew the damn things gave you cancer. It registered ninety-five. The old adrenaline kicked in, and he fought for calm. He turned on the engine, switched on the headlights, checked the rearview mirror, and gunned it onto the highway. It was a lovely machine, zero to sixty in no time at all. He checked his seat belt with one hand and then leaned back and floored the accelerator. The taillights grew closer. He was cruising at eighty-five. The car ahead slowed. He switched on the overheads and startled himself—a hangover from his pre-force days. That little kick of fear when you see rolling blues hit the road.

There were two, maybe three in the car. A classic, '57 Chevy. Some kids out for a joyride. *Well, it'll cost you boys.* He hit the siren, two short blasts. The car pulled away; he could smell oil and exhaust as the driver hammered the accelerator.

Sonofabitch, they were going to make a run for it. He set his jaw, felt the first nervous ticking in his chin. He felt like a kid himself again, dragging down this highway or another one very much like it. He might have a girl alongside, Bernice, or better yet Adrian, sweet Jesus how she loved speed, and they would run until the road won. It always had, with his old secondhand cars throwing up smoke that greased the windshield. But he had the car for it now. He had the excuse. He had all the time and road in the world and these kids were going to learn one hell of a lesson before he was through.

He goosed it, called dispatch. "Yeah, I'm in pursuit. On Frazier. Maybe ten miles to Baptiste, heading south. '57 Chevy, license plate number . . . hold on. No plate. Dark red chassis, white roof." He left the channel open, heard the dispatcher call the Highway Patrol as backup. He was doing ninety-five and still cooking. The road was sweet and clean, straight as the day was long. They were topping a hundred and five and the engine was just coming alive. Jackrabbits slewed in a blur from the road. He nosed up to the Chevy's fender. Two in the car, hit the siren again, saw the passenger, the smaller one jerk in the seat as if hit with a cattle prod. The Chevy inched away, hauling hard now. It was a classy rig—what he wouldn't have given for one like it as a kid, a lot of muscle, but old, and he could smell the oil.

Ahead, he thought he could make out a flash and sweep, blue lights like heat lightning, coming down in the distance, and he inched around the vehicle. He wasn't sure what he was going to do, maybe just take a

good look at the kids, maybe swerve at them a little and scare the beje-
sus out of them. Or maybe it was just the sheer joy of the engine humming under him and the road a level sweep and help just moments away
that turned it all into a sort of reckless game, and Ike would have his
skin for it, but that didn't matter. This was his collar and those kids were
going to know it. He glanced over at their window, grinning. He could
pick out the dip of cowboy hats, chins, and jutting noses. The passenger,
just a young kid, white-faced and out of his league, and Dan almost felt
sorry for him. And then they were swerving off, braking and skidding in
a glaze of dirt and hard grit, sliding into the field, and he looked ahead
in time to see *it* in the headlights and he thought as he caromed up, how
beautiful—with head lifted into the lights, eyes luminescent and full rack
grazing the hindquarters, and then it was levitating, lifting into the air,
swimming in the air that was all light and glass, and it hit the windshield,
the glass spidered, buckling in like a net, as if he were casting into water
and hauling in some huge glittering fish, and that was all Dan knew as
the legs drove through the windshield and a hoof took him in the neck,
snapping it at an angle so that his head bumped on his shoulder like a
baby who hadn't learned to lift it yet. The elk plowed through the cab,
hindquarters slewing through the passenger seat, toppling into the back
where it hung up, and the cruiser careened into the field, hit a rock,
canted, rolled onto its side. It flipped onto its roof and smeared a path
through sage and cactus, broadcasting bits of metal and glass until it
planted itself hood-first into the gouge it had shoveled out. And after a
small pause among the startled stampede of jackrabbits, it rocked back
down onto the flattened roof and rested with a final settling of bolts and
joints, the wheels spinning as if there were road yet to travel.

Ike got the call shortly after hanging up from Purvis. He drove out to
where Fred Elrose sat stunned in his cruiser and the Highway Patrol set
up detours. Elrose was shaken, said he'd gotten the call and being close
by had responded quickly. He'd seen two sets of headlights heading

down the road toward him, and then the one in the right lane swerved and shortly after that the left, and then he could see the left bumping and airborne it seemed, and then there was this. He'd gotten here as fast as he could. He didn't know what happened to the other car. He hadn't seen it after it had headed right. Maybe it cut across the field. Maybe it headed back down the highway. He didn't remember. He'd run out into the field, looked into the cruiser, and found himself sitting in the dirt with his eyes shut. There was Dan—and all that meat and blood—and then Fred was lowering his head again and breathing through his mouth.

It had to have been Purvis's Chevy. Everything happening, Ike reasoned, even as he was talking to Purvis. Dan was already dead, his neck snapped, the car flipping and stopping. All in the span of a phone call. Or no. It would have to have been earlier. Time enough for Elrose to arrive, witness the scene, recover, and call it in. The dispatcher getting over her first shock, calling Ike. There was an APB out on the car. An officer was dead.

It was all so senseless. Dan had been a good man. Ike would have to drive out to Dan's folks, tell them their son had died in the line of duty. They lived a good eighty miles away, on a small ranch that Dan had bragged himself lucky to escape—the small life, the boredom. And now he was dead and his parents, early in their middle years, would wake the rest of their days and know the relentless taste of grief as sharp and cold on their tongues as metal on a winter's morning.

The wrecker's winches growled and the cruiser bumped up while pieces—a fender, glass, some bits of metal—sprinkled down like a curious rain, and then the car was slowly rotating back onto wheels that had stopped and would never turn again. The ambulance stood by, its lights strobing red, crisscrossing the multiple blues that swept from the parked cruisers so that the entire area had a carnival aspect, even among the somber-faced deputies who stood in small packs at a distance and the wrecker crew trying to avoid looking inside the vehicle but unable not to, the rescue team studying how best to retrieve the body, and the ambulance attendants who had seen it all before, leaning against their van, smoking cigarettes, waiting for the door to be prised open so they could bag it and be gone, back to the tail end of their shift and home to wives or parents. And he tried to imagine how Dan's parents would take it, gowned and robed, in the living room politely waiting for the sheriff to speak, or by then sitting, though they would have known when they first caught sight of him at the door. And he wished he could spare them that—he on the doorstep under a lone lightbulb, sheriff's hat in hand, the truth already sinking in, limbs turning insubstantial, and realizing that *our Dan is dead.*

They fired up the Jaws of Life and the gas engine cut a swath through their voices. The attendants snuffed cigarettes. Ike moved just behind the rescue team, believing it important to witness, a friend among strangers. He had a fleeting image of Dan in his crisp uniform, all bluster as the others teased him about his spit-shined shoes. It was hard to make him out in the tangle, human and animal, and disconcerting the way his head rolled across the chest as they lifted him out. Elrose stood with his back to the scene and Ike was torn between doing right by the dead and dealing with the living. The attendants were skilled, already folding Dan into the body bag, and there were no jokes about the elk as he'd half expected, the size of the rack wedged between windshield frames, no death-site humor, so he went to where Elrose was looking out over the reaches as though he expected someone to come walking out of the dark. Elrose spoke. "I'm all right," he said. "I'll be fine." And Ike realized Elrose was speaking to himself, assuring himself his legs still worked and his heart still beat, and barring further catastrophe, would wake on the fortunate side of his bed in the morning.

"Go home," Ike said. "Can you drive?"

"Yeah," he said. "Sure. Slow as hell, you bet, but I'll make it all right." He shoved his hat back on his head, held his hands to his ears to warm them. Elrose's hands were trembling and he confined them to his pockets. "It's not like I haven't seen this kind of thing before," he said.

Ike gave him a moment. He glanced at his own hands and was surprised to see that they didn't hitch or jump, that other part of him taking over, inspecting the scene, distancing itself, preparing for the rest of the night.

Fred was nodding. "But this one was rough. I was so damned close," he said. "And Dan—what the hell was he doing? I mean, I was close. We could have run him to ground between us."

He blew a thin breath. "When I first shined my light in there, I didn't really expect to find him alive. Not with the mess, the speed they must have been traveling. I thought I was ready for it. But there was all that fur and bone. I mean, the Goddamned elk was glaring at me and Dan's head cheek-to-cheek with it so you couldn't make out at first what was what. Scared the hell out of me. Took me a moment." Elrose laughed softly. "I mean, I didn't expect *any* of this. And then this *thing* happened—like I was looking in a mirror and it was me hanging there with my neck broken, in my uniform, in my cruiser, and then I was just sitting and it was dark and"—he laughed again—"it was dark because I had my eyes closed, and when I opened them, I was sitting in the dirt and Dan was Dan and I was alive."

"I imagine it felt good," Ike said, laid his hand on Elrose's shoulder.

"You can't imagine."

"Yeah," Ike said. He looked around. "I'm going to send you home with one of the others. I know you're all right, you're fine. I'll send someone back out for your car. Lock it up, give me the keys, take a ride home and get some sleep."

The ambulance and rescue team pulled away. The wrecking crew was chaining the squad up to be loaded onto the flatbed. In an hour there would be nothing but the roadside scorch of flares, a scooped-out place in the dirt, some trinkets of glass and metal the pack rats would covet. In daylight, buzzards would feast on the elk carcass and a magpie might weave the hair in its nest. Ike made arrangements for Elrose's ride home, battened down the details before hitting the road himself. He had bad news to deliver. It was quarter past midnight.

The sheriff's office was buzzing when Purvis stepped in and then the noise fell to a hush and then silence. He felt it coming, something awful, like the news of his father's death, like the time Babs walked out on him and everything he did turned to shit. He braced himself in the chair.

Ike told Purvis the story, explained the wreck, his drive out to Dan's parents' place, and how later, in town, they'd found the Chevy and Joe Mattick.

"Oh God," Purvis said.

Ike rubbed his hands over his face. "Don't start wringing your hands now. I have put up with enough shit for one night. Joe's asking for you. His parents are with him now, and a lawyer. He claims he blacked out. Doesn't remember anything. If you're his friend—and he believes you still are—get that boy to talk."

Purvis nodded. He felt old, as if he'd just outlived his own life.

Joe looked small behind bars. A kid, on the point of being sick. His legs swung forward and back, one, then the other. The lawyer sat on a chair to the side, a yellow legal pad filled with scribbling on the floor next to him. Ike let Purvis into the cell, positioned himself next to the door. The kid looked up and quickly back down at his feet. His eyes were red and ringed with a sheen. His nose ran so that he swiped at it with his sleeve. Purvis offered his handkerchief and Joe took it.

Joe turned away, stared at the graffiti on the wall. *Hank was here.* Biblical quotes: *Bring my soul out of prison, that I might praise thy name.* And *Merry Fucking Christmas, December, 1984.* Purvis wondered what this young boy thought. He tried to see what it was in the kid he'd believed in.

Chas seldom drove into town now. There wasn't much to warrant it but boredom. He always drove past Taylor's house, kept an eye out for the wife, the tiny yapping dog. He'd idle past Coker's store, honk if he saw him and grin. They wanted to think him done with and over. He liked to think that too, sometimes. He wondered if Coker'd gotten a new dog yet.

Of course, he always watched for Pattiann. She'd been alongside her husband that day at his ranch. Chas had watched from the kitchen window, wringing his clothes in a basin of rinse water, while the sun picked out colors like blooms: blue sky, green jackets, gray, brown, a splash of red on Pattiann's shoulders where her hair wandered loose. Something satisfying about that. Watched her work the horse from a distance, a big gray. He'd wondered what she was thinking. If she thought of him at all, or watched for him as he watched for her, something inside her wringing each time he twisted the cloth in his fists.

He parked the rig next to the grocery. Foolish, but it was where he'd come across her before and that seemed enough reason to believe it could happen again. He stretched his legs and leaned his head against the window, squinting into the gray half-light this season was painful for, everything the hue of an unattended corpse: sidewalks, streets, cars and trucks, cinder block buildings, windows glazed like banks of sightless eyes. He felt immersed in gray, and looked at his pallid hands and believed if he could look through the flesh down his chest, he would see the cage of ribs dirtied to the bone. He felt chilled and thought of the store, its banks of fluorescent lights that hollowed eyes in people's skulls and spread its uniform blandness over the gaudy cans of food, the winter fruits, and the store's back wall with its coffin of meat brighter in dismemberment than in life. He stepped out of the rig, closed the door behind him, and waved himself into the store through the electric eye.

Johnny Cash groused through the overhead speakers—gone and shot another woman, Delia this time. Chas dipped his hat at the checkout girl, a woman of fifty who never raised her eyes from the conveyor belt of food but kept a running conversation with the customers as though she knew them by smell, and he could swear her nostrils flared and pinched as he walked by. She tolled the charges while a young housewife tried to look casual, fiddling her purse clasp like a thief fingering a combination. The owner, Ray Weldert, stood behind the customer service, watched the store's sole stock boy punch new labels over the old. Chas walked the abbreviated aisles: shampoo, hand soap, racks of makeup with packages sporting pouty women and slutty eyes. The end of the

aisle was a comedown: douches, pills for bloat, feminine hygiene products—a mountain of cotton wadding a woman would straddle before she
turned old. He picked up a package of tampons and tucked it under an
arm. He turned the corner and even as he did, he knew he would see
Pattiann. But there was only an old woman. Her head twitched toward
him, and she smiled in a way she must have imagined as coy. She
dropped a can of coffee in her cart and pushed it, one front wheel
thumping at a right angle to the others. He slipped the tampons in
among the instant coffees, snatched up, instead, a box of Earl Grey tea.
Tea with Pattiann. He would feed her orange slices. Then he was in the
pet section with its collars and leashes, flea powders, rubber bones, Kitty
Litter. Dried food, canned. He hefted a can of dog food, turning it over
in his hands.

His own good meat.

He laughed, could picture the neat slices of Alpo quick-browned in a
skillet. His own good meat on clean white dishes instead of slipping
down the gullet of some dissatisfied mutt who would blow a rank fart
that the owner would smell and never imagine what was behind the
smell: the sweet fields, grama grass and buffalo and sage. Never imagine
Chas of a summer night, standing in the field watching his cattle like so
many dark stars.

He made a circuit of the store. He was tired of it, thought Pattiann
selfish to keep him waiting in the aisles as if she must know they were to
meet today. At the end of his third walk through, before he passed the
customer service desk yet again, he tumbled the items in among the
refrigerated butter and eggs and walked through the register with a pack
of smokes. He paid out the price like he was pissing it, one coin at a
time. The checker said, "Have a nice day."

He stepped into the cold, looked up and down the street in hopes of
seeing Pattiann. No kids around, must be a weekday, school. Mostly
women, a stray one here and there. And it seemed to him they moved as
if in mourning, their coats buttoned to the neck, hands weighted with
packages, and still they stopped to stare in store windows, one blank

gaze meeting another, and maybe one sucked in a gut while another turned away like she'd seen more than the day allowed.

But no Pattiann. He could call her and that seemed reasonable. There was a phone booth across the street and he thought of dialing her number, out in the street, and he cut a diagonal across to the bar where there was a phone in the back hallway.

It was early, so Barry sat with his feet propped on the bartop. He read a book under a goose-necked lamp. The gray daylight filtered through the window in careful sips. Chas nodded, ordered a tap beer, and crossed through the room into the back hall. He filched out a quarter, fed it into the slot, and hung up when he realized he didn't know her number. The phone book dangled on a chain. Its upper edges were worn, a brown stain down the side. He flipped through: Ableson, Dilling, Latouse, Miller, N., O., P. He ran a finger down the directory: Pamier, Pape, Pappet. Parsons. Ike and Pattiann.

He committed the number to memory. He heard the coin drop, hit bottom. He moistened his lips, punched the number. She answered on the third ring.

"Yes?" she said.

"Yes," he agreed and cradled the phone on his shoulder.

"Who is this?"

And he was sure he could answer her, yet he didn't; he waited instead to hear her voice again. The open circuit hummed and the wall heater gave off a smell like burning hair. He should have had a beer first. And there was a dial tone. His quarter was gone and so was his stomach for it. He picked up the day's paper discarded on one of the back tables, drank the beer slowly, paid and left the bar.

He didn't know what he intended, but he drove to Pattiann's house, parked across the street. He imagined her in the kitchen, or showering, or making the bed. He sat with his hand on the truck's door handle. It would take a little push, a shove. Up the sidewalk, knock on the door. She would want to know what he wanted.

Good question.

He imagined her surprised at first, but then she'd invite him in. They were friends, after all. And maybe that was true. He approached the house, held his finger above the doorbell, enjoying the potential—if he did, if she were—and then he tried the door, unlocked, as he knew most doors in this small town were. He opened it a crack, and warmth eased out. He took in the first deep breath of her place: woodsmoke, lemon oil, bacon, something flowery, leather. He crossed the threshold, listened. He stepped into the hall, glanced in the mirror over a small chest in the entryway where he saw himself and the living room behind him reflected, rippling in the old glass as he moved from foot to foot. When he faced the room, its precision surprised him. The room was neat, snug with overstuffed furniture, a rocking chair with hand-embroidered seat covers alongside a fireplace. He tried to imagine Pattiann in the rocker with a sewing basket, and knew even as he thought it, that was not Pattiann. No. At the room's threshold was a boot tree, the hardwood floor scuffed where heels had clattered into the crotch. He vised his heel against the wedged back and pulled gently. The boot resisted and he stopped, stepped clear, and entered the living room.

He set the rocker in motion. He guessed the recliner was Ike's and so he settled himself into the plushy cushions, braced his heels on the ottoman. He tipped back his head and inhaled. He believed he could smell Pattiann, just like his daddy claimed he could his wife. Where was Pattiann anyway? On an errand? Or here, in the house? He hefted himself clear of the chair, whisked at the dirt newly smudging the ottoman, spat on a finger and rubbed the cloth, gave up with a shrug. He stepped quietly across the floor. The best part of it, he thought, would be surprising her around one corner or the next, an expectation that clenched him up in ways he hadn't known for awhile now. Not since the night he'd done the dogs.

In the kitchen, he could still smell the morning's bacon, and the coffeepot was half full. A cup was next to the pot and he ran his finger over the stain of lipstick. He raised the cup in a salute and sipped. Still liked her coffee black. He drank as he stepped off the kitchen's perimeter, opening drawers. He liked the mild disarray, towels mixed with dishrags, a potholder scorched but clean. The sink was chipped in a corner, and next to the sink was a thick cutting board. He picked up a filet knife. This too would be Pattiann—her tools in good order. He might have predicted this. He pressed the razor edge to the callused side of his hand, the skin lifting like a dull scale, an opaque sheet on the knife's shining surface. The clock above the sink ticked, the furnace blower kicked in with a hum, and sunlight through the window skewered his hand, the knife glowing and the skin curling over the blade, and then there was a noise upstairs. A squeak, shift, and back into quiet. He cocked his ear toward the ceiling. It was so still that he might have doubted himself had he not been sure from the start that *she was here,* as she was *intended* to be.

He set the knife down, and then he found himself on the stair and then in the upstairs hallway where he paused to study the portraits grouped on the wall: Pattiann as a younger woman, astride a horse; with her brother, branding calves. And Ike. His family farm. A young man milking a cow, forehead pressed to the ribs of the animal, face tilted toward the camera and smiling. Chas leaned closer. Parson's father, and Chas tried to imagine what it must have been to have lived Ike's life—the neat barns in the background, the cozy pens, the attention of the man in this photo. How delicately the fingers framed the cow's udder. Chas shook his head. He walked down the hall, glanced into the spare bedrooms, the bathroom, and at the head of the hallway he stopped before easing through the door. Pattiann was stretched out on the bed, fully clothed and sleeping. He waited in the doorway, just taking it in. He moved to the bedside and stood over her, as though he had the right.

The house was quiet, even the hum of the furnace had cut out, and sunlight sluiced through the window over her bed, kindling her hair, warming his skin. It was enough, he thought, to just stand here awhile and then leave—no one the wiser for it. He bent over, saw how the chenille spread dimpled her cheek, ran his hand over the still-warm depression from where she'd turned over. He sat on the edge of her bed, her body tilting with his weight. He stroked her cheek with a finger. She stirred and he could see how she rose out of the deeps of dreams, like a fish breaking the surface, her eyes flicking beneath the pale lids, the beginnings of a smile shaping itself on her face, a slow lovely gesture. Her eyes fluttered, opened, and grew larger with recognition and surprise, then narrowed. She lay still.

"Pattiann," he said.

She closed her eyes as if to send him back to the dreams she must believe she was still in. But when she opened them again, he could see the resignation there. "Chas," she said. She tipped up on an elbow, looked him in the eye. She held him with a stare for a long moment. He tried to read her.

He traced a ridge in the bedspread with a finger. "This don't need to be anything more than what you make of it," he said.

"What I make of 'it' is an invasion of privacy. Ike might give it another name—breaking and entering—you think of that, Chas?"

"Door was open." His finger followed the spread's fold to where her knee lay and he drew the finger back again. He folded his hands together in his lap. It was not a customary gesture and how strange—to find his hands so committed to nothing, so idle in his lap and primly posed. He crossed his arms, uncrossed them and let his hands drop.

"I didn't plan this, if that's what you're thinking," he said. "I didn't plan anything." He looked over the headboard, out the window to the gray sky, the blur of black branches against the gray, the scramble of twig and limb as the wind tussled the treetops. "Not even coming to town, or leaving the ranch, but here I am and if you asked me why, I couldn't say, except"—he rubbed a pant leg with his palm—"that there's *nothing* there at home. No one thing I *need* to do anymore."

"And so you just walk into my house, into my bedroom like that's the next natural thing?"

He studied the hand he was scrubbing down his pant leg, the palm reddened. "Yup. Go figure," he said.

She swung her legs off the other side of the bed, sat with her back to him. "Chas." Her voice was weary. "I am not now, and have not been a part of your life for a long time."

"Bullshit." He reached across the bed and grabbed her elbow. "Enough a part of your life you had to come out to the ranch and see for yourself. You may choose to think otherwise, but it was still a part of me you aimed for when you sighted on my cattle." She tugged her arm and he let go. She stood, brisked a hand down her shirt as if shaking off dust, and faced him. "All I want to know," he said, "is what I did that you should hate me so." He stayed seated on the bed, opened the bedside dresser drawer, looked in at the oiled rag neatly folded there. "Now, your husband, I can understand that, and that's not to say it was right, or just, or forgivable." He lifted the rag, sniffed it, tossed it back into the drawer. "Like two dogs staking out territory. I lift a leg, he lifts his a little higher." He smiled. "I had you first, but he has you last. Doesn't he?" he asked with his back still to her, his voice softening. "Doesn't he?"

"Oh Christ." Pattiann walked to the door. She crossed her hands over her chest. "This is an unlikely role for you: 'Oh no, honestly, it's really not about starving cattle, or even bad advice, but something much larger, something almost noble. Why, it's a struggle for love.' " She shook her head, nailed him with a finger. "Now we're really talking bullshit." She turned her back and disappeared down the hallway.

He followed.

Her voice trailed as she stomped down the stairs. "Ike saw your cattle and did what he had to. It's not a pissing match, Chas. But I suppose it's easier to live with if you think it has to do with something other than your own mistakes." She turned the corner into the kitchen.

He stopped short of the doorway. "What would you know about *my* mistakes? For three years"—he slapped the doorframe on either side—"you've lived the snug little life of the sheriff's wife. You keep a clean house, work your brother's cattle when you get bored. How nice for you." He clapped his hands. "No mistakes for Miss Pattiann, no siree. No sir-eeee." He walked over, and she stood her ground. "No mistakes. No dirty hands here." His fingers wrapped around her wrist and raised it to eye level.

She curled her hand into a fist. He folded it in his free hand, the small bones balled tight, felt the urge to crush them, compress bone on bone until it and the distance she kept folded in on itself like flesh. He leaned in toward her ear.

"Yes," he said. "I have made *mistakes*. Some of them . . . Listen, I have done things you would not want to hear of," he said. "And things . . . have not worked out as I *imagined*." He backed off, laughed softly. "Maybe," he said, "this is all just a failure of imagination. I look out my windows. Nothing. I walk the feedlot. *Poof.* All gone." He smiled. "Everything. Like a dream." He released her hand and it dropped slowly back to her side, the fist intact. He tugged at the fringe of hair over his forehead. "And so here I am, and by God, there you were, dreaming in the middle of the day."

She didn't answer and then he saw a softening come over her, a looseness of the neck, perhaps, or the way her cheeks suddenly appeared less drawn, and her eyes lowered and looked away. She turned on a heel and walked to the door. She stood with her hand on the doorknob. "You have to leave, Chas. You can't do this again."

He shifted from foot to foot, rocking in place so that the floorboards beneath him ground like old bones in a socket. He could feel the sag and rise, the flooring a gray and white checked linoleum, the old-fashioned type—one solid sheet—that dipped in a well-trod swale in front of the sink and window. The curtains fluttered briefly as the furnace blower cut in and the warm draft brushed across him. And only then did he realize he was already sweating under his heavy coat, the rank stickiness of fear and anger and embarrassment rising up through the layers and folds, lifting into the air, into the room, taking up residence alongside the work and sleep and rut of this couple. Just another breath in the house.

He crossed the kitchen and she was swinging the door open so that the chill flushed his heat and stink and he supposed he should be angry at how easily she rid herself of him. But it was all becoming so ordinary, so expected, almost boring. *Poof.* He's gone. Just like the cattle. He turned in the doorway, cupped a hand to the back of her head to stroke her hair—bright enough to heat his palm, he thought. Her feet were planted on the threshold and her eyes locked over his shoulder. He dropped his hand and turned to see Purvis standing at the roadway, watching. He smiled. "Your day for company," he said, and was gratified to see her composure slip. And then her head gave a tight nod toward the street, as if to a dog, as if to say *scat.*

It had taken awhile to convince Purvis to enter the house and sit down to a cup of coffee. "I'm not bothering you?" he kept asking. "I didn't mean to interrupt anything. . . ." That and other leading questions. But it was not in her to explain or defend what he'd witnessed. She was weary of men and their expectations, tired of being forced into a corner, one way or another, just because she was a woman. He would believe in her, or not. They were friends enough for that trust. Or not. She made fresh coffee. Purvis seated himself at the kitchen table, his gaze jumping over the counters, his shoulders tight. She sat across from him and they drank the first sips in silence. Purvis looked as if he were going to speak, but each time it was as though he'd lost track of his thoughts or the ability to shape them into speech. He sighed largely, once and then again. "Forgive me," he said. "It's been a hard morning."

And then Pattiann remembered. Dan was dead. She remembered Ike's grief, the loss of a good man and a friend—and having to inform the parents. And of course, there was no appeasing the loss of a child. But you could blunt it, for a while, maybe, by providing an honorable purpose to the death—*in the line of duty*—and arranging the police escort and graveside honors. It helped the family, he said. What he hadn't said, but she already knew, was it also helped that someone was in jail. The slowest healing, Ike always claimed, were the families and victims who had no one to fix blame on, finally coming to hate everyone and no one in specific. Or in some cases, ladling blame on themselves—*if only I'd been there, if only I'd warned him, if only I'd stopped him.* Providing answers to victims was part of his office, and mostly satisfying. But this time the answer was Joe Mattick.

Ike had stayed out all night, finally calling her at five in the morning, weary and stunned. "I wouldn't be surprised," he said, "if Purvis comes to see you." It had been offered as a caution. Preparing and then coaching her. "He'll need help. Some kindness."

She'd hung the phone up disappointed. He believed he had to tell her to be kind. What did he imagine her to be? What did he see when he looked at her?

But then, after all, there'd been a measure of accuracy in his doubt. Here Purvis was, and all Pattiann could think of was her own small difficulties, Chas's visit, her embarrassment. But then, it had always been the small acts of kindness she was most awkward at.

Life, as she understood it, was not kind. You never gave in to tears or asked for someone else's. It had always been that way. Rope burns, the come-along latch that snapped back, windburn, sunburn, frostbite, snakebite, insects, accidents. Keeping your hands to yourself was safe. Keeping your concerns to yourself was safe, because you had enough Goddamn troubles of your own. Silence was safe. Keeping your heart in your own hands was safest. And if a marriage or friendships worked, it was because you were responsible for this or that and you didn't interfere. Sometimes that translated to an unwillingness to risk any more than you had to. Even in love. Staying power was all.

So be it.

She found herself scratching circles on the oilcloth.

"You've heard about Joe?"

She braced the cup between both hands. "I'm sorry," she said. He looked older, used. She wanted to reach across the table and touch his hands. He was breathing as though he couldn't fill his lungs sufficiently. She became slowly aware of other sounds: the drip of water from the faucet, the wind at the windowpane. "I'm lousy at this," she said.

Purvis nodded his head. "Yes," he said. "You are." He let out a sigh and shrugged. "I sat across from Joe in his cell, and damned if I could find a way to make it easier for him. But then, wasn't that the problem? I made it too easy for him, and now he's in there because I trusted him, and somewhere inside I knew better. Shit." He rubbed his chin, a rasping sound of stubble against palm. "Ike warned me," he said. "I should have handed Joe over that first time, when he stole that money. But I let him off, so the next time he stole a car, and now a man's dead."

Pattiann tipped back in her seat. "No guarantee though that Joe would have gotten more than a slapped wrist. Or he might have done his time in juvenile and come out with no better prospects than what he'd learned from the other reform school boys." She found herself growing impatient. Her day had taken an off step somewhere, maybe by napping in the middle of the morning, giving dreams a foothold on the waking hours, and those hours becoming more and more unreal. First there was Chas who couldn't take responsibility, and then Purvis who couldn't let it go. And each of them coming to her as if she were the final arbiter, when what they really wanted from her was the very thing they couldn't find in themselves—a middle ground that found its logic outside of reason, that could love in spite of what they did or didn't do. Someone who could show them how to love themselves again. She thought how angered Purvis would be, to find himself compared to Chas, and how laughable Chas would find it. She would find it laughable herself, if the grief hadn't been so plainly written on both their faces. And of course, she did love them, in spite of it all. Chas and Purvis. And Ike.

She shook her head. "Damn. What could you have been thinking of? Taking him in after school to help around the clinic, showing him the prospects of real work and a paycheck, a way to make himself something other than a low-rent cowhand floating his way from job to job, season to season like his good buddy Lester. Jesus Christ, you ought to be horsewhipped." Her mouth snapped shut on the last syllable.

Purvis lifted an eyebrow at her.

She ducked her head, glanced to where sunlight buttered the counter surface. She looked back at him. Gave it a count of three. "More?" she asked, turning the coffee cup in her hands.

He leaned back in his seat, and his back and shoulders loosened. "Sometimes a good scolding cuts the crap," he said. "Women know that. My mother knew that." He got up, went to the counter, retrieved the pot, and poured them both fresh cups. He set the pot in the center of the table, then walked over to the sink where he stood looking out the window. "The thing is, there he was in jail, just a kid, wearing the same clothes he'd wear to school and saying he couldn't remember. But the keys were in *his* pocket and the car parked just down the street from where they found him." He turned around. Leaned against the sink. Pattiann watched him over the rim of her cup.

"What I can't really seem to get around," he said, "and maybe it's just me trying to pass the buck, but where's the justice? Who or what pits a fifteen-year-old boy against a world so much bigger, older and savvy? I mean, where's the mercy?"

Front-page news: OFFICER DEAD IN CAR CRASH AFTER CHASE. Chas imagined Ike laid out, meat for the renderer. There was some pleasure in the thought. He sat at the kitchen table, reading the paper he'd lifted from the bar: the sports pages with their petty ambitions and the classifieds—all the wants in the world. He imagined Ike dead, Pattiann grieving. He would console her. He would walk back into her life, like he'd walked into her house. That easy. And then he looked up, at the uncluttered room, thought about the empty feed yard. No. What he once had to offer her was gone.

He looked at the picture of the dead deputy and set it down, wondered if the guy had had any intuition of it the morning he'd waked. Did he feel God's hand shoving him through the day, directing him to *the* place at *the* time; did he notice the subtle realignment of landscape— moon here, barrow ditch there? An elk? God pulling the old sleight of hand—now you breathe, now you don't, and hiding behind scripture: "He maketh me to lie down," when what He really meant was *He maketh me to take it lying down.* He was a sucker for blood, a little sacrifice: lamb, sheep, goat, cattle.

Or your own son maybe. Like Chas's father holding him by the neck, next to the cat. Or like Abraham—You want this boy dead?

No, just testing, but would you have done it?

Of course, wouldn't You?

He fed the newspaper to the stove. He put on a coat, his hat, slipped into boots, and filled a bucket of water at the sink. It sloshed against his thigh and rang with a roiling chime against the jamb. The air was moist. The warmed fields steamed in the night air like a winding sheet. All the husk and meat gone. *Poof.* Just so much vapor. The night was gravid, his lungs packed with breath. Overhead clouds lowered the sky. Dark and darker. When he walked, he felt the new resilience of soil. Soon, there would be scrub feed on the ranges. He saw it as an impertinence—the first signs of reprieve so close on the heels of his cattle dragged to the waiting semis. A glut of warmth, rains saturating a land already gorged on snowmelt, turning the fields to soup, raising the reservoirs and creating of the hollows and low-lying fields a mirage of blue. And over his land the greeny growth would spread. A luxuriance of green. A wasteland of green. A spendthrift gesture like coins on the eyes of the dead.

He fumbled with the barn door and when it opened it was to a pitch darker than the night. He struck a kitchen match off his jeans and the flare was a bright hole he winced from. He lit the kerosene lantern next to the door and the flame glowed a weak amber through the sooty chimney. He was like a creature out of a fairy tale, a night visitor bearing gifts, his shadow stretched behind while a pale circle of light sketched his hands and lit the dirt at his feet. In the rafters there was a skittering. Wood dust bored by weevils fell like talcum on his clothes. He stopped, cocked his head, asked, "Where are You?"

He raised the lamp to the far corner, to the bolted stall that looked empty. But there was a wet breathing from the far corner, a cough and wheeze and then a heavy fumbling in the dirt and the slats of the stall thumped and groaned. It felt as though the air were an upwelling of expectation, the lamplight brittle, the birds salted to their perches.

Chas saw the wide blaze on the horse's face, its black eyes. The head slung over the door. The animal wheezed and finding its footing stood quiet as the accused in a witness box.

Chas set the pail down and the horse sniffed the air and nickered. "You." Chas said. He lifted the hat from his head, flagged it at the horse asking, "You in this horse?" The horse swung its head away from the hat, its nose jerking high in the air while its eyes rolled white. Then the horse lowered its head, pressed against the stall door, pushing at it, trying to get at the water. When it tired, it lowered its head so that the poll rested against Chas's chest. Chas spoke into its ear. "See, the way it really is, it ain't personal." He hefted the water pail over the half-door and into the stall. The horse backed up, then lowered its head to drink. "It's all just a pecking order. The sheriff's over me, *and* the judge *and* the bankers." He paused, looking about the barn.

"So if you think about it, it's not just me . . . and, of course, we can't be forgetting God—that sly old coot. Talk about dominion. Huh. You and me, we're all just jerking around at the end of our strings down here." He twitched a hand in the air, floated it up and down before his face. He took a couple of deep breaths and cupped his hands. He breathed into the hollow of his palms, stared into the dark there. "But in all that order of peck and pecked—you are the one thing left me."

The horse drank deeply, a sound issuing from its throat like an underground stream.

"You ain't listening to a thing I'm saying. Why do I bother, huh?" He draped his arms over the stall door, hung there idly. He thought of Patti-ann. Her neat little kitchen. How for that brief moment in the doorway her face had turned tender and he'd believed he was that close to getting back some of his own, but then she'd shagged him from her house like a dog. And now, here he was talking to a damn, spiny-backed nag. He clapped his hands against the stall door just to see the horse shy. The animal pivoted and swung into the corner. "Now I got your attention?" It watched Chas from the dark, the whites of its eyes shining.

"She wants responsibility . . . and by God, I can do that." He opened the door, stalked up to the horse, and the animal stayed riveted to the corner. He reached up, snatched its jaw in his hand, and pinched it between his fingers. With his other hand he grabbed the forelock and pulled the head down. "You don't know the meaning of hungry yet," he said. And then as if the anger in him were as easily calmed as the horse, it flickered and ebbed, and he leaned his forehead against the forehead of the horse, and he stood there like that a long while. And when he left the stall, it was as if the horse had understood him, and having given up hope of food had turned its back instead.

He hefted the lantern, blew it out, and let his eyes adjust to the dark, the trim square of starlight in the doorway. Chas stopped. The fields were heavy with permanence. It was the house that seemed insubstantial, a pale light moored in the darkness. His for a little while yet. He had no way to imagine it. This place separate from him. The cleft in his hand, the creek trough, the flat of his chest, the high pasture—the plat of the land like a map of his body. In the distance under some safer sky, he knew men dreamed of tomorrow. They fell through their days as they fell through sleep, heedless of God's inconstancies. He looked out over the far dark night, over the waking clay, the sage clumps where prairie hens clutched in sleep next to cattle bones. He looked to the far horizon he could not see.

Chapter Ten

The limousines, sheriffs' cars, Highway Patrol, and visiting delegates from other regional police enforcement wound slowly through Main Street, their overheads spiraling red and blue. People on the street doffed hats, bowed heads; the flag on City Hall hung at half-mast. As good a day as any to hold a funeral, better than some. Intermittent sun. Graveside, the mayor spoke, and then Ike, followed by a twenty-one-gun salute. Jimmy Matovich, in American Legion uniform, played Taps on a trumpet. The parents stood side by side. Dan's father accepted the folded flag, held it to his heart. To the side of the group ribboned flowers stiffened, their meaty petals turning translucent about the edges. Pattiann raised her eyes to the horizon and the Little Rockies. Her coat hung open. They'd turned a corner. She was sure of it. It *would* snow again, but it would be as transitory as the flowers on the grave. They'd come through the worst, and she felt guilty with relief, here, on this side of the grave while across from her Dan's mother's hands hung as though emptied of work for the last time. It was something perverse, this feeling that one woman's sacrifice spared another's, as though Pattiann had been given another chance.

The funeral director was inviting family members up for a final farewell. Pattiann leaned into Ike's hearing, whispered, "I'll see you at the hall," and picked her way through the mourners. She preferred to walk: through the old churchyard, and down two blocks to the Grange, where the town women were setting out food. At the outer edge of the mourners, Purvis stood alone. When she caught him by the elbow, he startled. "You should have stood with us," she said and hadn't meant to scold, but it sounded that way and she said more softly, "I'm always glad for your company."

He patted her fingers, turned to walk with her. "I know," he said. "I was late." He read a headstone. "Chambers," he said, and then another, "Samuel Walters and wife Christina." They found their way around the plots, some with short, spiked fences, headstones of granite, or sandstone, the oldest inscribed with origins from Scotland, Germany, Wales, like hopeful mile markers.

"Sometimes," he said, "I regret not having become a real doctor"—he waved his hand over the graves—"who might look at old Samuel back there and think, now there was a fine pain in the ass. Imagine seeing all the babies you'd delivered. It would give you hope." He put his hand over hers, squeezed it. "But when I was young like you, I didn't think of such things—hope was a given."

He led her into the shaded corner of the cemetery, behind the chapel, in a grove of stunted Russian olives. In summer they would rustle silver, drop their mealy fruit into the cheat grass and broom. Dogwood shrubs bordered the plot, their red canes a stab of color against the brown grasses. Purvis stepped carefully. "Right about here is Abigail Stubblefield."

Pattiann was hesitant to follow, though she was curious. It was the sorry back patch of the graveyard reserved for the poor, the abandoned. But the small white clapboarded church lent them some dignity. Purvis stood scratching the back of his head, his greatcoat shrugging up and down. "Here, I think."

"No marker?" Pattiann asked, but of course there wouldn't be one.

"Was one, once. I hadn't lived in town long at the time, but I used to take walks here. I suppose I thought the dead were easier to get to know back then. Found Avery here one day, pounding a cross into the head of her grave. A slapped-together thing. He resembled Chas, though thinner."

She picked her way through the sodden grass, past the odd stones with names and small concrete plat markers.

Purvis stepped around the area, checked the angle of the olive trees over his shoulder, and then the church window. "Picked up the shovel and drove it in up to the cross arm so that it made an X, like X marks the spot. Said, 'That ought to keep her,' and stalked off." Purvis kicked around in the weeds. "I'm glad it's gone."

"Hung herself, you know."

His eyes flitted from the grave to the trees. "I never know what to say to the dead. I can only trust they don't expect much."

"Doesn't look like anyone's been here in years. She must have hoped for better."

He took up her arm again, led them away from the grave site. "Well, hope's not enough in this world. The fact is I didn't become a medical doctor because I didn't have the stamina. And I wasn't a husband to my wife—yes, don't look so astounded, I was married for a brief time—but I wasn't a husband to my wife because I believed in the next day and the day after that, and all the time in the world, and what I didn't get done that day would surely get done the next. I was a dreamer. Back when I was young and immortal."

He wagged a finger in her face. "Oh hell. I should have, would have, could have. Moot points all of them. I've got to resign myself to the life lived. Surely there comes a time when a person can give over *wanting* and find some joy in what's been given?"

They stood at the crosswalk. The wind was picking up. Down two blocks and a short left was the Grange Hall where Ike and her family had filled plates with baked ham and rolls and potato salads, relishes. They'd be gathering in small groups, speaking in low voices, telling stories on one another, and soon there would be quiet laughter, because the living can't stay daunted by the dead for long. She buttoned her coat, knowing Purvis waited for an answer she didn't have. It seemed she only knew how to want as well. He nodded good day and turned away, but she snatched his sleeve and held him there.

"I don't know," she said. "Maybe it's in our nature to want more than we have." She looked up to where cirrus clouds scrawled across the blue. And she was struck by how much of her life had been determined by discontent, how at odds her dreams had always been with reality. She wondered if she would have been any happier had she gotten the ranch. She took a deep breath, let go of his coat.

He knocked a clump of dirt off his shoes into the curb. "My first muddy shoe of the season." He lifted his head and shook it. "It's all so damned human, isn't it? Here I am talking about resigning myself to the present and I can't help but think of spring." He lifted his nose to the air. "Do me a favor? Give Ed and Myrna my condolences. Tell them I'll come visit in a few days."

Pattiann tucked her hands in her pockets. "Ike's doing all he can for Joe."

Purvis nodded, and walked away.

Ike hated public speaking. Funerals were the worst. Give a man his due in ten minutes, console the family, heal the community, and call it duty. It was a good speech. He'd spent a long night writing it, but all through the delivery what he saw was Dan in his office a month prior, sitting awkwardly at attention in a straight-backed chair while Ike read him out for giving a young woman a "pleasure" ride in the cruiser. Though the office was cool, Dan's shirt leeched sweat under the armpits. There was chew in the young man's lower lip, and he swallowed his spit. He apologized, said it wouldn't happen again, ever, and confessed he was afraid of dismissal or suspension, of shaming his parents. "It'd kill them," he said. He was young enough to believe that, and new enough to not realize this was a perfunctory warning Ike had been compelled to give young men any number of times. Ike nodded tightly, said, "See it doesn't." And when he offered his hand, Dan shook it. "Yes, sir," he said, "yes, sir." And it seemed with the twenty-one-gun salute popping in his ears Ike could still feel that damp hand in his.

There was plenty to eat, and though he had little appetite he filled his

196

plate respectfully. In its practical way, the community offered what it could to stave grief: hot ham and biscuits, linked sausages, sliced beef with gravy, chickpeas, corn, wax beans, string beans, maple muffins, dilly bread, enough food to stagger a man. There were town people here, and ranchers who had traveled the length of the county toting covered dishes. And better than eulogies or twenty-one-gun salutes was that first bite of warm bread—acceptance for what is given as well as taken. It's what they do best, he thought.

Among the mourners, Jim Parker shook hands. Groups of men gathered to hear his lowered voice. Parker's bait to the commissioners had failed, quietly and quickly. The commissioners, old cowmen themselves, knew the state of Stubblefield's cattle. As Brett Handover one morning in his office had told Ike, "Parker's pulled his pants down on this one, but you might want to watch your back." And so the commissioners and by now most of the county knew Parker was making a bid for sheriff come the elections.

Let him. Ike didn't know how seriously he wanted the job anymore. He seated himself at the end of a long table, talked to fellow officers from neighboring townships, picked at his food between conversation. He sat next to Fred Elrose, who looked steady enough. Ike thought of the man as he'd seen him the night of the accident, still shaken and bewildered by the sight of the mangled car, elk, and body. When the table's attention was directed elsewhere, Fred said, "I wanted to thank you."

Ike speared a slice of ham onto his fork. "We were all shook that night."

"No," he said. "For talking to the captain. You must have called pretty early."

"I had a long night."

Fred nodded. "Me, too. He gave me a couple days off with pay to sort things out. I split wood, fixed the bathroom sink, talked to the wife and played with the kids. Read the help-wanted. By the end of the second day, I was ready to come back."

But he wasn't sure he'd done Fred a favor. It was getting to Ike—that responsibility for other lives, other families. The names on duty rosters weren't faceless. You felt their handshake for days after. They confessed their fears like sins in the after hours. They believed in you, and you were too human to qualify for that kind of trust, and sometimes the worst happened, and if they were young like Dan, you questioned your judgment in sending them, or if they were seasoned, you blamed yourself for not sensing the strain, and ultimately it didn't matter who it was, they were *all* at risk. And he was tired of it. How many dead did it take to bury you? He set his fork down. His plate was filled with food, the ham neatly sliced—*when did he do that?*

Ike felt Pattiann enter the hall before he saw her. He wondered why it was that he could sense her presence, lifting his head to see her suddenly appear in the quiet of his office or on a busy street, as though he knew her step that intimately, or the timbre of her breathing. It was one of the things he found most comforting, how love announced itself in familiarity.

She was making her way to him, hair tousled, and she raked through it with a hand as was her habit. Her cheeks were a high color and as she said her hellos to friends her eyes made contact briefly before moving on. She hesitated at the edge of a group that included Harley, several deputies, a few town people, and Jim Parker. Her back stiffened and to the side of her Harley shook his head. Then Harley was pushing his way into the center and Ike saw Pattiann extend a hand to stop Harley and then drop it at her side. Ike excused himself from the table.

"That's bullshit," Harley said, and at a nearby table the men turned in their chairs to see who spoke while the women frowned nervously or dipped more earnestly into their food.

Ike approached the group, looking over their heads to where Pattiann stood.

"You calling him a liar?" And Ike couldn't see who'd asked the question, but Parker backed up.

"I'm saying—" Harley's voice raised and Ike put a hand on his shoulder.

"Trouble, Harley?"

The deputy nailed Parker with a glare. Ike turned to the group.

"Maybe we ought to take this discussion outside, or hold it later. None of us wants to intrude on Ed and Myrna's grief."

"That's right," Parker said, stepping forward. "This is better discussed elsewhere—"

"Well, you brought it up," Harley persisted.

"Harley," Ike said and tightened his grip. He looked up at Pattiann, saw the stricken look.

"He's blaming you for Dan's death." Harley snapped off the last word.

At the surrounding tables cutlery stilled. Voices at the far tables droned on and children bolted from their seats to run outside. He wished he were out there himself, or fifty miles down the road and driving, and at that moment he was *willing* to leave everything and everyone. He saw Dan's father at the far edge of the group. The man was studying him, a slow appraisal. He met Ed's eyes and felt there was a reckoning coming that might be, finally, the thing that would send Ike on his way, out of this town and these lives. Nothing left to hold him in place. He'd welcome it. He angled his way toward Ed, felt Pattiann in the wake of people behind him.

Ed waited for Ike. He blew out a couple deep breaths, stared down at his feet. "My son," Ed said, cleared his throat. "He did good for you those years?"

"I never had a complaint," Ike said.

Ed nodded, tucked his hands inside his suit-coat pocket so that the corners pulled down and Ike could see the coat was one he didn't wear much, the material good but old, the narrow lapel resurrected now as stylish. He was ill at ease in the suit. He must hate it. "At the grave," Ed said, a hand gestured vaguely, "your words helped." He looked around. When he looked at Ike again, his focus was sharper. "I don't know what's all being said"—he glanced around the group—"but all those years at home, Dan was a good hand. And I may have given him more than he could handle, but I never gave him *less*. I like to think he respected that. I know he respected you." He jerked his head down, his face knotted above his tie. "That's all I got to say. Good day, Sheriff."

And he turned on his heel and worked his way to where his wife sat with friends, and as the group around Ike dissolved, he watched Ed offer his arm to her and lead her from the hall. And then Ike was alone and he felt Pattiann at his back. When he turned, he saw Harley was still there, red-faced but appeased. Parker was gone. Ike put Pattiann's hand off his sleeve, told Harley to stay put, and walked to the back door where he knew Parker had ducked out.

By the time Ike stepped outside, Parker was already nearing the far end of the parking lot. Ike walked briskly. A light wind spun grit and bits of litter around the cars. In the open bed of a pickup, a cow dog lifted its head, nosed into the wind, and yawned as though to eat the air before sliding back down into the bed with a grunt. A pop can rattled across his path and wedged against the tire of a '61 Oldsmobile—Paul Tinsley's car, and Ike wondered briefly if he'd gotten the taillight repaired. Parker turned.

"I don't like what you're doing, Jim. You got an ax to grind, bring it to me first," Ike said.

Parker smiled. "You offering your own neck? Or you got some other young kid like Dan to take it for you? Maybe that fool Harley."

"Take your complaints where they'll do some good—or, if you prefer, Joe Bridley at the feedlot, or Ben, Hank, Tom, and Arty chewing fat over at the elevators. The commissioners must have been a disappointment."

Parker prodded a finger into Ike's chest. "You don't know jack shit about us. We don't stay fooled for long."

Ike stared down at the finger, the plumping digit, the smooth nailbed that poked at his uniform coat. He was surprised by his lack of anger. He turned away from Parker, looked at the sky breaking blue, the clouds clumping like scattered thoughts. Or maybe he just didn't give a good Goddamn anymore? He could almost see them as the town must, squared off against each other. The dog snored in the truck bed. He cricked his neck to a side, said, "It's a damned beautiful day." He looked at Parker over his shoulder. "Why do funerals come on days like this?"

Parker's hand stopped fussing in the air, dropped to his side, and he stared at the sheriff, and then he lifted his head as if for a moment he too was struck with the incongruity of it. "Spring's coming," he said, and mumbled as an afterthought, "none too soon."

"Longest winter I've ever lived through." Ike scrubbed at his face with a hand. All he wanted was a clean pickup to lay himself down in in the sun. When he looked up, Parker was still there. "Why do you stay?" he asked. And as he asked Parker this, he knew he was asking more. He was asking why all of them stayed, through bad crops and indifferent weather, accidents and divorce, when all the country stirred around them changing households, cities, states, packing the roads with U-hauls and semis, industry shifting, leaving potholes in cities where rats flowered as suburbs grew like benign cankers and people rose from restless sleep to change beds, families, neighborhoods, and jobs, until change for its own sake was reason enough. Why did these people stay?

Parker smiled, a small shrug tilted his shoulders. "That's just the way it is." He inclined his head toward the sheriff. "What's your reason?"

Ike stooped to pick up a piece of paper that lodged against his shoe. It was a grocery receipt. On the back someone had scribbled: *pick up kids from dentist.* He hoped she'd remembered, been on time.

"Honestly? I don't know." He nodded good day and turned back to the hall.

As he neared the door, he realized he couldn't go back in. He saw Fran standing at the corner. She lifted a hand in a small gesture that might have been a wave, or a catch at the scarf that snapped in the wind. She was smiling, and he thought briefly of Pattiann before walking over.

"You look like you could use a drink," she said.

He tucked his head down and shook it. "Some fresh air maybe."

She led off. "It was a good speech. I stood in back. Dan would come into the café once in a while. He was polite. Left tips. I guess that's all it takes to ingratiate a person to me." She blinked as a quick gust flicked her hair across her eyes. She restrained it in her hands and tucked the ends into her collar. The scarf dangled from her fingers. "You all right?"

They stepped from the curb, turned away from the town center. A bell hammered from the single-story brick schoolhouse and there was a simmer of noise from inside and then the doors banged back on hinges and a stream of children boiled into the school yard, their noise mightier than their numbers. Girls with jump ropes swung them over their heads like lariats, and boys ran the length of the lot bunching fists in the air and shouting.

Fran scanned the playground, perhaps to see her own children and discover who they were when not with her.

"Your kids all right?" he asked.

"Yeah," she said. "Not much has changed for them. They live with me, see their father on weekends. They think of Jolene like some kind of older sister to keep clear of." They walked past the schoolyard, turned down a side street. "Were you the one took the papers out there?" she asked.

Ike nodded, thought about when yesterday he'd rung the bell and Jolene had answered the door, not slovenly as he'd hoped, but pert in a gingham apron which her hands kept brushing in a nervous gesture. She'd called Dave and he'd come into the living room with shaving cream still dappling one ear. Ike could smell dinner cooking, and to a side in the dining room he saw the flicker of candlelight. Dave seemed inordinately pleased with himself. Jolene appeared embarrassed.

"Delivered the papers late yesterday afternoon."

"How'd he take it?" She didn't look at Ike when she asked, but studied the pavement where the sidewalk had buckled over the cottonwood roots.

"Fine," he said. There had been that moment—Dave accepting the papers and his smile wearing thin before lifting a hand to Jolene's shoulder, squeezing it gently. He looked bolstered by the small woman, calling it finally "a relief" and joking, "thought you'd come to shoot my cattle."

He couldn't tell Fran this. How Dave had taken the paper and how his hand had rested on Jolene's shoulder. How happy they looked and how Ike, even for Dave's joke, couldn't dislike the pair—their happiness transparent as gingham and shaving cream.

"Well." Fran sighed, stopped where she stood as though she'd meant to be here, as far removed from her orderly day-to-day life as she was from her previous life on the ranch. "I guess that's the best of it. He's got what he wants."

"And you?" Ike asked.

They walked two blocks in silence, turned the corner, and found themselves on her street, standing opposite her house. "I make a good cup of coffee," she said. "Better than the diner's."

She was nervous. Her fingers picked at the coat buttons. But it was not in her nature to play Jolene's role, nor in his to be the man sitting across the table in candlelight, with shaving cream on his ear. That kind of love would be ponderous. "I would love a cup, Fran, but I'll have to pass."

"Well, then"–she pulled the scarf up about her head–"I'll see you at the diner sometime. Or in church maybe."

He watched her walk away, wondering why his feet refused to move.

Pattiann waited for Ike, but he didn't return. She helped with dishes while men stacked folding chairs and dropped the cleared tables with ricocheting bangs, carried them back into storage. Children were called in with yells and whistles, loaded into cars among the leftovers, and the numbers in the hall dwindled to a dozen and then a handful, and then there was finally only herself and the funeral director–keeper of the Grange Hall keys–who locked the door behind them. He stood on the step next to Pattiann trying to make conversation, and curiously, everything he said sounded like consolation, even his comment on the fine weather.

"It was a nice service," she said. "It's hard when they're so young."

They stood in the open air. He inhaled deeply. He smelled of cosmetics, powders and rouge.

"Would you like a ride?" he offered, the limousine at the curb.

He waited patiently as Pattiann did not answer, and then she asked, "Do you think there are deaths a person can't survive?" She looked at him, and she had the feeling he wanted to shake his head and walk away, an unfair question after all, but he steadied himself with a deep breath.

"I think there are some deaths we *believe* we cannot survive."

They stood near the hearse, beside the tinted windows where she saw reflected the roof of the Grange Hall edging up against a sky, bluer for the tint, and clouds that held still though the wind tumbled her hair, the world skating across that glib surface. She watched her hand gather the hair and shrug it into her coat collar. The undertaker looked away as if he'd witnessed something too private.

She turned from him. "I should be going," she said.

He fidgeted in his suit, as if wanting to say more, or ask what loss *she* believed she could not survive, but offered his hand instead. When she took it, he laid his other hand on top as though consoling her, as though it were her child who lay in the ground. He stepped off the curve, into the glare of sunlight on chrome, and dipped into the driver's side of the hearse. The big engine hummed alive, and Pattiann watched it pull away, and then she was alone and heading home.

She could drive to the ranch, saddle a horse, and ride out farther than the day's light would permit. But once home, she found herself doing odd chores, stopping now and again to lift the phone, to dial Ike's number at work before setting it back on the receiver. She polished furniture: the birch writing desk her father had given her as a young girl, the oak wardrobe Ike had found at a secondhand shop and refinished over two and a half years of "spare time," the dining-room table they'd bought together at an antique shop outside of Billings with a set of four cane chairs, worn in all the right places, as Ike liked to say. She worked in silence, as if all the creakings of the house were suspended so that the pipes did not rap and heaters did not tick and the wind outside avoided the eaves, and the only sounds were the small grunts as she wiped down the turned table legs, the pop her knees made when she stood suddenly. She was too restless for music. It was an irritation with herself she worked on, on her knees at the furniture, as if by becoming intimate with the chinks in the joints, the wood grains and inlays, she would understand what she and Ike had made of themselves.

She squatted on the living-room area rug that had been rubbed down in places to the weave beneath, a thing she was fond of for the graceful way it had withstood the abuse of years. Like people surviving in a land-scape that did not welcome them. Like losing the land that was never yours. She rubbed the oiled rag over her fingers, slid her wedding ring above the knuckle so that she could see the pale circle beneath.

She remembered Ed and Myrna graveside, neither touching the other, as if the air between them was a wedge as deep as the grave. They were strong, by God, and stood on their own two legs. Admirable. Ter-rifying. The stuff of everyday lives.

She looked about the living room. She settled herself into Ike's chair, the deep recliner where he rarely found the time to rest between work and community business. And of course, there were all the times she wouldn't have been home to see him, busy as she kept herself on her brother's place. Even now, she felt the old restlessness, the urge to get up and drive away. With Chas it had translated to a wildness that she was paying for these many years later. Wasn't that what had really drawn her to Ike? His solid, midwestern nature? A most ordinary man, who'd done a most extraordinary thing. A full year after she'd left the Midwest, he'd shown up on her doorstep wearing clean jeans and a shirt still wrin-kled from the traveling bag.

"You must be surprised," he'd said. "And maybe a little alarmed." He kept his distance across the threshold from her, his weight spread evenly on his feet, his hands composed at his side.

She'd studied him a long moment. She could see he watched her like a suspect, reading her body language, and in that quiet span of time she understood she'd never really stopped loving him. She saw that the root-edness within him did not depend on the familiarity of the ground he stood on. It was a quiet, unperturbed steadiness, even as he waited at her door like a supplicant, and she came to love him again, though it felt something more like hope.

"You missed me," she'd said, and he nodded. "You don't know what you're getting yourself into," she'd said. He shrugged, suggested that that was the case with waking up in the morning. He added it was prob-ably what made each day doable and how the the term "blissful igno-rance" had been coined. She suspected he was only half teasing. She'd thought on it a moment longer, then said, "Bliss." She cocked her head toward him. "Think we can manage that?" And then she'd invited him in and he'd accepted. They'd married shortly after, and she'd never regretted it. She wondered if he had.

Pattiann pushed herself up and out of Ike's chair, feeling the need to move about. She put her house in order, working through the changing light, the shadows of household objects shrinking, pivoting, stretching. She moved into the kitchen late afternoon, watched the last bit of sun ease over the backyard. She set a meal in the oven as though Ike would come home from work as he always did, trusting his love, and when, finally, the back door opened and he stepped in, she blessed again the ordinariness of the man, the habits that determined the smallest of his actions, like coming home, like hanging up his hat in her kitchen.

They ate between bits of conversation. He'd worked the rest of the day. There were some interesting results on the fingerprint tests they'd done on Purvis's car. He'd say no more until he knew more. A few of the visiting officers had stopped in after the funeral, compared similar accidents on their watches. They meant to be kind, he said.

"Did it help?" she asked.

He shrugged. "Maybe tomorrow, or the next day. Right now," he said, and looked down at the plate of food he'd been picking at, "I want to sleep, but I'm not tired."

Pattiann cleared their plates. He sat, rubbing his head with his hands, his eyes closed. She cleared the table, flipped on the stove light and turned off the overhead light. She moved behind him, bracing his head in the cleft of her breasts, moved her hands down to his neck, his shoulders, loosening the knotted muscles. "We don't have to stay here," she said.

He grunted softly as she found a tender spot. "We could go upstairs," he said, misunderstanding her meaning, which was to leave this place, this house and town, this land, but found she was relieved he'd taken it wrong, her heart hammering. She followed him, turning off lights as she went and enjoying the old comfort in knowing her way through the dark, following the sound of his steps through their house. It was a good house, she thought, generous in spite of her.

He sat in the dark on the edge of their bed. He looked surprised when she knelt on the floor, took each foot in her lap, and eased the shoes from them. She turned a sock back, down, and off his foot, cupped the foot in her hands. The skin was dry and strangely soft, and she could feel his embarrassment, at first, that she would take his feet and explore them with her fingers, the arch, the wide ball, the hollow beneath the toes, between each digit. But he gave over to the comfort, her fingers practiced from long years of kneading strained muscles in livestock. As she worked, he gathered her hair to his face and she felt the touch of his lips so lightly pressed she could not be sure, and when that ceased he sat perfectly still over her, his head suspended over her head in the dark with his feet in her hands, and she worked on until each foot was pliant and his breathing eased.

When at last she set his feet down, he touched her elbow, lifting her, drew her legs up and onto the bed, and laid her next to him. They let their eyes adjust to the dark—deeper than the starlit fields beyond the window, and his shirt a lesser black than the sweater he lifted over her breasts, the paired aureoles of her nipples dim as new moons against the pale skin, and his buckle a dim twinkling.

It was a marvel the way her hands revealed him. And how she had come to this place, after all these years, to find his body new—the cock in her hand, this shifting flesh that she had taken into herself countless times before and would again with such familiarity, having the same comfort as knowing a house this well, or the land whose ditches and hummocks only surprised you by their constancy and the stones you kicked over now were those same stones you had turned over as a child, and the earth itself was a skin that you wore on the soles of your feet, taking you into itself even as she took him, now, clothes turned back and down, wrung around their legs and arms, tangled in each other, her hips rising to his, the muted slap of flesh, and beyond the listening walls of the house the wind grew hushed in the fir bows, the croon of cats was silenced, the town extinguished beneath the brilliance of stars.

For the next week, Chas stayed on the ranch. He had no call to leave. He spent his waking hours between the house and the barn, and all the hours seemed waking now even when he slipped into his bed, the covers shedding like a snake's skin as he turned and turned, rising in what he believed were dreams only to discover he'd not been sleeping. He lived on the last of the flour mixed with water—a gruel that crusted and recrusted the kettles like highwater marks, and when it ran out he found that was okay too, having lost the taste for it anyway. He lived in what clothes were available—odd-paired socks, a shirt balled under the sheets, pants draped on doorknobs or kicked into the corner. He took on the smell of his clothes and his clothes the smell of him and the house was rank with it as though he wore the house as well. He chewed his fingernails, browsed the empty cupboards, spent long hours in the chair by the window. Each morning, he delivered a bucket of water to the horse, and returned with another in the evening. He idled the days between house and barn, and with the lack of sleep and food often found himself rising from his bed with no memory of having left the barn the evening before. One day he mistook sunrise for sunset and thought it a good joke when it took him hours to figure it out. Sometimes he thought he heard voices, or got dizzy if he stood up too quickly. The world became peculiar, and the peculiar became ordinary. There were few terrors left for him.

He stood in the barn, looking out the door at the land that was as empty and quiet as his own shriveled stomach. And that was a curious relief—how his gut no longer griped. He wondered briefly if the horse felt the same, or if it heard voices, too? If for the horse, the moon tracked backwards so that the sun set instead of rose? When he turned back to the interior, he heard the sound of small feet scrabbling about the loft, across the rafter. He stared up at the hand-hewn beam until his neck cricked, though the small pain proved a pleasant distraction now against the greater numbness.

Was this how his mama had come to feel, out here in the barn studying the rafter, all sensation bled from her limbs like her belief in Him, for wasn't that what her suicide was about? Despair. Having finally despaired of Him, or believing He had despaired of her—daughter of a preacher, granddaughter of a preacher. She with her missionary's heart; what a plum Avery must have appeared to be.

Better yet, he wondered how his father had felt coming into the barn, in the early dark, to the surprise awaiting him. Chas remembered. A spring morning. A Sunday. And he was a bare twelve years old, shuffling out of the house, wrestling his way into a jacket, when he saw his father coming out of the barn. He was leading the saddled piebald, the broad door banging shut on his heels. How many times had Chas tried to remember his father's face? His expression particular to that moment, having just saddled his horse in the shadow of his wife. Chas looked across the space. Not very wide where he'd have had to lead the animal past her. Did the horse nose her, or shy? He could almost see it. The horse bumping her, the stirrup catching her skirt. And the rope twisting, winding right and right, then slowing to a stop. The body beginning its slow spin to the left.

But what was it in his father's face? Nothing that would suggest what he'd seen. His face was as still, his focus as removed from Chas as it ever was. He'd handed the reins to Chas, told him to check the fences in the high country. "Be back before dark," he'd said. Nothing more, but sparing Chas the sight of his mother, or of the sheriff cutting her down. And just maybe that was the most merciful thing Avery had ever done. Albeit a cold kind of mercy.

In the stall, the animal drank, pausing often with the effort. A wind kicked up, gusted through the door, and Chas opened his jacket, letting the breeze air him out. He supposed he could clean the stall, but then we all died in shit, didn't we? The body purging itself as though dropping the ballast that kept it connected to the earth.

Then again, there was no need to die in more shit than necessary. He wasn't uncaring, after all. He chuckled. And what else did he have to do? The wind was moist with thawing earth, though the few grasses it ruffled in the feedlot were still reluctant and brown. The horse nickered, coughed, and as Chas turned, the animal lifted its head over the stall door and into the wind. It almost looked lively for a moment, a shake of head and mane before lowering again to drink. Chas hefted the pitch-fork, tapped his way across the dirt as a blind man uses a cane, and as happened fairly often now, the distance became elastic, the stall and horse moving away from him, as if viewed through the wrong end of a telescope. "Whoah, there," he said, and staggered to a stop. When the dizziness eased, he walked forward, thinking to count the paces to the stall. But he as quickly forgot that idea.

The horse waited. And he wondered if the animal comprehended it was going to die? And if that were the case, how did it pass these moments? Biding its time, Chas's own good time. "You still here?" he asked, and he gathered by the lack of an answer that He was. Waiting, biding His time, which was no time and all time, and Chas believed now, finally, he had an inkling of that trick, how a moment stretched to breaking, and next thing you knew it was dark of the next day, or maybe next week, and what did it matter because it was all pretty much one and the same thing. The horse dying here was already dead, and his cat-tle had always been just food for Taylor's dog.

He knocked the wood handle against a center post and the rap sounded clear and hard. "You here?"

He set aside the fork and entered the stall, prodded the horse's ribs with the wood handle, as if tapping at a door. The horse swung to the side, haunches swooning into the stall slats so that the head turned to look at its hindquarters as if they were just so much meat pieced together.

Chas scraped at the horse's shit, loose and black, packed into the dirt flooring. The smell of ammonia stung his eyes. The horse's piss was the color of straw, bright yellow. "Seems you're all the entertainment I got left."

He tossed the pitchfork over the stall, crossed to the horse. He stud-ied it, how the ribs labored like a bellows, the bones rising and floating in the skin. The coat was rubbed in patches down to pink skin. Its tail was a club of piss and shit. He leaned up to the horse's eye, stared into the pupil, large and black. He tried to see into the horse, past the glazy surface down into the hole of the horse where its stomach puckered like the empty sack of a castrated dog, to the intestines that shed skin and blood because it did not know how to stop pushing—he tried to see all of this and beyond it to that thing in the horse that was horse, some elusive, shining thing. He peeled back the eyelid with two fingers and the white rolled and flashed and Chas squinted so close that their eyes moistened with the nearness of the other, and the iris flickered and widened like a shutter, an aperture that opened on the dark of the barn, to the opened door beyond where shadows yawed over the muddied lots, and then, as if the two eyes had changed places, the lens pivoted on its axis, it was, he saw, the horse looking into him and he saw as the horse did—his own laboring heart and lungs, organs and bone, and he felt trapped there, squeamish with his own curiosity, and even as Chas jerked back from the horse's head, the horse raised its head to clamp teeth on his arm and held until the flesh tore and the teeth shivered across bone. Chas squeezed the bloody arm with his good hand and watched as the horse backed away.

And he heard that voice again, as he had off and on these last several days. *"Do you see?"* the voice asked.

Chas closed the stall behind him, walked out of the barn. "I'm not listening," he said.

Chapter Eleven

A cross the table from Ike sat the young boy—a nervous tic in one eyebrow. The nape and sides of his head were neatly trimmed. His hands were on top of the table, clean and clenched together. Bobby Acklin—Joe Mattick's best friend. Ike was in the boy's kitchen with the mother and father sitting at opposite ends of the table. A pie cooled on the counter and a puppy, the new family dog replacing the one they'd lost last month, paced the kitchen pausing now and again to lift its nose toward the dessert. They sat in silence, except for the occasional caution to the pup. The mother drummed her fingers. Ike had informed them the prints from Purvis's car included their son's. He'd been in trouble before.

The father, Kevin Acklin, rubbed his face in his hands. He was a rancher who ran a solid operation, a member of the Rotary who played fiddle with a small band at weddings and community dances. When Ike called, he'd been interrupted from practice for the Grange Hall dance to be held later that week. The fiddle sat on its back on the table looking outlandish, a delicate bracing of wood, gut, and wire on the white Formica top. "What the hell's next?" he said.

Rose stopped her fingers, looked from her husband to her son. "Tell me you didn't do this," she said.

"No," Kevin said. "Tell us what you did."

"Nothing," the boy said, and glanced over at the gangly-legged shepherd pup nosing the counter again.

Kevin stood, crossed the kitchen, and booted it away. "Go lay down," he said softly, and the pup retreated to a corner where it curled its nose into its tail and watched with nervous eyes. Kevin stood behind his son. The boy sat at attention. "You think I don't know a lie when I hear one?" Kevin asked.

The boy flinched and Ike found he had to look away—the mother shaking her head, the boy rigid in his chair. It was getting late. He had a long ride back and he was tired.

"I wasn't driving," the boy said softly.

"I can't hear you," Kevin said.

He repeated it louder. "I never planned on going," he said. "But we were drinking a little—"

"A lot," Kevin corrected.

The boy shrugged. He looked to Ike to save him. "I didn't know what I was getting into. Lester said we'd just take a short ride. Get the car back early."

"He gave you the alcohol?" Ike asked.

The boy nodded.

Kevin walked around the side of the table, sat at the head again. He pushed the violin aside; it wobbled on its back like a distressed turtle. He leaned across to Ike. "You nail that sonofabitch, you hear?"

"Who drove?" Ike asked. He wanted to hear the boy say the name.

"Lester. Found the keys on Joe. Joe passed out early on, in the back of Lester's truck. He can't hold his liquor," the boy giggled and stopped. He looked at his mother, but she kept her eyes averted. He did not look at his father.

"Joe was with you in the car?"

The boy shook his head. They'd driven around town, Lester stopping to pick up beer and then heading out toward the reservation. "Wanted to do him an Indian," Lester'd said, but Bobby confessed he didn't know exactly what Lester meant by that and they'd never made it onto the reservation. "And then there was this cop, and Lester tells me to hang on. I told him to stop." He turned to his mother who sat with her forehead in her hands. "Honest." He looked over at his father, who sat unflinching.

"A thief," Kevin said. "A damned thief."

The boy started to cry and neither parent moved to comfort him. Ike shifted in his seat. He waited for the boy to calm down. "So then what happened?"

The boy sighed. "Next thing I know, the cop's next to us and then Lester turns right and the car takes a ditch, bottoms out but keeps on going across a field, and then we're back on a road and I can't see anything behind us. No cop. Nothing." They'd driven back to town, parked the car, and hauled Joe out to the street where they left him with the keys in his pocket.

"Lester said to keep shut about it. Said he'd kill me if I talked."

They sat in silence again. The dog yawned in the corner and shut its eyes. Rose studied her son. "What happens now?" she asked Ike.

"Up to the courts."

Kevin sat back, shook his head. "He does time, you hear?" His finger moved across the table, pointed at his son. "By God . . ."

Ike pushed his chair back. "Can't say. I'll have to file a report, bring Bobby down for more questioning, and Joe."

"And Lester?" Kevin asked.

"I pick up Lester."

"Well, you'd better find a deep, dark place to put him, because if I see that sonofabitch, I'll shoot him."

Ike stood up, feeling strangely weary for the relief this should have been. "Mr. Acklin, I'd hate to have to jail you too. I'll take care of Lester."

Kevin stood, looked down at his son. "See you do." He spoke over his shoulder as Ike crossed to the door. "See you take care of that sonofabitch."

Rose held the door open for Ike. He looked down at her, his hat in his hand. "Good night, Mrs. Acklin, thank you for your hospitality."

She closed the door behind him without a word.

They had their first taste of spring, and while none of them was naive enough to believe it would last or that winter was done with them, still merchants had stock boys out on the sidewalks sweeping litter clear of their doors and the churches vied with seasonal quotes, the reformed church from New Testament, Mark: *So is the kingdom of God, as if a man should cast seed into the ground; and should sleep and rise night and day, and the seed should spring and grow up, he knoweth not how;* and the less forgiving from Old Testament, Proverbs: *The sluggard will not plow by reason of the cold; therefore shall he beg in harvest, and have nothing.*

Cattle were brought into the calving pens and children chucked outdoors to play. The days stretched and nights quickened. Men stomped the ground to hear how far the frost had receded. The cattleman's association prepared for its annual dance at the Grange Hall. It looked to be a good turnout, if the weather held, a last-ditch Canadian arctic system stalled north of them. They'd shake off winter, tipple away the cold. It was a chance to talk cattle and crops and be among the survivors again.

Ike was no different. It wasn't that he enjoyed dancing, but he liked the laughter, the easy bumping into folks he knew on the dance floor, the relief everyone exuded even in their tight-fitting best clothes, because the worst was past and any groundhog worth his spit knew that there were always six more weeks of winter and that was as it should be, and out here you could count on ten or more, but they'd come near the end of even that dour forecast, and the season's change was inevitable, and the people had come to the point where they could believe again.

He was an early arrival because Pattiann had been enlisted to help set up. She was spreading paper cloths over tables, lighting votive candles on each, and he liked to see the match flare, the way she touched light to the wicks with such single-minded concentration and how the glasses took on a glow until the room had a dozen or more flickering lights on white-cloaked tables.

The stage was a riser of boards and plywood that someone had covered with indoor/outdoor carpeting years ago. Two men on ladders were aiming spotlights, replacing gels—blue and red. His nephew Justin was testing the mikes, *check, one, check two,* and thumping the head with a finger. Ike watched the boy a long moment, wondered what it would be like when he moved in with them next fall, for they had agreed to his staying with them through the school terms, had told Harriet and Rob just a couple days ago. When they had told Justin, he'd taken it with his usual quiet good manners. "Thank you," he said, and then, "I won't be much of a bother." Ike had told them all how Pattiann had already been sizing up the extra room, moving furniture, clearing out the closet. He shook his head. "Next thing you know, she'll be sewing curtains," he said.

Pattiann had smiled, a lopsided grin. "Serve you right if I did," she said.

What he didn't tell them was how they'd both come to anticipate the idea of Justin living with them, the house snugging comfortably about the three of them. "Maybe it's time we learned how to make room for someone else in our lives?" Pattiann had said and Ike had begun to believe just maybe, she was right.

Justin moved to the next mike, waved to his grandfather who was off to a side with Kevin Acklin and Pete Wolfgram, tuning up their instruments.

Pattiann slipped up to his side and leaned down as if to tell a secret, hiding a kiss in the gesture before moving off. He fingered where her kiss had touched his cheek. What was he to make of it? This new Pattiann. They talked more. "Making up for lost time," she said. She was like someone coming out of a sleep, and when he told her this, she laughed. It was not as if she neglected her brother's ranch, but she rode out there less driven. He began to believe if he had to leave this place, it would not be alone.

Overhead the heating vent chuffed, and Ike leaned back, hands laced behind his head. The alternate banks of lights flicked off or dimmed, ceiling stains, pipes, and vents receding. There was a solitary clapping and Ike saw the room softened by candles, the blue stagelight brittle on the chrome drums. There was the chink of glassware as the bar opened on the far side of the room away from the temperate punchbowl the church deacons guarded.

He could name these people, recount their graces as well as sins, and it was a heady feeling, coming through the worst of it, a witness to their lives and they to his. How could he not feel new? As transformed as the hall. He thought he was close to laying a finger on what he needed, to be . . . content . . . and perhaps it would come to him in a moment longer, or a day, a month, an understanding of this place and these people in his care. And the truth as he saw it now, sitting in the Grange with the people filing in through the doors and the musicians tuning for the first set, he did not want to leave, would do what was in his power to stay. Let it be. Let it be spring, let the rains come and the grasses grow, let the wounds heal and the graves settle.

Before an hour was out, the hall was stifling, the old boiler throwing jets of hot air so that the dance floor smelled of Old Spice, Stetson, Canoe. Men shed suit coats and women piled their hair up. The fiddlers sawed, handkerchiefs bundled on chin rests to absorb the sweat, paused only to call out the tunes. Ike danced with Pattiann. The prettiest wife in the county, he called her.

"What about the single women?" she asked.

"Can't hold a candle," he said, tucked her closer, and they slewed out into the center of the floor where couples jigged the two-step and around the perimeter others processed clockwise, side by side, arms locked about waists.

Purvis showed up in a red suit coat, gray pants, and a bright yellow vest. "Christ," Ike had said. "All you need is a tuba and epaulets."

Purvis grinned, slapped Ike on the back. "I am a man of fashion."

"You're a bloody peacock."

Purvis nodded. "Damn right. I've decided to take my courting seriously, fan my feathers, jiggle my tail." He lifted a lapel. "Red's my color, don't you think?"

And now, from the dance floor, he could see Purvis still reclining by the bar, lifting his head back in guffaws as the men joked about his attire and the women contrived to get a closer look. Ike hoped it worked. It was good to see Purvis back on his feed now that the Mattick boy was home. Bobby Acklin would do time, but it would be minimal, Ike suspected, probation most likely, and he knew Purvis had already made an offer to the court to provide the boy with community service at the clinic, should the court feel so inclined, which Ike also suspected it would.

He nestled his hand lower on Pattiann's back, edging his finger nearer the crease of her buttocks. Her head snapped up in surprise, hitting his jaw. He drew his hand away to rub his chin. "Sorry," she whispered, but he could see she was amused. When the set ended, they joined Bill and Martha at a table. Purvis pulled up a chair and tipped a whiskey back.

"You going to dance with me, Martha? We could make out like Rome on fire while your husband fiddles," Purvis said.

Martha cocked an eyebrow at him. "Purvis, even if I could dance anymore, that coat's enough to give a woman the staggers."

"You like it? My father wore red long johns to bed. My parents enjoyed a long and fruitful marriage. He used to say, 'Red warms the cockles.' I misunderstood him for years."

"I think it's handsome," Pattiann said, and touched his sleeve.

Purvis waggled his brows at Ike. He leaned back in his seat, took a deep breath, and looked around. "Just what we needed," he said. "Good to see people when they're not on the far end of a cow. How's the herd, Bill?"

"Shop talk," Martha said, shaking her head.

"Might do all right, do better when the grass greens up." Bill paused. "And that's saying we get rain, the sun shines, and we don't get kidney-punched—"

"Listen to him," Martha said. "I for one have had enough, and if it means getting on the dance floor with Purvis to avoid it, I'll do that. Moreover, if God should see fit to strike me dead in midstep, at least I'll have gone out dancing." She pushed herself to her feet. "Where's the music?" she called out. She stood, looking down at her husband.

He finished his drink. "Order me another one, son," he said to Ike. "And you . . ." He leaned down to Purvis. "I'll be watching."

The band gathered. Bill, plucking up his fiddle, started playing "Waltzing Matilda" in a slowed tempo, the others picking up the tune as they joined him on stage. He kept them to that slow pace, his eye on his wife and hers on his, as she stepped into Purvis's arms and danced carefully. She was small and no longer nimble, her steps circumspect, and the other dancers on the floor kept their jostling to themselves, cutting them a space like the eye of a storm, upon which the lead fiddler smiled.

And when the song ended and Purvis escorted Martha back to the table, the company took up a romp, skirts bunched in hands, and boots beat a tattoo, couples changed partners, and some few abandoned the floor to the heat and sought the bar, or moved to the sidewalk in front of the hall and stood under the street lamps, their bodies steaming in the cold night air.

No cars moved about downtown. It seemed as if the entire county must have parked their rigs in the parking lot and down the long street. Businesses were shut, gas pumps locked. Down side streets, in well-lit homes, baby-sitters guarded sleeping children, an easy ten-buck night. Taylor's house was dark, and Chas Stubblefield walked up the back steps, tugged on the door. A small barking erupted at the side window. He waited but no lights came on. The dog chattered against the glass. Chas stepped next to the window, leaned his forehead against the glass. He could feel the heat of the house, and the small dog backed away. Chas pushed at the pane and the window eased upward. The dog crouched and whined.

"Hey, pooch," he said. "I should have brought you a treat, hmm?"

The dog, a small rag of an animal, whined, wagged its tail. Chas extended his hand and the animal sniffed it cautiously before twitching its tongue over the fingers. Chas snatched the neck, hauled it squealing over the sill by its scruff. The dog hung in his fingers, the whites bulging around the black of its eyes. He raised the dog to his face, sniffed. It smelled of canned food and shampoo.

He hung the slack-mouthed dog in front of his face. "Where's Daddy?" he asked. "Asleep?" He pounded against the side of the house with his free hand. "You in there, Taylor?" But all that came to him was the strangled breathing of the dog.

He shook his head. A fellow comes calling, nice and neighborly, and no one's home. Wouldn't you know it? "Even got cleaned up," he told the dog, then he lowered his arm so that the animal swung at his side. The night air was turning colder. Over the trees he saw the sky bit in half by a bank of clouds. Storm, he thought, and wished it so, believed he saw a flash of light, waited for the rumble. Seeing things. He felt light-headed, his body's hunger a distant distraction. Didn't remember when he'd last eaten. Days. A week? More? A fire would be nice. Kitchen curtains, carpets, furniture, drywall. His knuckles rapped down the clapboard side. He imagined squatting by the fire. He and the small dog. But Taylor wasn't home. Not him, not his wife. He raised the dog up and shook it. "I killed better dogs than you." And the dog seemed to agree, lolling from his bunched fist. He swung the animal back over the sill, closed the window behind it.

What had come to him these past days, in the silence of his fields and house, in the horse's complicated wasting away and his own gutted flesh, was a singular clarity of what and who he was—a man absolved of every last thing that held him bound to this earth or to the laws of man. And to God he neither spoke nor listened anymore.

He walked through the yard, turned down the street toward town, pausing now and again to peer into windows at hand-painted ceramic table lamps, walls with framed sunsets, the trophy elk or deer with their unconvincing glass eyes. He felt apart from this race who lived in tidy houses and bore children with sound teeth. He supposed he'd always been so, only now he knew it. He ticked the streets off on his fingers and kept an eye to the clouds stalled against the tide of stars. Working his way to the center of the town, he crossed the footbridge over Deer Creek where he stopped to listen to the water, heard music instead, and the sound of voices niggling through the air.

He followed it. He heard his own boot heels clapping off the brick storefronts as if they were another person's and looked over his shoulder to see who followed. Across from the Grange, he glanced in the bank windows, at his reflection—hair washed and combed, shirt and jeans cleaned for the occasion.

Beside him were parked cars, and across the reflected street, knots of men in red shirts and green, striped and checked. He breathed through his nose, watched as they talked or broke away to re-form new groups. When he turned to see them across the street, they looked nearer than in the glass. He stepped off the curb. He brushed past the men in front of the hall and he could tell they were grateful to be ignored. He stepped into the room and felt the wall of heat and noise roll over him like a weather front. Tables had been pushed back along the wall to enlarge the dance floor. When he walked in, it wasn't as if the seas parted, but he caused a ripple. A nodding of heads, a curt hello or two; more telling was the concerted effort not to acknowledge him. But how could they deny him? There came a crude lowing sound from a young teenage boy, and the call was taken up briefly by others in his circle until someone stepped in and silenced them. Chas walked heel to toe, between the tables. At the bar, Taylor froze mid-drink, but Chas looked through him and kept walking toward the dance floor. *Too big for his Goddamned britches* and *They shot the wrong one,* but he didn't pause to locate the speakers.

The dancers milled in a circle, colors all wrong in the blue and red light so that skin and clothes looked the same, and he could hear their breathing like the breath of a congregate animal. He stood at the edge and leaned on his toes, his grin loose and slipping on his face, and then someone was at his side, fingers on his sleeve, and he eased back on his heels and turned to her.

"Pattiann," he said.

"Chas?"

He bumped his head up and down. "Yes, yes," he said. He looked over his shoulder, didn't see the sheriff. "Come for my dance. Like the old days," he said. He tweaked a smile at her.

When Pattiann had first spotted Chas, she'd not recognized him. He looked hollowed out, like a child playing dress-up in clothes too large, or one of his own cattle lost in its skin. He moved like someone sleepwalking, his eyes moving back and forth. She touched the cuff of his shirt-sleeve, believing she could do this necessary thing, and it took a moment for his eyes to focus on her. "I haven't danced," he said. "All these years."

He turned to her, took her hand in his, and laid his other on her waist. He moved them out onto the floor. They stood there. "Am I doing all right?" he asked, and she nodded though they barely moved.

His hand was hot through her dress, and she thought he must be running a fever. "You been sick, Chas?"

"Sick?" he asked. "Yes." He shuffled to the side, his feet bumping hers.

The number of couples on the floor dwindled. Pattiann tried to ignore it, suggested they sit the dance out, and Chas nodded yes, but continued in the tight square he'd framed on the floor. "Nothing to it," he said. "One step in front of the other, just like I've moved my whole life." He stumbled and winced. "And sometimes," he said, "you step on someone's toes and that's nothing new either." He held her out in his arms. "Thought there was more." He stopped, looked around at the tables and the couples who had shuffled to a stop, and let go of her hands.

"They're staring," he said to Pattiann, giggled. "Must be I dance like shit. Must be I forgot to zip my fly," he said louder. There was a small commotion at the back of the room, and then a path opened and Ike was coming toward them.

Ike had been in the men's room, wiping a wet paper towel over the back of his neck trying to cool off, when Harley found him. He smiled into the mirror. There was a flaw in it, a black stain where the silver backing had corroded, leaving a thumb-sized hole in the reflection. Harley shifted.

"Hotter than Hades out there," Ike said.

"Getting hotter," Harley said. "Chas just come in."

Ike's hand stopped and water dripped over his collar. He tossed the paper towel in the wastebasket. "Trouble?"

"Hard to know, he's such a Goddamned spook. Might be drunk, wasn't walking real straight."

Ike tucked his shirt in. "What's he doing?"

"Dancing."

"No crime in that."

"With your wife."

Ike smoothed the hair down at his neck. "Not at gunpoint, I trust?" He patted Harley's shoulder. He saw the young man breathe easier and wished he could be as easily reassured. He just wanted the evening to go on as it had. A knot formed in his gut.

On the other side of the bathroom door, Taylor was waiting in a short queue that included Sam Coker and curious onlookers.

"That sonofabitch killed my dog," Coker was saying.

"Fuck your dog," Taylor said. "He junked my car." He turned to Ike. "You throw that sonofabitch out."

"Back off," he said.

"You don't tell me to fucking back off." Taylor leaned his face into Ike's. "I can break you, you sonofabitch—" He wagged a finger in Ike's face.

Ike snatched the finger, folded it back. "Get in line," he whispered. He dropped the hand, stepped past the group of men. An aisle opened to the dance floor where he saw Pattiann, her hair redder in the lights. She stood at arm's length in Chas's hands, staring at her feet. Ike strode up the opening, nodding to folks as he passed. Purvis appeared, and Ike urged him back with a firm hand to his elbow.

The back of Ike's neck felt sticky. The music never broke stride, and on stage the musicians watched even as they played. Chas had dropped Pattiann's hands. She looked tired, but brave, and he was alternately angry and proud of her.

Chas looked spit-polished. A slide guitar whined, drums gunned, and Ike thought it felt like the floor had turned slick. Chas sidestepped clear of Pattiann.

"How you doing, Chas?" Ike asked.

"Passable." Chas nodded his head slowly. "Passing queer, though, how this floor cleared soon as I got on it. Must know something we don't, Sheriff."

Ike tried to read the faces of the crowd. He knew the ranchers' feelings—the law had gone where none of them wanted to see it go, onto a man's property—but what Stubblefield had done was cruel. Worse, it was shoddy work, and they did not take that lightly. He had shamed them.

And there was fear, because it didn't take much—poor judgment, weather, accidents. He saw in those who refused to look at Chas a denial of that shameful possibility in themselves.

Ike wiped his forehead with a hand. "Hot in here." He looked over at Pattiann, jerked his head toward the hall's far end, then he turned away, cutting her off, focusing instead on Chas.

"Just dancing," Chas said, "and all of a sudden, *poof,* gone. Like so many cattle." He moved as if to follow Pattiann, but Ike's hand caught him gently by a cuff. He turned back to Ike. "I must carry the smell of pestilence," he said, and slapped his thigh. "You and me, Sheriff," he said. "Lepers. One of God's least amusing diseases. Weeping sores, bad breath."

He looked around him, then leaned into the sheriff's hearing. "But you got a temporary condition. Me? My fucking nose is falling off." He tweaked at his nose. He was suddenly steady on his feet and his words distinct.

Ike nudged at Chas's sleeve and he followed, across the floor. People shuffled aside. "You want something, Chas?" Ike asked.

Chas paused, considered. "A bell," he said. "Like they used to wear around their necks. Small ones for all the little lepers. A big one for you, me, and a fucking anchor for God."

Ike moved him on, through the hall, out the door, and into the cold night air. There was a sudden hush as the door shut behind them. "You drunk?"

"Haven't had a drop. Can't afford it. Pathetic, ain't it?" Chas nodded. "Nothing worse than a pathetic man. You know where my cattle are?" He stepped across the porch, settled a hand on the banister, leaned over the railing. The bank of clouds had closed in, low and black. The air smelled of moisture. "You know, some nights I see it—the trucks rolling across Montana, and Idaho, a convoy of meat high-balling to Spokane where they're chopped to meat and cooked down to feed somebody's dog. Think of it . . . my cattle—all of them, just yards on yards of little-dog shit." He reached over and squeezed Ike's arm.

"Christ, Chas, they were coyote food your way, what's the difference?" Ike asked.

"The difference," Chas said, "was this was all just so neat, wasn't it?" He clumped down off the porch. His feet wobbled in his boots. "You must feel clean when you go to bed. Your wife must like the smell of you." He danced off a few steps. "Nice music, huh?" He stopped, cocked his head to one side.

"You got something new to say to me?" Ike wanted to return to the warmth of the hall. Sweat was freezing in his armpits and down his back. His collar had frozen in a vise around his neck, but Chas was there, strung tight, contained for the moment; Ike couldn't release that inside. Not with his people in there. His wife.

"What's the difference, you say? Dead is dead, and my cattle are dead. So's my mama, and her husband. So's your deputy and tonight any number of people will die in their sleep, or while humping their wives or being humped. Fact is, we are populated by the dead and the about-to-be, so where's the difference?"

"Chas—"

"Parsons, you don't know *shit*." He squeezed his eyes shut. "The proceeds of your goodwill is just so much dung in Taylor's backyard." His eyes opened. He looked up at Ike on the steps. "Tell me, Sheriff. When you shot my cattle, did you look in their eyes first?"

"This is sick, Chas."

"No," Chas shouted. "Because if you had, you would know that the cattle, you, me, each fucking breathing thing is just so much meat for the Renderer and His big old meat hook in the sky.

"We are deceived," he added quietly.

"Deluded," Ike answered.

"That too," Chas agreed. "Fact is there's no real choice about it. We are handed our ends as blindly as we are handed our lives." Chas walked off a step, looked down the long street to where the blackness implied the vast sweep of land better than sunlight could. "I believe it's going to blow up a hell of a storm. One last stab at winter."

Under the streetlight, Chas was a man whittled to stick. He shook his head, looked up at Ike with a smile, and Ike was reminded of how after his father had sold the farm, he would come home from the factory, his body jangling with the noise of it all, and how he picked at his dinners, growing slight and slighter, his heart fodder for the machines, but still that same sweet smile had persisted. And Ike found he wanted to do something for Chas as he hadn't been able to do for his father, but Chas stood apart, under the solitary breach of light in the darkness as though he preferred it, or knew something beyond Ike's ability to know, even as Ike's father had seemed to before he died. And it came to Ike that Chas was as dead as his cattle.

Chas nodded, as if he'd read the sheriff's thoughts. His eyes were unblinking. "Still some final business left. Some loose ends," he said. "Paperwork, bills, forwarding address, things you can't imagine. But don't you worry, Sheriff, I'll have them cleaned up quick. Be gone in no time. Will you grieve to see me go, Sheriff?" He waited a beat. "I thought not."

Ike nodded. "I'm sorry, Chas," he said.

"Hell, yes," Chas agreed. "We are a sad and sorry lot, each last one of us."

Ike turned away and he heard Chas make a clicking noise with his tongue. "Hey, Sheriff," Chas said, and when Ike turned back around he saw Chas standing there, his finger pointed like a gun at Ike's head. "Bang," he said. He unfolded his hand, held it palm up. "Meat," he said. "Just that close to meat."

"That wouldn't be a threat?"

"No." Chas shook his head. "Just a friendly reminder."

Ike waited until Chas turned the corner. He stood on the porch debating whether or not he should follow or post someone to keep an eye on him. But then he thought of Chas under the light, how pathetic he had looked, and Ike knew what had become of the man was, in good part, Ike's own doing.

And Ike was a boy again, at the close of a summer's day, the light wan as a drawn-out sigh. His father was with him, outside the door of the milk house, sitting on upturned crates, scraping his boots. And Ike was a sixteen-year-old boy stuck in what he'd always known, while the world changed, the war ending in Vietnam, and his friends moved on to bigger lives somewhere out there. He was a young boy who felt caught in his father's life, trapped like the tic in his father's cheek.

And Ike made it his business to explain what it was his mother feared, dairy prices falling, the conglomerates pricing the family farms out of the market. His mother was the strong one, the levelheaded, the no-flights-of-fancy woman—sell the land to developers before the bottom drops, before the saturation of housing, none of them able to foresee there would *be* no saturation point, that family farms would continue to turn belly-up as the fields had once to the plows.

But logic and money talk never cut it with his father. "Don't you love us?" Ike asked instead. And that was the thing that still stung.

His father sat with his back against the stone walls, but his frame seemed to collapse on itself, and of course, he had agreed then, yes, he'd sell the farm. And Ike remembered how the nightjars kited through the great doors of the upper barn, and from within the lower barn with its damp fieldstone walls and its concrete catwalks and chain-scrubbed gutters, the cattle lowed in their stanchions, the sound rising like another moon that his father turned his face to, and that sound cutting of him a new silhouette as the moon does shadows, and what was it his father had said? *Was there ever a sweeter sound? Like the cry of angels.*

And Ike saw with an awful clarity that keeping the farm might be the ruin of them all, but losing it would be the ruin of his father, and how he could know this he could not say except that his father sat straighter, his bones knit tighter somehow in the wake of the cattle calling.

Ike looked up into the sky over the town, to the underbelly of a cloud dimly threatening. And now Chas. Purvis had seen it. That day Ike had driven with Purvis to see the animals and Purvis had suggested Ike turn his head the other way. Had there been another way around this all? Had he gone so far in service of the law that he'd overlooked a greater service underlying it?

The door opened behind him, and Pattiann stood there. "You all right?" she asked.

He looked down the street for Chas, but he was gone. Ike tugged at his shirt collar, stiffening in the cold.

Pattiann joined him. She gripped the railing. "I'm sorry," she said. "I didn't know what else to do."

Ike put his arm around her. She was shivering. He had the sudden urge to take her away from here, take her home where he could hold her for however long it took. Tell her how he had *seen* Chas in that brief moment under the streetlight. How he'd heard something in Chas's voice that had been so resonant that Ike had thought instead of his own father.

She was looking down at the porch floor, her brows drawn with worry. He smoothed the crease in her forehead with a thumb. "You did fine," he said. "You were kind." He pulled her to his chest and held her tight. "More than I can say for myself."

"Want to leave?" she asked.

He stroked her hair. Thought about the town people inside the hall. Waiting for his reassurance. He shook his head and gathered her elbow in his palm.

In the hall, Purvis tried to read Ike and Pattiann's faces. They'd reentered with arms about each other, smiling at the people who stood waiting as he did. Ike was putting off questions. Elsie Lager, a pert seventy-year-old who baked cakes for a hobby, said, "Shame on that boy," and wagged her head. Ike said he was eager to dance, and he was convincing enough so that Purvis thumped Harley on the back and offered to buy him a drink.

Harley countered, "I'll take that drink and raise you one."

They nursed their whiskey ditches at a table. Purvis watched Pattiann and Ike dancing. Times like this he thought of how it might have been for himself and Babs. Had they not married so young. If he'd known her now. Or if he found someone else. Times like this he almost believed he was not past having it yet.

Harley leaned into Purvis's arm, tugged on his sleeve. "Purvis, I'm in love," he said.

"Goddamn, this coat does wonders," Purvis said.

Harley slapped Purvis on the arm. "Not with you." He laughed. "You ain't got tit enough."

"A tit man? My father used to say, the only thing you could trust a tit man to know was where the milk came from. Not that he meant that disparagingly. He was a tit man too, my father. Admired the hell out of my mother's. But me, I prefer a good leg, I think. With a strong back and a weak mind."

"Purvis," Harley whined. "I'm trying to be *serious*. I'm thinking of popping *the question*."

"To whom?"

"Our dispatcher, Michelle Bonne Chance."

"Good luck."

Harley's brows beetled.

"Drink up, boy." He bumped Harley's elbow. "You owe me one."

"What if she says no?"

"You're not drunk, are you?" Purvis asked.

Harley shook his head.

"You've thought this over, deliberated soberly and judiciously?"

He nodded.

"Want to borrow my coat?"

Harley spit back some of the whiskey he'd sipped.

Purvis slapped him on the back. "You love this girl, you take her out on that dance floor in front of a hundred people, get on bended knee, and ask for her hand. Declare your undying love and undivided attention." He pulled Harley closer. "And then you live up to those words. Raise a passel of kids and send them to me for shots."

"My kids?"

"No, their pets. Every kid's got to have a pet." He hefted Harley to his feet. "Where is she?"

"Over there." Harley pointed vaguely.

"Well, go to it, boy. Go on."

They shook hands. Harley hitched his pants up and left. Purvis stayed long enough to watch the young man fumble his way to a table, speak into the ear of an honest-faced woman, then Purvis made his way to the door and out. He stood in the cold, wrapping his bright red coat tighter about him. It was, after all, a glorious night. He smiled to himself and crooned a few bars of "Oh Lonesome Me," before stepping down onto the sidewalk.

Chas retraced his steps to his truck. He rummaged about in the cab, grabbed a handful of oily rags. He hauled a can of gasoline from the back of the pickup. When he approached the house, the small dog yapped twice at the window, and when it saw who had come to call, jumped off the sill and retreated to its hidey hole under the stove. Chas tried the overhead garage door. Locked. He walked around back, wrapped his hand in the rags, and put a fist through the back door garage window. He let himself in, pressed his ear against the door connecting to the house, and smiled at the silence. "Good dog," he said.

He was still cold, though he no longer shivered. He sprinkled gasoline over rags and cardboard he found stacked in a corner. The small dog snuffled at the crack under the house door. Chas stepped back from the pile, struck a match, and dropped it. The *woof* of flames set him back on his heels and he snatched at the hair sizzling over his ears. "Oooee," he hooted, slapping at himself. "Damn near joined you, Mama." He crossed to the door, listened briefly to the fire's crackle before shutting the door and returning to his pickup. He pitched the empty can into a stand of brush, sniffed the gasoline on his hands, and started the engine. It would be satisfying to see the flames spread, better yet to have the luxury of waiting for Taylor to come home to a burning house. The twelve-gauge, side-by-side shotgun lay across the seat. He had a full night's work ahead, and damn, it felt good having something to occupy his time again. He drove slowly down the street. He would save the sheriff for later. Coker: that was the ticket. He watched Taylor's house dissolve into the dark of his rearview mirror, imagined the garage, the fire melting bike tires, gutting out the insulation, eating into the house. The little dog scrabbling at the window to get out. He hummed a tuneless song, and the wind gusted dirt at his lights. Overhead the stars had gone out, the cloudbank lowering with the temperature.

He didn't have far to walk, and the cold sobered him. Purvis shoved his hands into the sports-coat pockets, clenched and unclenched them. Down two blocks, past the mill and grain elevators, cut through the alley and across the cemetery to home. He'd fill the tub with hot water. He'd bundle up in his ratty bathrobe, light a fire in the woodstove, and contemplate his feet. He picked up to a jog but stopped when the cold made his lungs ache. Dirt lofted into the wind and he narrowed his eyes against it. The last dregs of winter. It would not be denied. Come spring rains, he would curse the gumbo mightily, but right now, by God, even that would seem like a blessing.

He laughed. His teeth chattered and he clamped them tighter. A red sports coat and yellow vest—always rains hardest on the peacock's tail. He was alone on the street, and he paused. He could turn around before he got any farther, warm himself with a woman's sweat on the dance floor and beg a ride home later. And then he saw someone over at Coker's mill, a pickup idling in the grain elevator yards. He ducked his head against the gritty wind. Maybe he could hitch. Though by then he realized the strangeness of it—a man on the loading docks, this time of night, everyone at the dance. Some fool kid, he thought, and Joe came to mind.

Purvis buttoned his coat over his belly and jogged down the street. He did not think what he would say or do. He tried to keep an eye on the man. The chill deepened. He was too old. Too nosy. His legs ached and his wind was short. By the time he got there, he'd be in no shape to do more than pant in the man's face. He slowed and recognized the pickup at the same moment the first flames erupted on the dock. "Stubblefield," he shouted, and the man turned.

It was the queerest thing. How the fire trickled a path across the dock. Not bright and leaping, but blue and low, as if tamped down by the cold, and then it reared upward with a *whoosh* into a stack mid-deck, and sent runners like a living thing, a branching tree, until there were four bright stacks lit against the walls and the walls themselves were fueling the fire. The wind huffed and the fires wavered and grew larger, and Stubblefield's figure rippled before them, as though the man himself had become part of the conflagration.

As Purvis ran toward the dock, the grain elevators bobbed up and down, a row of sedentary sentinels become animate, and he imagined he could already hear the suck of heat, the explosion from container to container taking out the homes around it. He could see Stubblefield in detail now—the curious smile on his face, *how nice to see you*—and the gun rising even as Purvis couldn't find it in his body to stop, as if he'd been lockstepped to this gravel lot from the first time he'd seen Stubblefield's cattle. In his coat, he looked like a stray flame in the dirt. He thought of the work he'd not gotten to. The work that never ended, cattle, calves, horses, the family dogs. He stopped short of the dock. He could feel the wave of heat and he withdrew his hands from his pockets and looked up at Stubblefield as if they shared a joke.

Stubblefield stood on the top step, his feet planted wide apart. A sportsman's stance. He tipped his head at an angle, sighted down the barrel. It should be Taylor, he thought, and for a moment willed it so, but the red coat kept tugging him back to the ridiculous vet, his country doctor ways. "Hot enough for you, Purvis?" he asked.

The wall of heat moved upward. There was a canopy of blue flames overhead. Chas took a step down, the gun barrel gravitating to the yellow vest. He flexed his shoulders and kept his attention on the spot pinpointed by the barrel, *like the finger of God,* he thought. And then there was a wail from the town's fire siren, long and protracted, while a wall behind Chas buckled, and the vet stood in the fire's light with his hands stretched out as if to warm them and the siren's wail raised higher, then fell, and rose again.

Purvis seemed relaxed and then he smiled at Chas with a dreaming look on his face, and Chas fired, and the body bent backward from the knees and toppled. The bright coat fanned open and the yellow vest turned black. Chas lowered the gun, jumped down from the last steps, and swayed on rubbery knees. He stood over the body. He lifted the hem of the jacket with the shotgun barrel, and wondered if Purvis had had some inkling when he put it on that he was dressing for his own funeral. Across the street, a young girl stood on the porch, outlined by the light of windows behind her. He waved her back into the house, and in the fire's parade of shadow and light, it looked like the porch she stood on was moving and she waving as if from a float. The siren halooed into the night, and soon people would be arriving. He felt the satisfying grab of heat, stack on stack of feed, straw bales, chemicals, and there was a small explosion behind him that lifted him to his toes and rocked him over Purvis's body, and standing on tiptoe, his arm wheeling for balance, hovering over the body, he saw Purvis's face and the eyes, empty as they were, shone in the firelight. He found he was trembling and he pivoted on his heels and fled across the parking lot to where his pickup idled. He threw the gun in on the seat and was pulling away before he'd closed his truck door. Down the block, he saw the first men running toward the fire. He turned his truck in a tight circle, headlights failing in the brighter glow of flames, and he had a quick glimpse of the red coat just before the truck bumped over the railroad spur and down a dark side street.

The dock fire spread quickly into the central building, warehouse, and retail shop. High winds rushed the flames across the roof, sparking down into the brushy lot, the tinder grass sizzling and popping. Children were the first on the scene. From across the way, the baby-sitter, who had called in the alarm, wrestled with a handful of her charges. She maneuvered herself between the children and the body. When the eldest boy at seven pulled free to look, she slapped his cheek, the sound lost in the popping fire. She hauled the startled boy back under her arms and moved them off the lot in a wedge about her body.

This was the sight that first greeted Ike: the building in flames, the children being herded back by a girl not much older than her charges. He helped the sitter move the children to safety across the street. She pointed to the gravel lot. "A man," she said. "In a old green Chevy pickup. He shot . . ." Her arm wavered. The fire trucks, hook and ladder were arriving, volunteers in party clothes, suiting up. The town hall siren had stopped but squads howled through the streets and trucks of volunteers squealed to the curbs. He looked where the young girl pointed, and from the corner of his eye, Ike saw the bit of color in the gravel. "Get the children out of here." He shook her gently, drawing her attention away from the gravel lot. "To the Grange Hall. You understand?"

She nodded.

"They'll help you out. Don't stop. Just get the kids there." She took a deep breath and straightened her back. She snagged the youngest boy by the back of his jeans and started moving off.

"An old green Chevy?" Ike shouted after her. She nodded. "Did the driver have dark hair?" he asked, and she shook her head. "Light," she shouted. "Blond hair," and then hustled the children down the street.

He covered the parking lot at a run, saw the scrap of red in the gravel, knew who and what it was before he approached. He felt for a pulse, found nothing. It had to have been a quick death. Parker arrived on Ike's heels, and Ike was grateful for the man's presence.

Ike released Purvis's hand. "We need to move the people out of these houses," he said. When there was no answer, he turned to Jim. "You hear me?" And then he realized that Parker had nodded but not spoken.

"I'll get on it," Parker said, but he remained staring. "Oh, Jesus," he said.

Ike squatted next to the body. "Get Harley, Turner, whoever else you can rustle up. We need a door-to-door. Evacuate them to the Grange, or

churches, friends, anywhere outside of this perimeter. If the grain elevators go—" He tried to estimate the proportion of a blast. "Make it three
square blocks."

Parker nodded. "Anything else?"

"We need to act on this fast. That's first priority. But keep an eye out
for Chas Stubblefield. Armed and dangerous."

Parker jogged across the lot to a waiting squad. He snatched Harley
on the way, waved Turner over, spoke a few words to each. They split up.

Teams of men beat at the grass with wet sacks in the back field. The
wind frisked across the lot and the stream of water from hoses turned at
a right angle. Ike studied the scene, tried to memorize it. Imagined the
gun aimed at Purvis's chest. Imagined Stubblefield aiming the gun.

Ike sat back on his heels. He'd cordon off the body, put out an all-
points, put his own men on it as soon as they'd evacuated the area, and
made sure the fire was controlled. The wind and cold would make it
tough. He needed photographs. When he looked up, Pattiann was
there.

He rose from his squat. He didn't touch her, but spoke into her ear,
his face buried in her blowing hair. "He's dead, Pattiann. There's nothing you can do here," he said. He put a hand under her elbow and
braced her arm. He could feel her shaking. "I want you to go with your
folks. Stay at their place, or Rob's. Are you listening?"

She nodded.

"I don't want you alone. Can you do that?"

She nodded again.

"You find someone to walk back to the hall with you, or I'll get you a
ride."

"No," she said. She stared at Purvis's body. "It was Chas, wasn't it?"

"I can't be sure," he said. "Seems likely."

"I could kill him," she said. Her voice cracked. "I could."

"Stop this. Go to Bill and Martha, now. Let me know you'll be okay,
so I can get on with my work. You understand? I can't do my job if I'm
worrying about you."

She pushed away.

"I don't have to lock you up for safekeeping?" He could see she was angry now, but relenting. He cupped her elbow tighter in his hand.

She nodded.

He turned away, called over a deputy, spoke to him, and as he met with the fire chief, he watched Pattiann make her way out of the lot, heading back toward the Grange.

She walked. Or at least her feet moved, one then the other. She was shaking. Maybe it was the cold that was settling deeper and deeper. Purvis was dead.

She crossed the street, stepping to the heartbeat in her ears. The town looked strange, glass and brick fronts rosy, the sky an outraged orange. She tasted wood ash. She could see the lit hall, the first of the children being led inside. "Puff the Magic Dragon" was being played, and she could hear children singing along, and she pictured it—the small faces pleased with the night's adventure. She stood on the stairway and tried to make sense of it. She looked over her shoulder at the bright corona in the night sky, and down at the blank windows and in the black glaze the tidy yellow squares of warm light reflected from the Grange. She felt remote. Culpable.

She couldn't imagine walking up those last two steps and going through the door, or talking to people. Telling her mother and father about Purvis. She could hear her father playing for the children, fiddling to keep them calm. Her own heart raced. She stepped away, down the street, angled across fenceless yards toward her house. They would need blankets, pillows, extra bedding at the hall. She jumped Deer Creek, slid, and soaked a foot. She'd change into jeans, boots, bring extra winter gear. She imagined tucking the children in, brewing coffee for the firefighters. She hoped the fire was contained, but found herself bracing for the blow that could come at any moment, the repercussive wave of hot air that would level her, make knives of every window.

She ran up the walk, opened the door, and locked it behind her. It was cool in the house. She turned the thermostat up and ran up the stairs, flipping on lights as she went. She gathered blankets, stripped the bed, and dumped the pile in the hall. She pulled on jeans, snugged a wool sweater over her head and arms. She pushed away the image of Purvis. She put on a down jacket and gathered the bedding in her arms.

It was good to have something to do. She wasn't ready for grief, wondered if she ever would be. Coming down the stairway she was surprised by the cold, wondered if the furnace pilot light had gone out. A newspaper fluttered on the sideboard at the base of the stairway. She hugged the bedding tighter. The back door was open.

And then she could smell the gunpowder. When she stepped off the riser facing the living room, he was there, in Ike's chair, waiting. The gun in his lap.

"Pattiann," he said.

"Chas," she answered. She dropped the bedding.

"I knocked," he said. "Knocked twice. Thought I might run into your husband before you."

"He's not here," Pattiann said.

He looked around, sniffed the air. He stood. "You disappointed in me, Pattiann?"

"Oh, Chas." She shook her head. She backed away, toward the kitchen, turned and ran. A chair fell behind her and there was the sound of heavy boots. She made it to the backyard before he caught her. He threw an arm around her neck, tackled her tight to him. He smelled of smoke and gasoline. "My truck's over there," he said, pointing with the gun in his free arm. She could see it parked on the dirt road off the corner of their lot. "You drive," he said, quirked a grin at her and lifted the gun higher. "I'll ride shotgun."

He directed her down back roads. He sat with his back braced against the passenger window, the gun angling up across his lap. He reached over, turned on the heat.

The fire's glow had lessened in the rearview, and she hoped it meant the worst was over. But there it was again—full blown in her head—Purvis dead. She was next. Her hands tightened on the wheel. What could she do? Wreck the truck? Wrestle the gun away? Shoot the sonofabitch? Was it in her to do such a thing? What was it she'd said? *I could kill him. I could.*

"Not a fit night," he said. "Damn." He slapped the dashboard and she jerked like a fish on a line. "Sorry about that, but I imagined this differently. Turn left, here." He nudged the gun toward her.

It was a gravel road, well off the highway. "Where are we going?" she asked.

He shrugged. "It's not like I planned this."

"And Purvis?"

"I didn't invite him to my bonfire. No. But it was fate, you know." He wagged his head. "God *will* stick His hand in where it don't belong. Best I could have hoped for, it would have been Coker, or Taylor." He paused. "Your husband maybe. Turn here again, right."

She slowed, did as he said. "This is all just getting worse, Chas. What are you going to gain by taking me?"

"Your sweet company, little girl. Like it used to be." He pushed his hair back, wiped sweat from his forehead though it was chilly in the cab. "Anyway, can't get much worse." He rested his elbow on the dash, his hand still snagged in his hair. "Killed a man . . . if only your husband had minded his own business."

"You *made* it his business. Goddamn it, Chas, Ike didn't make you kill Purvis. Ike didn't even kill your cattle–you did. You starved them until they were dropping dead in your fields."

"Well, he said that very same thing this evening, and all those fine, fine people in the hall straining to hear." Chas shook his head, clucked his tongue. "I know what they think of me," he whispered. He eased back, opened his jacket, tugged on the shirt at his neck, until the top button jettisoned, lightly banging off the windshield and falling into the dark at his feet. He settled the gun butt on the floor, his hand on the barrel, and the barrel alongside his cheek. He pointed to the next turn, and said, "What I do not know is what *you* think."

"I think you murdered Purvis."

He waved that away. "It wasn't as if I meant to." He looked out the side window, then back at Pattiann. "He was just there. Come out of nowhere, dressed like a clown. I warned him, I said, 'Is it hot enough for you, Purvis?' but he just stood there, warming his hands by my fire. Now don't you think that's a sorry-ass thing to do?"

"He didn't believe you'd shoot him."

"Oh, he *knew*. If you'd have seen his face . . . he was already dreaming of the other side, his smile kind as Christ's own, for all the good it did either of them." He leaned his head back against the glass, looked down on Pattiann.

The wind tugged at the car. She thought she saw a flash across the road, and then a few drops spattered the windshield with a slushy mix of ice and water and she heard the delayed rumble. If things could get worse, she thought. Freezing rain. A sleet storm. "It's going to get bad," she said.

"Pattiann," he said. "It's bad already. Don't you know that? Don't you know it's been bad forever?"

Pattiann took a firmer grip on the steering wheel, settled her left foot against the floorboard. She felt the rear end break loose, grab, and then she floored it. Chas was thrown back into the seat, and she grabbed the gun barrel with one hand and jammed it up toward the cab ceiling.

Chas reached across with his free hand, caught her by the collar. The truck wrenched to a side. "Brake," he yelled. He squeezed down on her neck; her hand on the gun was rammed tight against the dash. She kept her foot down. The tires gripped and slid, and then his leg was wedged between hers, his foot punching down on the brake pedal, and the engine screamed while the brakes locked, and the truck was skidding sideways toward the ditch. She hauled on the wheel and straightened it out, her foot lifting off the gas.

The truck slid to a side and swung two full circles before it jounced to a stop. He was still pressing down on her neck. The cab grew dark, darker. She could hear Chas at a distance but could not see him. She let go of the gun and wheel to pry at his hands. And then her head was rocking back, bounced against the side window. She heard the slap after the fact.

When she could see again, his face was close. "I've never given you reason to do this," she said.

"As if I needed one."

"I won't make it easy."

"Woman." He swung his head side to side. "There *is* nothing easier. All that keeps you suspended in the here and now is this thin skin of yours." He put his hand on her left breast, held tighter when she pulled back. "And this heartbeat."

He let go of her breast. He pushed back in his seat, lifted the shotgun into his lap. "It is *easier* to kill than you can imagine."

"Chas, you have no reason—"

"Reason? We put too much Goddamned almighty trust in reason. Why . . . why reason's just a justified whim, like lending money or not, shooting cattle or men. It's the *desire* that counts. There ain't a reason to keep on breathing day to day but that we desire to. And you don't need any more reason to kill than that you want to. Purvis knew that." He swung the gun barrel toward the road. "Now why don't you just drive on?"

The warehouse was gutted and a column of white steam bloomed over black boards. They plied water over the buildings and grasses, and sleet joined the barrage until fantastic ice shapes grew in the dark, stalactites and pillars and in the core of some the coals ebbed and glowed like small hearts beating. The men turned hoary with ice, gloved hands fused to firehoses, and others used their fists to break them free. They labored in shifts of quarter- and half-hours, de-icing gear, warming themselves with cups of hot coffee delivered from the Grange Hall. They bided their time at the fire and it would raise itself from time to time, flame jutting from a blown window or door, so that any number of false tongues wagged in reflection on slags of glass and ice.

Ike stayed until Purvis's body was removed and the homes surrounding the elevator had been evacuated. He regrouped his deputies in the hall's back office. Outside, the sleet kept falling—they could hear it on the boards and window. The highways and roads shone as if lacquered and Chas wouldn't get very far. Nor, of course, would they. He'd called in a vehicle description to the Highway Patrol, but they'd yet to report seeing it, and it was unlikely they would. Chas would keep to the little-traveled county roads.

In the room, chairs were banged open and scraped across the floor. There was a restlessness that transmitted itself through a hum of small movements. Men tugged at coats and raked fingers through their hair. The buzz was that Stubblefield had tried to burn Taylor's house as well, but Taylor had a sprinkler system in his home installed just last week. He'd come home to find a charred circle in the flooded garage interior.

Ike closed the door, shutting out the noise of children and a three-piece lullaby. Until the roads improved, they would keep the search down in numbers. Harley, Parker, and Ike. Work the back roads to Stubblefield's place. "If he goes to ground, it'll be there. Better chances are we'll find him spun off in a ditch. No heroics." Ike eyed Harley. "You spot him, call for backup. Just keep him in sight, that's all. Take foul-weather gear, blankets, a thermos of hot fluids. If you get stuck, it'll be a long night. Radio in and stay put." He ordered a rotation on dispatch and deputies ready to respond.

After he dismissed them, it didn't take long to discover that neither Bill nor Martha had seen Pattiann. Ike would not let himself be nervous, but he gathered his gear, made a radio check with the other units, and turned toward home. He kept his speed down, the Bronco holding a stable path on the streets. It would be slow going, torturous, and he could not imagine Chas's old pickup making any great distance. Tree limbs and powerlines already sagged under the ice. On the outskirts of town and nearing his home, it was quiet, no movement but for the downward sluicing of sleet. Ice filled the windshield well, the wipers skidding over the jelling mass. He pulled into the driveway and saw, with relief, the houselights were on.

He stopped just inside the front door, felt the cold. He believed he could smell smoke and gasoline and he hoped it was his own clothing, but knew it wasn't. He found the pile of bedding on the floor by the stairway, cut through the kitchen at a clip, and out the opened back door. He called her name. He stood in the yard, trying to see out to the street where Chas's truck might have parked, where he hoped it was still. When he turned back toward the house, the grass shattered under his feet.

He called it in to the dispatcher, to Harley and Parker. "He's got my wife," he said. And silence answered and then a muffled cursing from Harley, and a seasoned reassurance from Parker, and then Ike was inching his way out onto the roads, the house and town falling behind him.

"You just keep driving straight, unless I tell you. But you're doing real good." They'd been driving awhile now, though it was hard for Chas to say how long, everything seeming to be quick and slow at the same time with the ice crusting the side windows so that the world was a dark ripple and what was left them was the narrow beam of headlights, sleet falling into it as if the dark had quills. How could a body tell time in this elastic night, when all of Chas's life seemed a drop in that larger moment when he'd fingered the trigger and Purvis had dropped dead? He closed his eyes and played the moment out as he knew he would, again and again, for whatever time was left him—Purvis smiling and falling. Falling. Then there came a flash across his eyelids and a boom that startled Chas back to the here and now, but it was only lightning, and there was another fork of light and a lesser concussion and in the brief flash it seemed the land had turned to glass.

He looked over at Pattiann. She was focused on the road. Her eyes looked hollow in the dashboard's light, her lips a thin line. Her cheeks were dry. "You know what I find really strange?" he asked. "I don't think I've ever seen you cry. Not ever. Not back when we were together. Not now with your best friend dead . . . and you next, for all you know."

He smiled. "Not that I don't admire that," he said. "But strange, don't you think? You being a woman and all." He nudged her arm with a finger. "Don't pray either, do you?"

"What do you want me to say, Chas?"

"The truth."

"The truth," she said, her voice breaking, "is with the roads like this if you don't kill me, *I'll* probably kill us both."

"Hah!" he shouted. Lightning coursed across the sky and Chas slapped his thigh on the heels of the thunder. "That was a good one. Well, and I'd take over driving, but then you'd have to hold the gun." He grinned.

"Chas, if you cared for me at all—"

"If I did . . ." He looked out the side window, pressed his forehead against the glass so that the cold burned a path through his head. "Why," he said, straightening up with a smile, "I'd probably want you here with me. Right up to the end." And then his smile disappeared and he snatched the gun up, the barrel swiveling to her hairline. He pressed the bore against her temple. The truck hitched and slowed, and coasted to a crawl. The black night sealed them in, a shell forming around the doors and over the roof and hood, the antenna sheathed in ice, and they were pocketed in the green glow of dashlight while the wipers scratched at the windshield with a sound like a small animal at the back door. The gun bore eased up. "Just like a kiss, ain't it?" He slid it away.

"Keep driving," he said. "Did I tell you to slow?" And the truck eased forward. The cab silent except for the sound of slush in the wheel well, the hard pelting of sleet on the roof.

He lowered the gunstock to the floor again, his hand gripping the barrel like a divining rod. "I never asked for this, for any of this. The bankers, with all their money—*just take it,* they said—*this country's on the rise. Let us help you,* they said. Until I really needed their help. Until the drought settled in and the market bottomed out. Until I had more range than hands, and then more cattle than range, and there wasn't a soul I could turn to, not them, not God." He turned to her. "Not even you."

He was silent a long while and then Pattiann answered, "Purvis was right. You are a self-pitying sonofabitch."

He looked over at her, his eyes widened. "He say that?" He laughed softly. "Shit. I should have killed him twice."

She didn't have time to answer. There was a shape in the road, rushing out of the dark, large, square, and black, and she slammed on the brakes and as slow as they were traveling the truck swung in a pirouette once and then again, and they were sliding sideways past the cow and she could see its startled eyes, its head swinging to watch them pass, and then its kick before it bolted across the road and she thought she could see other cattle gathered in the field on the side of the road as the headlights circumscribed a wide circle and then the truck was canting sideways into a ditch and the front bumper slammed against the embankment, the wheels coming to a stop, and she was recoiling into her seat, feeling the punch of steering wheel to her breastbone. They rocked to a stop.

"Whooee," Chas said, and let go the dashboard. He leaned his head against the back window. He ran a hand over his face and neck, checked it for blood. "You think that was a real cow, or one of my own come back to haunt me?"

The headlights were a hot glare in the ditch. The truck had stalled and the last of the exhaust smoked over the light and vanished. "Start it up," he said.

The truck started. The wheels spun. She tried reverse. "Try rocking it," he said. The tires spun.

"You stay put," he said, and pulled on the door handle. The door was frozen shut. He hefted the gun out of the way, hunched his shoulder, and drove it into the door. There was a cracking sound as the ice shattered, and he was spilling out into the air.

He settled the gun in the bed and skated to the front wheels, holding on to the truck for balance. She could hear him pounding on the hubs, breaking the ice to lock them. She tried her own door. Frozen. Her chest throbbed. Chas was crossing in front of the headlights. He looked tidy, composed even, with the sleet beating on his face, his hair clinging to his scalp. He looked up at her through the windshield and bared his teeth in a grin. He mouthed something and then he was bending to the last hub. She heard it click in place. She threw the truck into compound gear and revved it forward, threw it into reverse, grinding the gear, back in compound, and Chas was beating his fist against her side of the door. She yanked on the wheel, eased off the gas, then down again, and the truck reared and she believed she would break free, but it was only shunting to a side, settling deeper in the ditch, and Chas was scrabbling over the ice on all fours, and then the truck tilted and held.

Chas picked up the gun on his way back. He opened his door and hauled himself into the cab, slammed it shut.

"We're stuck," he said. "We'll just have to wait."

She wondered for what, or whom, and she hoped for and against it being Ike. She began to appreciate how the storm had kept her attention elsewhere, her hands and mind occupied. Now she had time and more time, as much as Chas would allow, and the cab felt smaller for it so that she found her hands fussing at her coat and the seat belt. She fixed them on the wheel, ten and two, and waited.

Chas wrung water from his hair. Small clumps of ice dropped to his lap. "Cozy, huh?" he said, and looked around him as if the truck had changed in the short time he was outside.

Pattiann focused on her hands. "Why don't you let me go?" And then she looked out the windshield at the iced fences and grass.

He shook his head. "Boot you out into a storm like this? Damn. You wouldn't last an hour." He rubbed his hand down his pant leg. "It's been a rotten winter. Shit. It's been a craphouse life. Can you tell me what the attraction is? I mean, what keeps us living—besides being too scared to die?"

She lifted a hand from the wheel, ran it through her hair. She looked at him, and he was staring back. "Is there a point in my answering, Chas? Will it make you put the gun down? Turn yourself in?"

Their breath fogged the windows, and Chas wiped a clear circle, palm squeaking on the glass. "Never can tell," he said. "Can't hurt now, can it?"

A minute lapsed. Another. He clucked his tongue. "What is it about you, you got to make everything so difficult?" he asked.

She turned away, rubbed a clear circle on her side of the window, pressed her forehead against it.

246

"Maybe you can't help yourself? Maybe it's just in your nature to be obstinate. Some people are—like my father. Too stubborn to die. God damn. I thought he'd live forever." He laughed and it trailed off with a sigh. "My mother must have thought the same. For her, I think it just got to be more work to live."

Chas fell silent. He cranked down the side window, and as the glass eased into the door panel it left a pane of ice in its place. He rapped on the membrane. He pressed his face near, broke off a piece, and slid it into his mouth. He rolled the window back up. He sucked on the chunk of ice awhile and then said, "I never saw her cry either. Like you. A woman of few words . . . but a lot of prayer. She prayed for a sign, anything to let her know that He was still top dog. She made me pray along sometimes, but my heart wasn't in it. And to tell the truth, God wasn't speaking those days. Unless you count her hanging herself." He sighed again. "Aah, shit. She deserved better than that."

"And Purvis?" Pattiann asked. "Didn't he deserve better?"

His eyes were closed and his hand was gripping a knee. He shook his head. "God damn, but he looked the fool." When he opened his eyes again, he stared ahead at the windshield closing with ice. "Killing's easy. Doesn't take much. Point and squeeze." He rubbed his knee. "It's damn shabby, this body. Takes so little . . . effort. You know what you see when you look in the eyes of the dying?" He leaned closer to her. "I could *kill* you," he said. "And that terrifies you, doesn't it?"

She gripped the steering wheel. "Is that what you want? You want to frighten me, Chas? You want to see me cry?" She shook her head. She *was* scared. Terrified. But this was different from what she'd have expected—no rush of adrenaline, that first energy having deserted her now when she most needed it. Rather her arms felt weighted, her heart a brick in a chest too narrow to fill properly with air. Her mouth was dry. She wished she had the energy to break open the window as he had done. To suck on a sliver of ice until it melted, as if she were a child again, idling away thirst on a summer day. She became aware of how her hands cramped around the wheel, and she was amazed that he did not see, even in the dark of the cab, how her wedding band glowed against the unnatural white of her finger. "I don't . . ." she said. "There isn't . . ." she said. It pained her to realize how much time she'd spent, idling over the past, consumed with it, reinventing old grudges, distancing herself from family, from her husband. She thought of Ike, and longed for his gracious calm, the single steadiest, most precious gift he could have offered her, that quiet biding that *risks* everything, that offers itself with open hands and *demands* nothing. She looked over at that other ring of metal, the bore of the gun with its dimmer gleaming, Chas's hand white against the gunstock. Chas had been headed this way a long while, she realized. Only he'd never found his way out of it; he'd never found, as she had, another person who could turn the pain aside long enough for him to heal. No. He hadn't brought her here out of love, or regret, or even revenge.

She knew what it was he wanted, and she realized how alone he was, how utterly, devastatingly alone. "Chas, don't do this," she said. "Don't take me with you." And she saw how accurately she'd read him by the way he studied her face.

"Tell me why I shouldn't?"

"Because you don't have to," she said. "Because it's equally in your power not to do this." She took a deep breath. "Because," she removed her hands from the wheel, folded them in her lap, "I'm happy with my life." She waited a moment, then turned to see how he'd reacted. His cheek was resting against the gun barrel, his eyes staring out the side where he'd punched the hole in the ice, and that space already closed in with a new skin, a lighter wrinkling against the dark like an old scar. He rubbed his cheek up, then down the barrel, and it seemed to her that he was nodding to some voice she didn't hear and she heard his breath catch and realized how thoroughly cocooned they'd become in the ice, how the fierce wind and sleet drove soundless over the glassy surface.

When he finally stirred it was to throw his shoulder against the door, and the sudden noise and action startled Pattiann back against her own. And then he was lifting the handle, throwing his weight against the seal again, and the door opened. Sleet drove in the crack. "You stay dry," he said, a smile as if he'd told a joke on himself.

248

It took her a moment to react and one of his legs was already out the door. "Where are you going?" She reached across the seat, her hand stopping short of his.

He looked at her, at her hand. The sleet drove in with the wind so that she lost her breath, drenched in the chill. He shook his head. Shut the door behind him.

She watched him, gun over his shoulder, stumble up out of the ditch and into the field. She forced her window down and a sheet of sleet toppled into her lap. "Chas," she called, but the wind snatched her voice. She called again. She could not see. Icy water ran down her hair, her face. She swiped at her eyes with drenched hands and then raised the window against the cold and wet. She sat in the truck. She had a half tank of gas. She was shaking, as if all the cold and terror had just now taken hold, and her fingers fumbled at the ignition. She prayed the engine would catch, and when it did, she turned the heater on. She stared into the dark. There was nothing to be seen of Chas. Just the falling ice, the glazed fields.

It was Ike's old nightmare—every crossroad a decision and any one wrong decision carrying him farther away. He closed his eyes, breathed deeply, trying to lay out the land like a grid and imagine the turnings a madman might direct toward home. The other units called in with no news, and each time the radio stammered back into silence, Ike's heart stilled with it. Ike loosened his jacket. The ice and dark diffused the headlights and the sleet kept coming and he had to make another choice on which fork to take, and chances were that it would be the wrong one, that he would miss them, aiming parallel to them, or maybe the pickup had already stopped, or wrecked. He turned right.

He blamed himself for getting involved. The cattle were as good as dead before he'd gotten in the middle of it. What had he gained putting them down? "A mercy," Purvis had called it. And now Purvis was dead. And Pattiann? He concentrated on the road, invoking a discipline as old as setting one foot in front of the other.

When he first saw the truck in the distance, brake lights red in the ditch, he'd turned off his own headlights. He feathered the brakes, the Bronco's chains skittering, but the vehicle stopped several hundred feet short of the pickup. He'd work his way along the high end, well away from the truck lights, and hope to get a better view of the occupants. He prepared quickly: extra ammunition, gun loaded, safety on.

It was slow going, half crawling and sliding, and yes, it was Stubblefield's rig, and he couldn't make out anybody in the cab with the windows iced, but exhaust billowed. He eased his way toward the back of the truck, down the ditch on the driver's rear side, sliding hard, the shotgun punching into his ribs so that he lost his breath, and then he was on his hands and knees and the brake lights flashed again and the engine cut. He sat, collecting the calm he'd need. He kept his head low against the truck bed until he could see into the rear window. It looked to be one person. He thought he could make out Pattiann in the driver's seat. He eased up to the cleared side window, saw she was alone.

He rapped gently, and she startled, spread her hands on the glass as if to touch his face. Then she called through the ice and glass. "The door's frozen tight," she said. She pointed to the passenger's seat. "The other side . . ."

He slid around the front of the truck, eased himself into the seat next to her. He held her briefly, touched her wet cheeks. When he was convinced she was safe and well, he asked, "Where's Chas?"

"Gone," she said, pointed into the dark. "Out there. Somewhere."

Her hand snatched at his and he squeezed it gently. "You all right?" he asked.

She nodded. Her breath was a gulping and he knew she was close to hypothermia, shock, or both. He led her out, back to the Bronco where he pulled out the emergency blankets, dried her face and hair, wrapped her in their warmth. He studied the color of her skin, listened for her breathing to come back to normal. He wanted nothing more than to hold her. He cupped her face in his hands, pressed his forehead against hers, kissed her eyebrow. "You all right?" he asked again.

"Yes," she said, though her voice was small. So unlike her. She was trembling.

"How long's he been gone?" he asked.

She shook her head. She was crying. "Not sure." Her teeth still chattered and he snugged the blankets around her. "Maybe twenty minutes."

He reached into his pocket, pulled out keys and handed them to her. "There are more blankets, a thermos of coffee, some emergency supplies. A dry parka." He called dispatch, for backup, and then he pulled on a dry down-filled parka. He tucked two road flares into the inside pocket.

"You're not going?" She set down the thermos of coffee.

"Stubblefield's out there."

"Then wait for backup."

"That could be hours."

She shook her head. "No. Listen. You don't have to . . ." She wiped at her eyes, looked at her hands as if surprised to find tears, and he realized she'd been crying without knowing it.

He put his hand on the door handle.

She grabbed his free arm. "Goddamn it, Ike, he's still got the gun. He's half out of his head and wandering around. Don't you know, he's as good as dead out there?"

"Not if I find him first."

"Why? What do you gain? Revenge? Is that it? Because of me? Because of Purvis?"

"It's my job."

"Fuck your job." Her hand tightened on his wrist. "I'm sorry. I didn't mean that. But sometimes what's right and what's the law isn't the same."

Ike shook his head. "I can't just ignore what he's done, Pattiann." Ike flipped the hood up over his head. He grabbed the door handle.

Pattiann clasped his free hand. "He could have killed me, but he didn't. That should count for something." She squeezed his fingers. "Let the range take him. It would be a mercy, really. I'm not just pleading his side anymore. You don't know what it's like out there." She held tighter to his hand. "You go out there, it's not Chas you'll have to worry about. Chances are you'll never even find him. You'll wander around out there, get lost, die for nothing." She let go of his hand. "God damn it, what makes you so bullheaded?"

Ike smiled. He leaned over, buttoned her jacket closed at the neck. "A man less bullheaded wouldn't last around you." He fingered her cheek. "You know I *have* to do this."

She turned away to look out the side window. The door handle on his side clicked and the wind drove in.

"Ike," she called.

He leaned into the car one last time.

"The animals that survive keep moving. They outwalk the storm, keep the wind at their backs. Chas knows that."

Ike nodded, stepped back.

"I'll be here," she said. "Right here."

Chas slid and walked, and clods of ice built around his feet. He lowered himself between barbed strands in fences, his clothes cracking as he bent, spears of ice falling. He wished it was a clear, cold night. It would be nice to have the moon or a star to guide him.

But then, he was going no place in particular. He walked and walked until he couldn't feel his feet, nor most of his legs or his hands. When he tried to blink, found he couldn't. He'd walked for hours, he thought. Or minutes. It was that old shell game of time.

When he opened his mouth, he felt the ice crack across his cheek and jaws. He laughed, and it came out a muffled *mumph, mumph*. He kept the wind at his back. Like cattle, he thought, always moving ahead of the storm until they came to a fence and stopped. He was thirsty and he lifted a hand to his mouth and sucked at the crust that rimed his fingers.

"You here?" he asked, and listened to the wind, and then realized it was not the wind he heard through plugged ears but the booming of his own blood. He tried to nod, but his neck would not bend. Quite a night. He paused, looked around as if to get his bearings. Yes. Quite a night. Pulled out all the stops—killed a man. He laughed. That red coat, so absurdly bright—like a joke at a funeral.

He stumbled, slid to his knees, and thought his legs would snap. He teetered back on his haunches. He brushed at the ice that balled from his brows and hair, looked up. Not a damned star up there. "Couldn't give me that, I suppose?"

In the air around him there were creaks and groans and snappings, as the ice settled, layer over layer, and tiny fractures bloomed below and the crowned heads of sage shattered with weight and the wind skittered the tinkling shards across the glassy surface. He sat until his knees grew into painful knots. In the morning, he thought, he would see the sun rise through eyes frozen wide. He made a lowing sound deep in his throat. He felt the corners of his eyes sealing and could not tell if it was sleet or tears.

He believed he was warm, though he understood it was the numbness, and so he pushed himself back up to his feet. Moved on.

He still carried the gun, barrel pointed down, though almost certainly by now sealed tight over the chambers and the shot tucked within. He could have cast it away, but he did not. He kept it now simply because it had become a part of him—his hand fused to the stock.

The world was growing dimmer through the ice, and he closed his eyes, imagined it as he best loved it—the light coming over the fields. He was a boy again, flat on his back in the greening land, chewing the sweet stems of grama grass. Then he was a young man, and Pattiann was there with him, plucking wheat chaff from his hair, in the bed of straw where they'd just made love. And then he was a child, in his mother's arms, inhaling the earthiness of her skin, her hair. It smelled of iron and salt and a sticky sweetness like blood, and he saw Purvis, his eyes fixed and shining.

Chas discovered he'd stopped. "I'm cold," he said. "Tired."

Sleep.

"No," he said. There was something more. Some thing not done. He pushed himself. He thought of home. And when he looked up again, he saw that he was not alone.

Ike followed the iced track that led away from the truck. It was hard to see in the dim flashlight beam and driving sleet, and the tracks were filling in, glossing over. In another hour, maybe less, they would be gone. He looked up, to the far horizon, where he thought he could see a break in the storm, the glittering edge of stars. But it might have been wishful thinking and he trudged on, sliding and skating, his back wrenching with a missed step. He drew the parka's snorkel tight around his face. Kept his revolver pocketed and dry, the shotgun barrel pointed down and a canvas draped over the mechanism. He was warm and better prepared than Chas, though turning into the wind, that didn't make him feel any more assured. He stopped, looked back over his own tracks breaking through the ice, and somewhere, already out of sight, was the Bronco and Pattiann. What was it she had said? *Let the range take him.* Ike looked out over the level land. A dispassionate place. It just *was*. It gave you all the rope you could ever hope for with a vast, incomprehensible indifference. Ike skated his feet forward—the way he'd learned to walk the icy lakes back home as a kid—shuffle, shuffle, slide.

He remembered the ice storms of his childhood, every few years they would get hit with sleet, maybe once in a decade it would be as severe as this one was. Noise. That was what he remembered most vividly—the bang and concussion of maples exploding from the inside, the skreel of shredding limbs, or when the winds hit, the overhead shattering like wreckage in a glass shop. But here, it was so quiet—the small muttering of ice, the crunch of his feet breaking through.

He was scared. He could admit that. But he could not let that turn him aside. Why not? Revenge? And he believed he could honestly say, no. Though when Pattiann had asked, he'd doubted himself. His friend dead in the gravel. And his fear for Pattiann? So, wasn't at least a small part of

254

this pursuit inspired by something less than noble? He felt a cramp begin-ning in his fingers and switched the gun over to his other hand, flexed a fist, relaxed, flexed. He had a right to anger. He tried to see farther into the gloom, imagined Chas out there, trudging a path ahead of him.

But he had his duty as well. He was a man of the law. It was what he knew—as his father had known cattle. As Pattiann knew this land. The law. And wasn't part of the law justice, retribution? Punishment.

Jesus Christ. He could hardly stand to listen to himself.

He'd walked for a long while, or so it seemed to him, though when he checked his watch it had only been a little over a half-hour. Still he could see the storm was moving, the sky clearing, the faint points of stars swimming in the waning sleet, and at the skirt of clouds a brighter smudge where the moon must be. He cleared the ice from the flashlight lens, tracked the light's beam over the faint trail, though of course, he realized, it could very well not be Chas's at all. But perhaps a game trail. Or had he doubled back on his own? He could not afford to think about that. Instead, he opened the snorkel on his parka, took several deep breaths, and knocked off the clots of ice that dangled from the rim of the hood. He ran a check over his body, flexed his fingers. His hamstrings ached and the calves of his legs felt stretched, but all in all he was in pretty good shape. No lightheadedness, no dizziness. No major numb-ness, though his feet felt, he thought . . . distant.

Certainly no worse than Chas must be feeling. Assuming Chas was still on his feet, that he hadn't found someplace to hole up—a shed, a line shack, or old homestead.

He struck out again and for the next ten minutes he covered a fair amount of ground, believed the track looked fresher, as if he were gain-ing on who or what it was that walked ahead. And why not. Starved. That's how Chas had looked—hair slicked back, cheeks sunken, pants leashed tight. Hardly up to a trek like this. And then Ike's feet slid from under him and he landed hard on his hip and back, the air woofing out, the gun breaking free of his stiff fingers and clattering across the ice until it rucked up against a rock. It took a moment before he could start breathing again, and as he curled up onto his elbow he felt the bloom of pain at the back of his head and down his spine where it had hit. He rested a long minute, letting his vision clear, the pain ebb, and his breathing resume to normal. He checked his limbs, only now becoming aware of how close it was—a concussion, a broken bone—how deadly. He raised himself to a kneeling position and closed his eyes, waiting until the nausea subsided. And when he opened them it was to a world transformed, the moon sailing clear of the clouds, laying a roadway of light on the ice. And to the right of him the sleet was a storm of moonlight, silvered streamers pulling back in a curtain over the blackness. And maybe it was the hurt, the tailspin of emotions, or the brightness of the glazed fields with their faceted heads of sage and rocks, the spired bluestem and fused tumbleweed—a cathedral of light—so that he pinched his eyes against the sudden tears and a deeper confusion seated itself like a pain in his chest: loss, love, anger. And he felt the tingling in his legs, the ache in his hip, the nerveless absence of his toes. He plucked ice from his brows and rubbed his cheeks until they burned. What was it he'd come out here for, really? The end of a long ugly business? Justice? Not for Purvis— long past caring—nor for Pattiann—*Let the range take him*. For his own sake, then? For that thing done to him, back when Ike saw Chas's face transformed by a too familiar despair, and took pity.

And taking pity, turned him loose.

When he looked again, to the left he could see the triple strands of barb, sagging from pole to glittering pole stretching out and down into the shallow swale ahead where shadows inked against the indigo light, and he thought he could see a cluster of blacker shapes, up against the fence line, and listening he heard a dull thud and still another. He retrieved his gun and eased forward, until he could see the crisscrossing fences, and he could make out a half-dozen cattle stalled in the corner. And moving among them, he saw the smaller form of a man. His pale hair iced with light.

Confounded by the storm at their backs and the barbed wire in front, the cattle had stopped in a loose group. Chas moved among them as if he were caught in some recurring dream, back and forth he moved, between one cow and another. His first impulse had been to warm himself against their bulk, but they were sheathed in casings of ice like the carapace of outlandish beetles, their legs and hooves locked in place, their noses fused to the ground. A huffing steam rose through blowholes, like small thermal pools of warm breath. Their eyes were sealed. He used his fist on a cow, but it had no effect, and he could not feel his hand and so did not know how hard or soft his blows were. He tired and leaned over the back of a cow as if it were a bartop, his elbow skidding out from under him, so that finally he laid his cheek directly on the iced back where he could see air bubbles trapped among the hairs. When he felt strong enough he lifted away from the cow, and his clothes stuck, gave with a tearing sound. He patted himself as if expecting to find his skin exposed and then looked at his other hand, frozen to the gun. No pain. And for that matter, he realized he'd been relieved of his body in general, his feet, legs, thighs. His trunk just a dull presence. He punched the gunstock into the ice next to the cow's head, chipped away at it, the icy sheath shattering from the gun's mechanism, his own hand bleeding from the blows. He felt nothing, so he kept at it. He moved around the cow, moved on to another, and another, then back to the first. They were well sealed, and it didn't take much to exhaust him. He slid down next to the cow's head, rapped on the sealed eyelid, thought he saw the ear twitch beneath the ice.

"Now you're done for," he said. He pressed his cheek against the cow's. "But I don't blame you. Sometimes a fence is excuse enough." He leaned his head back. Easy enough to let go, here like this, use the fence as his own excuse. But it still seemed as if he'd misplaced some *thing,* some *purpose* that had been clear enough when the night had begun. Long before Purvis. Back in the barn with his father's horse, the last thing he owned on this earth beside his own skin. The dark had just begun settling into the window frames, and over the fields. In a short while, he would be gone, the door bolted from the outside, and already he could imagine the rats congregating, the coyotes circling the locked barn and abandoned house. He'd stood listening to the barn settle into the cold with creaks and groans like an old man hobbled to the lands. The air smelled burned clean.

The horse lay prone against the far side of the stall, where the wood was raw as a canker from the horse licking its breath's condensation. It was a genuine curiosity, he thought, what that animal had become. Eyes moving as if in a waking dream. Nothing could save this animal anymore—its stomach fallen in upon itself, intestines gone blue and useless. But still it struggled to live, and he watched amazed by the heart's labor, the lungs' need to fill and empty—until he almost believed it would rise and stand again. And then, when Chas saw the inevitable film growing over the open eye like a first frost, when he knew no amount of willpower would ever suffice to raise this beast again, then the legs began to move, churned the bedding in a slow, improbable gallop, as dogs will chase in dreams, and Chas wondered if this was death, was the animal running to or from it? Its wide, white face nodding over the dirt floor, then, my, how the skin had settled into each hollow and the ribs spread like an opening hand, releasing . . . what? That thing there is in all of us that desires its own end as much as fears it? And it seemed he could hear again the last breath, as if it was his own as well, and for the first time he had a sense of what loss might feel like—a true grief—that was not the vacuum, the nothingness he'd fingered all his life like a sore waiting for the pain to tell him he was still alive. He lowered his face into his hands.

"Put the gun down, Chas."

He might have imagined the voice for when he raised his head, he could not see, but then he remembered to open his eyes. It seemed he was ready for sleep, after all. The sleet had stopped. He wondered when that had happened? A moon, too—capping everything with an icy light. Even the sheriff.

"Do you hear me, Chas? Put the gun down." Ike kept his distance. It had taken him awhile to work his way close, his approach slow and circuitous, but now he could see how bad off Chas was and it was clearly a different kind of risk. He cautioned himself against pity, again.

"Sheriff," Chas said and nodded. He eased the gun up across his lap and the sheriff raised his own. "Is it me you're aiming at this time, Parsons, or the cows again?"

"You're in trouble, Chas. Put the gun down, slide it this way, and I'll help you back."

Chas shook his head. He could feel the weight of it, the last thing left him to feel. He smiled. "You are God's own fool for mercy, aren't you? I kill your friend, kidnap your wife . . . What's it take, Parsons?"

Ike kept the gun level, but raised his head away from the sights. "I don't know, Chas. More than I'd have guessed. Put the gun away. Let's go."

"No. I don't think so." Chas leaned his head back against the cow's leg, looked up into the clearing heavens. "There isn't a thing back there." He wagged his head. "Not a person. Goddamn," he said, lifted his hand over his eyes, "but that moon is bright."

And yes, it was bright and the light was amplified by all the ice so that shadows stretched as if for late afternoon, and Ike began to notice other things, how the feeling in his legs had vanished and how his arms shook holding the gun to his shoulder so that he wanted to ease it down, settle himself on the ice, back braced against a post, a cow, his face turned to the moon as Chas's. He simply wanted this to be done with, this question of what he should do, or what he was capable of. He felt an enormous fatigue lay hold of him, understood that he was chilled more deeply than he'd acknowledged—edging into hypothermia himself. If it took much longer, how much good would Ike be to Chas or himself?

Ike took a step closer and Chas lowered his face. "It could be, Parsons"—he spoke slowly, trying not to slur—"that you've . . ." and he raised the gun, but it was only to settle the stock against the ice, lean his cheek against the barrel. "Damn. Forgot. You find Pattiann?"

"Yes. She's fine," Ike said, lowered his gun.

"Obstinate woman," Chas said, grinning.

Ike nodded. "Chas—"

Chas waved him off. "This is one sorry-ass predicament, ain't it?" He tipped his head forward. "I mean, here you are, and here I am, and neither of us getting any nearer where we mean to be."

"Where's that, Chas?" Ike took another step closer.

"Parsons." Chas wagged his head. "Back off." He settled the gun bore under his own chin.

Ike put his gun down, took a step back. "You don't want to do this, Chas." And then another step when Chas's finger stretched down over the trigger. "Chas. Wait. Remember that day we first met? In the corral?"

Chas nodded, and the gunstock followed, sliding back and forth on the ice next to his leg.

"What was it you said about the cattle?"

Chas grinned. "Just so much meat," he said.

Ike nodded. "Yes. Not worth this, surely?" he asked. And suddenly he was no longer just interested in stalling for time. "Just meat," he repeated. And he wanted to know how it all might have been different. "Should I have given it over?" he asked. "Should I have left it alone? Your cattle?"

Chas laughed. "Would Purvis be alive, you mean? You accepting blame—or taking credit? You really think you had more say in this than I did?" He laughed and his chin bumped on the bore, but he did not feel it. That was encouraging. "Pattiann knows better. Fuck, Parsons. I *found* my way here. You're the only one thinks I'm lost."

"Chas . . ."

But Stubblefield shook his head as if to say enough, and his eyes squeezed shut as his finger squeezed the trigger and there was a loud click like teeth hitting on teeth and then silence. He pulled the bore away. "Damn," he said, swinging the barrel up, sighting down on Ike. "Chances are," Chas continued, "that this one won't fire. Or chances are it will. But I try this other shot on myself, and it doesn't work you'll drag my ass out of here. You'll *save* me." He clucked his tongue. He sighed. "But I shoot you dead, then I get to sit here and keep you company for as long as it takes."

Chas smiled and it was the earnest smile of a young boy again. "I *will* kill you, just like I killed Purvis. You going to just sit there and take it?" He steadied the barrel on Ike's chest even as Ike's gun swiveled over Chas's heart.

Ike looked down the barrel, his heart banging in his chest where the other bore centered. He struggled for another way out, but everything had turned to glass beneath him. He thought of Purvis. He thought of Pattiann. It seemed in the moonlight that while the earth had gone hard, Chas's face had softened, gone dreaming.

"Do you understand?" Chas asked.

Ike snugged the gun closer, took a deep breath, and even as he saw Chas's hand tighten, the facing barrel ease away from his chest, he heard the concussion from his own gun. There was a flash and it felt as if someone yanked his arm back, but still he watched and saw Chas fall to a side and lie still. He heard the booming in his ears, though it was like a faraway bellowing that rose up from under his feet, and then he understood that it was not the guns he heard, but the struggling of the frightened cows, their panicked cries venting from the airholes as if the land itself were hurting. And he stood riveted the long while it took for the cries to slow and when it was silent once again he put his gun down. He did not need to check a pulse to know he'd killed Chas. He saw the shadow lengthening down over the body, and he saw the sightless eyes staring moonward. He lowered his arms, felt warmth seeping into the palm of his left hand. He turned away from the body, to where the moonlight fired a hard path to the elusive horizon and the stars . . . the stars.

He heard shots firing in the near distance. He fumbled in his jacket, pulled out a flare, lit it, and propped it up on the ice. He slid to a seated position. The flare's light sputtered a hot pink across the icy floor and over the spindled weeds and sagebrush. It hurt Ike's eyes with its brightness so that he looked away. He roused to his knees, where he hunkered over, breathing through his mouth. In the distance, he believed he could see a set of small lights moving across the ice. He took off his belt, bound his arm to his side, and grunted when he pulled it tight, though he didn't think he'd felt any pain. He raised to his feet, shuffled across the short distance to where Chas lay.

In the light of the flare, he studied Chas, the ice beading down his hair, the hair still parted neatly to a side. The jacket open at the neck where a button was missing. A boot toed inward. It always startled Ike to see how small men looked in death. And then he was reminded of his friend Purvis, the same dark pool widening over the ground, eyes locked open to the heavens like a last avenue of escape. Or refuge.

He felt an immense weariness descend that he could not give in to yet. *Soon,* he told himself. In a short while, they would find him, and tend to his wound. He would make his way back to the squad where Pattiann waited. She'd look at him and know without asking of Chas's death. She'd embrace Ike, finger the crust of ice on his brow, worry over his arm, though that would not stop him from holding her close the rest of the long night and all the nights to follow. He knew that over the weeks and months and years to come he would question this night. He would question justice. And mercy. Whether he'd shot out of self-defense or compassion. Or anger. And on most sleepless nights, when he found himself striving to remember, trying to order and reorder the sequence of events, the sound and the flash, it would be the moon and the ice he remembered clearest, and that too, finally, he would come to see as a kindness. He looked out over the vast ice-locked landscape. The flare was guttering, its fierce light subdued so that Chas's body was a darker spot that jiggled at the side of Ike's vision, and beyond that the columns of ice that were the cattle glowed and dimmed against the blackness like the embers of a fire. He turned to the cattle and set to work, as Chas had before him, breaking them free.